BUSINESS LAW

TEXT AND CASES

AN ACCELERATED COURSE

Roger LeRoy Miller
Institute for University Studies
Arlington, Texas

CENGAGE
Learning·

Australia · Brazil · Japan · Mexico · Singapore · United Kingdom · United States

CENGAGE
Learning®

Business Law
TEXT and CASES

An Accelerated Course

Roger LeRoy Miller

Senior Vice President,
Global Product Management
Higher Education:
Jack W. Calhoun

Vice President and
General Manager,
Social Sciences
& Qualitative Business:
Erin Joyner

Product Director:
Michael Worls

Senior Product Manager:
Vicky True-Baker

Senior Content Developer:
Jan Lamar

Product Assistant:
Tristann Jones

Marketing Director:
Kristen Hurd

Senior Marketing Manager:
Robin LeFevre

Marketing Coordinator:
Chris Walz

Senior Art Director:
Michelle Kunkler

Senior Content Project Manager:
Ann Borman

Senior Media Developer:
Kristen Meere

Manufacturing Planner:
Kevin Kluck

Compositor:
Parkwood Composition Service

Cover and Internal Designer:
Red Hangar Design

Design Elements:
linen texture: Lisa-Blue/iStockphoto; justice scales:
imagedb.com/Shutterstock; gavel: koosen/Shutterstock;
media network: solarseven/Shutterstock; building
windows: Nneirda/Shutterstock; puzzle icon: Shebeko/
Shutterstock; spotlight: Ivan Lord/Shutterstock; ethics
scale: Lightspring/Shutterstock; magnifying glass icon:
sergign/Shutterstock; globe: mj007/Shutterstock;
compass: TADDEUS/Shutterstock; Insight Global globe:
evantravels/Shutterstock

> For product information and technology assistance, contact us at
> **Cengage Learning Customer & Sales Support**
> **1-800-354-9706**
>
> For permission to use material from this text or product,
> submit all requests online at
> **www.cengage.com/permissions**.
>
> Further permissions questions can be e-mailed to
> **permissionrequest@cengage.com**.

Library of Congress Control Number: 2013948832

ISBN-13: 978-1-285-77019-2

Cengage Learning
200 First Stamford Place, 4th Floor
Stamford, CT 06902
USA

Cengage Learning is a leading provider of customized learning solutions
with office locations around the globe, including Singapore, the United
Kingdom, Australia, Mexico, Brazil, and Japan. Locate your local office at:
www.cengage.com/global.

Cengage Learning products are represented in Canada
by Nelson Education, Ltd.

To learn more about Cengage Learning, visit **www.cengage.com**.

Purchase any of our products at your local college store
or at our preferred online store **www.cengagebrain.com**.

Printed in the United States of America
2 3 4 5 6 7 17 16 15 14

BRIEF CONTENTS

CONTENTS

CONCEPT SUMMARIES

EXHIBITS

Business Law: An Accelerated Course is an exciting, new textbook that has been tailor-made for those instructors who teach a condensed one-semester course of business law. This text is the result of repeated requests and recommendations from a wide variety of users of my best-selling textbook, *Business Law: Text and Cases,* for a smaller, more focused text on the basics of business law. This new textbook features a strong emphasis on contracts, sales, and business organizations.

I have spent a great deal of effort making *Business Law: An Accelerated Course* contemporary and accessible. Many features and special pedagogical devices focus on the legal, ethical, global, and e-commerce environments, while addressing core curriculum requirements.

UNIQUE DIGITAL LEARNING SYSTEMS

Before discussing the many aspects of this text, I wish to point out the exciting digital products offered in conjunction with *Business Law: An Accelerated Course.*

CengageNOW for Business Law: An Accelerated Course— Interactive Assignment System

CengageNOW™ is a powerful course management tool that provides control and customization to optimize the student learning experience and produce desired outcomes. The application features a variety of question types to test simple reading comprehension, complex critical thinking, legal reasoning, and case analysis skills.

CengageNOW includes:

- **An Interactive Book.**
- **Auto-Graded Homework** with the following consistent question types:
  - *Worksheets.* Interactive worksheets prepare students for class by ensuring reading and comprehension.
  - *Video Activities.* Real-world video exercises make business law engaging and relevant.
  - *Brief Hypotheticals.* These applications provide students practice in spotting the issue and applying the law in the context of a short, factual scenario.
  - *Case Problem Blueprints.* These case problems promote deeper critical thinking and legal reasoning by building on acquired knowledge to truly assess students' understanding of legal principles.
- **A Personalized Student Plan** with multimedia study tools and videos.
- **A *Test Bank.***
- **Reporting and Assessment Options.**

By using the optional *CengageNOW* system, students can complete the assignments online and can receive instant feedback on their answers. Instructors can utilize *CengageNOW* to upload their course syllabi, create and customize homework assignments, and keep track of their students' progress. Instructors can also communicate with their students about assignments and due dates, and create reports summarizing the data for an individual student or for the whole class.

CourseMate

CourseMate for *Business Law: An Accelerated Course* brings business law concepts to life with interactive learning, study, and exam-preparation tools that support the printed textbook. Built-in engagement-tracking tools allow instructors to assess the study activities of their students.

Additionally, *CourseMate* includes an interactive online textbook, which contains the complete content of the print textbook enhanced by the many advantages of a digital environment.

Cengage Learning Testing Powered by Cognero

Cengage Learning Testing Powered by Cognero is a flexible, online system that allows instructors to do the following:

- Author, edit, and manage *Test Bank* content from multiple Cengage Learning solutions.
- Create multiple test versions in an instant.
- Deliver tests from the Learning Management System, the classroom, or wherever an instructor wants.

START RIGHT AWAY! *Cengage Learning Testing Powered by Cognero* works on any operating system or browser.

- No special installs or downloads are needed.
- Create tests from school, home, the coffee shop—anywhere with Internet access.

WHAT YOU WILL FIND:

- *Simplicity at every step.* A desktop-inspired interface features drop-down menus and familiar intuitive tools that take you through content creation and management with ease.
- *Full-featured test generator.* Create ideal assessments with your choice of fifteen question types—including true-false, multiple choice, opinion scale/Likert, and essay). Multi-language support, an equation editor, and unlimited metadata help ensure your tests are complete and compliant.
- *Cross-compatible capability.* Import and export content into other systems.

A COMPLETE SUPPLEMENTS PACKAGE

Business Law: An Accelerated Course is accompanied by many teaching and learning supplements, which are available on the password-protected portion of the Instructor's Companion Web Site. The complete teaching/learning package offers numerous other supplements, including those listed below.

For further information on the *Business Law: An Accelerated Course* teaching/learning package, contact a local sales representative or visit the *Business Law: An Accelerated Course* Web site by going to **www.cengage.com** and entering ISBN 9781285770192.

Instructor's Companion Web Site

The Instructor's Companion Web Site includes the following supplements:

- ***Instructor's Manual.*** Contains sections entitled "Additional Cases Addressing This Issue" at the end of selected case synopses.
- ***Answers Manual.*** Provides answers to all questions presented in the text, including the questions in each case and feature.
- ***Test Bank.*** A comprehensive test bank that contains multiple-choice, true-false, and short essay questions.
- ***Case-Problem Cases.***
- ***Case Printouts.***
- ***PowerPoint Slides.***
- *Instructor's Manual* for the *Drama of the Law* video series.

Software, Video, and Multimedia Supplements

- ***Business Law Digital Video Library***—Provides access to ninety videos, including the *Drama of the Law* videos and video clips from actual Hollywood movies. Access to the digital library is available in an optional package with each new text at no additional cost. Instructors can access the *Business Law Digital Video Library*—along with corresponding *Video Questions* that are related to specific chapters in the text—at **www.cengagebrain.com**.
- ***CengageNOW***
- ***CourseMate***
- **Westlaw®**—Ten free hours for qualified adopters.

SPECIAL FEATURES AND PEDAGOGY

To make sure that *Business Law: An Accelerated Course* engages students, solidifies their understanding of legal concepts, and provides the best teaching tools available, the following items in this section are offered either in the text or in conjunction with the text.

Suggested answers to all of the questions and problems presented in the following features and pedagogy are included in both the *Instructor's Manual* and the *Answers Manual* for this text.

Managerial Strategy Features

Managerial Strategy features focus on the management aspects of business law. Special emphasis is given to sustainability, ethical trends, and changing managerial responsibilities.

Each feature includes a short section entitled *Managerial Implications* that provides concrete information for managers and connects the topic under discussion to operating a business. Each feature also concludes with two *Business Questions* that prompt students to further examine the issues discussed. Topics examined in these features include:

- Budget Cuts for State Courts Can Affect Businesses (Chapter 3)
- Facing Breach of Contract Issues (Chapter 16)

Examples and Case in Point Illustrations

The highlighted numbered *Examples* and *Cases in Point* features in every chapter are uniquely designed and consecutively numbered throughout each chapter for easy reference. *Examples* illustrate how the law applies in a specific situation. *Cases in Point* present the facts and issues of an actual case and then describe the court's decision and rationale.

The numbered *Examples* and *Cases in Point* features are integrated throughout the text to help students better understand how courts apply the principles in the real world.

Spotlight Cases and Spotlight Case Problems

For *Business Law: An Accelerated Course,* certain cases and case problems have been carefully chosen as exceptionally good teaching cases. *Spotlight Cases* and *Spotlight Case Problems* are labeled either by the name of one of the parties or by the subject involved. Some examples include a *Spotlight Case* on Amazon, the Seattle Mariners, commercial speech, and Internet porn.

Instructors will find these *Spotlight Cases* useful to illustrate the legal concepts under discussion. Students will enjoy studying these cases because the parties are often familiar and the cases involve interesting and memorable facts.

ExamPrep

A section called *ExamPrep* is included at the conclusion of each chapter. The section includes two *Issue Spotters,* which are related to the chapter's topics. The *Issue Spotters* facilitate student learning and provide a review of the materials. (Suggested answers to the *Issue Spotters* in every chapter are provided in Appendix B at the end of the text.)

Legal Reasoning Group Activities

For instructors who want their students to engage in group projects, each chapter includes a special *Legal Reasoning Group Activity.* Each activity begins by describing a business scenario and then requires each group of students to answer a specific question pertaining to the scenario based on the information that they learned in the chapter. These projects may be used in class to spur discussion or as homework assignments.

Insight into . . . Features

Insight into [E-Commerce, Ethics, the Global Environment, or Social Media] features appear in selected chapters. These features provide valuable insights into how the courts and the law are dealing with specific issues. Each of these features ends with a *Legal Critical Thinking* question that explores some cultural, environmental, or technological aspect of the issue.

The following are some of the topics explored in these features:

- *Insight into E-Commerce*—Do Computers Have Free Speech Rights? (Chapter 2)
- *Insight into the Global Environment*—Is It Legal to Resell Textbooks Purchased Abroad? (Chapter 5)
- *Insight into Social Media*—"Catfishing": Is That Online "Friend" Who You Think It Is? (Chapter 12)

Case Analysis Cases

In every chapter of *Business Law: An Accelerated Course,* there is one longer case excerpt—labeled *Case Analysis Case*—followed by four *Legal Reasoning Questions.* These questions are designed to guide students' analysis of the case and build their legal reasoning skills. These *Case Analysis Cases* may be used for case-briefing assignments and are also tied to the *Special Case Analysis* questions found in selected chapters.

The *Special Case Analysis* questions test students' ability to perform IRAC (Issue, Rule, Application, and Conclusion) case analysis. Students must identify the legal issue presented in the chapter's *Case Analysis Case,* understand the rule of law, determine how the rule applies to the facts of the case, and describe the court's conclusion. Instructors can assign these questions as homework or use them in class to elicit student participation and teach case analysis.

Emphasis on Business and Critical Thinking

Business Law: An Accelerated Course focuses on making the text more business related. To that end, I have carefully chosen cases, features, and problems that are relevant to operating a business. In addition, I recognize that today's business leaders must often think "outside the box" when making business decisions. For this reason, I have included numerous critical thinking and legal reasoning elements in this text. Almost all of the features and cases presented in the text conclude with some type of critical thinking question.

Cases may include one or more of the following critical thinking questions:

- *What If the Facts Were Different?*
- *The Ethical Dimension*
- *The E-Commerce Dimension*
- *The Global Dimension*
- *The Legal Environment Dimension*

In addition to the critical thinking questions, I have also included special case pedagogy at the end of selected cases that have particular importance for business managers. This section, called **Managerial Implications,** points out the significance of the court's ruling in the case for business owners and managers.

Reviewing . . . Features

I offer a *Reviewing . . .* feature at the end of every chapter to help solidify students' understanding of the chapter materials. Each *Reviewing . . .* feature presents a hypothetical scenario and then asks a series of questions that require students to identify the issues and apply the legal concepts discussed in the chapter.

These features are designed to help students review the chapter topics in a simple and interesting way and see how the legal principles discussed in the chapter affect the world in which they live. An instructor can use these features as the basis for in-class discussion or encourage students to use them for self-study before completing homework assignments.

Concept Summaries and Exhibits

When key areas of the law need additional emphasis, *Concept Summaries* are a popular pedagogical tool. This text includes twenty-five of these summaries. When appropriate, I also illustrate important aspects of the law in graphic form in exhibits. In all, more than forty exhibits are featured in *Business Law: An Accelerated Course.*

Case Problems

Every chapter includes a 2012 or 2013 case problem in its *Business Case Problems* section. These problems are designed to clarify how modern courts deal with the business issues discussed in the chapter. Every business scenario and case problem features a label that identifies the chapter topic to which the question relates. These labels make it easier for instructors who wish to assign only certain questions to their students.

In addition, page references to the text where the problem's answer can be found are also provided. I have also included two special problems—the *Spotlight Case Problems* (mentioned earlier), which are based on good teaching cases with interesting facts, and the *Business Case Problem with Sample Answer.*

Lastly, sample answers are available for each *Business Case Problem with Sample Answer.* The *Business Case Problem with Sample Answer* is based on an actual case, and students can access a sample answer in Appendix C.

BUSINESS LAW: AN ACCELERATED COURSE ON THE WEB

The Web site for *Business Law: An Accelerated Course* can be found by going to **www.cengagebrain.com** and entering ISBN 9781285770192. The Web site offers a broad array of teaching/learning resources, including the following:

- ***Practice quizzes*** for every chapter in this text.
- ***Interactive Flashcards*** and a ***Glossary*** for every chapter in this text.
- ***Legal reference materials,*** including a "Statutes" page that offers links to the full text of selected statutes referenced in the text, a Spanish glossary, and other important legal resources.
- ***CourseMate,*** which students can purchase access to, provides additional study tools, including an e-book, additional quizzes, Flashcards, key terms, and PowerPoint slides.

ACKNOWLEDGMENTS

I owe a debt of extreme gratitude to the numerous individuals who worked directly with me or at Cengage Learning. In particular, I wish to thank Vicky True-Baker, Rob Dewey, and Mike Worls for their helpful advice and guidance during all of the stages of this new textbook. I extend my thanks to Jan Lamar, my longtime senior content developer, for her many useful suggestions and for her efforts in coordinating the text and ensuring the timely and accurate publication of all supplemental materials. I am also indebted to Kristen Hurd for her excellent marketing advice.

My senior content project manager, Ann Borman, made sure that we came out with an error-free, visually attractive edition. I appreciate her efforts. I am also indebted to the staff at Parkwood Composition, the compositor. Their ability to generate the pages for this text quickly and accurately made it possible to meet an ambitious printing schedule.

I especially wish to thank Katherine Marie Silsbee for her management of the entire project, as well as for the application of her superb research and editorial skills. I also wish to thank William Eric Hollowell, who co-authored the *Instructor's Manual* and the *Test Bank,* for his excellent research efforts. I was fortunate enough to have the copyediting of Pat Lewis and the proofreading services of Jeanne Yost. I am also grateful for the efforts of Vickie Reierson and Roxanna Lee for their proofreading and other assistance, which helped to ensure an error-free text. Finally, thank you to Suzanne Jasin of K & M Consulting for her many special efforts on this project.

I welcome all comments about this new textbook and promise to respond promptly. By incorporating other ideas and suggestions, I can continue to write a business law text that is best for instructors and students.

Roger LeRoy Miller

Dedication

To Kim Kawaguchi,

You continue to amaze
me with your numerous
exploits, which of course,
I will never realize. But,
I keep trying!

Thanks for being a friend.

R. L. M.

AN ACCELERATED COURSE

MILLER

UNIT ONE

THE LEGAL ENVIRONMENT OF BUSINESS

CONTENTS

CHAPTER 1

LAW AND
LEGAL REASONING

One of the important functions of law in any society is to provide stability, predictability, and continuity so that people can know how to order their affairs. If any society is to survive, its citizens must be able to determine what is legally right and legally wrong. They must know what sanctions will be imposed on them if they commit wrongful acts. If they suffer harm as a result of others' wrongful acts, they must know how they can seek compensation. By setting forth the rights, obligations, and privileges of citizens, the law enables individuals to go about their business with confidence and a certain degree of predictability.

Although law has various definitions, they are all based on the general observation that **law** consists of *enforceable rules governing relationships among individuals and between individuals and their society*. These "enforceable rules" may consist of unwritten principles of behavior established by a nomadic tribe. They may be set forth in a law code, such as the Code of Hammurabi in ancient Babylon (c. 1780 B.C.E.) or the law code of one of today's European nations. They may consist of written laws and court decisions created by modern legislative and judicial bodies, as in the United States. Regardless of how such rules are created, they all have one thing in common: they establish rights, duties, and

privileges that are consistent with the values and beliefs of their society or its ruling group.

In this introductory chapter, we first look at an important question for any student reading this text: How does the legal environment affect business decision making? We next describe the major sources of American law, the common law tradition, and some basic schools of legal thought. We conclude the chapter with sections offering practical guidance on several topics, including how to find the sources of law discussed in this chapter (and referred to throughout the text) and how to read and understand court opinions.

BUSINESS ACTIVITIES AND THE LEGAL ENVIRONMENT

Laws and government regulations affect almost all business activities—from hiring and firing decisions to workplace safety, the manufacturing and marketing of products, business financing, and more. To make good business decisions, a basic knowledge of the laws and regulations governing these activities is beneficial—if not essential.

Realize also that in today's business world, a knowledge of "black-letter" law is not enough. Businesspersons are also pressured to make ethical decisions. Thus, the study of business law necessarily involves an ethical dimension.

Many Different Laws May Affect a Single Business Decision

As you will note, each chapter in this text covers specific areas of the law and shows how the legal rules in each area affect business activities. Though compartmentalizing the law in this fashion promotes conceptual clarity, it does not indicate the extent to which a number of different laws may apply to just one decision.

LESSONS FROM FACEBOOK When Mark Zuckerberg started Facebook as a Harvard student, he probably did not imagine all the legal challenges his company would face as a result of his business decisions.

• As you may know from the movie, *The Social Network*, shortly after Facebook was launched, others claimed that Zuckerberg had stolen their ideas for a social networking site. Their claims involved alleged theft of intellectual property (see Chapter 5), fraudulent misrepresentation (see Chapter 12), partnership law and securities law. Facebook ultimately paid a significant amount ($65 million) to settle those claims out of court (see Chapter 3).

- Facebook has also been sued repeatedly for violating users' privacy (such as by disseminating private information to third parties for commercial purposes—see Chapters 2 and 6).
- In 2012, a *class-action* lawsuit was filed against Facebook that seeks damages of $15 billion for violating users' privacy (and federal wiretapping law) by tracking their Web site usage.
- Facebook's business decisions have also come under scrutiny by federal regulators, such as the Federal Trade Commission (FTC) and the Securities and Exchange Commission (SEC).
- In 2011, the company settled a complaint filed by the FTC alleging that Facebook failed to keep "friends" lists and other user information private.
- In 2012, Facebook conducted a much-anticipated initial public offering (IPO) of its stock. The IPO did not go well, however, and many investors suffered losses. Facebook is facing dozens of lawsuits (including class actions) related to business decisions made with regard to the IPO and alleged violations of securities laws.
- The SEC is also investigating whether Facebook engaged in any wrongdoing with regard to its IPO and trading of stock.

POINTS TO CONSIDER A key to avoiding business disputes is to think ahead when starting or running a business or entering a contract. Learn what you can about the laws pertaining to that specific enterprise or transaction. Have some idea of the legal ramifications of your business decisions and seek the advice of counsel when in doubt. Exhibit 1–1 on the following page illustrates the various areas of law that may influence business decision making.

Ethics and Business Decision Making

Merely knowing the areas of law that may affect a business decision is not sufficient in today's business world. Businesspersons must also take ethics into account. As you will learn in Chapter 8, *ethics* gener-

ally is defined as the principles governing what constitutes right or wrong behavior.

Today, business decision makers need to consider not just whether a decision is legal, but also whether it is ethical. Often, as in several of the claims against Facebook discussed above, disputes arise in business because one party feels that he or she has been treated unfairly. Thus, the underlying reason for bringing some lawsuits is a breach of ethical duties (such as when a partner or employee attempts to secretly take advantage of a business opportunity).

Throughout this text, you will learn about the relationship between the law and ethics, as well as about some of the types of ethical questions that often arise in business. For example, we have included *Ethical Dimension* questions for selected cases that focus on ethical considerations in today's business climate and *Insight into Ethics* features that appear in selected chapters. A *Question of Ethics* case problem is included at the conclusion of every chapter to introduce you to the ethical aspects of specific cases involving real-life situations. Additionally, Chapter 8 offers a detailed look at the importance of business ethics.

SECTION 2
SOURCES OF AMERICAN LAW

There are numerous sources of American law. *Primary sources of law,* or sources that establish the law, include the following:

1. The U.S. Constitution and the constitutions of the various states.
2. Statutory law—including laws passed by Congress, state legislatures, or local governing bodies.
3. Regulations created by administrative agencies, such as the Food and Drug Administration.
4. Case law and common law doctrines.

We describe each of these important sources of law in the following pages.

Secondary sources of law are books and articles that summarize and clarify the primary sources of law. Examples include legal encyclopedias, treatises, articles in law reviews, and compilations of law, such as the *Restatements of the Law* (which will be discussed shortly). Courts often refer to secondary sources of law for guidance in interpreting and applying the primary sources of law discussed here.

EXHIBIT 1–1 Areas of the Law That May Affect Business Decision Making

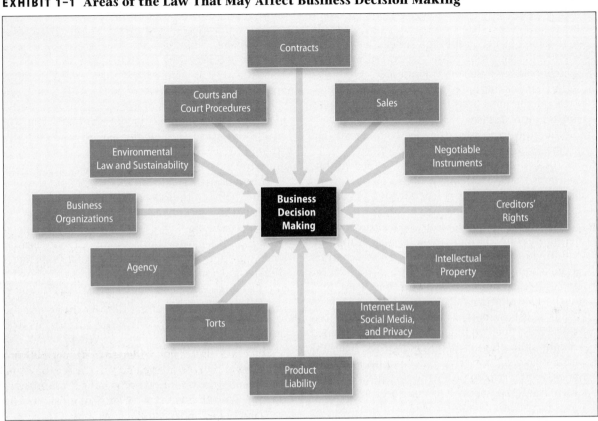

Constitutional Law

The federal government and the states have separate written constitutions that set forth the general organization, powers, and limits of their respective governments. **Constitutional law** is the law as expressed in these constitutions.

According to Article VI of the U.S. Constitution, the Constitution is the supreme law of the land. As such, it is the basis of all law in the United States. A law in violation of the Constitution, if challenged, will be declared unconstitutional and will not be enforced, no matter what its source. Because of its importance in the American legal system, we discuss the U.S. Constitution in depth in Chapter 2.

The Tenth Amendment to the U.S. Constitution reserves to the states all powers not granted to the federal government. Each state in the union has its own constitution. Unless it conflicts with the U.S. Constitution or a federal law, a state constitution is supreme within the state's borders.

Statutory Law

Laws enacted by legislative bodies at any level of government, such as statutes passed by Congress or by state legislatures, make up the body of law known as **statutory law.** When a legislature passes a statute, that statute ultimately is included in the federal code of laws or the relevant state code of laws (discussed later in this chapter).

Statutory law also includes local **ordinances**—statutes (laws, rules, or orders) passed by municipal or county governing units to govern matters not covered by federal or state law. Ordinances commonly have to do with city or county land use (zoning ordinances), building and safety codes, and other matters affecting the local community.

A federal statute, of course, applies to all states. A state statute, in contrast, applies only within the state's borders. State laws thus may vary from state to state. No federal statute may violate the U.S. Constitution, and no state statute or local ordinance may violate the U.S. Constitution or the relevant state constitution.

UNIFORM LAWS During the 1800s, the differences among state laws frequently created difficulties for businesspersons conducting trade and commerce among the states. To counter these problems, a group of legal scholars and lawyers formed the National Conference of Commissioners on Uniform State Laws (NCCUSL, **www.uniformlaws.org**) in 1892 to draft **uniform laws** (model statutes) for the states to consider adopting. The NCCUSL still exists today and continues to issue uniform laws.

Each state has the option of adopting or rejecting a uniform law. *Only if a state legislature adopts a uniform law does that law become part of the statutory law of that state.* Note that a state legislature may adopt all or part of a uniform law as it is written, or the legislature may rewrite the law however the legislature wishes. Hence, even though many states may have adopted a uniform law, those states' laws may not be entirely "uniform."

The earliest uniform law, the Uniform Negotiable Instruments Law, was completed by 1896 and adopted in every state by the 1920s (although not all states used exactly the same wording). Over the following decades, other acts were drawn up in a similar manner. In all, more than two hundred uniform acts have been issued by the NCCUSL since its inception. The most ambitious uniform act of all, however, was the Uniform Commercial Code.

THE UNIFORM COMMERCIAL CODE One of the most important uniform acts is the Uniform Commercial Code (UCC), which was created through the joint efforts of the NCCUSL and the American Law Institute.[1] The UCC was first issued in 1952 and has been adopted in all fifty states,[2] the District of Columbia, and the Virgin Islands.

The UCC facilitates commerce among the states by providing a uniform, yet flexible, set of rules governing commercial transactions. Because of its importance in the area of commercial law, we cite the UCC frequently in this text. We also present Article 2 of the UCC in Appendix A. From time to time, the NCCUSL revises the articles contained in the UCC and submits the revised versions to the states for adoption.

Administrative Law

Another important source of American law is **administrative law,** which consists of the rules,

orders, and decisions of administrative agencies. An **administrative agency** is a federal, state, or local government agency established to perform a specific function. Administrative law and procedures constitute a dominant element in the regulatory environment of business.

Rules issued by various administrative agencies now affect almost every aspect of a business's operations. Regulations govern a business's capital structure and financing, its hiring and firing procedures, its relations with employees and unions, and the way it manufactures and markets its products. Regulations enacted to protect the environment also often play a significant role in business operations.

FEDERAL AGENCIES At the national level, the cabinet departments of the executive branch include numerous **executive agencies.** The U.S. Food and Drug Administration, for example, is an agency within the U.S. Department of Health and Human Services. Executive agencies are subject to the authority of the president, who has the power to appoint and remove their officers.

There are also major **independent regulatory agencies** at the federal level, such as the Federal Trade Commission, the Securities and Exchange Commission, and the Federal Communications Commission. The president's power is less pronounced in regard to independent agencies, whose officers serve for fixed terms and cannot be removed without just cause.

STATE AND LOCAL AGENCIES There are administrative agencies at the state and local levels as well. Commonly, a state agency (such as a state pollution-control agency) is created as a parallel to a federal agency (such as the Environmental Protection Agency). Just as federal statutes take precedence over conflicting state statutes, federal agency regulations take precedence over conflicting state regulations.

Case Law and Common Law Doctrines

The rules of law announced in court decisions constitute another basic source of American law. These rules include interpretations of constitutional provisions, of statutes enacted by legislatures, and of regulations created by administrative agencies.

Today, this body of judge-made law is referred to as **case law.** Case law—the doctrines and principles announced in cases—governs all areas not covered by

---

1. This institute was formed in the 1920s and consists of practicing attorneys, legal scholars, and judges.
2. Louisiana has not adopted Articles 2 and 2A (covering contracts for the sale and lease of goods), however.

statutory law or administrative law and is part of our common law tradition. We look at the origins and characteristics of the common law tradition in some detail in the pages that follow.

See *Concept Summary 1.1* below for a review of the sources of American law.

SECTION 3
THE COMMON LAW TRADITION

Because of our colonial heritage, much of American law is based on the English legal system, which originated in medieval England and continued to evolve in the following centuries. Knowledge of this system is necessary to understanding the American legal system today.

Early English Courts

The origins of the English legal system—and thus the U.S. legal system as well—date back to 1066, when the Normans conquered England. William the Conqueror and his successors began the process of unifying the country under their rule. One of the means they used to do this was the establishment of the king's courts, or *curiae regis*.

Before the Norman Conquest, disputes had been settled according to the local legal customs and traditions in various regions of the country. The king's courts sought to establish a uniform set of customs for the country as a whole. What evolved in these courts was the beginning of the **common law**—a body of general rules that applied throughout the entire English realm. Eventually, the common law tradition became part of the heritage of all nations that were once British colonies, including the United States.

COURTS OF LAW AND REMEDIES AT LAW The early English king's courts could grant only very limited kinds of **remedies** (the legal means to enforce a right or redress a wrong). If one person wronged another in some way, the king's courts could award as compensation one or more of the following: (1) land, (2) items of value, or (3) money.

The courts that awarded this compensation became known as **courts of law,** and the three remedies were called **remedies at law.** (Today, the remedy at law normally takes the form of monetary **damages**— an amount given to a party whose legal interests have been injured.) This system made the procedure for settling disputes more uniform. When a complaining party wanted a remedy other than economic compensation, however, the courts of law could do nothing, so "no remedy, no right."

COURTS OF EQUITY *Equity* is a branch of law— founded on notions of justice and fair dealing—that seeks to supply a remedy when no adequate remedy at law is available. When individuals could not obtain an adequate remedy in a court of law, they petitioned the king for relief. Most of these petitions were decided by an adviser to the king, called a **chancellor,** who had the power to grant new and unique remedies. Eventually, formal chancery courts, or **courts of equity,** were established.

CONCEPT SUMMARY 1.1
Sources of American Law

SOURCE	DESCRIPTION
Constitutional Law	The law as expressed in the U.S. Constitution and the state constitutions. The U.S. Constitution is the supreme law of the land. State constitutions are supreme within state borders to the extent that they do not violate a clause of the U.S. Constitution or a federal law.
Statutory Law	Laws (statutes and ordinances) enacted by federal, state, and local legislatures and governing bodies. None of these laws can violate the U.S. Constitution or the relevant state constitution. Uniform laws, when adopted by a state, become statutory law in that state.
Administrative Law	The rules, orders, and decisions of federal, state, and local government administrative agencies.
Case Law and Common Law Doctrines	Judge-made law, including interpretations of constitutional provisions, of statutes enacted by legislatures, and of regulations created by administrative agencies.

REMEDIES IN EQUITY The remedies granted by the equity courts became known as **remedies in equity,** or equitable remedies. These remedies include specific performance, an injunction, and rescission. *Specific performance* involves ordering a party to perform an agreement as promised. An *injunction* is an order to a party to cease engaging in a specific activity or to undo some wrong or injury. *Rescission* is the cancellation of a contractual obligation. We will discuss these and other equitable remedies in more detail at appropriate points in the chapters that follow, particularly in Chapter 14.

As a general rule, today's courts, like the early English courts, will not grant equitable remedies unless the remedy at law—monetary damages—is inadequate. ▶ **Example 1.1** Ted forms a contract (a legally binding agreement—see Chapter 9) to purchase a parcel of land that he thinks will be perfect for his future home. The seller **breaches,** or fails to fulfill, this agreement. Ted could sue the seller for the return of any deposits or down payment he might have made on the land, but this is not the remedy he really seeks. What Ted wants is to have the court order the seller to perform the contract. In other words, Ted wants the court to grant the equitable remedy of specific performance because monetary damages are inadequate in this situation. ◀

EQUITABLE MAXIMS In fashioning appropriate remedies, judges often were (and continue to be) guided by so-called **equitable maxims**—propositions or general statements of equitable rules. Exhibit 1–2 below lists some important equitable maxims.

The last maxim listed in that exhibit—"Equity aids the vigilant, not those who rest on their rights"—merits special attention. It has become known as the equitable doctrine of **laches** (a term derived from the Latin *laxus,* meaning "lax" or "negligent"), and it can be used as a defense. A **defense** is an argument raised by the **defendant** (the party being sued) indicating why the **plaintiff** (the suing party) should not obtain the remedy sought. (Note that in equity proceedings, the party bringing a lawsuit is called the **petitioner,** and the party being sued is referred to as the **respondent.**)

The doctrine of laches arose to encourage people to bring lawsuits while the evidence was fresh. What constitutes a reasonable time, of course, varies according to the circumstances of the case. Time periods for different types of cases are now usually fixed by **statutes of limitations.** After the time allowed under a statute of limitations has expired, no action (lawsuit) can be brought, no matter how strong the case was originally.

Legal and Equitable Remedies Today

The establishment of courts of equity in medieval England resulted in two distinct court systems: courts of law and courts of equity. The courts had different sets of judges and granted different types of remedies. During the nineteenth century, however, most states in the United States adopted rules of procedure that resulted in the combining of courts of law and equity. A party now may request both legal and equitable remedies in the same action, and the trial court judge may grant either or both forms of relief.

The distinction between legal and equitable remedies remains relevant to students of business law, however, because these remedies differ. To seek the proper remedy for a wrong, one must know what

EXHIBIT 1–2 Equitable Maxims

1.	*Whoever seeks equity must do equity.* (Anyone who wishes to be treated fairly must treat others fairly.)
2.	*Where there is equal equity, the law must prevail.* (The law will determine the outcome of a controversy in which the merits of both sides are equal.)
3.	*One seeking the aid of an equity court must come to the court with clean hands.* (The plaintiff must have acted fairly and honestly.)
4.	*Equity will not suffer a wrong to be without a remedy.* (Equitable relief will be awarded when there is a right to relief and there is no adequate remedy at law.)
5.	*Equity regards substance rather than form.* (Equity is more concerned with fairness and justice than with legal technicalities.)
6.	*Equity aids the vigilant, not those who rest on their rights.* (Equity will not help those who neglect their rights for an unreasonable period of time.)

remedies are available. Additionally, certain vestiges of the procedures used when there were separate courts of law and equity still exist. For example, a party has the right to demand a jury trial in an action at law, but not in an action in equity. Exhibit 1–3 below summarizes the procedural differences (applicable in most states) between an action at law and an action in equity.

The Doctrine of *Stare Decisis*

One of the unique features of the common law is that it is *judge-made* law. The body of principles and doctrines that form the common law emerged over time as judges decided legal controversies.

CASE PRECEDENTS AND CASE REPORTERS When possible, judges attempted to be consistent and to base their decisions on the principles suggested by earlier cases. They sought to decide similar cases in a similar way and considered new cases with care because they knew that their decisions would make new law. Each interpretation became part of the law on the subject and thus served as a legal **precedent.** A precedent is a decision that furnishes an example or authority for deciding subsequent cases involving identical or similar legal principles or facts.

In the early years of the common law, there was no single place or publication where court opinions, or written decisions, could be found. By the fourteenth century, portions of the most important decisions from each year were being gathered together and recorded in *Year Books,* which became useful references for lawyers and judges. In the sixteenth century, the *Year Books* were discontinued, and other forms of case publication became available. Today, cases are published, or "reported," in volumes called **reporters,** or *reports*. We describe today's case reporting system in detail later in this chapter.

STARE DECISIS AND THE COMMON LAW TRADITION The practice of deciding new cases with reference to former decisions, or precedents, became a cornerstone of the English and American judicial systems. The practice formed a doctrine known as **stare decisis**[3] (a Latin phrase meaning "to stand on decided cases"). Under this doctrine, judges are obligated to follow the precedents established within their jurisdictions. The term *jurisdiction* refers to a geographic area in which a court or courts have the power to apply the law—see Chapter 3.

Once a court has set forth a principle of law as being applicable to a certain set of facts, that court must apply the principle in future cases involving similar facts. Courts of lower rank (within the same jurisdiction) must do likewise. Thus, *stare decisis* has two aspects:

1. A court should not overturn its own precedents unless there is a compelling reason to do so.
2. Decisions made by a higher court are binding on lower courts.

CONTROLLING PRECEDENTS Controlling precedents in a jurisdiction are referred to as binding authorities. A **binding authority** is any source of law that a court must follow when deciding a case. Binding authorities include constitutions, statutes, and regulations that govern the issue being decided, as well as court decisions that are controlling precedents within the jurisdiction. United States Supreme Court case decisions, no matter how old, remain controlling until they are overruled by a subsequent decision of the Supreme Court or changed by further legislation or a constitutional amendment.

STARE DECISIS AND LEGAL STABILITY The doctrine of *stare decisis* helps the courts to be more efficient because, if other courts have analyzed a similar case,

3. Pronounced *ster*-ay dih-*si*-ses.

EXHIBIT 1-3 Procedural Differences between an Action at Law and an Action in Equity

Procedure	Action at Law	Action in Equity
Initiation of lawsuit	By filing a complaint	By filing a petition
Parties	Plaintiff and defendant	Petitioner and respondent
Decision	By jury or judge	By judge (no jury)
Result	Judgment	Decree
Remedy	Monetary damages	Injunction, specific performance, or rescission

their legal reasoning and opinions can serve as guides. *Stare decisis* also makes the law more stable and predictable. If the law on a subject is well settled, someone bringing a case can usually rely on the court to rule based on what the law has been in the past.

DEPARTURES FROM PRECEDENT Although courts are obligated to follow precedents, sometimes a court will depart from the rule of precedent if it decides that the precedent should no longer be followed. If a court decides that a ruling precedent is simply incorrect or that technological or social changes have rendered the precedent inapplicable, the court might rule contrary to the precedent. Cases that overturn precedent often receive a great deal of publicity.

▶ **Case in Point 1.2** The United States Supreme Court expressly overturned precedent in the case of *Brown v. Board of Education of Topeka*.[4] The Court concluded that separate educational facilities for whites and blacks, which it had previously upheld as constitutional,[5] were inherently unequal. The Court's departure from precedent in this case received a tremendous amount of publicity as people began to realize the ramifications of this change in the law. ◀

Note that judges do have some flexibility in applying precedents. For instance, a lower court may avoid applying a precedent set by a higher court in its jurisdiction by distinguishing the two cases based on their facts. When this happens, the lower court's ruling stands unless it is appealed to a higher court and that court overturns the decision.

WHEN THERE IS NO PRECEDENT Occasionally, courts must decide cases for which no precedents exist, called cases of *first impression*. For instance, as you will read throughout this text, the extensive use of the Internet has presented many new and challenging issues for the courts to decide.

In deciding cases of first impression, courts often look at **persuasive authorities** (precedents from other jurisdictions) for guidance. A court may also consider legal principles and policies underlying previous court decisions or existing statutes. Other factors that courts look at include fairness, social values and customs, and **public policy** (governmental policy based on widely held societal values).

---

4. 347 U.S. 483, 74 S.Ct. 686, 98 L.Ed. 873 (1954). A later section in this chapter explains how to read legal citations.
5. See *Plessy v. Ferguson,* 163 U.S. 537, 16 S.Ct. 1138, 41 L.Ed. 256 (1896).

Stare Decisis and Legal Reasoning

In deciding what law applies to a given dispute and then applying that law to the facts or circumstances of the case, judges rely on the process of **legal reasoning.** Through the use of legal reasoning, judges harmonize their decisions with those that have been made before, as the doctrine of *stare decisis* requires.

Students of business law and the legal environment also engage in legal reasoning. For example, you may be asked to provide answers for some of the case problems that appear at the end of every chapter in this text. Each problem describes the facts of a particular dispute and the legal question at issue. If you are assigned a case problem, you will be asked to determine how a court would answer that question, and why. In other words, you will need to give legal reasons for whatever conclusion you reach.

We look next at the basic steps involved in legal reasoning and then describe some forms of reasoning commonly used by the courts in making their decisions.

BASIC STEPS IN LEGAL REASONING At times, the legal arguments set forth in court opinions are relatively simple and brief. At other times, the arguments are complex and lengthy. Regardless of the length of a legal argument, however, the basic steps of the legal reasoning process remain the same. These steps, which you can also follow when analyzing cases and case problems, form what is commonly referred to as the *IRAC method* of legal reasoning. IRAC is an acronym formed from the first letters of the following words: *Issue, Rule, Application,* and *Conclusion.*

To apply the IRAC method, you would ask the following questions:

1. **Issue**—*What are the key facts and issues?* Suppose that a plaintiff comes before the court claiming *assault* (words or acts that wrongfully and intentionally make another person fearful of immediate physical harm—see Chapter 4). The plaintiff claims that the defendant threatened her while she was sleeping. Although the plaintiff was unaware that she was being threatened, her roommate heard the defendant make the threat.

   The legal issue is whether the defendant's action constitutes the tort (civil wrong) of assault, given that the plaintiff was unaware of that action at the time it occurred.

2. **Rule**—*What rules of law apply to the case?* A rule of law may be a rule stated by the courts in previous decisions, a state or federal statute, or a state or federal administrative agency regulation. In our hypothetical case, the plaintiff **alleges** (claims) that the defendant committed a tort. Therefore, the applicable law is the common law of torts—specifically, tort law governing assault (see Chapter 4). Case precedents involving similar facts and issues thus would be relevant. Often, more than one rule of law will be applicable to a case.

3. **Application**—*How do the rules of law apply to the particular facts and circumstances of this case?* This step is often the most difficult because each case presents a unique set of facts, circumstances, and parties. Although cases may be similar, no two cases are ever identical in all respects. Normally, judges (and lawyers and law students) try to find **cases on point**—previously decided cases that are as similar as possible to the one under consideration. (Because of the difficulty—and importance—of this step in the legal reasoning process, we discuss it in more detail in the next subsection.)

4. **Conclusion**—*What conclusion should be drawn?* This step normally presents few problems. Usually, the conclusion is evident if the previous three steps have been followed carefully.

There Is No One "Right" Answer

Many people believe that there is one "right" answer to every legal question. In most legal controversies, however, there is no single correct result. Good arguments can usually be made to support either side of a legal controversy. Quite often, a case does not involve a "good" person suing a "bad" person. In many cases, both parties have acted in good faith in some measure or in bad faith to some degree.

Additionally, each judge has her or his own personal beliefs and philosophy (see the discussion in the next section), which shape the legal reasoning process, at least to some extent. This means that the outcome of a particular lawsuit before a court cannot be predicted with absolute certainty. Sometimes, even though the law would seem to favor one party's position, judges, through creative legal reasoning, have found ways to rule for the other party to prevent injustice.

Legal reasoning and other aspects of the common law tradition are reviewed in *Concept Summary 1.2* below.

The Common Law Today

Today, the common law derived from judicial decisions continues to be applied throughout the United States. Common law doctrines and principles, how-

---

CONCEPT SUMMARY 1.2
The Common Law Tradition

ASPECT	DESCRIPTION
Origins of the Common Law	The American legal system is based on the common law tradition, which originated in medieval England. Following the conquest of England in 1066 by William the Conqueror, king's courts were established throughout England, and the common law was developed in these courts.
Legal and Equitable Remedies	Remedies at law (money or items of value, such as land) and remedies in equity (including specific performance, injunction, and rescission of a contractual obligation) originated in the early English courts of law and courts of equity, respectively.
Case Precedents and the Doctrine of *Stare Decisis*	In the king's courts, judges attempted to make their decisions consistent with previous decisions, called precedents. This practice gave rise to the doctrine of *stare decisis*. This doctrine, which became a cornerstone of the common law tradition, obligates judges to abide by precedents established in their jurisdictions.
***Stare Decisis* and Legal Reasoning**	Legal reasoning is the reasoning process used by judges in applying the law to the facts and issues of specific cases. Legal reasoning involves becoming familiar with the key facts of a case, identifying the relevant legal rules, applying those rules to the facts, and drawing a conclusion.

ever, govern only areas *not* covered by statutory or administrative law. In a dispute concerning a particular employment practice, for instance, if a statute regulates that practice, the statute will apply rather than the common law doctrine that applied before the statute was enacted.

COURTS INTERPRET STATUTES Even in areas governed by statutory law, though, judge-made law continues to be important because there is a significant interplay between statutory law and the common law. For instance, many statutes essentially codify existing common law rules, and regulations issued by various administrative agencies usually are based, at least in part, on common law principles. Additionally, the courts, in interpreting statutory law, often rely on the common law as a guide to what the legislators intended.

Furthermore, how the courts interpret a particular statute determines how that statute will be applied. If you wanted to learn about the coverage and applicability of a particular statute, for example, you would necessarily have to locate the statute and study it. You would also need to see how the courts in your jurisdiction have interpreted and applied the statute. In other words, you would have to learn what precedents have been established in your jurisdiction with respect to that statute. Often, the applicability of a newly enacted statute does not become clear until a body of case law develops to clarify how, when, and to whom the statute applies.

***RESTATEMENTS OF THE LAW* CLARIFY AND ILLUSTRATE THE COMMON LAW** The American Law Institute (ALI) has published compilations of the common law called *Restatements of the Law,* which generally summarize the common law rules followed by most states. There are *Restatements of the Law* in the areas of contracts, torts, agency, trusts, property, restitution, security, judgments, and conflict of laws. The *Restatements,* like other secondary sources of law, do not in themselves have the force of law, but they are an important source of legal analysis and opinion. Hence, judges often rely on them in making decisions.

Many of the *Restatements* are now in their second, third, or fourth editions. We refer to the *Restatements* frequently in subsequent chapters of this text, indicating in parentheses the edition to which we are referring. For example, we refer to the third edition of the *Restatement of the Law of Contracts* as simply the *Restatement (Third) of Contracts.*

SECTION 4
SCHOOLS OF LEGAL THOUGHT

How judges apply the law to specific cases, including disputes relating to the business world, depends in part on their philosophical approaches to law. Thus, the study of law, or **jurisprudence,** involves learning about different schools of legal thought and how the approaches to law characteristic of each school can affect judicial decision making.

Clearly, a judge's function is not to *make* the laws—that is the function of the legislative branch of government—but to interpret and apply them. From a practical point of view, however, the courts play a significant role in defining the laws enacted by legislative bodies, which tend to be expressed in general terms. Judges thus have some flexibility in interpreting and applying the law. It is because of this flexibility that different courts can, and often do, arrive at different conclusions in cases that involve nearly identical issues, facts, and applicable laws.

The Natural Law School

An age-old question about the nature of law has to do with the finality of a nation's laws at a given point in time. What if a particular law is deemed to be a "bad" law by a substantial number of that nation's citizens? According to the **natural law** theory, a higher or universal law exists that applies to all human beings, and written laws should imitate these inherent principles. If a written law is unjust, then it is not a true (natural) law and need not be obeyed.

The natural law tradition is one of the oldest and most significant schools of jurisprudence. It dates back to the days of the Greek philosopher Aristotle (384–322 B.C.E.), who distinguished between natural law and the laws governing a particular nation. According to Aristotle, natural law applies universally to all humankind.

The notion that people have "natural rights" stems from the natural law tradition. Those who claim that a specific foreign government is depriving certain citizens of their human rights are implicitly appealing to a higher law that has universal applicability. The question of the universality of basic human rights also comes into play in the context of international business operations. ▶ **Example 1.3** U.S. companies that have operations abroad often hire foreign workers as employees. Should the same laws that protect

U.S. employees apply to these foreign employees? This question is rooted implicitly in a concept of universal rights that has its origins in the natural law tradition. ◄

The Positivist School

In contrast to natural law, *positive,* or national, law (the written law of a given society at a particular time) applies only to the citizens of that nation or society. Those who adhere to **legal positivism** believe that there can be no higher law than a nation's positive law.

According to the positivist school, there are no "natural rights." Rather, human rights exist solely because of laws. If the laws are not enforced, anarchy will result. Thus, whether a law is "bad" or "good" is irrelevant. The law is the law and must be obeyed until it is changed—in an orderly manner through a legitimate lawmaking process.

A judge with positivist leanings probably would be more inclined to defer to an existing law than would a judge who adheres to the natural law tradition.

The Historical School

The **historical school** of legal thought emphasizes the evolutionary process of law by concentrating on the origin and history of the legal system. This school looks to the past to discover what the principles of contemporary law should be. The legal doctrines that have withstood the passage of time—those that have worked in the past—are deemed best suited for shaping present laws. Hence, law derives its legitimacy and authority from adhering to the standards that historical development has shown to be workable.

Adherents of the historical school are more likely than those of other schools to strictly follow decisions made in past cases.

Legal Realism

In the 1920s and 1930s, a number of jurists and scholars, known as *legal realists,* rebelled against the historical approach to law. **Legal realism** is based on the idea that law is just one of many institutions in society and that it is shaped by social forces and needs. The law is a human enterprise, and judges should take social and economic realities into account when deciding cases.

Legal realists also believe that the law can never be applied with total uniformity. Given that judges are human beings with unique personalities, value systems, and intellects, different judges will obviously bring different reasoning processes to the same case. Female judges, for instance, might be more inclined than male judges to consider whether a decision might have a negative impact on the employment of women or minorities.

Legal realism strongly influenced the growth of what is sometimes called the **sociological school,** which views law as a tool for promoting justice in society. In the 1960s, for example, the justices of the United States Supreme Court helped advance the civil rights movement by upholding long-neglected laws calling for equal treatment for all Americans, including African Americans and other minorities. Generally, jurists who adhere to this philosophy of law are more likely to depart from past decisions than are jurists who adhere to other schools of legal thought.

Concept Summary 1.3 on the following page reviews the schools of jurisprudential thought.

SECTION 5
CLASSIFICATIONS OF LAW

The law may be broken down according to several classification systems. For example, one classification system divides law into substantive law and procedural law. **Substantive law** consists of all laws that define, describe, regulate, and create legal rights and obligations. **Procedural law** consists of all laws that outline the methods of enforcing the rights established by substantive law.

Note that many statutes contain both substantive and procedural provisions. ► **Example 1.4** A state law that provides employees with the right to *workers' compensation benefits* for on-the-job injuries is a substantive law because it creates legal rights. Procedural laws establish the method by which an employee must notify the employer about an on-the-job injury, prove the injury, and periodically submit additional proof to continue receiving workers' compensation benefits. ◄

Other classification systems divide law into federal law and state law, private law (dealing with relationships between private entities) and public law (addressing the relationship between persons and their governments), and national law and international law. Here we look at still another classification

---

CONCEPT SUMMARY 1.3
Schools of Jurisprudential Thought

SCHOOL OF THOUGHT	DESCRIPTION
Natural Law School	One of the oldest and most significant schools of legal thought. Those who believe in natural law hold that there is a universal law applicable to all human beings.
Positivist School	A school of legal thought centered on the assumption that there is no law higher than the laws created by the government.
Historical School	A school of legal thought that stresses the evolutionary nature of law and looks to doctrines that have withstood the passage of time for guidance in shaping present laws.
Legal Realism	A school of legal thought that advocates a less abstract and more realistic and pragmatic approach to the law and takes into account customary practices and the circumstances surrounding the particular transaction.

---

system, which divides law into civil law and criminal law, as well as at what is meant by the term *cyberlaw*.

Civil Law and Criminal Law

Civil law spells out the rights and duties that exist between persons and between persons and their governments, as well as the relief available when a person's rights are violated. Typically, in a civil case, a private party sues another private party who has failed to comply with a duty (note that the government can also sue a party for a civil law violation). Much of the law that we discuss in this text is civil law. Contract law, for example, covered in Chapters 9 through 14, is civil law. The whole body of tort law (see Chapter 4) is also civil law.

Criminal law, in contrast, is concerned with wrongs committed *against the public as a whole*. Criminal acts are defined and prohibited by local, state, or federal government statutes. Criminal defendants are thus prosecuted by public officials, such as a district attorney (D.A.), on behalf of the state, not by their victims or other private parties. (See Chapter 7 for a further discussion of the distinction between civil law and criminal law.)

Cyberlaw

As mentioned, the use of the Internet to conduct business transactions has led to new types of legal issues. In response, courts have had to adapt traditional laws to situations that are unique to our age.

Additionally, legislatures at both the federal and the state levels have created laws to deal specifically with such issues.

Frequently, people use the term **cyberlaw** to refer to the emerging body of law that governs transactions conducted via the Internet. Cyberlaw is not really a classification of law, nor is it a new *type* of law. Rather, it is an informal term used to refer to both new laws and modifications of traditional laws that relate to the online environment. Throughout this book, you will read how the law in a given area is evolving to govern specific legal issues that arise in the online context. We have also devoted Chapter 6 entirely to Internet law, social media, and privacy.

SECTION 6
HOW TO FIND PRIMARY SOURCES OF LAW

This text includes numerous references, or *citations,* to primary sources of law—federal and state statutes, the U.S. Constitution and state constitutions, regulations issued by administrative agencies, and court cases.

A **citation** identifies the publication in which a legal authority—such as a statute or a court decision or other source—can be found. In this section, we explain how you can use citations to find primary sources of law. Note that in addition to being published in sets of books, as described next, most federal and state laws and case decisions are available online.

Finding Statutory and Administrative Law

When Congress passes laws, they are collected in a publication titled *United States Statutes at Large.* When state legislatures pass laws, they are collected in similar state publications. Most frequently, however, laws are referred to in their codified form—that is, the form in which they appear in the federal and state codes. In these codes, laws are compiled by subject.

UNITED STATES CODE The *United States Code* (U.S.C.) arranges all existing federal laws by broad subject. Each of the fifty subjects is given a title and a title number. For instance, laws relating to commerce and trade are collected in Title 15, "Commerce and Trade." Titles are subdivided by sections.

A citation to the U.S.C. includes both title and section numbers. Thus, a reference to "15 U.S.C. Section 1" means that the statute can be found in Section 1 of Title 15. ("Section" may be designated by the symbol §, and "Sections," by §§.) In addition to the print publication, the federal government provides a searchable online database of the *United States Code* at **www.gpo.gov** (click on "Libraries" and then "Core Documents of Our Democracy" to find the U.S.C.).

Commercial publications of federal laws and regulations are also available. For instance, Legal Solutions from Thomson Reuters (formerly West Group) publishes the *United States Code Annotated* (U.S.C.A.). The U.S.C.A. contains the official text of the U.S.C., plus notes (annotations) on court decisions that interpret and apply specific sections of the statutes. The U.S.C.A. also includes additional research aids, such as cross-references to related statutes, historical notes, and library references. A citation to the U.S.C.A. is similar to a citation to the U.S.C.: "15 U.S.C.A. Section 1."

STATE CODES State codes follow the U.S.C. pattern of arranging law by subject. They may be called codes, revisions, compilations, consolidations, general statutes, or statutes, depending on the preferences of the states.

In some codes, subjects are designated by number. In others, they are designated by name. ▶ **Example 1.5** "13 Pennsylvania Consolidated Statutes Section 1101" means that the statute can be found in Title 13, Section 1101, of the Pennsylvania code. "California Commercial Code Section 1101" means that the statute can be found under the subject heading "Commercial Code" of the California code in Section 1101. Abbreviations are often used. For example, "13 Pennsylvania Consolidated Statutes Section 1101" is abbreviated "13 Pa. C.S. § 1101," and "California Commercial Code Section 1101" is abbreviated "Cal. Com. Code § 1101." ◀

ADMINISTRATIVE RULES Rules and regulations adopted by federal administrative agencies are initially published in the *Federal Register,* a daily publication of the U.S. government. Later, they are incorporated into the *Code of Federal Regulations* (C.F.R.).

Like the U.S.C., the C.F.R. is divided into fifty titles. Rules within each title are assigned section numbers. A full citation to the C.F.R. includes title and section numbers. ▶ **Example 1.6** A reference to "17 C.F.R. Section 230.504" means that the rule can be found in Section 230.504 of Title 17. ◀

Finding Case Law

Before discussing the case reporting system, we need to look briefly at the court system (which will be discussed in detail in Chapter 3). There are two types of courts in the United States, federal courts and state courts.

Both the federal and the state court systems consist of several levels, or tiers, of courts. *Trial courts,* in which evidence is presented and testimony given, are on the bottom tier (which also includes lower courts that handle specialized issues). Decisions from a trial court can be appealed to a higher court, which commonly is an intermediate *court of appeals,* or *appellate court.* Decisions from these intermediate courts of appeals may be appealed to an even higher court, such as a state supreme court or the United States Supreme Court.

STATE COURT DECISIONS Most state trial court decisions are not published in books (except in New York and a few other states, which publish selected trial court opinions). Decisions from state trial courts are typically filed in the office of the clerk of the court, where the decisions are available for public inspection. (Increasingly, they can be found online as well.)

Written decisions of the appellate, or reviewing, courts, however, are published and distributed (in print and online). As you will note, most of the state court cases presented in this textbook are from state appellate courts. The reported appellate decisions are published in volumes called *reports* or *reporters,* which are numbered consecutively. State appellate court decisions are found in the state reporters of that particular state. Official reports are published by the state, whereas unofficial reports are published by nongovernment entities.

Regional Reporters. State court opinions appear in regional units of the National Reporter System, published by West Group (now Thomson Reuters). Most lawyers and libraries have these reporters because they report cases more quickly and are distributed more widely than the state-published reporters. In fact, many states have eliminated their own reporters in favor of the National Reporter System.

The National Reporter System divides the states into the following geographic areas: *Atlantic* (A., A.2d, or A.3d), *North Eastern* (N.E. or N.E.2d), *North Western* (N.W. or N.W.2d), *Pacific* (P., P.2d, or P.3d), *South Eastern* (S.E. or S.E.2d), *South Western* (S.W., S.W.2d, or S.W.3d), and *Southern* (So., So.2d, or So.3d). (The *2d* and *3d* in the preceding abbreviations refer to *Second Series* and *Third Series,* respectively.) The states included in each of these regional divisions are indicated in Exhibit 1–4 on the following page, which illustrates the National Reporter System.

Case Citations. After appellate decisions have been published, they are normally referred to (cited) by the name of the case; the volume, name, and page number of the state's official reporter (if different from the National Reporter System); the volume, name, and page number of the National Reporter; and the volume, name, and page number of any other selected reporter. (Citing a reporter by volume number, name, and page number, in that order, is common to all citations. The year that the decision was issued is often included at the end in parentheses.) When more than one reporter is cited for the same case, each reference is called a *parallel citation.*

Note that some states have adopted a "public domain citation system" that uses a somewhat different format for the citation. For example, in Wisconsin, a Wisconsin Supreme Court decision might be designated "2013 WI 40," meaning that the case was decided in the year 2013 by the Wisconsin Supreme Court and was the fortieth decision issued by that court during that year. Parallel citations to the *Wisconsin Reports* and the *North Western Reporter* are still included after the public domain citation.

▶ **Example 1.7** Consider the following case citation: *Colbert v. Carr,* 140 Conn.App. 229, 57 A.3d. 878 (2013). We see that the opinion in this case can be found in Volume 140 of the official *Connecticut Appellate Court Reports,* on page 229. The parallel citation is to Volume 57 of the *Atlantic Reporter, Third Series,* page 878. ◀

When we present opinions in this text (starting in Chapter 3), in addition to the reporter, we give the name of the court hearing the case and the year of the court's decision. Sample citations to state court decisions are explained in Exhibit 1–5 on pages 17–18.

FEDERAL COURT DECISIONS Federal district (trial) court decisions are published unofficially in the *Federal Supplement* (F.Supp. or F.Supp.2d), and opinions from the circuit courts of appeals (reviewing courts) are reported unofficially in the *Federal Reporter* (F., F.2d, or F.3d). Cases concerning federal bankruptcy law are published unofficially in the *Bankruptcy Reporter* (Bankr. or B.R.).

The official edition of the United States Supreme Court decisions is the *United States Reports* (U.S.), which is published by the federal government. Unofficial editions of Supreme Court cases include the *Supreme Court Reporter* (S.Ct.) and the *Lawyers' Edition of the Supreme Court Reports* (L.Ed. or L.Ed.2d). Sample citations for federal court decisions are also listed and explained in Exhibit 1–5 on pages 17–19.

UNPUBLISHED OPINIONS Many court opinions that are not yet published or that are not intended for publication can be accessed through Westlaw® (abbreviated in citations as "WL"), an online legal database maintained by Thomson Reuters (formerly West Group). When no citation to a published reporter is available for cases cited in this text, we give the WL citation (see Exhibit 1–5 on page 19 for an example).

OLD CASE LAW On a few occasions, this text cites opinions from old, classic cases dating to the nineteenth century or earlier. Some of these are from the English courts. The citations to these cases may not conform to the descriptions just presented because the reporters in which they were originally published were often known by the names of the persons who compiled the reporters.

SECTION 7
HOW TO READ AND UNDERSTAND CASE LAW

The decisions made by the courts establish the boundaries of the law as it applies to almost all business relationships. It thus is essential that businesspersons know how to read and understand case law.

EXHIBIT 1-4 National Reporter System—Regional/Federal

Regional Reporters	Coverage Beginning	Coverage
Atlantic Reporter (A., A.2d, or A.3d)	1885	Connecticut, Delaware, District of Columbia, Maine, Maryland, New Hampshire, New Jersey, Pennsylvania, Rhode Island, and Vermont.
North Eastern Reporter (N.E. or N.E.2d)	1885	Illinois, Indiana, Massachusetts, New York, and Ohio.
North Western Reporter (N.W. or N.W.2d)	1879	Iowa, Michigan, Minnesota, Nebraska, North Dakota, South Dakota, and Wisconsin.
Pacific Reporter (P., P.2d, or P.3d)	1883	Alaska, Arizona, California, Colorado, Hawaii, Idaho, Kansas, Montana, Nevada, New Mexico, Oklahoma, Oregon, Utah, Washington, and Wyoming.
South Eastern Reporter (S.E. or S.E.2d)	1887	Georgia, North Carolina, South Carolina, Virginia, and West Virginia.
South Western Reporter (S.W., S.W.2d, or S.W.3d)	1886	Arkansas, Kentucky, Missouri, Tennessee, and Texas.
Southern Reporter (So., So.2d, or So.3d)	1887	Alabama, Florida, Louisiana, and Mississippi.
Federal Reporters		
Federal Reporter (F., F.2d, or F.3d)	1880	U.S. Circuit Courts from 1880 to 1912; U.S. Commerce Court from 1911 to 1913; U.S. District Courts from 1880 to 1932; U.S. Court of Claims (now called U.S. Court of Federal Claims) from 1929 to 1932 and since 1960; U.S. Courts of Appeals since 1891; U.S. Court of Customs and Patent Appeals since 1929; U.S. Emergency Court of Appeals since 1943.
Federal Supplement (F.Supp. or F.Supp.2d)	1932	U.S. Court of Claims from 1932 to 1960; U.S. District Courts since 1932; U.S. Customs Court since 1956.
Federal Rules Decisions (F.R.D.)	1939	U.S. District Courts involving the Federal Rules of Civil Procedure since 1939 and Federal Rules of Criminal Procedure since 1946.
Supreme Court Reporter (S.Ct.)	1882	United States Supreme Court since the October term of 1882.
Bankruptcy Reporter (Bankr.)	1980	Bankruptcy decisions of U.S. Bankruptcy Courts, U.S. District Courts, U.S. Courts of Appeals, and the United States Supreme Court.
Military Justice Reporter (M.J.)	1978	U.S. Court of Military Appeals and Courts of Military Review for the Army, Navy, Air Force, and Coast Guard.

NATIONAL REPORTER SYSTEM MAP

□ Pacific
□ North Western
□ South Western
■ North Eastern
□ Atlantic
□ South Eastern
■ Southern

EXHIBIT 1-5 How to Read Citations

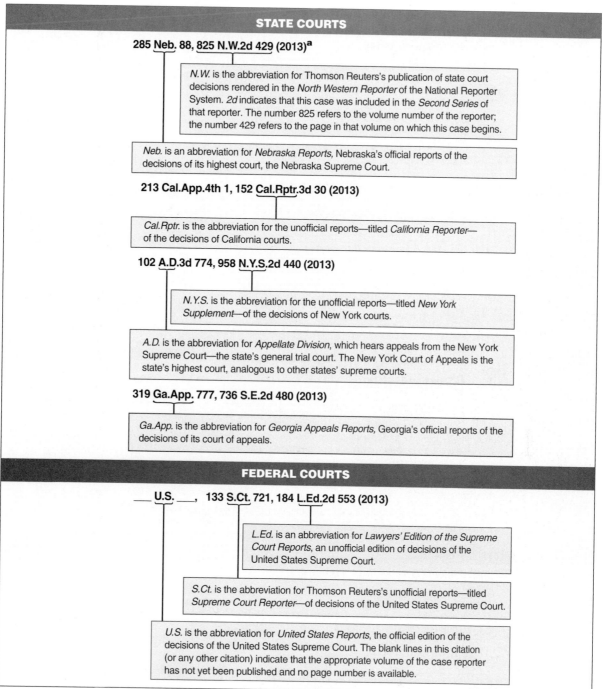

STATE COURTS

285 Neb. 88, 825 N.W.2d 429 (2013)[a]

N.W. is the abbreviation for Thomson Reuters's publication of state court decisions rendered in the *North Western Reporter* of the National Reporter System. *2d* indicates that this case was included in the *Second Series* of that reporter. The number 825 refers to the volume number of the reporter; the number 429 refers to the page in that volume on which this case begins.

Neb. is an abbreviation for *Nebraska Reports,* Nebraska's official reports of the decisions of its highest court, the Nebraska Supreme Court.

213 Cal.App.4th 1, 152 Cal.Rptr.3d 30 (2013)

Cal.Rptr. is the abbreviation for the unofficial reports—titled *California Reporter*—of the decisions of California courts.

102 A.D.3d 774, 958 N.Y.S.2d 440 (2013)

N.Y.S. is the abbreviation for the unofficial reports—titled *New York Supplement*—of the decisions of New York courts.

A.D. is the abbreviation for *Appellate Division,* which hears appeals from the New York Supreme Court—the state's general trial court. The New York Court of Appeals is the state's highest court, analogous to other states' supreme courts.

319 Ga.App. 777, 736 S.E.2d 480 (2013)

Ga.App. is the abbreviation for *Georgia Appeals Reports,* Georgia's official reports of the decisions of its court of appeals.

FEDERAL COURTS

___ U.S. ___, 133 S.Ct. 721, 184 L.Ed.2d 553 (2013)

L.Ed. is an abbreviation for *Lawyers' Edition of the Supreme Court Reports,* an unofficial edition of decisions of the United States Supreme Court.

S.Ct. is the abbreviation for Thomson Reuters's unofficial reports—titled *Supreme Court Reporter*—of decisions of the United States Supreme Court.

U.S. is the abbreviation for *United States Reports,* the official edition of the decisions of the United States Supreme Court. The blank lines in this citation (or any other citation) indicate that the appropriate volume of the case reporter has not yet been published and no page number is available.

a. The case names have been deleted from these citations to emphasize the publications. It should be kept in mind, however, that the name of a case is as important as the specific page numbers in the volumes in which it is found. If a citation is incorrect, the correct citation may be found in a publication's index of case names. In addition to providing a check on errors in citations, the date of a case is important because the value of a recent case as an authority is likely to be greater than that of older cases from the same court.

Continued

EXHIBIT 1–5 How to Read Citations—Continued

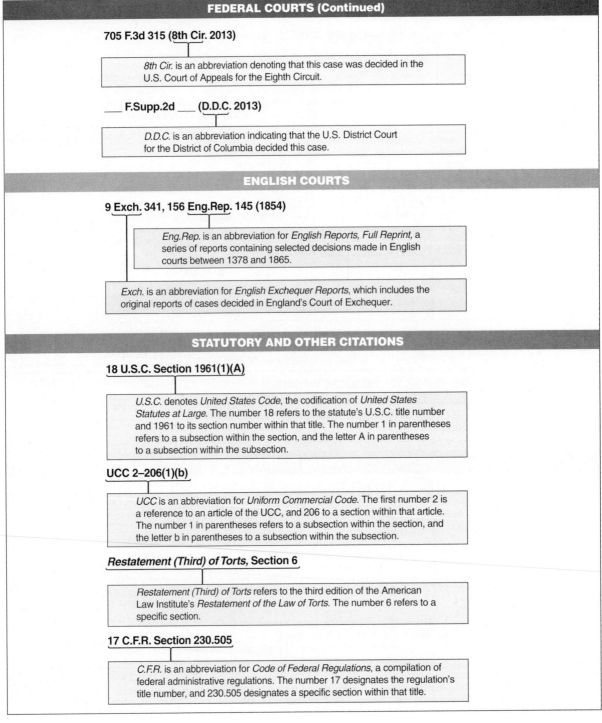

FEDERAL COURTS (Continued)

705 F.3d 315 (8th Cir. 2013)

8th Cir. is an abbreviation denoting that this case was decided in the U.S. Court of Appeals for the Eighth Circuit.

___ F.Supp.2d ___ (D.D.C. 2013)

D.D.C. is an abbreviation indicating that the U.S. District Court for the District of Columbia decided this case.

ENGLISH COURTS

9 Exch. 341, 156 Eng.Rep. 145 (1854)

Eng.Rep. is an abbreviation for *English Reports, Full Reprint,* a series of reports containing selected decisions made in English courts between 1378 and 1865.

Exch. is an abbreviation for *English Exchequer Reports*, which includes the original reports of cases decided in England's Court of Exchequer.

STATUTORY AND OTHER CITATIONS

18 U.S.C. Section 1961(1)(A)

U.S.C. denotes *United States Code*, the codification of *United States Statutes at Large*. The number 18 refers to the statute's U.S.C. title number and 1961 to its section number within that title. The number 1 in parentheses refers to a subsection within the section, and the letter A in parentheses to a subsection within the subsection.

UCC 2–206(1)(b)

UCC is an abbreviation for *Uniform Commercial Code*. The first number 2 is a reference to an article of the UCC, and 206 to a section within that article. The number 1 in parentheses refers to a subsection within the section, and the letter b in parentheses to a subsection within the subsection.

***Restatement (Third) of Torts,* Section 6**

Restatement (Third) of Torts refers to the third edition of the American Law Institute's *Restatement of the Law of Torts*. The number 6 refers to a specific section.

17 C.F.R. Section 230.505

C.F.R. is an abbreviation for *Code of Federal Regulations*, a compilation of federal administrative regulations. The number 17 designates the regulation's title number, and 230.505 designates a specific section within that title.

EXHIBIT 1–5 How to Read Citations—Continued

WESTLAW® CITATIONS[b]

2013 WL 285688

WL is an abbreviation for Westlaw. The number 2013 is the year of the document that can be found with this citation in the Westlaw database. The number 285688 is a number assigned to a specific document. A higher number indicates that a document was added to the Westlaw database later in the year.

UNIFORM RESOURCE LOCATORS (URLs)

web2.westlaw.com[c]

The suffix *com* is the top-level domain (TLD) for this Web site. The TLD *com* is an abbreviation for "commercial," which usually means that a for-profit entity hosts (maintains or supports) this Web site.

westlaw is the host name—the part of the domain name selected by the organization that registered the name. In this case, West Group (now Thomson Reuters) registered the name. This Internet site is the Westlaw database on the Web.

web2 describes Web sites that use software allowing users to interact and collaborate with each other in a social media dialogue, rather than limiting users to the passive viewing of static content.

http://www.uscourts.gov

This is "The Federal Judiciary Home Page." The host is the Administrative Office of the U.S. Courts. The TLD *gov* is an abbreviation for "government." This Web site includes information and links from, and about, the federal courts.

www is an abbreviation for "World Wide Web." The Web is a system of Internet servers that support documents formatted in *HTML* (hypertext markup language) and other formats as well.

http://www.law.cornell.edu/index.html

This part of a URL points to a Web page or file at a specific location within the host's domain. This page is a menu with links to documents within the domain and to other Internet resources.

This is the host name for a Web site that contains the Internet publications of the Legal Information Institute (LII), which is a part of Cornell Law School. The LII site includes a variety of legal materials and links to other legal resources on the Internet. The TLD *edu* is an abbreviation for "educational institution" (a school or a university).

http://www.ipl.org/div/news

This part of the Web site points to a static *news* page at this Web site, which provides links to online newspapers from around the world.

ipl is an abbreviation for "Internet Public Library," which is an online service that provides reference resources and links to other information services on the Web. The IPL is supported chiefly by the School of Information at the University of Michigan. The TLD *org* is an abbreviation for "organization" (normally nonprofit).

div is an abbreviation for "division," which is the way that the Internet Public Library tags the content on its Web site as relating to a specific topic.

b. Many court decisions that are not yet published or that are not intended for publication can be accessed through Westlaw, an online legal database.

c. The basic form for a URL is "service://hostname/path." The Internet service for all of the URLs in this text is *http* (hypertext transfer protocol). Because most Web browsers add this prefix automatically when a user enters a host name or a hostname/path, we have generally omitted the *http://* from the URLs listed in this text.

The cases that we present in this text have been condensed from the full text of the courts' opinions and are presented in a special format. In approximately two-thirds of the cases (including the cases designated as *Classic* and *Spotlight*), we have summarized the background and facts, as well as the court's decision and remedy, in our own words. In those cases, we have included only selected portions of the court's opinion ("in the language of the court"). In the remaining one-third of the cases (labeled "Case Analysis Cases"), we have provided a longer excerpt from the court's opinion without summarizing the background and facts or decision and remedy.

The following sections will provide useful insights into how to read and understand case law.

Case Titles and Terminology

The title of a case, such as *Adams v. Jones,* indicates the names of the parties to the lawsuit. The *v.* in the case title stands for *versus,* which means "against." In the trial court, Adams was the plaintiff—the person who filed the suit. Jones was the defendant. If the case is appealed, however, the appellate court will sometimes place the name of the party appealing the decision first, so the case may be called *Jones v. Adams* if Jones is appealing.

Because some appellate courts retain the trial court order of names, it is often impossible to distinguish the plaintiff from the defendant in the title of a reported appellate court decision. You must carefully read the facts of each case to identify the parties. Otherwise, the discussion by the appellate court may be difficult to understand.

The following terms, phrases, and abbreviations are frequently encountered in court opinions and legal publications.

PARTIES TO LAWSUITS As mentioned previously, the party initiating a lawsuit is referred to as the *plaintiff* or *petitioner,* depending on the nature of the action. The party against whom a lawsuit is brought is the *defendant* or *respondent.* Lawsuits frequently involve more than one plaintiff and/or defendant.

When a case is appealed from the original court or jurisdiction to another court or jurisdiction, the party appealing the case is called the **appellant.** The **appellee** is the party against whom the appeal is taken. (In some appellate courts, the party appealing a case is referred to as the petitioner, and the party against whom the suit is brought or appealed is called the respondent.)

JUDGES AND JUSTICES The terms *judge* and *justice* are usually synonymous and represent two designations given to judges in various courts. All members of the United States Supreme Court, for instance, are referred to as justices, and justice is the formal title often given to judges of appellate courts, although this is not always the case. In New York, a *justice* is a judge of the trial court (called the Supreme Court), and a member of the Court of Appeals (the state's highest court) is called a *judge.*

The term *justice* is commonly abbreviated to J., and *justices,* to JJ. A United States Supreme Court case might refer to Justice Sotomayor as Sotomayor, J., or to Chief Justice Roberts as Roberts, C.J.

DECISIONS AND OPINIONS Most decisions reached by reviewing, or appellate, courts are explained in written **opinions.** The opinion contains the court's reasons for its decision, the rules of law that apply, and the judgment. You may encounter several types of opinions as you read appellate cases, including the following:

- When all the judges (or justices) agree, a *unanimous opinion* is written for the entire court.
- When there is not unanimous agreement, a **majority opinion** is generally written. It outlines the views of the majority of the judges deciding the case.
- A judge who agrees (concurs) with the majority opinion as to the result but not as to the legal reasoning often writes a **concurring opinion.** In it, the judge sets out the reasoning that he or she considers correct.
- A **dissenting opinion** presents the views of one or more judges who disagree with the majority view.
- Sometimes, no single position is fully supported by a majority of the judges deciding a case. In this situation, we may have a **plurality opinion.** This is the opinion that has the support of the largest number of judges, but the group in agreement is less than a majority.
- Finally, a court occasionally issues a ***per curiam* opinion** (*per curiam* is Latin for "of the court"), which does not indicate which judge wrote the opinion.

A Sample Court Case

To illustrate the various elements contained in a court opinion, we present an annotated court opinion in Exhibit 1–6 starting on page 22. The opinion is from an actual case decided by a federal trial court located in California.

Background of the Case. In 2011, Amazon.com launched an Appstore for viewing and downloading applications to Android devices, such as the Kindle Fire. Apple products (iPads, iPhones, iPods) use the term APP STORE. In this case, Apple claims that Amazon's use of the name "Appstore" constitutes false advertising and trademark infringement (discussed in Chapter 5). The issue before the court here is whether Amazon's use of "Appstore" might mislead the public into thinking that Amazon's Appstore is affiliated with Apple and offers the same content.

Editorial Practice. You will note that triple asterisks (* * *) and quadruple asterisks (* * * *) frequently appear in the opinion. The triple asterisks indicate that we have deleted a few words or sentences from the opinion for the sake of readability or brevity. Quadruple asterisks mean that an entire paragraph (or more) has been omitted.

Additionally, when the opinion cites another case or legal source, the citation to the case or source has been omitted to save space and to improve the flow of the text. These editorial practices are continued in the other court opinions presented in this book. In addition, whenever we present a court opinion that includes a term or phrase that may not be readily understandable, a bracketed definition or paraphrase has been added.

Briefing Cases. Knowing how to read and understand court opinions and the legal reasoning used by the courts is an essential step in undertaking accurate legal research. A further step is "briefing," or summarizing, the case.

Legal researchers routinely brief cases by reducing the texts of the opinions to their essential elements. Generally, when you brief a case, you first summarize the background and facts of the case, as the authors have done for the cases presented in this text. You then indicate the issue (or issues) before the court. An important element in the case brief is, of course, the court's decision on the issue and the legal reasoning used by the court in reaching that decision.

THE SAMPLE COURT CASE STARTS ON THE FOLLOWING PAGE.

EXHIBIT 1-6 A Sample Court Case

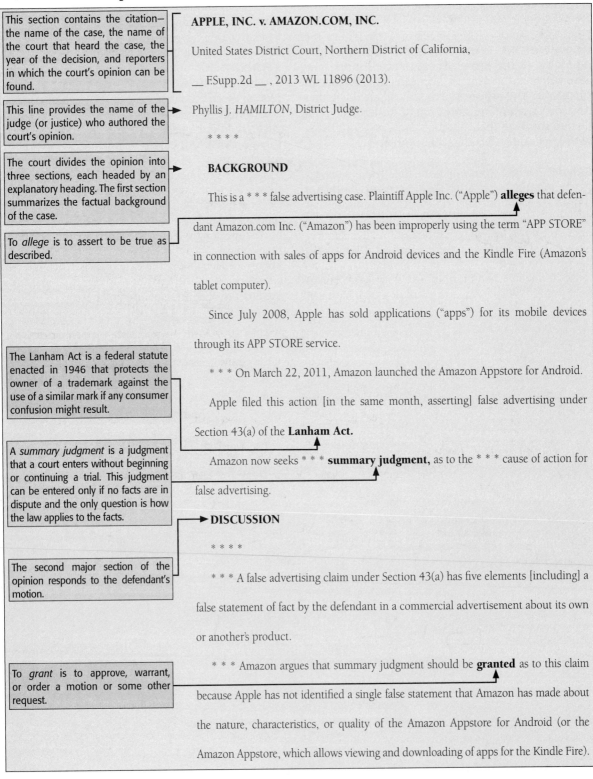

This section contains the citation— the name of the case, the name of the court that heard the case, the year of the decision, and reporters in which the court's opinion can be found.	**APPLE, INC. v. AMAZON.COM, INC.** United States District Court, Northern District of California, __ F.Supp.2d __ , 2013 WL 11896 (2013).
This line provides the name of the judge (or justice) who authored the court's opinion.	Phyllis J. *HAMILTON*, District Judge. * * * *
The court divides the opinion into three sections, each headed by an explanatory heading. The first section summarizes the factual background of the case.	**BACKGROUND** This is a * * * false advertising case. Plaintiff Apple Inc. ("Apple") **alleges** that defen-
To *allege* is to assert to be true as described.	dant Amazon.com Inc. ("Amazon") has been improperly using the term "APP STORE" in connection with sales of apps for Android devices and the Kindle Fire (Amazon's tablet computer). Since July 2008, Apple has sold applications ("apps") for its mobile devices through its APP STORE service.
The Lanham Act is a federal statute enacted in 1946 that protects the owner of a trademark against the use of a similar mark if any consumer confusion might result.	* * * On March 22, 2011, Amazon launched the Amazon Appstore for Android. Apple filed this action [in the same month, asserting] false advertising under Section 43(a) of the **Lanham Act.**
A *summary judgment* is a judgment that a court enters without beginning or continuing a trial. This judgment can be entered only if no facts are in dispute and the only question is how the law applies to the facts.	Amazon now seeks * * * **summary judgment,** as to the * * * cause of action for false advertising.
	DISCUSSION * * * *
The second major section of the opinion responds to the defendant's motion.	* * * A false advertising claim under Section 43(a) has five elements [including] a false statement of fact by the defendant in a commercial advertisement about its own or another's product.
To *grant* is to approve, warrant, or order a motion or some other request.	* * * Amazon argues that summary judgment should be **granted** as to this claim because Apple has not identified a single false statement that Amazon has made about the nature, characteristics, or quality of the Amazon Appstore for Android (or the Amazon Appstore, which allows viewing and downloading of apps for the Kindle Fire).

EXHIBIT 1-6 A Sample Court Case—Continued

Apple essentially alleges that by using the word "Appstore" in the name of Amazon's store, Amazon implies that its store is affiliated with or sponsored by Apple.

* * * *

Apple argues that * * * Amazon's service ("Appstore") does not possess the characteristics and qualities that the public has come to expect from the name APP STORE, based on their familiarity with Apple's service. For this reason, Apple argues, Amazon's use of "Appstore" misleads the public—in particular because (according to Apple) it "implies a false **equivalence** without cuing consumers to test this claim." Apple contends that because its APP STORE offers so many more apps than Amazon's Appstore, consumers will be misled into thinking that Amazon's Appstore will offer just as many.

An *equivalence* is a characteristic or quality corresponding in effect or function, or nearly equal or virtually identical, to another.

* * * The court finds no support for the proposition that Amazon has expressly or impliedly communicated that its Appstore for Android possesses the characteristics and qualities that the public has come to expect from the Apple APP STORE and/or Apple products.

That is, Apple has failed to establish that Amazon made any false statement (express or implied) of fact that actually deceived or had the tendency to deceive a substantial segment of its audience. The mere use of "Appstore" by Amazon to designate a site for viewing and downloading/purchasing apps cannot be **construed** as a representation that the nature, characteristics, or quality of the Amazon Appstore is the same as that of the Apple APP STORE. Apple has pointed to no advertisement by Amazon that qualifies as a false statement under Section 43(a) of the Lanham Act. Nor is there **sufficient evidence** to raise a **triable** issue.

To *construe* is to interpret or explain the sense of something according to judicial standards.

Sufficient evidence is evidence that is sufficient to satisfy an unprejudiced mind seeking the truth.

A *triable* issue is an issue that is subject to judicial examination and trial.

* * * If an advertisement is not false on its face (i.e., if there is no express or explicit false statement), the plaintiff must produce evidence, usually in the form of market research or consumer surveys, showing exactly what message was conveyed that was sufficient to constitute false advertising. Here, Apple has presented no evidence that

Continued

EXHIBIT 1–6 A Sample Court Case—Continued

consumers or customers understand "app store" to include specific qualities or characteristics or **attributes** of the Apple APP STORE, or that any customers were misled by Amazon's use of the term.

> In this context, *attribute* refers to the elements or properties of the App Store that are closely associated with Apple.

Apple asserts that its APP STORE offers many more apps than Amazon's does, and that the apps are **"seamlessly integrated"** with all Apple devices. However, there is no evidence that a consumer who accesses the Amazon Appstore would expect that it would be identical to the Apple APP STORE, particularly given that the Apple APP STORE sells apps solely for Apple devices, while the Amazon Appstore sells apps solely for Android and Kindle devices. Further, the integration of Apple devices has more to do with Apple's technology than it does with the nature, characteristics, or qualities of the APP STORE.

> Here, *seamlessly integrated* means coordinated to operate without any awkward transitions or interruptions.

Apple fails to make clear how [Amazon's use of Appstore] constitutes a "statement" that implies something false about the nature, characteristics, or qualities of Apple's APP STORE, because it has made no **showing** that such (implied) statement deceived or had a tendency to deceive users of Amazon's Appstore.

> *Showing* is the act of establishing through evidence and argument.

> In the third major section of the opinion, the court states its decision.

CONCLUSION

* * * Amazon's motion for summary judgment as to the * * * cause of action for false advertising is GRANTED.

Reviewing: Law and Legal Reasoning

Suppose that the California legislature passes a law that severely restricts carbon dioxide emissions from automobiles in that state. A group of automobile manufacturers files suit against the state of California to prevent the enforcement of the law. The automakers claim that a federal law already sets fuel economy standards nationwide and that fuel economy standards are essentially the same as carbon dioxide emission standards. According to the automobile manufacturers, it is unfair to allow California to impose more stringent regulations than those set by the federal law. Using the information presented in the chapter, answer the following questions.

1. Who are the parties (the plaintiffs and the defendant) in this lawsuit?
2. Are the plaintiffs seeking a legal remedy or an equitable remedy?
3. What is the primary source of the law that is at issue here?
4. Where would you look to find the relevant California and federal laws?

DEBATE THIS . . . *Under the doctrine of* stare decisis, *courts are obligated to follow the precedents established in their jurisdiction unless there is a compelling reason not to. Should U.S. courts continue to adhere to this common law principle, given that our government now regulates so many areas by statute?*

Terms and Concepts

administrative agency 5
administrative law 5
allege 10
appellant 20
appellee 20
binding authority 8
breach 7
case law 5
case on point 10
chancellor 6
citation 13
civil law 13
common law 6
concurring opinion 20
constitutional law 4
court of equity 6
court of law 6
criminal law 13
cyberlaw 13

damages 6
defendant 7
defense 7
dissenting opinion 20
equitable maxims 7
executive agency 5
historical school 12
independent regulatory agency 5
jurisprudence 11
laches 7
law 2
legal positivism 12
legal realism 12
legal reasoning 9
majority opinion 20
natural law 11
opinion 20
ordinance 4
persuasive authorities 9

per curiam opinion 20
petitioner 7
plaintiff 7
plurality opinion 20
precedent 8
procedural law 12
public policy 9
remedy 6
remedy at law 6
remedy in equity 6
reporter 8
respondent 7
sociological school 12
stare decisis 8
statute of limitations 7
statutory law 4
substantive law 12
uniform law 5

ExamPrep

Issue Spotters

1. Under what circumstances might a judge rely on case law to determine the intent and purpose of a statute? **(See page 5.)**

2. After World War II, several Nazis were convicted of "crimes against humanity" by an international court. Assuming that these convicted war criminals had not disobeyed any law of their country and had merely been following their government's orders, what law had they violated? Explain. **(See page 11.)**

• Check your answers to the Issue Spotters against the answers provided in Appendix B at the end of this text.

Before the Test

Go to **www.cengagebrain.com**, enter the ISBN 9781285770192, and click on "Find" to locate this textbook's Web site. Then, click on "Access Now" under "Study Tools," and select Chapter 1 at the top. There, you will find a Practice Quiz that you can take to assess your mastery of the concepts in this chapter, as well as Flashcards and a Glossary of important terms.

Business Scenarios

1–1. Binding versus Persuasive Authority. A county court in Illinois is deciding a case involving an issue that has never been addressed before in that state's courts. The Iowa Supreme Court, however, recently decided a case involving a very similar fact pattern. Is the Illinois court obligated to follow the Iowa Supreme Court's decision on the issue? If the United States Supreme Court had decided a similar case, would that decision be binding on the Illinois court? Explain. **(See page 8.)**

1–2. Sources of Law. This chapter discussed a number of sources of American law. Which source of law takes priority in the following situations, and why? **(See page 3.)**

(a) A federal statute conflicts with the U.S. Constitution.

(b) A federal statute conflicts with a state constitutional provision.

(c) A state statute conflicts with the common law of that state.

(d) A state constitutional amendment conflicts with the U.S. Constitution.

1–3. *Stare Decisis.* In the text of this chapter, we stated that the doctrine of *stare decisis* "became a cornerstone of the English and American judicial systems." What does *stare decisis* mean, and why has this doctrine been so funda-

mental to the development of our legal tradition? **(See page 8.)**

1–4. Remedies. Assume that Arthur Rabe is suing Xavier Sanchez for breaching a contract in which Sanchez promised to sell Rabe a painting by Vincent Van Gogh for $30 million. **(See page 6.)**

(a) In this lawsuit, who is the plaintiff and who is the defendant?

(b) Suppose that Rabe wants Sanchez to perform the contract as promised. What remedy would Rabe seek from the court?

(c) Now suppose that Rabe wants to cancel the contract because Sanchez fraudulently misrepresented the painting as an original Van Gogh when in fact it is a copy. What remedy would Rabe seek?

(d) Will the remedy Rabe seeks in either situation be a remedy at law or a remedy in equity? What is the difference between legal and equitable remedies?

(e) Suppose that the trial court finds in Rabe's favor and grants one of these remedies. Sanchez then appeals the decision to a higher court. On appeal, which party will be the appellant (or petitioner), and which party will be the appellee (or respondent)?

Business Case Problems

1–5. Spotlight on AOL—Common Law. AOL, LLC, mistakenly made public the personal information of 650,000 of its members. The members filed a suit, alleging violations of California law. AOL asked the court to dismiss the suit on the basis of a "forum-selection" clause in its member agreement that designates Virginia courts as the place where mem-

ber disputes will be tried. Under a decision of the United States Supreme Court, a forum-selection clause is unenforceable "if enforcement would contravene a strong public policy of the forum in which suit is brought." California courts have declared in other cases that the AOL clause contravenes a strong public policy. If the court applies the doctrine of *stare decisis,* will it dismiss the suit?

Explain. [*Doe 1 v. AOL LLC,* 552 F.3d 1077 (9th Cir. 2009)] **(See page 6.)**

1–6. BUSINESS CASE PROBLEM
WITH SAMPLE ANSWER—Reading Citations.

Assume that you want to read the entire court opinion in the case of United States v. Yi, *704 F.3d 800 (9th Cir. 2013). Refer to the subsection entitled "Finding Case Law" in this chapter, and then explain specifically where you would find the court's opinion.* **(See page 14.)**

• **For a sample answer to Problem 1–6, go to Appendix C at the end of this text.**

1–7. A QUESTION OF ETHICS—The Common Law Tradition.

On July 5, 1884, Dudley, Stephens, and Brooks—"all able-bodied English seamen"—and a teenage English boy were cast adrift in a lifeboat following a storm at sea. They had no water with them in the boat, and all they had for sustenance were two one-pound tins of turnips. On July 24, Dudley proposed that one of the four in the lifeboat be sacrificed to save the others. Stephens agreed with Dudley, but Brooks refused to consent—and the boy was never asked for his opinion. On July 25, Dudley killed the boy, and the three men then fed on the boy's body and blood. Four days later, a passing vessel rescued the men. They were taken to England and tried for the murder of the boy. If the men had not fed on the boy's body, they would probably have died of starvation within the four-day period. The boy, who was in a much weaker condition, would likely have died before the rest. [Regina v. Dudley and Stephens, *14 Q.B.D. (Queen's Bench Division, England) 273 (1884)]* **(See page 6.)**

(a) The basic question in this case is whether the survivors should be subject to penalties under English criminal law, given the men's unusual circumstances. Were the defendants' actions necessary but unethical? Explain your reasoning. What ethical issues might be involved here?

(b) Should judges ever have the power to look beyond the written "letter of the law" in making their decisions? Why or why not?

Legal Reasoning Group Activity

1–8. Court Opinions. Read through the subsection in this chapter entitled "Decisions and Opinions." **(See page 20.)**

(a) One group will explain the difference between a concurring opinion and a majority opinion.

(b) Another group will outline the difference between a concurring opinion and a dissenting opinion.

(c) A third group will explain why judges and justices write concurring and dissenting opinions, given that these opinions will not affect the outcome of the case at hand, which has already been decided by majority vote.

CHAPTER 2

BUSINESS AND THE CONSTITUTION

Laws that govern business have their origin in the lawmaking authority granted by the U.S. Constitution, which is the supreme law in this country. As mentioned in Chapter 1, neither Congress nor any state may pass a law that is in conflict with the Constitution.

Constitutional disputes frequently come before the courts. For instance, numerous states challenged the Obama administration's Affordable Care Act on constitutional grounds. The United States Supreme Court decided in 2012 that the provisions of this law, which require most Americans to have health insurance by 2014, did not exceed the constitutional authority of the federal government. The Court's decision in the matter continues to have a significant impact on the business environment.

In this chapter, we examine some basic constitutional concepts and clauses and their significance for businesspersons. We then look at certain freedoms guaranteed by the first ten amendments to the Constitution—the Bill of Rights—and discuss how these freedoms affect business activities.

SECTION 1
THE CONSTITUTIONAL POWERS OF GOVERNMENT

Following the Revolutionary War, the states adopted the Articles of Confederation. The Articles created a *confederal form of government* in which the states had the authority to govern themselves and the national government could exercise only limited powers. When problems arose because the nation was facing an economic crisis and state laws interfered with the free flow of commerce, a national convention was called, and the delegates drafted the U.S. Constitution. This document, after its ratification by the states in 1789, became the basis for an entirely new form of government.

A Federal Form of Government

The new government created by the U.S. Constitution reflected a series of compromises made by the convention delegates on various issues. Some delegates wanted sovereign power to remain with the states. Others wanted the national government alone to exercise sovereign power. The end result was a compromise—a **federal form of government** in which the national government and the states *share* sovereign power.

FEDERAL POWERS The Constitution sets forth specific powers that can be exercised by the national government. It further provides that the national government has the implied power to undertake actions necessary to carry out its expressly designated powers (or *enumerated powers*). All other powers are expressly "reserved" to the states under the Tenth Amendment to the U.S. Constitution.

REGULATORY POWERS OF THE STATES As part of their inherent **sovereignty** (independence), state governments have the authority to regulate affairs within their borders. As mentioned, this authority stems, in part, from the Tenth Amendment, which reserves all powers not delegated to the national government to the states or to the people.

State regulatory powers are often referred to as **police powers.** The term encompasses more than just the enforcement of criminal laws. Police powers also give state governments broad rights to regulate private activities to protect or promote the public order, health, safety, morals, and general welfare. Fire and building codes, antidiscrimination laws, parking regulations, zoning restrictions, licensing requirements, and thousands of other state statutes have been enacted pursuant to states' police powers.

Local governments, including cities, also exercise police powers.[1] Generally, state laws enacted pursuant to a state's police powers carry a strong presumption of validity.

Relations Among the States

The U.S. Constitution also includes provisions concerning relations among the states in our federal system. Particularly important are the *privileges and immunities clause* and the *full faith and credit clause*.

THE PRIVILEGES AND IMMUNITIES CLAUSE Article IV, Section 2, of the Constitution provides that the "Citizens of each State shall be entitled to all Privileges and Immunities of Citizens in the several States." This clause is often referred to as the interstate **privileges and immunities clause.**[2] It prevents a state from imposing unreasonable burdens on citizens of another state—particularly with regard to means of livelihood or doing business.

When a citizen of one state engages in basic and essential activities in another state (the "foreign state"), the foreign state must have a *substantial reason* for treating the nonresident differently from its own residents. Basic activities include transferring property, seeking employment, or accessing the court system. The foreign state must also establish that its reason for the discrimination is *substantially related* to the state's ultimate purpose in adopting the legislation or regulating the activity.[3]

THE FULL FAITH AND CREDIT CLAUSE Article IV, Section 1, of the U.S. Constitution provides that "Full Faith and Credit shall be given in each State to the public Acts, Records, and judicial Proceedings of every other State." This clause, which is referred to as the **full faith and credit clause,** applies only to civil matters. It ensures that rights established under deeds, wills, contracts, and similar instruments in one state will be honored by other states.

It also ensures that any judicial decision with respect to such property rights will be honored and enforced in all states.

▶ **Example 2.1** The legal issues raised by same-sex marriage involve, among other things, the full faith and credit clause because that clause requires each state to honor marriage decrees issued by another state. Therefore, if same-sex partners marry in Washington, which legalized same-sex marriage in 2012, and the couple later moves to another state, that state would be required to recognize the validity of their marriage. ◀

The full faith and credit clause has contributed to the unity of American citizens because it protects their legal rights as they move about from state to state. It also protects the rights of those to whom they owe obligations, such as a person who is awarded monetary damages by a court. The ability to enforce such rights is extremely important for the conduct of business in a country with a very mobile citizenry.

The Separation of Powers

To make it difficult for the national government to use its power arbitrarily, the Constitution provided for three branches of government. The legislative branch makes the laws, the executive branch enforces the laws, and the judicial branch interprets the laws. Each branch performs a separate function, and no branch may exercise the authority of another branch.

Additionally, a system of **checks and balances** allows each branch to limit the actions of the other two branches, thus preventing any one branch from exercising too much power. Some examples of these checks and balances include the following:

1. The legislative branch (Congress) can enact a law, but the executive branch (the president) has the constitutional authority to veto that law.
2. The executive branch is responsible for foreign affairs, but treaties with foreign governments require the advice and consent of the Senate.
3. Congress determines the jurisdiction of the federal courts, and the president appoints federal judges, with the advice and consent of the Senate. The judicial branch has the power to hold actions of the other two branches unconstitutional.[4]

---

1. Local governments derive their authority to regulate their communities from the state, because they are creatures of the state. In other words, they cannot come into existence unless authorized by the state to do so.
2. Interpretations of this clause commonly use the terms *privilege* and *immunity* synonymously. Generally, the terms refer to certain rights, benefits, or advantages enjoyed by individuals.
3. This test was first announced in *Supreme Court of New Hampshire v. Piper,* 470 U.S. 274, 105 S.Ct. 1272, 84 L.Ed.2d 205 (1985). For another example, see *Lee v. Miner,* 369 F.Supp.2d 527 (D.Del. 2005).

4. As will be discussed in Chapter 3, the power of judicial review was established by the United States Supreme Court in *Marbury v. Madison,* 5 U.S. (1 Cranch) 137, 2 L.Ed. 60 (1803).

The Commerce Clause

To prevent states from establishing laws and regulations that would interfere with trade and commerce among the states, the Constitution expressly delegated to the national government the power to regulate interstate commerce. Article I, Section 8, of the U.S. Constitution explicitly permits Congress "[t]o regulate Commerce with foreign Nations, and among the several States, and with the Indian Tribes." This clause, referred to as the **commerce clause,** has had a greater impact on business than any other provision in the Constitution. The commerce clause provides the basis for the national government's extensive regulation of state and even local affairs.

Initially, the courts interpreted the commerce clause to apply only to commerce between the states (*interstate* commerce) and not commerce within the states (*intrastate* commerce). In 1824, however, the United States Supreme Court decided the landmark case of *Gibbons v. Ogden.*[5] The Court held that commerce within the states could also be regulated by the national government as long as the commerce *substantially affected* commerce involving more than one state.

THE EXPANSION OF NATIONAL POWERS UNDER THE COMMERCE CLAUSE As the nation grew and faced new kinds of problems, the commerce clause became a vehicle for the additional expansion of the national government's regulatory powers. Even activities that seemed purely local in nature came under the regulatory reach of the national government if those activities were deemed to substantially affect interstate commerce. In 1942, the Supreme Court held that wheat production by an individual farmer intended wholly for consumption on his own farm was subject to federal regulation.[6]

▶ **Case in Point 2.2** In *Heart of Atlanta Motel v. United States,*[7] a landmark case decided in 1964, the Supreme Court upheld the federal government's authority under the commerce clause to prohibit racial discrimination nationwide in public facilities. The case was brought by an Atlanta motel owner who refused to rent rooms to African Americans, in violation of the Civil Rights Act of 1964. The Court concluded that local motels and restaurants do affect interstate commerce. The Court stated that "if it is interstate commerce that feels the pinch, it does

not matter how local the operation that applies the squeeze." ◀

THE COMMERCE CLAUSE TODAY Today, at least theoretically, the power over commerce authorizes the national government to regulate almost every commercial enterprise in the United States. The breadth of the commerce clause permits the national government to legislate in areas in which Congress has not explicitly been granted power.

In the last twenty years, the Supreme Court has on occasion curbed the national government's regulatory authority under the commerce clause. In 1995, the Court held—for the first time in sixty years—that Congress had exceeded its regulatory authority under the commerce clause. The Court struck down an act that banned the possession of guns within one thousand feet of any school because the act attempted to regulate an area that had "nothing to do with commerce."[8] Subsequently, the Court invalidated key portions of two other federal acts on the ground that they exceeded Congress's commerce clause authority.[9]

MEDICAL MARIJUANA AND THE COMMERCE CLAUSE In one notable case, however, the Supreme Court did allow the federal government to regulate noncommercial activities taking place wholly within a state's borders. ▶ **Case in Point 2.3** More than a dozen states, including California, have adopted laws that legalize marijuana for medical purposes. Marijuana possession, however, is illegal under the federal Controlled Substances Act (CSA).[10] After the federal government seized the marijuana that two seriously ill California women were using on the advice of their physicians, the women filed a lawsuit. They argued that it was unconstitutional for the federal statute to prohibit them from using marijuana for medical purposes that were legal within the state.

The Supreme Court, though, held that Congress has the authority to prohibit the *intrastate* possession and noncommercial cultivation of marijuana as part of a larger regulatory scheme (the CSA).[11] In other

---

5. 22 U.S. (9 Wheat.) 1, 6 L.Ed. 23 (1824).

6. *Wickard v. Filburn,* 317 U.S. 111, 63 S.Ct. 82, 87 L.Ed. 122 (1942).

7. 379 U.S. 241, 85 S.Ct. 348, 13 L.Ed.2d 258 (1964).

8. The Court held the Gun-Free School Zones Act of 1990 to be unconstitutional in *United States v. Lopez,* 514 U.S. 549, 115 S.Ct. 1624, 131 L.Ed.2d 626 (1995).

9. *Printz v. United States,* 521 U.S. 898, 117 S.Ct. 2365, 138 L.Ed.2d 914 (1997), involving the Brady Handgun Violence Prevention Act of 1993; and *United States v. Morrison,* 529 U.S. 598, 120 S.Ct. 1740, 146 L.Ed.2d 658 (2000), concerning the federal Violence Against Women Act of 1994.

10. 21 U.S.C. Sections 801 *et seq.*

11. *Gonzales v. Raich,* 545 U.S. 1, 125 S.Ct. 2195, 162 L.Ed.2d 1 (2005).

words, state medical marijuana laws do not insulate the users from federal prosecution. ◄

THE "DORMANT" COMMERCE CLAUSE The Supreme Court has interpreted the commerce clause to mean that the national government has the *exclusive* authority to regulate commerce that substantially affects trade and commerce among the states. This express grant of authority to the national government is often referred to as the "positive" aspect of the commerce clause. But this positive aspect also implies a negative aspect—that the states do *not* have the authority to regulate interstate commerce. This negative aspect of the commerce clause is often referred to as the "dormant" (implied) commerce clause.

The dormant commerce clause comes into play when state regulations affect interstate commerce. In this situation, the courts weigh the state's interest in regulating a certain matter against the burden that the state's regulation places on interstate commerce. Because courts balance the interests involved, it is difficult to predict the outcome in a particular case.

In the following case, the plaintiffs—a group of California wineries and others—contended that a Massachusetts statute discriminated against out-of-state wineries in violation of the dormant commerce clause. A federal district court agreed and enjoined (prevented) the enforcement of the statute. The commonwealth of Massachusetts appealed the trial court's decision.

CASE ANALYSIS

Case 2.1   Family Winemakers of California v. Jenkins[a]

United States Court of Appeals, First Circuit, 592 F.3d 1 (2010).

IN THE LANGUAGE OF THE COURT
LYNCH, Chief Judge.

* * * *

The ratification of the Twenty-first Amendment ended Prohibition[b] and gave states substantial control over the regulation of alcoholic beverages. Most states, including Massachusetts, then imposed a three-tier system to control the sale of alcoholic beverages within their territories. The hallmark of the three-tier system is a rigid, tightly regulated separation between producers, wholesalers, and retailers of alcoholic beverages. Producers can ordinarily sell alcoholic beverages only to licensed in-state wholesalers. Wholesalers then must obtain licenses to sell to retailers. Retailers, which

include stores, taverns, restaurants, and bars, must in turn obtain licenses to sell to consumers or to serve alcohol on their premises. Recently, as to wine, Massachusetts has adjusted the separation between these three tiers * * * .

* * * *

Wineries have heralded direct shipping as a supplemental avenue of distribution because of its economic advantages, especially for wineries that do not rank among the fifty to one hundred largest producers. Direct shipping lets consumers directly order wines from the winery, with access to their full range of wines, not just those a wholesaler is willing to distribute. Direct shipping also avoids added steps in the distribution chain, eliminating wholesaler and retailer price markups.

Before 2005, Massachusetts's * * * winery licensing law * * * allowed only in-state wineries to obtain licenses to combine distribution methods through wholesalers, retailers, and direct shipping to consumers. [After the United States Supreme Court] invalidated similar facially

discriminatory state laws, [the 2005 Massachusetts law] was held to be invalid under the Commerce Clause.

In 2006, the Massachusetts legislature enacted [a new law regulating wineries, which] does not distinguish on its face between in-state and out-of-state wineries' eligibility for direct shipping licenses, but instead distinguishes between "small" or "large" wineries through [a] 30,000 gallon cap.

* * * *

* * * All wineries producing over 30,000 gallons of wine—all of which are located outside Massachusetts—can apply for a "large winery shipment license[.]" * * * "Large" wineries can either choose to remain completely within the three-tier system and distribute their wines solely through wholesalers, or they can completely opt out of the three-tier system and sell their wines in Massachusetts exclusively through direct shipping [to consumers]. They cannot do both. * * * By contrast, "small" wineries can simultaneously use the traditional

CASE 2.1 CONTINUES ➧

---

a. The case was brought against Eddie J. Jenkins, the chair of the Massachusetts Alcoholic Beverages Control Commission, in his official capacity.

b. The Eighteenth Amendment to the U.S. Constitution, adopted in 1919, prohibited the sale of alcoholic beverages, giving rise to the so-called Prohibition Era. The Twenty-first Amendment, ratified in 1933, repealed the Eighteenth Amendment.

wholesaler distribution method, direct distribution to retailers, and direct shipping to reach consumers.

* * * *

* * * *Discrimination under the Commerce Clause* "means differential treatment of in-state and out-of-state economic interests that benefits the former and burdens the latter," as opposed to state laws that "regulate * * * evenhandedly with only incidental effects on interstate commerce[.]"* [Emphasis added.]

* * * Plaintiffs argue that Massachusetts's choice of 30,000 gallons as the demarcation [separation] point between "small" and "large" wineries, along with [a] production exception for fruit wine, has both a discriminatory effect and [a] purpose. The discriminatory effect is because [the law's] definition of "large" wineries encompasses the wineries which produce 98 percent of all wine in the United States, all of which are located out-of-state and all of which are deprived of the benefits of combining distribution methods. All wines produced in Massachusetts, on the other hand, are from "small" wineries that can use multiple distribution methods. Plaintiffs also say that [the law]

is discriminatory in purpose because the gallonage cap's particular features, along with legislators' statements and [the law's] process of enactment, show that [the law's] true purpose was to ensure that Massachusetts's wineries obtained advantages over their out-of-state counterparts.

* * * *

* * * State laws that alter conditions of competition to favor in-state interests over out-of-state competitors in a market have long been subject to invalidation.

* * * Here, the totality of the evidence introduced by plaintiffs demonstrates that [the law's] preferential treatment of "small" wineries that produce 30,000 gallons or less of grape wine is discriminatory. Its effect is to significantly alter the terms of competition between in-state and out-of-state wineries to the detriment of the out-of-state wineries that produce 98 percent of the country's wine.

[The 2006 law] confers a clear competitive advantage to "small" wineries, which include all Massachusetts's wineries, and creates a comparative disadvantage for "large" wineries, none of which are

in Massachusetts. "Small" wineries that obtain a * * * license can use direct shipping to consumers, retailer distribution, and wholesaler distribution simultaneously. Combining these distribution methods allows "small" wineries to sell their full range of wines at maximum efficiency because they serve complementary markets. "Small" wineries that produce higher-volume wines can continue distributing those wines through wholesaler relationships. They can obtain new markets for all their wines by distributing their wines directly to retailers, including individual bars, restaurants, and stores. They can also use direct shipping to offer their full range of wines directly to Massachusetts consumers, resulting in greater overall sales.

* * * *

We conclude that [the 2006 law] altered the competitive balance to favor Massachusetts's wineries and disfavor out-of-state competition by design.

* * * *

We *affirm* the judgment of the district court.

LEGAL REASONING QUESTIONS

1. The court held that the Massachusetts statute discriminated against out-of-state wineries "by design" (intentionally). How can a court determine legislative intent?

2. Suppose that most "small" wineries, as defined by the 2006 Massachusetts law, were located out of state. How could the law be discriminatory in that situation?

3. Suppose that the state had only required the out-of-state wineries to obtain a special license that was readily available. Would this have affected the outcome of the case? Explain.

4. When it is difficult to predict how the law might be applied—as in cases arising under the dormant commerce clause—what is the best course of conduct for a business?

The Supremacy Clause and Federal Preemption

Article VI of the U.S. Constitution, commonly referred to as the **supremacy clause,** provides that the Constitution, laws, and treaties of the United States are "the supreme Law of the Land." When there is a

direct conflict between a federal law and a state law, the state law is rendered invalid. Because some powers are *concurrent* (shared by the federal government and the states), however, it is necessary to determine which law governs in a particular circumstance.

When Congress chooses to act (legislate) exclusively in an area in which the federal government and the states have concurrent powers, **preemption** occurs. A valid federal statute or regulation will take precedence over a conflicting state or local law or regulation on the same general subject.

FEDERAL STATUTES MAY SPECIFY PREEMPTION Sometimes, the federal statute will include a preemption provision to make it clear that Congress intends the legislation to preempt any state laws on the matter. ▶ **Case in Point 2.4** A man who alleged that he had been injured by a faulty medical device (a balloon catheter that was inserted into his artery following a heart attack) sued the manufacturer.

The case ultimately came before the United States Supreme Court, which noted that the Medical Device Amendments of 1976 had included a preemption provision. The medical device had passed the U.S. Food and Drug Administration's rigorous premarket approval process. Therefore, the Court concluded that the federal regulation of medical devices preempted the injured party's state common law claims for negligence, strict liability, and implied warranty.[12] ◀

WHEN THE STATUTE DOES NOT EXPRESSLY MENTION PREEMPTION Often, it is not clear whether Congress, in passing a law, intended to preempt an entire subject area against state regulation. In those situations, the courts determine whether Congress intended to exercise exclusive power over a given area.

No single factor is decisive as to whether a court will find preemption. Generally, congressional intent to preempt will be found if a federal law regulating an activity is so pervasive, comprehensive, or detailed that the states have no room to regulate in that area. Also, when a federal statute creates an agency—such as the National Labor Relations Board—to enforce the law, matters that come within the agency's jurisdiction will likely preempt state laws.

The Taxing and Spending Powers

Article I, Section 8, of the U.S. Constitution provides that Congress has the "Power to lay and collect Taxes, Duties, Imposts, and Excises." Section 8 further requires uniformity in taxation among the states, and thus Congress may not tax some states while exempting others.

In the distant past, if Congress attempted to regulate indirectly, by taxation, an area over which it had

no authority, the courts would invalidate the tax. Today, however, if a tax measure is reasonable, it generally is held to be within the national taxing power. Moreover, the expansive interpretation of the commerce clause almost always provides a basis for sustaining a federal tax.

Article I, Section 8, also gives Congress its spending power—the power "to pay the Debts and provide for the common Defence and general Welfare of the United States." Congress can spend revenues not only to carry out its expressed powers but also to promote any objective it deems worthwhile, so long as it does not violate the Bill of Rights. The spending power necessarily involves policy choices, with which taxpayers (and politicians) may disagree.

SECTION 2

BUSINESS AND THE BILL OF RIGHTS

The importance of a written declaration of the rights of individuals caused the first Congress of the United States to submit twelve amendments to the U.S. Constitution to the states for approval. Ten of these amendments, known as the **Bill of Rights,** were adopted in 1791 and embody a series of protections for the individual against various types of interference by the federal government.[13]

The protections guaranteed by these ten amendments are summarized in Exhibit 2–1 on the following page. Some of these constitutional protections apply to business entities as well. For example, corporations exist as separate legal entities, or *legal persons,* and enjoy many of the same rights and privileges as *natural persons* do.

Limits on Federal and State Governmental Actions

As originally intended, the Bill of Rights limited only the powers of the national government. Over time, however, the United States Supreme Court "incorporated" most of these rights into the protections against state actions afforded by the Fourteenth Amendment to the Constitution.

---

12. *Riegel v. Medtronic, Inc.,* 552 U.S. 312, 128 S.Ct. 999, 169 L.Ed.2d 892 (2008).

13. Another of these proposed amendments was ratified more than two hundred years later (in 1992) and became the Twenty-seventh Amendment to the Constitution.

EXHIBIT 2–1 Protections Guaranteed by the Bill of Rights

First Amendment: Guarantees the freedoms of religion, speech, and the press and the rights to assemble peaceably and to petition the government.

Second Amendment: States that the right of the people to keep and bear arms shall not be infringed.

Third Amendment: Prohibits, in peacetime, the lodging of soldiers in any house without the owner's consent.

Fourth Amendment: Prohibits unreasonable searches and seizures of persons or property.

Fifth Amendment: Guarantees the rights to indictment by grand jury, to due process of law, and to fair payment when private property is taken for public use; prohibits compulsory self-incrimination and double jeopardy (being tried again for an alleged crime for which one has already stood trial).

Sixth Amendment: Guarantees the accused in a criminal case the right to a speedy and public trial by an impartial jury and with counsel. The accused has the right to cross-examine witnesses against him or her and to solicit testimony from witnesses in his or her favor.

Seventh Amendment: Guarantees the right to a trial by jury in a civil case involving at least twenty dollars.[a]

Eighth Amendment: Prohibits excessive bail and fines, as well as cruel and unusual punishment.

Ninth Amendment: Establishes that the people have rights in addition to those specified in the Constitution.

Tenth Amendment: Establishes that those powers neither delegated to the federal government nor denied to the states are reserved to the states and to the people.

a. Twenty dollars was forty days' pay for the average person when the Bill of Rights was written.

THE FOURTEENTH AMENDMENT The Fourteenth Amendment, passed in 1868 after the Civil War, provides, in part, that "[n]o State shall . . . deprive any person of life, liberty, or property, without due process of law." Starting in 1925, the Supreme Court began to define various rights and liberties guaranteed in the U.S. Constitution as constituting "due process of law," which was required of state governments under that amendment.

Today, most of the rights and liberties set forth in the Bill of Rights apply to state governments as well as the national government. In other words, neither the federal government nor state governments can deprive persons of those rights and liberties.

JUDICIAL INTERPRETATION The rights secured by the Bill of Rights are not absolute. Many of the rights guaranteed by the first ten amendments are set forth in very general terms. The Second Amendment states that people have a right to keep and bear arms, but it does not explain the extent of this right. As the Supreme Court noted in 2008, this does not mean that people can "keep and carry any weapon whatsoever in any manner whatsoever and for whatever purpose."[14] Legislatures can prohibit the carrying of concealed weapons or certain types of weapons, such as machine guns.

Ultimately, it is the United States Supreme Court, as the final interpreter of the Constitution, that gives meaning to these rights and determines their boundaries. Changing public views on controversial topics, such as privacy in an era of terrorist threats or the rights of gay men and lesbians, may affect the way the Supreme Court decides a case. On several occasions, justices on the Supreme Court have even mentioned that they have considered foreign laws in reaching a decision.

Freedom of Speech

A democratic form of government cannot survive unless people can freely voice their political opinions and criticize government actions or policies. Freedom of speech, particularly political speech, is thus a prized right, and traditionally the courts have protected this right to the fullest extent possible.

Symbolic speech—gestures, movements, articles of clothing, and other forms of expressive conduct— is also given substantial protection by the courts. The Supreme Court has held that the burning of the American flag as part of a peaceful protest is a constitutionally protected form of expression.[15] Similarly, wearing a T-shirt with a photo of a presidential candidate is a constitutionally protected form of expression. ▶ **Example 2.5** As a form of expression, Nate

---

14. *District of Columbia v. Heller,* 554 U.S. 570, 128 S.Ct. 2783, 171 L.Ed.2d 637 (2008).

15. *Texas v. Johnson,* 491 U.S. 397, 109 S.Ct. 2533, 105 L.Ed.2d 342 (1989).

has gang signs tattooed on his torso, arms, neck, and legs. If a reasonable person would interpret this conduct as conveying a message, then it might be a protected form of symbolic speech. ◄

An interesting topic in today's legal environment is whether computers should have free speech rights.

For a discussion of this issue, see this chapter's *Insight into E-Commerce* feature below.

REASONABLE RESTRICTIONS Expression—oral, written, or symbolized by conduct—is subject to reasonable restrictions. A balance must be struck between

INSIGHT INTO E-COMMERCE
Do Computers Have Free Speech Rights?

When you do a Web search using Bing, Google, or any other search engine, the program inherent in the engine gives you a list of results. When you use a document-creation program, such as Microsoft Word, it often guesses what you intend and corrects your misspellings automatically. Do computers that make such choices engage in "speech," and if so, do they enjoy First Amendment protection? This question is not as absurd as it may seem at first.

Are Google's Search Results "Speech"?

More than a decade ago, a company dissatisfied with its rankings in Google's search results sued. Google argued that its search results were constitutionally protected speech. The plaintiff, Search King, Inc., sought an injunction against Google, but a federal district court decided in Google's favor. The court ruled that the ranking of results when a search is undertaken "constitutes opinions protected by the First Amendment.... *Page Ranks* are opinions—opinions are the significance of particular Web sites as they correspond to a search query." Therefore, the First Amendment applied to the search results.[a]

Google versus the Federal Trade Commission

For the last few years, Google has been the dominant search engine. Yet in the 1990s, the federal government was worried that Microsoft's search engine was too dominant and was crushing the search engines of Yahoo!, AltaVista, and Lycos. Today, of course, AltaVista and Lycos no longer exist, and Microsoft's new search engine, Bing, is a relatively minor player in the field.

Fast-forward to 2011. The Federal Trade Commission (FTC) contemplated bringing charges against Google for favoring its own offerings, such as restaurant reviews, in its search results. Now it was Microsoft that was encouraging the FTC to proceed. After a nineteen-month investiga-

tion, in early 2013 the FTC announced that it would *not* prosecute Google. The FTC's decision was a blow to search engines that compete with Google, including Microsoft's Bing.

The First Amendment Protection Argument

Google commissioned Eugene Volokh and Donald Falk, two legal experts in this field, to research the issue of whether search engine results are protected by the First Amendment.[b] The researchers concluded that search engine results are the same as the editorial judgments that a newspaper makes in deciding which wire service stories to run and which op-ed and business columnists to feature. The authors further claim that free speech applies to editorial choices no matter what their format. Search engines are protected even when they are "unfair" in ranking search results. Whether the search engine uses a computerized algorithm to compile its rankings is irrelevant.

Columbia Law professor Tim Wu disagrees. He argues that the First Amendment was intended to protect humans against the evils of state censorship and that protecting a computer's speech is not related to that purpose. At best, he says, search engine results are *commercial speech,* which has always received limited protection under the First Amendment. After all, computers make trillions of invisible decisions each day. Is each of those decisions protected speech?

LEGAL CRITICAL THINKING
INSIGHT INTO SOCIAL MEDIA

Facebook has numerous computers, all programmed by humans, of course. If Facebook's computers make decisions that allow your private information to be shared without your knowledge, should the First Amendment protect Facebook? Why or why not?

---

a. *Search King, Inc. v. Google Technology, Inc.,* 2003 WL 21464568 (W.D.Okla. 2003). See also *Langdon v. Google, Inc.,* 474 F.Supp.2d 622 (D.Del. 2007).

b. Eugene Volokh and Donald Falk, "First Amendment Protection for Search Engine Search Results: White Paper Commissioned by Google" (UCLA School of Law Research Paper No. 12-22, April 20, 2012).

a government's obligation to protect its citizens and those citizens' exercise of their rights. Reasonableness is analyzed on a case-by-case basis.

Content-Neutral Laws. Laws that regulate the time, manner, and place, but not the content, of speech receive less scrutiny by the courts than do laws that restrict the content of expression. If a restriction imposed by the government is content neutral, then a court may allow it. To be content neutral, the restriction must be aimed at combatting some societal problem, such as crime or drug abuse, and not be aimed at suppressing the expressive conduct or its message. Courts have often protected nude dancing as a form of symbolic expression but typically allow content-neutral laws that ban all public nudity.

▶ **Case in Point 2.6** Ria Ora was charged with dancing nude at an annual "anti-Christmas" protest in Harvard Square in Cambridge, Massachusetts, under a statute banning public displays of open and gross lewdness. Ora argued that the statute was overbroad and unconstitutional, and a trial court agreed. On appeal, however, a state appellate court upheld the statute as constitutional in situations in which there was an unsuspecting or unwilling audience.[16] ◀

Laws That Restrict the Content of Speech. If a law regulates the content of the expression, it must serve a

compelling state interest and must be narrowly written to achieve that interest. Under the **compelling government interest** test, the government's interest is balanced against the individual's constitutional right to free expression. For the statute to be valid, there must be a compelling government interest that can be furthered only by the law in question.

The United States Supreme Court has held that schools may restrict students' speech at school events. ▶ **Case in Point 2.7** Some high school students held up a banner saying "Bong Hits 4 Jesus" at an off-campus but school-sanctioned event. The Supreme Court ruled that the school did not violate the students' free speech rights when school officials confiscated the banner and suspended the students for ten days. Because the banner could reasonably be interpreted as promoting drugs, the Court concluded that the school's actions were justified. Several justices disagreed, however, noting that the majority's holding creates an exception that will allow schools to censor any student speech that mentions drugs.[17] ◀

At issue in the following case was an Indiana state law that barred most sex offenders from using social networking sites such as Facebook, instant messaging services such as Twitter, and chat programs that the offenders knew were accessible to minors. Was this law unconstitutional under the First Amendment?

---

16. *Commonwealth v. Ora*, 451 Mass. 125, 883 N.E.2d 1217 (2008).

17. *Morse v. Frederick*, 551 U.S. 393, 127 S.Ct. 2618, 168 L.Ed.2d 290 (2007).

CASE 2.2

Doe[a] v. Prosecutor, Marion County, Indiana
United States Court of Appeals, Seventh Circuit, 705 F.3d 694 (2013).

BACKGROUND AND FACTS John Doe was convicted of child exploitation in Marion County, Indiana. After his release from prison, he was not subject to court supervision, but was required to register as a sex offender with the state. Under an Indiana statute that covered child exploitation and other sex offenses, Doe could not use certain Web sites and programs. Doe filed a suit in a federal district court against the Marion County prosecutor, alleging that the statute violated his right to freedom of speech under the First Amendment. Doe asked the court to issue an injunction to block enforcement of the law. The court held that "the regulation is narrowly tailored to serve a significant state interest" and entered a judgment for the defendant. Doe appealed to the U.S. Court of Appeals for the Seventh Circuit.

 IN THE LANGUAGE OF THE COURT
FLAUM, Circuit Judge.

* * * *

Indiana Code Section 35-42-4-12 prohibits certain sex offenders from "knowingly or intentionally using: a social networking Web site" or "an instant messaging or chat room program"

---

a. The names *John Doe* and *Jane Doe* are used as placeholders in litigation to represent a party whose true identity is either unknown or being with held for some reason.

CASE 2.2 CONTINUED that "the offender knows allows a person who is less than eighteen (18) years of age to access or use the Web site or program." The law applies broadly to all individuals required to register as sex offenders.

* * * *

This case presents a single legal question * * * . The statute clearly implicates Doe's First Amendment rights * * * . It not only precludes [prohibits] expression through the medium of social media, it also limits his right to receive information and ideas. The Indiana law, however, is content neutral because it restricts speech without reference to the expression's content. As such, it may impose reasonable time, place, or manner restrictions. To do so, the law * * * must be narrowly tailored to serve a significant governmental interest.

The state initially asserts an interest in "protecting public safety, and specifically in protecting minors from harmful online communications." Indiana is certainly justified in shielding its children from improper sexual communication.

* * * *

* * * The state agrees there is nothing dangerous about Doe's use of social media as long as he does not improperly communicate with minors. Further, there is no disagreement that illicit communication comprises a minuscule subset of the universe of social network activity. As such, *the Indiana law targets substantially more activity than the evil it seeks to redress.* * * * *Indiana has other methods to combat unwanted and inappropriate communication between minors and sex offenders.* For instance, [under Indiana Code Section 35-42-4-6] it is a felony in Indiana for persons over twenty-one to "solicit" children under sixteen "to engage in: (1) sexual intercourse; (2) deviate sexual conduct; or (3) any fondling intended to arouse or satisfy the sexual desires of either the child or the older person." A separate statute goes further. [Indiana Code Section 35-42-4-13] punishes mere "inappropriate communication with a child" and communication "with the intent to gratify the sexual desires of the person or the individual." Significantly, both statutes have enhanced penalties for using a computer network and better advance Indiana's interest in preventing harmful interaction with children (by going beyond social networks). They also accomplish that end more narrowly (by refusing to burden benign Internet activity). That is, they are neither over nor under-inclusive like the statute at issue here. [Emphasis added.]

* * * *

For the foregoing reasons, we REVERSE the district court's decision, and REMAND with instructions to enter judgment in favor of Doe and issue the injunction.

DECISION AND REMEDY *The U.S. Court of Appeals for the Seventh Circuit reversed the lower court's judgment in the defendant's favor and remanded the case for the entry of a judgment for Doe. A law that concerns rights under the First Amendment must be narrowly tailored to accomplish its objective. The blanket ban on social media in this case did not pass this test.*

THE LEGAL ENVIRONMENT DIMENSION *What is an injunction? What did the plaintiff in this case hope to gain by seeking an injunction?*

THE SOCIAL DIMENSION *Could a state effectively enforce a law that banned all communication between minors and sex offenders through social media sites? Why or why not?*

CORPORATE POLITICAL SPEECH Political speech by corporations also falls within the protection of the First Amendment. Many years ago, the United States Supreme Court struck down as unconstitutional a Massachusetts statute that prohibited corporations from making political contributions or expenditures that individuals were permitted to make.[18] The Court has also held that a law forbidding a corporation from including inserts with its bills to express its views on controversial issues violates the First Amendment.[19]

Corporate political speech continues to be given significant protection under the First Amendment. ▶ **Case in Point 2.8** In *Citizens United v. Federal*

---

18. *First National Bank of Boston v. Bellotti,* 435 U.S. 765, 98 S.Ct. 1407, 55 L.Ed.2d 707 (1978).

19. *Consolidated Edison Co. v. Public Service Commission,* 447 U.S. 530, 100 S.Ct. 2326, 65 L.Ed.2d 319 (1980).

Election Commission,[20] the Supreme Court issued a landmark decision that overturned a twenty-year-old precedent on campaign financing. The case involved Citizens United, a nonprofit corporation that has a *political action committee* (an organization that registers with the government and campaigns for or against political candidates).

Citizens United had produced a film called *Hillary: The Movie* that was critical of Hillary Clinton, who was seeking the Democratic nomination for presidential candidate. Campaign-finance law restricted Citizens United from broadcasting the movie, however. The Court ruled that the restrictions were unconstitutional and that the First Amendment, prevents limits from being placed on independent political expenditures by corporations. ◄

COMMERCIAL SPEECH The courts also give substantial protection to *commercial speech,* which consists of communications—primarily advertising and marketing—made by business firms that involve only their commercial interests. The protection given to commercial speech under the First Amendment is less extensive than that afforded to noncommercial speech, however.

_____

20. 558 U.S. 310, 130 S.Ct. 876, 175 L.Ed.2d 753 (2010).

A state may restrict certain kinds of advertising, for instance, in the interest of preventing consumers from being misled. States also have a legitimate interest in roadside beautification and therefore may impose restraints on billboard advertising. ▶ **Case in Point 2.9** Café Erotica, a nude dancing establishment, sued the state after being denied a permit to erect a billboard along an interstate highway in Florida. The state appellate court decided that because the law directly advanced a substantial government interest in highway beautification and safety, it was not an unconstitutional restraint on commercial speech.[21] ◄

Generally, a restriction on commercial speech will be considered valid as long as it meets three criteria:

1. It must seek to implement a substantial government interest.
2. It must directly advance that interest.
3. It must go no further than necessary to accomplish its objective.

At issue in the following case was whether a government agency had unconstitutionally restricted commercial speech when it prohibited the inclusion of a certain illustration on beer labels.

_____

21. *Café Erotica v. Florida Department of Transportation,* 830 So.2d 181 (Fla.App. 1 Dist. 2002); review denied by *Café Erotica We Dare to Bare v. Florida Department of Transportation,* 845 So.2d 888 (Fla. 2003).

SP TLIGHT on Beer Labels

Case 2.3 Bad Frog Brewery, Inc. v. New York State Liquor Authority

United States Court of Appeals, Second Circuit, 134 F.3d 87 (1998).

BACKGROUND AND FACTS Bad Frog Brewery, Inc., makes and sells alcoholic beverages. Some of the beverages feature labels that display a drawing of a frog making the gesture generally known as "giving the finger." Bad Frog's authorized New York distributor, Renaissance Beer Company, applied to the New York State Liquor Authority (NYSLA) for brand label approval, as required by state law before the beer could be sold in New York.

The NYSLA denied the application, in part, because "the label could appear in grocery and convenience stores, with obvious exposure on the shelf to children of tender age." Bad Frog filed a suit in a federal district court against the NYSLA, asking for, among other things, an injunction against the denial of the application. The court granted summary judgment in favor of the NYSLA. Bad Frog appealed to the U.S. Court of Appeals for the Second Circuit.

 IN THE LANGUAGE OF THE COURT
Jon O. *NEWMAN,* Circuit Judge:

* * * *

* * * To support its asserted power to ban Bad Frog's labels [NYSLA advances] * * * the State's interest in "protecting children from vulgar and profane advertising" * * * .

CASE 2.3 CONTINUED

[This interest is] substantial * * * . *States have a compelling interest in protecting the physical and psychological wellbeing of minors* * * * . [Emphasis added.]

* * * *

* * * NYSLA endeavors to advance the state interest in preventing exposure of children to vulgar displays by taking only the limited step of barring such displays from the labels of alcoholic beverages. *In view of the wide currency of vulgar displays throughout contemporary society, including comic books targeted directly at children, barring such displays from labels for alcoholic beverages cannot realistically be expected to reduce children's exposure to such displays to any significant degree.* [Emphasis added.]

* * * If New York decides to make a substantial effort to insulate children from vulgar displays in some significant sphere of activity, at least with respect to materials likely to be seen by children, NYSLA's label prohibition might well be found to make a justifiable contribution to the material advancement of such an effort, but its currently isolated response to the perceived problem, applicable only to labels on a product that children cannot purchase, does not suffice. * * * A state must demonstrate that its commercial speech limitation is part of a substantial effort to advance a valid state interest, not merely the removal of a few grains of offensive sand from a beach of vulgarity.

* * * *

* * * Even if we were to assume that the state materially advances its asserted interest by shielding children from viewing the Bad Frog labels, it is plainly excessive to prohibit the labels from all use, including placement on bottles displayed in bars and taverns where parental supervision of children is to be expected. Moreover, to whatever extent NYSLA is concerned that children will be harmfully exposed to the Bad Frog labels when wandering without parental supervision around grocery and convenience stores where beer is sold, that concern could be less intrusively dealt with by placing restrictions on the permissible locations where the appellant's products may be displayed within such stores.

DECISION AND REMEDY *The U.S. Court of Appeals for the Second Circuit reversed the judgment of the district court and remanded the case for the entry of a judgment in favor of Bad Frog. The NYSLA's ban on the use of the labels lacked a "reasonable fit" with the state's interest in shielding minors from vulgarity. In addition, the NYSLA had not adequately considered alternatives to the ban.*

WHAT IF THE FACTS WERE DIFFERENT? *If Bad Frog had sought to use the offensive label to market toys instead of beer, would the court's ruling likely have been the same? Why or why not?*

THE LEGAL ENVIRONMENT DIMENSION *Whose interests are advanced by the banning of certain types of advertising?*

UNPROTECTED SPEECH The United States Supreme Court has made it clear that certain types of speech will not be protected under the First Amendment. Speech that violates criminal laws (threatening speech and pornography, for example) is not constitutionally protected. Other unprotected speech includes fighting words, or words that are likely to incite others to respond violently. Speech that harms the good reputation of another, or defamatory speech (see Chapter 4), also is not protected under the First Amendment.

Obscene Speech. The First Amendment, as interpreted by the Supreme Court, also does not protect obscene speech. Establishing an objective definition of obscene speech has proved difficult, however, and

the Court has grappled from time to time with this problem. In *Miller v. California,*[22] the Supreme Court created a test for legal obscenity, including a set of requirements that must be met for material to be legally obscene. Under this test, material is obscene if all of the following are true:

1. The average person finds that it violates contemporary community standards.
2. The work taken as a whole appeals to a prurient (arousing or obsessive) interest in sex.
3. The work shows patently offensive sexual conduct.
4. The work lacks serious redeeming literary, artistic, political, or scientific merit.

---

22. 413 U.S. 15, 93 S.Ct. 2607, 37 L.Ed.2d 419 (1973).

Because community standards vary widely, the *Miller* test has had inconsistent applications, and obscenity remains a constitutionally unsettled issue. Numerous state and federal statutes make it a crime to disseminate obscene materials, including child pornography.

Online Obscenity. Congress's first two attempts at protecting minors from pornographic materials on the Internet—the Communications Decency Act (CDA) of 1996[23] and the Child Online Protection Act (COPA) of 1998[24]—failed. Ultimately, the United States Supreme Court struck down both the CDA and COPA as unconstitutional restraints on speech, largely because the wording of these acts was overbroad and would restrict nonpornographic materials.

In 2000, Congress enacted the Children's Internet Protection Act (CIPA),[25] which requires public schools and libraries to install **filtering software** on computers to keep children from accessing adult content. Such software is designed to prevent persons from viewing certain Web sites based on a site's Internet address or its **meta tags,** or key words. The CIPA was challenged on constitutional grounds, but in 2003 the Supreme Court held that the act does not violate the First Amendment. The Court concluded that because libraries can disable the filters for any patrons who ask, the system is reasonably flexible and does not burden free speech to an unconstitutional extent.[26]

Virtual Pornography. In 2003, Congress enacted the Prosecutorial Remedies and Other Tools to end the Exploitation of Children Today Act (Protect Act).[27] The act makes it a crime to knowingly advertise, present, distribute, or solicit "any material or purported material in a manner that reflects the belief, or that is intended to cause another to believe, that the material or purported material" depicts actual child pornography.

Thus, it is a crime to intentionally distribute virtual child pornography—which uses computer-generated images, not actual people—without indicating that it is computer generated. In a case challenging the constitutionality of the Protect Act, the Supreme Court held that the statute was valid because it does not prohibit a substantial amount of protected speech.[28] Rather, the act generally prohibits offers to provide, and requests to obtain, child pornography—both of which are unprotected speech. Nevertheless, because of the difficulties of policing the Internet, as well as the constitutional complexities of prohibiting online obscenity through legislation, it remains a problem worldwide.

Freedom of Religion

The First Amendment states that the government may neither establish any religion nor prohibit the free exercise of religious practices. The first part of this constitutional provision is referred to as the **establishment clause,** and the second part is known as the **free exercise clause.** Government action, both federal and state, must be consistent with this constitutional mandate.

THE ESTABLISHMENT CLAUSE The establishment clause prohibits the government from establishing a state-sponsored religion, as well as from passing laws that promote (aid or endorse) religion or show a preference for one religion over another. Although the establishment clause involves the separation of church and state, it does not require a complete separation.

Applicable Standard. Establishment clause cases often involve such issues as the legality of allowing or requiring school prayers, using state-issued vouchers to pay tuition at religious schools, and teaching creation theories versus evolution. Federal or state laws that do not promote or place a significant burden on religion are constitutional even if they have some impact on religion. For a government law or policy to be constitutional, it must not have the primary effect of promoting or inhibiting religion.

Religious Displays. Religious displays on public property have often been challenged as violating the establishment clause, and the United States Supreme Court has ruled on a number of such cases. Generally, the Court has focused on the proximity of the religious display to nonreligious symbols, such as reindeer and candy canes, or to symbols from different religions, such as a menorah (a nine-branched candelabrum used in celebrating Hanukkah). The Supreme Court

23. 47 U.S.C. Section 223(a)(1)(B)(ii).
24. 47 U.S.C. Section 231.
25. 17 U.S.C. Sections 1701–1741.
26. *United States v. American Library Association,* 539 U.S. 194, 123 S.Ct. 2297, 156 L.Ed.2d 221 (2003).
27. 18 U.S.C. Section 2252A(a)(5)(B).

28. *United States v. Williams,* 553 U.S. 285, 128 S.Ct. 1830, 170 L.Ed.2d 650 (2008).

took a slightly different approach when it held that public displays having historical, as well as religious, significance do not necessarily violate the establishment clause.[29]

▶ **Case in Point 2.10**   Mount Soledad is a prominent hill near San Diego. There has been a forty-foot cross on top of Mount Soledad since 1913. In the 1990s, a war memorial with six walls listing the names of veterans was constructed next to the cross. The site was privately owned until 2006, when Congress authorized the property's transfer to the federal government "to preserve a historically significant war memorial."

Steve Trunk and the Jewish War Veterans filed lawsuits claiming that the cross violated the establishment clause because it endorsed the Christian religion. A federal appellate court agreed, finding that the primary effect of the memorial as a whole sent a strong message of endorsement of Christianity and exclusion (of non-Christian veterans). Although the inclusion of a cross in a war memorial does not always violate the establishment clause, the cross in this case physically dominated the site. Also, the cross was originally dedicated to religious purposes, had a long history of religious use, and was the only portion visible to drivers on the freeway below.[30] ◄

THE FREE EXERCISE CLAUSE   The free exercise clause guarantees that a person can hold any religious belief that she or he wants, or a person can have no religious belief. The constitutional guarantee of personal freedom restricts only the actions of the government and not those of individuals or private businesses.

Restrictions Must Be Necessary.   The government must have a compelling state interest for restricting the free exercise of religion, and the restriction must be the only way to further that interest. ▶ **Case in Point 2.11**   Members of a particular Mennonite church must use horses and buggies for transportation, but they can use tractors to take their agricultural products to market. Their religion requires the tractors to have steel cleats on the tires, and they drove tractors with cleats on county roads for many years. Then the county passed an ordinance that prohibited the use of steel cleats because the cleats tend to damage newly surfaced roads.

When a member of the church received a citation for driving a tractor with cleats, he claimed that the

ordinance violated the church's right to freely exercise its religion. Ultimately, the court ruled in his favor. The county had not met its burden of showing that the ordinance served a compelling state interest and was the least restrictive means of attaining that interest. There was no evidence of how much the cleats harmed the roads, other events also harmed the roads, and the county had allowed the cleats to be used for many years. Therefore, the ordinance was not carefully tailored to achieve the stated objective of road preservation.[31] ◄

Public Welfare Exception.   When religious *practices* work against public policy and the public welfare, though, the government can act. For instance, the government can require that a child receive certain types of vaccinations or medical treatment if his or her life is in danger—regardless of the child's or parent's religious beliefs. When public safety is an issue, an individual's religious beliefs often have to give way to the government's interest in protecting the public.

▶ **Example 2.12**   In the Muslim faith, it is a religious violation for a woman to appear in public without a scarf over her head. Due to public safety concerns, many courts today do not allow any headgear to be worn in courtrooms. A courthouse in Georgia prevented a Muslim woman from entering because she refused to remove her scarf. As she left, she uttered an expletive at the court official and was arrested and brought before the judge, who ordered her to serve ten days in jail. ◄

Searches and Seizures

The Fourth Amendment protects the "right of the people to be secure in their persons, houses, papers, and effects." Before searching or seizing private property, law enforcement officers must usually obtain a **search warrant**—an order from a judge or other public official authorizing the search or seizure.

SEARCH WARRANTS AND PROBABLE CAUSE   To obtain a search warrant, law enforcement officers must convince a judge that they have reasonable grounds, or probable cause, to believe a search will reveal evidence of a specific illegality. To establish **probable cause,** the officers must have trustworthy evidence that would convince a reasonable person that the proposed search or seizure is more likely justified than not.

29. *Van Orden v. Perry,* 545 U.S. 677, 125 S.Ct. 2854, 162 L.Ed.2d 607 (2005).
30. *Trunk v. City of San Diego,* 629 F.3d 1099 (9th Cir. 2011).
31. *Mitchell County v. Zimmerman,* 810 N.W.2d 1 (Iowa Sup.Ct. 2012).

Furthermore, the Fourth Amendment prohibits *general* warrants. It requires warrants to include a particular description of whatever is to be searched or seized. General searches through a person's belongings are impermissible. The search cannot extend beyond what is described in the warrant. Although search warrants must be specific, if a warrant is issued for a person's residence, officers may search items found in that residence even though they belong to other individuals.

▶ **Case in Point 2.13** Paycom Billing Services, Inc., an online payment service, stores vast amounts of customer credit-card information. Christopher Adjani, a former Paycom employee, threatened to sell Paycom's confidential client information if the company did not pay him $3 million. Pursuant to an investigation, the Federal Bureau of Investigation (FBI) obtained a search warrant to search Adjani's person, automobile, and residence, including computer equipment. When the FBI agents served the warrant, they discovered evidence of the criminal scheme in the e-mail communications on a computer in Adjani's residence that belonged to Adjani's live-in girlfriend. The court held that the search of the computer was proper given the involvement of computers in the alleged crime.[32] ◀

SEARCHES AND SEIZURES IN THE BUSINESS CONTEXT
Because of the strong government interest in protecting the public, a warrant normally is not required for seizures of spoiled or contaminated food. Nor are warrants required for searches of businesses in such highly regulated industries as liquor, guns, and strip mining.

The standard used for highly regulated industries is sometimes applied in other contexts as well, such as screening for airline travel. ▶ **Case in Point 2.14** Christian Hartwell was attempting to board a flight from Philadelphia to Phoenix, Arizona. When he walked through the security checkpoint, he set off the alarm. Airport security took him aside and eventually discovered that he had two packages of crack cocaine in his pocket. When Hartwell was convicted of possession of drugs, he appealed, claiming that the airport search was suspicionless and violated his Fourth Amendment rights. A federal appellate court held that airports can be treated as highly regulated industries and that suspicionless checkpoint screening of airline passengers is constitutional.[33] ◀

Generally, however, government inspectors do not have the right to enter business premises without a warrant, although the standard of probable cause is not the same as that required in nonbusiness contexts. The existence of a general and neutral enforcement plan will normally justify issuance of the warrant. Lawyers and accountants frequently possess the business records of their clients, and inspecting these documents while they are out of the hands of their true owners also requires a warrant.

Self-Incrimination

The Fifth Amendment guarantees that no person "shall be compelled in any criminal case to be a witness against himself." Thus, in any court proceeding, an accused person cannot be forced to give testimony that might subject him or her to any criminal prosecution. The guarantee applies to both federal and state proceedings because the due process clause of the Fourteenth Amendment extends the protection to state courts.

The Fifth Amendment's guarantee against self-incrimination extends only to natural persons. Therefore, neither corporations nor partnerships receive Fifth Amendment protection. When a partnership is required to produce business records, it must do so even if the information provided incriminates the individual partners of the firm. In contrast, sole proprietors and sole practitioners (those who fully own their businesses) cannot be compelled to produce their business records. These individuals have full protection against self-incrimination because they function in only one capacity, and there is no separate business entity.

SECTION 3
DUE PROCESS AND EQUAL PROTECTION

Other constitutional guarantees of great significance to Americans are mandated by the *due process clauses* of the Fifth and Fourteenth Amendments and the *equal protection clause* of the Fourteenth Amendment.

Due Process

The Fifth and Fourteenth Amendments provide that no person shall be deprived "of life, liberty, or property, without due process of law." The

---

32. *United States v. Adjani,* 452 F.3d 1140 (9th Cir. 2006); *cert.* denied, 549 U.S. 1025, 127 S.Ct. 568, 166 L.Ed.2d 420 (2006).
33. *United States v. Hartwell,* 436 F.3d 174 (3d Cir. 2006).

due process clause of these constitutional amendments has two aspects—procedural and substantive. Note that the due process clause applies to "legal persons" (that is, corporations), as well as to individuals.

PROCEDURAL DUE PROCESS *Procedural* due process requires that any government decision to take life, liberty, or property must be made equitably. In other words, the government must give a person proper notice and an opportunity to be heard. Fair procedures must be used in determining whether a person will be subjected to punishment or have some burden imposed on her or him.

Fair procedure has been interpreted as requiring that the person have at least an opportunity to object to a proposed action before an impartial, neutral decision maker (which need not be a judge). ▶ **Example 2.15** Doyle Burns, a nursing student in Kansas, poses for a photograph standing next to a placenta used as a lab specimen. Although she quickly deletes the photo from her library, it ends up on Facebook. When the director of nursing sees the photo, Burns is expelled. She sues for reinstatement and wins. The school violated Burns's due process rights by expelling her from the nursing program for taking a photo without giving her an opportunity to present her side to school authorities. ◀

SUBSTANTIVE DUE PROCESS *Substantive* due process focuses on the content of legislation rather than the fairness of procedures. Substantive due process limits what the government may do in its legislative and executive capacities. Legislation must be fair and reasonable in content and must further a legitimate governmental objective. A city cannot, for instance, pass an ordinance that allows police officers to break up any group of two or more persons who are standing together if one of those persons is believed to be a gang member.

If a law or other governmental action limits a fundamental right, the state must have a legitimate and compelling interest to justify its action. Fundamental rights include interstate travel, privacy, voting, marriage and family, and all First Amendment rights. Thus, a state must have a substantial reason for taking any action that infringes on a person's free speech rights.

In situations not involving fundamental rights, a law or action does not violate substantive due process if it rationally relates to any legitimate government purpose. In these circumstances, only state conduct that is arbitrary or shocks the conscience will violate

substantive due process. Under this test, almost any business regulation will be upheld as reasonable.

Equal Protection

Under the Fourteenth Amendment, a state may not "deny to any person within its jurisdiction the equal protection of the laws." The United States Supreme Court has interpreted the due process clause of the Fifth Amendment to make the **equal protection clause** applicable to the federal government as well. Equal protection means that the government cannot enact laws that treat similarly situated individuals differently.

Equal protection, like substantive due process, relates to the substance of a law or other governmental action. When a law or action limits the liberty of *all* persons, it may violate substantive due process. When a law or action limits the liberty of *some* persons but not others, it may violate the equal protection clause. ▶ **Example 2.16** If a law prohibits all persons from buying contraceptive devices, it raises a substantive due process question. If it prohibits only unmarried persons from buying the same devices, it raises an equal protection issue. ◀

In an equal protection inquiry, when a law or action distinguishes between or among individuals, the basis for the distinction—that is, its classification—is examined. Depending on the classification, the courts apply different levels of scrutiny, or "tests," to determine whether the law or action violates the equal protection clause. The courts use one of three standards: strict scrutiny, intermediate scrutiny, or the "rational basis" test.

STRICT SCRUTINY If a law or action prohibits or inhibits some persons from exercising a fundamental right, the law or action will be subject to "strict scrutiny" by the courts. Under this standard, the classification must be necessary to promote a *compelling state interest*. Also, if the classification is based on a *suspect trait*—such as race, national origin, or citizenship status—it must be necessary to promote a compelling government interest.[34]

Compelling state interests include remedying past unconstitutional or illegal discrimination but do not include correcting the general effects of "society's discrimination." ▶ **Example 2.17** For a city to give preference to minority applicants in awarding

---

34. See *Johnson v. California*, 543 U.S. 499, 125 S.Ct. 1141, 160 L.Ed.2d 949 (2005).

construction contracts, it normally must identify past unconstitutional or illegal discrimination against minority construction firms. Because the policy is based on suspect traits (race and national origin), it will violate the equal protection clause *unless* it is necessary to promote a compelling state interest. ◄ Generally, few laws or actions survive strict-scrutiny analysis by the courts.

INTERMEDIATE SCRUTINY A higher standard, that of *intermediate scrutiny,* is applied in cases involving discrimination based on gender or discrimination against illegitimate children (children born out of wedlock). Laws using these classifications must be *substantially related to important government objectives.* For instance, an important government objective is preventing illegitimate teenage pregnancies. Because males and females are not similarly situated in this regard, a law that punishes men but not women for statutory rape will be upheld, even though it treats men and women unequally.

The state also has an important objective in establishing time limits (called *statutes of limitation*) for how long after an event a particular type of action can be brought. Nevertheless, the limitation period must be substantially related to the important objective of preventing fraudulent or outdated claims. ▶ **Example 2.18** A state law requires illegitimate children to bring paternity suits within six years of their births in order to seek support from their fathers. A court will strike down this law if legitimate children are allowed to seek support from their parents at any time. Distinguishing between support claims on the basis of legitimacy is not related to the important government objective of preventing fraudulent or outdated claims. ◄

THE "RATIONAL BASIS" TEST In matters of economic or social welfare, a classification will be considered valid if there is any conceivable *rational basis* on which the classification might relate to a legitimate government interest. It is almost impossible for a law or action to fail the rational basis test. ▶ **Example 2.19** A city ordinance prohibits all pushcart vendors, except a specific few, from operating in a particular area of the city. It will be upheld under the equal protection clause if the city provides a rational basis—such as reducing the traffic in the particular area—for the ordinance. ◄ In contrast, a law that provides unemployment benefits only to people over six feet tall would clearly fail the rational

basis test because it could not further any legitimate government objective.

SECTION 4
PRIVACY RIGHTS

The U.S. Constitution does not explicitly mention a general right to privacy. In a 1928 Supreme Court case, *Olmstead v. United States,*[35] Justice Louis Brandeis stated in his dissent that the right to privacy is "the most comprehensive of rights and the right most valued by civilized men." The majority of the justices at that time, however, did not agree with Brandeis.

It was not until the 1960s that the Supreme Court endorsed the view that the Constitution protects individual privacy rights. In a landmark 1965 case, *Griswold v. Connecticut,*[36] the Supreme Court held that a constitutional right to privacy was implied by the First, Third, Fourth, Fifth, and Ninth Amendments.

Federal Statutes Affecting Privacy Rights

In the 1960s, Americans were sufficiently alarmed by the accumulation of personal information in government files that they pressured Congress to pass laws permitting individuals to access their files. Congress responded in 1966 with the Freedom of Information Act, which allows any person to request copies of any information on her or him contained in federal government files.

In 1974, Congress passed the Privacy Act, which also gives persons the right to access such information. Since then, Congress has passed numerous other laws protecting individuals' privacy rights with respect to financial transactions, electronic communications, and other activities in which personal information may be gathered and stored by organizations.

Since the 1990s, one of the major concerns of individuals has been how to protect privacy rights in cyberspace and to safeguard private information that may be revealed online. The increasing value of personal information for online marketers has exacerbated the situation. Chapter 6 discusses online privacy in more detail.

PRETEXTING A *pretext* is a false motive put forth to hide the real motive, and *pretexting* is the process of

35. 277 U.S. 438, 48 S.Ct. 564, 72 L.Ed. 944 (1928).
36. 381 U.S. 479, 85 S.Ct. 1678, 14 L.Ed.2d 510 (1965).

obtaining information by false means. Pretexters may try to obtain personal data by claiming that they are taking a survey for a research firm, a political party, or even a charity. The Gramm-Leach-Bliley Act[37] makes pretexting to obtain financial information illegal, but it does not mention lying to obtain *nonfinancial* information (for purposes other than identity theft).

▶ **Example 2.20** To find out who had leaked confidential company information to the press, Patricia C. Dunn, the chair of Hewlett-Packard, hired private investigators. They used false pretenses to access individuals' personal cell phone records. Dunn claimed that she had not been aware of the investigators' methods and had assumed that they had obtained the information from a public record. Criminal charges were filed but later dropped. Nevertheless, the scandal was highly publicized, and several civil lawsuits followed. Hewlett-Packard wound up paying millions to settle these lawsuits, including $14.5 million in fines to settle a claim filed by the California attorney general. ◀

To clarify the law on pretexting to gain access to phone records, Congress enacted the Telephone Records and Privacy Protection Act.[38] This act makes it a federal crime to pretend to be someone else or to make false representations for the purpose of obtaining another person's confidential phone records. The Federal Trade Commission investigates and prosecutes violators, who can be fined and sentenced to up to ten years in prison.

MEDICAL INFORMATION Responding to the growing need to protect the privacy of individuals' health records—particularly computerized records—Congress passed the Health Insurance Portability and Accountability Act (HIPAA).[39] This act defines and limits the circumstances in which an individual's "protected health information" may be used or disclosed.

HIPAA also requires health-care providers and health-care plans, including certain employers who sponsor health plans, to inform patients of their privacy rights and of how their personal medical information may be used. The act also states that a person's medical records generally may not be used for purposes unrelated to health care—such as marketing,

for example—or disclosed to others without the individual's permission. Congress later expanded HIPAA's provisions to apply to vendors (those who maintain personal health records for health-care providers) and to electronic records shared by multiple medical providers. Congress also authorized the Federal Trade Commission to enforce HIPAA and pursue violators.

THE USA PATRIOT ACT The USA Patriot Act was passed by Congress in the wake of the terrorist attacks of September 11, 2001, and then reauthorized in 2006.[40] The Patriot Act has given government officials increased authority to monitor Internet activities (such as e-mail and Web site visits) and to gain access to personal financial information and student information. Law enforcement officials can now track the telephone and e-mail communications of one party to find out the identity of the other party or parties. Privacy advocates argue that this law adversely affects the constitutional rights of all Americans, and it has been widely criticized in the media.

To gain access to these communications, the government must certify that the information likely to be obtained by such monitoring is relevant to an ongoing criminal investigation. The government need not provide proof of any wrongdoing.[41]

▶ **Example 2.21** In 2012, General David Petraeus, who ran the wars in Iraq and Afghanistan, resigned as director of the Central Intelligence Agency after his extramarital affair with Paula Broadwell, his biographer, became public. Apparently, after Petraeus broke off the affair with Broadwell, she sent harassing e-mails to another woman. When she reported the harassment, the FBI investigated, accessed Petraeus's e-mail accounts, and discovered that he had communicated with Broadwell via messages left in a draft folder on his e-mail account. Although there was no evidence that Petraeus did anything illegal, he was urged to resign and did so. ◀

Other Laws Affecting Privacy

State constitutions and statutes also protect individuals' privacy rights, often to a significant degree. Privacy rights are also protected to some extent under

37. Also known as the Financial Services Modernization Act, Pub. L. No. 106-102 (1999), 113 Stat. 1338, codified in numerous sections of 12 U.S.C.A.
38. 18 U.S.C. Section 1039.
39. HIPAA was enacted as Pub. L. No. 104-191 (1996) and is codified in 29 U.S.C.A. Sections 1181 *et seq.*
40. The Uniting and Strengthening America by Providing Appropriate Tools Required to Intercept and Obstruct Terrorism Act of 2001, also known as the USA Patriot Act, was enacted as Pub. L. No. 107-56 (2001) and reauthorized by Pub. L. No. 109-173 (2006).
41. See, for example, *American Civil Liberties Union v. National Security Agency,* 493 F.3d 644 (6th Cir. 2007), in which a federal appeals court upheld the government's warrantless monitoring of electronic communications.

tort law (see Chapter 4), Internet law (see Chapter 6), and employment law. Additionally, the Federal Trade Commission has played an active role in protecting the privacy rights of online consumers.

Reviewing: Business and the Constitution

A state legislature enacted a statute that required any motorcycle operator or passenger on the state's highways to wear a protective helmet. Jim Alderman, a licensed motorcycle operator, sued the state to block enforcement of the law. Alderman asserted that the statute violated the equal protection clause because it placed requirements on motorcyclists that were not imposed on other motorists. Using the information presented in the chapter, answer the following questions.

1. Why does this statute raise equal protection issues instead of substantive due process concerns?
2. What are the three levels of scrutiny that the courts use in determining whether a law violates the equal protection clause?
3. Which standard of scrutiny, or test, would apply to this situation? Why?
4. Applying this standard, or test, is the helmet statute constitutional? Why or why not?

DEBATE THIS ... *Legislation aimed at "protecting people from themselves" concerns the individual as well as the public in general. Protective helmet laws are just one example of such legislation. Should individuals be allowed to engage in unsafe activities if they choose to do so?*

Terms and Concepts

Bill of Rights 33
checks and balances 29
commerce clause 30
compelling government interest 36
due process clause 43
equal protection clause 43
establishment clause 40

federal form of government 28
filtering software 40
free exercise clause 40
full faith and credit clause 29
meta tags 40
police powers 28
preemption 33

privileges and immunities clause 29
probable cause 41
search warrant 41
sovereignty 28
supremacy clause 32
symbolic speech 34

ExamPrep

Issue Spotters

1. Can a state, in the interest of energy conservation, ban all advertising by power utilities if conservation could be accomplished by less restrictive means? Why or why not? **(See page 38.)**

2. Suppose that a state imposes a higher tax on out-of-state companies doing business in the state than it imposes on in-state companies. Is this a violation of equal protection if the only reason for the tax is to protect the local firms from out-of-state competition? Explain. **(See page 31.)**

• Check your answers to the Issue Spotters against the answers provided in Appendix B at the end of this text.

Before the Test

Go to **www.cengagebrain.com**, enter the ISBN 9781285770192, and click on "Find" to locate this textbook's Web site. Then, click on "Access Now" under "Study Tools," and select Chapter 2 at the top. There, you will find a Practice Quiz that you can take to assess your mastery of the concepts in this chapter, as well as Flashcards and a Glossary of important terms.

Business Scenarios

2–1. Commerce Clause. A Georgia state law requires the use of contoured rear-fender mudguards on trucks and trailers operating within Georgia state lines. The statute further makes it illegal for trucks and trailers to use straight mudguards. In approximately thirty-five other states, straight mudguards are legal. Moreover, in Florida, straight mudguards are explicitly required by law. There is some evidence suggesting that contoured mudguards might be a little safer than straight mudguards. Discuss whether this Georgia statute violates any constitutional provisions. **(See page 30.)**

2–2. Freedom of Religion. Thomas worked in the nonmilitary operations of a large firm that produced both military and nonmilitary goods. When the company discontinued the production of nonmilitary goods, Thomas was transferred to a plant producing military equipment. Thomas left his job, claiming that it violated his religious principles to participate in the manufacture of goods to be used in destroying life. In effect, he argued, the transfer to the military equipment plant forced him to quit his job. He was denied unemployment compensation by the state because he had not been effectively "discharged" by the employer but had voluntarily terminated his employment. Did the state's denial of unemployment benefits to Thomas violate the free exercise clause of the First Amendment? Explain. **(See page 40.)**

2–3. Equal Protection. With the objectives of preventing crime, maintaining property values, and preserving the quality of urban life, New York City enacted an ordinance to regulate the locations of commercial establishments that featured adult entertainment. The ordinance expressly applied to female, but not male, topless entertainment. Adele Buzzetti owned the Cozy Cabin, a New York City cabaret that featured female topless dancers. Buzzetti and an anonymous dancer filed a suit in a federal district court against the city, asking the court to block the enforcement of the ordinance. The plaintiffs argued, in part, that the ordinance violated the equal protection clause. Under the equal protection clause, what standard applies to the court's consideration of this ordinance? Under this test, how should the court rule? Why? **(See page 43.)**

Business Case Problems

2–4. Spotlight on Plagiarism—Due Process. The Russ College of

Engineering and Technology of Ohio University announced in a press conference that it had found "rampant and flagrant plagiarism" in the theses of mechanical engineering graduate students. Faculty singled out for "ignoring their ethical responsibilities" included Jay Gunasekera, chair of the department. Gunasekera was prohibited from advising students. He filed a suit against Dennis Irwin, the dean of Russ College, for violating his due process rights. What does due process require in these circumstances? Why? [*Gunasekera v. Irwin*, 551 F.3d 461 (6th Cir. 2009)] **(See page 43.)**

2–5. Commerce Clause. Under the federal Sex Offender Registration and Notification Act (SORNA), sex offenders must register and update their registration as sex offenders when they travel from one state to another. David Hall, a convicted sex offender in New York, moved to Virginia, where he did not update his registration. He was charged with violating SORNA. He claimed that the statute is unconstitutional, arguing that Congress cannot criminalize interstate travel if no commerce is involved. Is that reasonable? Why or why not? [*United States v. Guzman*, 591 F.3d 83 (2d Cir. 2010)] **(See page 30.)**

2–6. BUSINESS CASE PROBLEM
WITH SAMPLE ANSWER: Establishment Clause.

Judge James DeWeese hung a poster in his courtroom showing the Ten Commandments. The American Civil Liberties Union (ACLU) filed a suit, alleging that the poster violated the estab- *lishment clause. DeWeese responded that his purpose was not to promote religion but to express his view about "warring" legal philosophies—moral relativism and moral absolutism. "Our legal system is based on moral absolutes from divine law handed down by God through the Ten Commandments." Does this poster violate the establishment clause? Why or why not?* [American Civil Liberties Union of Ohio Foundation, Inc. v. DeWeese, *633 F.3d 424 (6th Cir. 2011)*] **(See page 40.)**

- **For a sample answer to Problem 2–6, go to Appendix C at the end of this text.**

2–7. The Dormant Commerce Clause. In 2001, Puerto Rico enacted a law that requires specific labels on cement sold in Puerto Rico and imposes fines for any violations of these requirements. The law prohibits the sale or distribution of cement manufactured outside Puerto Rico that does not carry a required label warning that the cement may not be used in government-financed construction projects. Antilles Cement Corp., a Puerto Rican firm that imports foreign cement, filed a complaint in federal court, claiming that this law violated the dormant commerce clause. (The dormant commerce clause doctrine applies not only to commerce among the states and U.S. territories, but also to international commerce.) Did the 2001 Puerto Rican law violate the dormant commerce clause? Why or why not? [*Antilles Cement Corp. v. Fortuno*, 670 F.3d 310 (1st Cir. 2012)] **(See page 31.)**

2–8. Freedom of Speech. Mark Wooden sent an e-mail to an alderwoman for the city of St. Louis. Attached was a nineteen-minute audio file that compared her to the biblical character Jezebel. The audio said she was a "bitch in the Sixth Ward," spending too much time with the rich and powerful and too little time with the poor. In a menacing, maniacal tone, Wooden said that he was "dusting off a sawed-off shotgun," called himself a "domestic terrorist," and referred to the assassination of President John Kennedy, the murder of federal judge John Roll, and the shooting of Representative Gabrielle Giffords. Feeling threatened, the alderwoman called the police. Wooden was convicted of harassment under a state criminal statute. Was this conviction unconstitutional under the First Amendment? Discuss. [*State v. Wooden,* 388 S.W.3d 522 (Mo. 2013)] **(See page 34.)**

2–9. A QUESTION OF ETHICS: Defamation.

 Aric Toll owns and manages the Balboa Island Village Inn, a restaurant and bar in Newport Beach, California. Anne Lemen lives across from the inn. Lemen complained to the authorities

about the inn's customers, whom she called "drunks" and "whores." She referred to Aric's wife as "Madam Whore" and told neighbors that the owners were involved in illegal drugs and prostitution. Lemen told the inn's bartender Ewa Cook that Cook "worked for Satan." She repeated her statements to potential customers, and the inn's sales dropped more than 20 percent. The inn filed a suit against Lemen. [Balboa Island Village Inn, Inc. v. Lemen, *40 Cal.4th 1141, 156 P.3d 339 (2007)]* **(See page 39.)**

(a) Are Lemen's statements about the inn's owners, customers, and activities protected by the U.S. Constitution? Should such statements be protected? In whose favor should the court rule? Why?

(b) Did Lemen behave unethically in the circumstances of this case? Explain.

Legal Reasoning Group Activity

2–10. Free Speech and Equal Protection. For many years, New York City has had to deal with the vandalism and defacement of public property caused by unauthorized graffiti. In an effort to stop the damage, the city banned the sale of aerosol spray-paint cans and broad-tipped indelible markers to persons under twenty-one years of age. The new rules also prohibited people from possessing these items on property other than their own. Within a year, five people under age twenty-one were cited for violations of these regulations, and 871 individuals were arrested for actually making graffiti.

Lindsey Vincenty and other artists wished to create graffiti on legal surfaces, such as canvas, wood, and clothing. Unable to buy her supplies in the city or to carry them in the city if she bought them elsewhere, Vincenty and oth-

ers filed a lawsuit on behalf of themselves and other young artists against Michael Bloomberg, the city's mayor, and others. The plaintiffs claimed that, among other things, the new rules violated their right to freedom of speech.

(a) One group will argue in favor of the plaintiffs and provide several reasons why the court should hold that the city's new rules violate the plaintiffs' freedom of speech. **(See page 34.)**

(b) Another group will develop a counterargument that outlines the reasons why the new rules do not violate free speech rights. **(See page 34.)**

(c) A third group will argue that the city's ban violates the equal protection clause because it applies only to persons under age twenty-one. **(See page 43.)**

CHAPTER 3

COURTS AND ALTERNATIVE DISPUTE RESOLUTION

The United States has fifty-two court systems—one for each of the fifty states, one for the District of Columbia, and a federal system. Keep in mind that the federal courts are not superior to the state courts. They are simply an independent system of courts, which derives its authority from Article III, Section 2, of the U.S. Constitution. By the power given to it under the U.S. Constitution, Congress has extended the federal court system to U.S. territories such as Guam, Puerto Rico, and the Virgin Islands.[1]

As we shall see, the United States Supreme Court is the final controlling voice over all of these fifty-two systems, at least when questions of federal law are involved. The Supreme Court's decisions—whether on affirmative action, health-care reform, immigration, or same-sex marriage—represent the last word in the most controversial legal debates in our society. Nevertheless, many of the legal issues that arise in our daily lives, such as the use of social media by courts, employers, and law enforcement, have not yet come before the nation's highest court. The lower courts usually resolve such pressing matters, making these courts equally important in our legal system.

Although an understanding of our nation's court systems is beneficial for anyone, it is particularly crucial for businesspersons, who will likely face a lawsuit at some time during their careers. Anyone involved in business should be familiar with the basic requirements that must be met before a party can bring a lawsuit before a particular court. We discuss these requirements in this chapter. It is also increasingly important for businesspersons to understand the various methods of alternative dispute resolution, which are discussed at the end of this chapter.

---

1. In Guam and the Virgin Islands, territorial courts serve as both federal courts and state courts. In Puerto Rico, they serve only as federal courts.

THE JUDICIARY'S ROLE IN AMERICAN GOVERNMENT

As you learned in Chapter 1, the body of American law includes the federal and state constitutions, statutes passed by legislative bodies, administrative law, and the case decisions and legal principles that form the common law. These laws would be meaningless, however, without the courts to interpret and apply them. The essential role of the judiciary—the courts—in the American governmental system is to interpret the laws and apply them to specific situations.

Judicial Review

As the branch of government entrusted with interpreting the laws, the judiciary can decide, among other things, whether the laws or actions of the other two branches are constitutional. The process for making such a determination is known as **judicial review.** The power of judicial review enables the judicial branch to act as a check on the other two branches of government, in line with the system of checks and balances established by the U.S. Constitution.[2]

The Origins of Judicial Review in the United States

The power of judicial review is not mentioned in the U.S. Constitution (although many constitutional scholars believe that the founders intended

---

2. In a broad sense, judicial review occurs whenever a court "reviews" a case or legal proceeding—as when an appellate court reviews a lower court's decision. When discussing the judiciary's role in American government, however, the term *judicial review* refers to the power of the judiciary to decide whether the actions of the other two branches of government violate the U.S. Constitution.

49

the judiciary to have this power). The United States Supreme Court explicitly established this power in 1803 in the case *Marbury v. Madison*.[3] In that decision, the Court stated, "It is emphatically the province [authority] and duty of the Judicial Department to say what the law is. . . . If two laws conflict with each other, the courts must decide on the operation of each. . . . [I]f both [a] law and the Constitution apply to a particular case, . . . the Court must determine which of these conflicting rules governs the case. This is of the very essence of judicial duty." Since the *Marbury v. Madison* decision, the power of judicial review has remained unchallenged. Today, this power is exercised by both federal and state courts.

SECTION 2
BASIC JUDICIAL REQUIREMENTS

Before a lawsuit can be brought before a court, certain requirements must be met. These requirements relate to jurisdiction, venue, and standing to sue. We examine each of these important concepts here.

Jurisdiction

In Latin, *juris* means "law," and *diction* means "to speak." Thus, "the power to speak the law" is the literal meaning of the term **jurisdiction.** Before any court can hear a case, it must have jurisdiction over the person (or company) against whom the suit is brought (the defendant) or over the property involved in the suit. The court must also have jurisdiction over the subject matter of the dispute.

JURISDICTION OVER PERSONS OR PROPERTY
Generally, a particular court can exercise **in personam jurisdiction** (personal jurisdiction) over any person or business that resides in a certain geographic area. A state trial court, for example, normally has jurisdictional authority over residents (including businesses) of a particular area of the state, such as a county or district. A state's highest court (often called the state supreme court[4]) has jurisdictional authority over all residents within the state.

A court can also exercise jurisdiction over property that is located within its boundaries. This kind of jurisdiction is known as *in rem* **jurisdiction,** or "jurisdiction over the thing." ▶ **Example 3.1**   A dispute arises over the ownership of a boat in dry dock in Fort Lauderdale, Florida. The boat is owned by an Ohio resident, over whom a Florida court normally cannot exercise personal jurisdiction. The other party to the dispute is a resident of Nebraska. In this situation, a lawsuit concerning the boat could be brought in a Florida state court on the basis of the court's *in rem* jurisdiction. ◀

Long Arm Statutes and Minimum Contacts. Under the authority of a state **long arm statute,** a court can exercise personal jurisdiction over certain out-of-state defendants based on activities that took place within the state. Before a court can exercise jurisdiction, though, it must be demonstrated that the defendant had sufficient contacts, or *minimum contacts,* with the state to justify the jurisdiction.[5]

Generally, the minimum-contacts requirement means that the defendant must have sufficient connection to the state for the judge to conclude that it is fair for the state to exercise power over the defendant. For instance, if an out-of-state defendant caused an automobile accident within the state or breached a contract formed there, a court will usually find that minimum contacts exist to exercise jurisdiction over that defendant. Similarly, a state may exercise personal jurisdiction over a nonresident defendant that is sued for selling defective goods within the state.

▶ **Case in Point 3.2**   An Xbox game system caught fire in Bonnie Broquet's home in Texas and caused substantial personal injuries. Broquet filed a lawsuit in a Texas court against Ji-Haw Industrial Company, a nonresident company that made the Xbox components. Broquet alleged that Ji-Haw's components were defective and had caused the fire. Ji-Haw argued that the Texas court lacked jurisdiction over it, but a state appellate court held that the Texas long arm statute authorized the exercise of jurisdiction over the out-of-state defendant.[6] ◀

Corporate Contacts. Because corporations are considered legal persons, courts use the same principles to determine whether it is fair to exercise jurisdiction

---

3. 5 U.S. (1 Cranch) 137, 2 L.Ed. 60 (1803).
4. As will be discussed shortly, a state's highest court is often referred to as the state supreme court, but there are exceptions. For instance, in New York the supreme court is a trial court.

5. The minimum-contacts standard was first established in *International Shoe Co. v. State of Washington,* 326 U.S. 310, 66 S.Ct. 154, 90 L.Ed. 95 (1945).
6. *Ji-Haw Industrial Co. v. Broquet,* 2008 WL 441822 (Tex.App.—San Antonio 2008).

over a corporation.[7] A corporation normally is subject to personal jurisdiction in the state in which it is incorporated, has its principal office, and/or is doing business. Courts apply the minimum-contacts test to determine if they can exercise jurisdiction over out-of-state corporations.

The minimum-contacts requirement is usually met if the corporation advertises or sells its products within the state, or places its goods into the "stream of commerce" with the intent that the goods be sold in the state. ▶ **Example 3.3**   A business is incorporated under the laws of Maine but has a branch office and manufacturing plant in Georgia. The corporation also advertises and sells its products in Georgia. These activities would likely constitute sufficient contacts with the state of Georgia to allow a Georgia court to exercise jurisdiction over the corporation. ◀

Some corporations do not sell or advertise products or place any goods in the stream of commerce. Determining what constitutes minimum contacts in these situations can be more difficult. ▶ **Case in Point 3.4**   Independence Plating Corporation is a New Jersey corporation that provides metal-coating services. Its only office and all of its personnel are located in New Jersey, and it does not advertise out of state. Independence had a long-standing business relationship with Southern Prestige Industries, Inc., a North Carolina company. Eventually, Southern Prestige filed suit in North Carolina against Independence for defective workmanship. Independence argued that North Carolina did not have jurisdiction over it, but the court held that Independence had sufficient minimum contacts with the state to justify jurisdiction. The two parties had exchanged thirty-two separate purchase orders in a period of less than twelve months.[8] ◀

JURISDICTION OVER SUBJECT MATTER Subject-matter jurisdiction refers to the limitations on the types of cases a court can hear. Certain courts are empowered to hear certain kinds of disputes.

General and Limited Jurisdiction. In both the federal and the state court systems, there are courts of *general* (unlimited) *jurisdiction* and courts of *limited jurisdiction*. A court of general jurisdiction can decide cases involving a broad array of issues. An example of a court of general jurisdiction is a state trial court or a federal district court.

An example of a state court of limited jurisdiction is a probate court. **Probate courts** are state courts that handle only the disposition of a person's assets and obligations after that person's death, including issues relating to the custody and guardianship of children. An example of a federal court of limited subject-matter jurisdiction is a bankruptcy court. **Bankruptcy courts** handle only bankruptcy proceedings, which are governed by federal bankruptcy law.

A court's jurisdiction over subject matter is usually defined in the statute or constitution that created the court. In both the federal and the state court systems, a court's subject-matter jurisdiction can be limited by any of the following:

1. The subject of the lawsuit.
2. The sum in controversy.
3. Whether the case involves a felony (a more serious type of crime) or a misdemeanor (a less serious type of crime).
4. Whether the proceeding is a trial or an appeal.

Original and Appellate Jurisdiction. The distinction between courts of original jurisdiction and courts of appellate jurisdiction normally lies in whether the case is being heard for the first time. Courts having original jurisdiction are courts of the first instance, or trial courts. These are courts in which lawsuits begin, trials take place, and evidence is presented. In the federal court system, the *district courts* are trial courts. In the various state court systems, the trial courts are known by different names, as will be discussed shortly.

The key point here is that any court having original jurisdiction normally serves as a trial court. Courts having appellate jurisdiction act as reviewing, or appellate, courts. In general, cases can be brought before appellate courts only on appeal from an order or a judgment of a trial court or other lower courts.

JURISDICTION OF THE FEDERAL COURTS Because the federal government is a government of limited powers, the jurisdiction of the federal courts is limited. Federal courts have subject-matter jurisdiction in two situations: when a federal question is involved and when there is diversity of citizenship.

Federal Questions. Article III of the U.S. Constitution establishes the boundaries of federal judicial power. Section 2 of Article III states that "the judicial Power shall extend to all Cases, in Law and Equity, arising under this Constitution, the Laws of the United

---

7. In the eyes of the law, corporations are "legal persons"—entities that can sue and be sued.
8. *Southern Prestige Industries, Inc. v. Independence Plating Corp.,* 690 S.E.2d 768 (N.C. 2010).

States, and Treaties made, or which shall be made, under their Authority."

In effect, this clause means that whenever a plaintiff's cause of action is based, at least in part, on the U.S. Constitution, a treaty, or a federal law, a **federal question** arises. If a case involves a federal question, the case comes under the judicial power of the federal courts. A person who claims that her constitutional rights have been violated, for instance, can file the lawsuit in a federal court. Note that in a case based on a federal question, a federal court will apply federal law.

Diversity of Citizenship. Federal district courts can also exercise original jurisdiction over cases involving **diversity of citizenship.** The most common type of diversity jurisdiction[9] requires *both* of the following:

1. The plaintiff and defendant must be residents of different states.
2. The dollar amount in controversy must exceed $75,000.

_____

9. Diversity jurisdiction also exists in cases between (1) a foreign country and citizens of a state or of different states and (2) citizens of a state and citizens or subjects of a foreign country. Cases based on these types of diversity jurisdiction occur infrequently.

For purposes of diversity jurisdiction, a corporation is a citizen of both the state in which it is incorporated and the state in which its principal place of business is located. A case involving diversity of citizenship can be filed in the appropriate federal district court. If the case starts in a state court, it can sometimes be transferred, or "removed," to a federal court.

A large percentage of the cases filed in federal courts each year are based on diversity of citizenship. As noted before, a federal court will apply federal law in cases involving federal questions. In a case based on diversity of citizenship, in contrast, a federal court will apply the relevant state law (which is often the law of the state in which the court sits).

The following dispute focused on whether diversity jurisdiction existed. A boat owner was severely burned when his boat exploded after being filled with excessive fuel at a marina in the U.S. Virgin Islands. The owner filed a suit in a federal district court against the marina and sought a jury trial. The defendant argued that a plaintiff in an admiralty, or maritime (on the sea), case does not have a right to a jury trial unless the court has diversity jurisdiction. The defendant claimed that because it, like the plaintiff, was a citizen of the Virgin Islands, the court had no such jurisdiction.

CASE ANALYSIS

Case 3.1   Mala v. Crown Bay Marina, Inc.
United States Court of Appeals, Third Circuit, 704 F.3d 239 (2013).

IN THE LANGUAGE OF THE COURT
SMITH, Circuit Judge.
* * * *

Kelley Mala is a citizen of the United States Virgin Islands. * * * He went for a cruise in his powerboat near St. Thomas, Virgin Islands. When his boat ran low on gas, he entered Crown Bay Marina to refuel. Mala tied the boat to one of Crown Bay's eight fueling stations and began filling his tank with an automatic gas pump. Before walking to the cash register to buy oil, Mala asked a Crown Bay attendant to watch his boat.

By the time Mala returned, the boat's tank was overflowing and fuel

was spilling into the boat and into the water. The attendant manually shut off the pump and acknowledged that the pump had been malfunctioning in recent days. Mala began cleaning up the fuel, and at some point, the attendant provided soap and water. Mala eventually departed the marina, but as he did so, the engine caught fire and exploded. Mala was thrown into the water and was severely burned. His boat was unsalvageable.

* * * Mala sued Crown Bay in the District Court of the Virgin Islands. Mala's * * * complaint asserted * * * that Crown Bay negligently maintained its gas pump. [Negligence is

the failure to exercise the standard of care that a reasonable person would exercise in similar circumstances. Negligence is a tort—a breach of a legal duty that proximately causes harm or injury to another—that forms the basis for a claim subject to applicable state law.] The complaint also alleged that the District Court had admiralty and diversity jurisdiction over the case, and it requested a jury trial.
* * * *

* * * Crown Bay filed a motion to strike Mala's jury demand. Crown Bay argued that plaintiffs generally do not have a jury-trial right in admiralty cases—only when the court also has

CASE 3.1 CONTINUED

diversity jurisdiction. And Crown Bay asserted that the parties were not diverse in this case * * * . In response to this motion, the District Court ruled that both Mala and Crown Bay were citizens of the Virgin Islands. The court therefore struck Mala's jury demand, but nevertheless opted to empanel an advisory jury. [The court could accept or reject the advisory jury's verdict.]

* * * At the end of the trial, the advisory jury returned a verdict of $460,000 for Mala—$400,000 for pain and suffering and $60,000 in compensatory damages. It concluded that Mala was 25 percent at fault and that Crown Bay was 75 percent at fault. The District Court ultimately rejected the verdict and entered judgment for Crown Bay.

* * * *

This appeal followed.

* * * *

Mala * * * argues that the District Court improperly refused to conduct a jury trial. This claim ultimately depends on whether the District Court had diversity jurisdiction.

The Seventh Amendment [to the U.S. Constitution] creates a right to civil jury trials in federal court: "In Suits at common law * * * the right

of trial by jury shall be preserved." Admiralty suits are not "Suits at common law," which means that when a district court has only admiralty jurisdiction the plaintiff does not have a jury-trial right. But [a federal statute] allows plaintiffs to pursue state claims in admiralty cases as long as the district court also has diversity jurisdiction. In such cases [the statute] preserves whatever jury-trial right exists with respect to the underlying state claims.

Mala argues that the District Court had both admiralty and diversity jurisdiction. As a preliminary matter, the court certainly had admiralty jurisdiction. The alleged tort occurred on navigable water and bore a substantial connection to maritime activity.

The grounds for diversity jurisdiction are less certain. *District courts have jurisdiction only if the parties are completely diverse. This means that no plaintiff may have the same state or territorial citizenship as any defendant.* The parties agree that Mala was a citizen of the Virgin Islands. [Emphasis added.]

Unfortunately for Mala, the District Court concluded that Crown Bay also was a citizen of the Virgin Islands. Mala rejects this conclusion.

Mala bears the burden of proving that the District Court had diversity jurisdiction. Mala failed to meet that burden because he did not offer evidence that Crown Bay was anything other than a citizen of the Virgin Islands. Mala contends that Crown Bay admitted to being a citizen of Florida, but Crown Bay actually denied Mala's allegation.

Absent evidence that the parties were diverse, we are left with Mala's allegations. *Allegations are insufficient at trial. And they are especially insufficient on appeal,* where we review the District Court's underlying factual findings for clear error. Under this standard, we will not reverse unless we are left with the definite and firm conviction that Crown Bay was in fact a citizen of Florida. Mala has not presented any credible evidence that Crown Bay was a citizen of Florida— much less evidence that would leave us with the requisite firm conviction. [Emphasis added.]

* * * Accordingly, the parties were not diverse and Mala does not have a jury-trial right.

* * * *

* * * For these reasons we will affirm the District Court's judgment.

LEGAL REASONING QUESTIONS

1. What is "diversity of citizenship"?

2. How does the presence—or lack—of diversity of citizenship affect a lawsuit?

3. What did the court conclude with respect to the parties' "diversity of citizenship" in this case?

4. How did the court's conclusion affect the outcome?

EXCLUSIVE VERSUS CONCURRENT JURISDICTION

When cases can be tried only in federal courts or only in state courts, exclusive jurisdiction exists. Federal courts have **exclusive jurisdiction** in the following types of cases:

1. Federal crimes.

2. Bankruptcy.

3. Most patent and copyright claims.

4. Any lawsuits against the United States.

5. Some areas of admiralty law (law governing seaborne transportation and ocean waters).

State courts also have exclusive jurisdiction over certain subjects—for example, divorce and adoption.

When both federal and state courts have the power to hear a case, as is true in suits involving diversity of citizenship, **concurrent jurisdiction** exists. When concurrent jurisdiction exists, a party may choose to bring a suit in either a federal court or a state court.

Many factors can affect a party's decision to litigate in a federal versus a state court. Examples include the availability of different remedies, the distance to the respective courthouses, or the experience or reputation of a particular judge. For instance, if the dispute involves a trade secret, a party might conclude that a federal court—which has exclusive jurisdiction over copyrights and patents—would have more expertise in the matter. A party might also choose a federal court over a state court if a state court has a reputation for bias against certain types of cases or plaintiffs.

In contrast, a plaintiff might choose to litigate in a state court if the court has a reputation for awarding substantial amounts of damages or if the judge is perceived as being pro-plaintiff. The concepts of exclusive and concurrent jurisdiction are illustrated in Exhibit 3–1 below.

Jurisdiction in Cyberspace

The Internet's capacity to bypass political and geographic boundaries undercuts the traditional basis on which courts assert personal jurisdiction. This basis includes a party's contacts with a court's geographic jurisdiction.

As already discussed, for a court to compel a defendant to come before it, there must be at least minimum contacts—the presence of a salesperson within the state, for instance. When a defendant's only contacts with the state are through a Web site, however, it is more difficult to determine whether these contacts are sufficient for a court to exercise jurisdiction.

THE "SLIDING-SCALE" STANDARD The courts have developed a "sliding-scale" standard to determine when they can exercise personal jurisdiction over an out-of-state defendant based on the defendant's Web activities. The sliding-scale standard identifies three types of Internet business contacts and outlines the following rules for jurisdiction:

1. When the defendant conducts substantial business over the Internet (such as contracts and sales), jurisdiction is proper.
2. When there is some interactivity through a Web site, jurisdiction may be proper, depending on the circumstances. Even a single contact can satisfy the minimum-contacts requirement in certain situations.
3. When a defendant merely engages in passive advertising on the Web, jurisdiction is never proper.[10] An Internet communication is typically considered passive if people have to voluntarily access it to read the message and active if it is sent to specific individuals.

▶ **Case in Point 3.5** A Louisiana resident, Daniel Crummey, purchased a used recreational vehicle (RV) from sellers in Texas after viewing photos of it on eBay. The sellers' statements on eBay claimed that "Everything works great on this RV and will provide comfort and dependability for years to come. This RV will go to Alaska and back without problems!"

---

10. For a leading case on this issue, see *Zippo Manufacturing Co. v. Zippo Dot Com, Inc.,* 952 F.Supp. 1119 (W.D.Pa. 1997).

EXHIBIT 3–1 Exclusive and Concurrent Jurisdiction

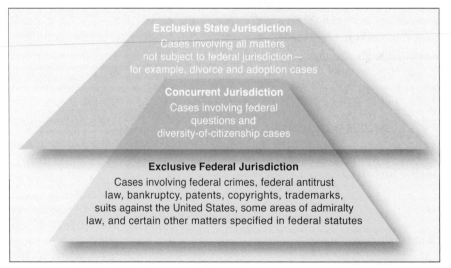

Crummey picked up the RV in Texas, but on the drive back to Louisiana, the RV quit working. He filed a suit in Louisiana against the sellers, alleging that the vehicle was defective. The sellers claimed that the Louisiana court lacked jurisdiction. The court found that Louisiana had jurisdiction because the sellers had used eBay to market and sell the RV to a Louisiana buyer—and had regularly used eBay to sell vehicles to remote parties in the past.[11] ◄

Concept Summary 3.1 reviews the various types of jurisdiction, including jurisdiction in cyberspace.

---

11. *Crummey v. Morgan,* 965 So.2d 497 (La.App. 1 Cir. 2007). But note that a single sale on eBay does not necessarily confer jurisdiction. Jurisdiction depends on whether the seller regularly uses eBay as a means for doing business with remote buyers. See *Boschetto v. Hansing,* 539 F.3d 1011 (9th Cir. 2008).

INTERNATIONAL JURISDICTIONAL ISSUES Because the Internet is international in scope, it obviously raises international jurisdictional issues. The world's courts seem to be developing a standard that echoes the requirement of minimum contacts applied by the U.S. courts.

Most courts are indicating that minimum contacts—doing business within the jurisdiction, for example—are enough to compel a defendant to appear and that a physical presence in the country is not necessary. The effect of this standard is that a business firm has to comply with the laws in any jurisdiction in which it targets customers for its products. This situation is complicated by the fact that many countries' laws on particular issues—free speech, for instance—are very different from U.S. laws.

CONCEPT SUMMARY 3.1
Jurisdiction

TYPE OF JURISDICTION	DESCRIPTION
Personal	Exists when a defendant is located in the territorial boundaries within which a court has the right and power to decide cases. Jurisdiction may be exercised over out-of-state defendants under state long arm statutes. Courts have jurisdiction over corporate defendants that do business within the state, as well as corporations that advertise, sell, or place goods into the stream of commerce in the state.
Property	Exists when the property that is subject to a lawsuit is located within the territorial boundaries within which a court has the right and power to decide cases.
Subject Matter	Limits the court's jurisdictional authority to particular types of cases. 1. *Limited jurisdiction*—Exists when a court is limited to a specific subject matter, such as probate or divorce. 2. *General jurisdiction*—Exists when a court can hear cases involving a broad array of issues.
Original	Exists with courts that have the authority to hear a case for the first time (trial courts).
Appellate	Exists with courts of appeal and review. Generally, appellate courts do not have original jurisdiction.
Federal	1. *Federal questions*—A federal court can exercise jurisdiction when the plaintiff's cause of action is based at least in part on the U.S. Constitution, a treaty, or a federal law. 2. *Diversity of citizenship*—A federal court can exercise jurisdiction in cases between citizens of different states when the amount in controversy exceeds $75,000 (or in cases between a foreign country and citizens of a state or of different states and in cases between citizens of a state and citizens or subjects of a foreign country).
Concurrent	Exists when both federal and state courts have authority to hear the same case.
Exclusive	Exists when only state courts or only federal courts have authority to hear a case.
Jurisdiction in Cyberspace	The courts have developed a sliding-scale standard to use in determining when jurisdiction over a Web site owner or operator in another state is proper.

The following case illustrates how federal courts apply a sliding-scale standard to determine if they can exercise jurisdiction over a foreign defendant whose only contact with the United States is through a Web site.

SP TLIGHT on Gucci

Case 3.2 Gucci America, Inc. v. Wang Huoqing

United States District Court, Northern District of California, ____ F.Supp.2d ____ (2011).

BACKGROUND AND FACTS Gucci America, Inc., is a New York corporation headquartered in New York City. Gucci manufactures and distributes high-quality luxury goods, including footwear, belts, sunglasses, handbags, and wallets, which are sold worldwide. In connection with its products, Gucci uses twenty-one federally registered trademarks (trademark law will be discussed in Chapter 5). Gucci also operates a number of boutiques, some of which are located in California.

Wang Huoqing, a resident of the People's Republic of China, operates numerous Web sites. When Gucci discovered that Wang Huoqing's Web sites offered for sale counterfeit goods—products bearing Gucci's trademarks but not genuine Gucci articles—it hired a private investigator in San Jose, California, to buy goods from the Web sites. The investigator purchased a wallet that was labeled Gucci but was counterfeit. Gucci filed a trademark infringement lawsuit against Wang Huoqing in a federal district court in California seeking damages and an injunction to prevent further infringement. Wang Huoqing was notified of the lawsuit via e-mail but did not appear in court. Gucci asked the court to enter a default judgment—that is, a judgment entered when the defendant fails to appear. First, however, the court had to determine whether it had personal jurisdiction over Wang Huoqing based on the Internet sales.

IN THE LANGUAGE OF THE COURT
Joseph C. *SPERO*, United States Magistrate Judge.

* * * *

* * * Under California's long-arm statute, federal courts in California may exercise jurisdiction to the extent permitted by the Due Process Clause of the Constitution. The Due Process Clause allows federal courts to exercise jurisdiction where * * * the defendant has had sufficient minimum contacts with the forum to subject him or her to the specific jurisdiction of the court. The courts apply a three-part test to determine whether specific jurisdiction exists:

> (1) The nonresident defendant must do some act or consummate some transaction with the forum or perform some act by which he purposefully avails himself of the privilege of conducting activities in the forum, thereby invoking the benefits and protections of its laws; (2) the claim must be one which arises out of or results from the defendant's forum-related activities; and (3) exercise of jurisdiction must be reasonable.

* * * *

In order to satisfy the first prong of the test for specific jurisdiction, a defendant must have either purposefully availed itself of [taken advantage of] the privilege of conducting business activities within the forum or purposefully directed activities toward the forum. *Purposeful availment typically consists of action taking place in the forum that invokes the benefits and protections of the laws of the forum, such as executing or performing a contract within the forum.* To show purposeful availment, a plaintiff must show that the defendant "engage[d] in some form of affirmative conduct allowing or promoting the transaction of business within the forum state." [Emphasis added.]

"In the Internet context, the Ninth Circuit utilizes a sliding scale analysis under which 'passive' websites do not create sufficient contacts to establish purposeful availment, whereas

CASE 3.2 CONTINUED interactive websites may create sufficient contacts, depending on how interactive the website is." * * * *Personal jurisdiction is appropriate where an entity is conducting business over the Internet and has offered for sale and sold its products to forum [California] residents.* [Emphasis added.]

Here, the allegations and evidence presented by Plaintiffs in support of the Motion are sufficient to show purposeful availment on the part of Defendant Wang Huoqing. Plaintiffs have alleged that Defendant operates "fully interactive Internet websites operating under the Subject Domain Names" and have presented evidence in the form of copies of web pages showing that the websites are, in fact, interactive. * * * Additionally, Plaintiffs allege Defendant is conducting counterfeiting and infringing activities within this Judicial District and has advertised and sold his counterfeit goods in the State of California. * * * Plaintiffs have also presented evidence of one actual sale within this district, made by investigator Robert Holmes from the website bag2do.cn. * * * Finally, Plaintiffs have presented evidence that Defendant Wang Huoqing owns or controls the twenty-eight websites listed in the Motion for Default Judgment. * * * Such commercial activity in the forum amounts to purposeful availment of the privilege of conducting activities within the forum, thus invoking the benefits and protections of its laws. Accordingly, the Court concludes that Defendant's contacts with California are sufficient to show purposeful availment.

DECISION AND REMEDY *The U.S. District Court for the Northern District of California held that it had personal jurisdiction over the foreign defendant, Wang Huoqing. The court entered a default judgment against Wang Huoqing and granted Gucci an injunction.*

WHAT IF THE FACTS WERE DIFFERENT? *Suppose that Gucci had not presented evidence that Wang Huoqing had made one actual sale through his Web site to a resident (the private investigator) of the court's district. Would the court still have found that it had personal jurisdiction over Wang Huoqing? Why or why not?*

THE LEGAL ENVIRONMENT DIMENSION *Is it relevant to the analysis of jurisdiction that Gucci America's principal place of business is in New York rather than California? Explain.*

Venue

Jurisdiction has to do with whether a court has authority to hear a case involving specific persons, property, or subject matter. **Venue**[12] is concerned with the most appropriate location for a trial. For instance, two state courts (or two federal courts) may have the authority to exercise jurisdiction over a case. Nonetheless, it may be more appropriate or convenient to hear the case in one court than in the other.

The concept of venue reflects the policy that a court trying a case should be in the geographic neighborhood (usually the county) where the incident occurred or where the parties reside. Venue in a civil case typically is where the defendant resides, whereas venue in a criminal case normally is where the crime occurred. Pretrial publicity or other factors, though, may require a change of venue to another community, especially in criminal cases in which the defendant's right to a fair and impartial jury has been impaired.

▶ **Example 3.6** Police raid a compound of religious polygamists in Texas and remove many children from the ranch. Authorities suspect that some of the girls were being sexually and physically abused. The raid receives a great deal of media attention, and people living in the nearby towns would likely be influenced by this publicity. If the government files criminal charges against a member of the religious sect, that individual may request a change of venue to another location. ◀

Note, though, that venue has lost some significance in today's world because of the Internet and 24/7 news reporting. Courts now rarely grant requests for a change of venue. Because everyone has instant access to all information about a purported crime, courts reason that no community is more or less informed or prejudiced for or against a defendant.

Standing to Sue

Before a party can bring a lawsuit to court, that party must have **standing to sue,** or a sufficient stake in

---

12. Pronounced *ven*-yoo.

a matter to justify seeking relief through the court system. Standing means that the party that filed the action in court has a legally protected interest at stake in the litigation. At times, a person can have standing to sue on behalf of another person, such as a minor (child) or a mentally incompetent person.

Standing can be broken down into three elements:

1. *Harm.* The party bringing the action must have suffered or will imminently suffer harm—an invasion of a legally protected interest. The controversy must be real and substantial rather than hypothetical.
2. *Causation.* There must be a causal connection between the conduct complained of and the injury.
3. *Remedy.* It must be likely, as opposed to merely speculative, that a favorable court decision will remedy, or make up for, the injury suffered.

▶ **Case in Point 3.7** The federal government's Legal Services Corporation (LSC) subsidizes legal services for people who cannot afford them. LSC restricts the use of its funds to certain purposes. In an attempt to cut costs, the state of Oregon tried to consolidate some of its legal assistance programs with similar programs provided by other organizations, including LSC. LSC did not approve, however, because Oregon's plan would integrate programs receiving federal funds with programs that engaged in restricted activities.

Oregon filed a suit against LSC, alleging that the state's ability to provide legal services to its citizens was frustrated, but the court dismissed the suit. Oregon had not accepted any federal funds and was not injured by the federal government's decision to subsidize certain private activities. The state had no standing to sue the federal government over federal subsidies to private parties.[13] ◄

SECTION 3

THE STATE AND FEDERAL COURT SYSTEMS

As mentioned earlier in this chapter, each state has its own court system. Additionally, there is a system of federal courts. Although no two state court systems are exactly the same, the right-hand side of Exhibit 3–2 below illustrates the basic organizational framework characteristic of the court systems in many states. The exhibit also shows how the federal court system is structured. We turn now to an examination of these court systems, beginning with the state courts.

The State Court Systems

Typically, a state court system includes several levels, or tiers, of courts, as shown in Exhibit 3–2. State courts may include (1) trial courts of limited jurisdiction, (2) trial courts of general jurisdiction, (3) appellate courts

---

13. *Oregon v. Legal Services Corp.,* 552 F.3d 965 (9th Cir. 2009).

EXHIBIT 3-2 The State and Federal Court Systems

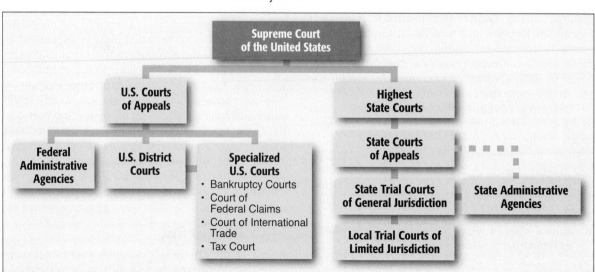

(intermediate appellate courts), and (4) the state's highest court (often called the state supreme court).

Generally, any person who is a party to a lawsuit has the opportunity to plead the case before a trial court and then, if he or she loses, before at least one level of appellate court. Finally, if the case involves a federal statute or federal constitutional issue, the decision of a state supreme court on that issue may be further appealed to the United States Supreme Court. (See this chapter's *Managerial Strategy* feature below for a discussion of how state budget cuts are making it more difficult to bring cases in some state courts.)

MANAGERIAL STRATEGY

Budget Cuts for State Courts Can Affect Businesses

In the United States, businesses use the courts far more than anyone else. Most civil court cases involve a business suing another business for breach of contract or fraud, for instance. Additionally, when one company fails to pay another company for products or services, the unpaid company will often turn to the court system. If that firm does not have ready access to the courts, its financial stability can be put at risk.

Court Budgets Have Been Reduced

According to the National Center for State Courts, since 2008 forty-two state legislatures have reduced funding for their state courts. California's courts have experienced the steepest cuts—$844 million from their annual budget since 2011. Recently, the Alabama legislature cut its court funding by almost 9 percent. As a result, the state's chief justice ordered courthouses to close on Fridays. The number of weeks that jury trials are available to civil litigants in Alabama has been reduced by 50 percent.

Intellectual Property Cases Take Longer to Resolve

Today, the value of a company's intellectual property, such as its copyrights and patents, often exceeds the value of its physical property. Not surprisingly, disputes over intellectual property have grown in number and importance. As a result of the court budget cuts, these disputes also take longer to resolve. In California, for example, a typical patent lawsuit used to last twelve months. Today, that same lawsuit might take three to five years.

Investors are reluctant to invest in a company that is the object of a patent or copyright lawsuit because they fear that if the company loses, it may lose the rights to its most valuable product. Consequently, when litigation drags on for years, some companies may suffer because investors abandon them even though the companies are otherwise healthy.

Other Types of Litigation Take Longer, Too

Other types of lawsuits are also taking longer to conclude. Now attorneys must tell businesses to consider not only the cost of bringing a lawsuit, but also the length of time involved. The longer the litigation lasts, the larger the legal bills and the greater the drain on company employees' time. Roy Weinstein, managing director of Micronomics in California, argues that the economic impact of court delays on businesses is substantial. During the years that a lawsuit can take, some businesses find that they cannot expand or hire new employees, and they are reluctant to spend on additional marketing and advertising.

In fact, it is not unusual for a company to win its case but end up going out of business. As a result of putting its business on hold for years, the company becomes insolvent.

Some Meritorious Cases Are Never Filed

Facing long delays in litigation with potential negative effects on their companies, business managers are becoming reluctant to bring lawsuits, even when their cases clearly have merit. In Alabama, for instance, the number of civil cases filed has dropped by more than a third in the last few years. Judge J. Scott Vowell of Jefferson County attributes this decline to delays and higher court costs.

MANAGERIAL IMPLICATIONS

Before bringing a lawsuit, a manager must now take into account the possibility of long delays before the case is resolved. A cost-benefit analysis for undertaking litigation must include the delays in the calculations. Managers can no longer just stand on principle because they know that they are right and that they will win a lawsuit. They have to look at the bigger picture, which includes substantial court delays.

BUSINESS QUESTIONS

1. *What are some of the costs of increased litigation delays caused by court budget cuts?*

2. *In response to budget cuts, many states have increased their filing fees. Is this fair? Why or why not?*

The states use various methods to select judges for their courts. Usually, voters elect judges, but in some states judges are appointed. For instance, in Iowa, the governor appoints judges, and then the general population decides whether to confirm their appointment in the next general election. The states usually specify the number of years that judges will serve. In contrast, as you will read shortly, judges in the federal court system are appointed by the president of the United States and, if they are confirmed by the Senate, hold office for life—unless they engage in blatantly illegal conduct.

TRIAL COURTS Trial courts are exactly what their name implies—courts in which trials are held and testimony is taken. State trial courts have either general or limited jurisdiction.

General Jurisdiction. Trial courts that have general jurisdiction as to subject matter may be called county, district, superior, or circuit courts.[14] State trial courts of general jurisdiction have jurisdiction over a wide variety of subjects, including both civil disputes and criminal prosecutions. In some states, trial courts of general jurisdiction may hear appeals from courts of limited jurisdiction.

Limited Jurisdiction. Courts of limited jurisdiction as to subject matter are generally inferior trial courts or minor judiciary courts. Limited jurisdiction courts might include local municipal courts (which could also have separate traffic courts and drug courts) and domestic relations courts (which handle divorce and child-custody disputes).

Small claims courts are inferior trial courts that hear only civil cases involving claims of less than a certain amount, such as $5,000 (the amount varies from state to state). Procedures in small claims courts are generally informal, and lawyers are not required (in a few states, lawyers are not even allowed). Decisions of small claims courts and municipal courts may sometimes be appealed to a state trial court of general jurisdiction.

A few states have also established Islamic law courts, which are courts of limited jurisdiction that serve the American Muslim community. These courts decide cases with reference to the *sharia*, a system of law used in most Islamic countries that is derived from the Qur'an and the sayings and doings of Muhammad and his followers.

Appellate, or Reviewing, Courts. Every state has at least one court of appeals (appellate court, or reviewing court), which may be an intermediate appellate court or the state's highest court. About three-fourths of the states have intermediate appellate courts.

Generally, courts of appeals do not conduct new trials, in which evidence is submitted to the court and witnesses are examined. Rather, an appellate court panel of three or more judges reviews the record of the case on appeal, which includes a transcript of the trial proceedings. The appellate court hears arguments from attorneys and determines whether the trial court committed an error.

Reviewing courts focus on questions of law, not questions of fact. A **question of fact** deals with what really happened in regard to the dispute being tried—such as whether a party actually burned a flag. A **question of law** concerns the application or interpretation of the law—such as whether flag-burning is a form of speech protected by the First Amendment to the U.S. Constitution. Only a judge, not a jury, can rule on questions of law.

Appellate courts normally defer (or give weight) to the trial court's findings on questions of fact because the trial court judge and jury were in a better position to evaluate testimony. The trial court judge and jury can directly observe witnesses' gestures, demeanor, and other nonverbal behavior during the trial. An appellate court cannot.

HIGHEST STATE COURTS The highest appellate court in a state is usually called the supreme court but may be designated by some other name. For instance, in both New York and Maryland, the highest state court is called the Court of Appeals. The highest state court in Maine and Massachusetts is the Supreme Judicial Court, and in West Virginia, it is the Supreme Court of Appeals.

The decisions of each state's highest court on all questions of state law are final. Only when issues of federal law are involved can the United States Supreme Court overrule a decision made by a state's highest court. ▶ **Example 3.8** A city enacts an ordinance that prohibits citizens from engaging in door-to-door advocacy without first registering with the mayor's office and receiving a permit. A religious group then sues the city, arguing that the law violates the freedoms of speech and religion guaranteed by the First Amendment. If the state supreme court upholds the law, the group could appeal the decision to the United States Supreme Court—because a constitutional (federal) issue is involved. ◀

---

14. The name in Ohio and Pennsylvania is Court of Common Pleas. The name in New York is Supreme Court, Trial Division.

The Federal Court System

The federal court system is basically a three-tiered model consisting of (1) U.S. district courts (trial courts of general jurisdiction) and various courts of limited jurisdiction, (2) U.S. courts of appeals (intermediate courts of appeals), and (3) the United States Supreme Court.

Unlike state court judges, who are usually elected, federal court judges—including the justices of the Supreme Court—are appointed by the president of the United States, subject to confirmation by the U.S. Senate. All federal judges receive lifetime appointments under Article III of the U.S. Constitution, which states that federal judges "hold their offices during good Behaviour." In the entire history of the United States, only seven federal judges have been removed from office through impeachment proceedings.

U.S. DISTRICT COURTS At the federal level, the equivalent of a state trial court of general jurisdiction is the district court. U.S. district courts have original jurisdiction in matters involving a federal question and concurrent jurisdiction with state courts when diversity jurisdiction exists. Federal cases typically originate in district courts. There are other federal courts with original, but special (or limited), jurisdiction, such as the federal bankruptcy courts and others shown in Exhibit 3–2 on page 58.

There is at least one federal district court in every state. The number of judicial districts can vary over time, primarily owing to population changes and corresponding changes in caseloads. Today there are ninety-four federal judicial districts. Exhibit 3–3 below shows the boundaries of both the U.S. district courts and the U.S. courts of appeals (discussed next).

U.S. COURTS OF APPEALS In the federal court system, there are thirteen U.S. courts of appeals—referred to as U.S. circuit courts of appeals. Twelve of the federal courts of appeals (including the Court of Appeals for the D.C. Circuit) hear appeals from the federal district courts located within their respective judicial circuits, or geographic boundaries (shown in Exhibit 3–3 on the

---

EXHIBIT 3-3 Geographic Boundaries of the U.S. Courts of Appeals and U.S. District Courts

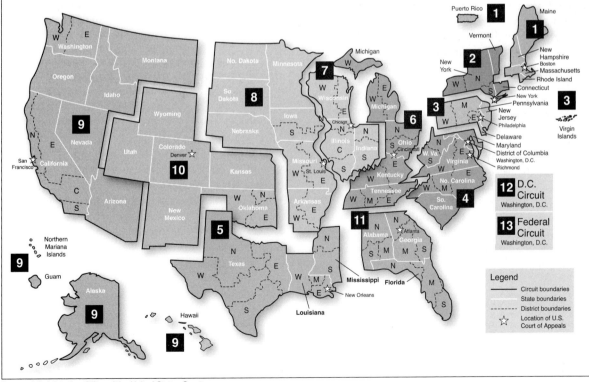

Source: Administrative Office of the United States Courts.

previous page).[15] The Court of Appeals for the Thirteenth Circuit, called the Federal Circuit, has national appellate jurisdiction over certain types of cases, such as those involving patent law and those in which the U.S. government is a defendant.

The decisions of a circuit court of appeals are binding on all courts within the circuit court's jurisdiction and are final in most cases, but appeal to the United States Supreme Court is possible.

THE UNITED STATES SUPREME COURT The highest level of the three-tiered federal court system is the United States Supreme Court. According to the U.S. Constitution, there is only one national Supreme Court. All other courts in the federal system are considered "inferior." Congress is empowered to create other inferior courts as it deems necessary. The inferior courts that Congress has created include the second tier in our model—the U.S. circuit courts of appeals—as well as the district courts and the various federal courts of limited, or specialized, jurisdiction.

The United States Supreme Court consists of nine justices. Although the Supreme Court has original, or trial, jurisdiction in rare instances (set forth in Article III, Sections 1 and 2), most of its work is as an appeals court. The Supreme Court can review any case decided by any of the federal courts of appeals. It also has appellate authority over cases involving federal questions that have been decided in the state courts. The Supreme Court is the final authority on the Constitution and federal law.

Appeals to the Supreme Court. To bring a case before the Supreme Court, a party requests the Court to issue a writ of *certiorari.*[16] A **writ of *certiorari*** is an order issued by the Supreme Court to a lower court requiring the latter to send it the record of the case for review. The Court will not issue a writ unless at least four of the nine justices approve of it. This is called the **rule of four.**

Whether the Court will issue a writ of *certiorari* is entirely within its discretion, and most petitions for writs are denied. (Although thousands of cases are filed with the Supreme Court each year, it hears, on average, fewer than one hundred of these cases.)[17] A

---

15. Historically, judges were required to "ride the circuit" and hear appeals in different courts around the country, which is how the name "circuit court" came about.
16. Pronounced sur-shee-uh-*rah*-ree.
17. From the mid-1950s through the early 1990s, the Supreme Court reviewed more cases per year than it has since then. In the Court's 1982–1983 term, for example, the Court issued written opinions in 151 cases. In contrast, during the Court's 2012–2013 term, the Court issued written opinions in only 79 cases.

denial of the request to issue a writ of *certiorari* is not a decision on the merits of the case, nor does it indicate agreement with the lower court's opinion. Also, denial of the writ has no value as a precedent. Denial simply means that the lower court's decision remains the law in that jurisdiction.

Petitions Granted by the Court. Typically, the Court grants petitions in cases that raise important constitutional questions or when the lower courts have issued conflicting decisions on a significant issue. The justices, however, never explain their reasons for hearing certain cases and not others, so it is difficult to predict which type of case the Court might select.

See *Concept Summary 3.2* on the next page to review the courts in the federal and state court systems.

SECTION 4
ALTERNATIVE DISPUTE RESOLUTION

Litigation—the process of resolving a dispute through the court system—is expensive and time consuming. Litigating even the simplest complaint is costly, and because of the backlog of cases pending in many courts, several years may pass before a case is actually tried. For these and other reasons, more and more businesspersons are turning to **alternative dispute resolution (ADR)** as a means of settling their disputes.

The great advantage of ADR is its flexibility. Methods of ADR range from the parties sitting down together and attempting to work out their differences to multinational corporations agreeing to resolve a dispute through a formal hearing before a panel of experts. Normally, the parties themselves can control how they will attempt to settle their dispute. They can decide what procedures will be used, whether a neutral third party will be present or make a decision, and whether that decision will be legally binding or nonbinding. ADR also offers more privacy than court proceedings and allows disputes to be resolved relatively quickly.

Today, more than 90 percent of civil lawsuits are settled before trial using some form of ADR. Indeed, most states either require or encourage parties to undertake ADR prior to trial. Many federal courts have instituted ADR programs as well. In the following pages, we examine the basic forms of ADR.

CONCEPT SUMMARY 3.2
Types of Courts

TYPE OF COURT	DESCRIPTION
Trial Courts	Trial courts are courts of original jurisdiction in which actions are initiated. 1. *State courts*—Courts of general jurisdiction can hear any case that has not been specifically designated for another court. Courts of limited jurisdiction include, among others, domestic relations courts, probate courts, municipal courts, and small claims courts. 2. *Federal courts*—The federal district court is the equivalent of the state trial court. Federal courts of limited jurisdiction include the bankruptcy courts and others shown in Exhibit 3–2 on page 58.
Intermediate Appellate Courts	Courts of appeals are reviewing courts. Generally, appellate courts do not have original jurisdiction. About three-fourths of the states have intermediate appellate courts. In the federal court system, the U.S. circuit courts of appeals are the intermediate appellate courts.
Supreme Courts	The highest state court is that state's supreme court, although it may be called by some other name. Appeal from state supreme courts to the United States Supreme Court is possible only if a federal question is involved. The United States Supreme Court is the highest court in the federal court system and the final authority on the Constitution and federal law.

Negotiation

The simplest form of ADR is **negotiation,** a process in which the parties attempt to settle their dispute informally, with or without attorneys to represent them. Attorneys frequently advise their clients to negotiate a settlement voluntarily before they proceed to trial. Parties may even try to negotiate a settlement during a trial or after the trial but before an appeal.

Negotiation traditionally involves just the parties themselves and (typically) their attorneys. The attorneys, though, are advocates—they are obligated to put their clients' interests first.

Mediation

In **mediation,** a neutral third party acts as a mediator and works with both sides in the dispute to facilitate a resolution. The mediator normally talks with the parties separately as well as jointly, emphasizes points of agreement, and helps the parties to evaluate their options.

Although the mediator may propose a solution (called a mediator's proposal), he or she does not make a decision resolving the matter. The mediator, who need not be a lawyer, usually charges a fee for his or her services (which can be split between the parties). States that require parties to undergo ADR before trial often offer mediation as one of the ADR options or (as in Florida) the only option.

One of the biggest advantages of mediation is that it is less adversarial than litigation. In mediation, the mediator takes an active role and attempts to bring the parties together so that they can come to a mutually satisfactory resolution. The mediation process tends to reduce the antagonism between the disputants, allowing them to resume their former relationship while minimizing hostility. For this reason, mediation is often the preferred form of ADR for disputes between business partners, employers and employees, or other parties involved in long-term relationships.

Arbitration

A more formal method of ADR is **arbitration,** in which an arbitrator (a neutral third party or a panel of experts) hears a dispute and imposes a resolution on the parties. Arbitration differs from other forms of ADR in that the third party hearing the dispute makes a decision for the parties. Exhibit 3–4 on the following page outlines the basic differences among the three traditional forms of ADR.

Usually, the parties in arbitration agree that the third party's decision will be *legally binding,* although the parties can also agree to *nonbinding* arbitration. (Arbitration that is mandated by the courts often is not binding on the parties.) In nonbinding arbitration, the parties can go forward with a lawsuit if they do not agree with the arbitrator's decision.

EXHIBIT 3–4 Basic Differences in the Traditional Forms of ADR

Type of ADR	Description	Neutral Third Party Present	Who Decides the Resolution
Negotiation	Parties meet informally with or without their attorneys and attempt to agree on a resolution. This is the simplest and least expensive method of ADR.	No	The parties themselves reach a resolution.
Mediation	A neutral third party meets with the parties and emphasizes points of agreement to bring them toward resolution of their dispute. 1. This method of ADR reduces hostility between the parties. 2. Mediation is preferred for resolving disputes between business partners, employers and employees, or others involved in long-term relationships.	Yes	The parties, but the mediator may suggest or propose a resolution.
Arbitration	The parties present their arguments and evidence before an arbitrator at a hearing, and the arbitrator renders a decision resolving the parties' dispute. 1. This ADR method is the most formal and resembles a court proceeding because some rules of evidence apply. 2. The parties are free to frame the issues and set the powers of the arbitrator. 3. If the parties agree that the arbitration is binding, then the parties' right to appeal the decision is limited.	Yes	The arbitrator imposes a resolution on the parties that may be either binding or nonbinding.

In some respects, formal arbitration resembles a trial, although usually the procedural rules are much less restrictive than those governing litigation. In a typical arbitration, the parties present opening arguments and ask for specific remedies. Both sides present evidence and may call and examine witnesses. The arbitrator then renders a decision.

THE ARBITRATOR'S DECISION The arbitrator's decision is called an **award.** It is is usually the final word on the matter. Although the parties may appeal an arbitrator's decision, a court's review of the decision will be much more restricted in scope than an appellate court's review of a trial court's decision. The general view is that because the parties were free to frame the issues and set the powers of the arbitrator at the outset, they cannot complain about the results. A court will set aside an award only in the event of one of the following:

1. The arbitrator's conduct or "bad faith" substantially prejudiced the rights of one of the parties.
2. The award violates an established public policy.
3. The arbitrator exceeded her or his powers—that is, arbitrated issues that the parties did not agree to submit to arbitration.

ARBITRATION CLAUSES Almost any commercial matter can be submitted to arbitration. Frequently, parties include an **arbitration clause** in a contract (a written agreement—see Chapter 9) specifying that any dispute arising under the contract will be resolved through arbitration rather than through the court system. Parties can also agree to arbitrate a dispute *after* it arises.

ARBITRATION STATUTES Most states have statutes (often based, in part, on the Uniform Arbitration Act of 1955) under which arbitration clauses will be enforced. Some state statutes compel arbitration of certain types of disputes, such as those involving public employees.

At the federal level, the Federal Arbitration Act (FAA), enacted in 1925, enforces arbitration clauses in contracts involving maritime activity and interstate commerce. Because of the breadth of the commerce clause (see Chapter 2), arbitration agreements involving transactions only slightly connected to the flow of interstate commerce may fall under the FAA. The FAA established a national policy favoring arbitration.

In the following case, the parties had agreed to arbitrate disputes involving their contract, but a state law allowed one party to void a contractual provision that required arbitration outside the state. The court had to decide if the FAA *preempted* (took priority over, or blocked—see Chapter 2) the state law.

CASE 3.3

Cleveland Construction, Inc. v. Levco Construction, Inc.
Court of Appeals of Texas, First District, 359 S.W.3d 843 (2012).

BACKGROUND AND FACTS Cleveland Construction, Inc. (CCI), was the general contractor on a project to build a grocery store in Houston, Texas. CCI hired Levco Construction, Inc., as a subcontractor to perform excavation and grading. The contract included an arbitration provision stating that any disputes would be resolved by arbitration in Ohio. When a dispute arose between the parties, Levco filed a suit against CCI in a Texas state court. CCI sought to compel arbitration in Ohio under the Federal Arbitration Act (FAA), but a Texas statute allows a party to void a contractual provision that requires arbitration outside Texas. The Texas court granted an emergency motion preventing arbitration. CCI appealed.

IN THE LANGUAGE OF THE COURT
Evelyn N. *KEYES,* Justice.

* * * *

[Texas] Business and Commerce Code section 272.001 provides:

If a contract contains a provision making * * * any conflict arising under the contract subject to * * * arbitration in another state, that provision is voidable by the party obligated by the contract to perform the construction * * * .

Levco argues * * * that it "exercised its option to void the requirement in the Contract to arbitrate in Lake County, Ohio."

*The FAA preempts all otherwise applicable inconsistent state laws * * * under the Supremacy Clause of the United States Constitution. The FAA declares written provisions for arbitration "valid, irrevocable, and enforceable, save upon such grounds as exist at law or in equity for the revocation of any contract."* [Emphasis added.]

* * * Applying section 272.001 as Levco asks us to do here would prevent us from enforcing a term of the parties' arbitration agreement—the venue—on a ground that is not recognized by the FAA or by general state-law contract principles. We hold that the FAA preempts application of this provision under the facts of this case. * * * By allowing a party to * * * declare void a previously bargained-for provision, application of section 272.001 would undermine the declared federal policy of rigorous enforcement of arbitration agreements.

DECISION AND REMEDY *The Texas appellate court reversed the trial court, holding that the FAA preempts the Texas statute. CCI could compel arbitration in Ohio.*

THE LEGAL ENVIRONMENT DIMENSION *How would business be affected if each state could pass a statute, like the one in Texas, allowing parties to void out-of-state arbitration?*

THE SOCIAL DIMENSION *Considering the relative bargaining power of the parties, was it fair to enforce the arbitration clause in this contract? Why or why not?*

THE ISSUE OF ARBITRABILITY The terms of an arbitration agreement can limit the types of disputes that the parties agree to arbitrate. Disputes can arise, however, when the parties do not specify limits or when the parties disagree on whether the particular matter is covered by their arbitration agreement.

When one party files a lawsuit to compel arbitration, it is up to the court to resolve the issue of *arbitrability.* That is, the court must decide whether the matter is one that must be resolved through arbitration.

If the court finds that the subject matter in controversy is covered by the agreement to arbitrate, then a party may be compelled to arbitrate the dispute. Usually, a court will allow the claim to be arbitrated if the court finds that the relevant statute (the state arbitration statute or the FAA) does not exclude such claims.

No party, however, will be ordered to submit a particular dispute to arbitration unless the court is convinced that the party has consented to do so. Additionally, the courts will not compel arbitration if it is clear that the arbitration rules and procedures are inherently unfair to one of the parties.

MANDATORY ARBITRATION IN THE EMPLOYMENT CONTEXT A significant question for businesspersons has concerned mandatory arbitration clauses in employment contracts. Many employees claim they are at a disadvantage when they are forced, as a condition of being hired, to agree to arbitrate all disputes and thus waive their rights under statutes designed to protect employees. The United States Supreme Court, however, has held that mandatory arbitration clauses in employment contracts are generally enforceable.

▶ **Case in Point 3.9** In a landmark decision, *Gilmer v. Interstate Johnson Lane Corp.,*[18] the Supreme Court held that a claim brought under a federal statute prohibiting age discrimination could be subject to arbitration. The Court concluded that the employee had waived his right to sue when he agreed, as part of a required application to be a securities representative, to arbitrate "any dispute, claim, or controversy" relating to his employment. ◀

Compulsory arbitration agreements often spell out the rules for a mandatory proceeding. For example, an agreement may address in detail the amount and payment of filing fees and other expenses. Employment-related agreements often require the parties to split the costs, but some courts have overturned those provisions when an individual worker lacked the ability to pay.[19]

Other Types of ADR

The three forms of ADR just discussed are the oldest and traditionally the most commonly used forms. In addition, a variety of new types of ADR have emerged in recent years, including those described here.

1. In **early neutral case evaluation,** the parties select a neutral third party (generally an expert in the subject matter of the dispute) and then explain their respective positions to that person. The case evaluator assesses the strengths and weaknesses of each party's claims.
2. In a **mini-trial,** each party's attorney briefly argues the party's case before the other party and a panel of representatives from each side who have the authority to settle the dispute. Typically, a neutral third party (usually an expert in the area being disputed) acts as an adviser. If the parties fail to reach an agreement, the adviser renders an opinion as to how a court would likely decide the issue.
3. Numerous federal courts now hold **summary jury trials,** in which the parties present their arguments and evidence and the jury renders a verdict. The jury's verdict is not binding, but it does act as a guide to both sides in reaching an agreement during the mandatory negotiations that immediately follow the trial.
4. Other alternatives being employed by the courts include summary procedures for commercial litigation and the appointment of special masters to assist judges in deciding complex issues.

Providers of ADR Services

Both government agencies and private organizations provide ADR services. A major provider of ADR services is the **American Arbitration Association (AAA).** The AAA was founded in 1926 and now handles more than 200,000 claims a year in its numerous offices worldwide.

Cases brought before the AAA are heard by an expert or a panel of experts in the area relating to the dispute and are usually settled quickly. Generally, about half of the panel members are lawyers. To cover its costs, the AAA charges a fee, paid by the party filing the claim. In addition, each party to the dispute pays a specified amount for each hearing day, as well as a special additional fee in cases involving personal injuries or property loss.

Hundreds of for-profit firms around the country also provide dispute-resolution services. Typically, these firms hire retired judges to conduct arbitration hearings or otherwise assist parties in settling their disputes. The judges follow procedures similar to those of the federal courts and use similar rules. Usually, each party to the dispute pays a filing fee and a designated fee for a hearing session or conference.

---

18. 500 U.S. 20, 111 S.Ct. 1647, 114 L.Ed.2d 26 (1991).
19. See, for example, *Davis v. O'Melveny & Myers, LLC,* 485 F.3d 1066 (9th Cir. 2007); and *Nagrampa v. MailCoups, Inc.,* 469 F.3d 1257 (9th Cir. 2006).

Online Dispute Resolution

An increasing number of companies and organizations are offering dispute-resolution services using the Internet. The settlement of disputes in these online forums is known as **online dispute resolution (ODR).** The disputes resolved in these forums have most commonly involved rights to domain names (Web site addresses—see Chapter 6) or the quality of goods sold via the Internet, including goods sold through Internet auction sites.

ODR may be best for resolving small- to medium-sized business liability claims, which may not be worth the expense of litigation or traditional ADR methods. Rules being developed in online forums may ultimately become a code of conduct for everyone who does business in cyberspace. Most online forums do not automatically apply the law of any specific jurisdiction. Instead, results are often based on general, more universal legal principles. As with offline methods of dispute resolution, any party may appeal to a court at any time if the ODR is nonbinding arbitration.

Some cities use ODR as a means of resolving claims against them. ▶ **Example 3.10**   New York City uses Cybersettle.com to resolve auto accident, sidewalk, and other personal-injury claims made against the city. Parties with complaints submit their demands, and the city submits its offers confidentially online. If an offer exceeds a demand, the claimant keeps half the difference as a bonus, plus the original claim. ◀

SECTION 5
INTERNATIONAL DISPUTE RESOLUTION

Businesspersons who engage in international business transactions normally take special precautions to protect themselves in the event that a party with whom they are dealing in another country breaches an agreement. Often, parties to international contracts include special clauses in their contracts providing for how disputes arising under the contracts will be resolved.

Forum-Selection and Choice-of-Law Clauses

As you will read in Chapter 15, parties to international transactions often include forum-selection and choice-of-law clauses in their contracts. These clauses designate the jurisdiction (court or country) where any dispute arising under the contract will be litigated and which nation's law will be applied.

When an international contract does not include such clauses, any legal proceedings arising under the contract will be more complex and attended by much more uncertainty. For instance, litigation may take place in two or more countries, with each country applying its own national law to the particular transactions.

Furthermore, even if a plaintiff wins a favorable judgment in a lawsuit litigated in the plaintiff's country, the defendant's country could refuse to enforce the court's judgment. The judgment may be enforced in the defendant's country for reasons of courtesy. The United States, for example, will generally enforce a foreign court's decision if it is consistent with U.S. national law and policy. Other nations, however, may not be as accommodating as the United States, and the plaintiff may be left empty-handed.

Arbitration Clauses

International contracts also often include arbitration clauses that require a neutral third party to decide any contract disputes. In international arbitration proceedings, the third party may be a neutral entity (such as the International Chamber of Commerce), a panel of individuals representing both parties' interests, or some other group or organization.

The United Nations Convention on the Recognition and Enforcement of Foreign Arbitral Awards[20] has been implemented in more than 145 countries, including the United States. This convention assists in the enforcement of arbitration clauses, as do provisions in specific treaties among nations. The American Arbitration Association provides arbitration services for international as well as domestic disputes.

International Treaties and Arbitration

International treaties—that is, formal agreements among several nations—sometimes also stipulate arbitration for resolving disputes. This is a tactic that has been used in the past to increase foreign investment. ▶ **Example 3.11** In the 1990s, Argentina encouraged foreign investment by forming bilateral investment treaties with other nations, including the United States and France. The treaties required Argentina to protect investors' property rights and provided that any grievances would be settled by arbitration at the

---

20. June 10, 1958, 21 U.S.T. 2517, T.I.A.S. No. 6997 (the "New York Convention").

International Centre for the Settlement of Investment Disputes (ICSID), which is part of the World Bank. Foreign investment in Argentina skyrocketed, in part, because companies had the security of knowing that disputes would be settled by the ICSID rather than by Argentina's courts.

After Argentina's economy collapsed in 2001, companies that had suffered significant losses filed claims against Argentina with the ICSID. The ICSID, however, resolved most claims in Argentina's favor. The few companies that won awards from the ICSID, such as Philip Morris International, then had to ask courts in Argentina to enforce the judgments. These problems have caused some nations to withdraw from the ICSID. Others, including Australia, have indicated that they will not enter any future trade agreements that require their domestic investors who invest in other countries to submit to arbitration. ◀

Reviewing: Courts and Alternative Dispute Resolution

Stan Garner resides in Illinois and promotes boxing matches for SuperSports, Inc., an Illinois corporation. Garner created the concept of "Ages" promotion—a three-fight series of boxing matches pitting an older fighter (George Foreman) against a younger fighter. The concept had titles for each of the three fights, including "Battle of the Ages." Garner contacted Foreman and his manager, who both reside in Texas, to sell the idea, and they arranged a meeting in Las Vegas, Nevada. During negotiations, Foreman's manager signed a nondisclosure agreement prohibiting him from disclosing Garner's promotional concepts unless the parties signed a contract. Nevertheless, after negotiations fell through, Foreman used Garner's "Battle of the Ages" concept to promote a subsequent fight. Garner filed a suit against Foreman and his manager in a federal district court located in Illinois, alleging breach of contract. Using the information presented in the chapter, answer the following questions.

1. On what basis might the federal district court in Illinois exercise jurisdiction in this case?
2. Does the federal district court have original or appellate jurisdiction?
3. Suppose that Garner had filed his action in an Illinois state court. Could an Illinois state court exercise personal jurisdiction over Foreman or his manager? Why or why not?
4. Assume that Garner had filed his action in a Nevada state court. Would that court have had personal jurisdiction over Foreman or his manager? Explain.

DEBATE THIS . . . *In this age of the Internet, when people communicate via e-mail, texts, tweets, Facebook, and Skype, is the concept of jurisdiction losing its meaning?*

Terms and Concepts

alternative dispute
  resolution (ADR) 62
American Arbitration
  Association (AAA) 66
arbitration 63
arbitration clause 64
award 64
bankruptcy court 51
concurrent jurisdiction 53
diversity of citizenship 52
early neutral case evaluation 66

exclusive jurisdiction 53
federal question 52
in personam jurisdiction 50
in rem jurisdiction 50
judicial review 49
jurisdiction 50
litigation 62
long arm statute 50
mediation 63
mini-trial 66
negotiation 63

online dispute resolution (ODR) 67
probate court 51
question of fact 60
question of law 60
rule of four 62
small claims court 60
standing to sue 57
summary jury trial 66
venue 57
writ of *certiorari* 62

ExamPrep

Issue Spotters

1. Sue uses her smartphone to purchase a video security system for her architectural firm from Tipton, Inc., a company that is located in a different state. The system arrives a month after the projected delivery date, is of poor quality, and does not function as advertised. Sue files a suit against Tipton in a state court. Does the court in Sue's state have jurisdiction over Tipton? What factors will the court consider? **(See page 50.)**

2. The state in which Sue resides requires that her dispute with Tipton be submitted to mediation or nonbinding arbitration. If the dispute is not resolved, or if either party disagrees with the decision of the media-

tor or arbitrator, will a court hear the case? Explain. **(See page 63.)**

- Check your answers to the Issue Spotters against the answers provided in Appendix B at the end of this text.

Before the Test

Go to **www.cengagebrain.com**, enter the ISBN 9781285770192, and click on "Find" to locate this textbook's Web site. Then, click on "Access Now" under "Study Tools," and select Chapter 3 at the top. There, you will find a Practice Quiz that you can take to assess your mastery of the concepts in this chapter, as well as Flashcards and a Glossary of important terms.

Business Scenarios

3–1. Standing. Jack and Maggie Turton bought a house in Jefferson County, Idaho, located directly across the street from a gravel pit. A few years later, the county converted the pit to a landfill. The landfill accepted many kinds of trash that cause harm to the environment, including major appliances, animal carcasses, containers with hazardous content warnings, leaking car batteries, and waste oil. The Turtons complained to the county, but the county did nothing. The Turtons then filed a lawsuit against the county alleging violations of federal environmental laws pertaining to groundwater contamination and other pollution. Do the Turtons have standing to sue? Why or why not? **(See pages 57 and 58.)**

3–2. Jurisdiction. Marya Callais, a citizen of Florida, was walking along a busy street in Tallahassee, Florida, when a large crate flew off a passing truck and hit her, causing numerous injuries. She experienced a great deal of pain and suffering, incurred significant medical expenses, and could not work for six months. She wants to sue the trucking firm for $300,000 in damages. The firm's headquarters are in Georgia, although the company does business in Florida. In what court might Callais bring suit—a Florida state court, a Georgia state court, or a federal court? What factors might influence her decision? **(See page 50.)**

Business Case Problems

3–3. BUSINESS CASE PROBLEM WITH SAMPLE ANSWER: Arbitration Clause.

 Kathleen Lowden sued cellular phone company T-Mobile USA, Inc., contending that its service agreements were not enforceable under Washington state law. Lowden requested that the court allow a class-action suit, in which her claims would extend to similarly affected customers. She contended that T-Mobile had improperly charged her fees beyond the advertised price of service and charged her for roaming calls that should not have been classified as roaming.

T-Mobile moved to force arbitration in accordance with the provisions that were clearly set forth in the service agreement. The agreement also specified that no class-action suit could be brought, so T-Mobile also asked the court to dismiss the request for a class-action suit. Was T-Mobile correct that Lowden's only course of action was to file for arbitration personally? Why or why not? [Lowden v. T-Mobile USA, Inc., 512 F.3d 1213 (9th Cir. 2008)] **(See page 64.)**

- For a sample answer to Problem 3–3, go to Appendix C at the end of this text.

3–4. Venue. Brandy Austin used powdered infant formula to feed her infant daughter shortly after her birth. Austin claimed that a can of Nestlé Good Start Supreme Powder Infant Formula was contaminated with *Enterobacter sakazakii* bacteria. The bacteria can cause infections of the bloodstream and central nervous system, in particular, meningitis (inflammation of the tissue surrounding the brain or spinal cord). Austin filed an action against Nestlé in Hennepin County District Court in Minnesota. Nestlé argued for a change of venue because the alleged tortious action on the part of Nestlé occurred in South Carolina. Austin is a South Carolina resident and gave birth to her daughter in that state. Should the case be transferred to a South Carolina venue? Why or why not? [*Austin v. Nestlé USA, Inc.,* 677 F.Supp.2d 1134 (D.Minn. 2009)] **(See page 57.)**

3–5. Arbitration. PRM Energy Systems owned patents licensed to Primenergy to use in the United States. Their contract stated that "all disputes" would be settled by arbitration. Kobe Steel of Japan was interested in using the technology represented by PRM's patents. Primenergy agreed to let Kobe use the technology in Japan without telling PRM. When PRM learned about the secret deal, the firm filed a suit against Primenergy for fraud and theft. Does this dispute go to arbitration or to trial? Why? [*PRM Energy Systems v. Primenergy*, 592 F.3d 830 (8th Cir. 2010)] **(See page 63.)**

3–6. Spotlight on the National Football League—Arbitration.

 Bruce Matthews played football for the Tennessee Titans. As part of his contract, he agreed to submit any dispute to arbitration. He also agreed that Tennessee law would determine all matters related to workers' compensation. After Matthews retired, he filed a workers' compensation claim in California. The arbitrator ruled that Matthews could pursue his claim in California but only under Tennessee law. Should this award be set aside? Explain. [*National Football League Players Association v. National Football League Management Council*, 2011 WL 1137334 (S.D.Cal. 2011)] **(See page 63.)**

3–7. Minimum Contacts. Seal Polymer Industries sold two freight containers of latex gloves to Med-Express, Inc., a company based in North Carolina. When Med-Express failed to pay the $104,000 owed for the gloves, Seal Polymer sued in an Illinois court and obtained a judgment against Med-Express. Med-Express argued that it did not have minimum contacts with Illinois and therefore the Illinois judgment based on personal jurisdiction was invalid. Med-Express stated that it was incorporated under North Carolina law, had its principal place of business in North Carolina, and therefore had no minimum contacts with Illinois. Was this statement alone sufficient to prevent the Illinois judgment from being collected against Med-Express in North Carolina? Why or why not? [*Seal Polymer Industries v. Med-Express, Inc.*, 725 S.E.2d 5 (N.C.App. 2012)] **(See pages 50 and 51.)**

3–8. Arbitration. Horton Automatics and the Industrial Division of the Communications Workers of America, the union that represented Horton's workers, negotiated a collective bargaining agreement. If an employee's discharge for a workplace-rule violation was submitted to arbitration, the agreement limited the arbitrator to determining whether the rule was reasonable and whether the employee violated it. When Horton discharged employee Ruben de la Garza, the union appealed to arbitration. The arbitrator found that de la Garza had violated a reasonable safety rule, but "was not totally convinced" that Horton should have treated the violation more seriously than other rule violations. The arbitrator ordered de la Garza reinstated. Can a court set aside this order? Explain. [*Horton Automatics v. The Industrial Division of the Communications Workers of America, AFL-CIO*, 2013 WL 59204 (5th Cir. 2013)] **(See page 63.)**

3–9. A QUESTION OF ETHICS: Agreement to Arbitrate.

 Nellie Lumpkin, who suffered from various illnesses, including dementia, was admitted to the Picayune Convalescent Center, a nursing home. Because of her mental condition, her daughter, Beverly McDaniel, filled out the admissions paperwork and signed the admissions agreement. It included a clause requiring parties to submit to arbitration any disputes that arose. After Lumpkin left the center two years later, she sued, through her husband, for negligent treatment and malpractice during her stay. The center moved to force the matter to arbitration. The trial court held that the arbitration agreement was not enforceable. The center appealed. [*Covenant Health & Rehabilitation of Picayune, LP v. Lumpkin*, 23 So.3d 1092 (Miss.App. 2009)] **(See page 63.)**

(a) Should a dispute involving medical malpractice be forced into arbitration? This is a claim of negligent care, not a breach of a commercial contract. Is it ethical for medical facilities to impose such a requirement? Is there really any bargaining over such terms? Discuss fully.

(b) Should a person with limited mental capacity be held to the arbitration clause agreed to by the next-of-kin who signed on behalf of that person? Why or why not?

Legal Reasoning Group Activity

3–10. Access to Courts. Assume that a statute in your state requires that all civil lawsuits involving damages of less than $50,000 be arbitrated. Such a case can be tried in court only if a party is dissatisfied with the arbitrator's decision. The statute also provides that if a trial does not result in an improvement of more than 10 percent in the position of the party who demanded the trial, that party must pay the entire costs of the arbitration proceeding. **(See page 63.)**

(a) One group will argue that the state statute violates litigants' rights of access to the courts and to trial by jury.

(b) Another group will argue that the statute does not violate litigants' rights of access to the courts.

(c) A third group will evaluate how the determination on rights of access would be changed if the statute was part of a pilot program and affected only a few judicial districts in the state.

CHAPTER 4

TORTS

Part of doing business today—and, indeed, part of everyday life—is the risk of being involved in a lawsuit. The list of circumstances in which businesspersons can be sued is long and varied. A customer who is injured by a security guard at a business establishment, for instance, may sue the business owner, claiming that the security guard's conduct was intentionally wrongful. The parents of a young girl who is bitten while feeding a dolphin may file a suit against Sea World, alleging *negligence* (to be explained later in this chapter).

Any time that one party's allegedly wrongful conduct causes injury to another, an action may arise under the law of *torts* (the word *tort* is French for "wrong"). Through tort law, society compensates those who have suffered injuries as a result of the wrongful conduct of others.

Many of the lawsuits brought by or against business firms are based on the tort theories discussed in this chapter and the next chapter, which covers strict liability and product liability. In addition, Chapter 6 discusses how tort law applies to wrongful actions in the online environment.

THE BASIS OF TORT LAW

Two notions serve as the basis of all **torts:** wrongs and compensation. Tort law is designed to compensate those who have suffered a loss or injury due to another person's wrongful act. In a tort action, one person or group brings a lawsuit against another person or group to obtain compensation (monetary damages) or other relief for the harm suffered.

The Purpose of Tort Law

Generally, the purpose of tort law is to provide remedies for the violation of various *protected interests*. Society recognizes an interest in personal physical safety. Thus, tort law provides remedies for acts that cause physical injury or that interfere with physical security and freedom of movement. Society recognizes an interest in protecting property, and tort law provides remedies for acts that cause destruction of or damage to property.

Damages Available in Tort Actions

Because the purpose of tort law is to compensate the injured party for the damage suffered, you need to have an understanding of the types of damages that plaintiffs seek in tort actions.

COMPENSATORY DAMAGES A plaintiff is awarded **compensatory damages** to compensate or reimburse the plaintiff for actual losses. Thus, the goal is to make the plaintiff whole and put her or him in the same position that she or he would have been in had the tort not occurred. Compensatory damages awards are often broken down into *special damages* and *general damages*.

Special damages compensate the plaintiff for quantifiable monetary losses. Such losses might include medical expenses, lost wages and benefits (now and in the future), extra costs, the loss of irreplaceable items, and the costs of repairing or replacing damaged property.

▶ **Case in Point 4.1** Seaway Marine Transport operates the *Enterprise*, a large cargo ship, which has twenty-two hatches for storing coal. When the *Enterprise* positioned itself to receive a load of coal on the shores of Lake Erie, in Ohio, it struck a land-based coal-loading machine operated by Bessemer & Lake Erie Railroad Company. A federal court found Seaway liable and awarded $522,000 in special damages to compensate Bessemer for the cost of repairing the damage to the loading boom.[1] ◄

General damages compensate individuals (not companies) for the nonmonetary aspects of the harm suffered, such as pain and suffering. A court might award general damages for physical or emotional pain and suffering, loss of companionship, loss of consortium (losing the emotional and physical benefits of a spousal relationship), disfigurement, loss of reputation, or loss or impairment of mental or physical capacity.

PUNITIVE DAMAGES Occasionally, the courts also award **punitive damages** in tort cases to punish the wrongdoer and deter others from similar wrongdoing. Punitive damages are appropriate only when the defendant's conduct was particularly egregious (reprehensible).

Usually, this means that punitive damages are available in *intentional* tort actions and only rarely in negligence lawsuits (negligence actions will be discussed later in this chapter). They may be awarded, however, in suits involving *gross negligence*. Gross negligence can be defined as an intentional failure to perform a manifest duty in reckless disregard of the consequences of such a failure for the life or property of another.

Courts exercise great restraint in granting punitive damages to plaintiffs in tort actions because punitive damages are subject to limitations under the due process clause of the U.S. Constitution (see Chapter 2). The United States Supreme Court has held that to the extent an award of punitive damages is grossly excessive, it furthers no legitimate purpose and violates due process requirements.[2] Consequently, an appellate court will sometimes reduce the amount of punitive damages awarded to a plaintiff on the ground that it is excessive and thereby violates the due process clause.[3]

Tort Reform

Tort law performs a valuable function by enabling injured parties to obtain compensation. Nevertheless, critics contend that certain aspects of today's tort law

encourage too many trivial and unfounded lawsuits, which clog the courts and add unnecessary costs. They say that damages awards are often excessive and bear little relationship to the actual damage suffered, which inspires more plaintiffs to file lawsuits. The result, in the critics' view, is a system that disproportionately rewards a few plaintiffs while imposing a "tort tax" on business and society as a whole. For instance, to avoid *medical malpractice* (see page 85) suits, physicians and hospitals often order more tests than necessary.

TYPES OF REFORMS The federal government and a number of states have begun to take some steps toward tort reform. Measures to reduce the number of tort cases can include any of the following:

1. Limiting the amount of both punitive damages and general damages that can be awarded.
2. Capping the amount that attorneys can collect in *contingency fees* (attorneys' fees that are based on a percentage of the damages awarded to the client).
3. Requiring the losing party to pay both the plaintiff's and the defendant's expenses.

FEDERAL REFORM At the federal level, the Class Action Fairness Act (CAFA) of 2005[4] shifted jurisdiction over large interstate tort and product liability class-action lawsuits from the state courts to the federal courts. (A *class action* is a lawsuit in which a large number of plaintiffs bring the suit as a group. *Product liability* suits involve the manufacture, sale, and distribution of dangerous and defective goods.)

The CAFA prevents plaintiffs' attorneys from *forum shopping*—looking for a state court known to be sympathetic to their clients' cause. Previously, some state courts had been predisposed to award large damages in class-action suits, even when the case had only a weak connection to that jurisdiction. State courts no longer have jurisdiction over class actions under the CAFA.

STATE REFORMS At the state level, more than half of the states have placed caps ranging from $250,000 to $750,000 on noneconomic general damages (for example, pain and suffering), especially in medical malpractice suits. More than thirty states have limited punitive damages, with some imposing outright bans.

Note that the supreme courts in about half a dozen states have declared their state's damages caps to be unconstitutional. ► **Case in Point 4.2** Naython

1. *Bessemer & Lake Erie Railroad Co. v. Seaway Marine Transport,* 357 F.3d 596 (6th Cir. 2010).
2. *State Farm Mutual Automobile Insurance Co. v. Campbell,* 538 U.S. 408, 123 S.Ct. 1513, 155 L.Ed.2d 585 (2003).
3. See, for example, *Buell-Wilson v. Ford Motor Co.,* 160 Cal.App.4th 1107, 73 Cal.Rptr.3d 277 (2008).
4. 28 U.S.C. Sections 1711–1715, 1453.

Watts was born with disabling brain injuries because Cox Medical Centers, in Missouri, and its associated physicians were negligent in providing health-care services. At the age of six, Naython cannot walk, talk, or feed himself; has the mental capacity of a two-year-old; suffers from seizures; and needs around-the-clock care. His mother, Deborah Watts, sued the medical center on his behalf. Watts won a $1.45 million jury award for noneconomic damages plus $3.37 million for future medical damages.

The trial court reduced the noneconomic damages award to $350,000—the statutory cap under Missouri's law. State law also required the trial court to split the future damages award into two parts, with half the amount payable in yearly installments for fifty years (Naython's life expectancy). Watts appealed. Missouri's highest court struck down the state's damages cap, holding that it violated the state constitution's right to trial by jury. The court reasoned that the amount of damages is a fact for the jury to determine, and the legislature cannot place caps on jury awards independent of the facts of a case.[5] ◄

Classification of Torts

There are two broad classifications of torts: *intentional torts* and *unintentional torts* (torts involving negligence). The classification of a particular tort depends largely on how the tort occurs (intentionally or negligently) and the surrounding circumstances. Intentional torts result from the intentional violation of person or property (fault plus intent). Negligence results from the breach of a duty to act reasonably (fault without intent).

Defenses

Even if a plaintiff proves all the elements of a tort, the defendant can raise a number of legally recognized *defenses* (reasons why the plaintiff should not obtain damages). The defenses available may vary depending on the specific tort involved. A common defense to intentional torts against persons, for instance, is *consent.* When a person consents to the act that damages her or him, there is generally no liability. The most widely used defense in negligence actions is *comparative negligence* (see page 90). A successful defense releases the defendant from partial or full liability for the tortious act.

---

5. *Watts v. Lester E. Cox Medical Centers,* 376 S.W.3d 633 (Mo. 2012).

INTENTIONAL TORTS AGAINST PERSONS

An **intentional tort,** as the term implies, requires intent. The **tortfeasor** (the one committing the tort) must intend to commit an act, the consequences of which interfere with another's personal or business interests in a way not permitted by law. An evil or harmful motive is not required—in fact, the person committing the action may even have a beneficial motive for doing what turns out to be a tortious act.

In tort law, *intent* means only that the person intended the consequences of his or her act or knew with substantial certainty that specific consequences would result from the act. The law generally assumes that individuals intend the *normal* consequences of their actions. Thus, forcefully pushing another—even if done in jest—is an intentional tort (if injury results), because the object of a strong push can ordinarily be expected to fall down.

In addition, intent can be transferred when a defendant intends to harm one individual, but unintentionally harms a second person. This is called **transferred intent. ► Example 4.3** Alex swings a bat intending to hit Blake but misses and hits Carson instead. Carson can sue Alex for the tort of battery (discussed shortly) because Alex's intent to harm Blake can be transferred to Carson. ◄

Assault

An **assault** is any intentional and unexcused threat of immediate harmful or offensive contact—words or acts that create a reasonably believable threat. An assault can occur even if there is no actual contact with the plaintiff, provided that the defendant's conduct creates a reasonable apprehension of imminent harm in the plaintiff. Tort law aims to protect individuals from having to expect harmful or offensive contact.

Battery

If the act that created the apprehension is *completed* and results in harm to the plaintiff, it is a **battery**— an unexcused and harmful or offensive physical contact *intentionally* performed. **► Example 4.4** Ivan threatens Jean with a gun and then shoots her. The pointing of the gun at Jean is an assault. The firing of the gun (if the bullet hits Jean) is a battery. ◄

The contact can be harmful, or it can be merely offensive (such as an unwelcome kiss). Physical injury need not occur. The contact can involve any part of the body or anything attached to it—for instance, a hat, a purse, or a jacket. The contact can be made by the defendant or by some force set in motion by the defendant, such as by throwing a rock. Whether the contact is offensive is determined by the *reasonable person standard*.[6]

If the plaintiff shows that there was contact, and the jury (or judge, if there is no jury) agrees that the contact was offensive, then the plaintiff has a right to compensation. A plaintiff may be compensated for the emotional harm or loss of reputation resulting from a battery, as well as for physical harm. A defendant may assert self-defense or defense of others in an attempt to justify his or her conduct.

False Imprisonment

False imprisonment is the intentional confinement or restraint of another person's activities without justification. False imprisonment interferes with the freedom to move without restraint. The confinement can be accomplished through the use of physical barriers, physical restraint, or threats of physical force. Moral pressure does not constitute false imprisonment. It is essential that the person being restrained does not wish to be restrained. (The plaintiff's consent to the restraint bars any liability.)

Businesspersons often face suits for false imprisonment after they have attempted to confine a suspected shoplifter for questioning. Under the "privilege to detain" granted to merchants in most states, a merchant can use *reasonable force* to detain or delay persons suspected of shoplifting and hold them for the police. Although laws pertaining to this privilege vary from state to state, generally any detention must be conducted in a *reasonable* manner and for only a *reasonable* length of time. Undue force or unreasonable detention can lead to liability for the business.

Cities and counties may also face lawsuits for false imprisonment if they detain individuals without reason. ▶ **Case in Point 4.5** Police arrested Adetokunbo Shoyoye for an unpaid subway ticket and for a theft that had been committed by someone who had stolen his identity. A court ordered him to be released, but a county employee mistakenly confused Shoyoye's paperwork with that of another person—who was scheduled to be sent to state prison. As a result, instead of being released, Shoyoye was held in county jail for more than two weeks. Shoyoye later sued the county for false imprisonment and won.[7] ◀

Intentional Infliction of Emotional Distress

The tort of *intentional infliction of emotional distress* involves an intentional act that amounts to extreme and outrageous conduct resulting in severe emotional distress to another. To be **actionable** (capable of serving as the ground for a lawsuit), the act must be extreme and outrageous to the point that it exceeds the bounds of decency accepted by society.

OUTRAGEOUS CONDUCT Courts in most jurisdictions are wary of emotional distress claims and confine them to situations involving truly outrageous behavior. Generally, repeated annoyances (such as those experienced by a person who is being stalked), coupled with threats, are enough. Acts that cause indignity or annoyance alone usually are not sufficient.

▶ **Example 4.6** A father attacks a man who has had consensual sexual relations with the father's nineteen-year-old daughter. The father handcuffs the man to a steel pole and threatens to kill him unless he leaves town immediately. The father's conduct may be sufficiently extreme and outrageous to be actionable as an intentional infliction of emotional distress. ◀

LIMITED BY THE FIRST AMENDMENT When the outrageous conduct consists of speech about a public figure, the First Amendment's guarantee of freedom of speech also limits emotional distress claims.

▶ **Case in Point 4.7** *Hustler* magazine once printed a false advertisement that showed a picture of the late Reverend Jerry Falwell and described him as having lost his virginity to his mother in an outhouse while he was drunk. Falwell sued the magazine for intentional infliction of emotional distress and won, but the United States Supreme Court overturned the decision. The Court held that creators of parodies of public figures are protected under the First Amendment from intentional infliction of emotional distress claims. (The Court used the same standards that apply to public figures in defamation lawsuits, discussed next.)[8] ◀

---

6. The *reasonable person standard* is an "objective" test of how a reasonable person would have acted under the same circumstances. See "The Duty of Care and Its Breach" later in this chapter.

7. *Shoyoye v. County of Los Angeles,* 203 Cal.App.4th 947, 137 Cal.Rptr.3d 839 (2012).

8. *Hustler Magazine, Inc. v. Falwell,* 485 U.S. 46, 108 S.Ct. 876, 99 L.Ed.2d 41 (1988). For another example of how the courts protect parody, see *Busch v. Viacom International, Inc.,* 477 F.Supp.2d 764 (N.D.Tex. 2007), involving a false endorsement of televangelist Pat Robertson's diet shake.

Defamation

As discussed in Chapter 2, the freedom of speech guaranteed by the First Amendment is not absolute. The courts are required to balance the vital guarantee of free speech against other pervasive and strong social interests, including society's interest in preventing and redressing attacks on reputation.

Defamation of character involves wrongfully hurting a person's good reputation. The law imposes a general duty on all persons to refrain from making false, defamatory *statements of fact* about others. Breaching this duty in writing or other permanent form (such as a digital recording) involves the tort of **libel.** Breaching this duty orally involves the tort of **slander.** The tort of defamation also arises when a false statement of fact is made about a person's product, business, or legal ownership rights to property.

To establish defamation, a plaintiff normally must prove the following:

1. The defendant made a false statement of fact.
2. The statement was understood as being about the plaintiff and tended to harm the plaintiff's reputation.
3. The statement was published to at least one person other than the plaintiff.
4. If the plaintiff is a public figure, she or he must prove *actual malice* (discussed on page 78).

STATEMENT-OF-FACT REQUIREMENT Often at issue in defamation lawsuits (including online defamation, which will be discussed later in this chapter) is whether the defendant made a statement of fact or a *statement of opinion*. Statements of opinion normally are not actionable because they are protected under the First Amendment.

In other words, making a negative statement about another person is not defamation unless the statement is false and represents something as a fact rather than a personal opinion. ▶ **Example 4.8** The statement "Lane cheats on his taxes," if false, can lead to liability for defamation. The statement "Lane is a jerk," however, cannot constitute defamation because it is an opinion. ◀

THE PUBLICATION REQUIREMENT The basis of the tort of defamation is the publication of a statement or statements that hold an individual up to contempt, ridicule, or hatred. *Publication* here means that the defamatory statements are communicated (either intentionally or accidentally) to persons

other than the defamed party. ▶ **Example 4.9** If Rodriques sends Andrews a private handwritten letter falsely accusing him of embezzling funds, the action does not constitute libel. If Peters falsely states that Gordon is dishonest and incompetent when no one else is around, the action does not constitute slander. In neither instance was the message communicated to a third party. ◀

The courts have generally held that even dictating a letter to a secretary constitutes publication, although the publication may be privileged (a concept that will be explained shortly). Moreover, if a third party merely overhears defamatory statements by chance, the courts usually hold that this also constitutes publication. Defamatory statements made via the Internet are actionable as well. Note also that any individual who repeats or republishes defamatory statements normally is liable even if that person reveals the source of the statements.

DAMAGES FOR LIBEL Once a defendant's liability for libel is established, general damages are presumed as a matter of law. General damages are designed to compensate the plaintiff for nonspecific harms such as disgrace or dishonor in the eyes of the community, humiliation, injured reputation, and emotional distress—harms that are difficult to measure. In other words, to recover damages, the plaintiff need not prove that he or she was actually harmed in any specific way as a result of the libelous statement.

DAMAGES FOR SLANDER In contrast to cases alleging libel, in a case alleging slander, the plaintiff must prove *special damages* to establish the defendant's liability. The plaintiff must show that the slanderous statement caused her or him to suffer actual economic or monetary losses.

Unless this initial hurdle of proving special damages is overcome, a plaintiff alleging slander normally cannot go forward with the suit and recover any damages. This requirement is imposed in slander cases because oral statements have a temporary quality. In contrast, a libelous (written) statement has the quality of permanence and can be circulated widely, especially through tweets and blogs. Also, libel usually results from some degree of deliberation by the author.

SLANDER *PER SE* Exceptions to the burden of proving special damages in cases alleging slander are made for certain types of slanderous statements. If a false statement constitutes "slander *per se*," it is actionable with no proof of special damages required. In most states, the following four types of declarations are considered to be slander *per se:*

1. A statement that another has a particular type of disease (such as a sexually transmitted disease or mental illness).
2. A statement that another has committed improprieties while engaging in a profession or trade.
3. A statement that another has committed or has been imprisoned for a serious crime.
4. A statement that a person (usually only unmarried persons and sometimes only women) is unchaste or has engaged in serious sexual misconduct.

DEFENSES TO DEFAMATION Truth is normally an absolute defense against a defamation charge. In other words, if a defendant in a defamation case can prove that the allegedly defamatory statements of fact were true, normally no tort has been committed.

Other defenses to defamation may exist if the speech is *privileged* or concerns a public figure. Note that the majority of defamation actions are filed in state courts, and state laws differ somewhat in the defenses they allow, such as privilege (discussed shortly).

At the heart of the following case were allegedly defamatory statements posted online that criticized a doctor for what the son of one of the doctor's patients perceived as rude and insensitive behavior.

CASE ANALYSIS

Case 4.1   McKee v. Laurion
Supreme Court of Minnesota, 825 N.W.2d 725 (2013).

IN THE LANGUAGE OF THE COURT
PAGE, Justice.

* * * *

On April 17, 2010, Kenneth Laurion, the father of Dennis Laurion (Laurion), was admitted to St. Luke's Hospital in Duluth [Minnesota] after suffering a hemorrhagic stroke. On April 19, Kenneth Laurion was transferred from the intensive care unit (ICU) of St. Luke's to a private room. The attending physician arranged for Dr. [David] McKee, a neurologist, to examine Kenneth Laurion. Dr. McKee had never met Kenneth Laurion before he examined him on April 19.

Three family members were present in Kenneth Laurion's hospital room when Dr. McKee's examination began: Laurion, his mother, and his wife. The examination lasted no longer than 20 minutes, during which time Dr. McKee made certain statements and acted in a manner that, as a whole, the Laurions perceived as rude and insensitive. After Kenneth

Laurion had been discharged from the hospital, Laurion posted the following statements regarding Dr. McKee on various "rate-your-doctor" websites:

My father spent 2 days in ICU after a hemorrhagic stroke. He saw a speech therapist and a physical therapist for evaluation. About 10 minutes after my father transferred from ICU to a ward room, Dr. McKee walked into a family visit with my dad. He seemed upset that my father had been moved. Never having met my father or his family, Dr. McKee said, "When you weren't in ICU, I had to spend time finding out if you transferred or died." When we gaped at him, he said, "Well, 44 percent of hemorrhagic strokes die within 30 days. I guess this is the better option." * * * When my father said his gown was just hanging from his neck without a back, Dr. McKee said, "That doesn't matter." My wife said, "It matters to us; let us go into the hall."

* * * *

After learning of Laurion's online postings from another patient, Dr.

McKee commenced this action [in a Minnesota state court] against Laurion, asserting claims for defamation * * * . Laurion moved for summary judgment seeking dismissal of Dr. McKee's lawsuit. The * * * court granted Laurion's motion * * * , concluding that * * * the statements were * * * substantially true.

The court of appeals * * * reversed the [lower] court * * * . The [appellate] court concluded that * * * there were genuine issues of material fact as to the statements' falsity.

* * * *

*Truth is a complete defense to a defamation action and true statements, however disparaging, are not actionable. * * * If the statement is true in substance, minor inaccuracies of expression or detail are immaterial. Minor inaccuracies do not amount to falsity so long as the substance, the gist, the sting, of the libelous charge is justified. A statement is substantially true if it would have the same effect on the mind of the reader or listener as that which the pleaded truth would have produced.*

CASE 4.1 CONTINUED

The plaintiff has the burden of proving falsity in order to establish a successful defamation claim. [Emphasis added.]

Viewing the evidence here in a light most favorable to Dr. McKee, we conclude that there is no genuine issue of material fact as to the falsity of [the] statements * * * . As to Statement 1 (Dr. McKee said he had to "spend time finding out if you transferred or died."), Dr. McKee described his account of the statement in his deposition testimony:

> I made a jocular [funny] comment * * * to the effect of I had looked for Kenneth Laurion up in the intensive care unit and was glad to find that, when he wasn't there, that he had been moved to a regular hospital bed, because you only go one of two ways when you leave the intensive care unit; you either have improved to the point where you're someplace like this or you leave because you've died.

In light of the substantial similarity between Statement 1 and Dr. McKee's account, we conclude that any differences between the two versions are nothing more than minor inaccuracies that cannot serve as a basis for satisfying the falsity element of a defamation claim. Here, the gist or sting of Laurion's and Dr. McKee's versions are the same. Both communicate the notion that patients in the intensive care unit who have suffered a hemorrhagic stroke leave the intensive care unit either because they have been transferred to a regular room or they have died. Therefore, the substance of Statement 1 is justified given the similarity of the two versions. In other words, Dr. McKee's account of what he said would produce the same effect on the mind of the reader as Statement 1. The minor inaccuracies of expression in Statement 1 as compared to Dr. McKee's version of what he said do not give rise to a genuine issue as to falsity. For these reasons, we conclude that there is no genuine issue of material fact as to the falsity of Statement 1.

As to Statement 2 (Dr. McKee said, "Well, 44 percent of hemorrhagic strokes die within 30 days. I guess this is the better option."), Dr. McKee acknowledged in his deposition that during the examination of Kenneth Laurion, he communicated to those present that some ICU patients die. However, he denies referencing a specific percentage. Thus, Dr. McKee posits that Statement 2 is false, or that, at the least, there is a genuine issue of material fact as to the falsity of Statement 2 because he never stated a specific percentage. The problem for Dr. McKee with respect to Statement 2 is that the gist or sting of Statement 2 is the mention of hemorrhagic stroke patients dying and not the percentage referenced. Statement 2 squarely satisfies the test for substantial truth because it would have the same effect on the reader regardless of whether a specific percentage is referenced (or whether the percentage is accurate). The presence or absence of a specific percentage within Statement 2, without more, has no bearing on how a reader would perceive the statement because the gist or sting of Dr. McKee's reference to death does not change based on the statistical reference. Nor does the presence, absence, or inaccuracy of the stated percentage, without more, cast Dr. McKee in a more negative light than does his discussion of patients dying. That is especially true when the reader is given no context for the statistics. Therefore, we conclude that there is no genuine issue of material fact as to the falsity of Statement 2.

As to Statement [3] (Dr. McKee said, "That doesn't matter" that the patient's gown did not cover his backside), Dr. McKee testified that he told the patient that the gown "looks like it's okay" because it did not appear that the gown was at risk of falling off. We are not persuaded that there is any meaningful difference between the two versions of the statements sufficient to create a genuine issue as to the falsity of Statement [3]. The substance or gist of the two versions is the same. Commenting that the gown "looks like it's okay" is another way of communicating that "it didn't matter" that the gown was not tied in the back. Thus, any inaccuracy of expression does not change the meaning of what Dr. McKee admits to having said. For these reasons, we conclude that Statement [3] is not actionable.

* * * *

Because the [three] statements at issue, viewed individually or in the context of the entire posting, are not actionable, we conclude that the [lower] court properly granted summary judgment in favor of Laurion.

Reversed.

LEGAL REASONING QUESTIONS

1. What are the required elements to establish a claim of defamation? Which party has to plead and prove these elements?

2. Which element of the claim is undercut by the "truth"?

3. How did the court's interpretation of the "truth" affect its decision in this case?

4. Suppose that Laurion had posted online, "When I mentioned Dr. McKee's name to a friend who is a nurse, she said, 'Dr. McKee is a real tool!'" Would this statement have been defamatory? Explain.

Privileged Communications. In some circumstances, a person will not be liable for defamatory statements because she or he enjoys a **privilege,** or immunity. Privileged communications are of two types: absolute and qualified.[9] Only in judicial proceedings and certain government proceedings is an *absolute privilege* granted. Thus, statements made by attorneys and judges in the courtroom during a trial are absolutely privileged, as are statements made by government officials during legislative debate.

In other situations, a person will not be liable for defamatory statements because he or she has a *qualified,* or *conditional, privilege.* An employer's statements in written evaluations of employees, for instance, are protected by a qualified privilege. Generally, if the statements are made in good faith and the publication is limited to those who have a legitimate interest in the communication, the statements fall within the area of qualified privilege.

▶ **Example 4.10** Jorge has worked at Sony Corporation for five years and is being considered for a management position. His supervisor, Lydia, writes a memo about Jorge's performance to those evaluating him for the position. The memo contains certain negative statements, which Lydia honestly believes are true. If Lydia limits the disclosure of the memo to company representatives, her statements will likely be protected by a qualified privilege. ◀

Public Figures. Politicians, entertainers, professional athletes, and others in the public eye are considered **public figures.** In general, public figures are considered "fair game," and false and defamatory statements about them that are published in the media will not constitute defamation unless the statements are made with **actual malice.**

To be made with actual malice, a statement must be made *with either knowledge of its falsity or a reckless disregard of the truth.*[10] Statements made about public figures, especially when they are communicated via a public medium, usually are related to matters of general public interest. Public figures generally have some access to a public medium for answering belittling falsehoods about themselves. For these reasons, public figures have a greater burden of proof in defa-

mation cases (to show actual malice) than do private individuals.

Invasion of Privacy

A person has a right to solitude and freedom from prying public eyes—in other words, to privacy. As mentioned in Chapter 2, the courts have held that certain amendments to the U.S. Constitution imply a right to privacy. Some state constitutions explicitly provide for privacy rights, as do a number of federal and state statutes. Tort law also safeguards these rights through the tort of *invasion of privacy.* Generally, to sue successfully for an invasion of privacy, a person must have a reasonable expectation of privacy, and the invasion must be highly offensive.

INVASION OF PRIVACY UNDER THE COMMON LAW
The following four acts qualify as an invasion of privacy under the common law:

1. *Intrusion into an individual's affairs or seclusion.* Invading someone's home or searching someone's briefcase or laptop without authorization is an invasion of privacy. This tort has been held to extend to eavesdropping by wiretap, unauthorized scanning of a bank account, compulsory blood testing, and window peeping. ▶ **Example 4.11** A female sports reporter for ESPN is digitally videoed while naked through the peephole in the door of her hotel room. She will probably win a lawsuit against the man who took the video and posted it on the Internet. ◀

2. *False light.* Publication of information that places a person in a false light is also an invasion of privacy. For instance, it is an invasions of privacy to write a story about a person that attributes ideas and opinions not held by that person. (Publishing such a story could involve the tort of defamation as well.) ▶ **Example 4.12** An Arkansas newspaper prints an article with the headline "Special Delivery: World's oldest newspaper carrier, 101, quits because she's pregnant!" Next to the article is a picture of a ninety-six-year-old woman who is not the subject of the article (and not pregnant). She sues the paper for placing her in a false light and probably will prevail. ◀

3. *Public disclosure of private facts.* This type of invasion of privacy occurs when a person publicly discloses private facts about an individual that an ordinary person would find objectionable or embarrassing. A newspaper account of a private

---

9. Note that the term *privileged communication* in this context is not the same as privileged communication between a professional, such as an attorney, and his or her client.

10. *New York Times Co. v. Sullivan,* 376 U.S. 254, 84 S.Ct. 710, 11 L.Ed.2d 686 (1964). As mentioned earlier, the First Amendment also protects the creator of a parody from liability for defamation of a public figure.

citizen's sex life or financial affairs could be an actionable invasion of privacy. This is so even if the information revealed is true, because it should not be a matter of public concern.

Note, however, that news reports about public figures' personal lives are often not actionable because a public figure's behavior *is* a legitimate public concern. For instance, when U.S. Congressman Anthony Weiner posted partially nude photos of himself on Twitter, his action was a matter of legitimate public concern. In contrast, the same online communications by a neighbor would likely not be a matter of public concern.

4. *Appropriation of identity.* Using a person's name, picture, likeness, or other identifiable characteristic for commercial purposes without permission is also an invasion of privacy. An individual's right to privacy normally includes the right to the exclusive use of her or his identity. ▶ **Example 4.13**   An advertising agency asks a singer with a distinctive voice and stage presence to do a marketing campaign for a new automobile. The singer rejects the offer. If the agency then uses someone who imitates the singer's voice and dance moves in the ad, it would be actionable as an appropriation of identity. ◄

APPROPRIATION STATUTES   Most states today have codified the common law tort of appropriation of identity in statutes that establish the distinct tort of appropriation or right of publicity. States differ as to the degree of likeness that is required to impose liability for appropriation, however.

Some courts have held that even when an animated character in a video or a video game is made to look like an actual person, there are not enough similarities to constitute appropriation. ▶ **Case in Point 4.14**   The Naked Cowboy, Robert Burck, is a street entertainer in New York City who performs for tourists wearing only a white cowboy hat, white cowboy boots, and white underwear. He carries a guitar strategically placed to give the illusion of nudity and has become famous. Burck sued Mars, Inc., the maker of M&Ms candy, over a video it showed on billboards in Times Square that depicted a blue M&M dressed exactly like The Naked Cowboy. The court, however, held that the use of Burck's signature costume did not amount to appropriation.[11] ◄

---

11. *Burck v. Mars, Inc.,* 571 F.Supp.2d 446 (S.D.N.Y. 2008).

Fraudulent Misrepresentation

A misrepresentation leads another to believe in a condition that is different from the condition that actually exists. Although persons sometimes make misrepresentations accidentally because they are unaware of the existing facts, the tort of **fraudulent misrepresentation,** or *fraud,* involves *intentional* deceit for personal gain. The tort includes several elements:

1. A misrepresentation of material facts or conditions with knowledge that they are false or with reckless disregard for the truth.
2. An intent to induce another party to rely on the misrepresentation.
3. A justifiable reliance on the misrepresentation by the deceived party.
4. Damages suffered as a result of that reliance.
5. A causal connection between the misrepresentation and the injury suffered.

For fraud to occur, more than mere **puffery,** or *seller's talk,* must be involved. Fraud exists only when a person represents as a fact something he or she knows is untrue. For instance, it is fraud to claim that the roof of a building does not leak when one knows that it does. Facts are objectively ascertainable, whereas seller's talk (such as "I am the best accountant in town") is not.

Normally, the tort of fraudulent misrepresentation occurs only when there is reliance on a *statement of fact.* Sometimes, however, reliance on a *statement of opinion* may involve the tort of fraudulent misrepresentation if the individual making the statement of opinion has superior knowledge of the subject matter. For instance, when a lawyer makes a statement of opinion about the law in a state in which the lawyer is licensed to practice, a court might treat it as a statement of fact.

Abusive or Frivolous Litigation

Tort law recognizes that people have a right not to be sued without a legally just and proper reason. It therefore protects individuals from the misuse of litigation. If the party that initiated a lawsuit did so out of malice and without a legitimate legal reason, and ended up losing that suit, the party can be sued for *malicious prosecution.*

Abuse of process can apply to any person using a legal process against another in an improper manner or to accomplish a purpose for which the process was not designed. The key difference between the torts of abuse of process and malicious prosecution is the level of proof. Abuse of process is not limited to prior litigation and does not require the plaintiff to prove malice. It can be based on the wrongful use of subpoenas, court orders to attach or seize real property, or other types of formal legal process.

Concept Summary 4.1 below reviews intentional torts against persons.

SECTION 3
BUSINESS TORTS

The torts known as *business torts* generally involve wrongful interference with another's business rights. Business torts involving wrongful interference generally fall into two categories: interference with a contractual relationship and interference with a business relationship.

Wrongful Interference with a Contractual Relationship

Three elements are necessary for wrongful interference with a contractual relationship to occur:

1. A valid, enforceable contract must exist between two parties.

2. A third party must know that this contract exists.
3. This third party must *intentionally induce* a party to the contract to breach the contract.

▶ **Case in Point 4.15**   A landmark case in this area involved an opera singer, Joanna Wagner, who was under contract to sing for a man named Lumley for a specified period of years. A man named Gye, who knew of this contract, nonetheless "enticed" Wagner to refuse to carry out the agreement, and Wagner began to sing for Gye. Gye's action constituted a tort because it interfered with the contractual relationship between Wagner and Lumley. (Of course, Wagner's refusal to carry out the agreement also entitled Lumley to sue Wagner for breach of contract.)[12] ◀

The body of tort law relating to wrongful interference with a contractual relationship has increased greatly in recent years. In principle, any lawful contract can be the basis for an action of this type. The contract could be between a firm and its employees or a firm and its customers. Sometimes, a competitor of a firm draws away one of the firm's key employees. Only if the original employer can show that the competitor knew of the contract's existence, and intentionally

---

12. *Lumley v. Gye,* 118 Eng.Rep. 749 (1853).

CONCEPT SUMMARY 4.1	
Intentional Torts against Persons	
NAME OF TORT	**DESCRIPTION**
Assault and Battery	Any unexcused and intentional act that causes another person to be apprehensive of immediate harm is an assault. An assault resulting in physical contact is a battery.
False Imprisonment	An intentional confinement or restraint of another person's movement without justification.
Intentional Infliction of Emotional Distress	An intentional act that amounts to extreme and outrageous conduct resulting in severe emotional distress to another.
Defamation (Libel or Slander)	A false statement of fact, not made under privilege, that is communicated to a third person and that causes damage to a person's reputation. For public figures, the plaintiff must also prove that the statement was made with actual malice.
Invasion of Privacy	Publishing or otherwise making known or using information relating to a person's private life and affairs, with which the public has no legitimate concern, without that person's permission or approval.
Fraudulent Misrepresentation (Fraud)	A false representation made by one party, through misstatement of facts or through conduct, with the intention of deceiving another and on which the other reasonably relies to his or her detriment.
Abusive or Frivolous Litigation	The filing of a lawsuit without legitimate grounds and with malice. Alternatively, the use of a legal process in an improper manner.

induced the breach, can damages be recovered from the competitor.

Wrongful Interference with a Business Relationship

Businesspersons devise countless schemes to attract customers. They are prohibited, however, from unreasonably interfering with another's business in their attempts to gain a greater share of the market.

There is a difference between *competitive practices* and *predatory behavior*—actions undertaken with the intention of unlawfully driving competitors completely out of the market. Attempting to attract customers in general is a legitimate business practice, whereas specifically targeting the customers of a competitor is more likely to be predatory.

▶ **Example 4.16** A shopping mall contains two athletic shoe stores: Joe's and Zappato's. Joe's cannot station an employee at the entrance of Zappato's to divert customers to Joe's by telling them that Joe's will beat Zappato's prices. Doing this would constitute the tort of wrongful interference with a business relationship because it would interfere with a prospective economic advantage. Such behavior is commonly considered to be an unfair trade practice. If this type of activity were permitted, Joe's would reap the benefits of Zappato's advertising. ◀

Generally, a plaintiff must prove that the defendant used predatory methods to intentionally harm an established business relationship or prospective economic advantage. The plaintiff must also prove that the defendant's interference caused the plaintiff to suffer economic harm.

Defenses to Wrongful Interference

A person will not be liable for the tort of wrongful interference with a contractual or business relationship if it can be shown that the interference was justified, or permissible. Bona fide competitive behavior—through aggressive marketing and advertising strategies, for instance—is a permissible interference even if it results in the breaking of a contract.

▶ **Example 4.17** Taylor Meats advertises so effectively that it induces Sam's Restaurant to break its contract with Burke's Meat Company. In that situation, Burke's Meat Company will be unable to recover against Taylor Meats on a wrongful interference theory. The public policy that favors free competition through advertising outweighs any possible instability that such competitive activity might cause in contractual relations. ◀

SECTION 4
INTENTIONAL TORTS AGAINST PROPERTY

Intentional torts against property include trespass to land, trespass to personal property, conversion, and disparagement of property. These torts are wrongful actions that interfere with individuals' legally recognized rights with regard to their land or personal property.

The law distinguishes real property from personal property. *Real property* is land and things permanently attached to the land, such as a house. *Personal property* consists of all other items, including cash and securities (stocks, bonds, and other ownership interests in companies).

Trespass to Land

A **trespass to land** occurs when a person, without permission, does any of the following:

1. Enters onto, above, or below the surface of land that is owned by another.
2. Causes anything to enter onto land owned by another.
3. Remains on land owned by another or permits anything to remain on it.

Actual harm to the land is not an essential element of this tort because the tort is designed to protect the right of an owner to exclusive possession.

Common types of trespass to land include walking or driving on another's land, shooting a gun over another's land, and throwing rocks at a building that belongs to someone else. Another common form of trespass involves constructing a building so that part of it extends onto an adjoining landowner's property.

ESTABLISHING TRESPASS Before a person can be a trespasser, the real property owner (or another person in actual and exclusive possession of the property, such as a renter) must establish that person as a trespasser. For instance, "posted" trespass signs expressly establish as a trespasser a person who ignores these signs and enters onto the property. A guest in your home is not a trespasser—unless he or she has been asked to leave and refuses. Any person who enters onto another's property to commit an illegal act (such as a thief entering a lumberyard at night to steal lumber) is established impliedly as a trespasser, without posted signs.

DAMAGES At common law, a trespasser is liable for any damage caused to the property and generally cannot hold the owner liable for injuries that the trespasser sustains on the premises. This common law rule is being abandoned in many jurisdictions, however, in favor of a *reasonable duty of care* rule that varies depending on the status of the parties.

For instance, a landowner may have a duty to post a notice that guard dogs patrol the property. Also, if young children were attracted to the property by some object, such a swimming pool or a sand pile, and were injured, the landowner may be held liable for their injuries. This is the so-called *attractive nuisance doctrine.* An owner can normally use reasonable force, however, to remove a trespasser from the premises—or detain the trespasser for a reasonable time—without liability for damages.

DEFENSES AGAINST TRESPASS TO LAND One defense to a claim of trespass is to show that the trespass was warranted—such as when a trespasser enters a building to assist someone in danger. Another defense exists when the trespasser can show that she or he had a *license* to come onto the land.

A **licensee** is one who is invited (or allowed to enter) onto the property of another for the licensee's benefit. A person who enters another's property to read an electric meter, for example, is a licensee. When you purchase a ticket to attend a movie or sporting event, you are licensed to go onto the property of another to view that movie or event.

Note that licenses to enter onto another's property are *revocable* by the property owner. If a property owner asks an electric meter reader to leave and she or he refuses to do so, the meter reader at that point becomes a trespasser.

Trespass to Personal Property

Whenever any individual wrongfully takes or harms the personal property of another or otherwise interferes with the lawful owner's possession and enjoyment of personal property, **trespass to personal property** occurs. This tort may also be called *trespass to chattels* or *trespass to personalty.*[13] In this context,

harm means not only destruction of the property, but also anything that diminishes its value, condition, or quality.

Trespass to personal property involves intentional meddling with a possessory interest (one arising from possession), including barring an owner's access to personal property. ▶ **Example 4.18** Kelly takes Ryan's business law book as a practical joke and hides it so that Ryan is unable to find it for several days before the final examination. Here, Kelly has engaged in a trespass to personal property (and also *conversion,* the tort discussed next). ◀

If it can be shown that trespass to personal property was warranted, then a complete defense exists. Most states, for instance, allow automobile repair shops to hold a customer's car (under what is called an *artisan's lien*) when the customer refuses to pay for repairs already completed.

Conversion

Any act that deprives an owner of personal property or of the use of that property without the owner's permission and without just cause can constitute **conversion.** Even the taking of electronic records and data may form the basis of a conversion claim. Often, when conversion occurs, a trespass to personal property also occurs because the original taking of the personal property from the owner was a trespass. Wrongfully retaining the property is conversion.

Conversion is the civil side of crimes related to theft, but it is not limited to theft. Even when the rightful owner consented to the initial taking of the property, so no theft or trespass occurred, a failure to return the property may still be conversion. ▶ **Example 4.19** Chen borrows Mark's iPad mini to use while traveling home from school for the holidays. When Chen returns to school, Mark asks for his iPad back, but Chen says that he gave it to his little brother for Christmas. In this situation, Mark can sue Chen for conversion, and Chen will have to either return the iPad or pay damages equal to its replacement value. ◀

Conversion can occur even when a person mistakenly believed that she or he was entitled to the goods. In other words, good intentions are not a defense against conversion. Someone who buys stolen goods, for instance, may be sued for conversion even if he or she did not know the goods were stolen. If the true owner brings a tort action against the buyer, the buyer must either return the property to the owner or pay the owner the full value of the property (despite having already paid the purchase price to the thief).

---

13. Pronounced *per-sun-ul-tee.*

Disparagement of Property

Disparagement of property occurs when economically injurious falsehoods are made about another's product or property rather than about another's reputation (as in the tort of defamation). *Disparagement of property* is a general term for torts that can be more specifically referred to as *slander of quality* or *slander of title.*

SLANDER OF QUALITY The publication of false information about another's product, alleging that it is not what its seller claims, constitutes the tort of **slander of quality,** or *trade libel.* To establish trade libel, the plaintiff must prove that the improper publication caused a third person to refrain from dealing with the plaintiff and that the plaintiff sustained economic damages (such as lost profits) as a result.

An improper publication may be both a slander of quality and a defamation of character. For instance, a statement that disparages the quality of a product may also, by implication, disparage the character of a person who would sell such a product.

SLANDER OF TITLE When a publication falsely denies or casts doubt on another's legal ownership of property, resulting in financial loss to the property's owner, the tort of **slander of title** occurs. Usually, this is an intentional tort in which someone knowingly publishes an untrue statement about another's ownership of certain property with the intent of discouraging a third person from dealing with the person slandered. For instance, it would be difficult for a car dealer to attract customers after competitors published a notice that the dealer's stock consisted of stolen automobiles.

See *Concept Summary 4.2* below for a review of intentional torts against property.

SECTION 5

UNINTENTIONAL TORTS (NEGLIGENCE)

The tort of **negligence** occurs when someone suffers injury because of another's failure to live up to a required *duty of care.* In contrast to intentional torts, in torts involving negligence, the tortfeasor neither wishes to bring about the consequences of the act nor believes that they will occur. The person's conduct merely creates a risk of such consequences. If no risk is created, there is no negligence. Moreover, the risk must be foreseeable. In other words, it must be such that a reasonable person engaging in the same activity would anticipate the risk and guard against it. In determining what is reasonable conduct, courts consider the nature of the possible harm.

Many of the actions giving rise to the intentional torts discussed earlier in the chapter constitute negligence if the element of intent is missing (or cannot be proved). ▶ **Example 4.20** Juan walks up to Maya and intentionally shoves her. Maya falls and breaks her arm as a result. In this situation, Juan is liable for the intentional tort of battery. If Juan carelessly bumps into Maya, however, and she falls and breaks her arm as a result, Juan's action constitutes

---

CONCEPT SUMMARY 4.2
Intentional Torts against Property

NAME OF TORT	DESCRIPTION
Trespass to Land	The invasion of another's real property without consent or privilege. Once a person is expressly or impliedly established as a trespasser, the property owner has specific rights, which may include the right to detain or remove the trespasser.
Trespass to Personal Property	The intentional interference with an owner's right to use, possess, or enjoy his or her personal property without the owner's consent.
Conversion	The wrongful possession or use of another person's personal property without just cause.
Disparagement of Property	Any economically injurious falsehood that is made about another's product or property; an inclusive term for the torts of *slander of quality* and *slander of title.*

negligence. In either situation, Juan has committed a tort. ◄

To succeed in a negligence action, the plaintiff must prove each of the following:

1. *Duty.* The defendant owed a duty of care to the plaintiff.
2. *Breach.* The defendant breached that duty.
3. *Causation.* The defendant's breach caused the plaintiff's injury.
4. *Damages.* The plaintiff suffered a legally recognizable injury.

The Duty of Care and Its Breach

Central to the tort of negligence is the concept of a **duty of care.** The basic principle underlying the duty of care is that people are free to act as they please so long as their actions do not infringe on the interests of others. When someone fails to comply with the duty to exercise reasonable care, a potentially tortious act may have been committed.

Failure to live up to a standard of care may be an act (accidentally setting fire to a building) or an omission (neglecting to put out a campfire). It may be a careless act or a carefully performed but, nevertheless, dangerous act that results in injury. Courts consider the nature of the act (whether it is outrageous or commonplace) and the manner in which the act is performed (carelessly versus cautiously). In addition, courts look at the nature of the injury (whether it is serious or slight) in determining whether the duty of care has been breached. Creating a very slight risk of a dangerous explosion might be unreasonable, whereas creating a distinct possibility of someone's burning his or her fingers on a stove might be reasonable.

THE REASONABLE PERSON STANDARD Tort law measures duty by the **reasonable person standard.** In determining whether a duty of care has been breached, the courts ask how a reasonable person would have acted in the same circumstances. The reasonable person standard is said to be objective. It is not necessarily how a particular person *would* act. It is society's judgment of how an ordinarily prudent person *should* act. If the so-called reasonable person existed, he or she would be careful, conscientious, even tempered, and honest.

The courts frequently use the hypothetical reasonable person standard in other areas of law as well. That individuals are required to exercise a reasonable standard of care in their activities is a pervasive con-

cept in business law. Many of the issues discussed in subsequent chapters of this text have to do with the duty of reasonable care.

In negligence cases, the degree of care to be exercised varies, depending on the defendant's occupation or profession, her or his relationship with the plaintiff, and other factors. Generally, whether an action constitutes a breach of the duty of care is determined on a case-by-case basis. The outcome depends on how the judge (or jury, if it is a jury trial) decides a reasonable person in the position of the defendant would have acted in the particular circumstances of the case.

THE DUTY OF LANDOWNERS Landowners are expected to exercise reasonable care to protect individuals coming onto their property from harm. In some jurisdictions, as mentioned earlier, landowners may even have a duty to protect trespassers against certain risks. Landowners who rent or lease premises to tenants are expected to exercise reasonable care to ensure that the tenants and their guests are not harmed in common areas, such as stairways, entryways, and laundry rooms.

The Duty to Warn Business Invitees of Risks. Retailers and other companies that explicitly or implicitly invite persons to come onto their premises have a duty to exercise reasonable care to protect these **business invitees.** The duty normally requires storeowners to warn business invitees of foreseeable risks, such as construction zones or wet floors, about which the owners knew or *should have known.*

▶ **Example 4.21** Liz enters a supermarket, slips on a wet floor, and sustains injuries as a result. If there was no sign or other warning that the floor was wet at the time Liz slipped, the supermarket owner would be liable for damages. A court would hold that the owner was negligent by failing to exercise a reasonable degree of care to protect customers against the foreseeable risk of injury from slipping on the wet floor. The owner should have taken care to avoid this risk or warn the customer of it (such as by posting a sign or setting out orange cones). ◄

The landowner also has a duty to discover and remove any hidden dangers that might injure a customer or other invitee. Hidden dangers might include uneven surfaces or defects in the pavement of a parking lot or a walkway. Store owners also have a duty to protect customers from slipping and injuring themselves on merchandise that has fallen off the shelves, for instance. Thus, the owners of business premises should evaluate and frequently reassess potential hazards on the property to ensure the safety of business invitees.

Obvious Risks Provide an Exception. Some risks, of course, are so obvious that an owner need not warn of them. For example, a business owner does not need to warn customers to open a door before attempting to walk through it. Other risks, however, even though they may seem obvious to a business owner, may not be so in the eyes of another, such as a child. In addition, even if a risk is obvious, that does not necessarily excuse a business owner from the duty to protect its customers from foreseeable harm.

▶ **Case in Point 4.22** Giorgio's Grill is a restaurant in Florida that becomes a nightclub after hours. At those times, traditionally, as the manager of Giorgio's knew, the staff and customers throw paper napkins into the air as the music plays. The napkins land on the floor, but no one picks them up. One night, Jane Izquierdo went to Giorgio's. Although she had been to the club on prior occasions and knew about the napkin-throwing tradition, she slipped and fell, breaking her leg. She sued Giorgio's for negligence, but lost at trial because a jury found that the risk of slipping on the napkins was obvious. A state appellate court reversed, however, holding that the obviousness of a risk does not discharge a business owner's duty to its invitees to maintain the premises in a safe condition.[14] ◀

THE DUTY OF PROFESSIONALS If an individual has knowledge or skill superior to that of an ordinary person, the individual's conduct must be consistent with that status. Professionals—including physicians, dentists, architects, engineers, accountants, and lawyers, among others—are required to have a standard minimum level of special knowledge and ability. Therefore, in determining what constitutes reasonable care in the case of professionals, the law takes their training and expertise into account. Thus, an accountant's conduct is judged not by the reasonable person standard, but by the reasonable accountant standard.

If a professional violates his or her duty of care toward a client, the client may bring a suit against the professional, alleging **malpractice,** which is essentially professional negligence. For instance, a patient might sue a physician for *medical malpractice*. A client might sue an attorney for *legal malpractice*.

Causation

Another element necessary to a negligence action is *causation*. If a person breaches a duty of care and someone suffers injury, the person's act must have caused the harm for it to constitute the tort of negligence.

COURTS ASK TWO QUESTIONS In deciding whether the requirement of causation is met, the court must address two questions:

1. *Is there causation in fact?* Did the injury occur because of the defendant's act, or would it have occurred anyway? If the injury would not have occurred without the defendant's act, then there is causation in fact.

    Causation in fact usually can be determined by use of the *but for* test: "but for" the wrongful act, the injury would not have occurred. This test determines whether there was an actual cause-and-effect relationship between the act and the injury suffered. In theory, causation in fact is limitless. One could claim, for example, that "but for" the creation of the world, a particular injury would not have occurred. Thus, as a practical matter, the law has to establish limits, and it does so through the concept of proximate cause.

2. *Was the act the proximate, or legal, cause of the injury?* **Proximate cause,** or *legal cause*, exists when the connection between an act and an injury is strong enough to justify imposing liability. Proximate cause asks whether the injuries sustained were foreseeable or were too remotely connected to the incident to trigger liability. Judges use proximate cause to limit the scope of the defendant's liability to a subset of the total number of potential plaintiffs that might have been harmed by the defendant's actions.

    ▶ **Example 4.23** Ackerman carelessly leaves a campfire burning. The fire not only burns down the forest but also sets off an explosion in a nearby chemical plant that spills chemicals into a river, killing all the fish for a hundred miles downstream and ruining the economy of a tourist resort. Should Ackerman be liable to the resort owners? To the tourists whose vacations were ruined? These are questions of proximate cause that a court must decide. ◀

Both of these causation questions must be answered in the affirmative for liability in tort to arise. If there is causation in fact but a court decides that the defendant's action is not the proximate cause of the plaintiff's injury, the causation requirement has not been

14. *Izquierdo v. Gyroscope, Inc.*, 946 So.2d 115 (Fla.App. 2007).

met. Therefore, the defendant normally will not be liable to the plaintiff.

FORESEEABILITY Questions of proximate cause are linked to the concept of foreseeability because it would be unfair to impose liability on a defendant unless the defendant's actions created a foreseeable risk of injury.

Probably the most cited case on the concept of foreseeability and proximate cause is the *Palsgraf* case, which is presented next. In determining the issue of proximate cause, the court addressed the following question: Does a defendant's duty of care extend only to those who may be injured as a result of a foreseeable risk, or does it also extend to a person whose injury could not reasonably be foreseen?

CLASSIC CASE 4.2

Palsgraf v. Long Island Railroad Co.
Court of Appeals of New York, 248 N.Y. 339, 162 N.E. 99 (1928).

BACKGROUND AND FACTS The plaintiff, Helen Palsgraf, was waiting for a train on a station platform. A man carrying a package was rushing to catch a train that was moving away from a platform across the tracks from Palsgraf. As the man attempted to jump aboard the moving train, he seemed unsteady and about to fall. A railroad guard on the car reached forward to grab him, and another guard on the platform pushed him from behind to help him board the train.

In the process, the man's package, which (unknown to the railroad guards) contained fireworks, fell on the railroad tracks and exploded. There was nothing about the package to indicate its contents. The repercussions of the explosion caused scales at the other end of the train platform to fall on Palsgraf, causing injuries for which she sued the railroad company. At the trial, the jury found that the railroad guards had been negligent in their conduct. The railroad company appealed. The appellate court affirmed the trial court's judgment, and the railroad company appealed to New York's highest state court.

IN THE LANGUAGE OF THE COURT
CARDOZO, C.J. [Chief Justice]

* * * *

The conduct of the defendant's guard, if a wrong in its relation to the holder of the package, was not a wrong in its relation to the plaintiff, standing far away. Relatively to her it was not negligence at all.

* * * *

* * * What the plaintiff must show is "a wrong" to herself; i.e., a violation of her own right, and not merely a wrong to someone else[.] * * * *The risk reasonably to be perceived defines the duty to be obeyed[.]* * * * Here, by concession, there was nothing in the situation to suggest to the most cautious mind that the parcel wrapped in newspaper would spread wreckage through the station. If the guard had thrown it down knowingly and willfully, he would not have threatened the plaintiff's safety, so far as appearances could warn him. His conduct would not have involved, even then, an unreasonable probability of invasion of her bodily security. Liability can be no greater where the act is inadvertent. [Emphasis added.]

* * * One who seeks redress at law does not make out a cause of action by showing without more that there has been damage to his person. If the harm was not willful, he must show that the act as to him had possibilities of danger so many and apparent as to entitle him to be protected against the doing of it though the harm was unintended. * * * The victim does not sue * * * to vindicate an interest invaded in the person of another. * * * He sues for breach of a duty owing to himself.

* * * [To rule otherwise] would entail liability for any and all consequences, however novel or extraordinary.

CASE 4.2 CONTINUED

DECISION AND REMEDY *Palsgraf's complaint was dismissed. The railroad had not been negligent toward her because injury to her was not foreseeable. Had the owner of the fireworks been harmed, and had he filed suit, there could well have been a different result.*

THE GLOBAL DIMENSION *What would be the advantages and disadvantages of a universal principle of proximate cause applied everywhere by all courts in all relevant cases? Discuss.*

IMPACT OF THIS CASE ON TODAY'S LAW *The Palsgraf case established foreseeability as the test for proximate cause. Today, the courts continue to apply this test in determining proximate cause—and thus tort liability for injuries. Generally, if the victim or the consequences of a harm done were unforeseeable, there is no proximate cause. Note, though, that in the online environment, distinctions based on physical proximity, such as that used by the court in this case, are largely inapplicable.*

The Injury Requirement and Damages

For a tort to have been committed, the plaintiff must have suffered a *legally recognizable* injury. To recover damages (receive compensation), the plaintiff must have suffered some loss, harm, wrong, or invasion of a protected interest. Essentially, the purpose of tort law is to compensate for legally recognized harms and injuries resulting from wrongful acts. If no harm or injury results from a given negligent action, there is nothing to compensate—and no tort exists.

For instance, if you carelessly bump into a passerby, who stumbles and falls as a result, you may be liable in tort if the passerby is injured in the fall. If the person is unharmed, however, there normally can be no suit for damages because no injury was suffered.

As mentioned at the start of this chapter, compensatory damages are the norm in negligence cases. Occasionally, though, a court will award punitive damages if the defendant's conduct was *grossly negligent*, meaning that the defendant intentionally failed to perform a duty with reckless disregard of the consequences to others.

Negligence *Per Se*

Certain conduct, whether it consists of an action or a failure to act, may be treated as **negligence *per se*** ("in or of itself"). Negligence *per se* may occur if an individual violates a statute or an ordinance providing for a criminal penalty and that violation causes another to be injured. The statute must be designed to prevent the type of injury that the plaintiff suffered and must clearly set out what standard of conduct is expected. The statute must also indicate when, where, and of whom that conduct is expected. The standard of conduct required by the statute is the duty that the

defendant owes to the plaintiff, and a violation of the statute is the breach of that duty.

▶ **Case in Point 4.24** A Delaware statute states that anyone "who operates a motor vehicle and who fails to give full time and attention to the operation of the vehicle" is guilty of inattentive driving. Michael Moore was cited for inattentive driving after he collided with Debra Wright's car when he backed a truck out of a parking space. Moore paid the ticket, which meant that he pleaded guilty to violating the statute. The day after the accident, Wright began having back pain, which eventually required surgery. She sued Moore for damages, alleging negligence *per se*. The court ruled that the inattentive driving statute sets forth a sufficiently specific standard of conduct to warrant application of negligence *per se*.[15] ◀

Good Samaritan Statutes

Most states now have what are called **Good Samaritan statutes**.[16] Under these statutes, someone who is aided voluntarily by another cannot turn around and sue the "Good Samaritan" for negligence. These laws were passed largely to protect physicians and medical personnel who volunteer their services in emergency situations to those in need, such as individuals hurt in car accidents.[17] Indeed, the California Supreme Court has interpreted that state's Good Samaritan statute to mean that a person who renders

---

15. *Wright v. Moore*, 931 A.2d 405 (Del.Supr. 2007).

16. These laws derive their name from the Good Samaritan story in the Bible. In the story, a traveler who had been robbed and beaten lay along the roadside, ignored by those passing by. Eventually, a man from the region of Samaria (the "Good Samaritan") stopped to render assistance to the injured person.

17. See, for example, the discussions of various state statutes in *Chamley v. Khokha*, 730 N.W.2d 864 (N.D. 2007), and *Mueller v. McMillian Warner Insurance Co.*, 2006 WI 54, 290 Wis.2d 571, 714 N.W.2d 183 (2006).

nonmedical aid is not immune from liability.[18] Thus, only medical personnel and persons rendering medical aid in emergencies are protected in California.

Dram Shop Acts

Many states have also passed **dram shop acts**,[19] under which a bar's owner or bartender may be held liable for injuries caused by a person who became intoxicated while drinking at the bar. The owner or bartender may also be held responsible for continuing to serve a person who was already intoxicated.

Some states' statutes also impose liability on *social hosts* (persons hosting parties) for injuries caused by guests who became intoxicated at the hosts' homes. Under these statutes, it is unnecessary to prove that the bar owner, bartender, or social host was negligent.

▶ **Example 4.25**   Jane hosts a Super Bowl party at which Brett, a minor, sneaks alcoholic drinks. Jane is potentially liable for damages resulting from Brett's drunk driving after the party. ◀

SECTION 6
DEFENSES TO NEGLIGENCE

Defendants often defend against negligence claims by asserting that the plaintiffs have failed to prove the existence of one or more of the required elements for negligence. Additionally, there are three basic *affirmative* defenses in negligence cases (defenses that a defendant can use to avoid liability even if the facts are as the plaintiff states): *assumption of risk, superseding cause,* and *contributory and comparative negligence.*

Assumption of Risk

A plaintiff who voluntarily enters into a risky situation, knowing the risk involved, will not be allowed to recover. This is the defense of **assumption of risk,** which requires:

1. Knowledge of the risk.
2. Voluntary assumption of the risk.

The defense of assumption of risk is frequently asserted when the plaintiff was injured during recreational activities that involve known risk, such as skiing and skydiving. Courts do not apply the assumption of risk doctrine in emergency situations. Note that assumption of risk can apply not only to participants in sporting events, but also to spectators and bystanders who are injured while attending those events.

In the following *Spotlight Case,* the issue was whether a spectator at a baseball game voluntarily assumed the risk of being hit by an errant ball thrown while the players were warming up before the game.

---

18. *Van Horn v. Watson,* 45 Cal.4th 322, 197 P.3d 164, 86 Cal.Rptr.3d 350 (2008).
19. Historically, a dram was a small unit of liquid, and distilled spirits (strong alcoholic liquor) were sold in drams. Thus, a dram shop was a place where liquor was sold in drams.

SP TLIGHT on the Seattle Mariners

Case 4.3   Taylor v. Baseball Club of Seattle, LP
Court of Appeals of Washington, 132 Wash.App. 32, 130 P.3d 835 (2006).

BACKGROUND AND FACTS   Delinda Taylor went to a Seattle Mariners baseball game at Safeco Field with her boyfriend and two minor sons. Their seats were four rows up from the field along the right field foul line. They arrived more than an hour before the game so that they could see the players warm up and get their autographs. When she walked in, Taylor saw that Mariners pitcher, Freddy Garcia, was throwing a ball back and forth with José Mesa right in front of their seats.

As Taylor stood in front of her seat, she looked away from the field, and a ball thrown by Mesa got past Garcia and struck her in the face, causing serious injuries. Taylor sued the Mariners for the allegedly

CASE 4.3 CONTINUED

negligent warm-up throw. The Mariners filed a motion for summary judgment in which they argued that Taylor, a longtime Mariners fan, was familiar with baseball and the inherent risk of balls entering the stands. Thus, the motion asserted, Taylor had assumed the risk of her injury. The trial court granted the motion and dismissed Taylor's case. Taylor appealed.

 **IN THE LANGUAGE OF THE COURT**
DWYER, J. [Judge]

* * * *

* * * For many decades, courts have required baseball stadiums to screen some seats—generally those behind home plate—to provide protection to spectators who choose it.

A sport spectator's assumption of risk and a defendant sports team's duty of care are accordingly discerned under the doctrine of primary assumption of risk. * * * "Implied *primary* assumption of risk arises where a plaintiff has impliedly consented (often in advance of any negligence by defendant) to relieve defendant of a duty to plaintiff regarding specific *known* and appreciated risks." [Emphasis in original.]

* * * *

Under this implied primary assumption of risk, defendant must show that plaintiff had full subjective understanding of the specific risk, both its nature and presence, and that he or she voluntarily chose to encounter the risk.

* * * It is undisputed that the warm-up is part of the sport, that spectators such as Taylor purposely attend that portion of the event, and that the Mariners permit ticket-holders to view the warm-up.

* * * We find the fact that Taylor was injured during warm-up is not legally significant because that portion of the event is necessarily incident to the game.

* * * *

Here, there is no evidence that the circumstances leading to Taylor's injury constituted an unusual danger. It is undisputed that it is the normal, every-day practice at all levels of baseball for pitchers to warm up in the manner that led to this incident. *The risk of injuries such as Taylor's are within the normal comprehension of a spectator who is familiar with the game.* Indeed, the possibility of an errant ball entering the stands is part of the game's attraction for many spectators. [Emphasis added.]

* * * The record contains substantial evidence regarding Taylor's familiarity with the game. She attended many of her sons' baseball games, she witnessed balls entering the stands, she had watched Mariners' games both at the Kingdome and on television, and she knew that there was no screen protecting her seats, which were close to the field. In fact, as she walked to her seat she saw the players warming up and was excited about being in an unscreened area where her party might get autographs from the players and catch balls.

DECISION AND REMEDY *The state intermediate appellate court affirmed the lower court's judgment. As a spectator who chose to sit in an unprotected area of seats, Taylor voluntarily undertook the risk associated with being hit by an errant baseball thrown during the warm-up before the game.*

WHAT IF THE FACTS WERE DIFFERENT? *Would the result in this case have been different if it had been Taylor's minor son, rather than Taylor herself, who had been struck by the ball? Should courts apply the doctrine of assumption of risk to children? Discuss.*

THE LEGAL ENVIRONMENT DIMENSION *What is the basis underlying the defense of assumption of risk? How does that basis support the court's decision in this case?*

Superseding Cause

An unforeseeable intervening event may break the causal connection between a wrongful act and an injury to another. If so, the intervening event acts as a **superseding cause**—that is, it relieves the defendant of liability for injuries caused by the intervening event.

▶ **Example 4.26** While riding his bicycle, Derrick negligently hits Julie, who is walking on the sidewalk. As a result of the impact, Julie falls and fractures her hip. While she is waiting for help to arrive, a small aircraft crashes nearby and explodes, and some of the fiery debris hits her, causing her to sustain severe burns. Derrick will be liable for the damages related to Julie's fractured hip, because the risk of injuring her with his bicycle was foreseeable. Normally, Derrick will not be liable for the burns caused by the plane crash—because the risk of a plane crashing nearby and injuring Julie was not foreseeable. ◀

Contributory Negligence

All individuals are expected to exercise a reasonable degree of care in looking out for themselves. In the past, under the common law doctrine of **contributory negligence,** a plaintiff who was also negligent (failed to exercise a reasonable degree of care) could not recover anything from the defendant. Under this rule, no matter how insignificant the plaintiff's negligence was relative to the defendant's negligence, the plaintiff would be precluded from recovering any damages. Today, only a few jurisdictions still hold to this doctrine.

Comparative Negligence

In most states, the doctrine of contributory negligence has been replaced by a **comparative negligence** standard. Under this standard, both the plaintiff's and the defendant's negligence are computed, and the liability for damages is distributed accordingly. Some jurisdictions have adopted a "pure" form of comparative negligence that allows the plaintiff to recover, even if the extent of his or her fault is greater than that of the defendant. Under pure comparative negligence, if the plaintiff was 80 percent at fault and the defendant 20 percent at fault, the plaintiff may recover 20 percent of his or her damages.

Many states' comparative negligence statutes, however, contain a "50 percent" rule that prevents the plaintiff from recovering any damages if she or he was more than 50 percent at fault. Under this rule, a plaintiff who is 35 percent at fault could recover 65 percent of his or her damages, but a plaintiff who is 65 percent (more than 50 percent) at fault could recover nothing.

Reviewing: Torts

Elaine Sweeney went to Ragged Mountain Ski Resort in New Hampshire with a friend. Elaine went snow tubing down a snow-tube run designed exclusively for snow tubers. There were no Ragged Mountain employees present in the snow-tube area to instruct Elaine on the proper use of a snow tube. On her fourth run down the trail, Elaine crossed over the center line between snow-tube lanes, collided with another snow tuber, and was injured. Elaine filed a negligence action against Ragged Mountain seeking compensation for the injuries that she sustained. Two years earlier, the New Hampshire state legislature had enacted a statute that prohibited a person who participates in the sport of skiing from suing a ski-area operator for injuries caused by the risks inherent in skiing. Using the information presented in the chapter, answer the following questions.

1. What defense will Ragged Mountain probably assert?
2. The central question in this case is whether the state statute establishing that skiers assume the risks inherent in the sport bars Elaine's suit. What would your decision be on this issue? Why?
3. Suppose that the court concludes that the statute applies only to skiing and not to snow tubing. Will Elaine's lawsuit be successful? Explain.
4. Now suppose that the jury concludes that Elaine was partly at fault for the accident. Under what theory might her damages be reduced in proportion to the degree to which her actions contributed to the accident and her resulting injuries?

DEBATE THIS . . . *Each time a state legislature enacts a law that applies the assumption of risk doctrine to a particular sport, participants in that sport suffer.*

Terms and Concepts

actionable 74

actual malice 78

assault 73

assumption of risk 88

battery 73

business invitee 84

causation in fact 85

comparative negligence 90

compensatory damages 71

contributory negligence 90

conversion 82

defamation 75

disparagement of property 83

dram shop act 88

duty of care 84

fraudulent misrepresentation 79

Good Samaritan statute 87

intentional tort 73

libel 75

licensee 82

malpractice 85

negligence 83

negligence *per se* 87

privilege 78

proximate cause 85

public figure 78

puffery 79

punitive damages 72

reasonable person standard 84

slander 75

slander of quality 83

slander of title 83

superseding cause 89

tort 71

tortfeasor 73

transferred intent 73

trespass to land 81

trespass to personal property 82

ExamPrep

Issue Spotters

1. Jana leaves her truck's motor running while she enters a Kwik-Pik Store. The truck's transmission engages, and the vehicle crashes into a gas pump, starting a fire that spreads to a warehouse on the next block. The warehouse collapses, causing its billboard to fall and injure Lou, a bystander. Can Lou recover from Jana? Why or why not? **(See page 84.)**

2. A water pipe bursts, flooding a Metal Fabrication Company utility room and tripping the circuit breakers on a panel in the room. Metal Fabrication contacts Nouri, a licensed electrician with five years' experience, to check the damage and turn the breakers back on. Without testing for short circuits, which Nouri knows that he should do, he tries to switch on a breaker. He is electrocuted, and his wife sues Metal Fabrication for damages, alleging negligence. What might the firm successfully claim in defense? **(See pages 84 and 90.)**

• **Check your answers to the Issue Spotters against the answers provided in Appendix B at the end of this text.**

Before the Test

Go to **www.cengagebrain.com**, enter the ISBN 9781285770192, and click on "Find" to locate this textbook's Web site. Then, click on "Access Now" under "Study Tools," and select Chapter 4 at the top. There, you will find a Practice Quiz that you can take to assess your mastery of the concepts in this chapter, as well as Flashcards and a Glossary of important terms.

Business Scenarios

4–1. Defamation. Richard is an employee of the Dun Construction Corp. While delivering materials to a construction site, he carelessly backs Dun's truck into a passenger vehicle driven by Green. This is Richard's second accident in six months. When the company owner, Dun, learns of this latest accident, a heated discussion ensues, and Dun fires Richard. Dun is so angry that he immediately writes a letter to the union of which Richard is a member and to all other construction companies in the community, stating that Richard is the "worst driver in the city" and that "anyone who hires him is asking for legal liability." Richard files a suit against Dun, alleging libel on the basis of the statements made in the letters. Discuss the results. **(See page 75.)**

4–2. Wrongful Interference. Lothar owns a bakery. He has been trying to obtain a long-term contract with the owner of Martha's Tea Salons for some time. Lothar starts a local advertising campaign on radio and television and in the newspaper. This advertising campaign is so persuasive that Martha decides to break the contract she has had with Harley's Bakery so that she can patronize Lothar's bakery. Is Lothar liable to Harley's Bakery for the tort of wrongful interference with a contractual relationship? Is Martha liable for this tort? Why or why not? **(See pages 80 and 81.)**

4–3. Liability to Business Invitees. Kim went to Ling's Market to pick up a few items for dinner. It was a stormy day, and the wind had blown water through the market's door each time it opened. As Kim entered through the door, she slipped and fell in the rainwater that had accumulated on the floor. The manager knew of the weather conditions but had not posted any sign to warn customers of the water hazard. Kim injured her back as a result of the fall and sued Ling's for damages. Can Ling's be held liable for negligence? Discuss. **(See page 84.)**

Business Case Problems

4–4. Spotlight on Intentional Torts—Defamation. Sharon Yeagle was an assistant to the vice president of student affairs at Virginia Polytechnic Institute and State University (Virginia Tech). As part of her duties, Yeagle helped students participate in the Governor's Fellows Program. The *Collegiate Times,* Virginia Tech's student newspaper, published an article about the university's success in placing students in the program. The article's text surrounded a block quotation attributed to Yeagle with the phrase "Director of Butt Licking" under her name. Yeagle sued the *Collegiate Times* for defamation. She argued that the phrase implied the commission of sodomy and was therefore actionable. What is *Collegiate Times's* defense to this claim? [*Yeagle v. Collegiate Times,* 497 S.E.2d 136 (Va. 1998)] **(See page 75.)**

4–5. Proximate Cause. Galen Stoller was killed at a railroad crossing when an AMTRAK train hit his car. The crossing was marked with a stop sign and a railroad-crossing symbol, but there were no flashing lights. Galen's parents filed a suit against National Railroad Passenger Corp. (AMTRAK) and Burlington Northern & Santa Fe Railroad Corp., alleging negligence in the design and maintenance of the crossing. The defendants argued that Galen had not stopped at the stop sign. Was AMTRAK negligent? What was the proximate cause of the accident? Discuss. [*Henderson v. National Railroad Passenger Corp.,* __ F.3d __ (10th Cir. 2011)] **(See page 85.)**

4–6. Business Torts. Medtronic, Inc., is a medical technology company that competes for customers with St. Jude Medical S.C., Inc. James Hughes worked for Medtronic as a sales manager. His contract prohibited him from working for a competitor for one year after leaving Medtronic. Hughes sought a position as a sales director for St. Jude. St. Jude told Hughes that his contract with Medtronic was unenforceable and offered him a job. Hughes accepted. Medtronic filed a suit, alleging wrongful interference. Which type of interference was most likely the basis for this suit? Did it occur here? Explain. [*Medtronic, Inc. v. Hughes,* __ N.W.2d __ (Minn.App. 2011)] **(See page 80.)**

4–7. Intentional Infliction of Emotional Distress. While living in her home country of Tanzania, Sophia Kiwanuka signed an employment contract with Anne Margareth Bakilana, a Tanzanian living in Washington, D.C. Kiwanuka traveled to the United States to work as a babysitter and maid in Bakilana's house. When Kiwanuka arrived, Bakilana confiscated her passport, held her in isolation, and forced her to work long hours under threat of having her deported. Kiwanuka worked seven days a week without breaks and was subjected to regular verbal and psychological abuse by Bakilana. Kiwanuka filed a complaint against Bakilana for intentional infliction of emotional distress, among other claims. Bakilana argued that Kiwanuka's complaint should be dismissed because the allegations were insufficient to show outrageous intentional conduct that resulted in severe emotional distress. If you were the judge, in whose favor would you rule? Why? [*Kiwanuka v. Bakilana,* 844 F.Supp.2d 107 (D.D.C. 2012)] **(See page 74.)**

4–8. BUSINESS CASE PROBLEM WITH SAMPLE ANSWER: Negligence.

 At the Weatherford Hotel in Flagstaff, Arizona, in Room 59, a balcony extends across thirty inches of the room's only window, leaving a twelve-inch gap with a three-story drop to the concrete below. A sign prohibits smoking in the room but invites guests to "step out onto the balcony" to smoke. Toni Lucario was a guest in Room 59 when she climbed out of the window and fell to her death. Patrick McMurtry, her estate's personal representative, filed a suit against the Weatherford. Did the hotel breach a duty of care to Locario? What might the Weatherford assert in its defense? Explain. [McMurtry v. Weatherford Hotel, Inc., 293 P.3d 520 (Ariz.App. 2013)] **(See page 83.)**

- **For a sample answer to Problem 4–8, go to Appendix C at the end of this text.**

4–9. A QUESTION OF ETHICS: Wrongful Interference with a Contractual Relationship.

 White Plains Coat & Apron Co. is a New York–based linen rental business. Cintas Corp. is a competitor. White Plains had five-year exclusive contracts with some of its customers. As a result of Cintas's soliciting of business, dozens of White Plains' customers breached their contracts and entered into rental agreements with Cintas. White Plains filed a suit against Cintas, alleging wrongful interference. [White Plains Coat & Apron Co. v. Cintas Corp., 8 N.Y.3d 422, 867 N.E.2d 381 (2007)] **(See page 80.)**

(a) What are the two important policy interests at odds in wrongful interference cases? Which of these interests should be accorded priority?

(b) The U.S. Court of Appeals for the Second Circuit asked the New York Court of Appeals to answer a question: Is a general interest in soliciting business for profit a sufficient defense to a claim of wrongful interference with a contractual relationship? What do you think? Why?

Legal Reasoning Group Activity

4–10. Negligence. Donald and Gloria Bowden hosted a cookout at their home in South Carolina, inviting mostly business acquaintances. Justin Parks, who was nineteen years old, attended the party. Alcoholic beverages were available to all of the guests, even those like Parks, who were between the ages of eighteen and twenty-one. Parks consumed alcohol at the party and left with other guests. One of these guests detained Parks at the guest's home to give Parks time to "sober up." Parks then drove himself from this guest's home and was killed in a one-car accident. At the time of death, he had a blood alcohol content of 0.291 percent, which exceeded the state's limit for driving a motor vehicle. Linda Marcum, Parks's mother, filed a suit in a South Carolina state court against the Bowdens and others, alleging that they were negligent. **(See page 83.)**

(a) The first group will present arguments in favor of holding the social hosts liable in this situation.

(b) The second group will formulate arguments against holding the social hosts liable based on principles in this chapter.

(c) The states vary widely in assessing liability and imposing sanctions in the circumstances described in this problem. The third group will determine the reasons why courts do not treat social hosts the same as parents who serve alcoholic beverages to their underage children.

CHAPTER 5

INTELLECTUAL PROPERTY RIGHTS

Intellectual property is any property that results from intellectual, creative processes—that is to say, the products of an individual's mind. Although it is an abstract term for an abstract concept, intellectual property is nonetheless familiar to almost everyone. The apps for your iPhone and iPad, the movies you see, and the music you listen to are all forms of intellectual property. More than two hundred years ago, the framers of the U.S. Constitution recognized the importance of protecting creative works in Article I, Section 8.

Statutory protection of these rights began in the 1940s and continues to evolve to meet the needs of modern society.

Of significant concern to businesspersons is the need to protect their rights in intellectual property, which in today's world may exceed the value of physical property, such as machines and buildings. Consider, for instance, the importance of intellectual property rights to technology companies, such as Apple, Inc. Intellectual property rights can be a company's most valuable

assets, which is why Apple sued rival Samsung Electronics Company. Apple claimed that Samsung's Galaxy line of mobile phones and tablets (those that run Google's Android software) copied the look, design, and user interface of Apple's iPhone and iPad. Although Apple is one of Samsung's biggest customers and buys many of its components from Samsung, Apple must also protect its iPhone and iPad revenues from competing Android products. You will read about the verdict in this case on page 101.

You will read about the verdict in this case on page 101.

SECTION 1

TRADEMARKS AND RELATED PROPERTY

A **trademark** is a distinctive mark, motto, device, or implement that a manufacturer stamps, prints, or otherwise affixes to the goods it produces so that they can be identified on the market and their origins made known. In other words, a trademark is a source indicator. At common law, the person who used a symbol or mark to identify a business or product was protected in the use of that trademark. Clearly, by using another's trademark, a business could lead consumers to believe that its goods were made by the other business. The law seeks to avoid this kind of confusion. In this section, we examine various aspects of the law governing trademarks.

In the following classic case concerning Coca-Cola, the defendants argued that the Coca-Cola trademark was entitled to no protection under the law because the term did not accurately represent the product.

CLASSIC CASE 5.1

The Coca-Cola Co. v. The Koke Co. of America
Supreme Court of the United States, 254 U.S. 143, 41 S.Ct. 113, 65 L.Ed.189 (1920).

COMPANY PROFILE John Pemberton, an Atlanta pharmacist, invented a caramel-colored, carbonated soft drink in 1886. His bookkeeper, Frank Robinson, named the beverage Coca-Cola after two of the ingredients, coca leaves and kola nuts. Asa Candler bought the Coca-Cola Company

CASE 5.1 CONTINUED

(**www.coca-colacompany.com**) in 1891, and within seven years, he had made the soft drink available throughout the United States, as well as in parts of Canada and Mexico. Candler continued to sell Coke aggressively and to open up new markets, reaching Europe before 1910. In doing so, however, he attracted numerous competitors, some of which tried to capitalize directly on the Coke name.

BACKGROUND AND FACTS The Coca-Cola Company sought to enjoin (prevent) the Koke Company of America and other beverage companies from, among other things, using the word Koke for their products. The Koke Company of America and other beverage companies contended that the Coca-Cola trademark was a fraudulent representation and that Coca-Cola was therefore not entitled to any help from the courts. The Koke Company and the other defendants alleged that the Coca-Cola Company, by its use of the Coca-Cola name, represented that the beverage contained cocaine (from coca leaves), which it no longer did. The trial court granted the injunction against the Koke Company, but the appellate court reversed the lower court's ruling. Coca-Cola then appealed to the United States Supreme Court.

IN THE LANGUAGE OF THE COURT
Mr. Justice *HOLMES* delivered the opinion of the Court.

* * * *

* * * Before 1900 the beginning of [Coca-Cola's] good will was more or less helped by the presence of cocaine, a drug that, like alcohol or caffeine or opium, may be described as a deadly poison or as a valuable [pharmaceutical item, depending on the speaker's purposes]. The amount seems to have been very small,[a] but it may have been enough to begin a bad habit and after the Food and Drug Act of June 30, 1906, if not earlier, long before this suit was brought, it was eliminated from the plaintiff's compound.

* * * Since 1900 the sales have increased at a very great rate corresponding to a like increase in advertising. The name now characterizes a beverage to be had at almost any soda fountain. It means a single thing coming from a single source, and well known to the community. It hardly would be too much to say that the drink characterizes the name as much as the name the drink. In other words *Coca-Cola probably means to most persons the plaintiff's familiar product to be had everywhere rather than a compound of particular substances.* * * * Before this suit was brought the plaintiff had advertised to the public that it must not expect and would not find cocaine, and had eliminated everything tending to suggest cocaine effects except the name and the picture of [coca] leaves and nuts, which probably conveyed little or nothing to most who saw it. It appears to us that it would be going too far to deny the plaintiff relief against a palpable [readily evident] fraud because possibly here and there an ignorant person might call for the drink with the hope for incipient cocaine intoxication. The plaintiff's position must be judged by the facts as they were when the suit was begun, not by the facts of a different condition and an earlier time. [Emphasis added.]

DECISION AND REMEDY *The district court's injunction was allowed to stand. The competing beverage companies were enjoined from calling their products Koke.*

WHAT IF THE FACTS WERE DIFFERENT? *Suppose that Coca-Cola had been trying to make the public believe that its product contained cocaine. Would the result in this case likely have been different? Why or why not?*

IMPACT OF THIS CASE ON TODAY'S LAW *In this early case, the United States Supreme Court made it clear that trademarks and trade names (and nicknames for those marks and names, such as the nickname "Coke" for "Coca-Cola") that are in common use receive protection under the common law. This holding is significant historically because it is the predecessor to the federal statute later passed to protect trademark rights—the Lanham Act of 1946, to be discussed next. In many ways, this act represented a codification of common law principles governing trademarks.*

---

a. In reality, until 1903 the amount of active cocaine in each bottle of Coke was equivalent to one "line" of cocaine.

Statutory Protection of Trademarks

Statutory protection of trademarks and related property is provided at the federal level by the Lanham Act of 1946.[1] The Lanham Act was enacted, in part, to protect manufacturers from losing business to rival companies that used confusingly similar trademarks.

The Lanham Act incorporates the common law of trademarks and provides remedies for owners of trademarks who wish to enforce their claims in federal court. Many states also have trademark statutes.

TRADEMARK DILUTION In 1995, Congress amended the Lanham Act by passing the Federal Trademark Dilution Act,[2] which allowed trademark owners to bring suits in federal court for trademark **dilution.** In 2006, Congress further amended the law on trademark dilution by passing the Trademark Dilution Revision Act (TDRA).[3]

Under the TDRA, to state a claim for trademark dilution, a plaintiff must prove the following:

1. The plaintiff owns a famous mark that is distinctive.
2. The defendant has begun using a mark in commerce that allegedly is diluting the famous mark.
3. The similarity between the defendant's mark and the famous mark gives rise to an *association* between the marks.
4. The association is likely to impair the distinctiveness of the famous mark or harm its reputation.

Trademark dilution laws protect "distinctive" or "famous" trademarks (such as Rolls Royce, McDonald's, and Apple) from certain unauthorized uses even when the use is on noncompeting goods or is unlikely to confuse. More than half of the states have also enacted trademark dilution laws.

SIMILAR MARKS MAY CONSTITUTE TRADEMARK DILUTION Note that a famous mark may be diluted by the use of an *identical* mark or by the use of a *similar* mark.[4] A similar mark is more likely to lessen the value of a famous mark when the companies using the marks provide related goods or compete against each other in the same market.

---

1. 15 U.S.C. Sections 1051–1128.
2. 15 U.S.C. Section 1125.
3. Pub. L. No. 103-312, 120 Stat. 1730 (2006).
4. See *Louis Vuitton Malletier S.A. v. Haute Diggity Dog, LLC,* 507 F.3d 252 (4th Cir. 2007); and *Moseley v. V Secret Catalogue, Inc.,* 537 U.S. 418, 123 S.Ct. 1115, 155 L.Ed.2d 1 (2003).

▶ **Case in Point 5.1** Samantha Lundberg opened "Sambuck's Coffeehouse," in Astoria, Oregon, even though she knew that "Starbucks" is one of the largest coffee chains in the nation. When Starbucks Corporation filed a dilution lawsuit, the federal court ruled that use of the "Sambuck's" mark constituted trademark dilution because it created confusion for consumers. Not only was there a "high degree" of similarity between the marks, but also both companies provided coffee-related services and marketed their services through "stand-alone" retail stores. Therefore, the use of the similar mark (Sambuck's) reduced the value of the famous mark (Starbucks).[5] ◀

Trademark Registration

Trademarks may be registered with the state or with the federal government. To register for protection under federal trademark law, a person must file an application with the U.S. Patent and Trademark Office in Washington, D.C. Under current law, a mark can be registered (1) if it is currently in commerce or (2) if the applicant intends to put it into commerce within six months.

In special circumstances, the six-month period can be extended by thirty months. Thus, the applicant would have a total of three years from the date of notice of trademark approval to make use of the mark and file the required use statement. Registration is postponed until the mark is actually used.

During this waiting period, any applicant can legally protect his or her trademark against a third party who previously has neither used the mark nor filed an application for it. Registration is renewable between the fifth and sixth years after the initial registration and every ten years thereafter (every twenty years for those trademarks registered before 1990).

Trademark Infringement

Registration of a trademark with the U.S. Patent and Trademark Office gives notice on a nationwide basis that the trademark belongs exclusively to the registrant. The registrant is also allowed to use the symbol ® to indicate that the mark has been registered. Whenever that trademark is copied to a substantial degree or used in its entirety by another, intentionally or unintentionally, the trademark has been *infringed* (used without authorization).

---

5. *Starbucks Corp. v. Lundberg,* 2005 WL 3183858 (D.Or. 2005).

When a trademark has been infringed, the owner of the mark has a cause of action against the infringer. To succeed in a trademark infringement action, the owner must show that the defendant's use of the mark created a likelihood of confusion about the origin of the defendant's goods or services. The owner need not prove that the infringer acted intentionally or that the trademark was registered (although registration does provide proof of the date of inception of the trademark's use).

The most commonly granted remedy for trademark infringement is an *injunction* to prevent further infringement. Under the Lanham Act, a trademark owner that successfully proves infringement can recover actual damages, plus the profits that the infringer wrongfully received from the unauthorized use of the mark. A court can also order the destruction of any goods bearing the unauthorized trademark. In some situations, the trademark owner may also be able to recover attorneys' fees.

Distinctiveness of the Mark

A trademark must be sufficiently distinctive to enable consumers to identify the manufacturer of the goods easily and to distinguish between those goods and competing products.

STRONG MARKS Fanciful, arbitrary, or suggestive trademarks are generally considered to be the most distinctive (strongest) trademarks. Marks that are fanciful, arbitrary, or suggestive are protected as inherently distinctive without demonstrating secondary meaning. These marks receive automatic protection because they serve to identify a particular product's source, as opposed to describing the product itself.

Fanciful and Arbitrary Trademarks. Fanciful trademarks are inherently distinctive and include invented words, such as "Xerox" for one manufacturer's copiers and "Google" for search engines. Arbitrary trademarks are those that use common words in an uncommon way that is nondescriptive, such as "Dutch Boy" as a name for paint.

Even a single letter used in a particular style can be an arbitrary trademark. ▶ **Case in Point 5.2** Sports entertainment company ESPN sued Quiksilver, Inc., a maker of youth-oriented clothing, alleging trademark infringement. ESPN claimed that Quiksilver's clothing had used the stylized "X" mark that ESPN uses in connection with the "X Games" (extreme action sports competitions). Quiksilver filed counterclaims for trademark infringement and dilution, arguing that it had a long history of using the stylized X on its products.

ESPN created the X Games in the mid-1990s, and Quiksilver has been using the X mark since 1994. ESPN asked the court to dismiss Quiksilver's counterclaims, but the court refused, holding that the X on Quiksilver's clothing is clearly an arbitrary mark. The court found that the two Xs are "similar enough that a consumer might well confuse them."[6] ◀

Suggestive Trademarks. Suggestive trademarks indicate something about a product's nature, quality, or characteristics, without describing the product directly. These marks require imagination on the part of the consumer to identify the characteristic. For example, "Dairy Queen" suggests an association between its products and milk, but it does not directly describe ice cream.

"Blu-ray" is a suggestive mark that is associated with the high-quality, high-definition video contained on a particular optical data storage disc. Although blue-violet lasers are used to read *blu-ray* discs, the term *blu-ray* does not directly describe the disc.

SECONDARY MEANING Descriptive terms, geographic terms, and personal names are not inherently distinctive and do not receive protection under the law until they acquire a secondary meaning. A secondary meaning may arise when customers begin to associate a specific term or phrase (such as *London Fog*) with specific trademarked items (coats with "London Fog" labels) made by a particular company.

▶ **Case in Point 5.3** Frosty Treats, Inc., sells frozen desserts out of ice cream trucks. The video game series Twisted Metal depicts an ice cream truck with a clown character on it that is similar to the clowns on Frosty Treats' trucks. In the last game of the series, the truck bears the label "Frosty Treats." Frosty sued the video game maker for trademark infringement. The court, however, held that "Frosty Treats" is a descriptive term and is not protected by trademark law unless it has acquired a secondary meaning.

To establish secondary meaning, Frosty Treats would have had to show that the public recognized its trademark and associated it with a single source. Because Frosty Treats failed to do so, the court entered a judgment in favor of the video game producer.[7] ◀

---

6. *ESPN, Inc. v. Quiksilver, Inc.,* 586 F.Supp.2d 219 (S.D.N.Y. 2008).
7. *Frosty Treats, Inc., v. Sony Computer Entertainment America, Inc.,* 426 F.3d 1001 (8th Cir. 2005).

Once a secondary meaning is attached to a term or name, a trademark is considered distinctive and is protected. Even a color can qualify for trademark protection, as did the color schemes used by some state university sports teams, including Ohio State University and Louisiana State University.[8]

GENERIC TERMS Generic terms that refer to an entire class of products, such as *bicycle* and *computer,* receive no protection, even if they acquire secondary meanings. A particularly thorny problem arises when a trademark acquires generic use. For instance, *aspirin* and *thermos* were originally the names of trademarked products, but today the words are used generically. Other trademarks that have acquired generic use are *escalator, trampoline, raisin bran, dry ice, lanolin, linoleum, nylon,* and *cornflakes.*

Service, Certification, and Collective marks

A **service mark** is essentially a trademark that is used to distinguish the *services* (rather than the products) of one person or company from those of another. For example, each airline has a particular mark or symbol associated with its name. Titles and character names used in radio and television are frequently registered as service marks.

Other marks protected by law include certification marks and collective marks. A **certification mark** is used by one or more persons, other than the owner, to certify the region, materials, mode of manufacture, quality, or other characteristic of specific goods or services. Certification marks include "Good Housekeeping Seal of Approval" and "UL Tested."

When used by members of a cooperative, association, or other organization, a certification mark is referred to as a **collective mark.** Collective marks appear at the ends of motion picture credits to indicate the various associations and organizations that participated in the making of the films. The union marks found on the tags of certain products are also collective marks.

Trade Dress

The term **trade dress** refers to the image and overall appearance of a product. Trade dress is a broad concept and can include either all or part of the total image or overall impression created by a product or its packaging.

▶ **Example 5.4** The distinctive decor, menu, layout, and style of service of a particular restaurant may be regarded as trade dress. Trade dress can also include the layout and appearance of a catalogue, the use of a lighthouse as part of the design of a golf hole, the fish shape of a cracker, or the G-shaped design of a Gucci watch. ◀

Basically, trade dress is subject to the same protection as trademarks. In cases involving trade dress infringement, as in trademark infringement cases, a major consideration is whether consumers are likely to be confused by the allegedly infringing use.

Counterfeit Goods

Counterfeit goods copy or otherwise imitate trademarked goods, but they are not the genuine trademarked goods. The importation of goods that bear counterfeit (fake) trademarks poses a growing problem for U.S. businesses, consumers, and law enforcement. In addition to the negative financial effects on legitimate businesses, certain counterfeit goods, such as pharmaceuticals and nutritional supplements, can present serious public health risks.

Although Congress has enacted statutes against counterfeit goods (discussed next), the United States cannot prosecute foreign counterfeiters because our national laws do not apply to them. Instead, one effective tool that U.S. officials use to combat online sales of counterfeit goods is to obtain a court order to close down the domain names of Web sites that sell such goods.

▶ **Example 5.5** In 2012, U.S. agents shut down 101 domain names on the Monday after Thanksgiving ("Cyber Monday," the online version of "Black Friday," the day after Thanksgiving when the holiday shopping season begins). Although the criminal enterprises may continue selling counterfeit versions of brand-name products under different domain names, shutting down the Web sites, particularly on key shopping days, prevents some counterfeit goods from entering the United States. ◀

THE STOP COUNTERFEITING IN MANUFACTURED GOODS ACT The Stop Counterfeiting in Manufactured Goods Act[9] (SCMGA) was enacted to combat counterfeit goods. The act makes it a crime to traffic inten-

---

8. *Board of Supervisors of Louisiana State University v. Smack Apparel Co.,* 438 F.Supp.2d 653 (E.D.La. 2006). See also *Abraham v. Alpha Chi Omega,* 781 F.Supp.2d 396 (N.D.Tex. 2011).

9. Pub. L. No. 109-181 (2006), which amended 18 U.S.C. Sections 2318–2320.

tionally in or attempt to traffic in counterfeit goods or services, or to knowingly use a counterfeit mark on or in connection with goods or services.

Before this act, the law did not prohibit the creation or shipment of counterfeit labels that were not attached to any product. Therefore, counterfeiters would make labels and packaging bearing another's trademark, ship the labels to another location, and then affix them to an inferior product to deceive buyers. The SCMGA closed this loophole by making it a crime to knowingly traffic in counterfeit labels, stickers, packaging, and the like, regardless of whether the items are attached to any goods.

PENALTIES FOR COUNTERFEITING Persons found guilty of violating the SCMGA may be fined up to $2 million or imprisoned for up to ten years (or more if they are repeat offenders). If a court finds that the statute was violated, it must order the defendant to forfeit the counterfeit products (which are then destroyed), as well as any property used in the commission of the crime. The defendant must also pay restitution to the trademark holder or victim in an amount equal to the victim's actual loss.

▶ **Case in Point 5.6** Wajdi Beydoun pleaded guilty to conspiring to import cigarette-rolling papers from Mexico that were falsely marked as "Zig-Zags" and selling them in the United States. The court sentenced Beydoun to prison and ordered him to pay $566,267 in restitution. On appeal, the court affirmed the prison sentence but reversed the restitution because the amount exceeded the actual loss suffered by the legitimate sellers of Zig-Zag rolling papers.[10] ◀

The United States has also joined with other nations in a new international agreement aimed at combating counterfeiting (see the discussion on page 111).

Trade Names

Trademarks apply to *products*. A **trade name** indicates part or all of a business's name, whether the business is a sole proprietorship, a partnership, or a corporation. Generally, a trade name is directly related to a business and its goodwill.

A trade name may be protected as a trademark if the trade name is also the name of the company's trademarked product—for example, Coca-Cola. Unless it is also used as a trademark or service mark, a trade name cannot be registered with the federal government. Trade names are protected under the common law,

but only if they are unusual or fancifully used. The word *Safeway,* for example, was sufficiently fanciful to obtain protection as a trade name for a grocery chain.

Licensing

One way to avoid litigation and still make use of another's trademark or other form of intellectual property is to obtain a license to do so. A **license** in this context is an agreement, or contract, permitting the use of a trademark, copyright, patent, or trade secret for certain purposes. The party that owns the intellectual property rights and issues the license is the *licensor,* and the party obtaining the license is the *licensee.*

A license grants only the rights expressly described in the license agreement. A licensor might, for example, allow the licensee to use the trademark as part of its company or domain name, but not otherwise use the mark on any products or services. Disputes frequently arise over licensing agreements, particularly when the license involves Internet uses.

▶ **Case in Point 5.7** George V Restauration S.A. and others owned and operated the Buddha Bar Paris, a restaurant with an Asian theme in Paris, France. One of the owners allowed Little Rest Twelve, Inc., to use the Buddha Bar trademark and its associated concept in New York City under the name *Buddha Bar NYC.* Little Rest paid royalties for its use of the Buddha Bar mark and advertised Buddha Bar NYC's affiliation with Buddha Bar Paris, a connection also noted on its Web site and in the media.

When a dispute arose, the owners of Buddha Bar Paris withdrew their permission for Buddha Bar NYC's use of their mark, but Little Rest continued to use it. The owners of the mark filed a suit in a New York state court against Little Rest. The court granted an injunction to prevent Little Rest from using the mark.[11] ◀

SECTION 2

PATENTS

A **patent** is a grant from the government that gives an inventor the exclusive right to make, use, or sell his or her invention for a period of twenty years. Patents for designs, as opposed to those for inventions, are given for a fourteen-year period. The applicant must

---

10. *United States v. Beydoun,* 469 F.3d 102 (5th Cir. 2006).

11. *George V Restauration S.A. v. Little Rest Twelve, Inc.,* 58 A.D.3d 428, 871 N.Y.S.2d 65 (2009).

demonstrate to the satisfaction of the U.S. Patent and Trademark Office that the invention, discovery, process, or design is novel, useful, and not obvious in light of current technology.

Until recently, U.S. patent law differed from the laws of many other countries because the first person to invent a product obtained the patent rights rather than the first person to file for a patent. It was often difficult to prove who invented an item first, however, which prompted Congress to change the system in 2011 by passing the America Invents Act.[12] Now the first person to file an application for a patent on a product or process will receive patent protection. In addition, the new law established a nine-month limit for challenging a patent on any ground.

The period of patent protection begins on the date the patent application is filed, rather than when the patent is issued, which may sometimes be years later. After the patent period ends (either fourteen or twenty years later), the product or process enters the public domain, and anyone can make, sell, or use the invention without paying the patent holder.

Searchable Patent Databases

A significant development relating to patents is the availability online of the world's patent databases. The Web site of the U.S. Patent and Trademark Office (**www.uspto.gov**) provides searchable databases covering U.S. patents granted since 1976. The Web site of the European Patent Office (**www.epo.org**) provides online access to 50 million patent documents in more than seventy nations through a searchable network of databases.

Businesses use these searchable databases in many ways. Because patents are valuable assets, businesses may need to perform patent searches to list or inventory their assets. Patent searches may also be conducted to study trends and patterns in a specific technology or to gather information about competitors in the industry.

What Is Patentable?

Under federal law, "[w]hoever invents or discovers any new and useful process, machine, manufacture, or composition of matter, or any new and useful improvement thereof, may obtain a patent therefor,

subject to the conditions and requirements of this title."[13] Thus, to be patentable, the applicant must prove that the invention, discovery, process, or design is *novel, useful,* and *not obvious* (in light of current technology).

In sum, almost anything is patentable, except the laws of nature, natural phenomena, and abstract ideas (including algorithms[14]). Even artistic methods and works of art, certain business processes, and the structures of storylines are patentable, provided that they are novel and not obvious.[15]

Plants that are reproduced asexually (by means other than from seed), such as hybrid or genetically engineered plants, are patentable in the United States, as are genetically engineered (or cloned) microorganisms and animals. ▶ **Case in Point 5.8** Monsanto, Inc., sells its patented genetically modified (GM) seeds to farmers as a way to achieve higher yields from crops using fewer pesticides. It requires farmers who buy GM seeds to sign licensing agreements promising to plant the seeds for only one crop and to pay a technology fee for each acre planted. To ensure compliance, Monsanto has many full-time employees whose job is to investigate and prosecute farmers who use the GM seeds illegally. Monsanto has filed nearly 150 lawsuits against farmers in the United States and has been awarded more than $15 million in damages (not including out-of-court settlement amounts).[16] ◀

Patent Infringement

If a firm makes, uses, or sells another's patented design, product, or process without the patent owner's permission, that firm commits the tort of patent infringement. Patent infringement may occur even though the patent owner has not put the patented product into commerce. Patent infringement may also occur even though not all features or parts of a product are copied. (To infringe the patent on a process, however, all steps or their equivalent must be copied.)

---

12. The full title of this law is the Leahy-Smith America Invents Act, Pub. L. No. 112-29 (2011), which amended 35 U.S.C. Sections 1, 41, and 321.

13. 35 U.S.C. Section 101.

14. An *algorithm* is a step-by-step procedure, formula, or set of instructions for accomplishing a specific task. An example is the set of rules used by a search engine to rank the listings contained within its index in response to a query.

15. For a United States Supreme Court case discussing the obviousness requirement, see *KSR International Co. v. Teleflex, Inc.,* 550 U.S. 398, 127 S.Ct. 1727, 167 L.Ed.2d 705 (2007).

16. See, for example, *Monsanto Co. v. Bowman,* 657 F.3d 1341 (Fed.Cir. 2011); and *Monsanto Co. v. Scruggs,* 2009 WL 1228318 (Fed.Cir. 2009).

PATENT INFRINGEMENT SUITS AND HIGH-TECH COMPANIES Obviously, companies that specialize in developing new technology stand to lose significant profits if someone "makes, uses, or sells" devices that incorporate their patented inventions. Because these firms are the holders of numerous patents, they are frequently involved in patent infringement lawsuits (as well as other types of intellectual property disputes).

Many companies that make and sell electronics and computer software and hardware are based in foreign nations (for example, Samsung Electronics Company is a Korean firm). Foreign firms can apply for and obtain U.S. patent protection on items that they sell within the United States. Similarly, U.S. firms can obtain protection in foreign nations where they sell goods.

Limitations on Exported Software. The United States Supreme Court has narrowly construed patent infringement as it applies to exported software. As a general rule, under U.S. law, no patent infringement occurs when a patented product is made and sold in another country.

▶ **Case in Point 5.9** AT&T Corporation holds a patent on a device used to digitally encode, compress, and process recorded speech. AT&T brought an infringement case against Microsoft Corporation, which admitted that its Windows operating system incorporated software code that infringed on AT&T's patent.

The case reached the United States Supreme Court on the question of whether Microsoft's liability extended to computers made in another country. The Court held that it did not. Microsoft was liable only for infringement in the United States and not for the Windows-based computers produced in foreign locations. The Court reasoned that Microsoft had not "supplied" the software for the computers but had only electronically transmitted a master copy, which the foreign manufacturers copied and loaded onto the computers.[17] ◀

Apple, Inc. v. Samsung Electronics Company. As mentioned in the chapter introduction, Apple sued Samsung alleging that Samsung's Galaxy mobile phones and tablets that use Google's HTC Android operating system infringe on Apple's patents. Apple has design patents that cover the graphical user interface (the display of icons on the home screen), the device's shell, and the screen and button design. Apple also has patents that cover the way information is displayed on iPhones and other devices, the way windows pop open, and the way information is scaled and rotated.

In 2012, a jury issued a verdict in favor of Apple and awarded more than $1 billion in damages—one of the largest awards ever made in a patent case (a judge later ruled that part of the damages had been incorrectly calculated, however).[18] The jury found that Samsung had willfully infringed five of Apple's patents. The case provides an important precedent for Apple in its legal battles against Android devices made by other companies worldwide. Nevertheless, litigation between the two companies has continued.

Remedies for Patent Infringement

If a patent is infringed, the patent holder may sue for relief in federal court. The patent holder can seek an injunction against the infringer and can also request damages for royalties and lost profits. In some cases, the court may grant the winning party reimbursement for attorneys' fees and costs. If the court determines that the infringement was willful, the court can triple the amount of damages awarded (treble damages).

In the past, permanent injunctions were routinely granted to prevent future infringement. In 2006, however, the United States Supreme Court ruled that patent holders are not automatically entitled to a permanent injunction against future infringing activities. The courts have discretion to decide whether equity requires it. According to the Court, a patent holder must prove that it has suffered irreparable injury and that the public interest would not be disserved by a permanent injunction.[19] This decision gives courts discretion to decide what is equitable in the circumstances and allows them to consider what is in the public interest rather than just the interests of the parties.

▶ **Case in Point 5.10** In the first case applying this rule, a court found that although Microsoft had infringed on the patent of a small software company, the latter was not entitled to an injunction. According to the court, the small company was not irreparably harmed and could be adequately compensated by monetary damages. Also, the public might suffer negative effects from an injunction because the

---

17. *Microsoft Corp. v. AT&T Corp.*, 550 U.S. 437, 127 S.Ct. 1746, 167 L.Ed.2d 737 (2007).

18. *Apple, Inc. v. Samsung Electronics Co.*, CV 11-1846 and CV 12-0630 (N.D.Cal. August 24, 2012). In 2013, a judge ruled that part of the damages awarded were incorrectly calculated and excessive, invalidating approximately $450.5 million of the jury's award. The judge ordered a new trial to determine the appropriate amount of damages. *Apple, Inc. v. Samsung Electronics Co.*, ___ F.Supp.2d ___, 2013 WL 772525 (N.D.Cal. 2013).

19. *eBay, Inc. v. MercExchange, LLC*, 547 U.S. 388, 126 S.Ct. 1837, 164 L.Ed.2d 641 (2006).

infringement involved part of Microsoft's widely used Office Suite software.[20] ◄

SECTION 3
COPYRIGHTS

A **copyright** is an intangible property right granted by federal statute to the author or originator of a literary or artistic production of a specified type. The Copyright Act of 1976,[21] as amended, governs copyrights. Works created after January 1, 1978, are automatically given statutory copyright protection for the life of the author plus 70 years. For copyrights owned by publishing houses, the copyright expires 95 years from the date of publication or 120 years from the date of creation, whichever comes first. For works by more than one author, the copyright expires 70 years after the death of the last surviving author.[22]

Copyrights can be registered with the U.S. Copyright Office (www.copyright.gov) in Washington, D.C. A copyright owner no longer needs to place the symbol © or the term *Copr.* or *Copyright* on the work to have the work protected against infringement. Chances are that if somebody created it, somebody owns it.

Generally, copyright owners are protected against the following:

1. Reproduction of the work.
2. Development of derivative works.
3. Distribution of the work.
4. Public display of the work.

What Is Protected Expression?

Works that are copyrightable include books, records, films, artworks, architectural plans, menus, music videos, product packaging, and computer software. To be protected, a work must be "fixed in a durable medium" from which it can be perceived, reproduced, or communicated. Protection is automatic. Registration is not required.

Section 102 of the Copyright Act explicitly states that it protects original works that fall into one of the following categories:

1. Literary works (including newspaper and magazine articles, computer and training manuals, catalogues, brochures, and print advertisements).
2. Musical works and accompanying words (including advertising jingles).
3. Dramatic works and accompanying music.
4. Pantomimes and choreographic works (including ballets and other forms of dance).
5. Pictorial, graphic, and sculptural works (including cartoons, maps, posters, statues, and even stuffed animals).
6. Motion pictures and other audiovisual works (including multimedia works).
7. Sound recordings.
8. Architectural works.

SECTION 102 EXCLUSIONS It is not possible to copyright an *idea*. Section 102 of the Copyright Act specifically excludes copyright protection for any "idea, procedure, process, system, method of operation, concept, principle, or discovery, regardless of the form in which it is described, explained, illustrated, or embodied." Thus, anyone can freely use the underlying ideas or principles embodied in a work.

What is copyrightable is the particular way in which an idea is *expressed*. Whenever an idea and an expression are inseparable, the expression cannot be copyrighted. Generally, anything that is not an original expression will not qualify for copyright protection. Facts widely known to the public are not copyrightable. Page numbers are not copyrightable because they follow a sequence known to everyone. Mathematical calculations are not copyrightable.

COMPILATIONS OF FACTS Unlike ideas, *compilations* of facts are copyrightable. Under Section 103 of the Copyright Act, a compilation is "a work formed by the collection and assembling of preexisting materials or data that are selected, coordinated, or arranged in such a way that the resulting work as a whole constitutes an original work of authorship."

The key requirement in the copyrightability of a compilation is originality. If the facts are selected, coordinated, or arranged in an original way, they can qualify for copyright protection. Therefore, the White Pages of a telephone directory do not qualify for copyright protection because they simply list alphabetically names and telephone numbers. The Yellow Pages of a directory can be copyrightable, provided the information is selected, coordinated, or arranged in an original way. Similarly, a compilation of infor-

---

20. *Z4 Technologies, Inc. v. Microsoft Corp.,* 434 F.Supp.2d 437 (E.D.Tex. 2006).
21. 17 U.S.C. Sections 101 *et seq.*
22. These time periods reflect the extensions of the length of copyright protection enacted by Congress in the Copyright Term Extension Act of 1998, 17 U.S.C. Section 302. The United States Supreme Court upheld the constitutionality of the act in 2003. See *Eldred v. Ashcroft,* 537 U.S. 186, 123 S.Ct. 769, 154 L.Ed.2d 683 (2003).

mation about yachts listed for sale has qualified for copyright protection.[23]

Copyright Infringement

Whenever the form or expression of an idea is copied, an infringement of copyright has occurred. The reproduction does not have to be exactly the same as the original, nor does it have to reproduce the original

in its entirety. If a substantial part of the original is reproduced, the copyright has been infringed.

In the following case, rapper Curtis Jackson—better known as "50 Cent"—was the defendant in a suit that claimed his album *Before I Self–Destruct*, and the companion film of the same name, infringed the copyright of Shadrach Winstead's book, *The Preacher's Son—But the Streets Turned Me into a Gangster.*

---

23. *BUC International Corp. v. International Yacht Council, Ltd.,* 489 F.3d 1129 (11th Cir. 2007).

CASE ANALYSIS

Case 5.2   Winstead v. Jackson
United States Court of Appeals, Third Circuit, 2013 WL 139622 (2013).

IN THE LANGUAGE OF THE COURT
PER CURIAM. [By the Whole Court]

* * * *

* * * Winstead filed his * * * complaint in the United States District Court for the District of New Jersey, claiming that Jackson's album/CD and film derived their contents from, and infringed the copyright of, his book.

* * * *

* * * The District Court dismissed Winstead's * * * complaint * * * , concluding that Jackson * * * did not improperly copy protected aspects of Winstead's book.

* * * *

Winstead appeals.

* * * *

Here, it is not disputed that Winstead is the owner of the copyrighted property * * * . However, *not all copying is copyright infringement, so even if actual copying is proven, the court must decide, by comparing the allegedly infringing work with the original work, whether the copying was unlawful. Copying may be proved inferentially by showing that the allegedly infringing work is substantially similar to the copyrighted work.* A court compares

the allegedly infringing work with the original work, and considers whether a "lay-observer" would believe that the copying was of protectable aspects of the copyrighted work. The inquiry involves distinguishing between the author's expression and the idea or theme that he or she seeks to convey or explore, because the former is protected and the latter is not. The court must determine whether the allegedly infringing work is similar because it appropriates the unique expressions of the original work, or merely because it contains elements that would be expected when two works express the same idea or explore the same theme. [Emphasis added.]

* * * A lay observer would not believe that Jackson's album/CD and film copied protectable aspects of Winstead's book. Jackson's album/CD is comprised of 16 individual songs, which explore drug-dealing, guns and money, vengeance, and other similar clichés of hip hop gangsterism. Jackson's fictional film is the story of a young man who turns to violence when his mother is killed in a drive-by shooting. The young man takes revenge by killing the man who killed his mother, and then gets

rich by becoming an "enforcer" for a powerful criminal. He takes up with a woman who eventually betrays him, and is shot to death by her boyfriend, who has just been released from prison. The movie ends with his younger brother vowing to seek vengeance. Winstead's book purports to be autobiographical and tells the story of a young man whose beloved father was a Bishop in the church. The protagonist was angry as a child because his stepmother abused him, but he found acceptance and self-esteem on the streets of Newark because he was physically powerful. He earned money robbing and beating people, went to jail, returned to crime upon his release, and then made even more money. The protagonist discusses his time at Rahway State Prison in great and compelling detail. The story ends when the protagonist learns that his father has passed away; he conveys his belief that this tragedy has led to his redemption, and he hopes that others might learn from his mistakes.

* * * Although Winstead's book and Jackson's works share similar themes and setting, the story of an angry and wronged protagonist who turns to a life of violence and crime

CASE 5.2 CONTINUES ➡

CASE 5.2 CONTINUED

has long been a part of the public domain [and is therefore not protected by copyright law]. Winstead argues * * * that a protagonist asking for God's help when his father dies, cutting drugs with mixing agents to maximize profits, and complaining about relatives who are addicts and steal the product, are protectable, but these things are not unique. To the extent that Jackson's works contain these elements, they are to be expected when two works express the same idea about "the streets" or explore the same theme. Winstead argues that not every protagonist whose story concerns guns, drugs, and violence in an urban setting winds up in prison or loses a parent, but this argument only serves to illustrate an important difference between his book and Jackson's film. Jackson's protagonist never spends any time in prison, whereas Winstead's protagonist devotes a considerable part of his story to his incarcerations.

In addition, Winstead's book and Jackson's works are different with respect to character, plot, mood, and sequence of events. Winstead's protagonist embarks on a life of crime at a very young age, but is redeemed by the death of his beloved father. Jackson's protagonist turns to crime when he is much older and only after his mother is murdered. He winds up dead at a young age, unredeemed. Winstead's book is hopeful; Jackson's film is characterized * * * by moral apathy. It is true that both works involve the loss of a parent and the protagonist's recognition of the parent's importance in his life, but nowhere does Jackson appropriate anything unique about Winstead's expression of this generic topic.

Winstead contends that direct phrases from his book appear in Jackson's film. * * * He emphasizes these phrases: "Yo, where is my money at," "I would never have done no shit like that to you," "my father, my strength was gone," "he was everything to me," and "I did not know what to do," but, like the phrases "putting the work in," "get the dope, cut the dope," "let's keep it popping," and "the strong take from the weak but the smart take from everybody," they are either common in general or common with respect to hip hop culture, and do not enjoy copyright protection. The average person reading or listening to these phrases in the context of an overall story or song would not regard them as unique and protectable. Moreover, words and short phrases do not enjoy copyright protection. The similarity between Winstead's book and the lyrics to Jackson's songs on the album/CD is even more tenuous. "Stretching the dope" and "bloodshot red eyes" are common phrases that do not enjoy copyright protection. A side-by-side comparison of Winstead's book and the lyrics from Jackson's album/CD do not support a claim of copyright infringement.

For the foregoing reasons, we will affirm the order of the District Court dismissing [Winstead's] complaint.

LEGAL REASONING QUESTIONS

1. Which expressions of an original work are protected by copyright law?

2. Is all copying copyright infringement? If not, what is the test for determining whether a creative work has been unlawfully copied?

3. How did the court in this case determine whether the defendant's work infringed on the plaintiff's copyright?

4. Is a claim of copyright infringement supported if two works share similar themes and setting, as well as words and short phrases? Explain.

REMEDIES FOR COPYRIGHT INFRINGEMENT Those who infringe copyrights may be liable for damages or criminal penalties. These range from actual damages or statutory damages, imposed at the court's discretion, to criminal proceedings for willful violations.

Actual damages are based on the harm caused to the copyright holder by the infringement, while statutory damages, not to exceed $150,000, are provided for under the Copyright Act. Criminal proceedings may result in fines and/or imprisonment. A court can also issue a permanent injunction against a defendant when the court deems it necessary to prevent future copyright infringement.

▶ **Case in Point 5.11** Rusty Carroll operated an online term paper business, R2C2, Inc., that offered up to 300,000 research papers for sale at nine Web sites. Individuals whose work was posted on these Web sites without their permission filed a lawsuit against Carroll for copyright infringement. Because Carroll had repeatedly failed to comply with court orders regarding discovery, the court found that the copyright infringement was likely to continue unless an injunction was issued. The court therefore issued a permanent injunction prohibiting Carroll and R2C2 from selling any term paper without sworn documentary evidence that the paper's author had given permission.[24] ◄

THE "FAIR USE" EXCEPTION An exception to liability for copyright infringement is made under the "fair use" doctrine. In certain circumstances, a person or organization can reproduce copyrighted material without paying royalties (fees paid to the copyright holder for the privilege of reproducing the copyrighted material). Section 107 of the Copyright Act provides as follows:

> [T]he fair use of a copyrighted work, including such use by reproduction in copies or phonorecords or by any other means specified by [Section 106 of the Copyright Act], for purposes such as criticism, comment, news reporting, teaching (including multiple copies for classroom use), scholarship, or research, is not an infringement of copyright. In determining whether the use made of a work in any particular case is a fair use the factors to be considered shall include—
>
> (1) the purpose and character of the use, including whether such use is of a commercial nature or is for nonprofit educational purposes;
>
> (2) the nature of the copyrighted work;
>
> (3) the amount and substantiality of the portion used in relation to the copyrighted work as a whole; and
>
> (4) the effect of the use upon the potential market for or value of the copyrighted work.

WHAT IS FAIR USE? Because these guidelines are very broad, the courts determine whether a particular use is fair on a case-by-case basis. Thus, anyone who reproduces copyrighted material may be committing a violation. In determining whether a use is fair, courts have often considered the fourth factor to be the most important.

► **Case in Point 5.12** BMG Music Publishing, an owner of copyrighted music, granted a license to Leadsinger, Inc., a manufacturer of karaoke devices. The license gave Leadsinger permission to reproduce the sound recordings, but not to reprint the song lyrics, which appeared at the bottom of a TV screen when the karaoke device was used.

BMG demanded that Leadsinger pay a "lyric reprint" fee and a "synchronization" fee. Leadsinger refused to pay, claiming that its use of the lyrics was educational and thus did not constitute copyright infringement under the fair use exception. A federal appellate court disagreed. The court held that Leadsinger's display of the lyrics was not a fair use because it would have a negative effect on the value of the copyrighted work.[25] ◄

The First Sale Doctrine

Section 109(a) of the Copyright Act provides that "the owner of a particular copy or phonorecord lawfully made under [the Copyright Act], or any person authorized by such owner, is entitled, without the authority of the copyright owner, to sell or otherwise dispose of the possession of that copy or phonorecord." This rule is known as the first sale doctrine.

Under this doctrine, once a copyright owner sells or gives away a particular copy of a work, the copyright owner no longer has the right to control the distribution of that copy. Thus, for example, a person who buys a copyrighted book can sell it to someone else.

In 2011, a court held that the first sale doctrine also applies to a person who receives promotional CDs, such as a music critic or radio programmer. ► **Case in Point 5.13** Universal Music Group (UMG) regularly ships promotional CDs to people in the music industry. Troy Augusto obtained some of these promotional CDs from various sources and sold them through online auction sites. UMG filed a copyright infringement lawsuit. Augusto argued that the music company had given up its right to control further distribution of the CDs under the first sale doctrine. Ultimately, a federal appellate court held in favor of Augusto. The promotional CDs were dispatched to the recipients without any prior arrangement as to those particular copies. Therefore, the court concluded that UMG had conveyed title of the copyrighted promotional CDs to the recipients.[26] ◄

In 2012, the United States Supreme Court heard the appeal of a case involving the resale of textbooks on eBay. To read about the Court's decision in this important case, see this chapter's *Insight into the Global Environment* feature on the following page.

Copyright Protection for Software

In 1980, Congress passed the Computer Software Copyright Act, which amended the Copyright Act of 1976 to include computer programs in the list of

---

24. *Weidner v. Carroll*, 2010 WL 310310 (S.D.Ill. 2010).

25. *Leadsinger, Inc. v. BMG Music Publishing*, 512 F.3d 522 (9th Cir. 2008).
26. *UMG Recordings, Inc. v. Augusto*, 628 F.3d 1175 (9th Cir. 2011).

INSIGHT INTO THE GLOBAL ENVIRONMENT
Is It Legal to Resell Textbooks Purchased Abroad?

Students and professors alike complain about the high price of college textbooks. Some enterprising students have found that if they purchase textbooks printed abroad, they can sometimes save enough to justify the shipping charges. Textbook prices are lower in other countries because (1) production costs are lower there and (2) average incomes are also lower, so students are unable to pay the higher prices that U.S. students face. (Also, neither students nor professors abroad have the full range of paper and digital supplements that are offered with most textbooks in the U.S.)

A Cornell University Student Starts a Side Business

Supap Kirtsaeng, a citizen of Thailand, started his studies at Cornell University in 1997 and then went on to a Ph.D. program at the University of Southern California. He enlisted friends and family in Thailand to buy copies of textbooks there and ship them to him in the United States. To pay for his education, Kirtsaeng resold the textbooks on eBay, where he eventually made about $100,000.

John Wiley & Sons, Inc., which had printed eight of those textbooks in Asia, sued Kirtsaeng in federal district court for copyright infringement under Section 602(a)(1) of the Copyright Act. Wiley claimed that it is impermissible to import a work "without the authority of the owner." Kirtsaeng's defense was that Section 109(a) of the Copyright Act allows the first purchaser-owner of a book to sell or otherwise dispose of it without the copyright owner's permission. Kirtsaeng did not prevail.[a]

Kirtsaeng Appeals the Verdict

Kirtsaeng appealed to the U.S. Court of Appeals for the Second Circuit, but the court upheld the lower court's judgment.[b] The majority held that the first sale doctrine of the Copyright Act refers specifically to works that are manufactured in the United States. Therefore, the doctrine does not apply to textbooks printed and sold abroad, and then resold in the United States. Kirtsaeng appealed to the United States Supreme Court.

The Supreme Court Weighs In

The Supreme Court had to decide this question: Can any copy of a book or CD or DVD that was legally produced abroad, acquired abroad, and then imported into the United States be resold in the United States without the copyright owner's permission? The answer to this question has implications for discount sellers, such as Costco, and online businesses, such as eBay and Google, all of which offer "good" prices on many products that were made abroad.

The Supreme Court ruled that in Kirtsaeng's favor, reversing the appellate court's decision.[c] The majority of the Court ruled that the first sale doctrine applies, even when the good was purchased abroad: " [T]he common-law history of the 'first-sale' doctrine . . . favors a non-geographical interpretation. We . . . doubt that Congress would have intended to create the practical copyright-related harms with which a geographical interpretation would threaten ordinary scholarly, artistic, commercial activities . . . ." As it turned out, much of the Court's decision concerned the potential consequences of what might occur if the Court did not reverse the appellate decision. Allowing that decision to stand would have meant that one "could prevent a buyer from domestically selling or even giving away copies of a video game made in Japan, a film made in Germany or a dress (with a design copyright) made in China."

LEGAL CRITICAL THINKING

INSIGHT INTO THE SOCIAL ENVIRONMENT

What options do textbook publishers face given this Supreme Court decision?

---

a. *John Wiley & Sons, Inc. v. Kirtsaeng*, 93 U.S.P.Q.2d 1432 (S.D.N.Y. 2009).
b. *John Wiley & Sons, Inc. v. Kirtsaeng*, 654 F.3d 210 (2d Cir. 2011).

c. *Kirtsaeng v. John Wiley & Sons, Inc.*, ___ U.S. ___, 133 S.Ct. 1351, 185 L.Ed.2d 392 (2013).

---

creative works protected by federal copyright law.[27] Generally, copyright protection extends to those parts of a computer program that can be read by humans, such as the "high-level" language of a source code.

Protection also extends to the binary-language object code, which is readable only by the computer, and to such elements as the overall structure, sequence, and organization of a program.

Not all aspects of software are protected, however. Courts typically have not extended copyright protec-

---

27. Pub. L. No. 96-517 (1980), amending 17 U.S.C. Sections 101, 117.

tion to the "look and feel"—the general appearance, command structure, video images, menus, windows, and other screen displays—of computer programs. ▶ **Example 5.14** MiTek develops a software program for laying out wood trusses (used in construction). Another company comes out with a different program that includes similar elements, such as the menu and submenu command tree-structures. MiTek cannot successfully sue for copyright infringement because the command structure of software is not protected. ◀ (Note that copying the "look and feel" of another's product may be a violation of trade dress or trademark laws, however.)

As will be explored in Chapter 6, technology has vastly increased the potential for copyright infringement via the Internet.

SECTION 4
TRADE SECRETS

The law of trade secrets protects some business processes and information that are not, or cannot be, patented, copyrighted, or trademarked against appropriation by competitors. A **trade secret** is basically information of commercial value, such as customer lists, plans, and research and development. Trade secrets may also include pricing information, marketing methods, production techniques, and generally anything that makes an individual company unique and that would have value to a competitor.

Unlike copyright and trademark protection, protection of trade secrets extends both to ideas and to their expression. (For this reason, and because there are no registration or filing requirements for trade secrets, trade secret protection may be well suited for software.) Of course, the secret formula, method, or other information must be disclosed to some persons, particularly to key employees. Businesses generally attempt to protect their trade secrets by having all employees who use a process or information agree in their contracts, or in confidentiality agreements, never to divulge it.

State and Federal Law on Trade Secrets

Under Section 757 of the *Restatement of Torts,* those who disclose or use another's trade secret, without authorization, are liable to that other party if:

1. They discovered the secret by improper means, or
2. Their disclosure or use constitutes a breach of a duty owed to the other party.

Stealing confidential business data by industrial espionage, such as by tapping into a competitor's computer, is a theft of trade secrets without any contractual violation and is actionable in itself.

Although trade secrets have long been protected under the common law, today most states' laws are based on the Uniform Trade Secrets Act,[28] which has been adopted in forty-seven states. Additionally, the Economic Espionage Act[29] (to be discussed in Chapter 7) makes the theft of trade secrets a federal crime.

Trade Secrets in Cyberspace

Computer technology is undercutting many business firms' ability to protect their confidential information, including trade secrets. For example, a dishonest employee could e-mail trade secrets in a company's computer to a competitor or a future employer. If e-mail is not an option, the employee might walk out with the information on a flash drive.

A former employee's continued use of a Twitter account after leaving the company may provide grounds for a suit alleging misappropriation of trade secrets. ▶ **Case in Point 5.15** Noah Kravitz worked for a company called PhoneDog for four years as a product reviewer and video blogger. PhoneDog provided him with the Twitter account "@PhoneDog_Noah." Kravitz's popularity grew, and he had approximately 17,000 followers by the time he quit. PhoneDog requested that Kravitz stop using the Twitter account. Although Kravitz changed his handle to "@noahkravitz," he continued to use the account. PhoneDog subsequently sued Kravitz for misappropriation of trade secrets, among other things. Kravitz moved for a dismissal, but the court found that the complaint adequately stated a cause of action for misappropriation of trade secrets and allowed the suit to continue.[30] ◀

For a comprehensive summary of trade secrets and the other forms of intellectual property discussed in this chapter, see Exhibit 5–1 on the following page.

28. The Uniform Trade Secrets Act, as drafted by the National Conference of Commissioners on Uniform State Laws (NCCUSL), can be found at **uniformlaws.org**.
29. 18 U.S.C. Sections 1831–1839.
30. *PhoneDog v. Kravitz,* 2011 WL 5415612 (N.D.Cal. 2011). See also *Mintel Learning Technology, Inc. v. Ambrow Education Holding Ltd.,* 2012 WL 762126 (N.D.Cal. 2012).

EXHIBIT 5-1 Forms of Intellectual Property

Form	Definition	How Acquired	Duration	Remedy for Infringement
Patent	A grant from the government that gives an inventor exclusive rights to an invention.	By filing a patent application with the U.S. Patent and Trademark Office and receiving its approval.	Twenty years from the date of the application; for design patents, fourteen years.	Monetary damages, including royalties and lost profits, *plus* attorneys' fees. Damages may be tripled for intentional infringements.
Copyright	The right of an author or originator of a literary or artistic work, or other production that falls within a specified category, to have the exclusive use of that work for a given period of time.	Automatic (once the work or creation is put in tangible form). Only the *expression* of an idea (and not the idea itself) can be protected by copyright.	For authors: the life of the author, plus 70 years. For publishers: 95 years after the date of publication or 120 years after creation.	Actual damages plus profits received by the party who infringed *or* statutory damages under the Copyright Act, *plus* costs and attorneys' fees in either situation.
Trademark (service mark and trade dress)	Any distinctive word, name, symbol, or device (image or appearance), or combination thereof, that an entity uses to distinguish its goods or services from those of others. The owner has the exclusive right to use that mark or trade dress.	1. At common law, ownership created by use of the mark. 2. Registration with the appropriate federal or state office gives notice and is permitted if the mark is currently in use or will be within the next six months.	Unlimited, as long as it is in use. To continue notice by registration, the owner must renew by filing between the fifth and sixth years, and thereafter, every ten years.	1. Injunction prohibiting the future use of the mark. 2. Actual damages plus profits received by the party who infringed (can be increased under the Lanham Act). 3. Destruction of articles that infringed. 4. *Plus* costs and attorneys' fees.
Trade Secret	Any information that a business possesses and that gives the business an advantage over competitors (including formulas, lists, patterns, plans, processes, and programs).	Through the originality and development of the information and processes that constitute the business secret and are unknown to others.	Unlimited, so long as not revealed to others. Once revealed to others, it is no longer a trade secret.	Monetary damages for misappropriation (the Uniform Trade Secrets Act also permits punitive damages if willful), *plus* costs and attorneys' fees.

INTERNATIONAL PROTECTION FOR INTELLECTUAL PROPERTY

For many years, the United States has been a party to various international agreements relating to intellectual property rights. For instance, the Paris Convention of 1883, to which about 173 countries are signatory, allows parties in one country to file for patent and trademark protection in any of the other member countries. Other international agreements in this area include the Berne Convention, the Trade-Related Aspects of Intellectual Property Rights (known as the TRIPS agreement), the Madrid Protocol, and the Anti-Counterfeiting Trade Agreement.

The Berne Convention

Under the Berne Convention of 1886, if a U.S. citizen writes a book, every country that has signed the convention must recognize the U.S. author's copyright in the book. Also, if a citizen of a country that has not signed the convention first publishes a book in one of the 165 countries that have signed, all other countries that have signed the convention must recognize that author's copyright. Copyright notice is not needed to gain protection under the Berne Convention for works published after March 1, 1989.

This convention and other international agreements have given some protection to intellectual property on a worldwide level. None of them, however, has been as significant and far reaching in scope as the TRIPS agreement, discussed in the next subsection.

In 2011, the European Union agreed to extend the period of royalty protection for musicians from fifty years to seventy years. This decision aids major record labels as well as performers and musicians who previously faced losing royalties from sales of their older recordings. The profits of musicians and record companies have been shrinking in recent years because of the sharp decline in sales of compact discs and the rise in illegal downloads.

In the following case, the United States Supreme Court had to decide if Congress had exceeded its authority under the U.S. Constitution when it enacted a law that restored copyright protection to many foreign works that were already in the public domain. (*Public domain* means that rights to certain intellectual property, such as songs and other published works, belong to everyone and are not protected by copyright or patent laws.)

CASE 5.3

Golan v. Holder

Supreme Court of the United States, ___ U.S. ___, 132 S.Ct. 873, 181 L.Ed.2d 835 (2012).

BACKGROUND AND FACTS The United States joined the Berne Convention in 1989, but it failed to give foreign copyright holders the same protections enjoyed by U.S. authors. Contrary to the Berne Convention, the United States did not protect any foreign work that had already entered the public domain.

In 1994, Congress enacted the Uruguay Round Agreements Act (URAA), which "restored" copyright protection for many foreign works that were already in the public domain. The URAA put foreign and domestic works on the same footing, allowing their copyrights to extend for the same number of years. Lawrence Golan, along with a group of musicians, conductors, and publishers, filed a suit against Eric Holder, in his capacity as the U.S. attorney general. These individuals had enjoyed free access to foreign works in the public domain before the URAA's enactment. They claimed that the URAA violated the copyright clause of the U.S. Constitution and thus that Congress had exceeded its constitutional authority in passing the URAA.

A federal appellate court held that Congress did not violate the copyright clause by passing the URAA. The petitioners appealed. The United States Supreme Court granted *certiorari* to resolve the matter.

IN THE LANGUAGE OF THE COURT
Justice *GINSBURG* delivered the opinion of the Court.

* * * *

* * * The Constitution states that "Congress shall have Power . . . to promote the Progress of Science . . . by securing for limited Times to Authors . . . the exclusive Right to their . . . Writings." Petitioners [Golan and others] find in this grant of authority an impenetrable [impassable] barrier to the extension of copyright protection to authors whose writings, for whatever reason, are in the public domain. We see no such barrier in the text of the Copyright Clause * * * .

* * * *

The text of the Copyright Clause does not exclude application of copyright protection to works in the public domain. * * * Petitioners' contrary argument relies primarily on the Constitution's confinement of a copyright's lifespan to a "limited Tim[e]." "Removing works from the public domain," they contend, "violates the 'limited times' restriction by turning a

CASE 5.3 CONTINUES ▶

CASE 5.3 CONTINUED fixed and predictable period into one that can be reset or resurrected at any time, even after it expires."

Our decision in [a prior case] is largely dispositive [capable of settling a dispute] of petitioners' limited-time argument.[a] There we addressed the question of whether Congress violated the Copyright Clause when it extended, by 20 years, the terms of existing copyrights. Ruling that Congress acted within constitutional bounds, we declined to infer from the text of the Copyright Clause "the command that a time prescription, once set, becomes forever 'fixed' or 'inalterable.'" *"The word 'limited,' we observed, "does not convey a meaning so constricted." Rather, the term is best understood to mean "confine[d] within certain bounds," "restrain[ed]," or "circumscribed."* The construction petitioners tender closely resembles the definition rejected in *Eldred* [the prior case] and is similarly infirm [weak]. [Emphasis added.]

＊ ＊ ＊ ＊

＊ ＊ ＊ In aligning the United States with other nations bound by the Berne Convention, and thereby according equitable treatment to once disfavored foreign authors, Congress can hardly be charged with a design to move stealthily toward a regime of perpetual copyrights.

DECISION AND REMEDY   *The United States Supreme Court affirmed the federal appellate court's ruling that the URAA does not violate the U.S. Constitution's copyright clause. Thus, Golan and the others could no longer use, without permission, any of the foreign works that were previously in the public domain. By passing the URAA in the United States, Congress, in effect, took those works out of the public domain and extended copyright protection to them. Henceforth, U.S. copyright and patent laws cover all such foreign intellectual property.*

THE GLOBAL DIMENSION   *What does the Court's decision in this case mean for copyright holders in the United States who want copyright protection in other countries? Will other nations be more or less inclined to protect U.S. authors? Explain.*

THE ECONOMIC DIMENSION   *Why did a group of musicians, conductors, publishers, and others file this suit? What did they hope to gain by a decision in their favor?*

---

a.   See *Eldred v. Ashcroft,* 537 U.S. 186, 123 S.Ct. 769, 154 L.Ed.2d 683 (2003).

The TRIPS Agreement

Representatives from more than one hundred nations signed the TRIPS agreement in 1994. The agreement established, for the first time, standards for the international protection of intellectual property rights, including patents, trademarks, and copyrights for movies, computer programs, books, and music. The TRIPS agreement provides that each member country of the World Trade Organization must include in its domestic laws broad intellectual property rights and effective remedies (including civil and criminal penalties) for violations of those rights.

Generally, the TRIPS agreement forbids member nations from discriminating against foreign owners of intellectual property rights (in the administration, regulation, or adjudication of such rights). In other words, a member nation cannot give its own nationals (citizens) favorable treatment without offering the same treatment to nationals of all other member countries. ▶ **Example 5.16**   A U.S. software manufacturer brings a suit for the infringement of intellectual property rights under Germany's national laws. Because Germany is a member of the TRIPS agreement, the U.S. manufacturer is entitled to receive the same treatment as a German manufacturer. ◀

Each member nation must also ensure that legal procedures are available for parties who wish to bring actions for infringement of intellectual property rights. Additionally, a related document established a mechanism for settling disputes among member nations.

The Madrid Protocol

In the past, one of the difficulties in protecting U.S. trademarks internationally was the time and expense required to apply for trademark registration in foreign countries. The filing fees and procedures for trademark registration vary significantly among individual countries. The Madrid Protocol, which was signed into law in 2003, may help to resolve these problems.

The Madrid Protocol is an international treaty that has been signed by eighty-six countries. Under its provisions, a U.S. company wishing to register its trademark abroad can submit a single application and designate other member countries in which the company would like to register its mark. The treaty was designed to reduce the costs of international trademark protection by more than 60 percent.

Although the Madrid Protocol may simplify and reduce the cost of trademark registration in foreign countries, it remains to be seen whether it will provide significant benefits to trademark owners. Even with an easier registration process, there are still questions as to whether all member countries will enforce the law and protect the mark.

The Anti-Counterfeiting Trade Agreement

In 2011 Australia, Canada, Japan, Korea, Morocco, New Zealand, Singapore, and the United States signed the Anti-Counterfeiting Trade Agreement (ACTA), an international treaty to combat global counterfeiting and piracy. The members of the European Union, Mexico, Switzerland, and other nations that support ACTA are still developing domestic procedures to comply with its provisions. Once a nation has adopted appropriate procedures, it can ratify the treaty.

PROVISIONS AND GOALS The goals of the treaty are to increase international cooperation, facilitate the best law enforcement practices, and provide a legal framework to combat counterfeiting. The treaty will have its own governing body.

ACTA applies not only to counterfeit physical goods, such as medications, but also to pirated copyrighted works being distributed via the Internet. The idea is to create a new standard of enforcement for intellectual property rights that goes beyond the TRIPS agreement and encourages international cooperation and information sharing among signatory countries.

BORDER SEARCHES Under ACTA, member nations are required to establish border measures that allow officials, on their own initiative, to search commercial shipments of imports and exports for counterfeit goods. The treaty neither requires nor prohibits random border searches of electronic devices, such as laptops, tablet devices, and smartphones, for infringing content. If border authorities reasonably believe that any goods in transit are counterfeit, the treaty allows them to keep the suspect goods unless the owner proves that the items are authentic and noninfringing.

The treaty allows member nations, in accordance with their own laws, to order online service providers to furnish information about (including the identity of) suspected trademark and copyright infringers.

Reviewing: Intellectual Property Rights

Two computer science majors, Trent and Xavier, have an idea for a new video game, which they propose to call "Hallowed." They form a business and begin developing their idea. Several months later, Trent and Xavier run into a problem with their design and consult a friend, Brad, who is an expert in designing computer source codes. After the software is completed but before Hallowed is marketed, a video game called Halo 2 is released for both the Xbox and the Playstation systems. Halo 2 uses source codes similar to those of Hallowed and imitates Hallowed's overall look and feel, although not all the features are alike. Using the information presented in the chapter, answer the following questions.

1. Would the name *Hallowed* receive protection as a trademark or as trade dress? Explain.
2. If Trent and Xavier had obtained a patent on Hallowed, would the release of Halo 2 have infringed on their patent? Why or why not?
3. Based only on the facts described above, could Trent and Xavier sue the makers of Halo 2 for copyright infringement? Why or why not?
4. Suppose that Trent and Xavier discover that Brad took the idea of Hallowed and sold it to the company that produced Halo 2. Which type of intellectual property issue does this raise?

DEBATE THIS ... *Congress has amended copyright law several times so that copyright holders now have protection for many decades. Was Congress right in extending these copyright time periods?*

Terms and Concepts

certification mark 98	intellectual property 94	trade dress 98
collective mark 98	license 99	trade name 99
copyright 102	patent 99	trade secret 107
dilution 96	service mark 98	trademark 94

ExamPrep

Issue Spotters

1. Roslyn is a food buyer for Organic Cornucopia Food Company when she decides to go into business for herself as Roslyn's Kitchen. She contacts Organic's suppliers, offering to buy their entire harvest for the next year, and Organic's customers, offering to sell her products for less than her ex-employer. Has Roslyn violated any of the intellectual property rights discussed in this chapter? Explain. **(See page 107.)**

2. Global Products develops, patents, and markets software. World Copies, Inc., sells Global's software without the maker's permission. Is this patent infringement? If so, how might Global save the cost of suing World for infringement and at the same time profit from World's sales? **(See page 100.)**

• Check your answers to the Issue Spotters against the answers provided in Appendix B at the end of this text.

Before the Test

Go to **www.cengagebrain.com**, enter the ISBN 9781285770192, and click on "Find" to locate this textbook's Web site. Then, click on "Access Now" under "Study Tools," and select Chapter 5 at the top. There, you will find a Practice Quiz that you can take to assess your mastery of the concepts in this chapter, as well as Flashcards and a Glossary of important terms.

Business Scenarios

5–1. Fair Use. Professor Wise is teaching a summer seminar in business torts at State University. Several times during the course, he makes copies of relevant sections from business law texts and distributes them to his students. Wise does not realize that the daughter of one of the textbook authors is a member of his seminar. She tells her father about Wise's copying activities, which have taken place without her father's or his publisher's permission. Her father sues Wise for copyright infringement. Wise claims protection under the fair use doctrine. Who will prevail? Explain. **(See page 105.)**

5–2. Patent Infringement. John and Andrew Doney invented a hard-bearing device for balancing rotors. Although they obtained a patent for their invention from the U.S. Patent and Trademark Office, it was never used as an automobile wheel balancer. Some time later, Exetron Corp. produced an automobile wheel balancer that used a hard-bearing device with a support plate similar to that of the Doneys' device. Given that the Doneys had not used their device for automobile wheel balancing, does Exetron's use of a similar device infringe on the Doneys' patent? Why or why not? **(See page 100.)**

Business Case Problems

5–3. Trade Secrets. Briefing.com offers Internet-based analyses of investment opportunities to investors. Richard Green is the company's president. One of Briefing. com's competitors is StreetAccount, LLC (limited liability company), whose owners include Gregory Jones and Cynthia Dietzmann. Jones worked for Briefing.com for six years until he quit in March 2003 and was a member of its board of directors until April 2003. Dietzmann worked for Briefing.com for seven years until she quit in March 2003. As Briefing.com employees, Jones and Dietzmann had access to confidential business data. For instance, Dietzmann developed a list of contacts through which Briefing.com obtained market information to display online. When Dietzmann quit, she did not return all of the contact information to the company. Briefing. com and Green filed a suit in a federal district court against Jones, Dietzmann, and StreetAccount, alleging that they had appropriated these data and other "trade secrets" to form a competing business. What are trade secrets? Why are they protected? Under what circumstances is a party liable at common law for their appropriation? How should these principles apply in this case?

[*Briefing.com v. Jones,* 2006 WY 16, 126 P.3d 928 (2006)]
(See page 107.)

5–4. Licensing. Redwin Wilchcombe composed, performed, and recorded a song called *Tha Weedman* at the request of Lil Jon, a member of Lil Jon & the East Side Boyz (LJESB), for LJESB's album *Kings of Crunk*. Wilchcombe was not paid, but was given credit on the album as a producer. After the album had sold 2 million copies, Wilchcombe filed a suit against LJESB, alleging copyright infringement. The defendants claimed that they had a license to use the song. Do the facts support this claim? Explain. [*Wilchcombe v. TeeVee Toons, Inc.,* 555 F.3d 949 (11th Cir. 2009)] **(See page 99.)**

5–5. BUSINESS CASE PROBLEM
WITH SAMPLE ANSWER: Trade Secrets.

 Jesse Edwards, an employee of Carbon Processing and Reclamation, LLC (CPR), put unmarked boxes of company records in his car. Edwards's wife, Channon, who suspected him of hiding financial information from her, gained access to the documents. William Jones, the owner of CPR, filed a suit, contending that Channon's unauthorized access to the files was a theft of trade secrets. Could the information in the documents be trade secrets? Should liability be imposed? Why or why not? [Jones v. Hamilton, 53 So.3d 134 (Ala.Civ.App. 2010)] **(See page 107.)**

• **For a sample answer to Problem 5–5, go to Appendix C at the end of this text.**

5–6. Spotlight on Macy's—Copyright Infringement. United

Fabrics International, Inc., bought a fabric design from an Italian designer and registered a copyright to it with the U.S. Copyright Office. When Macy's, Inc., began selling garments with a similar design, United filed a copyright infringement suit against Macy's. Macy's argued that United did not own a valid copyright to the design and so could not claim infringement. Does United have to prove that the copyright is valid to establish infringement? Explain. [*United Fabrics International, Inc. v. C&J Wear, Inc.,* 630 F.3d 1255 (9th Cir. 2011)] **(See page 103.)**

5–7. Theft of Trade Secrets. Hanjuan Jin, a citizen of the People's Republic of China, began working at Motorola in 1998. She worked as a software engineer in a division that created proprietary standards for cellular communications. In 2004 and 2005, contrary to Motorola's policies, Jin also began working as a consultant for Lemko Corp. Lemko introduced Jin to Sun Kaisens, a Chinese software company. During 2005, Jin returned to Beijing on several occasions and began working with Sun Kaisens and with the Chinese military. The following year, she started corresponding with Sun Kaisens's management about a possible full-time job in China. During this period, she took several medical leaves of absence from Motorola. In February 2007, after one of these medical leaves, she returned to Motorola.

During the next several days at Motorola, she accessed and downloaded thousands of documents on her personal laptop as well as on pen drives. On the following day, she attempted to board a flight to China but was randomly searched by U.S. Customs and Border Protection officials at Chicago's O'Hare International Airport. Ultimately, U.S. officials discovered the downloaded Motorola documents. Are there any circumstances under which Jin could avoid being prosecuted for theft of trade secrets? If so, what are these circumstances? Discuss fully. [*United States v. Hanjuan Jin,* 833 F.Supp.2d 977 (N.D.Ill. 2012)] **(See page 107.)**

5–8. Copyright Infringement. SilverEdge Systems Software hired Catherine Conrad to perform a singing telegram. SilverEdge arranged for James Bendewald to record Conrad's performance of her copyrighted song to post on its Web site. Conrad agreed to wear a microphone to assist in the recording, told Bendewald what to film, and asked for an additional fee only if SilverEdge used the video for a commercial purpose. Later, the company chose to post a video of a different performer's singing telegram instead. Conrad filed a suit in a federal district court against SilverEdge and Bendewald for copyright infringement. Are the defendants liable? Explain. [*Conrad v. Bendewald,* 2013 WL 310194 (7th Cir. 2013)] **(See page 103.)**

5–9. A QUESTION OF ETHICS: Copyright Infringement.

 Custom Copies, Inc., prepares and sells coursepacks, which contain compilations of readings for college courses. A teacher selects the readings and delivers a syllabus to the copy shop, which obtains the materials from a library, copies them, and binds the copies. Blackwell Publishing, Inc., which owns the copyright to some of the materials, filed a suit, alleging copyright infringement. [Blackwell Publishing, Inc. v. Custom Copies, Inc., 2006 WL 1529503 (N.D.Fla. 2006)] **(See page 103.)**

(a) Custom Copies argued, in part, that creating and selling did not "distribute" the coursepacks. Does a copy shop violate copyright law if it only copies materials for coursepacks? Does the copying fall under the "fair use" exception? Should the court grant the defendant's motion? Why or why not?

(b) What is the potential impact if copies of a book or journal are created and sold without the permission of, and the payment of royalties or a fee to, the copyright owner? Explain.

5–10. SPECIAL CASE ANALYSIS: Copyright Infringement.

 Go to Case Analysis Case 5.2, *Winstead v. Jackson,* on pages 103 and 104. Read the excerpt and answer the following questions.

(a) Issue: This case focused on an allegation of copyright infringement involving what parties and which creative works?

(b) Rule of Law: What is the test for determining whether a creative work infringes the copyright of another work?

(c) Applying the Rule of Law: How did the court determine whether the claim of copyright infringement was supported in this case?

(d) Conclusion: Was the defendant liable for copyright infringement? Why or why not?

Legal Reasoning Group Activity

5–11. Patents. After years of research, your company develops a product that might revolutionize the green (environmentally conscious) building industry. The product is made from relatively inexpensive and widely available materials combined in a unique way that can substantially lower the heating and cooling costs of residential and commercial buildings. The company has registered the trademark it intends to use on the product, and has filed a patent application with the U.S. Patent and Trademark Office. **(See page 99.)**

(a) One group should provide three reasons why this product does or does not qualify for patent protection.

(b) Another group should develop a four-step procedure for how your company can best protect its intellectual property rights (trademark, trade secret, and patent) and prevent domestic and foreign competitors from producing counterfeit goods or cheap knockoffs.

(c) Another group should list and explain three ways your company can utilize licensing.

CHAPTER 6

INTERNET LAW, SOCIAL MEDIA, AND PRIVACY

The Internet has changed our lives and our laws. Technology has put the world at our fingertips and now allows even the smallest business to reach customers around the globe. At the same time, the Internet presents a variety of challenges for the law. Courts are often in uncharted waters when deciding disputes that involve the Internet, social media, and online privacy. There may not be any common law precedents for judges to rely on when resolving a case. Long-standing principles of justice may be inapplicable. New rules are evolving, as we discuss in this chapter, but often not as quickly as technology.

SECTION 1
INTERNET LAW

A number of laws specifically address issues that arise only on the Internet. Three such issues are unsolicited e-mail, domain names, and cybersquatting, as we discuss here. We also discuss how the law is dealing with problems of trademark infringement and dilution online.

Spam

Businesses and individuals alike are targets of **spam.**[1] Spam is the unsolicited "junk e-mail" that floods virtual mailboxes with advertisements, solicitations, and other messages. Considered relatively harmless in the early days of the Internet, by 2013 spam accounted for roughly 75 percent of all e-mails.

STATE REGULATION OF SPAM In an attempt to combat spam, thirty-six states have enacted laws that prohibit or regulate its use. Many state laws that regulate spam require the senders of e-mail ads to instruct the recipients on how they can "opt out" of further e-mail ads from the same sources. For instance, in some states, an unsolicited e-mail must include a toll-free phone number or return e-mail address that the recipient can use to ask the sender to send no more unsolicited e-mails.

THE FEDERAL CAN-SPAM ACT In 2003, Congress enacted the Controlling the Assault of Non-Solicited Pornography and Marketing (CAN-SPAM) Act.[2] The legislation applies to any "commercial electronic mail messages" that are sent to promote a commercial product or service. Significantly, the statute preempts state antispam laws except for those provisions in state laws that prohibit false and deceptive e-mailing practices.

Generally, the act permits the sending of unsolicited commercial e-mail but prohibits certain types of spamming activities. Prohibited activities include the use of a false return address and the use of false, misleading, or deceptive information when sending e-mail. The statute also prohibits the use of "dictionary attacks"—sending messages to randomly generated e-mail addresses—and the "harvesting" of e-mail addresses from Web sites through the use of specialized software.

▶ **Example 6.1** Federal officials arrested Robert Alan Soloway, considered to be one of the world's most prolific spammers. Soloway, known as the "Spam King," had been using *botnets* (automated spamming networks) to send out hundreds of millions of unwanted e-mails. In 2008, Soloway pleaded guilty to mail fraud, spam, and failure to pay taxes. ◀

Arresting prolific spammers, however, has done little to curb spam, which continues to flow at a rate of 70 billion messages per day.

THE U.S. SAFE WEB ACT After the CAN-SPAM Act of 2003 prohibited false and deceptive e-mails originating in the United States, spamming from servers

---

1. The term *spam* is said to come from the lyrics of a Monty Python song that repeats the word *spam* over and over.

2. 15 U.S.C. 7701 *et seq.*

located in other nations increased. These cross-border spammers generally were able to escape detection and legal sanctions because the Federal Trade Commission (FTC) lacked the authority to investigate foreign spamming.

Congress sought to rectify the situation by enacting the U.S. Safe Web Act (also known as the Undertaking Spam, Spyware, and Fraud Enforcement with Enforcers Beyond Borders Act).[3] The act allows the FTC to cooperate and share information with foreign agencies in investigating and prosecuting those involved in spamming, spyware, and various Internet frauds and deceptions.

The Safe Web Act also provides a "safe harbor" for **Internet service providers (ISPs)**—that is, organizations that provide access to the Internet. The safe harbor gives ISPs immunity from liability for supplying information to the FTC concerning possible unfair or deceptive conduct in foreign jurisdictions.

Domain Names

As e-commerce expanded worldwide, one issue that emerged involved the rights of a trademark owner to use the mark as part of a domain name. A **domain name** is part of an Internet address, such as "**cengage.com.**"

STRUCTURE OF DOMAIN NAMES Every domain name ends with a generic top-level domain (TLD), which is the part of the name to the right of the period that often indicates the type of entity that operates the site. For instance, *com* is an abbreviation for *commercial,* and *edu* is short for *education.*

The second-level domain (SLD)—the part of the name to the left of the period—is chosen by the business entity or individual registering the domain name. Competition for SLDs among firms with similar names and products has led to numerous disputes. By using an identical or similar domain name, parties have attempted to profit from a competitor's **goodwill** (the nontangible value of a business). For instance, a party might use a similar domain name to sell pornography, offer for sale another party's domain name, or otherwise infringe on others' trademarks.

DISTRIBUTION SYSTEM The Internet Corporation for Assigned Names and Numbers (ICANN), a nonprofit corporation, oversees the distribution of domain names and operates an online arbitration system. Due to numerous complaints, ICANN completely overhauled the domain name distribution system.

In 2012, ICANN started selling new generic top-level domain names (gTLDs) for an initial price of $185,000 plus an annual fee of $25,000. Whereas TLDs were limited to only a few terms (such as "com," "net," and "org"), gTLDs can take any form. By 2013, many companies and corporations had acquired gTLDs based on their brands, such as .aol, .bmw, .canon, .gap, .target, .toyota, and .walmart. Some companies have numerous gTLDs. Google's gTLDs, for instance, include .android, .bing, .chrome, .gmail, .goog, and .YouTube.

Cybersquatting

One of the goals of the new gTLD system is to alleviate the problem of *cybersquatting*. **Cybersquatting** occurs when a person registers a domain name that is the same as, or confusingly similar to, the trademark of another and then offers to sell the domain name back to the trademark owner.

▶ **Case in Point 6.2** Apple, Inc., has repeatedly sued cybersquatters that registered domain names similar to its products, such as iphone4s.com and ipods.com. In 2012, Apple won a judgment in litigation at the World Intellectual Property Organization (WIPO) against a company that was squatting on the domain name iPhone5.com.[4] ◀

ANTICYBERSQUATTING LEGISLATION Because cybersquatting has led to so much litigation, Congress enacted the Anticybersquatting Consumer Protection Act (ACPA),[5] which amended the Lanham Act—the federal law protecting trademarks, discussed in Chapter 5. The ACPA makes cybersquatting illegal when both of the following are true:

1. The name is identical or confusingly similar to the trademark of another.
2. The one registering, trafficking in, or using the domain name has a "bad faith intent" to profit from that trademark.

THE ONGOING PROBLEM OF CYBERSQUATTING Despite the ACPA, cybersquatting continues to present a problem for businesses, largely because more TLDs and gTLDs are now available and many more companies are registering domain names. Indeed, domain name registrars have proliferated. Registrar companies

---

3. Pub. L. No. 109-455, 120 Stat. 3372 (2006), codified in various sections of 15 U.S.C. and 12 U.S.C. Section 3412.

4. WIPO Case No. D2012-0951.
5. 15 U.S.C. Section 1129.

charge a fee to businesses and individuals to register new names and to renew annual registrations (often through automated software). Many of these companies also buy and sell expired domain names.

All domain name registrars are supposed to relay information about these transactions to ICANN and other companies that keep a master list of domain names, but this does not always occur. The speed at which domain names change hands and the difficulty in tracking mass automated registrations have created an environment where cybersquatting can flourish. ▶ **Case in Point 6.3**   OnNet USA, Inc., owns the English-language rights to 9Dragons, a game with a martial arts theme, and operates a Web site for its promotion. When a party known as "Warv0x" began to operate a pirated version of the game at Play9D.com, OnNet filed an action under the ACPA in a federal court. OnNet was unable to obtain contact information for the owner of Play9D.com through its Australian domain name registrar, however, and thus could not complete *service of process*—that is, the delivery of a complaint and summons to a defendant. Therefore, the federal court allowed OnNet to serve the defendant by publishing a notice of the suit in a newspaper in Gold Coast, Australia.[6] ◀

TYPOSQUATTING   Cybersquatters have also developed new tactics, such as **typosquatting,** or registering a name that is a misspelling of a popular brand, such as googl.com or appple.com. Because many Internet users are not perfect typists, Web pages using these misspelled names receive a lot of traffic. More traffic generally means increased profit (advertisers often pay Web sites based on the number of unique visits, or hits), which in turn provides incentive for more cybersquatters. Also, if the misspelling is significant, the trademark owner may have difficulty proving that the name is identical or confusingly similar to the trademark of another as the ACPA requires.

Cybersquatting is costly for businesses, which must attempt to register all variations of a name to protect their domain name rights from would-be cybersquatters and typosquatters. Large corporations may have to register thousands of domain names across the globe just to protect their basic brands and trademarks.

APPLICABILITY AND SANCTIONS OF THE ACPA   The ACPA applies to all domain name registrations of trademarks. Successful plaintiffs in suits brought

under the act can collect actual damages and profits, or they can elect to receive statutory damages ranging from $1,000 to $100,000.

Although some companies have been successful suing under the ACPA, there are roadblocks to pursuing such lawsuits. Some domain name registrars offer privacy services that hide the true owners of Web sites, making it difficult for trademark owners to identify cybersquatters. Thus, before bringing a suit, a trademark owner has to ask the court for a subpoena to discover the identity of the owner of the infringing Web site. Because of the high costs of court proceedings, discovery, and even arbitration, many disputes over cybersquatting are settled out of court.

Meta Tags

Search engines compile their results by looking through a Web site's key-word field. As noted in Chapter 2, *meta tags* are key words that are inserted into the HTML (hypertext markup language) code to tell Internet browsers specific information about a Web page. Meta tags increase the likelihood that a site will be included in search engine results, even though the site may have nothing to do with the key words. Using this same technique, one site may appropriate the key words of other sites with more frequent hits so that the appropriating site will appear in the same search engine results as the more popular sites.

Using another's trademark in a meta tag without the owner's permission, however, normally constitutes trademark infringement. Some uses of another's trademark as a meta tag may be permissible if the use is reasonably necessary and does not suggest that the owner authorized or sponsored the use.

▶ **Case in Point 6.4**   Farzad and Lisa Tabari are auto brokers—the personal shoppers of the automotive world. They contact authorized dealers, solicit bids, and arrange for customers to buy from the dealer offering the best combination of location, availability, and price. The Tabaris offered this service at the Web sites **buy-a-lexus.com** and **buyorleaselexus.com**. Toyota Motor Sales U.S.A., Inc., the exclusive distributor of Lexus vehicles and the owner of the Lexus mark, objected to the Tabaris' practices. The Tabaris removed Toyota's photographs and logo from their site and added a disclaimer in large type at the top, but they refused to give up their domain names. Toyota sued for infringement. The court forced the Tabaris to stop using any "domain name, service mark, trademark,

---

6. *OnNet USA, Inc. v. Play9D.com,* ___F.Supp.2d ___, 2013 WL 120319 (N.D.Cal. 2013).

trade name, meta tag or other commercial indication of origin that includes the mark LEXUS."[7] ◄

Trademark Dilution in the Online World

As discussed in Chapter 5, trademark *dilution* occurs when a trademark is used, without authorization, in a way that diminishes the distinctive quality of the mark.

Unlike trademark infringement, a claim of dilution does not require proof that consumers are likely to be confused by a connection between the unauthorized use and the mark. For this reason, the products involved need not be similar, as the following *Spotlight Case* illustrates.

---

7. *Toyota Motor Sales, U.S.A., Inc. v. Tabari,* 610 F.3d 171 (9th Cir. 2011).

SPOTLIGHT on Internet Porn

Case 6.1   Hasbro, Inc. v. Internet Entertainment Group, Ltd.

United States District Court, Western District of Washington, ___ F.Supp.2d ___ (1996).

BACKGROUND AND FACTS In 1949, Hasbro, Inc.—then known as the Milton Bradley Company—published its first version of Candy Land, a children's board game. Hasbro is the owner of the trademark "Candy Land," which has been registered with the U.S. Patent and Trademark Office since 1951. Over the years, Hasbro has produced several versions of the game, including Candy Land puzzles, a travel version, a computer game, and a handheld electronic version. In the mid-1990s, Brian Cartmell and his employer, the Internet Entertainment Group, Ltd., used the term *candyland.com* as a domain name for a sexually explicit Internet site. Anyone who performed an online search using the word *candyland* was directed to this adult Web site. Hasbro filed a trademark dilution claim in a federal court, seeking a permanent injunction to prevent the defendants from using the Candy Land trademark.

 IN THE LANGUAGE OF THE COURT
DWYER, U.S. District Judge

* * * *

2. Hasbro has demonstrated a probability of proving that defendants Internet Entertainment Group, Ltd., Brian Cartmell and Internet Entertainment Group, Inc. (collectively referred to as "defendants") have been diluting the value of Hasbro's CANDY LAND mark by using the name CANDYLAND to identify a sexually explicit Internet site, and by using the name string "candyland.com" as an Internet domain name which, when typed into an Internet-connected computer, provides Internet users with access to that site.
* * * *

4. Hasbro has shown that defendants' use of the CANDY LAND name and the domain name candyland.com in connection with their Internet site is causing irreparable injury to Hasbro.

5. *The probable harm to Hasbro from defendants' conduct outweighs any inconvenience that defendants will experience if they are required to stop using the CANDYLAND name.* [Emphasis added.]
* * * *

THEREFORE, IT IS HEREBY ORDERED that Hasbro's motion for preliminary injunction is granted.

DECISION AND REMEDY *The federal district court granted Hasbro an injunction against the defendants, agreeing that the domain name candyland was "causing irreparable injury to Hasbro." The judge ordered the defendants to immediately remove all content from the candyland.com Web site and to stop using the Candy Land mark.*

THE ECONOMIC DIMENSION *How can companies protect themselves from others who create Web sites that have similar domain names, and what limits each company's ability to be fully protected?*

WHAT IF THE FACTS WERE DIFFERENT? *Suppose that the site using* candyland.com *had not been sexually explicit but had sold candy. Would the result have been the same? Explain.*

Licensing

Recall from Chapter 5 that a company may permit another party to use a trademark (or other intellectual property) under a license. A licensor might grant a license allowing its trademark to be used as part of a domain name, for example.

Indeed, licensing is ubiquitous in the online world. When you download an application on your smartphone, tablet, or other mobile device, for instance, you are typically entering into to a license agreement. You are obtaining only a *license* to use that app and not ownership rights in it. Apps published on Google Play, for instance, may use its licensing service to prompt users to agree to a license at the time of installation and use. Licensing agreements frequently include restrictions that prohibit licensees from sharing the file and using it to create similar software applications. The license may also limit the use of the application to a specific device or give permission to the user for a certain time period. For further discussion of licensing and e-contracts, see Chapter 10.

SECTION 2
COPYRIGHTS IN DIGITAL INFORMATION

Copyright law is probably the most important form of intellectual property protection on the Internet. This is because much of the material on the Internet (including software and database information) is copyrighted, and in order to transfer that material online, it must be "copied." Generally, whenever a party downloads software or music into a computer's random access memory, or RAM, without authorization, a copyright is infringed. Technology has vastly increased the potential for copyright infringement.

▶ **Case in Point 6.5**   A rap song that was included in the sound track of a movie had used only a few seconds from the guitar solo of another's copyrighted sound recording without permission. Nevertheless, a federal court held that digitally sampling a copyrighted sound recording of any length constitutes copyright infringement.[8] ◀

Some other federal courts have not found that digital sampling is always illegal. Some courts have allowed the defense of fair use (see Chapter 5), while others have not. ▶ **Example 6.6**   Hip hop stars Jay-Z and Kanye West were sued for digitally sampling music by soul musician Syl Johnson. Given the uncertain outcome of the litigation, they ended up settling the suit in 2012 for an undisclosed amount. ◀

Initially, criminal penalties for copyright violations could be imposed only if unauthorized copies were exchanged for financial gain. Yet much piracy of copyrighted materials online was "altruistic" in nature— unauthorized copies were made simply to be shared with others. Then, Congress amended the law and extended criminal liability for the piracy of copyrighted materials to persons who exchange unauthorized copies of copyrighted works without realizing a profit.

Digital Millennium Copyright Act

In 1998, Congress passed further legislation to protect copyright holders—the Digital Millennium Copyright Act (DMCA).[9] The DMCA gave significant protection to owners of copyrights in digital information. Among other things, the act established civil and criminal penalties for anyone who circumvents (bypasses) encryption software or other technological antipiracy protection. Also prohibited are the manufacture, import, sale, and distribution of devices or services for circumvention.

The DMCA provides for exceptions to fit the needs of libraries, scientists, universities, and others. In general, the law does not restrict the "fair use" of circumvention methods for educational and other noncommercial purposes. For instance, circumvention is allowed to test computer security, to conduct encryption research, to protect personal privacy, and

---

8. *Bridgeport Music, Inc. v. Dimension Films,* 410 F.3d 792 (6th Cir. 2005).
9. 17 U.S.C. Sections 512, 1201–1205, 1301–1332; and 28 U.S.C. Section 4001.

to enable parents to monitor their children's use of the Internet. The exceptions are to be reconsidered every three years.

The DMCA also limits the liability of Internet service providers (ISPs). Under the act, an ISP is not liable for copyright infringement by its customer *unless* the ISP is aware of the subscriber's violation. An ISP may be held liable only if it fails to take action to shut down the subscriber after learning of the violation. A copyright holder must act promptly, however, by pursuing a claim in court, or the subscriber has the right to be restored to online access.

MP3 and File-Sharing Technology

Soon after the Internet became popular, a few enterprising programmers created software to compress large data files, particularly those associated with music. The best-known compression and decompression system is MP3, which enables music fans to download songs or entire CDs onto their computers or onto portable listening devices, such as iPods. The MP3 system also made it possible for music fans to access other fans' files by engaging in file-sharing via the Internet.

METHODS OF FILE-SHARING File-sharing is accomplished through **peer-to-peer (P2P) networking.** The concept is simple. Rather than going through a central Web server, P2P networking uses numerous personal computers (PCs) that are connected to the Internet. Individuals on the same network can access files stored on one another's PCs through a **distributed network.** Parts of the network may be distributed all over the country or the world, which offers an unlimited number of uses. Persons scattered throughout the country or the world can work together on the same project by using file-sharing programs.

A newer method of sharing files via the Internet is **cloud computing**, which is essentially a subscription-based or pay-per-use service that extends a computer's software or storage capabilities. Cloud computing can deliver a single application through a browser to multiple users. Alternatively, cloud computing might be a utility program to pool resources and provide data storage and virtual servers that can be accessed on demand. Amazon, Facebook, Google, IBM, and Sun Microsystems are using and developing more cloud computing services.

SHARING STORED MUSIC FILES When file-sharing is used to download others' stored music files, copyright issues arise. Recording artists and their labels stand to lose large amounts of royalties and revenues if relatively few digital downloads or CDs are purchased and then made available on distributed networks. Anyone can get the music for free on these networks.

▶ **Case in Point 6.7** The issue of file-sharing infringement has been the subject of an ongoing debate since the highly publicized cases against two companies (Napster, Inc. and Grokster, Ltd.) that created software used for copyright infringement. In the first case, Napster operated a Web site with free software that enabled users to copy and transfer MP3 files via the Internet. Firms in the recording industry sued Napster. Ultimately, the court held that Napster was liable for contributory and vicarious[10] (indirect) copyright infringement.

As technology evolved, Grokster, Ltd., and several other companies created and distributed new types of file-sharing software. This software did not maintain a central index of content, but allowed P2P network users to share stored music files. The court held that because the companies distributed file-sharing software "with the object of promoting its use to infringe the copyright," they were liable for the resulting acts of infringement by the software's users.[11] ◀

In the following case, a group of recording companies sued an Internet user who had downloaded a number of copyrighted songs from the Internet. The user then shared the audio files with others via a P2P network. One of the issues before the court was whether the user was an "innocent infringer." In other words, was she innocent of copyright infringement because she was unaware that the works were copyrighted?

---

10. *Vicarious (indirect) liability* exists when one person is subject to liability for another's actions. A common example occurs in the employment context, when an employer is held vicariously liable by third parties for torts committed by employees in the course of their employment.

11. *A&M Records, Inc. v. Napster, Inc.,* 239 F.3d 1004 (9th Cir. 2001); and *Metro-Goldwyn-Mayer Studios, Inc. v. Grokster, Ltd.,* 545 U.S. 913, 125 S.Ct. 2764, 162 L.Ed.2d 781 (2005). Grokster, Ltd., later settled this dispute out of court and stopped distributing its software.

CASE 6.2

Maverick Recording Co. v. Harper
United States Court of Appeals, Fifth Circuit, 598 F.3d 193 (2010).

COMPANY PROFILE Recording star Madonna, others in the music business, and Time Warner created Maverick Records in 1992. Initially, the company saw great success with Alanis Morissette, The Prodigy, Candlebox, and the Deftones. It also created the sound track for the movie *The Matrix*. In a dispute over management of the company, Madonna and another co-owner were bought out. Today, Maverick is a wholly owned subsidiary of Warner Music Group.

BACKGROUND AND FACTS Maverick Recording Company and several other music-recording firms (the plaintiffs) hired MediaSentry to investigate the infringement of their copyrights over the Internet. During its investigation, MediaSentry discovered that Whitney Harper was using a file-sharing program to share digital audio files with other users of a peer-to-peer network. The shared audio files included a number of the plaintiffs' copyrighted works. The plaintiffs brought an action in a federal court against Harper for copyright infringement. They sought $750 per infringed work, the minimum amount of damages set forth in Section 504(c)(1) of the Copyright Act.

Harper asserted that her infringement was "innocent" and that therefore Section 504(c)(2) of the Copyright Act should apply. That section provides that when an infringer was not aware, and had no reason to believe, that his or her acts constituted copyright infringement, "the court in its discretion may reduce the award of statutory damages to a sum of not less than $200. "The trial court granted summary judgment for the plaintiffs on the issue of copyright infringement and enjoined Harper from further downloading and sharing of copyrighted works. The court, however, awarded the plaintiffs only $200 for each infringed work. Both parties appealed. Harper claimed that there was insufficient evidence of copyright infringement. The plaintiffs argued that the district court had erred by failing to rule out the innocent infringer defense as a matter of law.

IN THE LANGUAGE OF THE COURT
Edith *BROWN CLEMENT,* Circuit Judge:

* * * *

The uncontroverted [undisputed] evidence is more than sufficient to compel a finding that Harper had downloaded the files: there was no evidence from which a fact-finder could draw a reasonable inference that Harper had *not* downloaded them or that they were something other than audio files. * * * The district court properly rejected Harper's argument that the evidence of infringement was insufficient.

* * * *

* * * The district court held that there was a genuine issue of material fact as to whether Harper was an innocent infringer. * * * Harper averred [asserted] in an affidavit that she did not understand the nature of file-sharing programs and that she believed that listening to music from file-sharing networks was akin to listening to a noninfringing Internet radio station. The district court ruled that this assertion created a triable [capable of being tried before a judge or a jury] issue as to whether Harper's infringement was "innocent" under [Section 504(c)(2) of the Copyright Act].

* * * We hold that the defense was unavailable to her as a matter of law. *The innocent infringer defense is limited by [Section 402(d) of the Copyright Act]: with one exception not relevant here, when a proper copyright notice "appears on the published * * * phonorecords to which a defendant * * * had access, then no weight shall be given to such a defendant's interposition of a defense based on innocent infringement in mitigation of actual or statutory damages."* [Emphasis added.]

CASE 6.2 CONTINUES ▶

The district court acknowledged that Plaintiffs provided proper notice on each of the published phonorecords from which the audio files were taken. * * * Harper contended only that she was too young and naive to understand that the copyrights on published music applied to downloaded music.

These arguments are insufficient to defeat the interposition [interference] of the [Section 402(d)] limitation on the innocent infringer defense. Harper's reliance on her own understanding of copyright law—or lack thereof—is irrelevant in the context of [Section 402(d)]. *The plain language of the statute shows that the infringer's knowledge or intent does not affect its application. Lack of legal sophistication cannot overcome a properly asserted [Section 402(d)] limitation to the innocent infringer defense.* [Emphasis added.]

* * * *

In short, the district court found a genuine issue of fact as to whether Harper intended to infringe Plaintiffs' copyrights, but that issue was not material: [Section 402(d)] forecloses, as a matter of law, Harper's innocent infringer defense. Because the defense does not apply, Plaintiffs are entitled to statutory damages. And because Plaintiffs requested the minimum statutory damages under [Section 504(c)(1)], Harper's culpability is not an issue and there are no issues left for trial. Plaintiffs must be awarded statutory damages of $750 per infringed work.

DECISION AND REMEDY *The U.S. Court of Appeals for the Fifth Circuit affirmed the trial court's finding of copyright liability, reversed its finding that the innocent infringer defense presented an issue for trial, and remanded the case for further proceedings consistent with the court's opinion. The appellate court concluded that the district court had erred by awarding damages of $200 per infringement because Harper was not an innocent infringer.*

THE ETHICAL DIMENSION *In this and other cases involving similar rulings, the courts have held that when the published phonorecordings from which audio files were taken contained copyright notices, the innocent infringer defense does not apply. It is irrelevant that the notice is not provided in the online file. Is this fair? Explain.*

MANAGERIAL IMPLICATIONS *Owners and managers of firms in the business of recording and distributing music face a constant challenge in protecting their copyrights. This is particularly true for audio files in the online environment, where Internet users can easily download a copyrighted song and make it available to P2P file-sharing networks. Among other things, this means that recording companies must be ever vigilant in searching the Web to find infringing uses of any works distributed online. Today, it is not uncommon for companies to hire antipiracy firms to investigate the illegal downloading of their copyrighted materials.*

DVDs AND FILE-SHARING File-sharing also creates problems for the motion picture industry, which loses significant amounts of revenue annually as a result of pirated DVDs. Numerous Web sites offer software that facilitates the illegal copying of movies, such as BitTorrent, which enables users to download high-quality files from the Internet.

▶ **Case in Point 6.8** A popular BitTorrent indexing Web site, TorrentSpy, enabled users to locate and exchange files. The Motion Picture Association of America (MPAA) and Columbia Pictures, Inc., brought a lawsuit against the operators of TorrentSpy for facilitating copyright infringement. The MPAA also claimed that the operators had destroyed evidence that would reveal the identity of individual infringers. The operators had ignored a court order to keep server logs of the Internet addresses of people who facilitated the trading of files via the site. Because TorrentSpy's operators had willfully destroyed evidence, a federal court found in favor of the MPAA and ordered the defendants to pay a judgment of $111 million.[12] ◀

SECTION 3
SOCIAL MEDIA

Social media provide a means by which people can create, share, and exchange ideas and comments via the Internet. Social networking sites, such as Facebook, Google+, MySpace, LinkedIn, Pinterest, and Tumblr, have become ubiquitous. Studies show that Internet users spend more time on social networks than at any other sites. The amount of time people spend accessing social networks on their smartphones and other

---

12. *Columbia Pictures Industries, v. Bunnell,* 2007 WL 4877701 (C.D.Cal. 2007).

mobile devices has increased every year (by nearly 37 percent in 2012 alone).

▶ **Example 6.9** Facebook, which was launched in 2004, had more than a billion active users by 2013. Individuals of all ages use Facebook to maintain social contacts, update friends on events, and distribute images to others. Facebook members often share common interests based on their school, location, or recreational affiliation, such as a sports team. ◀

Legal Issues

The emergence of Facebook and other social networking sites has created a number of legal and ethical issues for businesses. For instance, a firm's rights in valuable intellectual property may be infringed if users post trademarked images or copyrighted materials on these sites without permission.

Social media posts now are routinely included in discovery in litigation because they can provide damaging information that establishes a person's intent or what she or he knew at a particular time. Like e-mail, posts on social networks can be the smoking gun that leads to liability.

Tweets and other social media posts can also be used to reduce damages awards. ▶ **Example 6.10** Omeisha Daniels sued for injuries she sustained in a car accident. She claimed that her injuries made it impossible for her to continue working as a hairstylist. The jury originally awarded her $237,000, but when the jurors saw Daniels's tweets and photographs of her partying in New Orleans and vacationing on the beach, they reduced the damages to $142,000. ◀

CRIMINAL INVESTIGATIONS Law enforcement uses social media to detect and prosecute criminals. ▶ **Example 6.11** A nineteen-year-old posts a message on Facebook bragging about how drunk he was on New Year's Eve and apologizing to the owner of the parked car that he hit. The next day, police officers arrest him for drunk driving and leaving the scene of an accident. ◀

ADMINISTRATIVE AGENCIES Federal regulators also use social media posts in their investigations into illegal activities. ▶ **Example 6.12** Reed Hastings, the top executive of Netflix, stated on Facebook that Netflix subscribers had watched a billion hours of video the previous month. This prompted a federal agency investigation. Because such a statement is considered to be material information to investors, it must be disclosed to all investors at the same time under securities law. ◀

The decision in a hearing before an administrative law judge can turn on the content of two Facebook posts, as occurred in the following case.

CASE ANALYSIS

Case 6.3 *In re* O'Brien

Superior Court of New Jersey, Appellate Division, 2013 WL 132508 (2013).

IN THE LANGUAGE OF THE COURT
PER CURIAM. [By the Whole Court]

* * * *

[Jennifer] O'Brien has been employed as a teacher in the [City of Paterson, New Jersey] schools since March 1998. She has a master's degree in education, and certifications as an elementary school teacher and supervisor.

* * * In December 2010, O'Brien was assigned to teach the first grade [at School No. 21].

* * * There were twenty-three students in O'Brien's first-grade class. Almost all were six years old. All were either Latino or African-American.

On March 28, 2011, O'Brien posted two statements on Facebook, an Internet social-networking site. The first statement was, "I'm not a teacher—I'm a warden for future criminals!" The second statement was, "They had a scared straight program in school—why couldn't I bring first graders?"

* * * *

On March 30, 2011, [Frank Puglise, the principal of School No. 21] confronted O'Brien about the postings.

According to Puglise, O'Brien insisted that she did not intend her comments to be offensive, but she was otherwise unrepentant [unapologetic]. O'Brien was suspended * * *, pending a complete investigation.

News of O'Brien's Facebook postings spread quickly throughout the district. * * * Two angry parents went to Puglise's office to express their outrage. One parent threatened to remove her child from the school. According to Puglise, the school received at least a dozen irate phone calls. * * * There was a protest outside

CASE 6.3 CONTINUES ▶

the school, attended by twenty to twenty-five persons.

The following day, reporters and camera crews from major news organizations descended upon the school and remained there until late in the afternoon. A larger-than-usual crowd attended the Home-School Council meeting that evening, and the meeting was principally devoted to the Facebook postings. Parents expressed their outrage concerning the postings, and Puglise reassured the attendees that O'Brien had been removed from the classroom.

On April 14, 2011, the deputy superintendent of schools filed a complaint against O'Brien, charging her with conduct unbecoming a teacher.

The charges were filed with the Commissioner of Education * * * , and the matter was referred to the Office of Administrative Law for a hearing before an Administrative Law Judge (ALJ).

* * * *

On October 31, 2011, the ALJ issued her initial decision. The ALJ rejected O'Brien's contention that her comments were protected by the First Amendment to the United States Constitution. The ALJ wrote that O'Brien's remarks were not addressing a matter of public concern, but were "a personal expression" of dissatisfaction with her job.

The ALJ also wrote that * * * her right to express her views was outweighed by the district's need to operate its schools efficiently. The ALJ stated that:

An Internet social-networking site such as Facebook is a questionable place to begin an earnest conversation about an important school issue such as classroom discipline. More to the point, a description of first-grade children as criminals with their teacher as their warden is intemperate and vituperative [insulting]. It becomes impossible for parents to cooperate with or have faith in a teacher who insults their children and trivializes legitimate educational concerns on the internet.

The ALJ added that, while First Amendment protections do not generally rise or fall on the public reactions to a person's statements, "in a public school setting thoughtless words can destroy the partnership between home and school that is essential to the mission of the schools."

The ALJ found that evidence supported the charges of conduct unbecoming a teacher. The ALJ determined that the evidence established that O'Brien failed to maintain a safe, caring, nurturing, educational environment * * * . The ALJ additionally determined that O'Brien breached her duty as a professional teacher * * * . In addition, the ALJ found that O'Brien's conduct endangered the mental well-being of the students.

The ALJ also determined O'Brien's actions warranted her removal * * * . The ALJ wrote,

If this was an aberrational [not normal] lapse in judgment, a reaction to an unusually bad day, I would have expected to have heard more genuine and passionate contrition in O'Brien's testimony. I needed to hear that she was terribly sorry she had insulted her young students; that she loved being their teacher; and that she wanted desperately to return to the classroom. I heard nothing of the sort. Rather, I came away with the impression that O'Brien remained somewhat befuddled by the commotion she had created, and that while she continued to maintain that her conduct was not inappropriate, she was sorry others thought differently.

The ALJ observed that, with some sensitivity training, and after some time to "reflect," O'Brien might successfully return to the classroom. The ALJ concluded, however, that O'Brien's relationship with the Paterson school community had been irreparably damaged, "not because the community thinks so, but because O'Brien fails to understand why it does." The ALJ ordered O'Brien's removal from her tenured position.

* * * The Acting Commissioner issued a final decision * * * . *The Acting Commissioner concluded that O'Brien's Facebook postings were not constitutionally protected; the evidence established that O'Brien engaged in conduct unbecoming a teacher; and removal was the appropriate penalty.* This appeal followed. [Emphasis added.]

* * * *

We * * * affirm the Acting Commissioner's final determination substantially for the reasons stated by the ALJ and the Acting Commissioner in their decisions.

* * * *

* * * We are satisfied that, in determining the appropriate penalty, the ALJ and Acting Commissioner considered all relevant factors and reasonably concluded that the seriousness of O'Brien's conduct warranted her removal from her tenured position in the district.

Affirmed.

LEGAL REASONING QUESTIONS

1. Certain interests of public employees and their employer are balanced to determine whether the First Amendment protects an employee's Facebook posts. What are those interests?

2. What did O'Brien do that constituted conduct unbecoming a tenured teacher?

3. What penalty did the administrative law judge impose? Why?

4. Would the outcome have been different if O'Brien had apologized? Discuss.

EMPLOYERS' SOCIAL MEDIA POLICIES Employees who use social media in a way that violates their employer's stated policies may be disciplined or fired from their jobs. (Many large corporations have established specific guidelines on creating a social media policy in the workplace.) Courts and employment agencies usually uphold an employer's right to terminate a person based on his or her violation of a social media policy.

▶ **Case in Point 6.13** Virginia Rodriquez worked for Wal-Mart Stores, Inc., for almost twenty years and had been promoted to management. Then she was disciplined for violating the company's policies by having a fellow employee use Rodriquez's password to alter the price of an item that she purchased. Under Wal-Mart's rules, another violation within a year would mean termination. Nine months later, on Facebook, Rodriquez publicly chastised employees under her supervision for calling in sick to go to a party. The posting violated Wal-Mart's "Social Media Policy," which was "to avoid public comment that adversely affects employees." Wal-Mart terminated Rodriquez. She filed a lawsuit, alleging discrimination, but the court issued a summary judgment in Wal-Mart's favor.[13] ◀ Note, however, that employees' posts on social media may be protected under labor law, as discussed in Chapter 8.

The Electronic Communications Privacy Act

The Electronic Communications Privacy Act (ECPA)[14] amended federal wiretapping law to cover electronic forms of communications. Although Congress enacted the ECPA many years before social media networks existed, it nevertheless applies to communications through social media.

The ECPA prohibits the intentional interception of any wire, oral, or electronic communication. It also prohibits the intentional disclosure or use of the information obtained by the interception.

EXCLUSIONS Excluded from the ECPA's coverage are any electronic communications through devices that an employer provides for its employee to use "in the ordinary course of its business." Consequently, if a company provides the electronic device (cell phone, laptop, tablet) to the employee for ordinary business

use, the company is not prohibited from intercepting business communications made on it.

This "business-extension exception" to the ECPA permits employers to monitor employees' electronic communications made in the ordinary course of business. It does not, however, permit employers to monitor employees' personal communications. Another exception allows an employer to avoid liability under the act if the employees consent to having their electronic communications monitored by the employer.

STORED COMMUNICATIONS Part of the ECPA is known as the Stored Communications Act (SCA).[15] The SCA prohibits intentional and unauthorized access to *stored* electronic communications and sets forth criminal and civil sanctions for violators. A person can violate the SCA by intentionally accessing a stored electronic communication. The SCA also prevents "providers" of communication services (such as cell phone companies and social media networks) from divulging private communications to certain entities and individuals.

▶ **Case in Point 6.14** Two restaurant employees, Brian Pietrylo and Doreen Marino, were fired after their manager uncovered their password-protected MySpace group. The group's communications, stored on MySpace's Web site, contained sexual remarks about customers and management, and comments about illegal drug use and violent behavior. One employee said the group's purpose was to "vent about any BS we deal with out of work without any outside eyes spying on us." The restaurant learned about the private MySpace group when a hostess showed it to a manager who requested access. The hostess was not explicitly threatened with termination but feared she would lose her job if she did not comply. The court allowed the employees' SCA claim, and the jury awarded them $17,003 in compensatory and punitive damages.[16] ◀

Protection of Social Media Passwords

In recent years, employees and applicants for jobs or colleges have sometimes been asked to divulge their social media passwords. Employers and schools have sometimes looked at an individual's Facebook or other account to see if it included controversial postings such as racially discriminatory remarks or photos

---

13. *Rodriquez v. Wal-Mart Stores, Inc.*, ___F.Supp.2d __, 2013 WL 102674 (N.D.Tex. 2013).
14. 18 U.S.C. Sections 2510–2521.
15. 18 U.S.C. Sections 2701–2711.
16. *Pietrylo v. Hillstone Restaurant Group*, 2009 WL 3128420 (D.N.J. 2009).

of drug parties. Such postings can have a negative effect on a person's prospects even though they were made years earlier or have been taken out of context.

By 2013, four states (California, Illinois, Maryland, and Michigan) had enacted legislation to protect individuals from having to disclose their social media passwords. Each state's law is slightly different. Some states, such as Michigan, prohibit employers from taking adverse action against an employee or job applicant based on what the person has posted online. Michigan's law also applies to e-mail and cloud storage accounts. The federal government is also considering legislation that would prohibit employers and schools from demanding passwords to social media accounts.

Even if legislation is passed, however, it will not completely prevent employers and others from taking actions against a person based on his or her social network postings. Management and human resources personnel are unlikely to admit that they looked at someone's Facebook page and that it influenced their decision. How would a person who does not get a job be able to prove that she or he was rejected because the employer accessed social media? Also, the employer or school may use private browsing, which enables people to keep their Web browsing activities confidential.

Company-wide Social Media Networks

Many companies, including Dell, Inc., and Nikon Instruments, form their own internal social media networks. Software companies offer a variety of systems, including Salesforce.com's Chatter, Microsoft's Yammer, and Cisco Systems' WebEx Social. Posts on these internal networks are quite different from the typical posts on Facebook, LinkedIn, and Twitter. Employees use these intranets to exchange messages about topics related to their work such as deals that are closing, new products, production flaws, how a team is solving a problem, and the details of customer orders. Thus, the tone is businesslike.

PROTECTION OF TRADE SECRETS An important advantage to using an internal system for employee communications is that the company can better protect its trade secrets. The company usually decides which employees can see particular intranet files and which employees will belong to each specific "social" group within the company. Companies providing internal social media networks often keep the resulting data on their own servers in secure "clouds."

OTHER ADVANTAGES Internal social media systems also offer additional benefits such as real-time information about important issues, such as production glitches. Additionally, posts can include tips on how to best sell new products or deal with difficult customers, as well as information about competitors' products and services.

Another major benefit of intranets is a significant reduction in the use of e-mail. Rather than wasting fellow employees' time reading mass e-mailings, workers can post messages or collaborate on presentations via the company's social network.

SECTION 4
ONLINE DEFAMATION

Cyber torts are torts that arise from online conduct. One of the most prevalent cyber torts is online defamation. Recall from Chapter 4 that defamation is wrongfully hurting a person's reputation by communicating false statements about that person to others. Because the Internet enables individuals to communicate with large numbers of people simultaneously (via a blog or tweet, for instance), online defamation has become a problem in today's legal environment.

▶ **Example 6.15** Courtney Love was sued for defamation based on remarks she posted about fashion designer Dawn Simorangkir on Twitter. Love claimed that her statements were opinion (rather than statements of fact, as required) and therefore were not actionable as defamation. Nevertheless, Love ended up paying $430,000 to settle the case out of court. ◀

Identifying the Author of Online Defamation

An initial issue raised by online defamation is simply discovering who is committing it. In the real world, identifying the author of a defamatory remark generally is an easy matter. Suppose, though, that a business firm has discovered that defamatory statements about its policies and products are being posted in an online forum. Such forums allow anyone—customers, employees, or crackpots—to complain about a firm that they dislike while remaining anonymous.

Therefore, a threshold barrier to anyone who seeks to bring an action for online defamation is discovering the identity of the person who posted the defamatory message. An Internet service provider (ISP) can disclose personal information about its customers only when ordered to do so by a court. Consequently, businesses and individuals are increasingly bringing lawsuits against "John Does" (John Doe, Jane Doe, and the like are fictitious names used in lawsuits when the identity of a party is not known or when a party wishes to conceal his or her name for privacy reasons). Then, using the authority of the courts, the plaintiffs can obtain from the ISPs the identity of the persons responsible for the defamatory messages.

Liability of Internet Service Providers

Recall from the discussion of defamation in Chapter 4 that normally one who repeats or otherwise republishes a defamatory statement is subject to liability as if he or she had originally published it. Thus, newspapers, magazines, and television and radio stations are subject to liability for defamatory content that they publish or broadcast, even though the content was prepared or created by others.

Applying this rule to cyberspace, however, raises an important issue: Should ISPs be regarded as publishers and therefore be held liable for defamatory messages that are posted by their users in online forums or other arenas?

GENERAL RULE The Communications Decency Act (CDA) states that "[n]o provider or user of an interactive computer service shall be treated as the publisher or speaker of any information provided by another information content provider."[17] Thus, under the CDA, ISPs usually are treated differently from publishers in print and other media and are not liable for publishing defamatory statements that come from a third party.

EXCEPTIONS Although the courts generally have construed the CDA as providing a broad shield to protect ISPs from liability for third party content, some courts have started establishing some limits to this immunity. ▶ **Case in Point 6.16** Roommate.com, LLC, operates an online roommate-matching Web site that helps individuals find roommates based on their descriptions of themselves and their room-

mate preferences. Users respond to a series of online questions, choosing from answers in drop-down and select-a-box menus.

Some of the questions asked users to disclose their sex, family status, and sexual orientation—which is not permitted under the federal Fair Housing Act. When a nonprofit housing organization sued Roommate.com, the company claimed it was immune from liability under the CDA. A federal appellate court disagreed and ruled that Roommate.com was not immune from liability. Roommate.com was ordered to pay nearly $500,000 for prompting discriminatory preferences from users and matching users based on these criteria in violation of federal law.[18] ◀

SECTION 5
PRIVACY

Facebook, Google, and Yahoo have all been accused of violating users' privacy rights. As discussed in Chapter 2, the courts have held that the right to privacy is guaranteed by the Bill of Rights, and some state constitutions guarantee it as well. To maintain a suit for the invasion of privacy, though, a person must have a reasonable expectation of privacy in the particular situation (see Chapter 4). People clearly have a reasonable expectation of privacy when they enter their personal banking or credit-card information online. They also have a reasonable expectation that online companies will follow their own privacy policies. But it is probably not reasonable to expect privacy in statements made on Twitter.

Sometimes, people are confused and mistakenly believe that they are making statements or posting photos in a private forum. ▶ **Example 6.17** Randi Zuckerberg, the older sister of Mark Zuckerberg (the founder of Facebook), used a mobile app called "Poke" to post a "private" photo on Facebook of their family gathering during the holidays. Poke allows the sender to decide how long the photo can be seen by others. Facebook allows users to configure their privacy settings to limit access to photos, which Randi thought she had done. Nonetheless, the photo showed up in the Facebook feed of Callie Schweitzer, who then put it on Twitter where it eventually went viral. Schweitzer apologized and removed the photo, but it had already gone public for the world to see. ◀

---

17. 47 U.S.C. Section 230.

18. *Fair Housing Council of San Fernando Valley v. Roommate.com, LLC,* 666 F.3d 1216 (9th Cir. 2012).

Data Collection and Cookies

Whenever a consumer purchases items from an online retailer, such as Amazon.com, or a retailer that sells both offline and online, such as Best Buy, the retailer collects information about the consumer. **Cookies** are invisible files that computers, smartphones, and other mobile devices create to track a user's Web browsing activities. Cookies provide detailed information to marketers about an individual's behavior and preferences, which is then used to personalize online services.

Over time, the retailer can amass considerable data about a person's shopping habits. Does collecting this information violate a consumer's right to privacy? Should retailers be able to pass on the data they have collected to their affiliates? Should they be able to use the information to predict what a consumer might want and then create online "coupons" customized to fit the person's buying history?

▶ **Example 6.18**   Facebook, Inc., recently settled a lawsuit over its use of a targeted advertising technique called "Sponsored Stories." An ad would display a Facebook friend's name, profile picture, and a statement that the friend "likes" the company sponsoring the advertisement, alongside the company's logo. A group of plaintiffs filed suit, claiming that Facebook had used their pictures for advertising without their permission. When a federal court refused to dismiss the case, Facebook agreed to settle. ◀

Internet Companies' Privacy Policies

The Federal Trade Commission (FTC) investigates consumer complaints of privacy violations. The FTC has forced many companies, including Google, Facebook, Twitter, and MySpace, to enter a consent decree that gives the FTC broad power to review their privacy and data practices. It can then sue companies that violate the terms of the decree.

▶ **Example 6.19**   In 2012, Google settled a suit brought by the FTC alleging that it had misused data from Apple's Safari users. Google allegedly had used cookies to trick the Safari browser on iPhones and iPads so that Google could monitor users who had blocked such tracking. This violated the consent decree with the FTC. Google agreed to pay $22.5 million to settle the suit without admitting liability. ◀

Facebook has faced a number of complaints about its privacy policy and has changed its policy several times to satisfy its critics and ward off potential government investigations. Other companies, including mobile app developers, have also changed their privacy policies to provide more information to consumers. Consequently, it is frequently the companies, rather than courts or legislatures, that are defining the privacy rights of their online users.

The Consumer Privacy Bill of Rights

To protect consumers' personal information, the Obama administration has proposed a consumer privacy bill of rights (see Exhibit 6–1 below). The goal is to ensure that personal information is safe online.

If this proposed privacy bill of rights becomes law, retailers will have to change some of their procedures. Retailers will have to give customers better choices about what data are collected and how the data are used for marketing. They may also have to take into account consumers' expectations about how their information will be used once it is collected.

EXHIBIT 6–1 The Proposed Consumer Privacy Bill of Rights

1. **Individual Control**—Consumers have a right to exercise control over what personal data organizations collect from them, and how they use it.

2. **Transparency**—Consumers have the right to easily understandable information about privacy and security practices.

3. **Respect for Context**—Consumers have a right to expect that organizations will collect, use, and disclose personal data in ways that are consistent with the context in which consumers provide the data.

4. **Security**—Consumers have the right to secure and responsible handling of personal data.

5. **Access and Accuracy**—Consumers have a right to access and correct personal data in usable formats, in a manner that is appropriate to the sensitivity of the data and the risk of adverse consequences to consumers if the data are inaccurate.

6. **Focus Collection**—Consumers have a right to reasonable limits on the personal data that companies collect and retain.

7. **Accountability**—Consumers have a right to have personal data handled by companies with appropriate measures in place to assure that they adhere to the Consumer Privacy Bill of Rights.

Reviewing: Internet Law, Social Media, and Privacy

While he was in high school, Joel Gibb downloaded numerous songs to his smartphone from an unlicensed file-sharing service. He used portions of the copyrighted songs when he recorded his own band and posted videos on YouTube and Facebook. Gibb also used BitTorrent to download several movies from the Internet. Now he has applied to Boston University. The admissions office has requested access to his Facebook password, and he has complied. Using the information presented in the chapter, answer the following questions.

1. What laws, if any, did Gibb violate by downloading the music and videos from the Internet?
2. Was Gibb's use of portions of copyrighted songs in his own music illegal? Explain.
3. Can individuals legally post copyrighted content on their Facebook pages? Why or why not?
4. Did Boston University violate any laws when it asked Joel to provide his Facebook password? Explain.

DEBATE THIS . . . *Internet service providers should be subject to the same defamation laws as newspapers, magazines, and television and radio stations.*

Terms and Concepts

cloud computing 120
cookie 128
cyber tort 126
cybersquatting 116

distributed network 120
domain name 116
goodwill 116
Internet service provider (ISP) 116

peer-to-peer (P2P) networking 120
social media 122
spam 115
typosquatting 117

ExamPrep

Issue Spotters

1. Karl self-publishes a cookbook titled *Hole Foods*, in which he sets out recipes for donuts, Bundt cakes, tortellini, and other foods with holes. To publicize the book, Karl designs the Web site **holefoods.com**. Karl appropriates the key words of other cooking and cookbook sites with more frequent hits so that **holefoods.com** will appear in the same search engine results as the more popular sites. Has Karl done anything wrong? Explain. **(See page 117.)**

2. Eagle Corporation began marketing software in 2001 under the mark "Eagle." In 2013, Eagle.com, Inc., a different company selling different products, begins to use *eagle* as part of its URL and registers it as a domain name. Can Eagle Corporation stop this use of *eagle*? If so, what must the company show? **(See page 118.)**

• Check your answers to the Issue Spotters against the answers provided in Appendix B at the end of this text.

Before the Test

Go to **www.cengagebrain.com**, enter the ISBN 9781285770192, and click on "Find" to locate this textbook's Web site. Then, click on "Access Now" under "Study Tools," and select Chapter 6 at the top. There, you will find a Practice Quiz that you can take to assess your mastery of the concepts in this chapter, as well as Flashcards and a Glossary of important terms.

Business Scenarios

6-1. Domain Names. Tony owns Antonio's, a pub in a small town in Iowa. Universal Dining, Inc., opens a chain of pizza parlors in California called "Antonio's." Without Tony's consent, Universal uses "antoniosincalifornia" as part of the domain name for the chain's Web site. Has Universal committed trademark dilution or any other violation of the law? Explain. **(See page 116.)**

6-2. Internet Service Providers. CyberConnect, Inc., is an Internet service provider (ISP). Pepper is a CyberConnect subscriber. Market Reach, Inc., is an online advertising company. Using sophisticated software, Market Reach directs its ads to those users most likely to be interested in a particular product. When Pepper receives one of the ads, she objects to the content. Further, she claims that CyberConnect should pay damages for "publishing" the ad. Is the ISP regarded as a publisher and therefore liable for the content of Market Reach's ad? Why or why not? **(See page 116.)**

6-3. Privacy. SeeYou, Inc., is an online social network. SeeYou's members develop personalized profiles to interact and share information—photos, videos, stories, activity updates, and other items—with other members. Members post the information that they want to share and decide with whom they want to share it. SeeYou launched a program to allow members to share with others what they do elsewhere online. For example, if a member rents a movie through Netflix, SeeYou will broadcast that information to everyone in the member's online network. How can SeeYou avoid complaints that this program violates its members' privacy? **(See page 127.)**

Business Case Problems

6-4. Copyrights in Digital Information. When she was in college, Jammie Thomas-Rasset wrote a case study on Napster, the online peer-to-peer (P2P) file-sharing network, and knew that it was shut down because it was illegal. Later, Capitol Records, Inc., which owns the copyrights to a large number of music recordings, discovered that "tereastarr"—a user name associated with Thomas-Rasset's Internet protocol address—had made twenty-four songs available for distribution on KaZaA, another P2P network. Capitol notified Thomas-Rasset that she had been identified as engaging in the unauthorized trading of music. She replaced the hard drive on her computer with a new drive that did not contain the songs in dispute. Is Thomas-Rasset liable for copyright infringement? Explain. [*Capitol Records, Inc. v. Thomas-Rasset*, 692 F.3d 899 (8th Cir. 2012)] **(See page 120.)**

6-5. Domain Names. Austin Rare Coins, Inc., buys and sells rare coins, bullion, and other precious metals through eight Web sites with different domain names. An unknown individual took control of Austin's servers and transferred the domain names to another registrant without Austin's permission. The new registrant began using the domain names to host malicious content—including hate letters to customers and fraudulent contact information—and to post customers' credit-card numbers and other private information, thereby tarnishing Austin's goodwill. Austin filed a suit in a federal district court against the new registrant under the Anticybersquatting Consumer Protection Act. Is Austin entitled to a transfer of the domain names? Explain. [*Austin Rare Coins, Inc. v. Acoins.com*, __ F.Supp.2d __, 2013 WL 85142 (E.D.Va. 2013)] **(See page 116.)**

6-6. BUSINESS CASE PROBLEM WITH SAMPLE ANSWER: Privacy.

 Using special software, South Dakota law enforcement officers found a person who appeared to possess child pornography at a specific Internet protocol address. The officers subpoenaed Midcontinent Communications, the service that assigned the address, for the personal information of its subscriber. With this information, the officers obtained a search warrant for the residence of John Rolfe, where they found a laptop that contained child pornography. Rolfe argued that the subpoenas violated his "expectation of privacy." Did Rolfe have a privacy interest in the information obtained by the subpoenas issued to Midcontinent? Discuss. [State of South Dakota v. Rolfe, 825 N.W.2d 901 (S.Dak. 2013)] **(See page 127.)**

• For a sample answer to Problem 6-6, go to Appendix C at the end of this text.

6-7. File-Sharing. Dartmouth College professor M. Eric Johnson, in collaboration with Tiversa, Inc., a company that monitors peer-to-peer networks to provide security services, wrote an article titled "Data Hemorrhages in the Health-Care Sector." In preparing the article, Johnson and Tiversa searched the networks for data that could be used to commit medical or financial identity theft. They found a document that contained the Social Security numbers, insurance information, and treatment codes for patients of LabMD, Inc. Tiversa notified LabMD of the find in order to solicit its business. Instead of hiring Tiversa, however, LabMD filed a suit in a federal district court against the company, alleging trespass, conversion, and violations of federal statutes. What do these facts indicate about the security of private information? Explain. How should the court rule? [*LabMD, Inc. v. Tiversa, Inc.*, 2013 WL 425983 (11th Cir. 2013)] **(See page 120.)**

6–8. A QUESTION OF ETHICS: Criminal Investigations.

 After the unauthorized release and posting of classified U.S. government documents to WikiLeaks.org, allegedly involving Bradley Manning, a U.S. Army private first class, the U.S. government began a criminal investigation. The government obtained a court order to require Twitter, Inc., to turn over subscriber information and communications to and from the e-mail addresses of Birgitta Jonsdottir and others. The court sealed the order and the other documents in the case, reasoning that "there exists no

right to public notice of all the types of documents filed in a . . . case." Jonsdottir and the others appealed this decision. [In re Application of the United States of America for an Order Pursuant to 18 U.S.C. Section 2703(d), *707 F.3d 283 (4th Cir. 2013)]* **(See page 123.)**

(a) Why would the government want to "seal" the documents of an investigation? Why would the individuals under investigation want those documents to be "unsealed"? What factors should be considered in striking a balance between these competing interests?

(b) How does law enforcement use social media to detect and prosecute criminals? Is this use of social media an unethical invasion of individuals' privacy? Discuss.

Legal Reasoning Group Activity

6–9. File-Sharing. James, Chang, and Sixta are roommates. They are music fans and frequently listen to the same artists and songs. They regularly exchange MP3 music files that contain songs from their favorite artists. **(See page 120.)**

(a) One group of students will decide whether the fact that the roommates are transferring files among

themselves for no monetary benefit precludes them from being subject to copyright law.

(b) The second group will consider an additional fact. Each roommate regularly buys CDs and rips them to his or her hard drive. Then the roommate gives the CDs to the other roommates to do the same.

CHAPTER 7

CRIMINAL LAW AND CYBER CRIME

Criminal law is an important part of the legal environment of business. Various sanctions are used to bring about a society in which individuals engaging in business can compete and flourish. These sanctions include damages for various types of tortious conduct (see Chapter 4), damages for breach of contract (to be discussed in Chapter 14), and the equitable remedies discussed in Chapter 1. Additional sanctions are imposed under criminal law. Indeed, many statutes regulating business provide for criminal as well as civil penalties.

In this chapter, after explaining some essential differences between criminal law and civil law, we look at how crimes are classified and at the elements that must be present for criminal liability to exist. We then examine the various categories of crimes, the defenses that can be raised to avoid criminal liability, and the rules of criminal procedure.

We conclude the chapter with a discussion of crimes that occur in cyberspace, which are often called *cyber crimes*. Cyber attacks are becoming all too common—even e-mail and data of government agencies and former U.S. presidents have been hacked. Smartphones are being infected by malicious software, which puts users' data at risk, as you will read in a feature later in this chapter.

SECTION 1
CIVIL LAW AND CRIMINAL LAW

Recall from Chapter 1 that *civil law* pertains to the duties that exist between persons or between persons and their governments. Criminal law, in contrast, has to do with crime. A **crime** can be defined as a wrong against society set forth in a statute and punishable by a fine and/or imprisonment—or, in some cases, death.

As mentioned in Chapter 1, because crimes are *offenses against society as a whole,* they are prosecuted by a public official, such as a district attorney (D.A.) or an attorney general (A.G.), not by the victims. Once a crime has been reported, the D.A.'s office decides whether to file criminal charges and to what extent to pursue the prosecution or carry out additional investigation.

Key Differences between Civil Law and Criminal Law

Because the state has extensive resources at its disposal when prosecuting criminal cases, there are numerous procedural safeguards to protect the rights of defendants. We look here at one of these safeguards—the higher burden of proof that applies in a criminal case—as well as the harsher sanctions for criminal acts compared with those for civil wrongs. Exhibit 7–1 on the following page summarizes these and other key differences between civil law and criminal law.

BURDEN OF PROOF In a civil case, the plaintiff usually must prove his or her case by a *preponderance of the evidence.* Under this standard, the plaintiff must convince the court that based on the evidence presented by both parties, it is more likely than not that the plaintiff's allegation is true.

In a criminal case, in contrast, the state must prove its case **beyond a reasonable doubt.** If the jury views the evidence in the case as reasonably permitting either a guilty or a not guilty verdict, then the jury's verdict must be not guilty. In other words, the government (prosecutor) must prove beyond a reasonable doubt that the defendant has committed every essential element of the offense with which she or he is charged.

If the jurors are not convinced of the defendant's guilt beyond a reasonable doubt, they must find

EXHIBIT 7-1 Key Differences between Civil Law and Criminal Law

Issue	Civil Law	Criminal Law
Party who brings suit	The person who suffered harm.	The state.
Wrongful act	Causing harm to a person or to a person's property.	Violating a statute that prohibits some type of activity.
Burden of proof	Preponderance of the evidence.	Beyond a reasonable doubt.
Verdict	Three-fourths majority (typically).	Unanimous (almost always).
Remedy	Damages to compensate for the harm or a decree to achieve an equitable result.	Punishment (fine, imprisonment, or death).

the defendant not guilty. Note also that in a criminal case, the jury's verdict normally must be unanimous—agreed to by all members of the jury—to convict the defendant.[1] (In a civil trial by jury, in contrast, typically only three-fourths of the jurors need to agree.)

CRIMINAL SANCTIONS The sanctions imposed on criminal wrongdoers are also harsher than those applied in civil cases. Remember from Chapter 4 that the purpose of tort law is to enable a person harmed by a wrongful act to obtain compensation from the wrongdoer, rather than to punish the wrongdoer. In contrast, criminal sanctions are designed to punish those who commit crimes and to deter others from committing similar acts in the future.

Criminal sanctions include fines as well as the much harsher penalty of the loss of one's liberty by incarceration in a jail or prison. Most criminal sanctions also involve probation and sometimes require performance of community service, completion of an educational or treatment program, or payment of restitution. The harshest criminal sanction is, of course, the death penalty.

Civil Liability for Criminal Acts

Some torts, such as assault and battery, provide a basis for a criminal prosecution as well as a civil action in tort. ▶ **Example 7.1** Jonas is walking down the street, minding his own business, when a person attacks him. In the ensuing struggle, the attacker stabs Jonas several times, seriously injuring him. A police officer restrains and arrests the assailant. In this situation, the attacker may be subject both to criminal prosecution by the state and to a tort lawsuit brought by Jonas to obtain compensation for his injuries. ◀

Exhibit 7–2 on the following page illustrates how the same wrongful act can result in both a civil (tort) action and a criminal action against the wrongdoer.

Classification of Crimes

Depending on their degree of seriousness, crimes are classified as felonies or misdemeanors. **Felonies** are serious crimes punishable by death or by imprisonment for more than one year.[2] Many states also define different degrees of felony offenses and vary the punishment according to the degree.[3] For instance, most jurisdictions punish a burglary that involves forced entry into a home at night more harshly than a burglary that involves breaking into a nonresidential building during the day.

Misdemeanors are less serious crimes, punishable by a fine or by confinement for up to a year. **Petty offenses** are minor violations, such as jaywalking or violations of building codes, considered to be a subset of misdemeanors. Even for petty offenses, however, a guilty party can be put in jail for a few days, fined, or both, depending on state or local law. Whether a crime is a felony or a misdemeanor can determine in which court the case is

---

1. A few states allow jury verdicts that are not unanimous. Arizona, for example, allows six of eight jurors to reach a verdict in criminal cases. Louisiana and Oregon have also relaxed the requirement of unanimous jury verdicts.

2. Some states, such as North Carolina, consider felonies to be punishable by incarceration for at least two years.

3. Although the American Law Institute issued the Model Penal Code in 1962, it is not a uniform code, and each state has developed its own set of laws governing criminal acts. Thus, types of crimes and prescribed punishments may differ from one jurisdiction to another.

EXHIBIT 7–2 Civil (Tort) Lawsuit and Criminal Prosecution for the Same Act

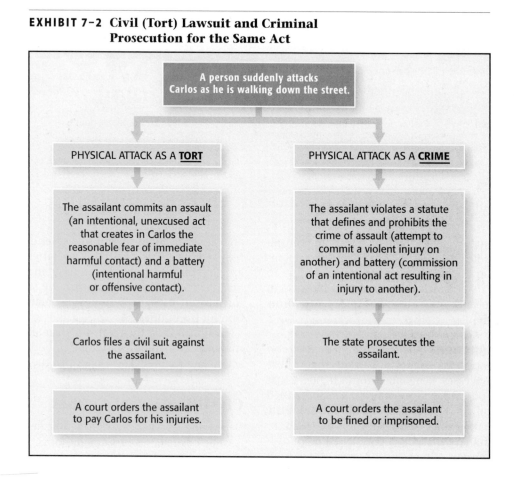

tried and, in some states, whether the defendant has a right to a jury trial.

SECTION 2
CRIMINAL LIABILITY

The following two elements normally must exist *simultaneously* for a person to be convicted of a crime:

1. The performance of a prohibited act *(actus reus).*
2. A specified state of mind, or intent, on the part of the actor *(mens rea).*

The Criminal Act

Every criminal statute prohibits certain behavior. Most crimes require an act of *commission*—that is, a person must *do* something in order to be accused of a crime. In criminal law, a prohibited act is referred to as the ***actus reus,***[4] or guilty act. In some instances, an act of omission can be a crime, but only when a person has a legal duty to perform the omitted act, such as filing a tax return.

The *guilty act* requirement is based on one of the premises of criminal law—that a person should be punished for harm done to society. For a crime to exist, the guilty act must cause some harm to a person or to property. Thinking about killing someone or about stealing a car may be morally wrong, but the thoughts do no harm until they are translated into action.

Of course, a person can be punished for *attempting* murder or robbery, but normally only if he or she has taken substantial steps toward the criminal objective. Additionally, the person must have specifically

---

4. Pronounced *ak*-tuhs *ray*-uhs.

intended to commit the crime to be convicted of an attempt.

State of Mind

A wrongful mental state, or **_mens rea,_**[5] also is typically required to establish criminal liability. The required mental state, or intent, is indicated in the applicable statute or law. Murder, for example, involves the guilty act of killing another human being, and the guilty mental state is the desire, or intent, to take another's life. For theft, the guilty act is the taking of another person's property. The mental state involves both the awareness that the property belongs to another and the desire to deprive the owner of it.

RECKLESSNESS A court can also find that the required mental state is present when a defendant's acts are reckless or criminally negligent. A defendant is _criminally reckless_ if he or she consciously disregards a substantial and unjustifiable risk.
▶ **Example 7.2** A fourteen-year-old New Jersey girl posts a Facebook message saying that she is going to launch a terrorist attack on her high school and asking if anyone wants to help. The police arrest the girl for the crime of making a terrorist threat. The statute requires the intent to commit an act of violence with "the intent to terrorize" or "in reckless disregard of the risk of causing" terror or inconvenience. Although the girl argues that she had no intent to cause harm, the police can prosecute her under the "reckless disregard" part of the statute. ◀

CRIMINAL NEGLIGENCE _Criminal negligence_ involves the mental state in which the defendant takes an unjustified, substantial, and foreseeable risk that results in harm. A defendant can negligent even if she or he was not actually aware of the risk but _should have been aware_ of it.[6]
A homicide is classified as _involuntary manslaughter_ when it results from an act of criminal negligence and there is no intent to kill. ▶ **Example 7.3** Dr. Conrad Murray, the personal physician of pop star Michael Jackson, was convicted of involuntary manslaughter in 2011 for prescribing the drug that led to Jackson's sudden death in 2009. Murray had given Jackson propofol, a powerful anesthetic normally used in sur-

gery, as a sleep aid on the night of his death, even though he knew that Jackson had already taken other sedatives. ◀

STRICT LIABILITY AND OVERCRIMINALIZATION An increasing number of laws and regulations impose criminal sanctions for strict liability crimes. Strict liability crimes are offenses that do not require a wrongful mental state to establish criminal liability.

Federal Crimes. The federal criminal code now lists more than four thousand criminal offenses, many of which do not require a specific mental state. There are also at least ten thousand federal rules that can be enforced through criminal sanctions, and many of these rules do not require intent.
▶ **Example 7.4** Eddie Leroy Anderson, a retired logger and former science teacher, and his son went digging for arrowheads near a campground in Idaho. They did not realize that they were on federal land and that it is a felony to remove artifacts from federal land without a permit. Although the crime carries as much as two years in prison, father and son pleaded guilty, and each received a sentence of probation and a $1,500 fine. ◀
Strict liability crimes are particularly common in environmental laws, laws aimed at combatting illegal drugs, and other laws affecting public health, safety, and welfare. Under federal law, for example, tenants can be evicted from public housing if a member of the household or a guest used illegal drugs. The eviction can occur regardless of whether the tenant knew or should have known about the drug activity.[7]

State Crimes. Many states have also enacted laws that punish behavior as criminal without the need to show criminal intent. ▶ **Example 7.5** In Arizona, a hunter who shoots an elk outside the area specified by the hunting permit has committed a crime. The hunter can be convicted of the crime regardless of her or his intent or knowledge of the law. ◀

Overcriminalization. Proponents of strict liability criminal laws argue that they are necessary to protect the public and the environment. Critics say laws that criminalize conduct without any required intent have led to _overcriminalization,_ or the use of criminal law as

---

5. Pronounced _mehns ray_-uh.
6. Model Penal Code Section 2.02(2)(d).

7. See, for example, _Department of Housing and Urban Development v. Rucker,_ 535 U.S. 125, 122 S.Ct. 1230, 152 L.Ed.2d 258 (2002).

the main tool to solve social problems, such as illegal drug use. They argue that when the requirement of intent is removed, people are more likely to commit crimes unknowingly—and perhaps even innocently. When an honest mistake can lead to a criminal conviction, the idea that crimes are a wrong against society is undermined.

Corporate Criminal Liability

A corporation is a legal entity created under the laws of a state. At one time, it was thought that a corporation could not incur criminal liability because, although a corporation is a legal person, it can act only through its agents (corporate directors, officers, and employees). Therefore, the corporate entity itself could not "intend" to commit a crime. Over time, this view has changed. Obviously, corporations cannot be imprisoned, but they can be fined or denied certain legal privileges (such as necessary licenses).

LIABILITY OF THE CORPORATE ENTITY Today, corporations normally are liable for the crimes committed by their agents and employees within the course and scope of their employment.[8] For liability to be imposed, the prosecutor generally must show that the corporation could have prevented the act or that a supervisor authorized or had knowledge of the act. In addition, corporations can be criminally liable for failing to perform specific duties imposed by law (such as duties under environmental laws or securities laws).

▶ **Case in Point 7.6** A prostitution ring, the Gold Club, was operating out of some motels in West Virginia. A motel manager, who was also a corporate officer, gave discounted rates to Gold Club prostitutes, and they paid him in cash. The corporation received a portion of the funds generated by the Gold Club's illegal operations. A jury found that the corporation was criminally liable because a supervisor within the corporation—the motel manager—had knowledge of the prostitution and the corporation had allowed it to continue.[9] ◀

LIABILITY OF THE CORPORATE OFFICERS AND DIRECTORS Corporate directors and officers are personally liable for the crimes they commit, regardless of whether the crimes were committed for their private benefit or on the corporation's behalf. Additionally, corporate directors and officers may be held liable for the actions of employees under their supervision. Under the *responsible corporate officer* doctrine, a court may impose criminal liability on a corporate officer who participated in, directed, or merely knew about a given criminal violation.

▶ **Case in Point 7.7** The Roscoe family owned the Customer Company, which operated an underground storage tank that leaked gasoline. An employee, John Johnson, reported the leak to the state environmental agency, and the Roscoes hired an environmental services firm to clean up the spill. The clean-up did not occur immediately, however. The state sent many notices to John Roscoe, a corporate officer, warning him that the company was violating federal and state environmental laws. Roscoe gave the letters to Johnson, who passed them on to the environmental services firm, but the spill was not cleaned up.

The state eventually filed criminal charges against the corporation and the Roscoes individually. They were convicted under the responsible corporate officer doctrine. The Roscoes were in positions of responsibility, they had influence over the corporation's actions, and their failure to act constituted a violation of environmental laws.[10] ◀

SECTION 3

TYPES OF CRIMES

Federal, state, and local laws provide for the classification and punishment of hundreds of thousands of different criminal acts. Generally, though, criminal acts can be grouped into five broad categories: violent crime (crimes against persons), property crime, public order crime, white-collar crime, and organized crime. Note also that many crimes may be committed in cyberspace, as well as the physical world. When they occur in the virtual world, we

---

8. See Model Penal Code Section 2.07.
9. As a result of the convictions, the motel manager was sentenced to fifteen months in prison, and the corporation was ordered to forfeit the motel property. *United States v. Singh*, 518 F.3d 236 (4th Cir. 2008).

10. The Roscoes and the corporation were sentenced to pay penalties of $2,493,250. *People v. Roscoe*, 169 Cal.App.4th 829, 87 Cal.Rptr.3d 187 (3 Dist. 2008).

refer to them as cyber crimes, as discussed later in the chapter.

Violent Crime

Certain crimes are called *violent crimes,* or crimes against persons, because they cause others to suffer harm or death. Murder is a violent crime. So is sexual assault, or rape. **Robbery**—defined as the taking of money, personal property, or any other article of value from a person by means of force or fear—is also a violent crime. Typically, states have more severe penalties for *aggravated robbery*—robbery with the use of a deadly weapon.

Assault and battery, which were discussed in Chapter 4 in the context of tort law, are also classified as violent crimes. ► **Example 7.8** Former rap star Flavor Flav (whose real name is William Drayton) was arrested in Las Vegas in 2012 on assault and battery charges. During an argument with his fiancée, Drayton allegedly threw her to the ground and then grabbed two kitchen knives and chased her son. ◄

Each violent crime is further classified by degree, depending on the circumstances surrounding the criminal act. These circumstances include the intent of the person committing the crime and whether a weapon was used. For crimes other than murder, the level of pain and suffering experienced by the victim is also a factor.

Property Crime

The most common type of criminal activity is property crime, in which the goal of the offender is some form of economic gain or the damaging of property. Robbery is a form of property crime, as well as a violent crime, because the offender seeks to gain the property of another. We look here at a number of other crimes that fall within the general category of property crime. (Note also that many types of cyber crime, discussed later in this chapter, are forms of property crime as well.)

BURGLARY Traditionally, **burglary** was defined as breaking and entering the dwelling of another at night with the intent to commit a felony. This definition was aimed at protecting an individual's home and its occupants. Most state statutes have eliminated some of the requirements found in the common law definition. The time of day at which the breaking and entering occurs, for example, is usually immaterial. State statutes frequently omit the element of breaking, and some states do not require that the building be a dwelling. When a deadly weapon is used in a burglary, the perpetrator can be charged with *aggravated burglary* and punished more severely.

LARCENY Under the common law, the crime of **larceny** involved the unlawful taking and carrying away of someone else's personal property with the intent to permanently deprive the owner of possession. Put simply, larceny is stealing, or theft. Whereas robbery involves force or fear, larceny does not. Therefore, picking pockets is larceny, not robbery. Similarly, taking company products and supplies home for personal use without permission is larceny. (Note that a person who commits larceny generally can also be sued under tort law because the act of taking possession of another's property involves a trespass to personal property.)

Most states have expanded the definition of property that is subject to larceny statutes. Stealing computer programs may constitute larceny even though the "property" is not physical (see the discussion of computer crime later in this chapter). So, too, can the theft of natural gas or Internet and television cable service.

OBTAINING GOODS BY FALSE PRETENSES Obtaining goods by means of false pretenses is a form of theft that involves trickery or fraud, such as using someone else's credit-card number without permission to purchase an iPad. Statutes dealing with such illegal activities vary widely from state to state. They often apply not only to property, but also to services and cash.

Sometimes, a statute consolidates the crime of obtaining goods by false pretenses with other property offenses, such as larceny and embezzlement, into a single crime called simply "theft." Under such a statute, it is not necessary for a defendant to be charged specifically with larceny, embezzlement, or obtaining goods by false pretenses. *Petty theft* is the theft of a small quantity of cash or low-value goods. *Grand theft* is the theft of a larger amount of cash or higher-value property. In the following case, the sales manager of a sports vehicle dealership was charged under a state statute with grand theft.

CASE ANALYSIS

Case 7.1 People v. Whitmer

Court of Appeal of California, Second District, Division 4, 213 Cal.App.4th 122, 152 Cal.Rptr.3d 216 (2013).

IN THE LANGUAGE OF THE COURT
MANELLA, J. [Judge]

* * * *

Jerome Gilding owned Temple City Power Sports, a business located in San Gabriel [California] that sold and serviced motorcycles, motorized dirt bikes [all terrain vehicles (ATVs)], and jet skis.

Customers of the dealership negotiated purchases with salespersons. The dealership made sales to customers who entered into financing agreements or paid with credit cards. In such cases, after the salesperson reached an agreement with the customer regarding an item and the manner of payment, the transaction was referred to the sales manager for approval. If approved, the transaction was sent to the dealership finance department, which collected the information necessary to process the financing agreement or credit card sale. When the dealership sold an item to a customer who failed to make the loan payments or used a bad credit card, the dealership incurred a "charge back," that is, took responsibility for the loss on the transaction. * * * To prevent charge backs, the dealership's policy was to require customers to make purchases in person and to present two forms of identification.

Ordinarily, when credit card purchases were made, the card was swiped through a credit card machine, which instantaneously sent information regarding the purchase to the pertinent bank. An approval or denial was received from the bank within a few seconds. In contrast, if the machine was set for an "offline" * * * sale, the machine recorded the transaction but sent no information to the bank. As a result, no immediate credit approval or denial was generated; instead,

information regarding the transaction was transmitted to the bank at the end of the business day. Gilding did not permit offline sales.

Associated with each vehicle sold by the dealership is a document known as the "manufacturer certificate of origin" (MSO). The vehicle's original MSO can be used to establish title to the vehicle in other states and countries. The dealership retained the original MSO after a sale unless the vehicle was sold to an out-of-state purchaser or transferred to another dealer. The dealership had contractual obligations to several manufacturers not to sell vehicles for exportation outside the United States.

In 2009 [Jeffrey Whitmer] was the dealership's sales manager, and Alex Barrera was employed as a salesperson. Eric Van Hek worked in the financial department until August or September 2009, when he was replaced by Richard Carlos. In late August or early September 2009, Gilding told [Whitmer] not to deal with Mordichi Mor, who had engaged in a fraudulent transaction at the dealership in 2008.

* * * *

* * * In the fall of 2009, * * * after meeting with Mordichi [Whitmer] directed Carlos to process sales transactions involving customers Carlos had never met * * * . Whenever the transaction involved a credit card [Whitmer] told Carlos to process it as an offline sale. Carlos prepared the paperwork for each transaction and gave it to [Whitmer] who returned the documents to him with the customer's signature. [Whitmer] directed other employees to deliver the purchased vehicles to Mordichi's home.

* * * *

[At Whitmer's request] Angela Wilcox, a dealership employee, * * * gave [Whitmer] original MSOs from

the dealership's files related to deals [Whitmer] arranged with Mor.

* * * In mid-December 2009, a credit card company told [Gilding] that credit card usage had increased at the dealership, and that he should expect charge backs. He initiated an inquiry that uncovered 20 potentially fraudulent sales of motorcycles, motorized dirt bikes, ATVs, and recreational vehicles at the dealership from August 4 to December 8, 2009. Barrera was the salesperson in all the sales, each of which involved one of seven purported buyers. * * * The dealership incurred a charge back on each sale ranging from $9,100 to $21,479.80, resulting in losses exceeding $250,000. In addition, the original MSOs for the vehicles in the dealership's files had been replaced by copies, even though the transactions were not of the type that required the dealership to transfer the original MSO to the purchaser.

Shortly after Gilding discovered the potential fraud, Barrera stopped appearing for work.

Later, [local] Police Department Detective Armando Valenzuela determined that the identification information provided for the buyers on the sales documents was false, and that the existence of the buyers could not be established. He also discovered that several of the vehicles had been shipped to Israel.

On February 16, 2010, Detective Valenzuela * * * arrested [Whitmer, who was charged with twenty counts of grand theft. A jury in a California state court convicted him on all counts. He appealed to a state intermediate appellate court, contending that he was unlawfully convicted.]

* * * We will affirm the convictions if there is substantial evidence to support a finding that each act of grand theft qualified as an independent offense.

CASE 7.1 CONTINUED

We conclude that the record discloses evidence sufficient to establish that appellant was properly convicted of 20 counts of grand theft. Each transaction involved a different vehicle. The 20 transactions occurred on 13 different dates. With the exception of two dates, whenever more than one transaction occurred on a single date, the transactions involved distinct fictitious buyers. On the two dates a fictitious buyer purportedly bought more than one vehicle, the transactions involved separate paperwork and documentation. This constituted substantial evidence that the 20 transactions constitute distinct offenses.

* * * In sum, appellant was properly convicted under the 20 counts of grand theft.

* * * *

* * * Appellant argues there was no direct evidence that he intentionally participated in the fraud activities related to the taking of each vehicle.

Appellant's argument misapprehends our role in reviewing the record for substantial evidence. We do not engage in independent factfinding, but instead affirm the jury's determinations if they are supported by any logical inferences grounded in the evidence. [Emphasis added.]

There was ample evidence that appellant directly perpetrated the thefts. * * * Appellant authorized the offline credit card sales and other violations of dealership policies, obtained the false signatures from the fictitious buyers on the sales documents, and arranged for the delivery of the vehicles. Furthermore, * * * appellant admitted that Mor had "gotten the ball rolling" on the thefts, that Van Hek had instructed appellant how to do offline transactions, and that appellant had participated for "personal gain." This evidence was sufficient to establish that appellant supervised and directed the thefts within the dealership.

* * * *

* * * The judgment is affirmed.

LEGAL REASONING QUESTIONS

1. What is the definition of the crime of obtaining goods by false pretenses? Do the facts in this case satisfy that definition? Explain.

2. Besides the defendant, who may have committed a crime in this case?

3. How might the dealership have prevented the crimes in this case?

4. Why do some states combine larceny, embezzlement, and obtaining goods by false pretenses into a single crime called theft? Discuss.

RECEIVING STOLEN GOODS It is a crime to receive goods that a person knows or should have known were stolen or illegally obtained. To be convicted, the recipient of such goods need not know the true identity of the owner or the thief, and need not have paid for the goods. All that is necessary is that the recipient knows or should know that the goods are stolen, which implies an intent to deprive the true owner of those goods.

ARSON The willful and malicious burning of a building (and, in some states, vehicles and other items of personal property) is the crime of **arson.** At common law, arson applied only to burning down another person's house. The law was designed to protect human life. Today, arson statutes have been extended to cover the destruction of any building, regardless of ownership, by fire or explosion.

Every state has a special statute that covers the act of burning a building for the purpose of collecting insurance. (Of course, the insurer need not pay the claim when insurance fraud is proved.)

FORGERY The fraudulent making or altering of any writing (including electronic records) in a way that changes the legal rights and liabilities of another is **forgery.** ▶ **Example 7.9** Without authorization, Severson signs Bennett's name to the back of a check made out to Bennett and attempts to cash it. Severson is committing forgery. ◀ Forgery also includes changing trademarks, falsifying public records, counterfeiting, and altering a legal document.

Public Order Crime

Historically, societies have always outlawed activities that are considered contrary to public values and morals. Today, the most common public order crimes include public drunkenness, prostitution, gambling, and illegal drug use. These crimes are sometimes referred to as *victimless crimes* because they normally harm only the offender. From a broader perspective, however, they are deemed detrimental to society as a whole because they may create an environment that gives rise to property and violent crimes.

▶ **Example 7.10** A man flying from Texas to California on a commercial airliner becomes angry and yells obscenities at a flight attendant when a beverage cart strikes his knee. After the pilot diverts the plane and makes an unscheduled landing at a nearby airport, police remove the passenger and arrest him. If the man is later found guilty of the public order crime of interfering with a flight crew, he may be sentenced to more than two years in prison. ◀

White-Collar Crime

Crimes occurring in the business context are popularly referred to as *white-collar crimes,* although this is not an official legal term. Ordinarily, **white-collar crime** involves an illegal act or series of acts committed by an individual or business entity using some nonviolent means to obtain a personal or business advantage.

Usually, this kind of crime takes place in the course of a legitimate business occupation. Corporate crimes fall into this category. Certain property crimes, such as larceny and forgery, may also be white-collar crimes if they occur within the business context. The crimes discussed next normally occur only in the business context.

EMBEZZLEMENT When a person who is entrusted with another person's property fraudulently appropriates it, **embezzlement** occurs. Typically, embezzlement is carried out by an employee who steals funds. Banks are particularly prone to this problem, but embezzlement can occur in any firm. Embezzlement is not larceny because the wrongdoer does not *physically* take the property from the possession of another, and it is not robbery because no force or fear is used. The intent to return the embezzled property—or its actual return—is not a defense to the crime of embezzlement.

Embezzlement occurs whether the embezzler takes the funds directly from the victim or from a third person. If the financial officer of a large corporation pockets checks from third parties that were given to her to deposit into the corporate account, she is embezzling.

Frequently, an embezzler takes a relatively small amount at one time but does so repeatedly over a long period. This might be done by underreporting income or deposits and embezzling the remaining amount or by creating fictitious persons or accounts and writing checks to them from the corporate account. Even an employer's failure to remit state withholding taxes that were collected from employee wages can constitute embezzlement.

MAIL AND WIRE FRAUD Among the most potent weapons against white-collar criminals are the federal laws that prohibit mail fraud[11] and wire fraud.[12] These laws make it a federal crime to devise any scheme that uses U.S. mail, commercial carriers (FedEx, UPS), or wire (telegraph, telephone, television, the Internet, e-mail) with the intent to defraud the public. These laws are often applied when persons send out advertisements or e-mails with the intent to fraudulently obtain cash or property by false pretenses.

▶ **Case in Point 7.11** Cisco Systems, Inc., offers a warranty program to authorized resellers of Cisco parts. Iheanyi Frank Chinasa and Robert Kendrick Chambliss devised a scheme to intentionally defraud Cisco with respect to this program and obtain replacement parts to which they were not entitled. The two men planned and used specific language in numerous e-mails and Internet service requests that they sent to Cisco to convince Cisco to ship them new parts via commercial carriers. Ultimately, Chinasa and Chambliss were convicted of mail and wire fraud, and conspiracy to commit mail and wire fraud.[13] ◀

The maximum penalty under these statutes is substantial. Persons convicted of mail, wire, and Internet fraud may be imprisoned for up to twenty years and/or fined. If the violation affects a financial institution or involves fraud in connection with emergency disaster-relief funds, the violator may be fined up to $1 million, imprisoned for up to thirty years, or both.

BRIBERY The crime of bribery involves offering to give something of value to a person in an attempt to influence that person, who is usually, but not always, a public official, to act in a way that serves a private interest. Three types of bribery are considered crimes: bribery of public officials, commercial bribery, and bribery of foreign officials. As an element of the crime of bribery, intent must be present and proved. The bribe itself can be anything the recipient considers to be valuable. Realize that the *crime of bribery occurs when the bribe is offered*—it is not required that the bribe be accepted. *Accepting a bribe* is a separate crime.

Commercial bribery involves corrupt dealings between private persons or businesses. Typically, people make commercial bribes to obtain proprietary information, cover up an inferior product, or secure

---

11. The Mail Fraud Act of 1990, 18 U.S.C. Sections 1341–1342.
12. 18 U.S.C. Section 1343.
13. *United States v. Chinasa,* 789 F.Supp.2d 691 (E.D.Va. 2011). See also *United States v. Lyons,* 569 F.3d 995 (9th Cir. 2009).

new business. Industrial espionage sometimes involves commercial bribes. ▶ **Example 7.12** Kent Peterson works at the firm of Jacoby & Meyers. He offers to pay Laurel, an employee in a competing firm, to give him that firm's trade secrets and pricing schedules. Peterson has committed commercial bribery. ◀ So-called kickbacks, or payoffs for special favors or services, are a form of commercial bribery in some situations.

BANKRUPTCY FRAUD Federal bankruptcy law allows individuals and businesses to be relieved of oppressive debt through bankruptcy proceedings. Numerous white-collar crimes may be committed during the many phases of a bankruptcy action. A creditor may file a false claim against the debtor, which is a crime. Also, a debtor may fraudulently transfer assets to favored parties before or after the petition for bankruptcy is filed. For instance, a company-owned automobile may be "sold" at a bargain price to a trusted friend or relative. Closely related to the crime of fraudulent transfer of property is the crime of fraudulent concealment of property, such as the hiding of gold coins.

INSIDER TRADING An individual who obtains "inside information" about the plans of a publicly listed corporation can often make stock-trading profits by purchasing or selling corporate securities based on this information. *Insider trading* is a violation of securities law. Basically, securities law prohibits a person who possesses inside information and has a duty not to disclose it to outsiders from trading on that information. A person may not profit from the purchase or sale of securities based on inside information until the information is made available to the public.

THEFT OF TRADE SECRETS AND OTHER INTELLECTUAL PROPERTY As discussed in Chapter 5, trade secrets constitute a form of intellectual property that for many businesses can be extremely valuable. The Economic Espionage Act[14] makes the theft of trade secrets a federal crime. The act also makes it a federal crime to buy or possess another person's trade secrets, knowing that the trade secrets were stolen or otherwise acquired without the owner's authorization.

Violations of the Economic Espionage Act can result in steep penalties: imprisonment for up to ten years and a fine of up to $500,000. A corporation or other organization can be fined up to $5 million. Additionally, the law provides that any property

---

14. 18 U.S.C. Sections 1831–1839.

acquired as a result of the violation, such as airplanes and automobiles, is subject to criminal forfeiture, or seizure by the government. Similarly, any property used in the commission of the violation, such as servers and other electronic devices, is subject to forfeiture. A theft of trade secrets conducted via the Internet, for instance, could result in the forfeiture of every computer or other device used to commit or facilitate the violation as well as any assets gained.

Organized Crime

White-collar crime takes place within the confines of the legitimate business world. *Organized crime,* in contrast, operates *illegitimately* by, among other things, providing illegal goods and services. Traditionally, the preferred markets for organized crime have been gambling, prostitution, illegal narcotics, and loan sharking (lending funds at higher-than-legal interest rates), along with more recent ventures into counterfeiting and credit-card scams.

MONEY LAUNDERING The profits from organized crime and illegal activities amount to billions of dollars a year. These profits come from illegal drug transactions and, to a lesser extent, from racketeering, prostitution, and gambling. Under federal law, banks, savings and loan associations, and other financial institutions are required to report currency transactions involving more than $10,000. Consequently, those who engage in illegal activities face difficulties in depositing their cash profits from illegal transactions.

As an alternative to storing cash from illegal transactions in a safe-deposit box, wrongdoers and racketeers launder "dirty" money through legitimate business to make it "clean." **Money laundering** is engaging in financial transactions to conceal the identity, source, or destination of illegally gained funds. ▶ **Example 7.13** Leo Harris, a successful drug dealer, becomes a partner with a restaurateur. Little by little, the restaurant shows increasing profits. As a partner in the restaurant, Harris is able to report the "profits" of the restaurant as legitimate income on which he pays federal and state taxes. He can then spend those funds without worrying that his lifestyle may exceed the level possible with his reported income. ◀

RACKETEERING To curb the entry of organized crime into the legitimate business world, Congress enacted the Racketeer Influenced and Corrupt

Organizations Act (RICO).[15] The statute makes it a federal crime to:

1. Use income obtained from racketeering activity to purchase any interest in an enterprise.
2. Acquire or maintain an interest in an enterprise through racketeering activity.
3. Conduct or participate in the affairs of an enterprise through racketeering activity.
4. Conspire to do any of the preceding activities.

Broad Application of RICO. The broad language of RICO has allowed it to be applied in cases that have little or nothing to do with organized crime. RICO incorporates by reference twenty-six separate types of federal crimes and nine types of state felonies.[16] If a person commits two of these offenses, he or she is guilty of "racketeering activity."

Under the criminal provisions of RICO, any individual found guilty is subject to a fine of up to $25,000 per violation, imprisonment for up to twenty years, or both. Additionally, any assets (property or cash) that were acquired as a result of the illegal activity or that were "involved in" or an "instrumentality of" the activity are subject to government forfeiture.

Civil Liability. In the event of a RICO violation, the government can seek civil penalties. The government can seek the divestiture of a defendant's interest in a business or the dissolution of the business. (Divestiture refers to the taking of possession—or forfeiture—of the defendant's interest and its subsequent sale.)

Moreover, in some cases, the statute allows private individuals to sue violators and potentially recover three times their actual losses (treble damages), plus attorneys' fees, for business injuries caused by a RICO violation. This is perhaps the most controversial aspect of RICO and one that continues to cause debate in the nation's federal courts. The prospect of receiving treble damages in civil RICO lawsuits has given plaintiffs a financial incentive to pursue businesses and employers for violations.

See *Concept Summary 7.1* on the following page for a review of the different types of crimes.

---

15. 18 U.S.C. Sections 1961–1968.
16. See 18 U.S.C. Section 1961(1)(A). The crimes listed in this section include murder, kidnapping, gambling, arson, robbery, bribery, extortion, money laundering, securities fraud, counterfeiting, dealing in obscene matter, dealing in controlled substances (illegal drugs), and a number of others.

DEFENSES TO CRIMINAL LIABILITY

Persons charged with crimes may be relieved of criminal liability if they can show that their criminal actions were justified under the circumstances. In certain situations, the law may also allow a person to be excused from criminal liability because she or he lacks the required mental state. We look at several defenses to criminal liability here.

Note that procedural violations (such as obtaining evidence without a valid search warrant) may also operate as defenses. Evidence obtained in violation of a defendant's constitutional rights may not be admitted in court. If the evidence is suppressed, then there may be no basis for prosecuting the defendant.

Justifiable Use of Force

Probably the best-known defense to criminal liability is **self-defense.** Other situations, however, also justify the use of force: the defense of one's dwelling, the defense of other property, and the prevention of a crime. In all of these situations, it is important to distinguish between deadly and nondeadly force. *Deadly force* is likely to result in death or serious bodily harm. *Nondeadly force* is force that reasonably appears necessary to prevent the imminent use of criminal force.

Generally speaking, people can use the amount of nondeadly force that seems necessary to protect themselves, their dwellings, or other property, or to prevent the commission of a crime. Deadly force can be used in self-defense only when the defender *reasonably believes* that imminent death or grievous bodily harm will otherwise result. In addition, normally the attacker must be using unlawful force, and the defender must not have initiated or provoked the attack.

Many states are expanding the situations in which the use of deadly force can be justified. Florida, for instance, allows the use of deadly force to prevent the commission of a "forcible felony," including robbery, carjacking, and sexual battery.

Necessity

Sometimes, criminal defendants can be relieved of liability by showing **necessity**—that a criminal act was necessary to prevent an even greater harm. ▶ **Example 7.14** Jake Trevor is a convicted felon and, as such, is legally prohibited from possessing a

---

CONCEPT SUMMARY 7.1
Types of Crimes

CRIME CATEGORY	DEFINITION AND EXAMPLES
Violent Crime	1. *Definition*—Crime that causes others to suffer harm or death. 2. *Examples*—Murder, assault and battery, sexual assault (rape), and robbery.
Property Crime	1. *Definition*—Crime in which the goal of the offender is some form of economic gain or the damaging of property; the most common form of crime. 2. *Examples*—Burglary, larceny, arson, receiving stolen goods, forgery, and obtaining goods by false pretenses.
Public Order Crime	1. *Definition*—Crime that is contrary to public values and morals. 2. *Examples*—Public drunkenness, prostitution, gambling, and illegal drug use.
White-Collar Crime	1. *Definition*—An illegal act or series of acts committed by an individual or business entity using some nonviolent means to obtain a personal or business advantage; usually committed in the course of a legitimate occupation. 2. *Examples*—Embezzlement, mail and wire fraud, bribery, bankruptcy fraud, insider trading, and the theft of intellectual property.
Organized Crime	1. *Definition*—A form of crime conducted by groups operating illegitimately to satisfy the public's demand for illegal goods and services (such as gambling and illegal narcotics). 2. *Money laundering*—Passing "dirty" money (obtained through criminal activities, such as illegal drug trafficking) through legitimate enterprises so as to "launder" it (make it appear to be legitimate income). 3. *RICO*—The Racketeer Influenced and Corrupt Organizations Act (RICO) makes it a federal crime to (a) use income obtained from racketeering activity to purchase any interest in an enterprise, (b) acquire or maintain an interest in an enterprise through racketeering activity, (c) conduct or participate in the affairs of an enterprise through racketeering activity, or (d) conspire to do any of the preceding activities. RICO provides for both civil and criminal liability.

---

firearm. While he and his wife are in a convenience store, a man draws a gun, points it at the cashier, and demands all the cash in the register. Afraid that the man will start shooting, Trevor grabs the gun and holds onto it until police arrive. In this situation, if Trevor is charged with possession of a firearm, he can assert the defense of necessity. ◀

Insanity

A person who suffers from a mental illness may be incapable of the state of mind required to commit a crime. Thus, insanity may be a defense to a criminal charge. Note that an insanity defense does not enable a person to avoid imprisonment. It simply means that if the defendant successfully proves insanity, she or he will be placed in a mental institution.

▶ **Example 7.15** James Holmes opened fire with an automatic weapon in a crowded Colorado movie theater during the screening of *The Dark Knight Rises,* killing twelve people and injuring more than fifty. Holmes had been a graduate student until he suffered from mental health problems. Before the incident, he had no criminal history. Holmes's attorneys are expected to assert the defense of insanity to try to avoid a possible death penalty. If the defense is successful, Holmes will be confined to a mental institution, rather than a prison. ◀

MODEL PENAL CODE The courts have had difficulty deciding what the test for legal insanity should be. Federal courts and some states use the substantial-capacity test set forth in the Model Penal Code:

> A person is not responsible for criminal conduct if at the time of such conduct as a result of mental disease or defect he or she lacks substantial capacity either to appreciate the wrongfulness of his [or her]

conduct or to conform his [or her] conduct to the requirements of the law.

M'NAGHTEN AND OTHER STATE RULES Some states use the *M'Naghten* test.[17] Under this test, a person is not responsible if, at the time of the offense, he or she did not know the nature and quality of the act or did not know that the act was wrong. Other states use the irresistible-impulse test. A person operating under an irresistible impulse may know an act is wrong but cannot refrain from doing it. Under any of these tests, proving insanity is extremely difficult. For this reason, the insanity defense is rarely used and usually is not successful. Four states have abolished the insanity defense.

Mistake

Everyone has heard the saying "Ignorance of the law is no excuse." Ordinarily, ignorance of the law or a mistaken idea about what the law requires is not a valid defense. A *mistake of fact,* however, as opposed to a *mistake of law,* can excuse criminal responsibility if it negates the mental state necessary to commit a crime.

▶ **Example 7.16** Oliver Wheaton mistakenly walks off with Julie Tyson's briefcase. If Wheaton genuinely thought that the case was his, there is no theft. Theft requires knowledge that the property belongs to another. (If Wheaton's act causes Tyson to incur damages, however, she may sue him in a civil action for trespass to personal property or conversion—torts that were discussed in Chapter 4.) ◀

Duress

Duress exists when the *wrongful threat* of one person induces another person to perform an act that he or she would not otherwise have performed. In such a situation, duress is said to negate the mental state necessary to commit a crime because the defendant was forced or compelled to commit the act.

Duress can be used as a defense to most crimes except murder. Both the definition of duress and the types of crimes that it can excuse vary among the states, however. Generally, to successfully assert duress as a defense, the defendant must reasonably have believed that he or she was in immediate danger,

and the jury (or judge) must conclude that the defendant's belief was reasonable.

Entrapment

Entrapment is a defense designed to prevent police officers or other government agents from enticing persons to commit crimes in order to later prosecute them for those crimes. In the typical entrapment case, an undercover agent *suggests* that a crime be committed and somehow pressures or induces an individual to commit it. The agent then arrests the individual for the crime.

For entrapment to be considered a defense, both the suggestion and the inducement must take place. The defense is not intended to prevent law enforcement agents from setting a trap for an unwary criminal. Rather, its purpose is to prevent them from pushing the individual into a criminal act. The crucial issue is whether the person who committed a crime was predisposed to commit the illegal act or did so only because the agent induced it.

Statute of Limitations

With some exceptions, such as the crime of murder, statutes of limitations apply to crimes just as they do to civil wrongs. In other words, the state must initiate criminal prosecution within a certain number of years. If a criminal action is brought after the statutory time period has expired, the accused person can raise the statute of limitations as a defense.

The running of the time period in a statute of limitations may be *tolled*—that is, suspended or stopped temporarily—if the defendant is a minor or is not in the jurisdiction. When the defendant reaches the age of majority or returns to the jurisdiction, the statutory time period begins to run again.

Immunity

Accused persons are understandably reluctant to give information if it will be used to prosecute them, and they cannot be forced to do so. The privilege against **self-incrimination** is guaranteed by a clause in the Fifth Amendment to the U.S. Constitution. The clause reads "nor shall [any person] be compelled in any criminal case to be a witness against himself."

When the state wishes to obtain information from a person accused of a crime, the state can grant *immunity* from prosecution. Alternatively, the state

---

17. A rule derived from *M'Naghten's* Case, 8 Eng.Rep. 718 (1843).

can agree to prosecute the accused for a less serious offense in exchange for the information. Once immunity is given, the person has an absolute privilege against self-incrimination and therefore can no longer refuse to testify on Fifth Amendment grounds.

Often, a grant of immunity from prosecution for a serious crime is part of the **plea bargaining** between the defending and prosecuting attorneys. The defendant may be convicted of a lesser offense, while the state uses the defendant's testimony to prosecute accomplices for serious crimes carrying heavy penalties.

SECTION 5
CRIMINAL PROCEDURES

Criminal law brings the force of the state, with all of its resources, to bear against the individual. Criminal procedures are designed to protect the constitutional rights of individuals and to prevent the arbitrary use of power on the part of the government.

The U.S. Constitution provides specific safeguards for those accused of crimes. The United States Supreme Court has ruled that most of these safeguards apply not only in federal court but also in state courts by virtue of the due process clause of the Fourteenth Amendment. These protections include the following:

1. The Fourth Amendment protection from unreasonable searches and seizures.
2. The Fourth Amendment requirement that no warrant for a search or an arrest be issued without probable cause.
3. The Fifth Amendment requirement that no one be deprived of "life, liberty, or property without due process of law."
4. The Fifth Amendment prohibition against **double jeopardy** (trying someone twice for the same criminal offense).[18]
5. The Fifth Amendment requirement that no person be required to be a witness against (incriminate) himself or herself.

6. The Sixth Amendment guarantees of a speedy trial, a trial by jury, a public trial, the right to confront witnesses, and the right to a lawyer at various stages in some proceedings.
7. The Eighth Amendment prohibitions against excessive bail and fines and against cruel and unusual punishment.

Fourth Amendment Protections

The Fourth Amendment protects the "right of the people to be secure in their persons, houses, papers, and effects." Before searching or seizing private property, normally law enforcement officers must obtain a **search warrant**—an order from a judge or other public official authorizing the search or seizure.

Advances in technology allow the authorities to track phone calls and vehicle movements with greater ease and precision. Nevertheless, the use of such technology can still constitute a search within the meaning of the Fourth Amendment. ▶ **Case in Point 7.17** Antoine Jones owned and operated a nightclub. Police suspected that he was also trafficking in narcotics. As part of their investigation, police obtained a warrant to attach a Global Positioning System (GPS) to his wife's car. Although the warrant specified that the GPS had to be attached within ten days, officers did not attach it until eleven days later.

Law enforcement then tracked the vehicle's movement for about a month, eventually arresting Jones for possession and intent to distribute cocaine. Jones was convicted. He appealed, arguing that police did not have a warrant for the GPS tracking. The United States Supreme Court held that the attachment of a GPS tracking device to a suspect's vehicle constitutes a Fourth Amendment search. The Court did not rule on whether the search in this case was unreasonable and required a warrant, however, and allowed Jones's conviction to stand.[19] ◀

PROBABLE CAUSE To obtain a search warrant, law enforcement officers must convince a judge that they have reasonable grounds, or **probable cause,** to believe a search will reveal a specific illegality. Probable cause requires the officers to have trustworthy evidence that would convince a reasonable person that the proposed search or seizure is more likely justified than not.

---

18. The prohibition against double jeopardy means that once a criminal defendant is found not guilty of a particular crime, the government may not indict that person again and retry him or her for the same crime. The prohibition does not preclude the crime victim from bringing a *civil* suit against that same person to recover damages, however. Additionally, a state's prosecution of a crime will not prevent a separate federal prosecution of the same crime, and vice versa.

19. *United States v. Jones,* __ U.S. __, 132 S.Ct. 945, 181 L.Ed.2d 911 (2012).

SCOPE OF WARRANT The Fourth Amendment prohibits general warrants. It requires a particular description of what is to be searched or seized. General searches through a person's belongings are impermissible. The search cannot extend beyond what is described in the warrant. Although search warrants require specificity, if a warrant is issued for a person's residence, items in that residence may be searched even if they do not belong to that individual.

In the following case, police officers obtained a search warrant and conducted a search for weapons in the home of a suspect's foster mother. A judge later ruled that the warrant was not supported by probable cause, and the homeowners sued individual police officers for executing an illegal search warrant.

CASE 7.2

Messerschmidt v. Millender

Supreme Court of the United States, ___ U.S. ___, 132 S.Ct. 1235, 182 L.Ed.2d 47 (2012).

BACKGROUND AND FACTS The Los Angeles County Sheriff's Department was protecting a woman from Jerry Ray Bowen, when he tried to kill her with a shotgun. The woman told the police that she and Bowen used to date, that Bowen was a gang member, and that she thought Bowen was staying at the home of Augusta Millender, his former foster mother. After investigating the incident further, the police prepared a warrant to search the home for all guns and gang-related material, and a magistrate approved it.

When the police, including Curt Messerschmidt, served the search warrant, they discovered that Bowen was not at the home, but they searched it anyway. The homeowners sued individual police officers in federal court for subjecting them to an illegal search. A federal appellate court held that the police lacked probable cause for such a broad search and that the police officers could be held personally liable. The police officers appealed. The United States Supreme Court granted *certiorari* to determine whether the police officers were immune from personal liability.

IN THE LANGUAGE OF THE COURT
Chief Justice *ROBERTS* delivered the opinion of the Court.

* * * *

The validity of the warrant is not before us. The question instead is whether Messerschmidt and [the other officers] are entitled to immunity from damages, even assuming that the warrant should not have been issued.

"The doctrine of qualified immunity protects government officials 'from liability for civil damages insofar as their conduct does not violate clearly established statutory or constitutional rights of which a reasonable person would have known.'" * * * "Whether an official protected by qualified immunity may be held personally liable for an allegedly unlawful official action generally turns on the 'objective legal reasonableness' of the action * * *."

Where the alleged Fourth Amendment violation involves a search or seizure pursuant to a warrant, the fact that a neutral magistrate has issued a warrant is the clearest indication that the officers acted in an objectively reasonable manner * * *. "Nonetheless, * * * we have recognized an exception allowing suit when 'it is obvious that no reasonably competent officer would have concluded that a warrant should issue.'" [Emphasis added.]

Our precedents make clear, however, that the threshold for establishing this exception is a high one, and it should be. * * * As we explained in [another case], "in the ordinary case, an officer cannot be expected to question the magistrate's probable-cause determination" because "it is the magistrate's responsibility to determine whether the officer's allegations establish probable cause and, if so, to issue a warrant comporting in form with the requirements of the Fourth Amendment."

DECISION AND REMEDY *The United States Supreme Court reversed the decision of the federal appellate court. It held that Messerschmidt and the other police officers were immune from personal liability.*

THE LEGAL ENVIRONMENT DIMENSION *How would police officers behave if they could always be held personally liable for executing unconstitutional warrants? Would they be more or less inclined to apply for and execute search warrants? Explain.*

CASE 7.2 CONTINUED **MANAGERIAL IMPLICATIONS** *The principles of this case would also apply in the context of searches of businesses. Businesses may be subject to warrantless administrative searches. Evidence gleaned from a search conducted in reasonable reliance on information that later proves to have been false may still be admissible in court in a case against the business.*

The Exclusionary Rule

Under what is known as the **exclusionary rule,** any evidence obtained in violation of the constitutional rights spelled out in the Fourth, Fifth, and Sixth Amendments generally is not admissible at trial. All evidence derived from the illegally obtained evidence is known as the "fruit of the poisonous tree," and such evidence normally must also be excluded from the trial proceedings. For instance, if a confession is obtained after an illegal arrest, the arrest is the "poisonous tree," and the confession, if "tainted" by the arrest, is the "fruit."

The purpose of the exclusionary rule is to deter police from conducting warrantless searches and engaging in other misconduct. The rule can sometimes lead to injustice, however. If the evidence of a defendant's guilt was obtained improperly (without a valid search warrant, for instance), it normally cannot be used against the defendant in court.

The *Miranda* Rule

An important question many courts faced in the 1950s and 1960s was not whether suspects had constitutional rights—that was not in doubt—but how and when those rights could be exercised. Could the right to be silent (under the Fifth Amendment's protection against self-incrimination) be exercised during pretrial interrogation proceedings or only during the trial? Were confessions obtained from suspects admissible in court if the suspects had not been advised of their right to remain silent and other constitutional rights?

To clarify these issues, the United States Supreme Court issued a landmark decision in 1966 in *Miranda v. Arizona,* which we present here. Today, the procedural rights required by the Court in this case are familiar to almost every American.

CLASSIC CASE 7.3

Miranda v. Arizona
Supreme Court of the United States, 384 U.S. 436, 86 S.Ct. 1602, 16 L.Ed.2d 694 (1966).

BACKGROUND AND FACTS On March 13, 1963, Ernesto Miranda was arrested at his home for the kidnapping and rape of an eighteen-year-old woman. Miranda was taken to a Phoenix, Arizona, police station and questioned by two officers. Two hours later, the officers emerged from the interrogation room with a written confession signed by Miranda. A paragraph at the top of the confession stated that the confession had been made voluntarily, without threats or promises of immunity, and "with full knowledge of my legal rights, understanding any statement I make may be used against me."

Miranda was never advised that he had a right to remain silent and a right to have a lawyer present. The confession was admitted into evidence at his trial, and Miranda was convicted and sentenced to prison for twenty to thirty years. Miranda appealed, claiming that he had not been informed of his constitutional rights. The Supreme Court of Arizona held that Miranda's constitutional rights had not been violated and affirmed his conviction. The *Miranda* case was subsequently reviewed by the United States Supreme Court.

 IN THE LANGUAGE OF THE COURT
Mr. Chief Justice *WARREN* delivered the opinion of the Court.

The cases before us raise questions which go to the roots of our concepts of American criminal jurisprudence; the restraints society must observe consistent with the Federal Constitution in prosecuting individuals for crime.

CASE 7.3 CONTINUES ▶

CASE 7.3 CONTINUED

* * * *

At the outset, if a person in custody is to be subjected to interrogation, he must first be informed in clear and unequivocal terms that he has the right to remain silent.

* * * *

The warning of the right to remain silent must be accompanied by the explanation that anything said can and will be used against the individual in court. This warning is needed in order to make him aware not only of the privilege, *but also of the consequences of forgoing it.* [Emphasis added.]

The circumstances surrounding in-custody interrogation can operate very quickly to overbear the will of one merely made aware of his privilege by his interrogators. Therefore the right to have counsel present at the interrogation is indispensable to the protection of the Fifth Amendment privilege under the system we delineate today.

* * * *

In order fully to apprise a person interrogated of the extent of his rights under this system then, it is necessary to warn him not only that he has the right to consult with an attorney, but also that if he is indigent [without funds] a lawyer will be appointed to represent him. * * * The warning of a right to counsel would be hollow if not couched in terms that would convey to the indigent—the person most often subjected to interrogation—the knowledge that he too has a right to have counsel present.

DECISION AND REMEDY *The United States Supreme Court held that Miranda could not be convicted of the crime on the basis of his confession because his confession was inadmissible as evidence. For any statement made by a defendant to be admissible, the defendant must be informed of certain constitutional rights prior to police interrogation. If the accused waives his or her rights to remain silent and to have counsel present, the government must demonstrate that the waiver was made knowingly, voluntarily, and intelligently.*

THE GLOBAL DIMENSION *The right to remain silent has long been a legal hallmark in Great Britain as well as in the United States. In 1994, however, the British Parliament passed an act that provides that a criminal defendant's silence may be interpreted as evidence of his or her guilt. British police officers are now required, when making an arrest, to inform the suspect, "You do not have to say anything. But if you do not mention now something which you later use in your defense, the court may decide that your failure to mention it now strengthens the case against you. A record will be made of everything you say, and it may be given in evidence if you are brought to trial." Should U.S. law also be changed to allow a defendant's silence during questioning to be considered as an indication of guilt? Why or why not?*

IMPACT OF THIS CASE ON TODAY'S LAW *Despite considerable criticism and later attempts to overrule the* Miranda *decision through legislation, the requirements stated in this case continue to provide the benchmark by which criminal procedures are judged today. Police officers routinely advise suspects of their "Miranda rights" on arrest. When Ernesto Miranda himself was later murdered, the suspected murderer was "read his Miranda rights."*

Exceptions to the *Miranda* Rule

Although the Supreme Court's decision in the *Miranda* case was controversial, it has survived several attempts by Congress to overrule it. Over time, however, the Supreme Court has made a number of exceptions to the *Miranda* ruling. For instance, the Court has recognized a "public safety" exception that allows certain statements to be admitted even if the defendant was not given *Miranda* warnings. A defendant's statements that reveal the location of a weapon would be admissible under this exception.

Additionally, a suspect must unequivocally and assertively ask to exercise her or his right to counsel in order to stop police questioning. Saying, "Maybe I should talk to a lawyer" during an interrogation after being taken into custody is not enough.

Criminal Process

As mentioned earlier in this chapter, a criminal prosecution differs significantly from a civil case in several respects. These differences reflect the desire to safeguard the rights of the individual against the state. Exhibit 7–3 below summarizes the major steps in processing a criminal case. We now discuss three phases of the criminal process—arrest, indictment or information, and trial—in more detail.

ARREST Before a warrant for arrest can be issued, there must be probable cause to believe that the individual in question has committed a crime. As discussed earlier in this chapter, *probable cause* can be defined as a substantial likelihood that the person has committed or is about to commit a crime. Note that probable cause involves a likelihood, not just a possibility. Arrests can be made without a warrant if there is no time to get one, but the action of the arresting officer is still judged by the standard of probable cause.

INDICTMENT OR INFORMATION Individuals must be formally charged with having committed specific

EXHIBIT 7–3 Major Procedural Steps in a Criminal Case

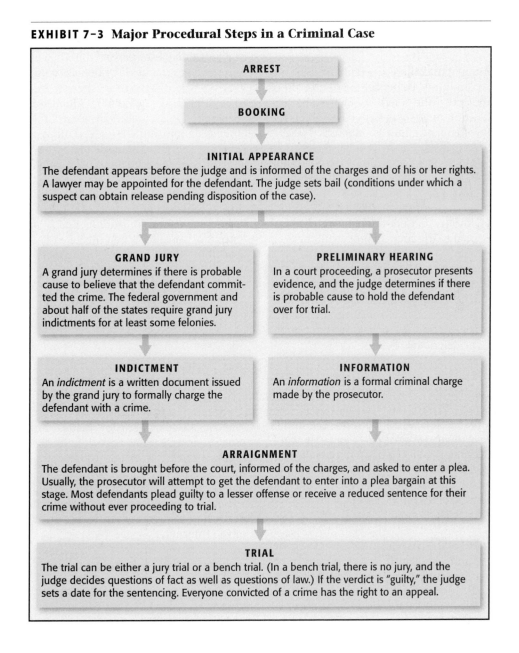

ARREST

BOOKING

INITIAL APPEARANCE
The defendant appears before the judge and is informed of the charges and of his or her rights. A lawyer may be appointed for the defendant. The judge sets bail (conditions under which a suspect can obtain release pending disposition of the case).

GRAND JURY
A grand jury determines if there is probable cause to believe that the defendant committed the crime. The federal government and about half of the states require grand jury indictments for at least some felonies.

PRELIMINARY HEARING
In a court proceeding, a prosecutor presents evidence, and the judge determines if there is probable cause to hold the defendant over for trial.

INDICTMENT
An *indictment* is a written document issued by the grand jury to formally charge the defendant with a crime.

INFORMATION
An *information* is a formal criminal charge made by the prosecutor.

ARRAIGNMENT
The defendant is brought before the court, informed of the charges, and asked to enter a plea. Usually, the prosecutor will attempt to get the defendant to enter into a plea bargain at this stage. Most defendants plead guilty to a lesser offense or receive a reduced sentence for their crime without ever proceeding to trial.

TRIAL
The trial can be either a jury trial or a bench trial. (In a bench trial, there is no jury, and the judge decides questions of fact as well as questions of law.) If the verdict is "guilty," the judge sets a date for the sentencing. Everyone convicted of a crime has the right to an appeal.

crimes before they can be brought to trial. If issued by a grand jury, such a charge is called an **indictment.**[20] A **grand jury** does not determine the guilt or innocence of an accused party. Rather, its function is to hear the state's evidence and to determine whether a reasonable basis (probable cause) exists for believing that a crime has been committed and that a trial ought to be held.

Usually, grand juries are called in cases involving serious crimes, such as murder. For lesser crimes, an individual may be formally charged with a crime by an **information,** or criminal complaint. An information will be issued by a government prosecutor if the prosecutor determines that there is sufficient evidence to justify bringing the individual to trial.

TRIAL At a criminal trial, the accused person does not have to prove anything. The entire burden of proof is on the prosecutor (the state). As mentioned earlier, the prosecution must show that, based on all the evidence, the defendant's guilt is established *beyond a reasonable doubt.* If there is reasonable doubt as to whether a criminal defendant committed the crime with which she or he has been charged, then the verdict must be "not guilty." A verdict of "not guilty" is not the same as stating that the defendant is innocent. It merely means that not enough evidence was properly presented to the court to prove guilt beyond a reasonable doubt.

Courts have complex rules about what types of evidence may be presented and how the evidence may be brought out in criminal cases, especially in jury trials. These rules are designed to ensure that evidence presented at trials is relevant, reliable, and not prejudicial toward the defendant.

Federal Sentencing Guidelines

The Sentencing Reform Act created the U.S. Sentencing Commission, which performs the task of standardizing sentences for *federal* crimes. The commission's guidelines establish a range of possible penalties for each federal crime. Originally, the guidelines were mandatory, in that the judge was required to select a sentence from within the set range and was not allowed to deviate from it.

PROBLEMS WITH CONSTITUTIONALITY In 2005, the United States Supreme Court held that certain provisions of the federal sentencing guidelines were unconstitutional. ▶ **Case in Point 7.18** Freddie Booker

was arrested with 92.5 grams of crack cocaine in his possession. Booker admitted to police that he had sold an additional 566 grams of crack cocaine, but he was never charged with, or tried for, possession of this additional quantity. Nevertheless, under the federal sentencing guidelines the judge was required to sentence Booker to twenty-two years in prison. The Court ruled that this sentence was unconstitutional because a jury did not find beyond a reasonable doubt that Booker had possessed the additional 566 grams of crack.[21] ◀

Essentially, the Court's ruling changed the federal sentencing guidelines from mandatory to advisory. Depending on the circumstances of the case, a federal trial judge may now depart from the guidelines if she or he believes that it is reasonable to do so.

FACTORS THAT INCREASE CRIMINAL PENALTIES Sentencing guidelines still exist and provide for enhanced punishment for certain types of crimes. Penalties can be enhanced for white-collar crimes, violations of the Sarbanes-Oxley Act (mentioned in Chapter 8), and violations of securities laws.[22]

The sentencing judge must take into account the various sentencing factors that apply to an individual defendant before concluding that a particular sentence is reasonable. When the defendant is a business firm, these factors include the company's history of past violations, management's cooperation with federal investigators, and the extent to which the firm has undertaken specific programs and procedures to prevent criminal activities by its employees.

CYBER CRIME

The U.S. Department of Justice broadly defines **computer crime** as any violation of criminal law that involves knowledge of computer technology for its perpetration, investigation, or prosecution. Many computer crimes fall under the broad label of **cyber crime,** which describes any criminal activity occurring via a computer in the virtual community of the Internet.

---

20. Pronounced in-*dyte*-ment.

21. *United States v. Booker,* 543 U.S. 220, 125 S.Ct. 738, 160 L.Ed.2d 621 (2005).

22. The sentencing guidelines were amended in 2003, as required under the Sarbanes-Oxley Act of 2002, to impose stiffer penalties for corporate securities fraud.

Most cyber crimes are simply existing crimes, such as fraud and theft of intellectual property, in which the Internet is the instrument of wrongdoing. ▶ **Example 7.19** Richard O'Dwyer ran TVShack.net, a Web site with links directing users to copyrighted TV shows and movies. U.S. authorities seized his .net domain name, claiming that the site was nothing more than a search engine for pirated content. O'Dwyer simply moved the site to a .cc domain over which the United States apparently has no authority. ◀

Here we look at several types of activities that constitute cyber crimes against persons or property. (Of course, just as computers and the Internet have expanded the scope of crime, they have also provided new ways of detecting and combatting crime. For instance, police are using social media as an investigative tool, as discussed in Chapter 6.)

Cyber Fraud

As pointed out in Chapter 4, fraud is any misrepresentation knowingly made with the intention of deceiving another and on which a reasonable person would and does rely to her or his detriment. **Cyber fraud** is fraud committed over the Internet.

ONLINE AUCTION FRAUD Online auction fraud, in its most basic form, is a simple process. A person puts up an expensive item for auction, on either a legitimate or a fake auction site, and then refuses to send the product after receiving payment. Or, as a variation, the wrongdoer may send the purchaser an item that is worth less than the one offered in the auction.

The larger online auction sites, such as eBay, try to protect consumers against such schemes by providing warnings about deceptive sellers or offering various forms of insurance. It is nearly impossible to completely block fraudulent auction activity on the Internet, however. Because users can assume multiple identities, it is very difficult to pinpoint fraudulent sellers—they will simply change their screen names with each auction.

ONLINE RETAIL FRAUD Somewhat similar to online auction fraud is online retail fraud, in which consumers pay directly (without bidding) for items that are never delivered. As with other forms of online fraud, it is difficult to determine the actual extent of online sales fraud, but anecdotal evidence suggests that it is a substantial problem.
▶ **Case in Point 7.20** Jeremy Jaynes grossed more than $750,000 per week selling nonexistent or worth-

less products such as "penny stock pickers" and "Internet history erasers." By the time he was arrested, he had amassed an estimated $24 million from his various fraudulent schemes.[23] ◀

Cyber Theft

In cyberspace, thieves are not subject to the physical limitations of the "real" world. A thief can steal data stored in a networked computer with Internet access from anywhere on the globe. Only the speed of the connection and the thief's computer equipment limit the quantity of data that can be stolen.

IDENTITY THEFT Not surprisingly, there has been a marked increase in identity theft in recent years. **Identity theft** occurs when the wrongdoer steals a form of identification—such as a name, date of birth, or Social Security number—and uses the information to access the victim's financial resources.

The Internet has provided even easier access to private data, as we discussed in Chapter 6. Frequent Web surfers surrender a wealth of information about themselves without knowing it. Most Web sites use "cookies" to collect data on those who visit their sites. Web browsers often store information such as the consumer's name and e-mail address. Finally, every time a purchase is made online, the item is linked to the purchaser's name.

PHISHING A distinct form of identity theft known as **phishing** has added a different wrinkle to the practice. In a phishing attack, the perpetrator "fishes" for financial data and passwords from consumers by posing as a legitimate business, such as a bank or credit-card company. The "phisher" sends an e-mail asking the recipient to update or confirm vital information, often with the threat that an account or some other service will be discontinued if the information is not provided. Once the unsuspecting individual enters the information, the phisher can use it to masquerade as that person or to drain his or her bank or credit account.
▶ **Example 7.21** Customers of Wachovia Bank (now owned by Wells Fargo) received official-looking e-mails telling them to type in personal information on a Web form to complete a mandatory installation of a new Internet security certificate. But the Web site was bogus. When people filled out the forms, their

---

23. *Jaynes v. Commonwealth of Virginia*, 276 Va.App. 443, 666 S.E.2d 303 (2008).

computers were infected and funneled their data to a computer server. The cyber criminals then sold the data. ◄

EMPLOYMENT FRAUD Cyber criminals also look for victims at online job-posting sites. Claiming to be an employment officer in a well-known company, the criminal sends bogus e-mail messages to job seekers. The messages ask the unsuspecting job seekers to reveal enough information to allow for identity theft. As the unemployment rate has remained high, cyber criminals have found many opportunities for employment fraud.

▶ **Example 7.22**   The job site Monster.com once asked 4.5 million users to change their passwords. Cyber thieves had broken into its databases and stolen user identities, passwords, and other data in one of Britain's largest cyber theft cases. ◄

CREDIT-CARD NUMBERS Companies take risks by storing their online customers' credit-card numbers. Although the consumer can make a purchase more quickly without entering a lengthy card number, the electronic warehouses that store the numbers are targets for cyber thieves. Stolen credit-card numbers are much more likely to hurt merchants and credit-card issuers (such as banks) than consumers. In most situations, the legitimate holders of credit cards are not held responsible for the costs of purchases made with a stolen number.

Hacking

A **hacker** is someone who uses one computer to break into another. The danger posed by hackers has increased significantly because of **botnets,** or networks of computers that have been appropriated by hackers without the knowledge of their owners. A hacker may secretly install a program on thousands, if not millions, of personal computer "robots," or "bots," that allows him or her to forward transmissions to an even larger number of systems.

▶ **Example 7.23**   When a hacker broke into Sony Corporation's PlayStation 3 video gaming and entertainment networks, the company had to temporarily shut down its online services. This single hacking incident affected more than 100 million online accounts that provide gaming, chat, and music streaming services. ◄

MALWARE Botnets are one of the latest forms of **malware**, a term that refers to any program that is harmful to a computer or, by extension, a computer user. A **worm,** for example, is a software program that is capable of reproducing itself as it spreads from one computer to the next.

▶ **Example 7.24**   Within three weeks, the computer worm called "Conflicker" spread to more than a million personal computers around the world. It was transmitted to some computers through the use of Facebook and Twitter. This worm also infected servers and devices plugged into infected computers, via USB ports, such as iPads, iPhones, and flash drives. ◄

A **virus,** another form of malware, is also able to reproduce itself, but must be attached to an "infested" host file to travel from one computer network to another. For instance, hackers are now capable of corrupting banner ads that use Adobe's Flash Player. When an Internet user clicks on the banner ad, a virus is installed. Worms and viruses can be programmed to perform a number of functions, such as prompting host computers to continually "crash" and reboot, or otherwise infect the system. (For a discussion of how malware is now affecting smartphones, see this chapter's *Insight into the Global Environment* feature on the following page.)

SERVICE-BASED HACKING Today, many companies offer "software as a service." Instead of buying software to install on a computer, the user connects to Web-based software. The user can write e-mails, edit spreadsheets, or perform other tasks using his or her Web browser. Cyber criminals have adapted this distribution method to provide "crimeware as a service."

A would-be thief no longer has to be a computer hacker to create a botnet, or steal banking information and credit-card numbers. He or she can rent the online services of cyber criminals to do the work for a small price. Fake security software (also known as scareware) is a common example. The thief can even target individual groups, such as U.S. physicians or British attorneys.

CYBERTERRORISM Cyberterrorists, as well as hackers, may target businesses. The goals of a hacking operation might include a wholesale theft of data, such as a merchant's customer files, or the monitoring of a computer to discover a business firm's plans and transactions. A cyberterrorist might also want to insert false codes or data. For instance, the process-

INSIGHT INTO THE GLOBAL ENVIRONMENT
Even Smartphones Are Vulnerable to International Cyber Attacks

Recent statistics show that the number of bank robberies occurring annually is on the decline. Criminals have learned that it is easier, less risky, and more profitable to steal via the Internet. Advances in the speed and use of the Internet have fostered the growth of a relatively new criminal industry that uses malware to conduct espionage and profit from crime.

Who Are the Creators of Malware?

While any smart teenager can buy prepackaged hacking software on the Internet, the malware that businesses and governments are worried about is much more sophisticated. There is evidence that malware that can be used for international diplomatic espionage as well as industrial espionage is most often developed by so-called cyber mercenaries. According to Steve Sachs of the cyber security firm FireEye, "There are entire little villages dedicated to malware in Russia, villages in China, very sophisticated, very organized, very well-funded."

Flame Malware

The most sophisticated globally created and propagated malware has been labeled Flame. Flame was discovered in 2012, although experts believe that it was lying dormant in thousands of computers worldwide for at least five years.

Flame can record screen shots, keyboard strokes, network traffic, and audio. It can also record Skype conversations. It can even turn infected computers into Bluetooth beacons, which can then attempt to download contact information from nearby Bluetooth-enabled devices.

The Malware Can Infect Smartphones

Many smartphone owners are unaware that their Apple, Nokia, and Microsoft Windows mobile phones can be infected with Flame malware or variants of it without

their knowledge. The information that is hacked from smartphones can then be sent on to a series of command-and-control servers and ultimately to members of international criminal gangs.

Once a computer or smartphone is infected with this malware, all information in the device can be transferred. Additionally, files can be deleted, and furthermore, files that have been erased on hard drives can be resurrected. This malware has been responsible for stealing e-mail databases from Microsoft's e-mail program Outlook and has even been able to capture e-mail from remote servers.[a] Until recently, most attacks involved diplomatic espionage, but cyber technicians at large business enterprises are now worried that industrial espionage may be taking place. In fact, an extensive hacking operation was uncovered in 2013 that was linked to a Chinese military unit (the "Comment Crew"). The wide-ranging cyber attacks involved the theft of hundreds of terabytes of data and intellectual property of more than 140 corporations in twenty different industries. The goal of the attacks was to help Chinese companies better compete against U.S. and foreign firms.[b]

LEGAL CRITICAL THINKING

INSIGHT INTO THE TECHNOLOGICAL ENVIRONMENT

What entities might pay "cyber mercenaries" to create some of the malware described in this feature?

---

a. Mark Stevens, "CWI Cryptanalyst Discovers New Cryptographic Attack Variant in Flame Spy Malware," June 7, 2012, www.cwi.nl/news.

b. David E. Sanger, David Barboza, and Nicole Perlroth, "Chinese Army Unit Is Seen as Tied to Hacking Against U.S.," www.nytimes.com.

ing control system of a food manufacturer could be changed to alter the levels of ingredients so that consumers of the food would become ill.

A cyberterrorist attack on a major financial institution, such as the New York Stock Exchange or a large bank, could leave securities or money markets in flux and seriously affect the daily lives of millions of citizens. Similarly, any prolonged disruption of computer, cable, satellite, or telecommunications sys-

tems due to the actions of expert hackers would have serious repercussions on business operations—and national security—on a global level.

Prosecuting Cyber Crime

Cyber crime has raised new issues in the investigation of crimes and the prosecution of offenders. Determining the "location" of a cyber crime and identifying a criminal in cyberspace present significant challenges for law enforcement.

JURISDICTION AND IDENTIFICATION CHALLENGES A threshold issue is, of course, jurisdiction. Jurisdiction is normally based on physical geography, as discussed in Chapter 3. Each state and nation has jurisdiction, or authority, over crimes committed within its boundaries. But geographic boundaries simply do not apply in cyberspace. A person who commits an act against a business in California, where the act is a cyber crime, might never have set foot in California but might instead reside in New York, or even in Canada, where the act may not be a crime.

Identifying the wrongdoer can also be difficult. Cyber criminals do not leave physical traces, such as fingerprints or DNA samples, as evidence of their crimes. Even electronic "footprints" can be hard to find and follow. For instance, e-mail may be sent through a remailer, an online service that guarantees that a message cannot be traced to its source.

For these reasons, laws written to protect physical property are often difficult to apply in cyberspace. Nonetheless, governments at both the state and the federal level have taken significant steps toward controlling cyber crime. California, for instance, which has the highest identity theft rate in the nation, has established a new eCrime unit to investigate and prosecute cyber crimes. Other states, including Florida,

Louisiana, and Texas, also have special law enforcement units that focus solely on Internet crimes.

THE COMPUTER FRAUD AND ABUSE ACT Perhaps the most significant federal statute specifically addressing cyber crime is the Counterfeit Access Device and Computer Fraud and Abuse Act.[24] This act is commonly known as the Computer Fraud and Abuse Act (CFAA).

Among other things, the CFAA provides that a person who accesses a computer online, without authority, to obtain classified, restricted, or protected data (or attempts to do so) is subject to criminal prosecution. Such data could include financial and credit records, medical records, legal files, military and national security files, and other confidential information. The data can be located in government or private computers. The crime has two elements: accessing a computer without authority and taking the data.

This theft is a felony if it is committed for a commercial purpose or for private financial gain, or if the value of the stolen data (or computer time) exceeds $5,000. Penalties include fines and imprisonment for up to twenty years. A victim of computer theft can also bring a civil suit against the violator to obtain damages, an injunction, and other relief.

---

24. 18 U.S.C. Section 1030.

Reviewing: Criminal Law and Cyber Crime

Edward Hanousek worked for Pacific & Arctic Railway and Navigation Company (P&A) as a roadmaster of the White Pass & Yukon Railroad in Alaska. Hanousek was responsible "for every detail of the safe and efficient maintenance and construction of track, structures and marine facilities of the entire railroad," including special projects. One project was a rock quarry, known as "6-mile," above the Skagway River. Next to the quarry, and just beneath the surface, ran a high-pressure oil pipeline owned by Pacific & Arctic Pipeline, Inc., P&A's sister company. When the quarry's backhoe operator punctured the pipeline, an estimated 1,000 to 5,000 gallons of oil were discharged into the river. Hanousek was charged with negligently discharging a harmful quantity of oil into a navigable water of the United States in violation of the criminal provisions of the Clean Water Act (CWA). Using the information presented in the chapter, answer the following questions.

1. Did Hanousek have the required mental state (*mens rea*) to be convicted of a crime? Why or why not?
2. Which theory discussed in the chapter would enable a court to hold Hanousek criminally liable for violating the statute if he participated in, directed, or merely knew about the specific violation?
3. Could the backhoe operator who punctured the pipeline also be charged with a crime in this situation? Explain.

4. Suppose that at trial, Hanousek argued that he should not be convicted because he was not aware of the requirements of the CWA. Would this defense be successful? Why or why not?

DEBATE THIS... *Because of overcriminalization, particularly by the federal government, Americans may be breaking the law regularly without knowing it. Should Congress rescind many of the more than four thousand federal crimes now on the books?*

Terms and Concepts

actus reus 134
arson 139
beyond a reasonable doubt 132
botnet 152
burglary 137
computer crime 150
crime 132
cyber crime 150
cyber fraud 151
double jeopardy 145
duress 144
embezzlement 140
entrapment 144

exclusionary rule 147
felony 133
forgery 139
grand jury 150
hacker 152
identity theft 151
indictment 150
information 150
larceny 137
malware 152
mens rea 135
misdemeanor 133
money laundering 141

necessity 142
petty offense 133
phishing 151
plea bargaining 145
probable cause 145
robbery 137
search warrant 145
self-defense 142
self-incrimination 144
virus 152
white-collar crime 140
worm 152

ExamPrep

Issue Spotters

1. Dana takes her roommate's credit card without permission, intending to charge expenses that she incurs on a vacation. Her first stop is a gas station, where she uses the card to pay for gas. With respect to the gas station, has she committed a crime? If so, what is it? **(See page 137.)**

2. Without permission, Ben downloads consumer credit files from a computer belonging to Consumer Credit Agency. He then sells the data to Dawn. Has Ben committed a crime? If so, what is it? **(See page 154.)**

• Check your answers to the Issue Spotters against the answers provided in Appendix B at the end of this text.

Before the Test

Go to **www.cengagebrain.com**, enter the ISBN 97812851770192, and click on "Find" to locate this textbook's Web site. Then, click on "Access Now" under "Study Tools," and select Chapter 7 at the top. There, you will find a Practice Quiz that you can take to assess your mastery of the concepts in this chapter, as well as Flashcards and a Glossary of important terms.

Business Scenarios

7–1. Types of Cyber Crimes. The following situations are similar, but each represents a variation of a particular crime. Identify the crime and point out the differences in the variations. **(See pages 150–153.)**

(a) Chen, posing fraudulently as Diamond Credit Card Co., sends an e-mail to Emily, stating that the company has observed suspicious activity in her account and has frozen the account. The e-mail asks her to reregister her credit-card number and password to re-open the account.

(b) Claiming falsely to be Big Buy Retail Finance Co., Conner sends an e-mail to Dino, asking him to confirm or update his personal security information to prevent his Big Buy account from being discontinued.

(c) Felicia posts her résumé on GotWork.com, an online job-posting site, seeking a position in business and managerial finance and accounting. Hayden, who misrepresents himself as an employment officer with International Bank & Commerce Corp., sends her an e-mail asking for more personal information.

7–2. Property Crimes. Which, if any, of the following crimes necessarily involves illegal activity on the part of more than one person? **(See page 137.)**

(a) Bribery.

(b) Forgery.

(c) Embezzlement.

(d) Larceny.

(e) Receiving stolen property.

7–3. Cyber Scam. Kayla, a student at Learnwell University, owes $20,000 in unpaid tuition. If Kayla does not pay the tuition, Learnwell will not allow her to graduate. To obtain the funds to pay the debt, she sends e-mails to people that she does not personally know asking for financial help to send Milo, her disabled child, to a special school. In reality, Kayla has no children. Is this a crime? If so, which one? **(See page 151.)**

Business Case Problems

7–4. Cyber Crime. Jiri Klimecek was a member of a group that overrode copyright protection in movies, video games, and software, and made them available for download online. Klimecek bought and installed hardware and software to set up a computer server and paid half of the monthly service charges to connect the server to the Internet. He knew that users around the world could access the server to upload and download copyrighted works. He obtained access to Czech movies and music to make them available. Klimecek was indicted in a federal district court for copyright infringement. He claimed that he did not understand the full scope of the operation. Did Klimecek commit a crime? If so, was he a "minor participant" entitled to a reduced sentence? Explain. [*United States v. Klimecek,* ___F.3d ___ (7th Cir. 2009)] **(See page 150.)**

7–5. Fourth Amendment. Three police officers, including Maria Trevizo, were on patrol in Tucson, Arizona, near a neighborhood associated with the Crips gang, when they pulled over a car with suspended registration. Each officer talked to one of the three occupants. Trevizo spoke with Lemon Johnson, who was wearing clothing consistent with Crips membership. Visible in his jacket pocket was a police scanner, and he said that he had served time in prison for burglary. Trevizo asked him to get out of the car and patted him down "for officer safety." She found a gun. Johnson was charged in an Arizona state court with illegal possession of a weapon. What standard should apply to an officer's patdown of a passenger during a traffic stop? Should a search warrant be required? Could a search proceed solely on the basis of probable cause? Would a reasonable suspicion short of probable cause be sufficient? Discuss. [*Arizona v. Johnson,* 555 U.S. 323, 129 S.Ct. 781, 172 L.Ed.2d 694 (2009)] **(See page 145.)**

7–6. Searches. Charles Byrd was in a minimum-security jail awaiting trial. A team of sheriff's deputies took several inmates into a room for a strip search without any apparent justification. Byrd was ordered to remove all of his clothing except his boxer shorts. A female deputy searched Byrd while several male deputies watched. One of the male deputies videotaped the search. Byrd filed a suit against the sheriff's department. Did the search violate Byrd's rights? Discuss. [*Byrd v. Maricopa County Sheriff's Department,* 629 F.3d. 1135 (9th Cir. 2011)] **(See page 145.)**

7–7. Credit-Card Theft. Jacqueline Barden was shopping for school clothes with her children when her purse and automobile were taken. In Barden's purse were her car keys, credit and debit cards for herself and her children, as well as the children's Social Security cards and birth certificates needed for enrollment at school. Immediately after the purse and car were stolen, Rebecca Mary Turner attempted to use Barden's credit card at a local Exxon gas station, but the card was declined. The gas station attendant recognized Turner because she had previously written bad checks and used credit cards that did not belong to her.

Turner was later arrested while attempting to use one of Barden's checks to pay for merchandise at a Wal-Mart—where the clerk also recognized Turner from prior criminal activity. Turner claimed that she had not stolen Barden's purse or car, and that a friend had told her he had some checks and credit cards and asked her to try using them at Wal-Mart. Turner was convicted at trial. She appealed, claiming that there was insufficient evidence that she committed credit- and debit-card theft. Was the evidence sufficient to uphold her conviction? Why or why not? [*Turner v. State of Arkansas,* 2012 Ark.App. 150 (2012)] **(See page 134.)**

7–8. BUSINESS CASE PROBLEM WITH SAMPLE ANSWER: Criminal Liability.

 During the morning rush hour, David Green threw bottles and plates from a twenty-sixth-floor hotel balcony overlooking Seventh Avenue in New York City. A video of the incident also showed him doing cartwheels while holding a beer bottle and sprinting toward the balcony while holding a glass steadily in his hand. When he saw police on the street below and on the roof of the building

across the street, he suspended his antics but resumed tossing objects off the balcony after the police left. He later admitted that he could recall what he had done, but claimed to have been intoxicated and said his only purpose was to amuse himself and his friends. Did Green have the mental state required to establish criminal liability? Discuss. [State of New York v. Green, *104 A.D.3d 126, 958 N.Y.S.2d 138 (1 Dept. 2013)]* **(See page 134.)**

- **For a sample answer to Problem 7–8, go to Appendix C at the end of this text.**

7–9. A QUESTION OF ETHICS: Identity Theft.

 Twenty-year-old Davis Omole had good grades in high school, where he played on the football and chess teams, and went on to college. Omole worked at a cell phone store where he stole customers' personal information. He used the stolen identities to create a hundred different accounts on eBay, and held more than three hundred auctions listing for sale items that he did not own *(including cell phones, plasma televisions, and stereos). From these auctions, he collected $90,000. To avoid getting caught, he continuously closed and opened the eBay accounts, activated and deactivated cell phone and e-mail accounts, and changed mailing addresses and post office boxes. Omole, who had previously been convicted in a state court for Internet fraud, was convicted in a federal district court of identity theft and wire fraud.* [United States v. Omole, *523 F.3d 691 (7th Cir. 2008)]* **(See page 151.)**

(a) Omole displayed contempt for the court and ridiculed his victims, calling them stupid for having been cheated. What does this behavior suggest about Omole's ethics?

(b) Under federal sentencing guidelines, Omole could have been imprisoned for more than eight years. He received only three years, however, two of which comprised the mandatory sentence for identity theft. Was this sentence too lenient? Explain.

Legal Reasoning Group Activity

7–10. Cyber Crime. Cyber crime costs consumers millions of dollars per year, and it costs businesses, including banks and other credit-card issuers, even more. Nonetheless, when cyber criminals are caught and convicted, they are rarely ordered to pay restitution or sentenced to long prison terms. **(See page 150.)**

(a) One group should argue that stiffer sentences would reduce the amount of cyber crime.

(b) A second group should determine how businesspersons can best protect themselves from cyber crime and avoid the associated costs.

CHAPTER 8

BUSINESS ETHICS

One of the most complex issues businesspersons and corporations face is ethics. It is not as well defined as the law, and yet it can have tremendous impacts on a firm's finances and reputation. Consider, for instance, the experience of the Chick-fil-A restaurant chain in 2012 when its chief operating officer made several statements about the company's commitment to supporting traditional marriage.

After those comments were made, it became public knowledge that Chick-fil-A had made donations to Christian organizations perceived to be opposed to same-sex marriage. Opponents of same-sex marriage held support rallies and Chick-fil-A appreciation days. Supporters of same-sex marriage held "kiss-ins" at local Chick-fil-A restaurants. Some politicians denounced Chick-fil-A's position and said that they would block expansion of the company in their cities. Eventually, Chick-fil-A issued a statement saying that it had ceased donations to any organization that promotes discrimination in any way. Chick-fil-A no longer sponsors charities that discriminate against same-sex couples or those who identify as gay, lesbian, bisexual, or transgendered.

Chick-fil-A was not accused of violating any laws, but its actions raised questions about the role of corporations and the effect of corporate ethics on profit. This chapter addresses some of those same questions. First, we look at business ethics—its definitions, its importance, and its relationship to the law. Next, we examine the philosophical bases for making ethical decisions. Finally, we discuss the application of business ethics to global situations.

BUSINESS ETHICS

At the most basic level, the study of **ethics** is the study of what constitutes right or wrong behavior. It is a branch of philosophy focusing on morality and the way moral principles are derived and implemented. Ethics has to do with the fairness, justness, rightness, or wrongness of an action.

The study of **business ethics** typically looks at the decisions businesses make or have to make and whether those decisions are right or wrong. It has to do with how businesspersons apply moral and ethical principles in making their decisions. Those who study business ethics also evaluate what duties and responsibilities exist or should exist for businesses.

Why Is Studying Business Ethics Important?

Over the last two hundred years, the public perception of the corporation has changed from an entity that primarily generates revenues for its owners to an entity that participates in society as a corporate citizen. Originally, the only goal or duty of a corporation was to maximize profits. Although many people today may view this idea as greedy or inhumane, the rationale for the profit-maximization theory is still valid.

PROFIT MAXIMIZATION In theory, if all firms strictly adhere to the goal of profit maximization, resources flow to where they are most highly valued by society. Corporations can focus on their strengths, and other entities that are better suited to deal with social problems and perform charitable acts can specialize in those activities. The government, through taxes and other financial allocations, can shift resources to those other entities to perform public services. Thus, in an ideal world, profit maximization leads to the most efficient allocation of scarce resources.

THE RISE OF CORPORATE CITIZENSHIP Over the years, as resources were not sufficiently reallocated to cover the costs of social needs, many people became dissatisfied with the profit-maximization theory. Investors and others began to look beyond profits and dividends and to consider the **triple bottom line**—a corporation's profits, its impact on people, and its impact on the planet. Magazines and Web sites began to rank companies based on their environmental impacts and their ethical decisions. The corporation came to be viewed as a "citizen" that was expected to participate in bettering communities and society.

Even so, many still believe that corporations are fundamentally money-making entities that should have no responsibility other than profit maximization.

The Importance of Ethics in Making Business Decisions

Whether one believes in the profit-maximization theory or corporate citizenship, ethics is important in making business decisions. Corporations should strive to be "good citizens." When making decisions, a business should evaluate:

1. The legal implications of each decision.
2. The public relations impact.
3. The safety risks for consumers and employees.
4. The financial implications.

This analysis will assist the firm in making decisions that not only maximize profits but also reflect good corporate citizenship.

LONG-RUN PROFIT MAXIMIZATION In attempting to maximize profits, however, corporate executives and employees have to distinguish between *short-run* and *long-run* profit maximization. In the short run, a company may increase its profits by continuing to sell a product, even though it knows that the product is defective. In the long run, though, because of lawsuits, large settlements, and bad publicity, such unethical conduct will cause profits to suffer. Thus, business ethics is consistent only with long-run profit maximization. An overemphasis on short-term profit maximization is the most common reason that ethical problems occur in business.

▶ **Case in Point 8.1** When the powerful narcotic painkiller OxyContin was first marketed, its manufacturer, Purdue Pharma, claimed that it was unlikely to lead to drug addiction or abuse. Internal company documents later showed that the company's executives knew that OxyContin could be addictive, but kept this risk a secret to boost sales and maximize short-term profits.

Subsequently, Purdue Pharma and three former executives pleaded guilty to criminal charges that they misled regulators, patients, and physicians about OxyContin's risks of addiction. Purdue Pharma agreed to pay $600 million in fines and other payments. The three former executives agreed to pay $34.5 million in fines and were barred from federal health programs for a period of fifteen years. Thus, the company's focus on maximizing profits in the short run led to unethical conduct that hurt profits in the long run.[1] ◀

THE INTERNET CAN RUIN REPUTATIONS In the past, negative information or opinions about a company might remain hidden. Now, however, cyberspace provides a forum where disgruntled employees, unhappy consumers, or special interest groups can post derogatory remarks. Thus, the Internet has increased the potential for a major corporation (or other business) to suffer damage to its reputation or loss of profits through negative publicity.

Wal-Mart and Nike in particular have been frequent targets for advocacy groups that believe that those corporations exploit their workers. Although some of these assertions may be unfounded or exaggerated, the courts generally have refused to consider them *defamatory* (the tort of defamation will be discussed in Chapter 4). Most courts regard online attacks as simply the expression of opinion and therefore a form of speech protected by the First Amendment. Even so, corporations often incur considerable expense in running marketing campaigns to thwart bad publicity and may even face legal costs (if the complaint leads to litigation).

IMAGE IS EVERYTHING The study of business ethics is concerned with the purposes of a business and how that business achieves those purposes. Thus, business ethics is concerned with the image of the business and the impacts that the business has on the environment, customers, suppliers, employees, and the global economy.

Unethical corporate decision making can negatively affect suppliers, consumers, the community, and society as a whole. It can also have a negative

---

1. *United States v. Purdue Frederick Co.*, 495 F.Supp.2d 569 (W.D.Va. 2007).

impact on the reputation of the company and the individuals who run that company. Hence, an in-depth understanding of business ethics is important to the long-run viability of any corporation today.

The Relationship of Law and Ethics

Because the law does not codify all ethical requirements of all persons, compliance with the law is not always sufficient to determine "right" behavior. Laws have to be general enough to apply in a variety of circumstances. Laws are broad in their purpose and their scope. They prohibit or require certain actions to avoid significant harm to society.

When two competing companies secretly agree to set prices on products, for instance, society suffers harm—typically, the companies will charge higher prices than they could if they continued to compete. This harm inflicted on consumers has negative consequences for the economy, and so colluding to set prices is an illegal activity. Similarly, when a company is preparing to issue stock, the law requires certain disclosures to potential investors. This requirement is meant to avoid harms that come with uninformed investing, such as occurred in the 1920s and contributed to the stock market crash and the Great Depression.

MORAL MINIMUM Compliance with the law is sometimes called the **moral minimum.** If people and entities merely comply with the law, they are acting at the lowest ethical level society will tolerate. The study of ethics goes beyond those legal requirements to evaluate what is right for society.

Businesspersons must remember that just because an action is legal does not mean it is ethical. For instance, no law specifies the salaries that publicly held corporations (companies that sell their shares to the public) can pay their officers (executive employees). Nevertheless, if a corporation pays its officers an excessive amount relative to other employees, or relative to what officers at other corporations are paid, the executives' compensation might be viewed as unethical.

In the following case, the court had to determine if a repair shop was entitled to receive full payment of an invoice or a lesser amount given its conduct in the matter.

CASE 8.1

Johnson Construction Co. v. Shaffer
Court of Appeal of Louisiana, Second Circuit, 87 So.3d 203 (2012).

BACKGROUND AND FACTS A truck owned by Johnson Construction Company needed repairs. John Robert Johnson, Jr., the company's president, took the truck with its attached fifteen-ton trailer to Bubba Shaffer, doing business as Shaffer's Auto and Diesel Repair. The truck was supposedly fixed, and Johnson paid the bill. The truck continued to leak oil and water. Johnson returned the truck to Shaffer, who again claimed to have fixed the problem. Johnson paid the second bill. The problems with the truck continued, however, so Johnson returned the truck and trailer a third time. Shaffer gave a verbal estimate of $1,000 for the repairs, but he ultimately sent an invoice for $5,863.49. Johnson offered to settle for $2,480, the amount of the initial estimate ($1,000), plus the costs of parts and shipping. Shaffer refused the offer and would not return Johnson's truck or trailer until full payment was made. Shaffer also charged Johnson a storage fee of $50 a day and 18 percent interest on the $5,863.49.

Johnson Construction filed a suit against Shaffer alleging unfair trade practices. The trial court determined that Shaffer had acted deceptively and wrongfully in maintaining possession of the trailer, on which no work had been performed. The trial court awarded Johnson $3,500 in general damages, plus $750 in attorneys' fees. Shaffer was awarded the initial estimate of $1,000 and appealed.

 **IN THE LANGUAGE OF THE COURT**
LOLLEY, J. [Judge]

* * * *

* * * At the outset, we point out that Mr. Johnson maintained he had a verbal agreement with Bubba Shaffer, the owner of Shaffer's Auto Diesel and Repair, that the repairs to the truck would cost $1,000. Mr. Johnson also testified that he was not informed otherwise.

CASE 8.1 CONTINUED   The existence or nonexistence of a contract is a question of fact, and the finder of fact's determination may not be set aside unless it is clearly wrong.

* * * *

* * * At the trial of the matter, the trial court was presented with testimony from Mr. Johnson, Mr. Shaffer, and Michael Louton, a mechanic employed by Shaffer. * * * The trial court did not believe Mr. Johnson was informed of the cost for the additional work.

* * * We cannot say that the trial court was clearly wrong in its determination. * * * The trial court viewed Mr. Shaffer's testimony on the issue as "disingenuous" and we cannot see where that was an error.

As for the amount that Shaffer contends is due for storage, had it invoiced Mr. Johnson the amount of the original estimate in the first place, there would have been no need to store the truck or trailer. * * * We cannot see how Shaffer would be entitled to any payment for storage when it failed to return the truck and trailer where an offer of payment for the agreed upon price had been conveyed.

* * * *

* * * So considering, we see no error in the trial court's characterization of Shaffer's actions with the trailer as holding "hostage in an effort to force payment for unauthorized repairs." * * * . Shaffer had no legal right to retain possession of the trailer * * * . *Thus, the trial court did not err in its determination that Shaffer's retention of Johnson Construction's trailer [for four years!] was a deceptive conversion of the trailer.* [Emphasis added.]

DECISION AND REMEDY *The state appellate court affirmed the judgment of the trial court in favor of Johnson Construction Company. It affirmed the award of $3,500, plus $750 in attorneys' fees, as well as Shaffer's original award of $1,000.*

WHAT IF THE FACTS WERE DIFFERENT? *Suppose that Shaffer had invoiced Johnson for only $1,500. Would the outcome have been different?*

THE ETHICAL DIMENSION *Would it have been ethical for Shaffer's mechanic to lie to support his employer's case? Discuss.*

ETHICS AND PRIVATE LAW Most companies attempt to link ethics and law through the creation of internal codes of ethics. Company codes are not law. Instead, they are rules that the company sets forth that it can also enforce (by terminating an employee who does not follow them, for instance). Codes of conduct typically outline the company's policies on particular issues and indicate how employees are expected to act.

▶ **Example 8.2** Google's code of conduct starts with the motto "Don't be evil." The code then makes general statements about how Google promotes integrity, mutual respect, and the highest standard of ethical business conduct. Google's code also provides specific rules on a number of issues, such as privacy, drugs and alcohol, conflicts of interest, co-worker relationships, and confidentiality—it even has a dog policy. The company takes a stand against employment discrimination that goes further than the law requires. It prohibits discrimination based on sexual orientation, gender identity or expression, and veteran status. ◀

Numerous industries have also developed their own codes of ethics. The American Institute of Certified Public Accountants (AICPA) has a comprehensive Code of Professional Conduct for the ethical practicing of accounting. The American Bar Association has model rules of professional conduct for attorneys, and the American Nurses Association has a code of ethics that applies to nurses. These codes can give guidance to decision makers facing ethical questions. Violation of a code may result in discipline of an employee or sanctions against a company from the industry organization. Remember, though, that these internal codes are not laws, so their effectiveness is determined by the commitment of the industry or company leadership to enforcing the codes.

ETHICAL UNCERTAINTY Ethics can be a difficult subject for corporate officers to fully understand. Because it is often highly subjective and subject to change over time without any sort of formal process, ethics is less certain than law.

The law can also be uncertain, however, and contains numerous "gray areas" that make it difficult to predict with certainty how a court will apply a given law to a particular action. Uncertainty can make decision making difficult, especially when a law requires a court to determine what is "foreseeable" or "reasonable" in a particular situation. Because a business has no way of predicting how a specific court will decide these issues, decision makers need to proceed with caution and evaluate an action and its consequences from an ethical perspective.

Ethics is based more on judgment than research. A company that can show it acted ethically, responsibly, and in good faith (honestly) has a better chance of succeeding in a dispute than one that cannot make such a showing.

In the following case, the court concluded that the employer's response to complaints about a hostile work environment was so inadequate that it not only violated the employee's rights but was unethical enough to warrant a large penalty against the corporation. Notice the court's language about the company's behavior.

CASE 8.2

May v. Chrysler Group, LLC
United States Court of Appeals, Seventh Circuit, 692 F.3d 734 (2012).

COMPANY PROFILE Chrysler Group, LLC, is the parent company of Fiat, Chrysler, Dodge, Jeep, and several other automobile manufacturers. (An LLC is a limited liability company.) Chrysler Group was created in 2009 to manage the consolidation of the different automobile companies during the economic downturn of the late 2000s. The company employs more than 64,000 people at thirty-two manufacturing facilities. Its 2013 revenue was estimated to be $60 billion.

BACKGROUND AND FACTS Between 2002 and 2005, Otto May, Jr., a pipefitter at Chrysler's Belvedere Assembly Plant, was the target of more than fifty racist, homophobic, and anti-Semitic messages and graffiti. He found six death-threat notes in his toolbox, his bike and car tires were punctured, and someone poured sugar into the gas tank of his car twice. At one point, a dead bird wrapped in toilet paper to look like a member of the Ku Klux Klan (including the white pointed hat) was left at his work station. May complained to Chrysler. The director of human resources met with May, documented the complaints, and initiated an internal investigation. As part of that investigation, records were checked to determine who was in the building when the incidents occurred, and the handwriting on the notes and graffiti was analyzed.

The director held two meetings with about sixty employees (out of more than a thousand plant employees). At the meetings, the director reminded the workers that harassment was not acceptable. The harassers were never caught, and the harassment continued after the meetings. Chrysler's headquarters became involved only after the Anti-Defamation League wrote a letter on May's behalf. May sued Chrysler for hostile work environment harassment and was awarded $709,000 in compensatory damages and $3.5 million in punitive damages (or punishment). The judge overturned the punitive damages award, and May appealed.

 IN THE LANGUAGE OF THE COURT
TINDER, Circuit Judge.

* * * *

May can recover punitive damages only if he presented sufficient evidence for the jury to conclude that Chrysler acted with "malice or with reckless indifference to [his] federally protected rights." * * * *No evidence of "egregious" or "outrageous" conduct by the employer is required, although, of course, such a showing could support a conclusion that the employer acted with the requisite mental state.* [Emphasis added.]

We have already explained why it was appropriate for Chrysler to be held responsible for the hostile work environment. Its response was shockingly thin as measured against the gravity of May's harassment.

CASE 8.2 CONTINUED

* * * *

* * *[A]lthough the district court did not rule on whether the jury's $3.5 million award of punitive damages is "grossly excessive" and therefore violates due process, * * * we asked the parties for supplemental briefing so that we might consider that question now. After reviewing the parties' submissions, we are convinced that the punitive damage award does not violate the Constitution and should therefore be reinstated in full. The award is substantial— five times the original compensatory damages and eleven times the remitted amount—but Chrysler's long-term recklessness in the face of repeated threats of violence against May and his family is sufficiently reprehensible [shameful] to support it.

DECISION AND REMEDY   *The federal appellate court reinstated the punitive damages award based on the reprehensible and unethical nature of Chrysler's failure to sufficiently address the harassment.*

THE ETHICAL DIMENSION   *Does an organization have an ethical obligation to secure a safe and harassment-free workplace for its employees? Why or why not? Discuss.*

MANAGERIAL IMPLICATIONS   *It is clear from this opinion that employers have a significant duty to take complaints of harassment seriously. Even if Chrysler believed that May was harassing himself (perhaps in order to obtain compensation from the company), as the company implied at the trial, it had an obligation to do a serious investigation, to set up clear policies and procedures, and to follow those procedures when a complaint was made.*

SECTION 2

BUSINESS ETHICS AND SOCIAL MEDIA

Although most young people think of social media— Facebook, Twitter, Pinterest, Google+, MySpace, LinkedIn, and the like—as simply ways to communicate rapidly, businesses face ethical issues with respect to these same social media platforms.

Hiring Procedures

In the past, to learn about a prospective employee, the employer would ask the candidate's former employers for references. Today, employers are likely to also conduct Internet searches to discover what job candidates have posted on their Facebook pages, blogs, and tweets. Nevertheless, many people believe that judging a job candidate based on what she or he does outside the work environment is unethical.

Sometimes, too, the opposite situation occurs, and job candidates are rejected because they *do not* participate in any social media. Given that the vast majority of younger people do use social media, some employers have decided that the failure to do so raises a red flag. Some consider this employer behavior to be unethical as well.

The Use of Social Media to Discuss Work-Related Issues

Because so many Americans use social media many times a day, they often discuss work-related issues there. Numerous companies have provided strict guidelines about what is appropriate and inappropriate when making posts at one's own or others' social media accounts. A number of companies have fired employees for such activities as criticizing other employees or managers through social media outlets. Until recently, such disciplinary measures were considered ethical and legal.

Today, in contrast, a ruling by the National Labor Relations Board (NLRB—the federal agency that investigates unfair labor practices) has changed the legality of such actions. ▶ **Example 8.3** Costco's social media policy specified that its employees should not make statements that would damage the company, harm another person's reputation, or violate the company's policies. Employees who violated these rules were subject to discipline and could be fired.

In 2012, the NLRB ruled that Costco's social media policy violated federal labor law, which protects employees' right to engage in "concerted activities." Employees can freely associate with each other and have conversations about common workplace issues without employer interference. This right extends to social media posts. Therefore, Costco cannot broadly prohibit its employees from criticizing the company or co-workers, supervisors, or managers via social media. ◀

Ethics in Reverse

While most of the discussion in this chapter involves business ethics, employee ethics is also an important issue. For instance, is it ethical for employees to make negative posts in social media about other employees or, more commonly, about managers? After all, negative comments about managers reflect badly on those managers, who often are reluctant to respond via social media to such criticism. Disgruntled employees may exaggerate the negative qualities of managers whom they do not like.

Some may consider the latest decision by the National Labor Relations Board outlined in *Example 8.3* to be too lenient toward employees and too stringent toward management. There is likely to be an ongoing debate about how to balance employees' right to free expression against employers' right to prevent inaccurate negative statements being spread across the Internet.

SECTION 3

ETHICAL PRINCIPLES AND PHILOSOPHIES

As Dean Krehmeyer, executive director of the Business Roundtable's Institute for Corporate Ethics, once said, "Evidence strongly suggests being ethical—doing the right thing—pays." Instilling ethical business decision making into the fabric of a business organization is no small task, even if ethics "pays." How do business decision makers decide whether a given action is the "right" one for their firms? What ethical standards should be applied?

Broadly speaking, **ethical reasoning**—the application of morals and ethics to a situation—applies to businesses just as it does to individuals. As businesses make decisions, they must analyze the alternatives in a variety of ways, one of which is the ethical implications.

Generally, the study of ethics is divided into two major categories—duty-based ethics and outcome-based ethics. **Duty-based ethics** is rooted in the idea that every person has certain duties to others, including both humans and the planet. Those duties may be derived from religious principles or from other

philosophical reasoning. **Outcome-based ethics** focuses on the impacts of a decision on society or on key *stakeholders*.

Duty-Based Ethics

Duty-based ethics focuses on the obligations of the corporation. It deals with standards for behavior that traditionally were derived from revealed truths, religious authorities, or philosophical reasoning. These standards involve concepts of right and wrong, and duties owed and rights to be protected.

Corporations today often describe these values or duties in their mission statements or strategic plans. Some companies base their statements on a nonreligious rationale, but others still derive their values from religious doctrine (such as the statements of Chick-fil-A, discussed in the introduction to this chapter).

RELIGIOUS ETHICAL PRINCIPLES Nearly every religion has principles or beliefs about how one should treat others. In the Judeo-Christian tradition, which is the dominant religious tradition in the United States, the Ten Commandments of the Old Testament establish these fundamental rules for moral action. The principles of the Muslim faith are set out in the Qur'an, and Hindus find their principles in the four Vedas.

Religious rules generally are absolute with respect to the behavior of their adherents. ▶ **Example 8.4** The commandment "Thou shalt not steal" is an absolute mandate for a person who believes that the Ten Commandments reflect revealed truth. Even a benevolent motive for stealing (such as Robin Hood's) cannot justify the act because the act itself is inherently immoral and thus wrong. ◀

For businesses, religious principles can be a unifying force for employees or a rallying point to increase employee motivation. They can also be problematic, however, because different owners, suppliers, employees, and customers may all have different religious backgrounds. As the introduction to this chapter illustrated, taking an action based on religious principles, especially when those principles address socially or politically controversial topics, can lead to negative publicity and even to protests or boycotts.

PRINCIPLES OF RIGHTS Another view of duty-based ethics focuses on basic rights. The principle that human beings have certain fundamental rights (to life, freedom, and the pursuit of happiness, for example) is deeply embedded in Western culture. As discussed in Chapter 1, the natural law tradition embraces the concept that certain actions (such as killing another person) are morally wrong because they are contrary to nature (the natural desire to continue living).

Those who adhere to this **principle of rights,** or "rights theory," believe that a key factor in determining whether a business decision is ethical is how that decision affects the rights of others. These others include the firm's owners, its employees, the consumers of its products or services, its suppliers, the community in which it does business, and society as a whole.

Conflicting Rights. A potential dilemma for those who support rights theory, however, is that they may disagree on which rights are most important. When considering all those affected by a business decision to downsize a firm, for example, how much weight should be given to employees relative to shareholders? Which employees should be laid off first—those with the highest salaries or those who have worked there for less time (and have less seniority)? How should the firm weigh the rights of customers relative to the community, or employees relative to society as a whole?

Resolving Conflicts. In general, rights theorists believe that whichever right is stronger in a particular circumstance takes precedence. ▶ **Example 8.5** Murray Chemical Corporation has to decide whether to keep a chemical plant in Utah open, thereby saving the jobs of a hundred and fifty workers, or shut it down. Closing the plant will avoid contaminating a river with pollutants that would endanger the health of tens of thousands of people. In this situation, a rights theorist can easily choose which group to favor because the value of the right to health and well-being is obviously stronger than the basic right to work. (Not all choices are so clear-cut, however.) ◀

KANTIAN ETHICAL PRINCIPLES Duty-based ethical standards may also be derived solely from philosophical reasoning. The German philosopher Immanuel Kant (1724–1804) identified some general guiding principles for moral behavior based on what he thought to be the fundamental nature of human beings. Kant believed that human beings are qualitatively different from other physical objects and are endowed with moral integrity and the capacity to reason and conduct their affairs rationally.

People Are Not a Means to an End. Based on this view of human beings, Kant said that when people are treated merely as a means to an end, they are being treated as the equivalent of objects and are being denied their basic humanity. For instance, a manager who treats subordinates as mere profit-making tools is less likely to retain motivated and loyal employees than a manager who respects his or her employees. Management research has shown that employees who feel empowered to share their thoughts, opinions, and solutions to problems are happier and more productive.

Categorical Imperative. When a business makes unethical decisions, it often rationalizes its action by saying that the company is "just one small part" of the problem or that its decision would have "only a small impact." A central theme in Kantian ethics is that individuals should evaluate their actions in light of the consequences that would follow if everyone in society acted in the same way. This **categorical imperative** can be applied to any action. ▶ **Example 8.6** CHS Fertilizer is deciding whether to invest in expensive equipment that will decrease profits but will also reduce pollution from its factories. If CHS has adopted Kant's categorical imperative, the decision makers will consider the consequences if every company invested in the equipment (or if no company did so). If the result would make the world a better place (less polluted), CHS's decision would be clear. ◀

Outcome-Based Ethics: Utilitarianism

In contrast to duty-based ethics, outcome-based ethics focuses on the consequences of an action, not on the nature of the action itself or on any set of preestablished moral values or religious beliefs. Outcome-based ethics looks at the impacts of a decision in an attempt to maximize benefits and minimize harms. The premier philosophical theory for outcome-based decision making is **utilitarianism,** a philosophical theory developed by Jeremy Bentham (1748–1832) and modified by John Stuart Mill (1806–1873)—both British philosophers.

"The greatest good for the greatest number" is a paraphrase of the major premise of the utilitarian approach to ethics.

COST-BENEFIT ANALYSIS Under a utilitarian model of ethics, an action is morally correct, or "right," when, among the people it affects, it produces the greatest amount of good for the greatest number or creates the least amount of harm for the fewest people. When an action affects the majority adversely, it is morally wrong. Applying the utilitarian theory thus requires the following steps:

1. A determination of which individuals will be affected by the action in question.
2. A **cost-benefit analysis,** which involves an assessment of the negative and positive effects of alternative actions on these individuals.
3. A choice among alternative actions that will produce maximum societal utility (the greatest positive net benefits for the greatest number of individuals).

Thus, if expanding a factory would provide hundreds of jobs but generate pollution that could endanger the lives of thousands of people, a utilitarian analysis would find that saving the lives of thousands creates greater good than providing jobs for hundreds.

PROBLEMS WITH THE UTILITARIAN APPROACH There are problems with a strict utilitarian analysis. In some situations, an action that products the greatest good for the most people may not seem to be the most ethical. ▶ **Example 8.7** Phazim Company is producing a drug that will cure a disease in 85 percent of patients, but the other 15 percent will experience agonizing side effects and a horrible, painful death. A quick utilitarian analysis would suggest that the drug should be produced and marketed because the majority of patients will benefit. Many people, however, have significant concerns about manufacturing a drug that will cause such harm to anyone. ◀

Corporate Social Responsibility

In pairing duty-based concepts with outcome-based concepts, strategists and theorists developed the idea of the corporate citizen. **Corporate social responsibility (CSR)** combines a commitment to good citizenship with a commitment to making ethical decisions, improving society, and minimizing environmental impact.

CSR is a relatively new concept in the history of business, but a concept that becomes more important every year. Although CSR is not imposed on corporations by law, it does involve a commitment to self-regulation in a way that attends to the text and intent of the law, ethical norms, and global standards. A survey of U.S. executives undertaken by the Boston College Center for Corporate Citizenship found that more than 70 percent of those polled agreed that cor-

porate citizenship must be treated as a priority. More than 60 percent said that good corporate citizenship added to their companies' profits.

CSR can be an incredibly successful strategy for companies, but corporate decision makers must not lose track of the two descriptors in the title: *corporate* and *social.* The company must link the responsibility of citizenship with the strategy and key principles of the business. Incorporating both the social and the corporate components of CSR and making ethical decisions can help companies grow and prosper.

THE SOCIAL ASPECTS OF CSR First, the social aspect requires that corporations demonstrate that they are promoting goals that society deems worthwhile and are moving toward solutions to social problems. Because business controls so much of the wealth and power of this country, business, in turn, has a responsibility to society to use that wealth and power in socially beneficial ways. Companies may be judged on how much they donate to social causes, as well as how they conduct their operations with respect to employment discrimination, human rights, environmental concerns, and similar issues.

Some corporations publish annual social responsibility reports, which may also be called corporate sustainability (referring to the capacity to endure) or citizenship reports. ▶ **Example 8.8** The Hitachi Group has Web pages dedicated to its CSR initiatives and includes reports outlining its environmental strategies, its human rights policies, and its commitment to diversity. The software company Symantec Corporation issues corporate responsibility reports to demonstrate its focus on critical environmental, social, and governance issues. In its 2012 report, Symantec pointed out that 88 percent of facilities it owns or leases on a long-term basis are certified as environmentally friendly by the LEED program. LEED stands for Leadership in Energy and Environmental Design. Certification requires the achievement of high standards for energy efficiency, material usage in construction, and other environmental qualities. ◀

THE CORPORATE ASPECTS OF CSR Arguably, any socially responsible activity will benefit a corporation. The corporation may see an increase in goodwill from the local community for creating a park. Corporations may see increases in sales if they are viewed as good citizens.

At times, the benefit may not be immediate. Constructing a new plant that meets the high LEED standards may cost more initially. Nevertheless, over the life of the building, the savings in maintenance and utilities may more than make up for the extra cost of construction.

Surveys of college students about to enter the job market confirm that young people are looking for socially responsible employers. Socially responsible activities may cost a corporation now, but may lead to more impressive, and more committed employees. Corporations that engage in meaningful social activities retain workers longer, particularly younger ones.

Corporate responsibility is most successful when a company undertakes activities that are significant and related to its business operations. ▶ **Example 8.9** In 2012, the Walt Disney Company announced that in an effort to curb childhood obesity, it was issuing strict nutritional standards for all products advertised through its media outlets. In addition to focusing on a major social issue, the initiative was intended to clarify Disney's mission and values, as well as enhance its reputation as a trustworthy, family-friendly company. The initiative has been praised by commentators and politicians and is expected to increase Disney's revenue in the long term. ◀

STAKEHOLDERS One view of CSR stresses that corporations have a duty not just to shareholders, but also to other groups affected by corporate decisions—called **stakeholders.** The rationale for this "stakeholder view" is that, in some circumstances, one or more of these other groups may have a greater stake in company decisions than the shareholders do.

Under this approach, a corporation considers the impact of its decisions on its employees, customers, creditors, suppliers, and the community in which it operates. Stakeholders could also include advocacy groups such as environmental groups and animal rights groups. To avoid making a decision that may be perceived as unethical and result in negative publicity or protests, a corporation should consider the impact of its decision on the stakeholders. The most difficult aspect of the stakeholder analysis is determining which group's interests should receive greater weight if the interests conflict.

For instance, during the last few years, layoffs numbered in the millions. Nonetheless, some corporations succeeded in reducing labor costs without layoffs. To avoid slashing their workforces, these employers turned to alternatives such as (1) four-day workweeks, (2) unpaid vacations and voluntary furloughs, (3) wage freezes, (4) pension cuts, and (5) flexible work schedules. Some companies asked their workers to accept wage cuts to prevent layoffs, and the workers agreed.

Companies finding alternatives to layoffs included Dell (extended unpaid holidays), Cisco Systems (four-day end-of-year shutdowns), Motorola (salary cuts), and Honda (voluntary unpaid vacation time).

S E C T I O N 4
MAKING ETHICAL BUSINESS DECISIONS

Even if officers, directors, and others in a company want to make ethical decisions, it is not always clear what is ethical in a given situation. Thinking beyond things that are easily measured, such as profits, can be challenging. Although profit projections are not always accurate, they are more objective than considering the personal impacts of decisions on employees, shareholders, customers, and even the community. But this subjective component to decision making potentially has a great influence on a company's profits.

Companies once considered leaders in their industry, such as Enron and the worldwide accounting firm Arthur Andersen, were brought down by the unethical behavior of a few. A two-hundred-year-old British investment banking firm, Barings Bank, was destroyed by the actions of one employee and a few of his friends. Clearly, ensuring that all employees get on the ethical business decision-making "bandwagon" is crucial in today's fast-paced world.

Individuals entering the global corporate community, even in entry-level positions, must be prepared to make hard decisions. Sometimes, there is no "good" answer to the questions that arise. Therefore, it is important to have tools to help in the decision-making process and a framework for organizing those tools. Business decisions can be complex and may involve legal concerns, financial questions, possibly health and safety concerns, and ethical components.

A Systematic Approach

Organizing the ethical concerns and issues and approaching them systematically can help a businessperson eliminate various alternatives and identify the strengths and weaknesses of the remaining alternatives. Ethics consultant Leonard H. Bucklin of Corporate-Ethics.US™ has devised a procedure that he calls Business Process Pragmatism™. It involves five steps.

STEP 1: INQUIRY First, the decision maker must understand the problem. To do this, one must identify the parties involved (the stakeholders) and collect the relevant facts. Once the ethical problem or problems are clarified, the decision maker lists any relevant legal and ethical principles that will guide the decision.

STEP 2: DISCUSSION In this step, the decision maker lists possible actions. The ultimate goals for the decision are determined, and each option is evaluated using the laws and ethical principles listed in Step 1.

STEP 3: DECISION In this step, those participating in the decision making work together to craft a consensus decision or consensus plan of action for the corporation.

STEP 4: JUSTIFICATION In this step, the decision maker articulates the reasons for the proposed action or series of actions. Generally these reasons should come from the analysis done in Step 3. This step essentially results in documentation to be shared with stakeholders explaining why the proposal is an ethical solution to the problem.

STEP 5: EVALUATION This final step occurs once the decision has been made and implemented. The solution should be analyzed to determine if it was effective. The results of this evaluation may be used in making future decisions.

The Importance of Ethical Leadership

Talking about ethical business decision making is meaningless if management does not set standards.

Furthermore, managers must apply the same standards to themselves as they do to the company's employees.

ATTITUDE OF TOP MANAGEMENT One of the most important ways to create and maintain an ethical workplace is for top management to demonstrate its commitment to ethical decision making. A manager who is not totally committed to an ethical workplace rarely succeeds in creating one. Management's behavior, more than anything else, sets the ethical tone of a firm. Employees take their cues from management. ▶ **Example 8.10** Devon, a BioTek employee, observes his manager cheating on her expense account. Later, when Devon is promoted to a managerial position, he "pads" his expense account as well, knowing that he is unlikely to face sanctions for doing so. ◀

Managers who set unrealistic production or sales goals increase the probability that employees will act unethically. If a sales quota can be met only through high-pressure, unethical sales tactics, employees will try to act "in the best interest of the company" and will continue to behave unethically.

A manager who looks the other way when she or he knows about an employee's unethical behavior also sets an example—one indicating that ethical transgressions will be accepted. Managers have found that discharging even one employee for ethical reasons has a tremendous impact as a deterrent to unethical behavior in the workplace. This is true even if the company has a written code of ethics. If management does not enforce the company code, the code is essentially nonexistent.

The following case demonstrates the types of situations that can occur when management demonstrates a lack of concern about ethics.

CASE ANALYSIS

Case 8.3   Moseley v. Pepco Energy Services, Inc.
United States District Court, District of New Jersey, 2011 WL 1584166 (2011).

IN THE LANGUAGE OF THE COURT
Joseph H. *RODRIGUEZ*, District Judge.

* * * Plaintiff Moseley is an employee of Defendant Pepco Energy Services, Inc. ("PES"). He has been employed

by PES or its corporate predecessors for over twenty-five years. PES, a subsidiary of Defendant Pepco Holdings, Inc. ("PHI"), provides deregulated energy and energy-related services for residential, small business, and large commercial customers.
* * * *

In 1998, Thomas Herzog held the position of Vice President of CTS. * * * In or around 2002, CTS merged with Potomic Electric Power Company, Inc., and each company became a subsidiary of PHI. Following the merger, according to Plaintiff, he continued to work for PHI, still as

Maintenance Manager at Midtown Thermal, until December 31, 2009.

* * * *

Following the 2002 merger with PHI, employees were required to complete an annual ethics survey. By March of 2007, Plaintiff and two co-workers had discussed their respective observations of Herzog's conduct, which they deemed questionable and possibly unethical. Specifically, they felt that Herzog improperly used company assets and improperly hired immediate family members and friends who did not appear on the payroll. The three decided to disclose this information on PHI's annual "Ethics Survey."

The three planned to reveal that Herzog employed his daughter, Laurie, as his secretary in the summer of 2005 and the beginning of 2006 without posting the position first and in violation of PHI's anti-nepotism policy.

* * * *

Next, Herzog hired his girlfriend's daughter as his secretary after his daughter had gone back to school. Plaintiff believed this was in violation of Company policy because the position again was not posted. Herzog also hired his son as a project manager, again through a third party independent contractor, Walter Ratai. Plaintiff thought this was wrong because (1) Herzog circumvented the Company's hiring process, (2) it violated Company policy, and (3) Herzog's son was being paid $75.00/hr, which was more than Plaintiff was making. * * * In addition, Plaintiff had learned that Herzog was improperly using the Company's Eagles' tickets for personal use. Finally, Herzog had leased a new SUV with Company funds, but which was not approved by the Company.

* * * *

[After the surveys were completed, an] investigation ensued. Following the investigation, effective on or about May 10, 2007, Herzog was escorted out of the building. * * * On

March 8, 2008, Plaintiff received his annual performance evaluation * * *; for the first time in twenty-three years, Plaintiff's performance review was negative. Plaintiff feels that this negative performance review was a further act of retaliation for his disclosure of Herzog's conduct.

* * * *

On or about June 11, 2008 the Plant/Operations Manager position was posted * * *. Plaintiff applied for the position, but it was offered to [another person]. Plaintiff alleges that he "was not promoted to the position of Plant/Operations Manager despite his experience performing the job for the previous two and a half years, qualifications for same and seniority, as a direct and proximate result of his prior complaints and/or disclosures regarding the Herzog illegal conduct and activities."

* * * *

The New Jersey Legislature enacted the Conscientious Employee Protection Act (CEPA) to "protect and encourage employees to report illegal or unethical workplace activities." * * * CEPA prohibits a New Jersey employer from taking "retaliatory action" against an employee who objects to "any activity, policy or practice which the employee reasonably believes" is in violation of applicable law. * * * "To prevail on a claim under this provision, a plaintiff must establish that: (1) he reasonably believed that [the complained-of] conduct was violating a law or rule or regulation promulgated pursuant to law; (2) he objected to the conduct; (3) an adverse employment action was taken against him; and (4) a causal connection exists between the whistleblowing activity and the adverse employment action.

* * * *

The first element of the prima facie case [a case sufficient to be sent to the jury] under CEPA is that the Plaintiff reasonably believed that the complained-of conduct (1) was violat-

ing a "law, rule, or regulation promulgated pursuant to law, including any violation involving deception of, or misrepresentation to, any shareholder, investor, client, patient, customer, employee, former employee, retiree or pensioner of the employer or any governmental entity"; or "(2) is fraudulent or criminal, including any activity, policy or practice of deception or misrepresentation which the employee reasonably believes may defraud any shareholder, investor, client, patient, customer, employee, former employee, retiree or pensioner of the employer or any governmental entity."

Although Defendants have argued that Plaintiff merely disclosed a violation of Company policy, Moseley has testified that in March 2007, he reported what he believed to be "unethical conduct, misappropriation of company funds, and theft" by his direct supervisor. * * * *Moreover, a plaintiff need not demonstrate that there was a violation of the law or fraud, but instead that he "reasonably believed" that to be the case.* The facts in this case support an objectively reasonable belief that a violation of law or fraudulent conduct was being committed by Plaintiff's supervisor. [Emphasis added.]

Regarding the causal connection between Plaintiff's whistleblowing activity and the negative adverse employment actions taken against him, Plaintiff stresses that he was employed by the Defendants for twenty-five years without a negative employment evaluation or any form of discipline until immediately after he disclosed the wrongful conduct of his supervisor. Not only did Plaintiff then receive a negative performance evaluation, but the posted position of Plant Manager was given to [another], despite [the other's] alleged past negative history and despite that Plaintiff asserts he had been acting in that job for over two years. Plaintiff contends that this is sufficient evidence of pretext.

The Court is unable to find as a matter of law that Defendants' inferences

CASE 8.3 CONTINUES ▶

prevail or that a jury could not reasonably adopt a contrary inference of retaliation. There are questions of fact as to how much the individuals responsible for Plaintiff's negative performance evaluations knew about Plaintiff's complaints. "[A] finding of the required causal connection may

be based solely on circumstantial evidence that the person ultimately responsible for an adverse employment action was aware of an employee's whistle-blowing activity." Because jurors may infer a causal connection from the surrounding circumstances, as well as temporal proximity, the

Court will not grant summary judgment. [Emphasis added.]

* * * *

IT IS ORDERED on this 26th day of April, 2011 that Defendants' motion for summary judgment is hereby DENIED.

LEGAL REASONING QUESTIONS

1. Using duty-based ethical principles, what facts or circumstances in this case would lead Moseley to disclose Herzog's behavior?

2. Using outcome-based ethical principles, what issues would Moseley have to analyze in making the decision to report Herzog's behavior? What would be the risks to Moseley? The benefits?

3. Under the Business Process Pragmatism™ steps, what alternatives might Moseley have had in this situation?

4. Regardless of who wins this case at trial, in performing Step 5 (Evaluation) of the Business Process Pragmatism™ procedure, what changes should the company take with regard to the complaint process?

BEHAVIOR OF OWNERS AND MANAGERS Business owners and managers sometimes take more active roles in fostering unethical and illegal conduct. This may indicate to their co-owners, co-managers, employees, and others that unethical business behavior will be tolerated. Business owners' misbehavior can have negative consequences for themselves and their business. Not only can a court sanction the owners and managers, but it can also issue an injunction that prevents them from engaging in similar patterns of conduct in the future.

▶ **Example 8.11** Lawyer Samir Zia Chowhan posted a help-wanted ad on Craigslist seeking an "energetic woman" for the position of legal secretary. The ad stated that the position included secretarial and paralegal work, as well as "additional duties" for two lawyers in the firm. Applicants were asked to send pictures and describe their physical features.

When a woman applied for the job, Chowhan sent her an e-mail saying that "in addition to the legal work, you would be required to have sexual interaction with me and my partner, sometimes together sometimes separate." He also explained that she would need to perform sexual acts at the job interview so that he and his partner could determine whether she would be able to handle these duties. The woman filed a complaint with the Illinois Bar Association, which suspended Chowhan's law license for a year for making false statements about the ad. Because the bar association's ethics rules prohibited attorneys from having sex with their clients, but not with potential employees, Chowhan could only be disciplined for lying. ◀

THE SARBANES-OXLEY ACT The Sarbanes-Oxley Act of 2002[2] requires companies to set up confidential systems so that employees and others can "raise red flags" about suspected illegal or unethical auditing and accounting practices.

Some companies have implemented online reporting systems to accomplish this goal. In one such system, employees can click on an icon on their computers that anonymously links them with NAVEX, an organization based in Lake Oswego, Oregon. Through NAVEX Global, employees can report suspicious accounting practices, sexual harassment, and other possibly unethical behavior. NAVEX Global, in turn, alerts management personnel or an audit committee at the designated company to the possible problem. Those who have used the system say that it is less inhibiting than calling a company's toll-free number.

SECTION 5
GLOBAL BUSINESS ETHICS

Just as different religions have different moral codes, different countries, regions and even states have different ethical expectations and priorities. Some of these differences are based in religious values, whereas others are cultural in nature. As a result of the various

---

2. 15 U.S.C. Sections 7201 *et seq.*

cultures and religions throughout the world, making ethical business decisions can be even more difficult.

For instance, in certain countries the consumption of alcohol and specific foods is forbidden for religious reasons. It would be considered unethical for a U.S. business to build a factory to produce alcohol and employee local workers in a culture in which alcohol is forbidden.

International transactions often involve issues related to employment and financing. Congress has addressed some of these issues, not eliminating the ethical components but clarifying some of the conflicts between the ethics of the United States and the ethics of other nations. For example, the Civil Rights Act of 1964 and the Foreign Corrupt Practices Act (discussed in more detail below) have clarified the U.S. ethical position on employment issues and bribery in foreign nations. (Other nations, including Mexico, have also enacted laws that prohibit bribery, as discussed in this chapter's *Insight into the Global Environment* feature on the following page.)

The Monitoring of Employment Practices of Foreign Suppliers

Many businesses contract with companies in developing nations to produce goods, such as shoes and clothing, because the wage rates in those nations are significantly lower than those in the United States. Yet what if a foreign company hires women and children at below-minimum-wage rates, for example, or requires its employees to work long hours in a workplace full of health hazards? What if the company's supervisors routinely engage in workplace conduct that is offensive to women? What if plants located abroad routinely violate labor and environmental standards?

▶ **Example 8.12** Apple, Inc., owns Pegatron Corporation, a subsidiary company based in China, which supplies parts for iPads and other Apple products. In December 2011, there was an explosion at a Pegatron factory in Shanghai. Dozens of employees were injured when aluminum dust from polishing cases for iPads caught fire and caused the explosion. Allegations surfaced that the conditions at the factory violated labor and environmental standards. California-based Apple did not comment on the issue. ◀

Given today's global communications network, few companies can assume that their actions in other nations will go unnoticed by "corporate watch" groups that discover and publicize unethical corporate behavior. As a result, U.S. businesses today usu-

ally take steps to avoid such adverse publicity—either by refusing to deal with certain suppliers or by arranging to monitor their suppliers' workplaces to make sure that the employees are not being mistreated.

The Foreign Corrupt Practices Act

Another ethical problem in international business dealings has to do with the legitimacy of certain side payments to government officials. In the United States, the majority of contracts are formed within the private sector. In many foreign countries, however, government officials make the decisions on most major construction and manufacturing contracts because of extensive government regulation and control over trade and industry.

Side payments to government officials in exchange for favorable business contracts are not unusual in such countries, nor are they considered to be unethical. In the past, U.S. corporations doing business in these nations largely followed the dictum "When in Rome, do as the Romans do."

In the 1970s, however, the U.S. media uncovered a number of business scandals involving large side payments by U.S. corporations to foreign representatives for the purpose of securing advantageous international trade contracts. In response to this unethical behavior, in 1977 Congress passed the Foreign Corrupt Practices Act[3] (FCPA), which prohibits U.S. businesspersons from bribing foreign officials to secure beneficial contracts.

PROHIBITION AGAINST THE BRIBERY OF FOREIGN OFFICIALS The first part of the FCPA applies to all U.S. companies and their directors, officers, shareholders, employees, and agents. This part prohibits the bribery of most officials of foreign governments if the purpose of the payment is to motivate the official to act in his or her official capacity to provide business opportunities.

The FCPA does not prohibit payment of substantial sums to minor officials whose duties are ministerial. A ministerial action is a routine activity such as the processing of paperwork with little or no discretion involved in the action. These payments are often referred to as "grease," or facilitating payments. They are meant to accelerate the performance of administrative services that might otherwise be carried out at a slow pace. Thus, for instance, if a firm makes a payment to a minor official to speed up an import licensing process, the firm has not violated the FCPA.

---

3. 15 U.S.C. Sections 78dd-1 *et seq.*

INSIGHT INTO THE GLOBAL ENVIRONMENT
Bribery and the Foreign Corrupt Practices Act

Many countries have followed in the footsteps of the United States by passing their own anticorruption laws, some of which are similar to our Foreign Corrupt Practices Act. Nevertheless, some countries are still not diligent in weeding out corruption—of government officials, for instance.

Mexico Faces a Corruption Issue

Recently, Mexico passed an anticorruption law that prevents hospital administrators from approving contracts. Medical device supplier Orthofix International NV, based in Texas, faced a problem after passage of the new law. It wanted to continue providing bone-repair products to Mexico. It therefore bribed regional government officials instead of hospital administrators. Over several years, Orthofix paid more than $300,000 in bribes to Mexican officials to retain government health-care contracts. Employees at Orthofix called these bribes "chocolates." The contracts generated almost $8.7 million in revenues for the company.

The Bribing Process

Before the anticorruption law was enacted, Orthofix's Mexican subsidiary, Promeca, regularly offered cash and gifts, such as vacation packages, televisions, and laptops, to hospital employees in order to secure sales contracts. These employees then submitted falsified receipts for imaginary expenses such as meals and new car tires. When the bribes became too large to hide in this manner, Promeca's employees falsely attributed the payments to promotional and training expenses. After the new law was passed, Mexico formed a special national committee to approve medical contracts. Promeca employees then sim-ply bribed committee members to ensure that the company was awarded the contracts.

No Compliance Policy or Training to Prevent Violations

As it turned out, Orthofix did not provide any training in how to prevent violations of the Foreign Corrupt Practices Act or have a compliance policy in place in Mexico. Orthofix did create a code of ethics and antibribery training materials, but they were only distributed in English. When Orthofix managers found out about Promeca's overbudget expenses, they questioned the amounts, but initially took no further steps.

The U.S. Government Investigates

Sometime after Orthofix learned of the payments, it self-reported them to the U.S. Securities and Exchange Commission (SEC). After negotiations with the SEC, Orthofix agreed to terminate the Promeca executives who had engaged in the bribery and to end Promeca's operations. Orthofix required mandatory training for all employees and strengthened its auditing of company payments. In addition, the company paid more than $7 million in penalties.

LEGAL CRITICAL THINKING
INSIGHT INTO THE LEGAL ENVIRONMENT

Because managers are potentially responsible for all actions of their foreign subsidiaries whether or not they knew of the illegal conduct, what actions should Orthofix's upper management have taken before this corruption scandal came to light?

Generally, the act, as amended, permits payments to foreign officials if such payments are lawful within the foreign country. Payments to private foreign companies or other third parties are permissible—unless the U.S. firm knows that the payments will be passed on to a foreign government in violation of the FCPA. The U.S. Department of Justice also uses the FCPA to prosecute foreign companies suspected of bribing officials outside the United States.

ACCOUNTING REQUIREMENTS To prevent bribes from being concealed in the corporate financial records, the second part of the FCPA is directed toward accountants. All companies must keep detailed records that "accurately and fairly" reflect their financial activities. Their accounting systems must provide "reasonable assurance" that all transactions entered into by the companies are accounted for and legal. These requirements assist in detecting illegal bribes. The FCPA prohibits any person from making false statements to accountants or false entries in any record or account.

PENALTIES FOR VIOLATIONS The FCPA provides that business firms that violate the act may be fined up to $2 million. Individual officers or directors who violate the FCPA may be fined up to $100,000 (the fine cannot be paid by the company) and may be imprisoned for up to five years.

Reviewing: Business Ethics

James Stilton is the chief executive officer (CEO) of RightLiving, Inc., a company that buys life insurance policies at a discount from terminally ill persons and sells the policies to investors. RightLiving pays the terminally ill patients a percentage of the future death benefit (usually 65 percent) and then sells the policies to investors for 85 percent of the value of the future benefit. The patients receive the cash to use for medical and other expenses, the investors are "guaranteed" a positive return on their investment, and RightLiving profits on the difference between the purchase and sale prices. Stilton is aware that some sick patients might obtain insurance policies through fraud (by not revealing the illness on the insurance application). Insurance companies that discover this will cancel the policy and refuse to pay. Stilton believes that most of the policies he has purchased are legitimate, but he knows that some probably are not. Using the information presented in this chapter, answer the following questions.

1. Would a person who adheres to the principle of rights consider it ethical for Stilton not to disclose the potential risk of cancellation to investors? Why or why not?
2. Using Immanuel Kant's categorical imperative, are the actions of RightLiving, Inc. ethical? Why or why not?
3. Under utilitarianism, are Stilton's actions ethical? Why or why not? What difference does it make if most of the policies are legitimate and will be paid rather than being fraudulently procured and void?
4. Using the Business Process Pragmatism™ steps discussed in this chapter, discuss the decision process Stilton should use in deciding whether to disclose the risk of fraudulent policies to potential investors.

DEBATE THIS . . . *Executives in large corporations are ultimately rewarded if their companies do well, particularly as evidenced by rising stock prices. Consequently, should we let those who run corporations decide what level of negative side effects of their goods or services is "acceptable"?*

Terms and Concepts

business ethics 158
categorical imperative 165
corporate social
responsibility (CSR) 166
cost-benefit analysis 166

duty-based ethics 164
ethical reasoning 164
ethics 158
moral minimum 160
outcome-based ethics 164

principle of rights 165
stakeholders 167
triple bottom line 159
utilitarianism 165

ExamPrep

Issue Spotters

1. News, Inc., is always looking for ways to increase the number of its viewers. Recently, it was the first network to interview surviving witnesses on location after a tragic school shooting. Are there ethical concerns about putting traumatized children on the news immediately after an event like this? Why or why not? **(See pages 164–166.)**
2. Johnny Sport is a world-famous athlete. He is careful to avoid using any performance-enhancing drugs that

are banned by his sport's oversight organization. Is it ethical for Johnny to take a performance-enhancing drug that has not been banned? Why or why not? **(See pages 160–162.)**

• **Check your answers to the Issue Spotters against the answers provided in Appendix B at the end of this text.**

Before the Test

Go to **www.cengagebrain.com**, enter the ISBN 9781285770192, and click on "Find" to locate this textbook's Web site. Then, click on "Access Now" under "Study Tools," and select Chapter 8 at the top. There, you will find a Practice Quiz that you can take to assess your

mastery of the concepts in this chapter, as well as Flash-cards and a Glossary of important terms.

Business Scenarios

8–1. Business Ethics. Jason Trevor owns a commercial bakery in Blakely, Georgia, that produces a variety of goods sold in grocery stores. Trevor is required by law to perform internal tests on food produced at his plant to check for contamination. On three occasions, the tests of food products containing peanut butter were positive for salmonella contamination. Trevor was not required to report the results to U.S. Food and Drug Administration officials, however, so he did not. Instead, Trevor instructed his employees to simply repeat the tests until the results were negative. Meanwhile, the products that had originally tested positive for salmonella were eventually shipped out to retailers. Five people who ate Trevor's baked goods that year became seriously ill, and one person died from a salmonella infection. Even though Trevor's conduct was legal, was it unethical for him to sell goods that had once tested positive for salmonella? Why or why not? **(See page 167.)**

8–2. Ethical Conduct. Internet giant Zoidle, a U.S. company, generated sales of £2.5 billion in the United Kingdom in 2013 (approximately $4 billion in U.S. dollars). Its net

profits before taxes on these sales were £200 million, and it paid £6 million in corporate tax, resulting in a tax rate of 3 percent. The corporate tax rate in the United Kingdom is between 20 percent and 24 percent.

The CEO of Zoidle held a press conference stating that he was proud of his company for taking advantage of tax loopholes and for sheltering profits in other nations to avoid paying taxes. He called this practice "capitalism at its finest." He further stated that it would be unethical for Zoidle not to take advantage of loopholes and that it would be borderline illegal to tell shareholders that the company paid more taxes than it had to pay because it felt that it should. Zoidle receives significant benefits for doing business in the United Kingdom, including tremendous sales tax exemptions and some property tax breaks. The United Kingdom relies on the corporate income tax to provide services to the poor and to help run the agency that regulates corporations. Is it ethical for Zoidle to avoid paying taxes? Why or why not? **(See page 167.)**

Business Case Problems

8–3. Spotlight on Pfizer, Inc.—Corporate Social Responsibility. Methamphetamine (meth) is an addictive drug made chiefly in small toxic labs (STLs) in homes, tents, barns, or hotel rooms. The manufacturing process is dangerous and often results in explosions, burns, and toxic fumes. Government entities spend time and resources to find and destroy STLs, imprison meth dealers and users, treat addicts, and provide services for affected families. Meth cannot be made without ingredients that are also used in cold and allergy medications. Arkansas has one of the highest numbers of STLs in the United States. To recoup the costs of fighting the meth epidemic, twenty counties in Arkansas filed a suit against Pfizer, Inc., which makes cold and allergy medications. What is Pfizer's ethical responsibility here, and to whom is it owed? Why? [*Ashley County, Arkansas v. Pfizer, Inc.,* 552 F.3d. 659 (8th Cir. 2009)] **(See page 166.)**

8–4. Ethical Leadership. David Krasner, who worked for HSH Nordbank AG, complained that his supervisor, Roland Kiser, fostered an atmosphere of sexism that was demeaning to women. Among other things, Krasner

claimed that career advancement was based on "sexual favoritism." He objected to Kiser's relationship with a female employee, Melissa Campfield, who was promoted before more qualified employees, including Krasner. How do a manager's attitudes and actions affect the workplace? [*Krasner v. HSH Nordbank AG,* 680 F.Supp.2d 502 (S.D.N.Y. 2010)] **(See page 168.)**

8–5. BUSINESS CASE PROBLEM WITH SAMPLE ANSWER: Online Privacy.

Facebook, Inc., launched a program called "Beacon" that automatically updated the profiles of users on Facebook's social networking site when those users had any activity on Beacon "partner" sites. For example, one partner site was Blockbuster.com. When a user rented or purchased a movie through Blockbuster.com, the user's Facebook profile would be updated to share the purchase. The Beacon program was set up as a default setting, so users never consented to the program, but they could opt out. What are the ethical implications of an opt-in program versus an opt-out program in social media? [Lane v. Facebook, Inc., 696 F.3d 811 (9th Cir. 2011)] **(See page 163.)**

• For a sample answer to Problem 8–5, go to Appendix C at the end of this text.

8–6. Business Ethics on a Global Scale. After the fall of the Soviet Union, the new government of Azerbaijan began converting certain state-controlled industries to private ownership. Ownership in these companies could be purchased through a voucher program. Frederic Bourke, Jr., and Viktor Kozeny wanted to purchase the Azerbaijani oil company, SOCAR, but it was unclear whether the Azerbaijani president would allow SOCAR to be put up for sale. Kozeny met with one of the vice presidents of SOCAR (who was also the son of the president of Azerbaijan) and other Azerbaijani leaders to discuss the sale of SOCAR. To obtain their cooperation, Kozeny set up a series of parent and subsidiary companies through which the Azerbaijani leaders would eventually receive two-thirds of the SOCAR profits without ever investing any of their own funds. In return, the Azerbaijani leaders would attempt to use their influence to convince the president to put SOCAR up for sale. Assume that Bourke and Kozeny are operating out of a U.S. company. Discuss the ethics of this scheme, both in terms of the Foreign Corrupt Practices Act (FCPA) and as a general ethical issue. What duties did Kozeny have under the FCPA? [*United States v. Kozeny,* 667 F.3d 122 (2d Cir. 2011)] **(See page 170.)**

8–7. Business Ethics. Mark Ramun worked as a manager for Allied Erecting and Dismantling Co., where he had a tense relationship with his father, who was Allied's president. After more than ten years, Mark left Allied, taking 15,000 pages of Allied's documents on DVDs and CDs, which constituted trade secrets. Later, he joined Allied's competitor, Genesis Equipment & Manufacturing, Inc. Genesis soon developed a piece of equipment that incorporated elements of Allied equipment. How might business ethics have been violated in these circumstances? Discuss. [*Allied Erecting and Dismantling Co. v. Genesis Equipment & Manufacturing, Inc.,* 2013 WL 85907 (6th Cir. 2013)] **(See page 167.)**

8–8. A QUESTION OF ETHICS: Consumer Rights.

Best Buy, a national electronics retailer, offered a credit card that allowed users to earn "reward points" that could be redeemed for discounts on Best Buy goods. After reading a newspaper advertisement for the card, Gary Davis applied for, and was given, a credit card. As part of the application process, he visited a Web page containing Frequently Asked Questions as well as terms and conditions for the card. He clicked on a button affirming that he understood the terms and conditions. When Davis received his card, it came with seven brochures about the card and the reward point program. As he read the brochures, he discovered that a $59 annual fee would be charged for the card. Davis went back to the Web pages he had visited and found a statement that the card "may" have an annual fee. Davis sued, claiming that the company did not adequately disclose the fee. [Davis v. HSBC Bank Nevada, N.A., 691 F.3d 1152 (9th Cir. 2012)] **(See pages 164–166.)**

(a) Online applications frequently have click-on buttons or check boxes for consumers to acknowledge that they have read and understand the terms and conditions of applications or purchases. Often, the terms and conditions are so long that they cannot all be seen on one screen and users must scroll to view the entire document. Is it unethical for companies to put terms and conditions, especially terms that may cost the consumer, in an electronic document that is too long to read on one screen? Why or why not? Does this differ from having a consumer sign a hard-copy document with terms and conditions printed on it? Why or why not?

(b) The Truth-in-Lending Act requires that credit terms be clearly and conspicuously disclosed in application materials. Assuming that the Best Buy credit-card materials had sufficient legal disclosures, discuss the ethical aspects of businesses strictly following the language of the law as compared to following the intent of the law.

Legal Reasoning Group Activity

8–9. Global Business Ethics. Pfizer, Inc., developed a new antibiotic called Trovan (trovafloxacinmesylate). Tests showed that in animals Trovan had life-threatening side effects, including joint disease, abnormal cartilage growth, liver damage, and a degenerative bone condition. Several years later, an epidemic of bacterial meningitis swept across Nigeria. Pfizer sent three U.S. physicians to test Trovan on children who were patients in Nigeria's Infectious Disease Hospital. Pfizer did not obtain the patients' consent, alert them to the risks, or tell them that Médecins Sans Frontières (Doctors without Borders) was providing an effective conventional treatment at the same site. Eleven children died in the experiment, and others were left blind, deaf, paralyzed, or brain damaged. Rabi Abdullahi and other Nigerian children filed a suit in a U.S. federal court against Pfizer, alleging a violation of a customary international law norm prohibiting involuntary medical experimentation on humans. **(See page 170.)**

(a) One group should use the principles of ethical reasoning discussed in this chapter to develop three arguments that Pfizer's conduct was a violation of ethical standards.

(b) A second group should take a pro-Pfizer position and argue that the company did not violate any ethical standards (and counter the first group).

(c) A third group should come up with proposals for what Pfizer might have done differently to avert the consequences.

Unit Two

Contracts

Contents

CHAPTER 9

NATURE AND TERMINOLOGY

The noted legal scholar Roscoe Pound once said that "[t]he social order rests upon the stability and predictability of conduct, of which keeping promises is a large item."[1] Contract law deals with, among other things, the formation and keeping of promises. A **promise** is a declaration by a person (the *promisor*) to do or not to do a certain act. As a result, the person to whom the promise is made (the *promisee*) has a right to expect or demand that something either will or will not happen in the future.

Like other types of law, contract law reflects our social values, interests, and expectations at a given point in time. It shows, for instance, to what extent our society allows people to make promises or commitments that are legally binding. It distinguishes between promises that create only *moral* obligations (such as a promise to take a friend to lunch) and promises that are legally binding (such as a promise to pay for merchandise purchased).

Contract law also demonstrates which excuses our society accepts for breaking certain types of promises. In addition, it indicates which promises are considered to be contrary to public policy—against the interests of society as a whole—and therefore legally invalid. When the person making a promise is a child or is mentally incompetent, for example, a question will arise as to whether the promise should be enforced. Resolving such questions is the essence of contract law.

1. Roscoe Pound, *Jurisprudence*, Vol. 3 (St. Paul, Minn.: West Publishing Co., 1959), p. 162.

SECTION 1
AN OVERVIEW OF CONTRACT LAW

Before we look at the numerous rules that courts use to determine whether a particular promise will be enforced, it is necessary to understand some fundamental concepts of contract law. In this section, we describe the sources and general function of contract law and introduce the objective theory of contracts.

Sources of Contract Law

The common law governs all contracts except when it has been modified or replaced by statutory law, such as the Uniform Commercial Code (UCC),[2] or by administrative agency regulations. Contracts relating to services, real estate, employment, and insurance, for instance, generally are governed by the common law of contracts.

Contracts for the sale and lease of goods, however, are governed by the UCC—to the extent that the UCC has modified general contract law. The relationship between general contract law and the law governing sales and leases of goods will be explored in detail in Chapter 15. In the discussion of general contract law that follows, we indicate in footnotes the areas in which the UCC has significantly altered common law contract principles.

The Function of Contract Law

No aspect of modern life is entirely free of contractual relationships. You acquire rights and obligations, for example, when you borrow funds, buy or lease a house, obtain insurance, and purchase goods or services. Contract law is designed to provide stability and predictability, as well as certainty, for both buyers and sellers in the marketplace.

2. See Chapters 1 and 15 for further discussions of the significance and coverage of the UCC. Article 2 of the UCC is presented in Appendix A at the end of this book.

Contract law assures the parties to private agreements that the promises they make will be enforceable. Clearly, many promises are kept because the parties involved feel a moral obligation to keep them or because keeping a promise is in their mutual self-interest. The **promisor** (the person making the promise) and the **promisee** (the person to whom the promise is made) may also decide to honor their agreement for other reasons. In business agreements, the rules of contract law are often followed to avoid potential disputes.

By supplying procedures for enforcing private contractual agreements, contract law provides an essential condition for the existence of a market economy. Without a legal framework of reasonably assured expectations within which to make long-run plans, businesspersons would be able to rely only on the good faith of others. Duty and good faith are usually sufficient to obtain compliance with a promise. When price changes or adverse economic factors make compliance costly, however, these elements may not be enough. Contract law is necessary to ensure compliance with a promise or to entitle the innocent party to some form of relief.

The Definition of a Contract

A **contract** is "a promise or a set of promises for the breach of which the law gives a remedy, or the performance of which the law in some way recognizes as a duty."[3] Put simply, a contract is an agreement that can be enforced in court. It is formed by two or more parties who agree to perform or to refrain from performing some act now or in the future.

Generally, contract disputes arise when there is a promise of future performance. If the contractual promise is not fulfilled, the party who made it is subject to the sanctions of a court (see Chapter 14). That party may be required to pay damages for failing to perform the contractual promise. In a few instances, the party may be required to perform the promised act.

---

3. *Restatement (Second) of Contracts,* Section 1. As mentioned in Chapter 1, *Restatements of the Law* are scholarly books that restate the existing common law principles distilled from court opinions as a set of rules on a particular topic. Courts often refer to the *Restatements* for guidance. The *Restatement of the Law of Contracts* was compiled by the American Law Institute in 1932. The *Restatement,* which is now in its second edition (a third edition is being drafted), will be referred to throughout the following chapters on contract law.

The Objective Theory of Contracts

In determining whether a contract has been formed, the element of intent is of prime importance. In contract law, intent is determined by what is called the **objective theory of contracts,** not by the personal or subjective intent, or belief, of a party. (We will also look at the objective theory of contracts in Chapter 10, in the context of contract formation.)

FACTS AS INTERPRETED BY A REASONABLE PERSON
The theory is that a party's intention to enter into a legally binding agreement, or contract, is judged by outward, objective facts. The facts are as interpreted by a *reasonable* person, rather than by the party's own secret, subjective intentions. Objective facts may include:

1. What the party said when entering into the contract.
2. How the party acted or appeared (intent may be manifested by conduct as well as by oral or written words).
3. The circumstances surrounding the transaction.

▶ **Case in Point 9.1** Linear Technology Corporation (LTC) makes and sells integrated circuits for use in cell phones and computers. LTC sued its competitor, Micrel, Inc., for infringement of a patent on a particular chip. In its defense, Micrel claimed that LTC's patent was invalid because LTC had offered to sell the chip commercially before the date on which it could be legally sold. The issue was whether LTC had entered into sales contracts when it solicited input on pricing and accepted distributors' purchase orders using a "will advise" procedure before the critical date. The court ruled that under the objective theory of contracts, no reasonable customer could interpret LTC's requests for information about pricing and potential orders as an offer that could bind LTC to a sale. Therefore, LTC did not violate the ban on sales and could continue its suit against Micrel for patent infringement.[4] ◀

UNDERLYING MOTIVE NOT IMPORTANT A party may have many reasons for entering into an agreement—obtaining real property, goods, or services, for example, and profiting from the deal. Any of these purposes may provide a motivation for performing the contract. In the following case, however, one party failed to perform and claimed that he had not intended to enter into the contract when he signed it.

---

4. *Linear Technology Corp. v. Micrel, Inc.,* 275 F.3d 1040 (Fed.Cir. 2001).

CASE ANALYSIS

Case 9.1 Pan Handle Realty, LLC v. Olins

Appellate Court of Connecticut, 140 Conn.App. 556, 59 A.3d 842 (2013).

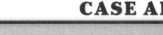

IN THE LANGUAGE OF THE COURT
SHELDON, J. [Judge]

* * * *

* * * The plaintiff is a Connecticut limited liability company [a form of business organization] * * * , which constructed a luxury home at 4 Pan Handle Lane in Westport [Connecticut] (the property). * * * The defendant [Robert Olins] expressed an interest in leasing the property from the plaintiff for a period of one year. In pursuit of that interest, he submitted an application proposing to rent the property from the plaintiff at the rate of $12,000 per month, together with an accompanying financial statement. The plaintiff responded to the defendant's proposal by preparing a draft lease for his review, which the defendant promptly forwarded to his attorney.

On January 17, 2009, the defendant and his real estate agent, Laura Sydney, met with Irwin Stillman, then acting as the plaintiff's representative, to discuss the draft lease (January 17 meeting). At that meeting, the defendant and Irwin Stillman agreed to several revisions to the draft lease that had been proposed by the defendant's attorney, then incorporated the revisions into the lease and signed it. The resulting lease, which was dated January 19, 2009, specified a lump sum annual rent of $138,000. At the time of the signing, the defendant gave the plaintiff a postdated check for $138,000 * * * . The lease agreement required the plaintiff to make certain modifications to the property prior to the occupancy date, including the removal of all of the furnishings from the leased premises.

On January 21, 2009, the plaintiff's real estate broker informed it that, according to Sydney, the defendant planned to move into the property

on January 28, 2009. The next day, the defendant requested information from the plaintiff for his renter's insurance policy, which the plaintiff duly provided. By that time, the plaintiff had also completed the modifications requested by the defendant at the January 17 meeting and agreed to in the lease agreement, including the removal of the furniture. The defendant's check, which was postdated January 26, 2009, was deposited by the plaintiff on that date.

The following day, however, Citibank advised the plaintiff that the defendant had issued a stop payment order on his postdated rental check and explained that the check would not be honored. The plaintiff subsequently received a letter from the defendant's attorney stating that "[the defendant] is unable to pursue any further interest in the property." Thereafter, the plaintiff made substantial efforts to secure a new tenant for the property, listing the property with a real estate broker, advertising its availability and expending $80,000 to restage it. Although, by these efforts, the plaintiff generated several offers to lease the property, it was never able to find a qualified tenant, or, for that reason, to enter into an acceptable lease agreement with anyone for all or any part of the one year period of the defendant's January 19, 2009 lease.

Thereafter, on March 6, 2009, the plaintiff filed this action [in a Connecticut state court], alleging that the defendant had breached an enforceable lease agreement. The plaintiff further alleged that, despite its efforts to mitigate [lessen] its damages, it had sustained damages as a result of the defendant's breach, including unpaid rental payments it was to have received under the lease, brokerage commissions it incurred to rent the

property again and the cost of modifications to the property that were completed at the defendant's request.

* * * The court issued a memorandum of decision resolving the merits of the case in favor of the plaintiff (May 11 decision). In that decision, the court found, more particularly, that the plaintiff had met its burden of proving that the parties had entered into an enforceable lease agreement, that the defendant had breached that agreement, and that the breach had caused the plaintiff damages in lost rent and utility bills incurred during the lease period * * * . On the basis of these findings, the court awarded the plaintiff compensatory damages in the amount of $146,000—$138,000 in unpaid rent for the term of the lease and $8,000 in utility fees incurred by the plaintiff during the lease period—plus interest, and attorney's fees.

* * * This appeal followed.
* * * *

The defendant's * * * claim on appeal is that the court improperly determined that the parties entered into a valid lease agreement. The defendant contends that because "material terms were still being negotiated and various issues were unresolved," there was no meeting of the minds, which is required to form a contract.
* * * *

In order for an enforceable contract to exist, the court must find that the parties' minds had truly met. * * * *If there has been a misunderstanding between the parties, or a misapprehension by one or both so that their minds have never met, no contract has been entered into by them and the court will not make for them a contract which they themselves did not make.* [Emphasis added.]

There was evidence in the record to support the court's finding that the parties entered into a valid lease agreement because there was a true meeting of the parties' minds as to the essential terms of the agreement. Prior to the January 17 meeting, the plaintiff had provided the defendant with a draft lease agreement, which the defendant had forwarded to his attorney for review. The defendant testified that at the January 17 meeting, he and the plaintiff's representative discussed the revisions proposed by the defendant's attorney, made the revisions and signed the lease. It was then that the defendant tendered a check, post-dated to the start of the lease period, on which he noted payment for a one-year lease of the premises.

There is no evidence in the record to support the defendant's conten-

tion that he did not intend to be bound by the lease when he signed it or that terms of the lease were still being negotiated at that time. Pursuant to the lease, the plaintiff was obligated to make modifications to the premises and the defendant was required to tender a security deposit [and] procure renter's insurance * * * . The defendant's apparent unilateral change of heart regarding the lease agreement does not negate the parties' prior meeting of the minds that occurred at the time the lease was executed. There is ample evidence in the record evincing [showing] the intent of the parties to be bound by the lease when they signed it and, thus, to support the court's find-

ing that "the lease agreement was a valid and binding contract which the defendant * * * has breached."

* * * *

* * * As in any other contract action the measure of damages is that the award should place the injured party in the same position as he would have been in had the contract been fully performed. * * * As a consequence, the unpaid rent * * * may be used by the court in computing the losses suffered by the plaintiff by reason of the defendant's breach of contract of lease.

* * * *

The judgment is affirmed.

LEGAL REASONING QUESTIONS

1. What is the objective theory of contracts?

2. How did the objective theory of contracts affect the result in this case? Explain.

3. The defendant never moved into the house. Why then did the court find that he breached the lease?

4. On finding that the defendant breached the lease, what did the court impose as a sanction? How was this determined?

SECTION 2

ELEMENTS OF A CONTRACT

The many topics that will be discussed in the following chapters on contract law require an understanding of the basic elements of a valid contract and the way in which a contract is created. It is also necessary to understand the types of circumstances in which even legally valid contracts will not be enforced.

Requirements of a Valid Contract

The following list briefly describes the four requirements that must be met before a valid contract exists. If any of these elements is lacking, no contract will have been formed. (Each requirement will be explained more fully in subsequent chapters.)

1. *Agreement.* An agreement to form a contract includes an *offer* and an *acceptance*. One party

must offer to enter into a legal agreement, and another party must accept the terms of the offer.

2. *Consideration.* Any promises made by the parties to the contract must be supported by legally sufficient and bargained-for *consideration* (something of value received or promised, such as money, to convince a person to make a deal).

3. *Contractual capacity.* Both parties entering into the contract must have the contractual *capacity* to do so. The law must recognize them as possessing characteristics that qualify them as competent parties.

4. *Legality.* The contract's purpose must be to accomplish some goal that is legal and not against public policy.

Defenses to the Enforceability of a Contract

Even if all of the requirements listed above are satisfied, a contract may be unenforceable if certain requirements are not met. As you will read in

Chapter 12, the following requirements typically are raised as *defenses* to the enforceability of an otherwise valid contract:

1. *Voluntary consent.* The consent of both parties must be voluntary. For instance, if a contract was formed as a result of fraud, undue influence, mistake, or duress, the contract may not be enforceable.
2. *Form.* The contract must be in whatever form the law requires. Some contracts must be in writing to be enforceable.

SECTION 3
TYPES OF CONTRACTS

There are many types of contracts. They are categorized based on legal distinctions as to their formation, performance, and enforceability.

Contract Formation

Contracts can be classified according to how and when they are formed. Exhibit 9–1 below shows three such classifications, and the following subsections explain them in greater detail.

BILATERAL VERSUS UNILATERAL CONTRACTS Every contract involves at least two parties. The **offeror** is the party making the offer. The **offeree** is the party to whom the offer is made. Whether the contract is classified as *bilateral* or *unilateral* depends on what the offeree must do to accept the offer and bind the offeror to a contract.

Bilateral Contracts. If the offeree can accept simply by promising to perform, the contract is a **bilateral contract.** Hence, a bilateral contract is a "promise for a promise." No performance, such as payment of funds or delivery of goods, need take place for a bilateral contract to be formed. The contract comes into existence at the moment the promises are exchanged.

▶ **Example 9.2** Javier offers to buy Ann's smartphone for $200. Javier tells Ann that he will give her the $200 for the smartphone next Friday, when he gets paid. Ann accepts Javier's offer and promises to give him the smartphone when he pays her on Friday. Javier and Ann have formed a bilateral contract. ◀

Unilateral Contracts. If the offer is phrased so that the offeree can accept the offer only by completing the contract performance, the contract is a **unilateral contract.** Hence, a unilateral contract is a "promise for an act."[5] In other words, a unilateral contract is formed not at the moment when promises are exchanged but at the moment when the contract is *performed.* ▶ **Example 9.3** Reese says to Celia, "If you drive my car from New York to Los Angeles, I'll give you $1,000." Only on Celia's completion of the act—bringing the car to Los Angeles—does she fully accept Reese's offer to pay $1,000. If she chooses not to accept the offer to drive the car to Los Angeles, there are no legal consequences. ◀

Contests, lotteries, and other competitions involving prizes are examples of offers to form unilateral

---

5. The phrase *unilateral contract,* if read literally, is a contradiction in terms. A contract cannot be one sided because, by definition, an agreement implies the existence of two or more parties.

EXHIBIT 9–1 Classifications Based on Contract Formation

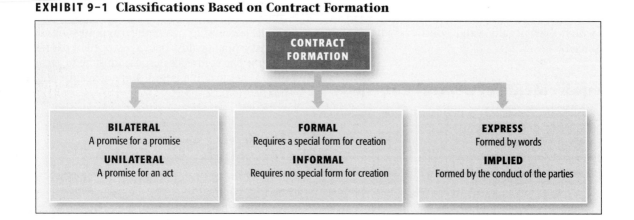

CONTRACT FORMATION		
BILATERAL A promise for a promise	**FORMAL** Requires a special form for creation	**EXPRESS** Formed by words
UNILATERAL A promise for an act	**INFORMAL** Requires no special form for creation	**IMPLIED** Formed by the conduct of the parties

contracts. If a person complies with the rules of the contest—such as by submitting the right lottery number at the right place and time—a unilateral contract is formed. The organization offering the prize is then bound to a contract to perform as promised in the offer. If the person fails to comply with the contest rules, however, no binding contract is formed. (See this chapter's *Insight into Ethics* feature below for a discussion of whether a company can change a contest prize from what it originally advertised.)

Revocation of Offers for Unilateral Contracts. A problem arises in unilateral contracts when the promisor attempts to *revoke* (cancel) the offer after the promisee has begun performance but before the act has been completed. ▶ **Example 9.4**   Seiko offers to buy Jin's sailboat, moored in San Francisco, on delivery of the boat to Seiko's dock in Newport Beach, three hundred miles south of San Francisco. Jin rigs the boat and sets sail. Shortly before his arrival at Newport Beach, Jin receives a message from Seiko withdrawing her offer. Seiko's offer was for a unilateral contract, which could be accepted only by Jin's delivery of the sailboat at her dock. ◀

In contract law, offers are normally *revocable* (capable of being taken back, or canceled) until accepted. Under the traditional view of unilateral contracts, Seiko's revocation would terminate the offer. Because of the harsh effect on the offeree of the revocation of an offer to form a unilateral contract, the modern-day view is different. Today, once performance has been *substantially* undertaken, the offeror cannot revoke the offer. Thus, in *Example 9.4*, even though Jin has not yet accepted the offer by complete performance, Seiko is normally prohibited from revoking it. Jin can deliver the boat and bind Seiko to the contract.

FORMAL VERSUS INFORMAL CONTRACTS Another classification system divides contracts into formal contracts and informal contracts. **Formal contracts** are contracts that require a special form or method of creation (formation) to be enforceable.[6] One example is *negotiable instruments*, which include checks, drafts,

---

6. See *Restatement (Second) of Contracts,* Section 6, which explains that formal contracts include (1) contracts under seal, (2) recognizances, (3) negotiable instruments, and (4) letters of credit.

INSIGHT INTO ETHICS
Can a Company That Sponsors a Contest Change the Prize from What It Originally Offered?

Courts have historically treated contests as unilateral contracts, which typically cannot be modified by the offeror after the offeree has begun to perform. But this principle may not always apply to contest terms or advertisements.

John Rogalski entered a poker tournament conducted by Little Poker League, LLC (LPL).The tournament lasted several months as players competed for spots in a winner-take-all final event. During the final event, Rogalski and the other contestants signed a "World Series of Poker (WSOP) Agreement," which stated that LPL would pay the $10,000 WSOP entry fee on the winner's behalf and provide $2,500 for travel-related expenses. The agreement also stated that if the winner did not attend the WSOP, he or she would relinquish the WSOP seat and return the expense money to LPL.

Rogalski won and took the $2,500 for travel expenses, but did not attend the WSOP. He then filed a suit for $10,000 against LPL, arguing that it had advertised that the winner could choose to receive the cash value of the prizes ($12,500) instead of going to the WSOP. Rogalski

claimed that, by participating in the tournament, he had accepted the advertised offer to take the cash in lieu of entering the WSOP. He further claimed that the later agreement was an invalid contract modification. LPL filed a counterclaim to recover the $2,500 in expenses. The court ruled in favor of LPL, finding that the contract was not formed when Rogalski began participating in the contest. Rather, it was formed when he signed the WSOP agreement. Under the contest rules as stated in the WSOP agreement, Rogalski had to return the $2,500 of expenses to LPL.[a]

LEGAL CRITICAL THINKING
INSIGHT INTO THE SOCIAL ENVIRONMENT

Why would a company that changes its advertised prizes have to worry about its reputation?

---

a. *Rogalski v. Little Poker League, LLC,* 2011 WL 589636 (Minn.App. 2011).

promissory notes, bills of exchange, and certificates of deposit. Negotiable instruments are formal contracts because, under the Uniform Commercial Code (UCC), a special form and language are required to create them.

Letters of credit, which are frequently used in international sales contracts, are another type of formal contract. Letters of credit are agreements to pay contingent on the purchaser's receipt of invoices and *bills of lading* (documents evidencing receipt of, and title to, goods shipped).

Informal contracts (also called *simple contracts*) include all other contracts. No special form is required (except for certain types of contracts that must be in writing), as the contracts are usually based on their substance rather than their form. Typically, businesspersons put their contracts in writing to ensure that there is some proof of a contract's existence should disputes arise.

EXPRESS VERSUS IMPLIED CONTRACTS Contracts may also be categorized as *express* or *implied.* In an **express contract,** the terms of the agreement are fully and explicitly stated in words, oral or written. A signed lease for an apartment or a house is an express written contract. If one classmate calls another on the phone and agrees to buy her textbooks from last semester for $300, an express oral contract has been made.

A contract that is implied from the conduct of the parties is called an **implied contract** (or sometimes an *implied-in-fact contract*). This type of contract differs from an express contract in that the conduct of the parties, rather than their words, creates and defines the terms of the contract.

Requirements for Implied Contracts. For an implied contract to arise, certain requirements must be met. Normally, if the following conditions exist, a court will hold that an implied contract was formed:

1. The plaintiff furnished some service or property.
2. The plaintiff expected to be paid for that service or property, and the defendant knew or should have known that payment was expected.
3. The defendant had a chance to reject the services or property and did not.

▶ **Example 9.5** Oleg, a small-business owner, needs an accountant to complete his tax return. He drops by a local accountant's office, explains his situation to the accountant, and learns what fees she charges. The next day, he returns and gives the receptionist all of the necessary documents to com-plete his return. Then he walks out without saying anything further to the accountant. In this situation, Oleg has entered into an implied contract to pay the accountant the usual fees for her services. The contract is implied because of Oleg's conduct and hers. She expects to be paid for completing the tax return, and by bringing in the records she will need to do the job, Oleg has implied an intent to pay her. ◀

Contracts with Express and Implied Terms. Note that a contract may be a mixture of an express contract and an implied contract. In other words, a contract may contain some express terms, while others are implied. During the constructions of a home, for instance, the homeowner often asks the builder to make changes in the original specifications.

▶ **Case in Point 9.6** Lamar Hopkins hired Uhrhahn Construction & Design, Inc., for several projects in building his home. For each project, the parties signed a written contract that was based on a cost estimate and specifications and that required changes to the agreement to be in writing. While the work was in progress, however, Hopkins repeatedly asked Uhrhahn to deviate from the contract specifications, which Uhrhahn did. None of these requests was made in writing.

One day, Hopkins asked Uhrhahn to use Durisol blocks instead of the cinder blocks specified in the original contract, indicating that the cost would be the same. Uhrhahn used the Durisol blocks but demanded extra payment when it became clear that the Durisol blocks were more complicated to install. Although Hopkins had paid for the other deviations from the contract that he had orally requested, he refused to pay Uhrhahn for the substitution of the Durisol blocks. Uhrhahn sued for breach of contract. The court found that Hopkins, through his conduct, had waived the provision requiring written contract modification and created an implied contract to pay the extra cost of installing the Durisol blocks.[7] ◀

Contract Performance

Contracts are also classified according to the degree to which they have been performed. A contract that has been fully performed on both sides is called an **executed contract.** A contract that has not been fully performed by the parties is called an **executory contract.** If one party has fully performed but the

---

7. *Uhrhahn Construction & Design, Inc. v. Hopkins,* 179 P.3d 808 (Utah App. 2008).

other has not, the contract is said to be executed on the one side and executory on the other, but the contract is still classified as executory.

▶ **Example 9.7** Jackson, Inc., agreed to buy ten tons of coal from the Northern Coal Company. Northern delivered the coal to Jackson's steel mill, where it is being burned. At this point, the contract is executed on the part of Northern and executory on Jackson's part. After Jackson pays Northern, the contract will be executed on both sides. ◀

Contract Enforceability

A **valid contract** has the elements necessary to entitle at least one of the parties to enforce it in court. Those elements, as mentioned earlier, consist of (1) an agreement (offer and acceptance) (2) supported by legally sufficient consideration (3) made by parties who have the legal capacity to enter into the contract, and (4) a legal purpose.

As you can see in Exhibit 9–2 below, valid contracts may be enforceable, voidable, or unenforceable. Additionally, a contract may be referred to as a *void contract.* We look next at the meaning of the terms *voidable, unenforceable,* and *void* in relation to contract enforceability.

VOIDABLE CONTRACTS A **voidable contract** is a valid contract but one that can be avoided at the option of one or both of the parties. The party having the option can elect either to avoid any duty to perform or to *ratify* (make valid) the contract. If the

contract is avoided, both parties are released from it. If it is ratified, both parties must fully perform their respective legal obligations.

As you will read in Chapter 11, contracts made by minors generally are voidable at the option of the minor (with certain exceptions). Contracts made by mentally incompetent persons and intoxicated persons may also be voidable. Additionally, contracts entered into under fraudulent conditions are voidable at the option of the defrauded party. Contracts entered into under legally defined duress or undue influence are also voidable (see Chapter 12).

UNENFORCEABLE CONTRACTS An **unenforceable contract** is one that cannot be enforced because of certain legal defenses against it. It is not unenforceable because a party failed to satisfy a legal requirement of the contract. Rather, it is a valid contract rendered unenforceable by some statute or law. For instance, certain contracts must be in writing (see Chapter 12), and if they are not, they will not be enforceable except in certain exceptional circumstances.

VOID CONTRACTS A **void contract** is no contract at all. The terms *void* and *contract* are contradictory. None of the parties have any legal obligations if a contract is void. A contract can be void because one of the parties was determined by a court to mentally incompetent, for instance, or because the purpose of the contract was illegal (see Chapter 11).

To review the various types of contracts, see *Concept Summary 9.1* on the following page.

EXHIBIT 9–2 Enforceable, Voidable, Unenforceable, and Void Contracts

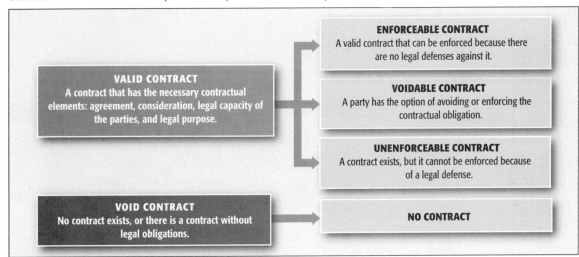

CONCEPT SUMMARY 9.1
Types of Contracts

ASPECT	DEFINITION
Formation	1. *Bilateral*—A promise for a promise.
	2. *Unilateral*—A promise for an act (acceptance is the completed performance of the act).
	3. *Formal*—Requires a special form for creation.
	4. *Informal*—Requires no special form for creation.
	5. *Express*—Formed by words (oral, written, or a combination).
	6. *Implied*—Formed by the conduct of the parties.
Performance	1. *Executed*—A fully performed contract.
	2. *Executory*—A contract not fully performed.
Enforceability	1. *Valid*—The contract has the necessary contractual elements: agreement (offer and acceptance), consideration, legal capacity of the parties, and legal purpose.
	2. *Voidable*—One party has the option of avoiding or enforcing the contractual obligation.
	3. *Unenforceable*—A contract exists, but it cannot be enforced because of a legal defense.
	4. *Void*—No contract exists, or there is a contract without legal obligations.

SECTION 4
QUASI CONTRACTS

Quasi contracts, or contracts *implied in law,* are not actual contracts. Express contracts and implied contracts are actual or true contracts formed by the words or actions of the parties. The word *quasi* is Latin for "as if" or "analogous to." Quasi contracts are not true contracts because they do not arise from any agreement, express or implied, between the parties themselves. Rather, quasi contracts are fictional contracts that courts can impose on the parties "as if" the parties had entered into an actual contract. They are equitable rather than legal contracts.

Usually, quasi contracts are imposed to avoid the *unjust enrichment* of one party at the expense of another. The doctrine of unjust enrichment is based on the theory that individuals should not be allowed to profit or enrich themselves inequitably at the expense of others. When the court imposes a quasi contract, a plaintiff may recover in **quantum meruit,**[8] a Latin phrase meaning "as much as he or she deserves." *Quantum meruit* essentially describes the extent of compensation owed under a contract implied in law.

In the following case, the parties did not have an express contract, but one party enjoyed the benefits of the other party's services. The court had to decide if the parties had a quasi contract.

---

8. Pronounced *kwahn*-tuhm *mehr*-oo-wit.

CASE 9.2

Seawest Services Association v. Copenhaver
Court of Appeals of Washington, 166 Wash.App. 1006 (2012).

BACKGROUND AND FACTS   Seawest Services Association owned and operated a water distribution system that served homes both inside and outside a housing development. Seawest had two classes of members. "Full members" owned property in the housing development, and "limited members" received water services for homes outside the development. Both full and limited members paid water bills and, as necessary, assessments for work performed on the water system. In 2001, the Copenhavers

CASE 9.2 CONTINUED   purchased a home outside the housing development. They did not have an express contract with Seawest, but they paid water bills for eight years and paid one $3,950 assessment for water system upgrades. In 2009, a dispute arose between the parties, and the Copenhavers began refusing to pay their water bills and assessments. Seawest sued the Copenhavers in a Washington state court. The trial court found that the Copenhavers were limited members of Seawest and thus were liable for the unpaid water bills and assessments. The Copenhavers appealed.

 IN THE LANGUAGE OF THE COURT
LAU, J. [Judge]

* * * *

* * * *The essential elements of unjust enrichment are " 'a benefit conferred upon the defendant by the plaintiff; an appreciation or knowledge by the defendant of the benefit; and the acceptance or retention by the defendant under such circumstances as to make it inequitable for the defendant to retain the benefit without the payment of its value.' "* [Emphasis added.]

Undisputed evidence * * * shows that the Copenhavers * * * have utilized the Seawest system and have paid, without objection until litigation ensued, all water use, water maintenance, and assessment base charges to Seawest.

* * * *

* * * The Copenhavers would be unjustly enriched if they could retain benefits provided by Seawest without paying for them. The Copenhavers obtained property that carried with it a water share. They knew that no property owner is entitled to receive water without membership in Seawest.

We conclude that the undisputed record supports a contract implied in law.

DECISION AND REMEDY   *The Washington appellate court affirmed the trial court's judgment. It held that the Copenhavers were liable to Seawest because the parties had a quasi contract.*

THE ETHICAL DIMENSION   *In recognizing quasi contracts, does the law try to correct for unethical behavior? Why or why not?*

THE ECONOMIC DIMENSION   *Could the Copenhavers have successfully argued that by forcing them to pay a price to which they had not agreed, Seawest was unjustly enriched at their expense?*

Limitations on Quasi-Contractual Recovery

Although quasi contracts exist to prevent unjust enrichment, the party obtaining the enrichment is not held liable in some situations. In general, a party who has conferred a benefit on someone else unnecessarily or as a result of misconduct or negligence cannot invoke the principle of quasi contract. The enrichment in those situations will not be considered "unjust."

▶ **Case in Point 9.8**   Qwest Wireless, LLC, provides wireless phone services in Arizona and thirteen other states. Qwest marketed and sold handset insurance to its customers, although it did not have a license to sell insurance in Arizona or in any other state. Patrick and Vicki Van Zanen sued Qwest for unjust enrichment based on its receipt of sales commissions for the handset insurance. The court agreed that Qwest had

violated the insurance-licensing statute. Nevertheless, the court found that the commissions did not constitute unjust enrichment because the customers had, in fact, received the insurance. Qwest had not retained a benefit (the commissions) without paying for it (providing insurance).[9] ◀

When an Actual Contract Exists

The doctrine of quasi contract generally cannot be used when there is an *actual contract* that covers the matter in controversy. A remedy already exists if a party is unjustly enriched as a result of a breach of contract: the nonbreaching party can sue the breaching party for breach of contract.

▶ **Example 9.9**   Fung contracts with Cameron to deliver a furnace to a building owned by Grant. Fung

---

9. *Van Zanen v. Qwest Wireless, LLC,* 522 F.3d 1127 (10th Cir. 2008).

delivers the furnace, but Cameron never pays Fung. Grant has been unjustly enriched in this situation, to be sure. Fung, however, cannot recover from Grant in quasi contract because Fung had an actual contract with Cameron. Fung already has a remedy—he can sue for breach of contract to recover the price of the furnace from Cameron. The court does not need to impose a quasi contract in this situation to achieve justice. ◀

SECTION 5
INTERPRETATION OF CONTRACTS

Sometimes, parties agree that a contract has been formed but disagree on its meaning or legal effect. One reason this may happen is that one of the parties is not familiar with the legal terminology used in the contract. To an extent, *plain language* laws (enacted by the federal government and a majority of the states) have helped to avoid this difficulty. Sometimes, though, a dispute may arise over the meaning of a contract simply because the rights or obligations under the contract are not expressed clearly—no matter how "plain" the language used.

In this section, we look at some common law rules of contract interpretation. These rules, which have evolved over time, provide the courts with guidelines for deciding disputes over how contract terms or provisions should be interpreted. Exhibit 9–3 below provides a brief graphic summary of how these rules are applied.

The Plain Meaning Rule

When a contract's writing is clear and unequivocal, a court will enforce it according to its obvious terms. The meaning of the terms must be determined from the *face of the instrument*—from the written document alone. This is sometimes referred to as the *plain meaning rule.*

The words—and their plain, ordinary meaning—determine the intent of the parties at the time that they entered into the contract. A court is bound to give effect to the contract according to this intent.

AMBIGUITY A court will consider a contract to be ambiguous (unclear) in the following situations:

1. When the intent of the parties cannot be determined from the contract's language.
2. When the contract lacks a provision on a disputed term.
3. When a term is susceptible to more than one interpretation.
4. When there is uncertainty about a provision.

EXTRINSIC EVIDENCE If a contract term is ambiguous, a court can consider *extrinsic evidence* (evidence outside the contract), or it may interpret the ambiguity against the party who drafted the term. **Extrinsic evidence** is any evidence not contained in the document itself—such as the testimony of parties and witnesses, additional agreements or communications, or other relevant information.

EXHIBIT 9–3 Rules of Contract Interpretation

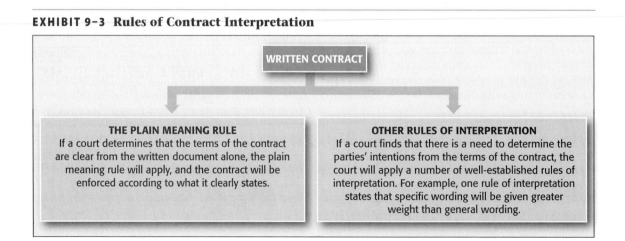

The admissibility of extrinsic evidence can significantly affect the court's interpretation of ambiguous contractual provisions and thus the outcome of litigation. When a contract is clear and unambiguous, a court cannot consider extrinsic evidence. The following case illustrates these points.

SP TLIGHT on Columbia Pictures

Case 9.3   Wagner v. Columbia Pictures Industries, Inc.

California Court of Appeal, Second District, 146 Cal.App.4th 586, 52 Cal.Rptr.3d 898 (2007).

BACKGROUND AND FACTS   Actor Robert Wagner entered into an agreement with Spelling-Goldberg Productions (SGP) "relating to *Charlie's Angels* (herein called the 'series')." The contract entitled Wagner to 50 percent of the net profits that SGP received from broadcasting the series and from all ancillary, music, and subsidiary rights in connection with the series. SGP hired Ivan Goff and Ben Roberts to write the series, under a contract subject to the Writers Guild of America Minimum Basic Agreement (MBA).[a] The MBA stipulates that the writer of a television show retains the right to make and market films based on the material, subject to the producer's right to buy this right if the writer decides to sell it within five years.

The first *Charlie's Angels* episode aired in 1976. In 1982, SGP sold its rights to the series to Columbia Pictures Industries, Inc. Thirteen years later, Columbia bought the movie rights to the material from Goff's and Roberts's heirs. In 2000 and 2003, Columbia produced and distributed two *Charlie's Angels* films. Wagner filed a suit in a California state court against Columbia, claiming a share of the profits from the films. The court granted Columbia's motion for summary judgment. Wagner appealed to a state intermediate appellate court.

IN THE LANGUAGE OF THE COURT
JOHNSON, Acting P.J. [Presiding Judge]

* * * *

Wagner contends the "subsidiary rights" provision in the agreement with SGP entitles him * * * to 50 percent of the net profits from the two "Charlie's Angels" films.

* * * *

Wagner introduced evidence of the history of the negotiations underlying the "Charlie's Angels" contract in support of his [contention].

This history begins with a contract the Wagners [Wagner and his wife, Natalie Wood] entered into with SGP to star in a television movie-of-the-week, "Love Song." As compensation for Wagner and Wood acting in "Love Song," SGP agreed to pay them a fixed amount plus one-half the net profits * * * .

* * * *

In the * * * "Love Song" contract net profits were not limited to monies received "for the right to exhibit the Photoplay." Instead they were defined as the net of "all monies received by Producer as consideration for the right to exhibit the Photoplay, and exploitation of all ancillary, music and subsidiary rights in connection therewith."

* * * *

Wagner's argument is simple and straightforward. The net profits provision in the "Love Song" agreement was intended to give the Wagners a one-half share in the net profits received by SGP "from all sources" without limitation as to source or time. The "Charlie's Angels" agreement was based on the "Love Song" agreement and defines net profits in identical language. Therefore, the "Charlie's Angels" agreement should also be interpreted as providing the Wagners with a 50 percent share in SGP's income "from all sources" without limitation

---

a. The Writers Guild of America is an association of screen and television writers that negotiates industry-wide agreements with motion picture and television producers.

CASE 9.3 CONTINUES ▶

CASE 9.3 CONTINUED as to source or time. Since Columbia admits it stands in SGP's shoes with respect to SGP's obligations under the "Charlie's Angels" agreement, Columbia is obligated to pay Wagner * * * 50 percent of the net profits derived from the "Charlie's Angels" movies.
      * * * *

The problem with Wagner's extrinsic evidence is that it does not explain the ["Charlie's Angels"] contract language, it contradicts it. *Under the parol evidence rule,*[b] *extrinsic evidence is not admissible to contradict express terms in a written contract or to explain what the agreement was. The agreement is the writing itself. Parol evidence cannot be admitted to show intention independent of an unambiguous written instrument.* [Emphasis added.]

Even if the Wagners and SGP intended the Wagners would share in the net profits "from any and all sources" they did not say so in their contract. What they said in their contract was the Wagners would share in "all monies actually received by Producer, as consideration for the right to exhibit photoplays of the series, and from the exploitation of all ancillary, music and subsidiary rights in connection therewith." For a right to be "subsidiary" or "ancillary," meaning supplementary or subordinate, there must be a primary right to which it relates. The only primary right mentioned in the contract is "the right to exhibit photoplays of the series." Thus the Wagners were entitled to share in the profits from the exploitation of the movie rights to "Charlie's Angels" if those rights were exploited by Columbia as ancillary or subsidiary rights of its primary "right to exhibit photoplays of the series" but not if those rights were acquired by Columbia independently from its right to exhibit photoplays.

DECISION AND REMEDY *The state intermediate appellate court affirmed the lower court's summary judgment in favor of Columbia. The contract "unambiguously" stated the conditions under which the parties were to share the films' profits, and those conditions had not occurred.*

WHAT IF THE FACTS WERE DIFFERENT? *How might the result in this case have been different if the court had admitted Wagner's evidence of the "Love Song" contract?*

THE LEGAL ENVIRONMENT DIMENSION *Under what circumstances would Wagner have been entitled to a share of the profits from the* Charlie's Angels *movies even though the evidence of the* Love Song *contract was irrelevant?*

---

b. The *parol evidence rule* prohibits the parties from introducing in court evidence of an oral agreement that contradicts the written terms of a contract (see Chapter 12).

Other Rules of Interpretation

Generally, a court will interpret the language to give effect to the parties' intent as *expressed in their contract*. This is the primary purpose of the rules of interpretation—to determine the parties' intent from the language used in their agreement and to give effect to that intent. A court normally will not make or remake a contract, nor will it interpret the language according to what the parties *claim* their intent was when they made it.

RULES THE COURTS USE The courts use the following rules in interpreting contractual terms:

1. As far as possible, a reasonable, lawful, and effective meaning will be given to all of a contract's terms.

2. A contract will be interpreted as a whole. Individual, specific clauses will be considered subordinate to the contract's general intent. All writings that are a part of the same transaction will be interpreted together.

3. Terms that were the subject of separate negotiation will be given greater consideration than standardized terms and terms that were not negotiated separately.

4. A word will be given its ordinary, commonly accepted meaning, and a technical word or term will be given its technical meaning, unless the parties clearly intended something else.

5. Specific and exact wording will be given greater consideration than general language.

6. Written or typewritten terms will prevail over preprinted ones.

7. Because a contract should be drafted in clear and unambiguous language, a party who uses ambiguous expressions is held to be responsible for the ambiguities. Thus, when the language has more than one meaning, it will be interpreted against the party who drafted the contract.

8. Evidence of *usage of trade, course of dealing,* and *course of performance* may be admitted to clarify the meaning of an ambiguously worded contract. (These terms will be defined and discussed in more detail in Chapter 15.)

EXPRESS TERMS USUALLY GIVEN THE MOST WEIGHT Express terms (terms expressly stated in the contract) are given the greatest weight, followed by course of performance, course of dealing, and custom and usage of trade—in that order. When considering custom and usage, a court will look at the trade customs and usage common to the particular business or industry and to the locale in which the contract was made or is to be performed.

▶ **Case in Point 9.10** Jessica Robbins bought a house in Tennessee. U.S. Bank financed the purchase, and Tennessee Farmers Mutual Insurance Company issued the homeowner's insurance policy. The policy included a clause that promised payment to the bank unless the house was lost due to an "increase in hazard" that the bank knew about but did not tell the insurer. When Robbins fell behind on her mortgage payments, the bank started foreclosure proceedings. No one told the insurer. Robbins filed for bankruptcy, which postponed foreclosure.

Meanwhile, the house was destroyed in a fire. The bank filed a claim under the policy, but the insurer refused to pay because it had not been told by the bank of an "increase in hazard"—the foreclosure. The bank then filed a lawsuit. The court found that the plain meaning of the words "increase in hazard" in the policy referred to physical conditions on the property that posed a risk, not to events such as foreclosure. Thus, the bank was not required to notify the insurer under the terms of the policy, and the lack of notice did not invalidate the coverage.[10] ◀

10. *U.S. Bank, N.A. v. Tennessee Farmers Mutual Insurance Co.,* 277 S.W.3d 381 (Tenn.Sup.Ct. 2009).

Reviewing: Nature and Terminology

Mitsui Bank hired Ross Duncan as a branch manager in one of its Southern California locations. At that time, Duncan received an employee handbook informing him that Mitsui would review his performance and salary level annually. In 2012, Mitsui decided to create a new lending program to help financially troubled businesses stay afloat. It hired Duncan to be the credit development officer (CDO) and gave him a written compensation plan. Duncan's compensation was to be based on the program's success and involved a bonus and commissions based on the volume of new loans and sales. The written plan also stated, "This compensation plan will be reviewed and potentially amended after one year and will be subject to such review and amendment annually thereafter."

Duncan's efforts as CDO were successful, and the business-lending program he developed grew to represent 25 percent of Mitsui's business in 2013 and 40 percent in 2014. Nevertheless, Mitsui refused to give Duncan a raise in 2013. Mitsui also amended his compensation plan to significantly reduce his compensation and to change his performance evaluation schedule to every six months. When he had still not received a raise by 2014, Duncan resigned as CDO and filed a lawsuit alleging breach of contract. Using the information presented in the chapter, answer the following questions.

1. What are the four requirements of a valid contract?
2. Did Duncan have a valid contract with Mitsui for employment as CDO? If so, was it a bilateral or a unilateral contract?
3. What are the requirements of an implied contract?
4. Can Duncan establish an implied contract based on the employment manual or the written compensation plan? Why or why not?

DEBATE THIS . . . *Companies should be able to make or break employment contracts whenever and however they wish.*

Terms and Concepts

bilateral contract 182

contract 179

executed contract 184

executory contract 184

express contract 184

extrinsic evidence 188

formal contract 183

implied contract 184

informal contract 184

objective theory of contracts 179

offeree 182

offeror 182

promise 178

promisee 179

promisor 179

quantum meruit 186

quasi contract 186

unenforceable contract 185

unilateral contract 182

valid contract 185

void contract 185

voidable contract 185

ExamPrep

Issue Spotters

1. Joli receives a letter from Kerin saying that he has a book at a certain price. Joli signs and returns the letter to Kerin. When Kerin delivers the book, Joli sends it back, claiming that they do not have a contract. Kerin claims they do. What standard determines whether these parties have a contract? **(See page 179.)**

2. Dyna tells Ed that she will pay him $1,000 to set fire to her store so that she can collect under a fire insurance policy. Ed sets fire to the store, but Dyna refuses to pay. Can Ed recover? Why or why not? **(See page 185.)**

• Check your answers to the Issue Spotters against the answers provided in Appendix B at the end of this text.

Before the Test

Go to **www.cengagebrain.com**, enter the ISBN 9781285770192, and click on "Find" to locate this textbook's Web site. Then, click on "Access Now" under "Study Tools," and select Chapter 9 at the top. There, you will find a Practice Quiz that you can take to assess your mastery of the concepts in this chapter, as well as Flashcards and a Glossary of important terms.

Business Scenarios

9–1. Unilateral Contract. Rocky Mountain Races, Inc., sponsors the "Pioneer Trail Ultramarathon" with an advertised first prize of $10,000. The rules require the competitors to run 100 miles from the floor of Blackwater Canyon to the top of Pinnacle Mountain. The rules also provide that Rocky reserves the right to change the terms of the race at any time. Monica enters the race and is declared the winner. Rocky offers her a prize of $1,000 instead of $10,000. Did Rocky and Monica have a contract? Explain. **(See page 182.)**

9–2. Implied Contract. Janine was hospitalized with severe abdominal pain and placed in an intensive care unit. Her doctor told the hospital personnel to order around-the-clock nursing care for Janine. At the hospital's request, a nursing services firm, Nursing Services Unlimited, provided two weeks of in-hospital care and, after Janine was sent home, an additional two weeks of at-home care. During the at-home period of care, Janine was fully aware that she

was receiving the benefit of the nursing services. Nursing Services later billed Janine $4,000 for the nursing care, but Janine refused to pay on the ground that she had never contracted for the services, either orally or in writing. In view of the fact that no express contract was ever formed, can Nursing Services recover the $4,000 from Janine? If so, under what legal theory? Discuss. **(See page 184.)**

9–3. Contract Classification. For employment with the Firestorm Smokejumpers—a crew of elite paratroopers who parachute into dangerous situations to fight fires—applicants must complete a series of tests. The crew chief sends the most qualified applicants a letter stating that they will be admitted to Firestorm's training sessions if they pass a medical exam. Jake Kurzyniec receives the letter and passes the exam, but a new crew chief changes the selection process and rejects him. Is there a contract between Kurzyniec and Firestorm? If there is a contract, what type of contract is it? **(See pages 182–184.)**

Business Case Problems

9–4. Spotlight on Taco Bell—Implied Contract. Thomas Rinks and Joseph Shields developed Psycho Chihuahua, a caricature of a Chihuahua dog with a "do-not-back-down" attitude. They promoted and marketed the character through

their company, Wrench, L.L.C. Ed Alfaro and Rudy Pollak, representatives of Taco Bell Corp., learned of Psycho Chihuahua and met with Rinks and Shields to talk about using the character as a Taco Bell "icon." Wrench sent artwork, merchandise, and marketing ideas to Alfaro, who promoted the character within Taco Bell. Alfaro asked Wrench to propose terms for Taco Bell's use of Psycho Chihuahua. Taco Bell did not accept Wrench's terms, but Alfaro continued to promote the character within the company. Meanwhile, Taco Bell hired a new advertising agency, which proposed an advertising campaign involving a Chihuahua. When Alfaro learned of this proposal, he sent the Psycho Chihuahua materials to the agency. Taco Bell made a Chihuahua the focus of its marketing but paid nothing to Wrench. Wrench filed a suit against Taco Bell in a federal court claiming that it had an implied contract with Taco Bell and that Taco Bell breached that contract. Do these facts satisfy the requirements for an implied contract? Why or why not? [*Wrench, L.L.C. v. Taco Bell Corp.,* 256 F.3d 446 (6th Cir. 2001), cert. denied, 534 U.S. 1114, 122 S.Ct. 921, 151 L.Ed.2d 805 (2002)] **(See page 184.)**

9–5. Quasi Contract. Kim Panenka asked to borrow $4,750 from her sister, Kris, to make a mortgage payment. Kris deposited a check for that amount into Kim's bank account. Hours later, Kim asked to borrow another $1,100. Kris took a cash advance on her credit card and deposited this amount into Kim's account. When Kim did not repay the amounts, Kris filed a suit, arguing that she had "loaned" Kim the money. Can the court impose a contract between the sisters? Explain. [*Panenka v. Panenka,* 331 Wis.2d 731, 795 N.W.2d 493 (2011)] **(See page 186.)**

9–6. Interpretation of Contracts. Lisa and Darrell Miller had a son, Landon. When the Millers divorced, they entered into a "Joint Plan" (JP). Under the JP, Darrell agreed to "begin setting funds aside for Landon to attend college." After Landon's eighteenth birthday, Lisa asked a court to order Darrell to pay the boy's college expenses based on the JP. Darrell contended that the JP was not clear on this point. Do the rules of contract interpretation support Lisa's request or Darrell's contention? Explain. [*Miller v. Miller,* 1 So.3d 815 (La.App. 2009)] **(See page 188.)**

**9–7. BUSINESS CASE PROBLEM
WITH SAMPLE ANSWER: Quasi Contract.**

Robert Gutkowski, a sports marketing expert, met numerous times with George Steinbrenner, the owner of the New York Yankees, to discuss the Yankees Entertainment and Sports Network (YES). Gutkowski was paid as a consultant. Later, he filed a suit, seeking an ownership share in YES. There was no written contract for the share, but he claimed that there were discussions about his being a part owner. Does Gutkowski have a valid claim for

payment? Discuss. [Gutkowski v. Steinbrenner, 680 *F.Supp.2d 602 (S.D.N.Y. 2010)]* **(See page 186.)**

- **For a sample answer to Problem 9–7, go to Appendix C at the end of this text.**

9–8. Implied Contract. Ralph Ramsey insured his car with Allstate Insurance Co. He also owned a house on which he maintained a homeowner's insurance policy with Allstate. Bank of America had a mortgage on the house and paid the insurance premiums on the homeowner's policy from Ralph's account. After Ralph died, Allstate canceled the car insurance. Ralph's son Douglas inherited the house. The bank continued to pay the premiums on the homeowner's policy, but from Douglas's account, and Allstate continued to renew the insurance. When a fire destroyed the house, Allstate denied coverage, however, claiming that the policy was still in Ralph's name. Douglas filed a suit in a federal district court against the insurer. Was Allstate liable under the homeowner's policy? Explain. [*Ramsey v. Allstate Insurance Co.,* 2013 WL 467327 (6th Cir. 2013)] **(See page 184.)**

9–9. A QUESTION OF ETHICS: Unilateral Contract.

International Business Machines Corp. (IBM) hired Niels Jensen in 2000 as a software sales representative. According to the brochure on IBM's "Sales Incentive Plan" (SIP), "the more you sell, the more earnings for you." But "the SIP program does not constitute a promise by IBM. IBM reserves the right to modify the program at any time." Jensen was given a "quota letter" that said he would be paid $75,000 as a base salary and, if he attained his quota, an additional $75,000 as incentive pay. Jensen closed a deal worth more than $24 million to IBM. When IBM paid him less than $500,000 as a commission, Jensen filed a suit. He argued that the SIP was a unilateral offer that became a binding contract when he closed the sale. [Jensen v. International Business Machines Corp., 454 F.3d 382 (4th Cir. 2006)] **(See page 182.)**

(a) Would it be fair to the employer for the court to hold that the SIP brochure and the quota letter created a unilateral contract if IBM did not *intend* to create such a contract? Would it be fair to the employee to hold that *no* contract was created? Explain.

(b) The "Sales Incentives" section of IBM's brochure included a clause providing that "management will decide if an adjustment to the payment is appropriate" when an employee closes a large transaction. Does this affect your answers to the above questions? From an ethical perspective, would it be fair to hold that a contract exists despite these statements? Why or why not?

Legal Reasoning Group Activity

9–10. Contracts. Review the basic requirements for a valid contract listed at the beginning of this chapter. Now consider the relationship created when a student enrolls in a college or university. **(See page 181.)**

(a) One group should analyze and discuss whether a contract has been formed between the student and the college or university.

(b) A second group should assume that there is a contract and explain whether it is bilateral or unilateral.

CHAPTER 10

AGREEMENT IN TRADITIONAL AND E-CONTRACTS

Contract law developed over time to meet society's need to know with certainty what kinds of promises, or contracts, will be enforced and the point at which a valid and binding contract is formed. For a contract to be considered valid and enforceable, the requirements listed in Chapter 9 must be met. In this chapter, we look closely at the first of these requirements, *agreement*.

Agreement is required to form a contract, whether it is formed in the traditional way (on paper) or online. In today's world, many contracts are formed via the Internet—even from smartphones, tablets, and other mobile devices. We discuss online offers and acceptances and examine some laws that have been created to apply to electronic contracts, or *e-contracts,* in the latter part of this chapter.

AGREEMENT

An essential element for contract formation is **agreement**—the parties must agree on the terms of the contract and manifest to each other their *mutual assent* (agreement) to the same bargain. Ordinarily, agreement is evidenced by two events: an *offer* and an *acceptance*. One party offers a certain bargain to another party, who then accepts that bargain.

The agreement does not necessarily have to be in writing. Both parties, however, must manifest their assent, or voluntary consent, to the same bargain. Once an agreement is reached, if the other elements of a contract (consideration, capacity, and legality—discussed in Chapter 11) are present, a valid contract is formed. Generally, the contract creates enforceable rights and duties between the parties.

Because words often fail to convey the precise meaning intended, the law of contracts generally adheres to the *objective theory of contracts,* as discussed in Chapter 9. Under this theory, a party's words and conduct are held to mean whatever a reasonable person in the offeree's position would think they meant.

Requirements of the Offer

An **offer** is a promise or commitment to do or refrain from doing some specified action in the future. As mentioned in Chapter 9, the parties to a contract are the *offeror,* the one who makes an offer or proposal to another party, and the *offeree,* the one to whom the offer or proposal is made. Under the common law, three elements are necessary for an offer to be effective:

1. The offeror must have a serious intention to become bound by the offer.
2. The terms of the offer must be reasonably certain, or definite, so that the parties and the court can ascertain the terms of the contract.
3. The offer must be communicated to the offeree.

Once an effective offer has been made, the offeree's acceptance of that offer creates a legally binding contract (providing the other essential elements for a valid and enforceable contract are present).

INTENTION The first requirement for an effective offer is a serious intent on the part of the offeror. Serious intent is not determined by the subjective intentions, beliefs, and assumptions of the offeror. Rather, it is determined by what a reasonable person in the offeree's position would conclude that the offeror's words and actions meant. Offers made in obvious anger, jest, or undue excitement do not meet the serious-and-objective-intent test because a reasonable person would realize that a serious offer was not being made. Because these offers are not effective, an offeree's acceptance does not create an agreement.

▶ **Example 10.1**   Linda and Dena ride to school each day in Dena's new automobile, which has a market value of $20,000. One cold morning, they get into the car, but the car will not start. Dena yells in anger, "I'll sell this car to anyone for $500!" Linda drops $500 on Dena's lap. A reasonable person—taking into consideration Dena's frustration and the obvious difference in value between the market price of the car and the proposed purchase price—would realize that Dena's offer was not made with serious and objective intent. No agreement is formed. ◀

In the classic case presented next, the court considered whether an offer made "after a few drinks" met the serious-and-objective-intent requirement.

CLASSIC CASE 10.1

Lucy v. Zehmer
Supreme Court of Appeals of Virginia, 196 Va. 493, 84 S.E.2d 516 (1954).

BACKGROUND AND FACTS   W. O. Lucy, the plaintiff, filed a suit against A. H. and Ida Zehmer, the defendants, to compel the Zehmers to transfer title of their property, known as the Ferguson Farm, to the Lucys (W. O. and his wife) for $50,000, as the Zehmers had allegedly agreed to do. Lucy had known A. H. Zehmer for fifteen or twenty years and for the last eight years or so had been anxious to buy the Ferguson Farm from him. One night, Lucy stopped to visit the Zehmers in the combination restaurant, filling station, and motor court they operated. While there, Lucy tried to buy the Ferguson Farm once again. This time he tried a new approach. According to the trial court transcript, Lucy said to Zehmer, "I bet you wouldn't take $50,000 for that place." Zehmer replied, "Yes, I would too; you wouldn't give fifty." Throughout the evening, the conversation returned to the sale of the Ferguson Farm for $50,000. All the while, the men continued to drink whiskey and engage in light conversation.

Eventually, Lucy enticed Zehmer to write up an agreement to the effect that the Zehmers would sell the Ferguson Farm to Lucy for $50,000 complete. Later, Lucy sued Zehmer to compel him to go through with the sale. Zehmer argued that he had been drunk and that the offer had been made in jest and hence was unenforceable. The trial court agreed with Zehmer, and Lucy appealed.

 IN THE LANGUAGE OF THE COURT
BUCHANAN, J. [Justice] delivered the opinion of the court.

* * * *

In his testimony, Zehmer claimed that he "was high as a Georgia pine," and that the transaction "was just a bunch of two doggoned drunks bluffing to see who could talk the biggest and say the most." That claim is inconsistent with his attempt to testify in great detail as to what was said and what was done.

* * * *

The appearance of the contract, the fact that it was under discussion for forty minutes or more before it was signed; Lucy's objection to the first draft because it was written in the singular, and he wanted Mrs. Zehmer to sign it also; the rewriting to meet that objection and the signing by Mrs. Zehmer; the discussion of what was to be included in the sale, the provision for the examination of the title, the completeness of the instrument that was executed, the taking possession of it by Lucy with no request or suggestion by either of the defendants that he give it back, are facts which furnish persuasive evidence that the execution of the contract was a serious business transaction rather than a casual, jesting matter as defendants now contend.

* * * *

In the field of contracts, as generally elsewhere, *we must look to the outward expression of a person as manifesting his intention rather than to his secret and unexpressed intention*. The law imputes to a person an intention corresponding to the reasonable meaning of his words and acts. [Emphasis added.]

CASE 10.1 CONTINUES ▶

* * * *

Whether the writing signed by the defendants and now sought to be enforced by the complainants was the result of a serious offer by Lucy and a serious acceptance by the defendants, or was a serious offer by Lucy and an acceptance in secret jest by the defendants, in either event it constituted a binding contract of sale between the parties.

DECISION AND REMEDY *The Supreme Court of Appeals of Virginia determined that the writing was an enforceable contract and reversed the ruling of the lower court. The Zehmers were required by court order to follow through with the sale of the Ferguson Farm to the Lucys.*

WHAT IF THE FACTS WERE DIFFERENT? *Suppose that the day after Lucy signed the purchase agreement for the farm, he decided that he did not want it after all, and Zehmer sued Lucy to perform the contract. Would this change in the facts alter the court's decision that Lucy and Zehmer had created an enforceable contract? Why or why not?*

IMPACT OF THIS CASE ON TODAY'S LAW *This is a classic case in contract law because it illustrates so clearly the objective theory of contracts with respect to determining whether a serious offer was intended. Today, the courts continue to apply the objective theory of contracts and routinely cite* Lucy v. Zehmer *as a significant precedent in this area.*

SITUATIONS WHEN INTENT MAY BE LACKING The concept of intention can be further clarified through an examination of types of statements that are *not* offers. We look at these expressions and statements in the subsections that follow.

Expressions of Opinion. An expression of opinion is not an offer. It does not indicate an intention to enter into a binding agreement.

▶ **Case in Point 10.2** George Hawkins took his son to McGee, a physician, and asked McGee to operate on the son's hand. McGee said that the boy would be in the hospital three or four days and that the hand would *probably* heal a few days later. The son's hand did not heal for a month, but the father did not win a suit for breach of contract. The court held that McGee had not made an offer to heal the son's hand in a few days. He had merely expressed an opinion as to when the hand would heal.[1] ◀

Statements of Future Intent. A statement of an intention to do something in the future is not an offer.
▶ **Example 10.3** Samir says, "I *plan* to sell my stock in Novation, Inc., for $150 per share." If John "accepts" and tenders the $150 per share for the stock, no contract is created. Samir has merely expressed his intention to enter into a future contract for the sale of the stock. No contract is formed because a reasonable person would conclude that

Samir was only *thinking about* selling his stock, not *promising* to sell it. ◀

Preliminary Negotiations. A request or invitation to negotiate is not an offer. It only expresses a willingness to discuss the possibility of entering into a contract. Statements such as "Will you sell Blythe Estate?" or "I wouldn't sell my car for less than $5,000" are examples. A reasonable person in the offeree's position would not conclude that these statements indicated an intention to enter into a binding obligation.

Likewise, when the government or private firms require construction work, they invite contractors to submit bids. The *invitation* to submit bids is not an offer, and a contractor does not bind the government or private firm by submitting a bid. (The bids that the contractors submit are offers, however, and the government or private firm can bind the contractor by accepting the bid.)

Advertisements. In general, advertisements (including representations made in mail-order catalogues, price lists, and circulars) are treated not as offers to contract but as invitations to negotiate.[2] ▶ **Case in Point 10.4** An advertisement on the *Science NOW* Web site asked readers to submit "news tips," which the organization would investigate for possible inclusion in its magazine or on the Web site. Erik Trell, a professor and physician, submitted a manuscript

---

1. *Hawkins v. McGee*, 84 N.H. 114, 146 A. 641 (1929).

2. *Restatement (Second) of Contracts*, Section 26, Comment b.

in which he claimed to have solved a famous mathematical problem.

When *Science NOW* did not publish the solution, Trell filed a lawsuit for breach of contract. He claimed that the *Science NOW* ad was an offer, which he had accepted by submitting his manuscript. The court dismissed Trell's suit, holding that the ad was not an offer, but merely an invitation to offer. Responses to the ad were not acceptances. Trell's submission of the manuscript for publication was the offer, which *Science NOW* did not accept.[3] ◄

Price lists are another form of invitation to negotiate or trade. A seller's price list is not an offer to sell at that price. It merely invites the buyer to offer to buy at that price. In fact, the seller usually puts "prices subject to change" on the price list. Only in rare circumstances will a price quotation be construed as an offer.

Although most advertisements and price lists are treated as invitations to negotiate, this does not mean that they can never be an offer. On some occasions, courts have construed advertisements to be offers because the ads contained definite terms that invited acceptance (such as an ad offering a reward for the return of a lost dog).

Online Auctions. The most familiar type of auction today takes place on the Internet. Online auction sites, such as eBay, eBid, and WebStore, provide a forum for buyers and sellers to find or sell almost anything. Like advertisements and price lists, "offers" to sell an item on these sites generally are treated as invitations to negotiate. Unlike live auctions (discussed next), online auctions are automated. Buyers can enter incremental bids on an item (without approving each price increase) up to a specified amount or without a limit, if they want to be assured of making the winning bid.

Live Auctions. In a live auction, a seller "offers" goods for sale through an auctioneer, but this is not an offer to form a contract. Rather, it is an invitation asking bidders to submit offers. In the context of an auction, a bidder is the offeror, and the auctioneer is the offeree. The offer is accepted when the auctioneer strikes the hammer. Before the fall of the hammer, a bidder may revoke (take back) her or his bid, or the auctioneer may reject that bid or all bids. Typically, an auctioneer will reject a bid that is below the price the seller is willing to accept.

When the auctioneer accepts a higher bid, he or she rejects all previous bids. Because rejection terminates an offer (as will be discussed later), those bids represent offers that have been terminated. Thus, if the highest bidder withdraws her or his bid before the hammer falls, none of the previous bids is reinstated. If the bid is not withdrawn or rejected, the contract is formed when the auctioneer announces, "Going once, going twice, sold!" (or something similar) and lets the hammer fall.

Auctions with and without Reserve. Auctions traditionally have been referred to as either "with reserve" or "without reserve." In an auction with reserve, the seller (through the auctioneer) may withdraw the goods at any time before the auctioneer closes the sale by announcement or by the fall of the hammer.

All auctions are assumed to be auctions with reserve unless the terms of the auction are explicitly stated to be *without reserve*. In an auction without reserve, the goods cannot be withdrawn by the seller and must be sold to the highest bidder. In auctions with reserve, the seller may reserve the right to confirm or reject the sale even after "the hammer has fallen." In this situation, the seller is obligated to notify those attending the auction that sales of goods made during the auction are not final until confirmed by the seller.[4]

Agreements to Agree. Traditionally, agreements to agree—that is, agreements to agree to the material terms of a contract at some future date—were not considered to be binding contracts. The modern view, however, is that agreements to agree may be enforceable agreements (contracts) if it is clear that the parties intended to be bound by the agreements. In other words, under the modern view the emphasis is on the parties' intent rather than on form.

▶ **Case in Point 10.5** After a person was injured and nearly drowned on a water ride at one of its amusement parks, Six Flags, Inc., filed a lawsuit against the manufacturer that had designed the ride. The defendant manufacturer claimed that the parties did not have a binding contract but had only engaged in preliminary negotiations that were never formalized in a construction contract. The court, however, held that the evidence was sufficient to show an intent to be bound. The evidence included a faxed document specifying the details of the water ride, along with the parties' subsequent actions (beginning

---

3. *Trell v. American Association for the Advancement of Science,* ___ F.Supp.2d ___ (W.D.N.Y. 2007).

4. These rules apply under both the common law of contracts and the Uniform Commercial Code (UCC)—see UCC 2–328.

construction and handwriting notes on the fax). The manufacturer was required to provide insurance for the water ride at Six Flags. Its insurer was required to defend Six Flags in the personal-injury lawsuit that arose out of the incident.[5] ◀

Preliminary Agreements. Increasingly, the courts are holding that a preliminary agreement constitutes a binding contract if the parties have agreed on all essential terms and no disputed issues remain to be resolved. In contrast, if the parties agree on certain major terms

but leave other terms open for further negotiation, a preliminary agreement is not binding. The parties are bound only in the sense that they have committed themselves to negotiate the undecided terms in good faith in an effort to reach a final agreement.

In the following *Spotlight Case,* the dispute was over an agreement to settle a case during the trial. One party claimed that the agreement formed via e-mail was binding. The other party claimed the e-mail exchange was merely an agreement to work out the terms of a settlement in the future. Can an exchange of e-mails create a complete and unambiguous agreement?

---

5. *Six Flags, Inc. v. Steadfast Insurance Co.,* 474 F.Supp.2d 201 (D.Mass. 2007).

SP TLIGHT on Amazon.com

Case 10.2   Basis Technology Corp. v. Amazon.com, Inc.
Appeals Court of Massachusetts, 71 Mass.App.Ct. 29, 878 N.E.2d 952 (2008).

BACKGROUND AND FACTS Basis Technology Corporation created software and provided technical services for a Japanese-language Web site belonging to Amazon.com, Inc. The agreement between the two companies allowed for separately negotiated contracts for additional services that Basis might provide to Amazon. At the end of 1999, Basis and Amazon entered into stock-purchase agreements. Later, Amazon objected to certain actions related to the securities that Basis sold. Basis sued Amazon for various claims involving these securities and for failing to pay for services performed by Basis that were not included in the original agreement. During the trial, the two parties appeared to reach an agreement to settle out of court via a series of e-mail exchanges outlining the settlement. When Amazon reneged, Basis served a motion to enforce the proposed settlement. The trial judge entered a judgment against Amazon, which appealed.

 IN THE LANGUAGE OF THE COURT
SIKORA, J. [Judge]

* * * *

* * * On the evening of March 23, after the third day of evidence and after settlement discussions, Basis counsel sent an e-mail with the following text to Amazon counsel:

> [Amazon counsel]—This e-mail confirms the essential business terms of the settlement between our respective clients * * *. Basis and Amazon agree that they promptly will take all reasonable steps to memorialize in a written agreement, to be signed by individuals authorized by each party, the terms set forth below, as well as such other terms that are reasonably necessary to make these terms effective.
> * * * *
> [Amazon counsel], please contact me first thing tomorrow morning if this e-mail does not accurately summarize the settlement terms reached earlier this evening.
> See you tomorrow morning when we report this matter settled to the Court.

At 7:26 A.M. on March 24, Amazon counsel sent an e-mail with a one-word reply: "correct." Later in the morning, in open court and on the record, both counsel reported the result of a settlement without specification of the terms.

On March 25, Amazon's counsel sent a facsimile of the first draft of a settlement agreement to Basis's counsel. The draft comported with all the terms of the e-mail exchange, and added some implementing and boilerplate [standard contract provisions] terms.

* * * *

[Within a few days, though,] the parties were deadlocked. On April 21, Basis served its motion to enforce the settlement agreement. Amazon opposed. * * * The motion and opposition presented the issues whether the e-mail terms were sufficiently complete and definite to form an agreement and whether Amazon had intended to be bound by them.

* * * *

We examine the text of the terms for the incompleteness and indefiniteness charged by Amazon. *Provisions are not ambiguous simply because the parties have developed different interpretations of them.* [Emphasis added.]

* * * *

We must interpret the document as a whole. In the preface to the enumerated terms, Basis counsel stated that the "e-mail confirms the essential business terms of the settlement between our respective clients," and that the parties "agree that they promptly will take all reasonable steps to memorialize" those terms. Amazon counsel concisely responded, "correct." Thus the "essential business terms" were resolved. The parties were proceeding to "memorialize" or record the settlement terms, not to create them.

* * * *

To ascertain intent, a court considers the words used by the parties, the agreement taken as a whole, and surrounding facts and circumstances. The essential circumstance of this disputed agreement is that it concluded a trial.

* * * As the trial judge explained in her memorandum of decision, she "terminated" the trial; she did not suspend it for exploratory negotiations. She did so in reliance upon the parties' report of an accomplished agreement for the settlement of their dispute.

* * * *

In sum, the deliberateness and the gravity attributable to a report of a settlement, especially during the progress of a trial, weigh heavily as circumstantial evidence of the intention of a party such as Amazon to be bound by its communication to the opposing party and to the court.

DECISION AND REMEDY *The Appeals Court of Massachusetts affirmed the trial court's finding that Amazon intended to be bound by the terms of the March 23 e-mail. That e-mail constituted a complete and unambiguous statement of the parties' desire to be bound by the settlement terms.*

WHAT IF THE FACTS WERE DIFFERENT? *Suppose that the attorneys for both sides had simply had a phone conversation that included all of the terms to which they actually agreed in their e-mail exchanges. Would the court have ruled differently? Why or why not?*

THE LEGAL ENVIRONMENT DIMENSION *What does the result in this case suggest that a businessperson should do before agreeing to a settlement of a legal dispute?*

DEFINITENESS OF TERMS The second requirement for an effective offer involves the definiteness of its terms. An offer must have reasonably definite terms so that a court can determine if a breach has occurred and give an appropriate remedy.[6] The specific terms required depend, of course, on the type of contract. Generally, a contract must include the following terms, either expressed in the contract or capable of being reasonably inferred from it:

1. The identification of the parties.
2. The identification of the object or subject matter of the contract (also the quantity, when appropriate), including the work to be performed, with specific identification of such items as goods, services, and land.
3. The consideration to be paid.
4. The time of payment, delivery, or performance.

An offer may invite an acceptance to be worded in such specific terms that the contract is made definite. ▶ **Example 10.6** Nintendo of America, Inc.,

6. *Restatement (Second) of Contracts,* Section 33.

contacts your Play 2 Win Games store and offers to sell "from one to twenty-five Nintendo 3DS gaming systems for $75 each. State number desired in acceptance." You agree to buy twenty systems. Because the quantity is specified in the acceptance, the terms are definite, and the contract is enforceable. ◀

When the parties have clearly manifested an intent to form a contract, courts sometimes are willing to supply a missing term in a contract, especially a sales contract.[7] But a court will not rewrite a contract if the parties' expression of intent is too vague or uncertain to be given any precise meaning.

COMMUNICATION The third requirement for an effective offer is communication—the offer must

---

7. See UCC 2–204. Note that Article 2 of the UCC specifies different rules relating to the definiteness of terms used in a contract for the sale of goods. In essence, Article 2 modifies general contract law by requiring *less* specificity.

be communicated to the offeree. Ordinarily, one cannot agree to a bargain without knowing that it exists. ▶ **Example 10.7**   Tolson advertises a reward for the return of her lost cat. Dirk, not knowing of the reward, finds the cat and returns it to Tolson. Usually, Dirk cannot recover the reward because an essential element of a reward contract is that the one who claims the reward must have known it was offered. A few states would allow recovery of the reward, but not on contract principles. Dirk would be allowed to recover on the basis that it would be unfair to deny him the reward just because he did not know about it. ◀

In the following case, a woman hit by a bus signed documents that clearly released her claims against the bus company in exchange for the payment of $1 million from the company's insurer. Did the documents have to be delivered to the company or its insurer for the release and settlement to be binding?

CASE ANALYSIS

Case 10.3   Gyabaah v. Rivlab Transportation Corp.
New York Supreme Court, Appellate Division, First Department, 102 A.D.3d 451, 958 N.Y.S.2d 109 (2013).

IN THE LANGUAGE OF THE COURT
TOM, J.P. [Judge Presiding], ANDRIAS, RENWICK, DEGRASSE, ABDUS-SALAAM, JJ. [Judges]

* * * *

[Adwoa Gyabaah was hit by a bus owned by Rivlab Transportation Corporation. She retained attorney Jeffrey Aronsky to represent her in negotiations with Rivlab, its insurer National Casualty Company, and their attorneys. Gyabaah agreed to pay Aronsky a contingency fee of one-third of the amount of her recovery. Aronsky] commenced this personal injury action on plaintiff's behalf on August 25, 2010 [against Rivlab]. By letter to Aronsky dated October 1, 2010, defendant's carrier tendered its $1 million policy limits for purposes of settlement. Aronsky explained the proposal to plaintiff who, at that time, chose to accept the settlement.

Accordingly, plaintiff executed a general release on October 5, 2010 * * *. Aronsky advised plaintiff that he would hold the release pending receipt of * * * advice from plaintiff as to whether she preferred to have the settlement structured [paid over a period of time rather than in one lump sum].

By December 9, 2010, plaintiff had retained new counsel, Kenneth A. Wilhelm, Esq. [Esquire]. On that date, Wilhelm advised Aronsky that plaintiff did not wish to settle the case or have the release sent to defendant. Aronsky moved the court below for an order enforcing what he contended was a $1 million settlement and setting his firm's contingency fee at one-third of the recovery pursuant to plaintiff's retainer agreement. In making his motion, Aronsky did not allege that acceptance of the offer was ever communicated to defendant or

its carrier. This omission is fatal to Aronsky's claim of a settlement for reasons that follow. Aronsky maintained that "plaintiff's signing of the General Release constituted a binding legal contract." The court denied the motion and vacated the release in what it perceived to be the interest of justice.

* * * The application of contract law * * * required the denial of Aronsky's motion. A general release is governed by principles of contract law. * * * *It is essential in any bilateral contract that the fact of acceptance be communicated to the offeror. Therefore, this action was not settled because the executed release was never forwarded to defendant nor was acceptance of the offer otherwise communicated to defendant or its carrier.* This record does not contain a single affidavit by anyone asserting that either occurred. * * * We do not share the * * * view that an October 6,

CASE 10.3 CONTINUED

2010 letter from defendant's counsel to Aronsky "evidenced" an agreement to settle. Defense counsel's statement in the letter that he was "advised" of a settlement does not suffice as evidence that such a settlement was effected. * * * Because there has been no settlement, the amount of Aronsky's fee should be determined upon the disposition of this action [as a percentage of the fee recovered by the Wilhelm firm based on the *pro rata* share of the work the two attorneys performed in obtaining the recovery]. [Emphasis added.]

* * * We see no need for a hearing to determine whether Aronsky was discharged for cause. The record discloses that plaintiff has not made a *prima facie* showing of any cause for Aronsky's discharge. Plaintiff stated in her affidavit that she signed the release * * * because she felt "pressured" to do so. Plaintiff made no mention of what the pressure consisted of or, more importantly, what professional misconduct, if any, brought it about. To be sure, a hearing was not warranted by plaintiff's untenable [indefensible] argument that Aronsky disobeyed her instructions by making the instant motion albeit [although] after he had already been discharged as her attorney.

[The order of the lower court denying Aronsky's motion insofar as it sought to enforce a purported settlement and set Aronsky's fee accordingly is affirmed.]

LEGAL REASONING QUESTIONS

1. Why did the court conclude that the parties in this case were not bound by the settlement and release documents signed by Gyabaah?

2. Why did Aronsky fail to deliver the signed documents to Rivlab or its insurer?

3. What is the most likely reason that Gyabaah did not wish to settle the case with Rivlab or its insurer according to their terms?

4. If Aronsky had informed Rivlab or its insurer that Gyabaah had agreed to the settlement, would her later "change of heart" have been sufficient to set aside the agreement?

Termination of the Offer

The communication of an effective offer to an offeree gives the offeree the power to transform the offer into a binding, legal obligation (a contract) by an acceptance. This power of acceptance does not continue forever, though. It can be terminated either by action of the parties or by operation of law.

TERMINATION BY ACTION OF THE PARTIES An offer can be terminated by action of the parties in any of three ways: by revocation, by rejection, or by counteroffer.

Revocation. The offeror's act of withdrawing (revoking) an offer is known as **revocation.** Unless an offer is irrevocable, the offeror usually can revoke the offer, as long as the revocation is communicated to the offeree before the offeree accepts. Revocation may be accomplished by either of the following:

1. Express repudiation of the offer (such as "I withdraw my previous offer of October 17").

2. Performance of acts that are inconsistent with the existence of the offer and are made known to the offeree (for instance, selling the offered property to another person in the presence of the offeree).

In most states, a revocation becomes effective when the offeree or the offeree's *agent* (a person acting on behalf of the offeree) actually receives it. Therefore, a revocation sent via FedEx on April 1 and delivered at the offeree's residence or place of business on April 3 becomes effective on April 3.

An offer made to the general public can be revoked in the same manner that the offer was originally communicated. ▶ **Example 10.8** An electronics retailer offers a $10,000 reward to anyone who provides information leading to the arrest of the individuals who broke into its store. The offer is published on the Web sites and in the printed editions of three local papers and of four papers in nearby communities. To revoke the offer, the retailer must publish the revocation in all seven papers in which it published the offer. ◀

Irrevocable Offers. Although most offers are revocable, some can be made irrevocable—that is, they cannot be revoked. Increasingly, courts refuse to allow an offeror to revoke an offer when the offeree has changed position because of justifiable reliance on the offer.

(The courts apply the doctrine of *detrimental reliance,* or *promissory estoppel,* which will be discussed in Chapter 11.) In some circumstances, "firm offers" made by merchants may also be considered irrevocable—see the discussion of a "merchant's firm offer" in Chapter 15.

Another form of irrevocable offer is an **option contract.** An option contract is created when an offeror promises to hold an offer open for a specified period of time in return for a payment (consideration) given by the offeree. An option contract takes away the offeror's power to revoke the offer for the period of time specified in the option.

Option contracts are frequently used in conjunction with the sale or lease of real estate. ▶ **Example 10.9** Tyrell agrees to lease a house from Jackson, the property owner. The lease contract includes a clause stating that Tyrell is paying an additional $15,000 for an option to purchase the property within a specified period of time. If Tyrell decides not to purchase the house after the specified period has lapsed, he loses the $15,000, and Jackson is free to sell the property to another buyer. ◀

Rejection. If the offeree rejects the offer—by words or by conduct—the offer is terminated. Any subsequent attempt by the offeree to accept will be construed as a new offer, giving the original offeror (now the offeree) the power of acceptance. Like a revocation, a rejection of an offer is effective only when it is actually received by the offeror or the offeror's agent.

Merely inquiring about an offer does not constitute rejection. When the offeree merely inquires as to the "firmness" of the offer, there is no reason to presume that he or she intends to reject it. ▶ **Example 10.10** Raymond offers to buy Francie's iPhone 5 for $200, and Francie responds, "Is that your best offer?" or "Will you pay me $275 for it?" A reasonable person would conclude that Francie did not reject the offer but merely made an inquiry about it. She can still accept and bind Raymond to the $200 purchase price. ◀

Counteroffer. A **counteroffer** is a rejection of the original offer and the simultaneous making of a new offer. ▶ **Example 10.11** Burke offers to sell his home to Lang for $270,000. Lang responds, "Your price is too high. I'll offer to purchase your house for $250,000." Lang's response is called a counteroffer because it rejects Burke's offer to sell at $270,000 and creates a new offer by Lang to purchase the home at a price of $250,000. ◀

At common law, the **mirror image rule** requires the offeree's acceptance to match the offeror's offer exactly—to mirror the offer. Any change in, or addition to, the terms of the original offer automatically terminates that offer and substitutes the counteroffer. The counteroffer, of course, need not be accepted, but if the original offeror does accept the terms of the counteroffer, a valid contract is created.[8]

TERMINATION BY OPERATION OF LAW The power of the offeree to transform the offer into a binding, legal obligation can be terminated by operation of law through the occurrence of any of the following events:

1. Lapse of time.
2. Destruction of the specific subject matter of the offer.
3. Death or incompetence of the offeror or the offeree.
4. Supervening illegality of the proposed contract. (A statute or court decision that makes an offer illegal automatically terminates the offer.)

Lapse of Time. An offer terminates automatically by law when the period of time *specified in the offer* has passed. If the offer states that it will be left open until a particular date, then the offer will terminate at midnight on that day. If the offer states that it will be open for a number of days, this time period normally begins to run when the offeree *receives* the offer (not when it is formed or sent).

If the offer does not specify a time for acceptance, the offer terminates at the end of a *reasonable* period of time. What constitutes a reasonable period of time depends on the subject matter of the contract, business and market conditions, and other relevant circumstances. An offer to sell farm produce, for example, will terminate sooner than an offer to sell farm equipment because farm produce is perishable. Produce is also subject to greater fluctuations in market value.

Destruction of the Subject Matter. An offer is automatically terminated if the specific subject matter of the offer (such as a smartphone or a house) is destroyed before the offer is accepted.[9] ▶ **Example 10.12** John-

---

8. The mirror image rule has been greatly modified in regard to sales contracts. Section 2–207 of the UCC provides that a contract is formed if the offeree makes a definite expression of acceptance (such as signing the form in the appropriate location), even though the terms of the acceptance modify or add to the terms of the original offer (see Chapter 20).

9. *Restatement (Second) of Contracts,* Section 36.

son offers to sell his prize greyhound to Rizzo. If the dog dies before Rizzo can accept, the offer is automatically terminated. Johnson does not have to tell Rizzo that the animal has died for the offer to terminate. ◀

Death or Incompetence of the Offeror or Offeree. An offeree's power of acceptance is terminated when the offeror or offeree dies or is legally incapacitated— *unless the offer is irrevocable.* ▶ **Example 10.13** Sybil Maven offers to sell commercial property to Westside Investment for $2 million. In June, Westside pays Maven $5,000 in exchange for her agreement to hold the offer open for ten months (forming an option contract). If Maven dies in July, her offer is not terminated because it is irrevocable. Westside can purchase the property anytime within the ten-month period. ◀

A revocable offer is personal to both parties and cannot pass to the heirs, guardian, or estate of either party. This rule applies whether or not the other party had notice of the death or incompetence.

Supervening Illegality of the Proposed Contract. A statute or court decision that makes an offer illegal automatically terminates the offer.[10] ▶ **Example 10.14** Lee offers to lend Kim $10,000 at an annual interest rate

---

10. *Restatement (Second) of Contracts,* Section 36.

of 15 percent. Before Kim can accept the offer, a law is enacted that prohibits interest rates higher than 12 percent. Lee's offer is automatically terminated. (If the statute is enacted after Kim accepts the offer, a valid contract is formed, but the contract may still be unenforceable—see Chapter 11.) ◀

Concept Summary 10.1 below provides a review of the ways in which an offer can be terminated.

Acceptance

Acceptance is a voluntary act by the offeree that shows assent (agreement) to the terms of an offer. The offeree's act may consist of words or conduct. The acceptance must be unequivocal and must be communicated to the offeror. Generally, only the person to whom the offer is made or that person's agent can accept the offer and create a binding contract.

UNEQUIVOCAL ACCEPTANCE To exercise the power of acceptance effectively, the offeree must accept unequivocally. This is the *mirror image rule* previously discussed. An acceptance may be unequivocal even though the offeree expresses dissatisfaction with the contract. For instance, "I accept the offer, but can you give me a better price?" is an effective acceptance.

CONCEPT SUMMARY 10.1
Methods by Which an Offer Can Be Terminated

BY ACTION OF THE PARTIES—

1. *Revocation*—Unless the offer is irrevocable, it can be revoked at any time before acceptance without liability. Revocation is not effective until received by the offeree or the offeree's agent. Some offers, such as a merchant's firm offer and option contracts, are irrevocable. Also, in some situations, an offeree's detrimental reliance or partial performance will cause a court to rule that the offeror cannot revoke the offer.
2. *Rejection*—Accomplished by words or actions that demonstrate a clear intent not to accept the offer; not effective until received by the offeror or the offeror's agent.
3. *Counteroffer*—A rejection of the original offer and the making of a new offer.

BY OPERATION OF LAW—

1. *Lapse of time*—The offer terminates at the end of the time period specified in the offer or, if no time period is stated in the offer, at the end of a reasonable time period.
2. *Destruction of the subject matter*—When the specific subject matter of the offer is destroyed before the offer is accepted, the offer automatically terminates.
3. *Death or incompetence of the offeror or offeree*—If the offeror or offeree dies or becomes incompetent, this offer terminates (unless the offer is irrevocable).
4. *Supervening illegality*—When a statute or court decision makes the proposed contract illegal, the offer automatically terminates.

An acceptance cannot impose new conditions or change the terms of the original offer. If it does, the acceptance may be considered a counteroffer, which is a rejection of the original offer. For instance, the statement "I accept the offer but only if I can pay on ninety days' credit" is a counteroffer and not an unequivocal acceptance.

Certain terms, when included in an acceptance, will not change the offer sufficiently to constitute rejection. ▶ **Example 10.15** In response to an art dealer's offer to sell a painting, the offeree, Ashton Gibbs, replies, "I accept. Please send a written contract." Gibbs is requesting a written contract but is not making it a condition for acceptance. Therefore, the acceptance is effective without the written contract. In contrast, if Gibbs replies, "I accept *if* you send a written contract," the acceptance is expressly conditioned on the request for a writing, and the statement is not an acceptance but a counteroffer. (Notice how important each word is!)[11] ◀

SILENCE AS ACCEPTANCE Ordinarily, silence cannot constitute acceptance, even if the offeror states, "By your silence and inaction, you will be deemed to have accepted this offer." An offeree should not be obligated to act affirmatively to reject an offer when no consideration (nothing of value) has passed to the offeree to impose such a duty.

In some instances, however, the offeree does have a duty to speak and her or his silence or inaction will operate as an acceptance. Silence may constitute an acceptance in the following circumstances:

1. When an offeree takes the benefit of offered services even though he or she had an opportunity to reject them and knew that they were offered with the expectation of compensation. ▶ **Example 10.16** John is a student who earns extra income by washing store windows. John taps on the window of a store, catches the attention of the store's manager, and points to the window and raises his cleaner, signaling that he will be washing the window. The manager does nothing to stop him. Here, the store manager's silence constitutes an acceptance, and an implied contract is created. The store is bound to pay a reasonable value for John's work. ◀
2. When the offeree has had prior dealings with the offeror. For instance, a merchant routinely receives shipments from a certain supplier and

always notifies that supplier when defective goods are rejected. The merchant's silence regarding a particular shipment (failure to reject the goods) will constitute acceptance.

COMMUNICATION OF ACCEPTANCE In a bilateral contract, acceptance is in the form of a promise (not performance). Because bilateral contracts are formed when the promise is made (rather than when the act is performed), communication of acceptance is necessary. Communication of acceptance may not be necessary if the offer dispenses with the requirement, however, or if the offer can be accepted by silence.

▶ **Case in Point 10.17** Powerhouse Custom Homes, Inc., owed $95,260.42 to 84 Lumber Company under a credit agreement. When Powerhouse failed to pay, 84 Lumber filed a suit to collect. During mediation, the parties agreed to a deadline for objections to whatever agreement they might reach. If there were no objections, the agreement would be binding. Powerhouse then offered to pay less than the amount owed, and 84 Lumber did not respond. Powerhouse argued that 84 Lumber accepted the offer by not objecting to it within the deadline. The court, however, held that for a contract to be formed, an offer must be accepted unequivocally. Although Powerhouse had made an offer of a proposed settlement, 84 Lumber did not communicate its acceptance. Thus, the court reasoned that the parties did not reach an agreement on the proposed settlement.[12] ◀

Because a unilateral contract calls for the full performance of some act, acceptance is usually evident, and notification is therefore unnecessary. Nevertheless, exceptions do exist, such as when the offeror requests notice of acceptance or has no way of determining whether the requested act has been performed.

MODE AND TIMELINESS OF ACCEPTANCE In bilateral contracts, acceptance must be timely. The general rule is that acceptance in a bilateral contract is timely if it is made before the offer is terminated. Problems may arise, though, when the parties involved are not dealing face to face. In such situations, the offeree should use an authorized mode of communication.

The Mailbox Rule. Acceptance takes effect, thus completing formation of the contract, at the time the offeree sends or delivers the communication via the mode expressly or impliedly authorized by the offeror. This is the so-called **mailbox rule,** also called

---

11. As noted in footnote 8, in regard to sales contracts, the UCC provides that an acceptance may still be valid even if some terms are added. The new terms are simply treated as proposed additions to the contract.

12. *Powerhouse Custom Homes, Inc. v. 84 Lumber Co.,* 307 Ga.App. 605, 705 S.E.2d 704 (2011).

the *deposited acceptance rule,* which the majority of courts follow. Under this rule, if the authorized mode of communication is the mail, then an acceptance becomes valid when it is dispatched (placed in the control of the U.S. Postal Service)—*not* when it is received by the offeror. (Note, however, that if the offer stipulates when acceptance will be effective, then the offer will not be effective until the time specified.)

The mailbox rule does not apply to instantaneous forms of communication, such as when the parties are dealing face to face, by telephone, by fax, and usually by e-mail. Under the Uniform Electronic Transactions Act (UETA—discussed later in this chapter), e-mail is considered sent when it either leaves the control of the sender or is received by the recipient. This rule takes the place of the mailbox rule when the parties have agreed to conduct transactions electronically and allows an e-mail acceptance to become effective when sent.

Authorized Means of Acceptance. A means of communicating acceptance can be expressly authorized by the offeror or impliedly authorized by the facts and circumstances of the situation.[13] An acceptance sent by means not expressly or impliedly authorized normally is not effective until it is received by the offeror.

When an offeror specifies how acceptance should be made (for example, by overnight delivery), *express authorization* is said to exist. The contract is not formed unless the offeree uses that specified mode of acceptance. Moreover, both offeror and offeree are bound in contract the moment this means of acceptance is employed. ▶ **Example 10.18** Motorola Mobility, Inc., offers to sell 144 Atrix 4G smartphones and 72 Lapdocks to Call Me Plus phone stores. The offer states that Call Me Plus must accept the offer via FedEx overnight delivery. The acceptance is effective (and a binding contract is formed) the moment that Call Me Plus gives the overnight envelope containing the acceptance to the FedEx driver. ◀

If the offeror does not expressly authorize a certain mode of acceptance, then acceptance can be made by *any reasonable means.*[14] Courts look at the prevailing business usages and the surrounding circumstances to determine whether the mode of acceptance used was reasonable. Usually, the offeror's choice of a particular means in making the offer implies that the offeree can use the *same or a faster means* for acceptance. Thus, if

the offer is made via Priority U.S. mail, it would be reasonable to accept the offer via Priority mail or by a faster method, such as signed scanned documents sent as attachments via e-mail or overnight delivery.

Substitute Method of Acceptance. Sometimes, the offeror authorizes a particular method of acceptance, but the offeree accepts by a different means. In that situation, the acceptance may still be effective if the substituted method serves the same purpose as the authorized means.

The acceptance by a substitute method is not effective on dispatch, though, and no contract will be formed until the acceptance is received by the offeror. For instance, an offer specifies acceptance by FedEx overnight delivery, but the offeree instead accepts by overnight delivery from another carrier. The substitute method of acceptance will still be effective, but the contract will not be formed until the offeror receives it.

SECTION 2
AGREEMENT IN E-CONTRACTS

Numerous contracts are formed online. Electronic contracts, or **e-contracts,** must meet the same basic requirements (agreement, consideration, contractual capacity, and legality) as paper contracts. Disputes concerning e-contracts, however, tend to center on contract terms and whether the parties voluntarily agreed to those terms.

Online contracts may be formed not only for the sale of goods and services but also for *licensing.* As mentioned in Chapter 6, the purchase of software generally involves a license, or a right to use the software, rather than the passage of title (ownership rights) from the seller to the buyer. ▶ **Example 10.19** Galynn downloads an app on her iPad that enables her to work on spreadsheets. During the transaction, she has to select "I agree" several times to indicate that she understands that she is purchasing only the right to use the software under specific terms. After she agrees to these terms (the licensing agreement), she can use the application. ◀

Online Offers

Sellers doing business via the Internet can protect themselves against contract disputes and legal liability by creating offers that clearly spell out the terms

---

13. *Restatement (Second) of Contracts,* Section 30, provides that an offer invites acceptance "by any medium reasonable in the circumstances," unless the offer specifies the means of acceptance.

14. *Restatement (Second) of Contracts,* Section 30. This is also the rule under UCC 2–206(1)(a).

that will govern their transactions if the offers are accepted. All important terms should be conspicuous and easy to view.

DISPLAYING THE OFFER The seller's Web site should include a hypertext link to a page containing the full contract so that potential buyers are made aware of the terms to which they are assenting. The contract generally must be displayed online in a readable format, such as a twelve-point typeface.

All provisions should be reasonably clear. ▶ **Example 10.20** Netquip sells a variety of heavy equipment, such as trucks and trailers, on its Web site. Because Netquip's pricing schedule is very complex, the schedule must be fully provided and explained on the Web site. In addition, the terms of the sale (such as any warranties and the refund policy) must be fully disclosed. ◀

PROVISIONS TO INCLUDE An important rule to keep in mind is that the offeror (the seller) controls the offer and thus the resulting contract. The seller should therefore anticipate the terms he or she wants to include in a contract and provide for them in the offer. In some instances, a standardized contract form may suffice. At a minimum, an online offer should include the following provisions:

1. *Acceptance of terms.* A clause that clearly indicates what constitutes the buyer's agreement to the terms of the offer, such as a box containing the words "I accept" that the buyer can click. (Mechanisms for accepting online offers will be discussed in detail later in the chapter.)

2. *Payment.* A provision specifying how payment for the goods (including any applicable taxes) must be made.

3. *Return policy.* A statement of the seller's refund and return policies.

4. *Disclaimer.* Disclaimers of liability for certain uses of the goods. For example, an online seller of business forms may add a disclaimer that the seller does not accept responsibility for the buyer's reliance on the forms rather than on an attorney's advice.

5. *Limitation on remedies.* A provision specifying the remedies available to the buyer if the goods are found to be defective or if the contract is otherwise breached. Any limitation of remedies should be clearly spelled out.

6. *Privacy policy.* A statement indicating how the seller will use the information gathered about the buyer.

7. *Dispute resolution.* Provisions relating to dispute settlement, such as an arbitration clause or a *forum-selection clause* (discussed next).

DISPUTE-SETTLEMENT PROVISIONS Online offers frequently include provisions relating to dispute settlement. For example, the offer might include an arbitration clause specifying that any dispute arising under the contract will be arbitrated in a designated forum.

Forum-Selection Clause. Many online contracts contain a **forum-selection clause** indicating the forum, or location (such as a court or jurisdiction), in which contract disputes will be resolved. As discussed in Chapter 3, significant jurisdictional issues may arise when parties are at a great distance, as they often are when they form contracts via the Internet. A forum-selection clause will help to avert future jurisdictional problems and also help to ensure that the seller will not be required to appear in court in a distant state.

▶ **Case in Point 10.21** Before advertisers can place ads through Google, Inc., they must agree to certain terms that are displayed in an online window. These terms include a forum-selection clause, which provides that any dispute is to be "adjudicated in Santa Clara County, California." Lawrence Feldman, who advertised through Google, complained that he was overcharged and filed a lawsuit against Google in a federal district court in Pennsylvania. The court held that Feldman had agreed to the forum-selection clause in Google's online contract and transferred the case to a court in Santa Clara County.[15] ◀

Choice-of-Law Clause. Some online contracts may also include a *choice-of-law clause* specifying that any contract dispute will be settled according to the law of a particular jurisdiction, such as a state or country. Choice-of-law clauses are particularly common in international contracts, but they may also appear in e-contracts to specify which state's laws will govern in the United States.

Online Acceptances

The *Restatement (Second) of Contracts*, which, as noted earlier, is a compilation of common law contract principles, states that parties may agree to a contract "by written or spoken words or by other action or by failure

---

15. *Feldman v. Google, Inc.,* 513 F.Supp.2d 229 (E.D.Pa. 2007).

to act."[16] The Uniform Commercial Code (UCC), which governs sales contracts, has a similar provision. Section 2–204 of the UCC states that any contract for the sale of goods "may be made in any manner sufficient to show agreement, including conduct by both parties which recognizes the existence of such a contract."

CLICK-ON AGREEMENTS The courts have used the *Restatement* and UCC provisions to conclude that a binding contract can be created by conduct. This includes the act of clicking on a box indicating "I accept" or "I agree" to accept an online offer. The agreement resulting from such an acceptance is often called a **click-on agreement** (sometimes referred to as a *click-on license* or *click-wrap agreement*). Exhibit 10–1 below shows a portion of a typical click-on agreement that accompanies a software package.

Generally, the law does not require that the parties have read all of the terms in a contract for it to be effective. Therefore, clicking on a box that states "I agree" to certain terms can be enough. The terms may be contained on a Web site through which the buyer is obtaining goods or services. They may also appear on a screen when software is loaded from a CD-ROM or DVD or downloaded from the Internet.

▶ **Case in Point 10.22** The "Terms of Use" that govern Facebook users' accounts include a forum-selection clause that provides for the resolution of all disputes in a court in Santa Clara County, California. To sign up for a Facebook account, a person must click on a box indicating that he or she has agreed to this term.

Mustafa Fteja was an active user of face-book.com when his account was disabled. He sued Facebook in a federal court in New York, claiming that it had disabled his Facebook page without justification and for discriminatory reasons. Facebook filed a motion to transfer the case to California under the forum-selection clause. The court found that the clause in Facebook's online contract was binding and transferred the case. When Fteja clicked on the button to accept the "Terms of Use" and become a Facebook user, he agreed to resolve all disputes with Facebook in Santa Clara County, California.[17] ◀

SHRINK-WRAP AGREEMENTS With a **shrink-wrap agreement** (or *shrink-wrap license*), the

terms are expressed inside the box in which the goods are packaged. (The term *shrink-wrap* refers to the plastic that covers the box.) Usually, the party who opens the box is told that she or he agrees to the terms by keeping whatever is in the box. Similarly, when a purchaser opens a software package, he or she agrees to abide by the terms of the limited license agreement.

▶ **Example 10.23** Ava orders a new iMac from Big Dog Electronics, which ships it to her. Along with the iMac, the box contains an agreement setting forth the terms of the sale, including what remedies are available. The document also states that Ava's retention of the iMac for longer than thirty days will be construed as an acceptance of the terms. ◀

In most instances, a shrink-wrap agreement is not between a retailer and a buyer, but between the manufacturer of the hardware or software and the ultimate buyer-user of the product. The terms generally concern warranties, remedies, and other issues associated with the use of the product.

Shrink-Wrap Agreements and Enforceable Contract Terms. In some cases, the courts have enforced the terms of shrink-wrap agreements in the same way as the terms of other contracts. These courts have reasoned that by including the terms with the product, the seller proposed a contract. The buyer could accept this contract by using the product after having an opportunity to read the terms. Thus, a buyer's failure to object to terms contained within a shrink-wrapped software package may constitute an acceptance of the terms by conduct.

EXHIBIT 10–1 A Click-On Agreement Sample

This exhibit illustrates an online offer to form a contract. To accept the offer, the user simply scrolls down the page and clicks on the "I Accept" button.

---

16. *Restatement (Second) of Contracts*, Section 19.
17. *Fteja v. Facebook, Inc.*, 841 F.Supp.2d 829 (S.D.N.Y. 2012).

Shrink-Wrap Terms That May Not Be Enforced. Sometimes, however, the courts have refused to enforce certain terms included in shrink-wrap agreements because the buyer did not expressly consent to them. An important factor is when the parties formed their contract.

If a buyer orders a product over the telephone, for instance, and is not informed of an arbitration clause or forum-selection clause at that time, the buyer clearly has not expressly agreed to these terms. If the buyer discovers the clauses *after* the parties entered into a contract, a court may conclude that those terms were proposals for additional terms and were not part of the contract.

BROWSE-WRAP TERMS Like the terms of click-on agreements, **browse-wrap terms** can occur in transactions conducted over the Internet. Unlike click-on agreements, however, browse-wrap terms do not require Internet users to assent to the terms before downloading or using certain software. In other words, a person can install the software without clicking "I agree" to the terms of a license. Browse-wrap terms are often unenforceable because they do not satisfy the agreement requirement of contract formation.[18]

▶ **Example 10.24** BrowseNet Corporation provides free downloadable software called "QuickLoad" on its Web site. Users must indicate, by clicking on a designated box, that they wish to obtain it. On the Web site's download page is a reference to a license agreement that users can view only by scrolling to the next screen. In other words, the user does not have to agree to the terms of the license before downloading the software. One of the license terms requires all disputes to be submitted to arbitration in California. If a user sues BrowseNet in Washington state, the arbitration clause might not be enforceable because users were not required to indicate their assent to the agreement. ◀

E-Signature Technologies

Today, numerous technologies allow electronic documents to be signed. An **e-signature** has been defined as "an electronic sound, symbol, or process attached to or logically associated with a record and executed or adopted by a person with the intent to sign the record."[19] Thus, e-signatures include encrypted digital signatures, names (intended as signatures) at the end of e-mail messages, and clicks on a Web page if the click includes some means of identification.

Federal Law on E-Signatures and E-Documents

In 2000, Congress enacted the Electronic Signatures in Global and National Commerce Act (E-SIGN Act),[20] which provides that no contract, record, or signature may be "denied legal effect" solely because it is in electronic form. In other words, under this law, an electronic signature is as valid as a signature on paper, and an e-document can be as enforceable as a paper one.

For an e-signature to be enforceable, the contracting parties must have agreed to use electronic signatures. For an electronic document to be valid, it must be in a form that can be retained and accurately reproduced.

The E-SIGN Act does not apply to all types of documents. Contracts and documents that are exempt include court papers, divorce decrees, evictions, foreclosures, health-insurance terminations, prenuptial agreements, and wills. Also, the only agreements governed by the UCC that fall under this law are those covered by Articles 2 and 2A (sales and lease contracts) and UCC 1–107 and 1–206. Despite these limitations, the E-SIGN Act significantly expanded the possibilities for contracting online.

Partnering Agreements

One way that online sellers and buyers can prevent disputes over signatures in their e-contracts, as well as disputes over the terms and conditions of those contracts, is to form partnering agreements. In a **partnering agreement,** a seller and a buyer who frequently do business with each other agree in advance on the terms and conditions that will apply to all transactions subsequently conducted electronically. The partnering agreement can also establish special access and identification codes to be used by the parties when transacting business electronically.

A partnering agreement reduces the likelihood that disputes will arise under the contract because the parties have agreed in advance to the terms and conditions that will accompany each sale. Furthermore, if a dispute does arise, a court or arbitration forum will be able to refer to the partnering agreement when determining the parties' intent.

---

18. See, for example, *Jesmer v. Retail Magic, Inc.,* 863 N.Y.S.2d 737 (2008).
19. This definition is from the Uniform Electronic Transactions Act, which will be discussed later in this chapter.
20. 15 U.S.C. Sections 7001 *et seq.*

SECTION 3
THE UNIFORM ELECTRONIC TRANSACTIONS ACT

Although most states have laws governing e-signatures and other aspects of electronic transactions, these laws vary. In an attempt to create more uniformity among the states, in 1999 the National Conference of Commissioners on Uniform State Laws and the American Law Institute promulgated the Uniform Electronic Transactions Act (UETA). The UETA has been adopted, at least in part, by forty-eight states. Among other things, the UETA declares that a signature may not be denied legal effect or enforceability solely because it is in electronic form.

The primary purpose of the UETA is to remove barriers to e-commerce by giving the same legal effect to electronic records and signatures as is given to paper documents and signatures. As mentioned earlier, the UETA broadly defines an *e-signature* as "an electronic sound, symbol, or process attached to or logically associated with a record and executed or adopted by a person with the intent to sign the record."[21] A **record** is "information that is inscribed on a tangible medium or that is stored in an electronic or other medium and is retrievable in perceivable [visual] form."[22]

The Scope and Applicability of the UETA

The UETA does not create new rules for electronic contracts but rather establishes that records, signatures, and contracts may not be denied enforceability solely due to their electronic form. The UETA does not apply to all writings and signatures. It covers only electronic records and electronic signatures *relating to a transaction*. A *transaction* is defined as an interaction between two or more people relating to business, commercial, or governmental activities.[23]

The act specifically does not apply to wills or testamentary trusts or to transactions governed by the UCC (other than those covered by Articles 2 and 2A).[24] In addition, the provisions of the UETA allow the states to exclude its application to other areas of law.

The UETA does not apply to a transaction unless each of the parties has previously agreed to conduct transactions by electronic means. The agreement need not be explicit, however. It can be implied by the conduct of the parties and the surrounding circumstances, such as negotiating a contract via e-mail.[25] The parties can agree to opt out of all or some of the terms of the UETA, but if they do not, then the UETA terms will govern their electronic transactions.

The Federal E-SIGN Act and the UETA

Congress passed the E-SIGN Act in 2000, a year after the UETA was presented to the states for adoption. Thus, a significant issue was to what extent the federal E-SIGN Act preempted the UETA as adopted by the states.

The E-SIGN Act[26] refers explicitly to the UETA and provides that if a state has enacted the uniform version of the UETA, it is not preempted by the E-SIGN Act. In other words, if the state has enacted the UETA without modification, state law will govern. The problem is that many states have enacted nonuniform (modified) versions of the UETA, usually to exclude other areas of state law from the UETA's terms. The E-SIGN Act specifies that those exclusions will be preempted to the extent that they are inconsistent with the E-SIGN Act's provisions.

The E-SIGN Act explicitly allows the states to enact alternative requirements for the use of electronic records or electronic signatures. Generally, however, the requirements must be consistent with the provisions of the E-SIGN Act, and the state must not give greater legal status or effect to one specific type of technology. Additionally, if a state enacts alternative requirements after the E-SIGN Act was adopted, the state law must specifically refer to the E-SIGN Act. The relationship between the UETA and the E-SIGN Act is illustrated in Exhibit 10–2 on the following page.

Signatures on Electronic Records

Under the UETA, if an electronic record or signature is the act of a particular person, the record or signature may be attributed to that person. If a person types her or his name at the bottom of an e-mail purchase order, for instance, that name would qualify as a "signature." The signature would therefore be attributed to the person whose name appeared.

---

21. UETA 102(8).
22. UETA 102(15).
23. UETA 2(12) and 3.
24. UETA 3(b).

25. UETA 5(b), and Comment 4B.
26. 15 U.S.C. Section 7002(2)(A)(i).

EXHIBIT 10-2 The E-SIGN Act and the UETA

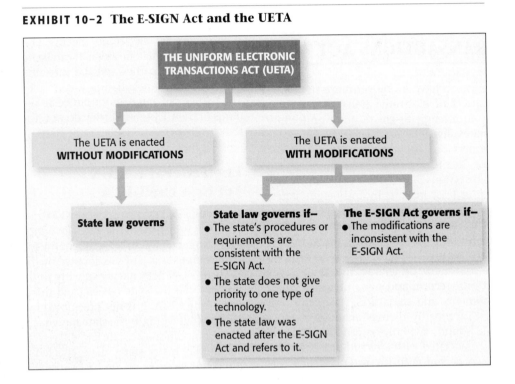

The UETA does not contain any express provisions about what constitutes fraud or whether an agent is authorized to enter a contract. Under the UETA, other state laws control if any issues relating to agency, authority, forgery, or contract formation arise. If existing state law requires a document to be notarized, the UETA provides that this requirement is satisfied by the electronic signature of a notary public or other person authorized to verify signatures.

The Effect of Errors

The UETA encourages, but does not require, the use of security procedures (such as encryption) to verify changes to electronic documents and to correct errors. It does this by providing a benefit to parties who have agreed to a security procedure. If one of the parties does not detect an error because he or she did not follow the procedure, the other party can legally avoid the effect of the change or error. When the parties have not agreed to use a security procedure, then other state laws (including contract law governing mistakes—see Chapter 12) will determine the effect of the error.

To avoid the effect of errors, a party must promptly notify the other party of the error and of her or his intent not to be bound by the error. In addition, the party must take reasonable steps to return any benefit received: parties cannot avoid a transaction if they have benefited.

Timing

An electronic record is considered *sent* when it is properly directed to the intended recipient in a form readable by the recipient's computer system. Once the electronic record leaves the control of the sender or comes under the control of the recipient, the UETA deems it to have been sent. An electronic record is considered *received* when it enters the recipient's processing system in a readable form—*even if no individual is aware of its receipt.*

SECTION 4

INTERNATIONAL TREATIES AFFECTING E-CONTRACTS

Today, much of the e-commerce conducted on a worldwide basis involves buyers and sellers from the United States. The preeminence of U.S. law in this area is likely to be challenged in the future, however, as Internet use continues to expand worldwide. Already, several international organizations have created their own regulations for global Internet transactions.

The United Nations Convention on the Use of Electronic Communications in International Contracts improves commercial certainty by determining an Internet user's location for legal purposes. The convention also establishes standards for creating functional equivalence between electronic communications and paper documents. The convention also provides that e-signatures will be treated as the equivalent of signatures on paper documents.

Another treaty relevant to e-contracts is the Hague Convention on the Choice of Court Agreements. Although it does not specifically mention e-commerce, this convention provides more certainty regarding jurisdiction and recognition of judgments by other nations' courts, thereby facilitating both offline and online transactions.

Reviewing: Agreement in Traditional and E-Contracts

Shane Durbin wanted to have a recording studio custom-built in his home. He sent invitations to a number of local contractors to submit bids on the project. Rory Amstel submitted the lowest bid, which was $20,000 less than any of the other bids Durbin received. Durbin called Amstel to ascertain the type and quality of the materials that were included in the bid and to find out if he could substitute a superior brand of acoustic tiles for the same bid price. Amstel said he would have to check into the price difference. The parties also discussed a possible start date for construction. Two weeks later, Durbin changed his mind and decided not to go forward with his plan to build a recording studio. Amstel filed a suit against Durbin for breach of contract. Using the information presented in the chapter, answer the following questions.

1. Did Amstel's bid meet the requirements of an offer? Explain.
2. Was there an acceptance of the offer? Why or why not?
3. Suppose that the court determines that the parties did not reach an agreement. Further suppose that Amstel, in anticipation of building Durbin's studio, had purchased materials and refused other jobs so that he would have time in his schedule for Durbin's project. Under what theory discussed in the chapter might Amstel attempt to recover these costs?
4. How is an offer terminated? Assuming that Durbin did not inform Amstel that he was rejecting the offer, was the offer terminated at any time described here? Explain.

DEBATE THIS . . . *The terms and conditions in click-on agreements are so long and detailed that no one ever reads the agreements. Therefore, the act of clicking on "I agree" is not really an acceptance.*

Terms and Concepts

acceptance 203
agreement 194
browse-wrap terms 208
click-on agreement 207
counteroffer 202
e-contract 205

e-signature 208
forum-selection clause 206
mailbox rule 204
mirror image rule 202
offer 194
option contract 202

partnering agreement 208
record 209
revocation 201
shrink-wrap agreement 207

ExamPrep

Issue Spotters

1. Fidelity Corporation offers to hire Ron to replace Monica, who has given Fidelity a month's notice of intent to quit. Fidelity gives Ron a week to decide whether to accept. Two days later, Monica decides not to quit and signs an employment contract with Fidelity for another year. The next day, Monica tells Ron of the new contract. Ron immediately faxes a formal letter of acceptance to Fidelity. Do Fidelity and Ron have a contract? Why or why not? **(See page 201.)**

2. Applied Products, Inc., does business with Beltway Distributors, Inc., online. Under the Uniform Electronic Transactions Act, what determines the effect of the electronic documents evidencing the parties' deal? Is a party's "signature" necessary? Explain. **(See page 209.)**

• Check your answers to the Issue Spotters against the answers provided in Appendix B at the end of this text.

Before the Test

Go to **www.cengagebrain.com**, enter the ISBN 9781285770192, and click on "Find" to locate this textbook's Web site. Then, click on "Access Now" under "Study Tools," and select Chapter 10 at the top. There, you will find a Practice Quiz that you can take to assess your mastery of the concepts in this chapter, as well as Flashcards and a Glossary of important terms.

Business Scenarios

10–1. Agreement. Ball e-mails Sullivan and inquires how much Sullivan is asking for a specific forty-acre tract of land Sullivan owns. Sullivan responds, "I will not take less than $60,000 for the forty-acre tract as specified." Ball immediately sends Sullivan a fax stating, "I accept your offer for $60,000 for the forty-acre tract as specified." Discuss whether Ball can hold Sullivan to a contract for the sale of the land. **(See page 196.)**

10–2. Offer and Acceptance. Schmidt, the owner of a small business, has a large piece of used farm equipment for sale. He offers to sell the equipment to Barry for $10,000. Discuss the legal effects of the following events on the offer: **(See page 203.)**

(a) Schmidt dies prior to Barry's acceptance, and at the time he accepts, Barry is unaware of Schmidt's death.

(b) The night before Barry accepts, fire destroys the equipment.

(c) Barry pays $100 for a thirty-day option to purchase the equipment. During this period, Schmidt dies, and later Barry accepts the offer, knowing of Schmidt's death.

(d) Barry pays $100 for a thirty-day option to purchase the equipment. During this period, Barry dies, and Barry's estate accepts Schmidt's offer within the stipulated time period.

10–3. Online Acceptance. Anne is a reporter for *Daily Business Journal,* a print publication consulted by investors and other businesspersons. She often uses the Internet to perform research for the articles that she writes for the publication. While visiting the Web site of Cyberspace Investments Corp., Anne reads a pop-up window that states, "Our business newsletter, *E-Commerce Weekly,* is available at a one-year subscription rate of $5 per issue. To subscribe, enter your e-mail address below and click 'SUBSCRIBE.' By subscribing, you agree to the terms of the subscriber's agreement. To read this agreement, click 'AGREEMENT.' " Anne enters her e-mail address, but does not click on "AGREEMENT" to read the terms. Has Anne entered into an enforceable contract to pay for *E-Commerce Weekly?* Explain. **(See page 206.)**

Business Case Problems

10–4. Spotlight on Crime Stoppers—Communication. The

Baton Rouge Crime Stoppers (BCS) offered a reward for information about the "South Louisiana Serial Killer." The information was to be provided via a hot line. Dianne Alexander had survived an attack by a person suspected of being the killer. She identified a suspect in a police photo lineup and later sought to collect the reward. BCS refused to pay because she did not provide information to them via the hot line. Did Alexander comply with the terms of the offer? Explain. [*Alexander v. Lafayette Crime Stoppers, Inc.,* 38 So.3d 282 (La.App. 3 Dist. 2010) **(See page 200.)**

10–5. BUSINESS CASE PROBLEM WITH SAMPLE ANSWER: Offer and Acceptance.

While gambling at Prairie Meadows Casino, Troy Blackford became angry and smashed a slot machine. He was banned from the premises. Despite the ban, he later gambled at the casino and won

$9,387. When he tried to collect his winnings, the casino refused to pay. Blackford filed a suit for breach of contract, arguing that he and the casino had a contract because he had accepted its offer to gamble. Did the casino and Blackford have a contract? Discuss. [Blackford v. Prairie Meadows Racetrack and Casino, 778 N.W.2d 184 (Sup.Ct. Iowa 2010)] **(See page 194.)**

- For a sample answer to Problem 10–5, go to Appendix C at the end of this text.

10–6. Shrink-Wrap Agreements. TracFone Wireless, Inc., sells phones and wireless service. The phones are sold for less than their cost, which TracFone recoups by selling prepaid airtime for their use on its network. Software in the phones prohibits their use on other networks. The phones are sold subject to the condition that the buyer agrees "not to tamper with or alter the software." This is printed on the packaging. Bequator Corp. bought at least 18,616 of the phones, disabled the software so that they could be used on other networks, and resold them. Is Bequator liable for breach of contract? Explain. [*TracFone Wireless, Inc. v. Bequator Corp.,* __ F.Supp.2d __ (S.D.Fla. 2011)] **(See page 207.)**

10–7. Online Acceptances. Heather Reasonover opted to try Internet service from Clearwire Corp. Clearwire sent her a confirmation e-mail that included a link to its Web site. Clearwire also sent her a modem. In the enclosed written materials, at the bottom of a page, in small type was the Web site URL. When Reasonover plugged in the modem, an "I accept terms" box appeared. Without clicking on the box, Reasonover quit the page. A clause in Clearwire's "Terms of Service," accessible only through its Web site, required its subscribers to submit any dispute to arbitration. Is Reasonover bound to this clause? Why or why not? [*Kwan v. Clearwire Corp.,* 2012 WL 32380 (W.D.Wash. 2012)] **(See page 206.)**

10–8. Acceptance. Judy Olsen, Kristy Johnston, and their mother, Joyce Johnston, owned seventy-eight acres of real property on Eagle Creek in Meagher County, Montana. When Joyce died, she left her interest in the property to Kristy. Kristy wrote to Judy, offering to buy Judy's interest or to sell her own interest to Judy. The letter said to "please respond to Bruce Townsend." In a letter to Kristy—not to Bruce—Judy accepted Kristy's offer to sell her interest. By that time, however, Kristy had made the same offer to sell her interest to their brother Dave, and he had accepted. Did Judy and Kristy have an enforceable binding contract? Or did Kristy's offer specifying one exclusive mode of acceptance mean that Judy's reply was not effective? Discuss. [*Olsen v. Johnston,* 368 Mont. 347, __ P.3d __, (2013)] **(See page 203.)**

10–9. A QUESTION OF ETHICS: E-Contract Disputes.

 Dewayne Hubbert, Elden Craft, Chris Grout, and Rhonda Byington bought computers from Dell Corp. through its Web site. Before buying, Hubbert and the others configured their own computers. To make a purchase, each buyer completed forms on five Web pages. On each page, Dell's "Terms and Conditions of Sale" were accessible by clicking on a blue hyperlink. A statement on three of the pages read, "All sales are subject to Dell's Term[s] and Conditions of Sale," but a buyer was not required to click an assent to the terms to complete a purchase. The terms were also printed on the backs of the invoices and on separate documents contained in the shipping boxes with the computers. Among those terms was a "Binding Arbitration" clause.

The computers contained Pentium 4 microprocessors, which Dell advertised as the fastest, most powerful Intel Pentium processors then available. In 2002, Hubbert and the others filed a suit in an Illinois state court against Dell, alleging that this marketing was false, misleading, and deceptive. The plaintiffs claimed that the Pentium 4 microprocessor was slower and less powerful, and provided less performance, than either a Pentium III or an AMD Athlon, and at a greater cost. Dell asked the court to compel arbitration. [Hubbert v. Dell Corp., 359 Ill.App.3d 976, 835 N.E.2d 113, 296 Ill.Dec. 258 (5 Dist. 2005)] **(See page 205.)**

- **(a)** Should the court enforce the arbitration clause in this case? If you were the judge, how would you rule on this issue?
- **(b)** Do you think shrink-wrap, click-on, and browse-wrap terms impose too great a burden on purchasers? Why or why not?
- **(c)** An ongoing complaint about shrink-wrap, click-on, and browse-wrap terms is that sellers (often large corporations) draft them and buyers (typically individual consumers) do not read them. Should purchasers be bound in contract by terms that they have not even read? Why or why not?

Legal Reasoning Group Activity

10–10. E-Contracts. To download a specific application (app) to your smartphone or tablet device, usually you have to check a box indicating that you agree to the company's terms and conditions. Most individuals do so without ever reading those terms and conditions. Print out a specific set of terms and conditions from a downloaded app to use in this assignment. **(See page 205.)**

- **(a)** One group will determine which of these terms and conditions are favorable to the company.
- **(b)** Another group will determine which of these terms and conditions conceivably will be favorable to the individual.
- **(c)** A third group will determine which terms and conditions, on net, favor the company too much.

CHAPTER 11

CONSIDERATION, CAPACITY, AND LEGALITY

Courts generally want contracts to be enforceable, and much of the law is devoted to aiding the enforceability of contracts. Before a court will enforce a contractual promise, however, it must be convinced that there was some exchange of consideration underlying the bargain. Furthermore, "liberty of contract" is not absolute. In other words, not all people can make legally binding contracts at all times. Contracts entered into by persons lacking the capacity to do so may be voidable. Similarly, contracts calling for the performance of an illegal act are illegal and thus void—they are not contracts at all. In this chapter, we first examine the requirement of consideration and then look at contractual capacity and legality.

CONSIDERATION

The fact that a promise has been made does not mean the promise can or will be enforced. Under Roman law, a promise was not enforceable without a *causa*—that is, a reason for making the promise that was also deemed to be a sufficient reason for enforcing it. Under the common law, a primary basis for the enforcement of promises is consideration. **Consideration** usually is defined as the value (such as cash) given in return for a promise (in a bilateral contract) or in return for a performance (in a unilateral contract).

Elements of Consideration

Often, consideration is broken down into two parts: (1) something of *legally sufficient value* must be given in exchange for the promise, and (2) there must be a *bargained-for exchange*.

LEGALLY SUFFICIENT VALUE To be legally sufficient, consideration must be something of value in the eyes of the law. The "something of legally sufficient value" may consist of the following:

1. A promise to do something that one has no prior legal duty to do.

2. The performance of an action that one is otherwise not obligated to undertake.

3. The refraining from an action that one has a legal right to undertake (called a **forbearance**).

Consideration in bilateral contracts normally consists of a promise in return for a promise, as explained in Chapter 9. In a contract for the sale of goods, for instance, the seller promises to ship specific goods to the buyer, and the buyer promises to pay for those goods. Each of these promises constitutes consideration for the contract.

In contrast, unilateral contracts involve a promise in return for a performance. ▶ **Example 11.1** Anita says to her neighbor, "When you finish painting the garage, I will pay you $800." Anita's neighbor paints the garage. The act of painting the garage is the consideration that creates Anita's contractual obligation to pay her neighbor $800. ◀

BARGAINED-FOR EXCHANGE The second element of consideration is that it must provide the basis for the bargain struck between the contracting parties. The item of value must be given or promised by the promisor (offeror) in return for the promisee's promise, performance, or promise of performance.

This element of bargained-for exchange distinguishes contracts from gifts. ▶ **Example 11.2** Sheng-Li says to his son, "In consideration of the fact that you are not as wealthy as your brothers, I will pay you $5,000." The fact that the word *consideration* is used does not, by itself, mean that consideration has been given. Indeed, Sheng-Li's promise is not enforceable because the son does not have to do anything in order to receive the $5,000 promised. Because the son does not need to give Sheng-Li something of legal value in return for his promise, there is no bargained-for exchange. Rather, Sheng-Li has simply stated his motive for giving his son a gift. ◀

Adequacy of Consideration

Adequacy of consideration involves how much consideration is given. Essentially, adequacy of consideration concerns the fairness of the bargain.

THE GENERAL RULE On the surface, when the items exchanged are of unequal value, fairness would appear to be an issue. In general, however, a court will not question the adequacy of consideration based solely on the comparative value of the things exchanged.

In other words, the determination of whether consideration exists does not depend on a comparison of the values of the things exchanged. Something need not be of direct economic or financial value to be considered legally sufficient consideration. In many situations, the exchange of promises and potential benefits is deemed to be sufficient consideration.

Under the doctrine of freedom of contract, courts leave it up to the parties to decide what something is worth, and parties are usually free to bargain as they wish. If people could sue merely because they had entered into an unwise contract, the courts would be overloaded with frivolous suits.

WHEN VOLUNTARY CONSENT MAY BE LACKING When there is a large disparity in the amount or value of the consideration exchanged, it may raise a red flag for a court to look more closely at the bargain. Shockingly inadequate consideration can indicate that fraud, duress, or undue influence was involved. It may also cause a judge to question whether the contract is so one sided that it is *unconscionable*,[1] a concept that will be discussed later in this chapter on page 228.

For instance, an experienced appliance dealer induces a consumer to sign a contract written in complicated legal language. If the contract requires the consumer to pay twice the market value of the appliance, the disparity in value may indicate that the

sale involved undue influence or fraud. A judge would thus want to make sure that the person voluntarily entered into this agreement.

Agreements That Lack Consideration

Sometimes, one of the parties (or both parties) to an agreement may think that consideration has been exchanged when, in fact, it has not. Here, we look at some situations in which the parties' promises or actions do not qualify as contractual consideration.

PREEXISTING DUTY Under most circumstances, a promise to do what one already has a legal duty to do does not constitute legally sufficient consideration. The preexisting legal duty may be imposed by law or may arise out of a previous contract. A sheriff, for instance, has a duty to investigate crime and to arrest criminals. Hence, a sheriff cannot collect a reward for providing information leading to the capture of a criminal.

Likewise, if a party is already bound by contract to perform a certain duty, that duty cannot serve as consideration for a second contract. ▶ **Example 11.3** Ajax Contractors begins construction on a seven-story office building and after three months demands an extra $75,000 on its contract. If the extra $75,000 is not paid, the contractor will stop working. The owner of the land, finding no one else to complete the construction, agrees to pay the extra $75,000. The agreement is unenforceable because it is not supported by legally sufficient consideration. Ajax Contractors had a preexisting contractual duty to complete the building. ◀

Unforeseen Difficulties. The rule regarding preexisting duty is meant to prevent extortion and the so-called holdup game. Nonetheless, if, during performance of a contract, extraordinary difficulties arise that were totally unforeseen at the time the contract was formed, a court may allow an exception to the rule. The key is whether the court finds the modification is fair and equitable in view of circumstances not anticipated by the parties when the contract was made.[2]

Suppose that in *Example 11.3*, Ajax Contractors had asked for the extra $75,000 because it encountered a rock formation that no one knew existed. If the landowner agrees to pay the extra $75,000 to excavate the rock and the court finds that it is fair to do so,

---

1. Pronounced un-*kon*-shun-uh-bul.

2. *Restatement (Second) of Contracts*, Section 73.

Ajax Contractors can enforce the agreement. If rock formations are common in the area, however, the court may determine that the contractor should have known of the risk. In that situation, the court may choose to apply the preexisting duty rule and prevent Ajax Contractors from obtaining the extra $75,000.

Rescission and New Contract. The law recognizes that two parties can mutually agree to rescind, or cancel, their contract, at least to the extent that it is *executory* (still to be carried out). **Rescission**[3] is the unmaking of a contract so as to return the parties to the positions they occupied before the contract was made.

Sometimes, parties rescind a contract and make a new contract at the same time. When this occurs, it is often difficult to determine whether there was consideration for the new contract, or whether the parties had a preexisting duty under the previous contract. If a court finds there was a preexisting duty, then the new contract will be invalid because there was no consideration.

PAST CONSIDERATION Promises made in return for actions or events that have already taken place are unenforceable. These promises lack consideration in that the element of bargained-for exchange is missing. In short, you can bargain for something to take place now or in the future but not for something that has already taken place. Therefore, **past consideration** is no consideration.

▶ **Case in Point 11.4** Jamil Blackmon became friends with Allen Iverson when Iverson was a high school student who showed tremendous promise as an athlete. One evening, Blackmon suggested that Iverson use "The Answer" as a nickname in the summer league basketball tournaments. Blackmon said that Iverson would be "The Answer" to all of the National Basketball Association's woes. Later that night, Iverson said that he would give Blackmon 25 percent of any proceeds from the merchandising of products that used "The Answer" as a logo or a slogan. Because Iverson's promise was made in return for past consideration, it was unenforceable. In effect, Iverson stated his intention to give Blackmon a gift.[4] ◀

In a variety of situations, an employer will often ask an employee to sign a *noncompete agreement,* also called a *covenant not to compete.* Under such an agreement, the employee agrees not to compete with the employer for a certain period of time after the employment relationship ends. When a current employee is required to sign a noncompete agreement, his or her employment is not sufficient consideration for the agreement because the individual is already employed. To be valid, the agreement requires new consideration.

In the following case, the court had to decide if new consideration supported a noncompete agreement between physicians and a medical clinic.

---

3. Pronounced reh-*sih*-zhen.

4. *Blackmon v. Iverson,* 324 F.Supp.2d 602 (E.D.Pa. 2003).

CASE ANALYSIS

Case 11.1 Baugh v. Columbia Heart Clinic, P.A.[a]
Court of Appeals of South Carolina, 402 S.C. 1, 738 S.E.2d 480 (2013).

**IN THE LANGUAGE
OF THE COURT**
THOMAS, J. [Judge]
* * * *

Columbia Heart [Clinic, P.A., in Columbia, South Carolina] is a corporate medical practice that provides comprehensive cardiology services. Its physicians are all cardiologists.

J. Kevin Baugh, M.D., and Barry J. Feldman, M.D., * * * are cardiologists who had been shareholders and employees of Columbia Heart since before 2000.
* * * *

When [Baugh and Feldman] became shareholders, they each entered employment agreements that forfeited money payable to them upon termination if they competed with Columbia Heart in Lexington and Richland Counties within a year. These agreements contained no other provisions that discouraged competi-

tion, and their consideration was a compensation system.

In 2004, Columbia Heart's shareholders embarked on the construction of a new medical office building in Lexington County through a limited liability company (the LLC). The LLC was almost entirely owned by the shareholder-physicians of Columbia Heart. * * * Each member of the LLC signed personal obligations on the project debt in pro-

---

a. *P.A.* means "Professional Organization."

CASE 11.1 CONTINUED

portion to their equity [ownership share] in the LLC. Because of (1) the investment and liabilities undertaken by Columbia Heart's shareholders as members of the LLC and (2) a recent departure of a large number of Columbia Heart physicians, Columbia Heart sought to bind its shareholder-physicians more tightly to the medical practice. Thus, in July 2004 Columbia Heart's shareholder-physicians entered into * * * [non-compete] agreements.

* * * *

* * * Article 5 [of the agreements] says the following:

Physician, in the event of termination * * * for any reason, during the twelve (12) month period immediately following the date of termination * * * shall not Compete * * * with Columbia Heart.

Section 5.2 defines specific terms "for purposes of Article 5":

"Compete" means directly or indirectly, on his own behalf or on behalf of any other Person, other than at the direction of Columbia Heart and on behalf of Columbia Heart: (A) organizing or owning any interest in a business which engages in the Business in the Territory; (B) engaging in the Business in the Territory; and (C) assisting any Person (as director, officer, employee, agent, consultant, lender, lessor or otherwise) to engage in the Business in the Territory.

"Business" is defined as "the practice of medicine in the field of cardiology." "Territory" is defined as "the area within a twenty (20) mile radius of any Columbia Heart office at which Physician routinely provided services during the year prior to the date of termination."

No separate monetary consideration was paid to any shareholder-physician to sign the Agreements, nor did the Agreements change the [established] compensation system.

* * * *

Columbia Heart opened a new office in the LLC's building in December 2005. In April 2006, [Baugh and Feldman] left Columbia Heart.

Within a month after departing, [Baugh and Feldman] opened a new practice, Lexington Heart Clinic, where they treated patients in cardiology and hired a number of Columbia Heart's administrative and medical support staff. Lexington Heart was on the same campus as Columbia Heart's Lexington office, separated by an approximate distance of 300 yards. Columbia Heart's * * * office closed in September 2006 because of fiscal unsustainability.

[Baugh and Feldman] filed suit against Columbia Heart [in a South Carolina state court] * * * seeking * * * a ruling that the Agreements contain unenforceable non-competition provisions.

The trial court * * * held the Agreements' non-competition provisions unenforceable * * * . This appeal followed.

* * * *

[Baugh and Feldman] contend * * * that the Agreements are unenforceable because they are not supported by new consideration. We disagree.

*When a covenant not to compete is entered into after the inception of employment, separate consideration, in addition to continued * * * employment, is necessary in order for the covenant to be enforceable. There is no consideration when the contract containing the covenant is exacted after several years' employment and the employee's duties and position are left unchanged.* [Emphasis added.]

[Baugh and Feldman] executed the Agreements after they became employed by Columbia Heart, and the Agreements did not change the general compensation system agreed to by the parties under their prior employment contracts. However, * * * Article 4 of the Agreements provides the following:

Physician shall be paid Five Thousand and No/100 Dollars ($5,000.00) per month for each of the twelve (12) months following termination, so long as the Physician is not in violation of Article 5 of this Agreement.

This language established that Columbia Heart promised to pay [Baugh and Feldman] each * * * a total of $60,000 over twelve months after termination so long as they did not violate the non-competition provision in Article 5. * * * Consequently, the Agreements are supported by new consideration.

* * * *

We reverse the trial court's finding that the non-competition provisions in Article 5 and Article 4 are unenforceable.

LEGAL REASONING QUESTIONS

1. What is consideration?

2. When a noncompete agreement is entered into *before* employment, would additional compensation (beyond the basic salary for the position) constitute sufficient consideration for the agreement? Why or why not?

3. When a noncompete agreement is entered into *after* employment has begun, would continued employment constitute sufficient consideration for the agreement? Explain.

4. In this case, did the court hold that the noncompete agreement at the heart of the dispute was supported by consideration? Why or why not?

ILLUSORY PROMISES If the terms of the contract express such uncertainty of performance that the promisor has not definitely promised to do anything, the promise is said to be *illusory*—without consideration and unenforceable. A promise is illusory when it fails to bind the promisor.

▶ **Example 11.5** The president of Tuscan Corporation says to her employees, "If profits continue to be high, everyone will get a 10 percent bonus at the end of the year—if management agrees." This is an *illusory promise,* or no promise at all, because performance depends solely on the discretion of the president (management). There is no bargained-for consideration. The statement indicates only that management may or may not do something in the future. Therefore, even though the employees work hard and profits remain high, the company is not obligated to pay the bonus now or later. ◀

Option-to-Cancel Clauses. Sometimes, option-to-cancel clauses in contracts present problems in regard to consideration. When the promisor has the option to cancel the contract before performance has begun, the promise is illusory. ▶ **Example 11.6** Abe contracts to hire Chris for one year at $5,000 per month, reserving the right to cancel the contract at any time. On close examination of these words, you can see that Abe has not actually agreed to hire Chris, as Abe could cancel without liability before Chris started performance. This contract is therefore illusory.

But if Abe instead reserves the right to cancel the contract at any time *after* Chris has begun performance by giving Chris *thirty days' notice,* the promise is not illusory. Abe, by saying that he will give Chris thirty days' notice, is relinquishing the opportunity (legal right) to hire someone else instead of Chris for a thirty-day period. If Chris works for one month and Abe then gives him thirty days' notice, Chris has an enforceable claim for two months' salary ($10,000). ◀

Requirements and Output Contracts. Problems with consideration may also arise in other types of contracts because of uncertainty of performance. Uncertain performance is characteristic of requirements and output contracts, for instance. In a *requirements contract,* a buyer and a seller agree that the buyer will purchase from the seller all of the goods of a designated type that the buyer needs, or requires. In an *output contract,* the buyer and seller agree that the buyer will purchase from the seller all of what the seller produces, or the seller's output. These types of sales contracts will be discussed further in Chapter 15.

Concept Summary 11.1 on the following page provides a convenient summary of the main aspects of consideration.

Settlement of Claims

Businesspersons and others often enter into contracts to settle legal claims. It is important to understand the nature of consideration given in these kinds of settlement agreements, or contracts. Claims are commonly settled through an *accord and satisfaction,* in which a debtor offers to pay a lesser amount than the creditor purports to be owed. Claims may also be settled by the signing of a *release* or a *covenant not to sue.*

ACCORD AND SATISFACTION In an **accord and satisfaction,** a debtor offers to pay, and a creditor accepts, a lesser amount than the creditor originally claimed was owed. The *accord* is the agreement. In the accord, one party undertakes to give or perform, and the other to accept, in satisfaction of a claim, something other than that on which the parties originally agreed. *Satisfaction* is the performance (usually payment) that takes place after the accord is executed.

A basic rule is that there can be no satisfaction unless there is first an accord. For accord and satisfaction to occur, the amount of the debt *must be in dispute.*

Liquidated Debts. If a debt is *liquidated,* accord and satisfaction cannot take place. A **liquidated debt** is one whose amount has been ascertained, fixed, agreed on, settled, or exactly determined. ▶ **Example 11.7** Barbara Kwan signs an installment loan contract with her bank. In the contract, Kwan agrees to pay a set rate of interest on a specified amount of borrowed funds at monthly intervals for two years. Because both parties know the precise amount of the total obligation, it is a liquidated debt. ◀

In the majority of states, acceptance of a lesser sum than the entire amount of a liquidated debt is *not* satisfaction, and the balance of the debt is still legally owed. The reason for this rule is that the debtor has given no consideration to satisfy the obligation of paying the balance to the creditor. The debtor had a preexisting legal obligation to pay the entire debt. (Of course, even with liquidated debts, creditors often do negotiate debt settlement agreements with debtors for a lesser amount than was originally owed. Creditors sometimes even forgive or write off a liquidated debt as uncollectable.)

Unliquidated Debts. An **unliquidated debt** is the opposite of a liquidated debt. The amount of the debt

---

CONCEPT SUMMARY 11.1
Consideration

Elements of Consideration	Consideration is the value given in exchange for a promise. A contract cannot be formed without sufficient consideration. Consideration is often broken down into two elements: 1. *Legal value*—Something of legally sufficient value must be given in exchange for a promise. This may consist of a promise, a performance, or a forbearance. 2. *Bargained-for exchange*—There must be a bargained-for exchange.
Adequacy of Consideration	Adequacy of consideration relates to how much consideration is given and whether a fair bargain was reached. Courts will inquire into the adequacy of consideration (if the consideration is legally sufficient) only when fraud, undue influence, duress, or the lack of a bargained-for exchange may be involved.
Agreements That Lack Consideration	Consideration is lacking in the following situations: 1. *Preexisting duty*—Consideration is not legally sufficient if one is either by law or by contract under a *preexisting duty* to perform the action being offered as consideration for a new contract. 2. *Past consideration*—Actions or events that have already taken place do not constitute legally sufficient consideration. 3. *Illusory promises*—When the nature or extent of performance is too uncertain, the promise is rendered illusory and unenforceable.

---

is *not* settled, fixed, agreed on, ascertained, or determined, and reasonable persons may differ over the amount owed. In these circumstances, acceptance of a lesser sum operates as satisfaction, or discharge, of the debt because there is valid consideration. The parties give up a legal right to contest the amount in dispute.

RELEASE A **release** is a contract in which one party forfeits the right to pursue a legal claim against the other party. It bars any further recovery beyond the terms stated in the release.

A release will generally be binding if it meets the following requirements:

1. The agreement is made in good faith (honesty).
2. The release contract is in a signed writing (required in many states).
3. The contract is accompanied by consideration.[5]

Clearly, an individual is better off knowing the extent of his or her injuries or damages before signing a release. ▶ **Example 11.8** Lupe's car is damaged in an automobile accident caused by Dexter's

negligence. Dexter offers to give her $3,000 if she will release him from further liability resulting from the accident. Lupe agrees and signs the release.

If Lupe later discovers that it will cost $4,200 to repair her car, she cannot recover the additional amount from Dexter. Lupe is limited to the $3,000 specified in the release. Lupe and Dexter both voluntarily agreed to the terms in the release, which was in a signed writing, and sufficient consideration was present. The consideration was the legal right Lupe forfeited to sue to recover damages, should they be more than $3,000, in exchange for Dexter's promise to give her $3,000. ◀

COVENANT NOT TO SUE Unlike a release, a **covenant not to sue** does not always bar further recovery. The parties simply substitute a contractual obligation for some other type of legal action based on a valid claim. Suppose in *Example 11.8*, that Lupe agrees with Dexter not to sue for damages in a tort action if he will pay for the damage to her car. If Dexter fails to pay for the repairs, Lupe can bring an action against him for breach of contract.

As the following case illustrates, a covenant not to sue can form the basis for a dismissal of the claims of either party to the covenant.

---

5. Under the Uniform Commercial Code (UCC), a written, signed waiver or renunciation by an aggrieved party discharges any further liability for a breach, even without consideration.

SP TLIGHT on Nike

Case 11.2   Already, LLC v. Nike, Inc.
Supreme Court of the United States, __ U.S. __, 133 S.Ct. 721, 184 L.Ed.2d 553 (2013).

BACKGROUND AND FACTS   Nike, Inc., designs, makes, and sells athletic footwear, including a line of shoes known as "Air Force 1." Already, LLC, also designs and markets athletic footwear, including the "Sugar" and "Soulja Boy" lines. Nike filed a suit in a federal district court against Already, alleging that Soulja Boys and Sugars infringed the Air Force 1 trademark. Already filed a counterclaim, contending that the Air Force 1 trademark was invalid. While the suit was pending, Nike issued a covenant not to sue, promising not to raise any trademark claims against Already or any affiliated entity based on Already's existing footwear designs, or any future Already designs that constituted a "colorable imitation" of Already's current products. Nike then filed a motion to dismiss its own claims and to dismiss Already's counterclaim. Already opposed the dismissal of its counterclaim, but the court granted Nike's motion. The U.S. Court of Appeals for the Second Circuit affirmed. Already appealed to the United States Supreme Court.

IN THE LANGUAGE OF THE COURT
Chief Justice *ROBERTS* delivered the opinion of the Court.

* * * *

* * * A defendant cannot automatically moot a case simply by ending its unlawful conduct once sued. Otherwise, a defendant could engage in unlawful conduct, stop when sued to have the case declared moot [of no legal relevance], then pick up where he left off, repeating this cycle until he achieves all his unlawful ends. Given this concern, * * * *a defendant claiming that its voluntary compliance moots a case bears the formidable burden of showing that it is absolutely clear the allegedly wrongful behavior could not reasonably be expected to recur.* [This is the voluntary cessation test. Emphasis added.]

* * * *

We begin our analysis with the terms of the covenant:

[Nike] unconditionally and irrevocably covenants to refrain from making *any* claim(s) or demand(s) * * * against Already or *any* of its * * * related business entities * * * [including] distributors * * * and employees of such entities and *all* customers * * * on account of any *possible* cause of action based on or involving trademark infringement * * * relating to the NIKE Mark based on the appearance of *any* of Already's current and/or previous footwear product designs, and *any* colorable imitations thereof, regardless of whether that footwear is produced * * * or otherwise used in commerce.

The breadth of this covenant suffices to meet the burden imposed by the voluntary cessation test.

In addition, Nike originally argued that the Sugars and Soulja Boys infringed its trademark; in other words, Nike believed those shoes were "colorable imitations" of the Air Force 1s. Nike's covenant now allows Already to produce all of its existing footwear designs—including the Sugar and Soulja Boy—and any "colorable imitation" of those designs. * * * It is hard to imagine a scenario that would potentially infringe Nike's trademark and yet not fall under the covenant. Nike, having taken the position in court that there is no prospect of such a shoe, would be hard pressed to assert the contrary down the road. If such a shoe exists, the parties have not pointed to it, there is no evidence that Already has dreamt of it, and we cannot conceive of it. It sits, as far as we can tell, on a shelf between Dorothy's ruby slippers and Perseus's winged sandals.

* * * *

* * * Given the covenant's broad language, and given that Already has asserted no concrete plans to engage in conduct not covered by the covenant, we can conclude the case is moot because the challenged conduct cannot reasonably be expected to recur.

DECISION AND REMEDY   *The United States Supreme Court affirmed the judgment of the lower court. Under the covenant not to sue, Nike could not file a claim for trademark infringement against Already, and Already could not assert that Nike's trademark was invalid.*

CASE 11.2 CONTINUED **THE ECONOMIC DIMENSION** *Why would any party agree to a covenant not to sue?*

THE LEGAL ENVIRONMENT DIMENSION *Which types of contracts are similar to a covenant not to sue? Explain.*

Exceptions to the Consideration Requirement

There are some exceptions to the rule that only promises supported by consideration are enforceable. The following types of promises may be enforced despite the lack of consideration:

1. Promises that induce detrimental reliance, under the doctrine of *promissory estoppel.*
2. Promises to pay debts that are barred by a statute of limitations.
3. Promises to make charitable contributions.

PROMISSORY ESTOPPEL Sometimes, individuals rely on promises to their detriment, and their reliance may form a basis for a court to infer contract rights and duties. Under the doctrine of **promissory estoppel** (also called *detrimental reliance*), a person who has reasonably and substantially relied on the promise of another may be able to obtain some measure of recovery.

Promissory estoppel is applied in a wide variety of contexts in which a promise is otherwise unenforceable, such as when a promise made *without consideration.* Under this doctrine, a court may enforce an otherwise unenforceable promise to avoid the injustice that would otherwise result.

Requirements to State a Claim. For the promissory estoppel doctrine to be applied, the following elements are required:

1. There must be a clear and definite promise.
2. The promisor should have expected that the promisee would rely on the promise.
3. The promisee reasonably relied on the promise by acting or refraining from some act.
4. The promisee's reliance was definite and resulted in substantial detriment.
5. Enforcement of the promise is necessary to avoid injustice.

If these requirements are met, a promise may be enforced even though it is not supported by consideration.[6] In essence, the promisor will be **estopped**

(prevented) from asserting the lack of consideration as a defense.

Promissory estoppel is similar in some ways to the doctrine of quasi contract that was discussed in Chapter 9. In both situations, a court, acting in the interests of equity, imposes contract obligations on the parties to prevent unfairness even though no actual contract exists. The difference is that with quasi contract, no promise was made at all. In contrast, with promissory estoppel, a promise was made and relied on, but it was unenforceable.

Application of the Doctrine. Promissory estoppel was originally applied to situations involving gifts (I promise to pay you $1,000 a week so that you will not have to work) and donations to charities (I promise to contribute $50,000 a year to the Raising Giants orphanage). Later, courts began to apply the doctrine to avoid inequity or hardship in other situations, including business transactions, some employment relationships, and even disputes among family members.

▶ **Case in Point 11.9** Jeffrey and Kathryn Dow own 125 acres of land in Corinth, Maine. The Dows regarded the land as their children's heritage, and the subject of the children's living on the land was often discussed within the family. With the Dows' permission, their daughter Teresa installed a mobile home and built a garage on the land. After Teresa married Jarrod Harvey, the Dows agreed to finance the construction of a house on the land for the couple. When Jarrod died in a motorcycle accident, however, Teresa financed the house with his life insurance proceeds. The construction cost about $200,000. Her father, Jeffrey, performed a substantial amount of carpentry and other work on the house.

Teresa then asked her parents for a deed to the property so that she could obtain a mortgage. They refused. Teresa sued her parents for promissory estoppel. Maine's highest court ruled in favor of Teresa's promissory estoppel claim. The court reasoned that the Dows' support and encouragement of their daughter's construction of a house on the land "conclusively demonstrated" their intent to transfer. For years, they had made general promises to convey the land to their children, including Teresa. Teresa had

---

6. *Restatement (Second) of Contracts,* Section 90.

reasonably relied on their promise in financing construction of a house to her detriment ($200,000). The court concluded that enforcing the promise was the only way to avoid injustice in this situation.[7] ◄

STATUTE OF LIMITATIONS Statutes of limitations in all states require a creditor to sue within a specified period to recover a debt. If the creditor fails to sue in time, recovery of the debt is barred by the statute of limitations.

A debtor who promises to pay a previous debt even though recovery is barred by the statute of limitations makes an enforceable promise. *The promise needs no consideration.* (Some states, however, require that it be in writing.) In effect, the promise extends the limitations period, and the creditor can sue to recover the entire debt or at least the amount promised. The promise can be implied if the debtor acknowledges the barred debt by making a partial payment.

CHARITABLE SUBSCRIPTIONS A charitable subscription is a promise to make a donation to a religious, educational, or charitable institution. Traditionally, such promises were unenforceable because they are not supported by legally sufficient consideration. A gift, after all, is the opposite of bargained-for consideration. The modern view, however, is to make exceptions to the general rule by applying the doctrine of promissory estoppel.

▶ **Example 11.10** A church solicits and receives pledges (commitments to contribute funds) from church members to erect a new church building. On the basis of these pledges, the church purchases land, hires architects, and makes other contracts that change its position. Because of the church's detrimental reliance, a court may enforce the pledges under the theory of promissory estoppel. Alternatively, a court may find consideration in the fact that each promise was made in reliance on the other promises of support or that the church trustees, by accepting the subscriptions, impliedly promised to complete the proposed undertaking. ◄

SECTION 2
CONTRACTUAL CAPACITY

In addition to agreement and consideration, for a contract to be deemed valid, the parties to the contract must have **contractual capacity**—the legal ability to enter into a contractual relationship. Courts generally presume the existence of contractual capacity, but in some situations, as when a person is young or mentally incompetent, capacity may be lacking or questionable.

A person who has been determined by a court to be mentally incompetent, for instance, cannot form a legally binding contract with another party. In other situations, a party may have the capacity to enter into a valid contract but also have the right to avoid liability under it. Minors—or *infants,* as they are commonly referred to in legal terminology—usually are not legally bound by contracts.

In this section, we look at the effect of youth (minority), intoxication, and mental incompetence on contractual capacity.

Minors

Today, in almost all states, the **age of majority** (when a person is no longer a minor) for contractual purposes is eighteen years.[8] In addition, some states provide for the termination of minority on marriage.

Minority status may also be terminated by a minor's **emancipation,** which occurs when a child's parent or legal guardian relinquishes the legal right to exercise control over the child. Normally, minors who leave home to support themselves are considered emancipated. Several jurisdictions permit minors themselves to petition a court for emancipation. For business purposes, a minor may petition a court to be treated as an adult.

The general rule is that a minor can enter into any contract that an adult can, except contracts prohibited by law for minors (for example, the purchase of tobacco or alcoholic beverages). A contract entered into by a minor, however, is voidable at the option of that minor, subject to certain exceptions. To exercise the option to avoid a contract, a minor need only manifest (clearly show) an intention not to be bound by it. The minor "avoids" the contract by disaffirming it.

DISAFFIRMANCE The legal avoidance, or setting aside, of a contractual obligation is referred to as **disaffirmance.** To disaffirm, a minor must express his or her intent, through words or conduct, not to be bound to the contract. The minor must disaffirm the entire contract, not merely a portion of it. For

---

7. *Harvey v. Dow,* 2011 ME 4, 11 A.3d 303 (2011).

8. The age of majority may still be twenty-one for other purposes, such as the purchase and consumption of alcohol.

instance, the minor cannot decide to keep part of the goods purchased under a contract and return the remaining goods.

▶ **Case in Point 11.11** Fifteen-year-old Morgan Kelly was a cadet in her high school's Navy Junior Reserve Officer Training Corps. As part of the program, she visited a U.S. Marine Corps training facility. To enter the camp, she was required to sign a waiver that exempted the Marines from all liability for any injuries arising from her visit. While participating in activities on the camp's confidence-building course, Kelly fell from the "Slide for Life" and suffered serious injuries. She filed a suit to recover her medical costs. The Marines asserted that she had signed their waiver of liability. Kelly claimed that she had disaffirmed the waiver when she filed suit. The court ruled in Kelly's favor. Liability waivers are generally enforceable contracts, but a minor can avoid a contract by disaffirming it.[9] ◀

Note that an adult who enters into a contract with a minor cannot avoid his or her contractual duties on the ground that the minor can do so. Unless the minor exercises the option to disaffirm the contract, the adult party normally is bound by it. On disaffirming a contract, a minor can recover any property that he or she transferred to the adult as consideration, even if the property is in the possession of a third party.[10]

Must Be within a Reasonable Time. A contract can ordinarily be disaffirmed at any time during minority[11] or for a reasonable period after reaching majority. What constitutes a "reasonable" time may vary. If an individual fails to disaffirm an executed contract (fully performed) within a reasonable time after reaching the age of majority, a court will likely hold that the contract has been ratified (*ratification* will be discussed shortly).

Minor's Obligations on Disaffirmance. Although all states' laws permit minors to disaffirm contracts (with certain exceptions), states differ on the extent of a minor's obligations on disaffirmance. Courts in most states hold that the minor need only return the goods (or other consideration) subject to the contract, provided the goods are in the minor's possession or con-

trol. Even if the minor returns damaged goods, the minor often is entitled to disaffirm the contract and obtain a full refund of the purchase price.

Courts in a growing number of states place an additional duty on the minor to restore the adult party to the position she or he held before the contract was made. These courts may hold a minor responsible for damage, ordinary wear and tear, and depreciation of goods that the minor used prior to disaffirmance.

▶ **Case in Point 11.12** Sixteen-year-old Joseph Dodson bought a pickup truck from a used-car dealer. Although the truck developed mechanical problems nine months later, Dodson continued to drive it until it stopped running. Then Dodson disaffirmed the contract and attempted to return the truck to the dealer for a full refund. When the dealer refused to accept the pickup or refund the purchase price, Dodson filed a suit. Ultimately, the Tennessee Supreme Court allowed Dodson to disaffirm the contract but required him to compensate the seller for the depreciated value—not the purchase price—of the pickup.[12] ◀

EXCEPTIONS TO A MINOR'S RIGHT TO DISAFFIRM

State courts and legislatures have carved out several exceptions to a minor's right to disaffirm. Marriage contracts and contracts to enlist in the armed services, for instance, cannot be avoided for public-policy reasons. Some contracts may not be disaffirmed for other reasons, including those discussed here.

Misrepresentation of Age. Ordinarily, minors can disaffirm contracts even when they have misrepresented their age (claimed to be twenty-one years old when they were not). Nevertheless, a growing number of states have enacted laws to prohibit disaffirmance in such situations. In some states, misrepresentation of age is enough to prevent disaffirmance. Other states prohibit disaffirmance by minors who misrepresented their age while engaged in business as an adult.

Contracts for Necessaries. A minor who enters into a contract for necessaries may disaffirm the contract but remains liable for the reasonable value of the goods. **Necessaries** are basic needs, such as food, clothing, shelter, and medical services. What is a necessary for one minor, however, may be a luxury for another, depending on the minors' customary living standard. Contracts for necessaries are enforceable only to the

---

9. *Kelly v. United States,* 809 F.Supp.2d 429 (E.D.N.C. 2011).

10. Section 2–403(1) of the Uniform Commercial Code (UCC) allows an exception if the third party is a "good faith purchaser for value." See Chapter 15.

11. In some states, however, a minor who enters into a contract for the sale of land cannot disaffirm the contract until she or he reaches the age of majority.

12. *Dodson v. Shrader,* 824 S.W.2d 545 (Tenn.Sup.Ct. 1992) is a seminal case on this subject. See also *Restatement (Third) of Restitution,* Sections 16 and 33.

level of value needed to maintain the minor's standard of living.

RATIFICATION In contract law, **ratification** is the act of accepting and giving legal force to an obligation that previously was not enforceable. A minor who has reached the age of majority can ratify a contract expressly or impliedly. *Express* ratification takes place when the individual, on reaching the age of majority, states orally or in writing that he or she intends to be bound by the contract. *Implied* ratification takes place when the minor, on reaching the age of majority, indicates an intent to abide by the contract.

▶ **Example 11.13** Lin enters into a contract to sell her laptop to Andrew, a minor. If, on reaching the age of majority, Andrew e-mails Lin stating that he still agrees to buy the laptop, he has *expressly* ratified the contract. If, instead, Andrew takes possession of the laptop as a minor and continues to use it well after reaching the age of majority, he has *impliedly* ratified the contract. ◀

If a minor fails to disaffirm a contract within a reasonable time after reaching the age of majority, then the court must determine whether the conduct constitutes ratification or disaffirmance. Generally, courts presume that executed contracts (fully performed) are ratified and that executory contracts (not yet fully performed by both parties) are disaffirmed.

PARENTS' LIABILITY As a general rule, parents are not liable for contracts made by minor children acting on their own. As a consequence, businesses ordinarily require parents to cosign any contract made with a minor. The parents then become personally obligated under the contract to perform the conditions of the contract, even if their child avoids liability. (Parents can sometimes be held liable for a minor's torts, however, depending on state law.)

Concept Summary 11.2 below reviews the rules relating to contracts by minors.

Intoxication

Intoxication is a condition in which a person's normal capacity to act or think is inhibited by alcohol or some other drug. A contract entered into by an intoxicated person can be either voidable or valid (and thus enforceable).[13]

If the person was sufficiently intoxicated to lack mental capacity, then the agreement may be voidable even if the intoxication was purely voluntary. If, despite intoxication, the person understood the legal consequences of the agreement, the contract will be enforceable.

Courts look at objective indications of the intoxicated person's condition to determine if he or she possessed or lacked the required capacity. It is difficult to prove that a person's judgment was so severely impaired that he or she could not comprehend the legal consequences of entering into a contract. Therefore, courts rarely permit contracts to be avoided due to intoxication.

---

13. Note that if an alcoholic makes a contract while sober, there is no lack of capacity. See *Wright v. Fisher,* 32 N.W. 605 (Mich. 1887).

CONCEPT SUMMARY 11.2
Contracts by Minors

CONCEPT	DESCRIPTION
General Rule	Contracts entered into by minors are *voidable* at the option of the minor.
Rules of Disaffirmance	A minor may disaffirm the contract at any time while still a minor and within a reasonable time after reaching the age of majority. Most states do not require restitution.
Exceptions to Basic Rules of Disaffirmance	1. *Misrepresentation of age (or fraud)*—In many jurisdictions, misrepresentation of age prohibits the right of disaffirmance. 2. *Necessaries*—Minors remain liable for the reasonable value of necessaries (goods and services). 3. *Ratification*—After reaching the age of majority, a person can ratify a contract that he or she formed as a minor, thereby becoming fully liable for it.

DISAFFIRMANCE If a contract is voidable because one party was intoxicated, that person has the option of disaffirming it while intoxicated and for a reasonable time after becoming sober. The person claiming intoxication typically must be able to return all consideration received unless the contract involved necessaries. Contracts for necessaries are voidable, but the intoxicated person is liable in quasi contract for the reasonable value of the consideration received.

RATIFICATION An intoxicated person, after becoming sober, may ratify a contract expressly or impliedly, just as a minor may do on reaching majority. Implied ratification occurs when a person enters into a contract while intoxicated and fails to disaffirm the contract within a *reasonable* time after becoming sober. Acts or conduct inconsistent with an intent to disaffirm—such as the continued use of property purchased under a voidable contract—will also ratify the contract.

See *Concept Summary 11.3* below for a review of the rules relating to contracts by intoxicated persons.

Mental Incompetence

Contracts made by mentally incompetent persons can be void, voidable, or valid. We look here at the circumstances that determine when each of these classifications applies.

WHEN THE CONTRACT WILL BE VOID If a court has previously determined that a person is mentally incompetent, any contract made by that person is *void*—no contract exists. On determining that someone is mentally incompetent, the court appoints a guardian to represent the individual. Only the guardian can enter into binding legal obligations on behalf of the mentally incompetent person.

WHEN THE CONTRACT WILL BE VOIDABLE If a court has not previously judged a person to be mentally incompetent but the person was incompetent at the time the contract was formed, the contract may be voidable. A contract is *voidable* if the person did not know he or she was entering into the contract or lacked the mental capacity to comprehend its nature, purpose, and consequences. In such situations, the contract is voidable (or can be ratified) at the option of the mentally incompetent person but not at the option of the other party.

▶ **Example 11.14** Larry agrees to sell his stock in Google, Inc., to Sergey for substantially less than its market value. At the time of the deal, Larry is confused about the purpose and details of the transaction, but he has not been declared incompetent. Nonetheless, if a court finds that Larry did not understand the nature and consequences of the contract due to a lack of mental capacity, he can avoid the sale. ◀

WHEN THE CONTRACT WILL BE VALID A contract entered into by a mentally incompetent person (whom a court has not previously declared incompetent) may also be *valid* if the person had capacity *at the time the contract was formed*. Some people who are incompetent due to age or illness have *lucid intervals*—temporary periods of sufficient intelligence, judgment, and will. During such intervals,

---

CONCEPT SUMMARY 11.3
Contracts by Intoxicated Persons

CONCEPT	DESCRIPTION
General Rules	If a person was sufficiently intoxicated to lack the mental capacity to comprehend the legal consequences of entering into the contract, the contract may be *voidable* at the option of the intoxicated person. If, despite intoxication, the person understood these legal consequences, the contract will be enforceable.
Disaffirmance	An intoxicated person may disaffirm the contract at any time while intoxicated and for a reasonable time after becoming sober but must make full restitution. Contracts for necessaries are voidable, but the intoxicated person is liable for the reasonable value of the goods or services.
Ratification	After becoming sober, a person can ratify a contract that she or he formed while intoxicated, thereby becoming fully liable for it.

they will be considered to have legal capacity to enter into contracts.

See *Concept Summary 11.4* below for a review of the rules relating to contracts entered into by mentally incompetent persons.

SECTION 3
LEGALITY

Legality is the fourth requirement for a valid contract to exist. For a contract to be valid and enforceable, it must be formed for a legal purpose. A contract to do something that is prohibited by federal or state statutory law is illegal and, as such, void from the outset and thus unenforceable. Additionally, a contract to commit a tortious act—such as an agreement to engage in fraudulent misrepresentation (see Chapter 4)—is contrary to public policy and therefore illegal and unenforceable.

Contracts Contrary to Statute

Statutes often set forth rules specifying which terms and clauses may be included in contracts and which are prohibited. We now examine several ways in which contracts may be contrary to statute and thus illegal.

CONTRACTS TO COMMIT A CRIME Any contract to commit a crime is in violation of a statute. Thus, a contract to sell illegal drugs in violation of criminal laws is unenforceable, as is a contract to cover up a corporation's violation of the Dodd-Frank Wall Street Reform and Consumer Protection Act. Similarly, a contract to

smuggle undocumented workers from another country into the United States for an employer is illegal, as is a contract to dump hazardous waste in violation of environmental laws.

Sometimes, the object or performance of a contract is rendered illegal by a statute *after* the parties entered into the contract. In that situation, the contract is considered to be discharged by law. (See the discussion of impossibility or impracticability of performance in Chapter 13.)

USURY Almost every state has a statute that sets the maximum rate of interest that can be charged for different types of transactions, including ordinary loans. A lender who makes a loan at an interest rate above the lawful maximum commits **usury.** Although usurious contracts are illegal, most states simply limit the interest that the lender may collect on the contract to the lawful maximum interest rate in that state. In a few states, the lender can recover the principal amount of the loan but no interest.

Usury statutes place a ceiling on allowable rates of interest, but states can make exceptions to facilitate business transactions. For instance, many states exempt corporate loans from the usury laws, and nearly all states allow higher interest rate loans for borrowers who could not otherwise obtain funds. In reaction to the latest economic recession, the federal government placed some restrictions on the interest rates and fees that banks and credit-card companies can legally charge consumers.[14]

---

14. The Credit Card Accountability, Responsibility, and Disclosure Act of 2009, Pub. L. No. 111-24, 123 Stat. 1734.

CONCEPT SUMMARY 11.4
Contracts by Mentally Incompetent Persons

CONCEPT	DESCRIPTION
Void	If a court has declared a person to be mentally incompetent and has appointed a legal guardian, any contract made by that person is void from the outset.
Voidable	If a court has *not* declared a person mentally incompetent, but that person lacked the capacity to comprehend the subject matter, nature, and consequences of the agreement, then the contract is voidable at that person's option.
Valid	If a court has *not* declared a person mentally incompetent and that person was able to understand the nature and effect of the contract at the time it was formed, then the contract is valid and enforceable.

GAMBLING Gambling is the creation of risk for the purpose of assuming it. Any scheme that involves the distribution of property by chance among persons who have paid valuable consideration for the opportunity (chance) to receive the property is gambling. Traditionally, the states have deemed gambling contracts illegal and thus void. It is sometimes difficult, however, to distinguish a gambling contract from the risk sharing inherent in almost all contracts.

All states have statutes that regulate gambling, and many states allow certain forms of gambling, such as betting on horse races, poker machines, and charity-sponsored bingo. In addition, nearly all states allow state-operated lotteries as well as gambling on Native American reservations. Even in states that permit certain types of gambling, though, courts often find that gambling contracts are illegal.

▶ **Case in Point 11.15** Video poker machines are legal in Louisiana, but their use requires the approval of the state video gaming commission. Gaming Venture, Inc., did not obtain this approval before agreeing with Tastee Restaurant Corporation to install poker machines in some of its restaurants. For this reason, when Tastee allegedly reneged on the deal by refusing to install the machines, a state court held that their agreement was an illegal gambling contract and therefore void.[15] ◀

LICENSING STATUTES All states require members of certain professions—including physicians, lawyers, real estate brokers, accountants, architects, electricians, and stockbrokers—to have licenses. Some licenses are obtained only after extensive schooling and examinations, which indicate to the public that a special skill has been acquired. Others require only that the applicant be of good moral character and pay a fee.

Whether a contract with an unlicensed person is legal and enforceable depends on the purpose of the licensing statute. If the statute's purpose is to protect the public from unauthorized practitioners (such as unlicensed attorneys and electricians, for instance), then a contract involving an unlicensed practitioner is generally illegal and unenforceable. If the statute's purpose is merely to raise government revenues, however, a court may enforce the contract and fine the unlicensed person.

▶ **Case in Point 11.16** The United Arab Emirates (UAE) held a competition for the design of an embassy in Washington, D.C. Elena Sturdza—an architect not licensed in the District of Columbia—won. Sturdza and the UAE exchanged proposals, but then the UAE stopped communicating with her. Two years later, Sturdza learned that the UAE had contracted with a District of Columbia architect to use his design. Sturdza filed a suit against the UAE, alleging breach of contract. The court, however, held that an architect cannot recover on a contract to perform architectural services in the District of Columbia if he or she lacks a District of Columbia license. For the safety of those who work in and visit buildings in the District of Columbia, and the safety of neighboring buildings, the architects who design the buildings and oversee their construction should be qualified and licensed in the District of Columbia.[16] ◀

Contracts Contrary to Public Policy

Although contracts involve private parties, some are not enforceable because of the negative impact they would have on society. These contracts are said to be *contrary to public policy.* Examples include a contract to commit an immoral act, such as selling a child, and a contract that prohibits marriage. We look here at certain types of business contracts that are often found to be against public policy.

CONTRACTS IN RESTRAINT OF TRADE Contracts in restraint of trade (anticompetitive agreements) usually adversely affect the public policy that favors competition in the economy. Typically, such contracts also violate one or more federal or state antitrust statutes.[17]

An exception is recognized when the restraint is reasonable and is contained in an ancillary (secondary or subordinate) clause in a contract. Such restraints often are included in contracts for the sale of an ongoing business and employment contracts.

Covenants Not to Compete and the Sale of an Ongoing Business. Many contracts involve a type of restraint called a **covenant not to compete,** or a restrictive covenant (promise). A covenant not to compete may be created when a seller of a store agrees not to open a new store in a certain geographic area surrounding

15. *Gaming Venture, Inc. v. Tastee Restaurant Corp.,* 996 So.2d 515 (La. App. 5 Cir. 2008).
16. *Sturdza v. United Arab Emirates,* 11 A.3d 251 (D.C. 2011).
17. Federal statutes include the Sherman Antitrust Act, the Clayton Act, and the Federal Trade Commission Act.

the old business. The agreement enables the purchaser to buy, and the seller to sell, the goodwill and reputation of an ongoing business without having to worry that the seller will open a competing business a block away. Provided the restrictive covenant is reasonable and is an ancillary part of the sale of an ongoing business, it is enforceable.

Covenants Not to Compete in Employment Contracts. Sometimes, agreements not to compete (also referred to as *noncompete agreements*) are included in employment contracts. People in middle- or upper-level management positions commonly agree not to work for competitors or not to start competing businesses for a specified period of time after termination of employment.

Such agreements are legal in most states so long as the specified period of time (of restraint) is not excessive in duration and the geographic restriction is reasonable. What constitutes a reasonable time period may be shorter in the online environment than in conventional employment contracts because the restrictions apply worldwide.

To be reasonable, a restriction on competition must protect a legitimate business interest and must not be any greater than necessary to protect that interest. ▶ **Case in Point 11.17**   Safety and Compliance Management, Inc. (SCMI), provides drug- and alcohol-testing services. When SCMI hired Angela to pick up test specimens, she signed a covenant not to compete "in any area of SCMI business." Angela later quit SCMI's employ to work in a hospital where she sometimes collected patient specimens. SCMI claimed this was a breach of their noncompete agreement. A court ruled that the covenant was unreasonable because it imposed a greater restriction on Angela than necessary to protect SCMI.[18] ◀

Enforcement Problems.   The laws governing the enforceability of covenants not to compete vary significantly from state to state. In some states, including Texas, such a covenant will not be enforced unless the employee has received some benefit in return for signing the noncompete agreement. This is true even if the covenant is reasonable as to time and area. If the employee receives no benefit, the covenant will be deemed void. California prohibits altogether the enforcement of covenants not to compete.

Occasionally, depending on the jurisdiction, courts will *reform* covenants not to compete. If a covenant is found to be unreasonable in time or geographic area, the court may convert the terms into reasonable ones and then enforce the reformed covenant. Such court actions present a problem, though, in that the judge implicitly becomes a party to the contract. Consequently, courts usually resort to contract **reformation** only when necessary to prevent undue burdens or hardships.

UNCONSCIONABLE CONTRACTS OR CLAUSES   A court ordinarily does not look at the fairness or equity of a contract (or inquire into the adequacy of consideration, as discussed earlier in this chapter). Persons are assumed to be reasonably intelligent, and the courts will not come to their aid just because they have made an unwise or foolish bargain.

In certain circumstances, however, bargains are so oppressive that the courts relieve innocent parties of part or all of their duties. Such bargains are deemed **unconscionable** because they are so unscrupulous or grossly unfair as to be "void of conscience."

The Uniform Commercial Code (UCC) incorporates the concept of unconscionability in its provisions with regard to the sale and lease of goods.[19] A contract can be unconscionable on either procedural or substantive grounds, as discussed in the following subsections and illustrated graphically in Exhibit 11–1 on the next page.

Procedural Unconscionability.   *Procedural* unconscionability often involves inconspicuous print, unintelligible language ("legalese"), or the lack of an opportunity to read the contract or ask questions about its meaning. This type of unconscionability typically arises when a party's lack of knowledge or understanding of the contract terms deprived him or her of any meaningful choice.

Procedural unconscionability can also occur when there is such disparity in bargaining power between the two parties that the weaker party's consent is not voluntary. This type of situation often involves an *adhesion* contract (see Chapter 12), which is a contract written exclusively by one party and presented to the other on a take-it-or-leave-it basis.[20] In other words, the party to whom the contract is presented (usually a buyer or borrower) has no opportunity to

---

18. *Stultz v. Safety and Compliance Management, Inc.,* 285 Ga.App. 799, 648 S.E.2d 129 (2007).

19. See UCC 2–302 and 2A–719.

20. For a classic case involving an adhesion contract, see *Henningsen v. Bloomfield Motors, Inc.,* 32 N.J. 358, 161 A.2d 69 (1960).

EXHIBIT 11-1 Unconscionability

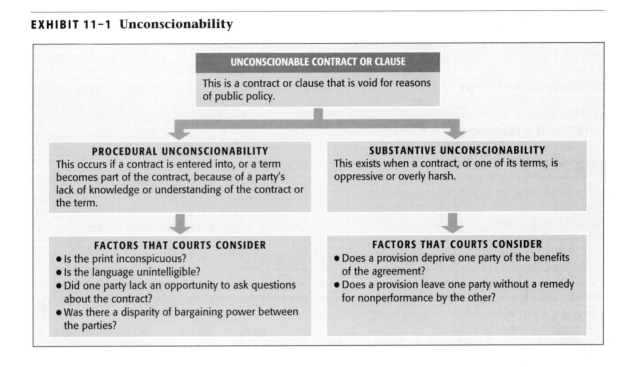

negotiate its terms. Not all adhesion contracts are unconscionable, only those that unreasonably favor the drafter.[21]

Substantive Unconscionability. *Substantive* unconscionability occurs when contracts, or portions of contracts, are oppressive or overly harsh. Courts generally focus on provisions that deprive one party of the benefits of the agreement or leave that party without a remedy for nonperformance by the other.

Substantive unconscionability can arise in a wide variety of business contexts. For instance, a contract clause that gives the business entity free access to the courts but requires the other party to arbitrate any dispute with the firm may be unconscionable.[22] Similarly, contracts drafted by cell phone providers and insurance companies have been found substantively unconscionable when they included provisions that were overly harsh or one sided.[23]

EXCULPATORY CLAUSES Often closely related to the concept of unconscionability are **exculpatory clauses,** which release a party from liability in the event of monetary or physical injury *no matter who is at fault.* Indeed, courts sometimes refuse to enforce such clauses on the ground that they are unconscionable.

Exculpatory Clauses Often Violate Public Policy. Most courts view exculpatory clauses with disfavor. Exculpatory clauses found in rental agreements for commercial property are frequently held to be contrary to public policy, and such clauses are almost always unenforceable in residential property leases. Courts also usually hold that exculpatory clauses are against public policy in the employment context. Thus, employers frequently cannot enforce exculpatory clauses in contracts with employees or independent contractors (see Chapter 17) to avoid liability for work-related injuries.

▶ **Case in Point 11.18** Speedway SuperAmerica, LLC, hired Sebert Erwin to work for its convenience stores. The company required Erwin, who had an eighth-grade education, to sign a contract stating that he was not an employee and had no right to workers' compensation. The contract also included a clause

21. See, for example, *Thibodeau v. Comcast Corp.,* 2006 PA Super. 346, 912 A.2d 874 (2006).
22. See, for example, *Wisconsin Auto Title Loans, Inc. v. Jones,* 290 Wis.2d 514, 714 N.W.2d 155 (2006).
23. See, for example, *Gatton v. T-Mobile USA, Inc.,* 152 Cal.App.4th 571, 61 Cal.Rptr.3d 344 (2007); *Kinkel v. Cingular Wireless, LLC,* 223 Ill.2d 1, 857 N.E.2d 250, 306 Ill.Dec. 157 (2006); and *Aul v. Golden Rule Insurance Co.,* 737 N.W.2d 24 (Wis.App. 2007).

under which Erwin promised not to hold Speedway liable for anything that happened to him while working for the company. When Erwin was later injured on the job and sued Speedway for damages, the court held that the exculpatory clause was invalid because it was against public policy.[24] ◄

When Courts Will Enforce Exculpatory Clauses. Courts do enforce exculpatory clauses if they are reasonable, do not violate public policy, and do not protect parties from liability for intentional misconduct. The language used must not be ambiguous, and the parties must have been in relatively equal bargaining positions.

---

24. *Speedway SuperAmerica, LLC v. Erwin*, 250 S.W.3d 339 (Ky. 2008).

Businesses such as health clubs, racetracks, amusement parks, skiing facilities, horse-rental operations, golf-cart concessions, and skydiving organizations frequently use exculpatory clauses to limit their liability for patrons' injuries. Because these services are not essential, the companies offering them have no relative advantage in bargaining strength, and anyone contracting for their services does so voluntarily. Courts also may enforce reasonable exculpatory clauses in loan documents, real estate contracts, and trust agreements.

In the following case, the court considered whether an exculpatory clause that released "any Event sponsors and their agents and employees" from liability for future negligence was ambiguous.

CASE 11.3

Holmes v. Multimedia KSDK, Inc.
Missouri Court of Appeals, Eastern District, 2013 WL 150809 (2013).

BACKGROUND AND FACTS Colleen Holmes signed an entry form for the 2009 Susan G. Komen Race for the Cure to be held on Saturday, June 13, 2009, in St. Louis, Missouri. The form included a "RACE WAIVER AND RELEASE" under which Holmes agreed to "release . . . any Event sponsors and their agents and employees . . . for any injury or damages I might suffer in connection with my participation in this Event . . . . This release applies to any . . . negligence of the [sponsors]." Later, Multimedia KSDK, Inc., agreed to be one of the sponsors of the event. KSDK also broadcast the race. During the event, Holmes was injured when she tripped and fell over an audiovisual box. KSDK employees had placed the box on the ground without barricades or warnings of its presence. Holmes and her husband, Rick, filed a suit in a Missouri state court against KSDK. The court entered a judgment in the defendant's favor. The plaintiffs appealed.

IN THE LANGUAGE OF THE COURT
Kathianne Knaup *CRANE*, Presiding Judge.

* * * *

The release described the individuals and entities to be released in the following language:

The St. Louis Affiliate of Susan G. Komen for the Cure, their affiliates, and any affiliated individuals, any Event sponsors and their agents and employees, and all other persons or entities associated with this Event. * * *

Plaintiffs argue that the * * * language is ambiguous because it does not specifically name the individuals and entities being released. They contend that such specificity is required in a prospective release.

We have routinely held that the word "any" when used with a class in a release is all-inclusive, it excludes nothing, and it is not ambiguous. * * * *A release that releases claims against "any and all persons" is unambiguous and enforceable to bar claims against third parties who were not parties to the release, and it is not necessary that the release identify those persons by name or otherwise.* Thus, * * * the release of "any Event sponsors" unambiguously releases all Event sponsors without exclusion, and it is not necessary that each sponsor be named. [Emphasis added.]

CASE 11.3 CONTINUED

However, plaintiffs argue that this reasoning does not apply to the use of "any" with classes of persons in a prospective release for future acts of negligence because courts require more specificity in a prospective release. We disagree.

Public policy disfavors but does *not* prohibit releases of future negligence. * * * To be enforceable in Missouri, exculpatory clauses must contain clear, unambiguous, unmistakable, and conspicuous language in order to release a party from his or her own future negligence. The exculpatory language must effectively notify a party that he or she is releasing the other party from claims arising from the other party's own negligence. * * * The words "negligence" or "fault" or their equivalents must be used conspicuously so that a clear and unmistakable waiver and shifting of risk occurs. There must be no doubt that a reasonable person agreeing to an exculpatory clause actually understands what future claims he or she is waiving.

* * * *

* * * [It is] not required that for a release of liability for future negligence to be effective, it must identify every individual sought to be released by name.

The release of "any Event sponsors and their agents and employees" from liability for future negligence clearly releases all Event sponsors and their agents and employees without exclusion. It is not ambiguous because it does not name each individual Event sponsor it purported to release from liability.

DECISION AND REMEDY *A state intermediate appellate court affirmed the lower court's judgment in favor of KSDK. The appellate court held that the language used in the exculpatory clause clearly released all sponsors and their agents and employees without exclusion from liability for future negligence.*

THE SOCIAL DIMENSION *At the time Holmes had signed the release, KSDK had not yet become a sponsor of the event. Should this fact have rendered the clause unenforceable? Explain.*

THE LEGAL DIMENSION *Was the exculpatory clause at issue in this case enforceable? Why or why not?*

DISCRIMINATORY CONTRACTS Contracts in which a party promises to discriminate on the basis of race, color, national origin, religion, gender, age, or disability are contrary to both statute and public policy. They are also unenforceable.[25] For instance, if a property owner promises in a contract not to sell the property to a member of a particular race, the contract is unenforceable. The public policy underlying these prohibitions is very strong, and the courts are quick to invalidate discriminatory contracts.

Exhibit 11–2 on the next page illustrates the types of contracts that may be illegal because they are contrary to statute or public policy.

Effect of Illegality

In general, an illegal contract is void—that is, the contract is deemed never to have existed, and the courts will not aid either party. In most illegal contracts,

both parties are considered to be equally at fault—*in pari delicto*.[26] If the contract is executory (not yet fulfilled), neither party can enforce it. If it has been executed, neither party can recover damages.

The courts are usually not concerned if one wrongdoer in an illegal contract is unjustly enriched at the expense of the other—except under certain circumstances. The main reason for this hands-off attitude is the belief that a plaintiff who has broken the law by entering into an illegal bargain should not be allowed to obtain help from the courts. Another justification is the hoped-for deterrent effect: a plaintiff who suffers a loss because of an illegal bargain will presumably be deterred from entering into similar illegal bargains in the future.

There are exceptions to the general rule that neither party to an illegal bargain can sue for breach and neither party can recover for performance rendered. We look at these exceptions next.

---

25. The major federal statute prohibiting discrimination is the Civil Rights Act of 1964, 42 U.S.C. Sections 2000e–2000e-17.

26. Pronounced in-*pah*-ree deh-*lick*-tow.

EXHIBIT 11-2 Contract Legality

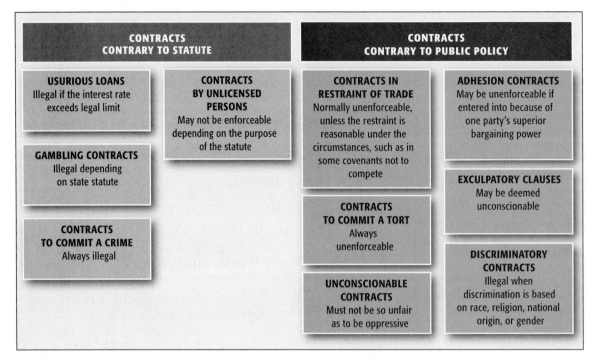

CONTRACTS CONTRARY TO STATUTE

USURIOUS LOANS
Illegal if the interest rate exceeds legal limit

CONTRACTS BY UNLICENSED PERSONS
May not be enforceable depending on the purpose of the statute

GAMBLING CONTRACTS
Illegal depending on state statute

CONTRACTS TO COMMIT A CRIME
Always illegal

CONTRACTS CONTRARY TO PUBLIC POLICY

CONTRACTS IN RESTRAINT OF TRADE
Normally unenforceable, unless the restraint is reasonable under the circumstances, such as in some covenants not to compete

ADHESION CONTRACTS
May be unenforceable if entered into because of one party's superior bargaining power

EXCULPATORY CLAUSES
May be deemed unconscionable

CONTRACTS TO COMMIT A TORT
Always unenforceable

DISCRIMINATORY CONTRACTS
Illegal when discrimination is based on race, religion, national origin, or gender

UNCONSCIONABLE CONTRACTS
Must not be so unfair as to be oppressive

JUSTIFIABLE IGNORANCE OF THE FACTS When one of the parties is relatively innocent (has no reason to know that the contract is illegal), that party can often recover any benefits conferred in a partially executed contract. In this situation, the courts will not enforce the contract but will allow the parties to return to their original positions.

A court may sometimes permit an innocent party who has fully performed under the contract to enforce the contract against the guilty party. ▶ **Example 11.19**   A trucking company contracts with Gillespie to carry crates filled with goods to a specific destination for the normal fee of $5,000. The trucker delivers the crates and later finds out that they contained illegal goods. Although the law specifies that the shipment, use, and sale of the goods were illegal, the trucker, being an innocent party, can still legally collect the $5,000 from Gillespie. ◀

MEMBERS OF PROTECTED CLASSES When a statute is clearly designed to protect a certain class of people, a member of that class can enforce a contract in violation of the statute even though the other party cannot. ▶ **Example 11.20**   Statutes prohibit certain employees (such as flight attendants and pilots) from working more than a certain number of hours per month. An employee who is required to work more than the maximum can recover for those extra hours of service. ◀

Other examples of statutes designed to protect a particular class of people are state statutes that regulate the sale of insurance. If an insurance company violates a statute when selling insurance, the purchaser can still enforce the policy and recover from the insurer.

WITHDRAWAL FROM AN ILLEGAL AGREEMENT If the illegal part of a bargain has not yet been performed, the party rendering performance can withdraw from the contract and recover the performance or its value. ▶ **Example 11.21**   Sam and Jim decide to wager (illegally) on the outcome of a boxing match. Each deposits cash with a stakeholder, who agrees to pay the winner of the bet. At this point, each party has performed part of the agreement, but the illegal element of the agreement will not occur until the funds are paid to the winner. Before that payment occurs, either party is entitled to withdraw from the bargain by giving notice of repudiation to the stakeholder. ◀

CONTRACT ILLEGAL THROUGH FRAUD, DURESS, OR UNDUE INFLUENCE Often, one party to an illegal contract is more at fault than the other. When one party uses fraud, duress, or undue influence to induce another party to enter into an illegal bargain, the second party will be allowed to recover for the performance or its value.

SEVERABLE, OR DIVISIBLE, CONTRACTS A contract that is *severable,* or divisible, consists of distinct parts that can be performed separately, with separate consideration provided for each part. With an *indivisible* contract, in contrast, complete performance by each party is essential, even if the contract contains a number of seemingly separate provisions.

If a contract is divisible into legal and illegal portions, a court may enforce the legal portion but not the illegal one, so long as the illegal portion does not affect the essence of the bargain. This approach is consistent with the courts' basic policy of enforcing the legal intentions of the contracting parties whenever possible.

▶ **Example 11.22** Cole signs an employment contract that includes an overly broad and thus illegal covenant not to compete. In that situation, a court might allow the employment contract to be enforceable but reform the unreasonably broad covenant by converting its terms into reasonable ones. Alternatively, the court could declare the covenant illegal (and thus void) and enforce the remaining employment terms. ◀

Reviewing: Consideration, Capacity, and Legality

Renee Beaver started racing go-karts competitively in 2012, when she was fourteen. Many of the races required her to sign an exculpatory clause to participate, which she or her parents regularly signed. In 2014, right before her sixteenth birthday, she participated in the annual Elkhart Grand Prix, a series of races in Elkhart, Indiana. During the event in which she drove, a piece of foam padding used as a course barrier was torn from its base and ended up on the track. A portion of the padding struck Beaver in the head, and another portion was thrown into oncoming traffic, causing a multikart collision during which she sustained severe injuries. Beaver filed an action against the race organizers for negligence. The race organizers could not locate the exculpatory clause that Beaver had supposedly signed. The organizers argued that she must have signed one to enter the race, but even if she had not signed one, her actions showed her intent to be bound by its terms. Using the information presented in the chapter, answer the following questions.

1. Did Beaver have the contractual capacity to enter a contract with an exculpatory clause? Why or why not?
2. Assuming that Beaver did, in fact, sign the exculpatory clause, did she later disaffirm or ratify the contract? Explain.
3. Now assume that Beaver stated that she was eighteen years old at the time that she signed the exculpatory clause. How might this affect Beaver's ability to disaffirm or ratify the contract?
4. If Beaver did not actually sign the exculpatory clause, could a court conclude that she impliedly accepted its terms by participating in the race? Why or why not?

DEBATE THIS . . . *After agreeing to an exculpatory clause or purchasing some item, such as a computer, minors often seek to avoid the contracts. Today's minors are far from naïve and should not be allowed to avoid their contractual obligations.*

Terms and Concepts

accord and satisfaction 218
age of majority 222
consideration 214

contractual capacity 222
covenant not to compete 227
covenant not to sue 219

disaffirmance 222
emancipation 222
estopped 221

ExamPrep

Issue Spotters

1. Joan, who is sixteen years old, moves out of her parents' home and signs a one-year lease for an apartment at Kenwood Apartments. Joan's parents tell her that she can return to live with them at any time. Unable to pay the rent, Joan moves back to her parents' home two months later. Can Kenwood enforce the lease against Joan? Why or why not? **(See pages 222 and 223.)**

2. In September, Sharyn agrees to work for Totem Productions, Inc., at $500 a week for a year beginning January 1. In October, Sharyn is offered the same work at $600 a week by Umber Shows, Ltd. When Sharyn tells Totem about the other offer, they tear up their contract and agree that Sharyn will be paid $575. Is the new contract binding? Explain. **(See page 216.)**

- Check your answers to the Issue Spotters against the answers provided in Appendix B at the end of this text.

Before the Test

Go to **www.cengagebrain.com**, enter the ISBN 9781285770192, and click on "Find" to locate this textbook's Web site. Then, click on "Access Now" under "Study Tools," and select Chapter 11 at the top. There, you will find a Practice Quiz that you can take to assess your mastery of the concepts in this chapter, as well as Flashcards and a Glossary of important terms.

Business Scenarios

11–1. Covenants Not to Compete. A famous New York City hotel, Hotel Lux, is noted for its food as well as its luxury accommodations. Hotel Lux contracts with a famous chef, Chef Perlee, to become its head chef at $30,000 per month. The contract states that should Perlee leave the employment of Hotel Lux for any reason, he will not work as a chef for any hotel or restaurant in New York, New Jersey, or Pennsylvania for a period of one year. During the first six months of the contract, Hotel Lux heavily advertises Perlee as its head chef, and business at the hotel is excellent. Then a dispute arises between the hotel's management and Perlee, and Perlee terminates his employment. One month later, he is hired by a famous New Jersey restaurant just across the New York state line. Hotel Lux learns of Perlee's employment through a large advertisement in a New York City newspaper. It seeks to enjoin (prevent) Perlee from working in that restaurant as a chef for one year. Discuss how successful Hotel Lux will be in its action. **(See pages 227 and 228.)**

11–2. Capacity. Joanne is a seventy-five-year-old widow who survives on her husband's small pension. Joanne has become increasingly forgetful, and her family worries that she may have Alzheimer's disease (a brain disorder that seriously affects a person's ability to carry out daily activities). No physician has diagnosed her, however, and no court has ruled on Joanne's legal competence. One day while she is out shopping, Joanne stops by a store that is having a sale on pianos and enters into a fifteen-year installment contract to buy a grand piano. When the piano arrives the next day, Joanne seems confused and repeatedly asks the delivery person why a piano is being delivered. Joanne claims that she does not recall buying a piano. Explain whether this contract is void, voidable, or valid. Can Joanne avoid her contractual obligation to buy the piano? If so, how? **(See page 225.)**

11–3. Illusory Promises. Costello hired Sagan to drive his racing car in a race. Sagan's friend Gideon promised to pay Sagan $3,000 if she won the race. Sagan won the race, but Gideon refused to pay. Gideon contended that no legally binding contract had been formed because he had received no consideration from Sagan in exchange for his promise to pay the $3,000. Sagan sued Gideon for breach of contract, arguing that winning the race was the consideration given in exchange for Gideon's promise to pay the $3,000. What rule of law discussed in this chapter supports Gideon's claim? **(See page 218.)**

Business Case Problems

11–4. Rescission. Farrokh and Scheherezade Sharabianlou signed a purchase agreement to buy a building owned by Berenstein Associates for $2 million. They deposited $115,000 toward the purchase. Before the deal closed, an environmental assessment of the property indicated the presence of chemicals used in dry cleaning. This substantially reduced the property's value. Do the Sharabianlous have a good argument for the return of their deposit and rescission of the contract? Explain your answer. [*Sharabianlou v. Karp,* 181 Cal.App.4th 1133, 105 Cal. Rptr.3d 300 (1st Dist. 2010)] **(See page 216.)**

11–5. BUSINESS CASE PROBLEM WITH SAMPLE ANSWER: Unconscionable Clauses.

 Geographic Expeditions, Inc. (GeoEx), which guided climbs up Mount Kilimanjaro, required climbers to sign a release to participate in an expedition. The form mandated the arbitration of any dispute in San Francisco and limited damages to the cost of the trip. GeoEx told climbers that the terms were nonnegotiable and were the same as terms imposed by other travel firms. Jason Lhotka died on a GeoEx climb. His mother filed a suit against GeoEx. GeoEx sought arbitration. Was the arbitration clause unconscionable? Why or why not? [Lhotka v. Geographic Expeditions, Inc., *181 Cal.App.4th 816, 104 Cal.Rptr.3d 844 (1 Dist. 2010)]* **(See page 228.)**

- For a sample answer to Problem 11–5, go to Appendix C at the end of this text.

11–6. Mental Incompetence. Dorothy Drury suffered from dementia and chronic confusion. When she became unable to manage her own affairs, including decisions about medical and financial matters, her son Eddie arranged for her move to an assisted living facility. During admission, she signed a residency agreement, which included an arbitration clause. After she sustained injuries in a fall at the facility, a suit was filed to recover damages. The facility asked the court to compel arbitration. Was Dorothy bound to the residency agreement? Discuss. [*Drury v. Assisted Living Concepts, Inc.,* 245 Or.App. 217, 262 P.3d 1162 (2011)] **(See page 225.)**

11–7. Minors. D.V.G. (a minor) was injured in a one-car auto accident in Hoover, Alabama. The vehicle was covered by an insurance policy issued by Nationwide Mutual Insurance Co. Stan Brobston, D.V.G.'s attorney, accepted Nationwide's offer of $50,000 on D.V.G.'s behalf. Before the settlement could be submitted to an Alabama state court for approval, D.V.G. died from injuries received in a second, unrelated auto accident. Nationwide argued that it was not bound to the settlement because a minor lacks the capacity to contract and so cannot enter into a binding settlement without court approval. Should Nationwide be bound to the settlement? Why or why not? [*Nationwide Mutual Insurance Co. v. Wood,* __ So.3d __, 2013 WL 646468 (Ala. 2013)] **(See page 222.)**

11–8. Consideration. On Brenda Sniezek's first day of work for the Kansas City Chiefs Football Club, she signed a document that purported to compel arbitration of any disputes that she might have with the Chiefs. In the document, Sniezek agreed to comply at all times with and be bound by the constitution and bylaws of the National Football League (NFL). She agreed to refer all disputes to the NFL commissioner for a binding decision. On the commissioner's decision, she agreed to release the Chiefs and others from any related claims. Nowhere in the document did the Chiefs agree to do anything. Was there consideration for the arbitration provision? Explain. [*Sniezek v. Kansas City Chiefs Football Club,* 402 S.W.3d 580 (Mo. App. W.D. 2013)] **(See page 214.)**

11–9. A QUESTION OF ETHICS: Promissory Estoppel. *Claudia Aceves borrowed from U.S. Bank to buy a home. Two years later, she could no longer afford the monthly payments. The bank notified her that it planned to foreclose (take possession of and sell) on her home. Aceves filed for bankruptcy. The bank offered to modify Aceves's mortgage if she would forgo bankruptcy. She agreed. Once she withdrew the filing, however, the bank foreclosed.* [Aceves v. U.S. Bank, N.A., *192 Cal.App.4th 218, 120 Cal.Rptr.3d 507 (2 Dist. 2011)]* **(See page 221.)**

(a) Could Aceves succeed on a claim of promissory estoppel? Why or why not?

(b) Did Aceves or U.S. Bank behave unethically? Discuss.

Legal Reasoning Group Activity

11–10. Covenants Not to Compete. Assume that you are part of a group of executives at a large software corporation. The company is considering whether to incorporate covenants not to compete into its employment contracts. You know that there are some issues with the enforceability of these covenants and want to make an informed decision. **(See pages 227 and 228.)**

(a) One group should make a list of what interests are served by enforcing covenants not to compete.

(b) A second group should create a list of what interests are served by refusing to enforce covenants not to compete.

(c) A third group should discuss whether a court should reform (and then enforce) a covenant not to compete that it determines is illegal, and create an argument for and against reformation.

CHAPTER 12

DEFENSES TO CONTRACT ENFORCEABILITY

An otherwise valid contract may still be unenforceable if the parties have not genuinely agreed to its terms. As mentioned in Chapter 9, a lack of voluntary consent (assent) can be used as a *defense* to a contract's enforceability.

Voluntary consent may be lacking because of a *mistake, fraudulent misrepresentation, undue influence,* or *duress.* Generally, a party who demonstrates that he or she did not truly agree to the terms of a contract can choose either to carry out the contract or to rescind (cancel) it and thus avoid the entire transaction.

A contract that is otherwise valid may also be unenforceable if it is not in the proper form. For example, certain types of contracts are required to be in writing or evidenced by a memorandum, note, or electronic record (*record* was defined in Chapter 10). The writing requirement does not mean that an agreement must be a formal written contract. All that is necessary is some written proof that a contract exists, such as an e-mail exchange evidencing the agreement.

Under what is called the *Statute of Frauds,* certain agreements are required

by law to be in writing or evidenced by a record. If there is no written evidence of the contract, it may not be enforceable.

In this chapter, we first examine the kinds of factors that may indicate a lack of voluntary consent and cause a court to refuse to enforce a contract. We then consider what types of contracts require a writing under the Statute of Frauds. The chapter concludes with a discussion of the *parol evidence rule,* under which courts determine the admissibility at trial of evidence extraneous (external) to written contracts.

SECTION 1
MISTAKES

We all make mistakes, so it is not surprising that mistakes are made when contracts are formed. In certain circumstances, contract law allows a contract to be avoided on the basis of mistake. It is important to distinguish between *mistakes of fact* and *mistakes of value or quality.* Only a mistake of fact makes a contract voidable. Also, the mistake must involve some *material fact*—a fact that a reasonable person would consider important when determining his or her course of action.

▶ **Example 12.1**   Sung buys a violin from Bev for $250. Although the violin is very old, neither party believes that it is valuable. Later, however, an antiques dealer informs the parties that the violin is rare and worth thousands of dollars. Here, both parties were mistaken, but the mistake is a mistake of *value* rather than a mistake of *fact* that warrants contract rescission. Therefore, Bev cannot rescind the contract. ◀

Mistakes of fact occur in two forms—*unilateral* and *bilateral.* A unilateral mistake is made by only *one* of the parties. A bilateral, or mutual, mistake is made by *both* of the contracting parties. We look next at these two types of mistakes and illustrate them graphically in Exhibit 12–1 on the following page.

Unilateral Mistakes of Fact

A unilateral mistake is made by only one of the parties. In general, a unilateral mistake does not give the mistaken party any right to relief from the contract. Normally, the contract is enforceable.

▶ **Example 12.2**   Elena intends to sell her jet ski for $2,500. When she learns that Chin is interested in buying a used jet ski, she sends him an e-mail offering to sell the jet ski to him. When typing the e-mail, however, she mistakenly keys in the price of $1,500. Chin immediately sends Elena an e-mail reply accepting her offer. Even though Elena intended to sell her personal jet ski for $2,500, she has made a unilateral mistake and is bound by the contract to sell it to Chin for $1,500. ◀

EXHIBIT 12-1 Mistakes of Fact

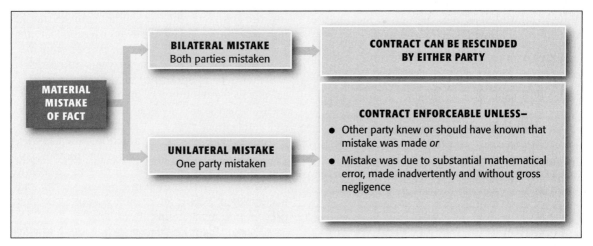

This general rule has at least two exceptions.[1] The contract may be enforceable if:

1. The *other* party to the contract knows or should have known that a mistake of fact was made.
2. The error was due to a substantial mathematical mistake in addition, subtraction, division, or multiplication and was made inadvertently and without gross (extreme) negligence. If, for instance, a contractor's bid was significantly low because he or she made a mistake in addition when totaling the estimated costs, any contract resulting from the bid normally may be rescinded.

Of course, in both situations, the mistake must still involve some material fact.

Bilateral (Mutual) Mistakes of Fact

A bilateral mistake is a "mutual misunderstanding concerning a basic assumption on which the contract was made."[2] When both parties are mistaken about the same material fact, the contract can be rescinded by either party.

A word or term in a contract may be subject to more than one reasonable interpretation. If the parties to the contract attach materially different meanings to the term, a court may allow the contract to be rescinded because there has been no true "meeting of the minds."

Mistakes of Value

If a mistake concerns the future market value or quality of the object of the contract, the mistake is one of *value,* and the contract normally is enforceable. The reason for this is that value is variable. Depending on the time, place, and other circumstances, the same item may be worth considerably different amounts.

When parties form a contract, their agreement establishes the value of the object of their transaction—for the moment. Each party is considered to have assumed the risk that the value will change in the future or prove to be different from what he or she thought. Without this rule, almost any party who did not receive what she or he considered a fair bargain could argue mistake.

SECTION 2
FRAUDULENT MISREPRESENTATION

Although fraud is a tort (see Chapter 4), it also affects the authenticity of the innocent party's consent to the contract. When an innocent party is fraudulently induced to enter into a contract, the contract normally can be avoided because that party has not *voluntarily* consented to its terms.[3] Ordinarily, the innocent party can either rescind the contract and be restored to her or his original position or enforce the contract and seek damages for any harms resulting from the fraud.

---

1. The *Restatement (Second) of Contracts,* Section 153, liberalizes the general rule to take into account the modern trend of allowing avoidance even though only one party has been mistaken.
2. *Restatement (Second) of Contracts,* Section 152.

3. *Restatement (Second) of Contracts,* Sections 163 and 164.

Generally, fraudulent misrepresentation refers only to misrepresentation that is consciously false and is intended to mislead another. The person making the fraudulent misrepresentation knows or believes that the assertion is false or knows that she or he does not have a basis (stated or implied) for the assertion.[4] Typically, fraudulent misrepresentation consists of the following elements:

1. A misrepresentation of a material fact must occur.
2. There must be an intent to deceive.
3. The innocent party must justifiably rely on the misrepresentation.
4. To collect damages, a party must have been harmed as a result of the misrepresentation.

Misrepresentation Has Occurred

The first element of proving fraud is to show that misrepresentation of a material fact has occurred. This misrepresentation can occur by words or actions. For instance, the statement "This sculpture was created by Michelangelo" is a misrepresentation of fact if another artist sculpted the statue. Similarly, if a customer asks to see only paintings by the decorative artist Paul Wright and the gallery owner immediately leads the customer over to paintings that were not done by Wright, the owner's actions can be a misrepresentation.

MISREPRESENTATION BY CONDUCT Misrepresentation also occurs when a party takes specific action to conceal a fact that is material to the contract.[5] Therefore, if a seller, by her or his actions, prevents a buyer from learning of some fact that is material to the contract, such behavior constitutes misrepresentation by conduct.
▶ **Case in Point 12.3** Actor Tom Selleck contracted to purchase a horse named Zorro for his daughter from Dolores Cuenca. Cuenca acted as though Zorro was fit to ride in competitions, when in reality the horse suffered from a medical condition. Selleck filed a lawsuit against Cuenca for wrongfully concealing the horse's condition and won. A jury awarded Selleck more than $187,000 for Cuenca's misrepresentation by conduct.[6] ◀

STATEMENTS OF OPINION Statements of opinion and representations of future facts (predictions) gener-

ally are not subject to claims of fraud. Every person is expected to exercise care and judgment when entering into contracts. The law will not come to the aid of one who simply makes an unwise bargain. Statements such as "This land will be worth twice as much next year" or "This car will last for years and years" are statements of opinion, not fact. Contracting parties should recognize them as opinions and not rely on them. A fact is objective and verifiable, whereas an opinion is usually subject to debate.

Nevertheless, in certain situations, such as when a naïve purchaser relies on an opinion from an expert, the innocent party may be entitled to rescission or reformation. (As discussed in Chapter 11, *reformation* occurs when a court alters the terms of a contract to prevent undue hardships or burdens.)
▶ **Case in Point 12.4** In a classic case, an instructor at an Arthur Murray dance school told Audrey Vokes, a widow without family, that she had the potential to become an accomplished dancer. The instructor sold her 2,302 hours of dancing lessons for a total amount of $31,090.45 (equivalent to $142,000 in 2014). When it became clear to Vokes that she did not, in fact, have the potential to be an excellent dancer, she sued the school for fraudulent misrepresentation. The court held that because the dance school had superior knowledge about a person's dance potential, the instructor's statements could be considered statements of fact rather than opinion.[7] ◀

MISREPRESENTATION OF LAW Misrepresentation of law *ordinarily* does not entitle a party to relief from a contract. ▶ **Example 12.5** Camara has a parcel of property that she is trying to sell to Pike. Camara knows that a local ordinance prohibits the construction of anything higher than three stories on the property. Nonetheless, she tells Pike, "You can build a condominium a hundred stories high on this land if you want to." Pike buys the land and later discovers that Camara's statement was false. Normally, Pike cannot avoid the contract because people are assumed to know state and local laws. ◀

Exceptions to this rule occur when the misrepresenting party is in a profession that is known to require greater knowledge of the law than the average citizen possesses. For instance, if Camara, in *Example 12.5*, had been a lawyer or a real estate broker, her willful misrepresentation of the area's zoning laws probably would have constituted fraud.

---

4. *Restatement (Second) of Contracts*, Section 162.
5. *Restatement (Second) of Contracts*, Section 160.
6. *Selleck v. Cuenca*, Case No. GIN056909, North County of San Diego, California, decided September 9, 2009.
7. *Vokes v. Arthur Murray, Inc.*, 212 So.2d 906 (Fla.App. 1968).

MISREPRESENTATION BY SILENCE   Ordinarily, neither party to a contract has a duty to come forward and disclose facts. Therefore, courts typically do not set aside contracts because a party did not volunteer pertinent information.   ▶ **Example 12.6**   Jim is selling a car that has been in an accident and has been repaired. He does not need to volunteer this information to a potential buyer. If, however, the purchaser asks Jim if the car has had extensive bodywork and Jim lies, he has committed a fraudulent misrepresentation.   ◀

In general, if a seller knows of a serious potential problem that the buyer cannot reasonably be expected to discover, the seller may have a duty to speak. Generally, the seller must disclose only **latent defects**—that is, defects that could not readily be ascertained. Because a buyer of a house could easily discover the presence of termites through an inspection, for instance, termites may not qualify as a latent defect. Also, when the parties are in a *fiduciary relationship*—one of trust, such as partners, physician and patient, or attorney and client—they have a duty to disclose material facts. Failure to do so may constitute fraud.

In the following case, a real estate investor claimed that misrepresentation by silence had occurred when a seller of property failed to disclose material facts about its value.

CASE 12.1

Fazio v. Cypress/GR Houston I, LP

Court of Appeals of Texas, First Division, ____ S.W.3d ____ (2012).

BACKGROUND AND FACTS   Peter Fazio began talks with Cypress/GR Houston I, LP, to buy retail property whose main tenant was a Garden Ridge store. In performing a background investigation, Fazio and his agents became concerned about Garden Ridge's financial health. Nevertheless, after being assured that Garden Ridge had a positive financial outlook, Fazio sent Cypress a letter of intent to buy the property for $7.67 million "based on the currently reported absolute net income of $805,040." Cypress then agreed to provide all information in its possession, but it failed to disclose that:

1. A consultant for Garden Ridge had recently requested a $240,000 reduction in the annual rent as part of a restructuring of the company's real estate leases.
2. Cypress's bank was so concerned about Garden Ridge's financial health that it had required a personal guaranty of the property's loan.

The parties entered into a purchase agreement, but Garden Ridge went into bankruptcy shortly after the deal closed. Fazio sued Cypress for fraud after he was forced to sell the property for only $3.75 million. A jury found in Fazio's favor, but the trial court awarded judgment *n.o.v.* (notwithstanding the verdict) to Cypress. Fazio appealed.

   IN THE LANGUAGE OF THE COURT
Evelyn V. *KEYES*, Justice.

* * * *

We * * * *hold that Fazio's claims clearly fall within the category of claims for which an action for fraudulent inducement lies.* [Emphasis added.]

Cypress knew from the express representation in the LOI [letter of intent] that Fazio was willing to pay the requested purchase price of $7,667,000 for the Property "based on the currently reported absolute net income of $805,040." It further knew that this income was generated by rental income received from Garden Ridge. Fazio agreed in the LOI to conduct due diligence [background investigation], and, in accepting the LOI, Cypress agreed to "provide Buyer with all information in [its] possession * * * ." Fazio, an experienced real estate investor, and his experienced agents conducted reasonable due diligence before Fazio signed the Purchase Agreement, including requesting and reviewing all economic information about the Property in Cypress's possession. When Fazio discovered disturbing information about Garden Ridge in the financial statements provided to him, he conducted further investigations with

CASE 12.1 CONTINUES ▶

CASE 12.1 CONTINUED both Garden Ridge and Cypress. He was repeatedly assured that all was well and that Garden Ridge anticipated strong sales * * * .

A reasonable person in Fazio's position would clearly have attached importance to the facts that approximately eight months before he purchased the Property in September 2003, Garden Ridge had retained [a consultant] to assist it in restructuring and renegotiating Garden Ridge's real estate leases; [the consultant] had prepared a letter for Garden Ridge to send to landlords; a copy of that letter, stating that Garden Ridge was restructuring and that as part of its restructuring it needed to reduce its occupancy costs at certain stores, including the Garden Ridge store on the Property, was sent to Cypress's President, Maguire, on March 5, 2003; and [the consultant] had contacted Cypress's Director of Finance and others at Cypress on at least three other occasions to discuss the proposed rent relief, seeking an annual rent reduction of 30% for the Property, or $241,512.

A reasonable real estate investor who had signed an LOI to purchase the Property for $7,667,000 on September 2, 2003 would also attach importance to and be induced to act on the information that, on August 14, 2003, Cypress's lender, Guaranty Bank, had requested that Cypress's President execute a personal guaranty of the balance of $4,500,000 on the $5,704,000 loan secured by the Property because the bank was concerned about Garden Ridge's financial condition.

* * * We * * * hold that Cypress's active concealment of this material information, which it was under a duty to disclose as financial information material to the real estate transaction in its possession, was fraudulent as a matter of law.

DECISION AND REMEDY *The Texas appellate court reversed the trial court and held that Cypress was liable to Fazio for fraud.*

THE ETHICAL DIMENSION *Was Cypress's conduct unethical? Why or why not?*

THE SOCIAL DIMENSION *What does the decision in this case suggest to sellers of commercial real estate and others who engage in business negotiations?*

Intent to Deceive

The second element of fraud is knowledge on the part of the misrepresenting party that facts have been falsely represented. This element, normally called ***scienter***,[8] or "guilty knowledge," signifies that there was an *intent to deceive*. *Scienter* clearly exists if a party knows a fact is not as stated. *Scienter* also exists if a party makes a statement that he or she believes is not true or makes a statement recklessly, without regard to whether it is true or false. Finally, this element is met if a party says or implies that a statement is made on some basis, such as personal knowledge or personal investigation, when it is not.

▶ **Case in Point 12.7** Robert Sarvis applied for a position as a business law professor two weeks after his release from prison. On his résumé, he said that he had been a corporate president for fourteen years and had taught business law at another college. After he was hired, his probation officer alerted the school to Sarvis's criminal history. The school immediately fired him. When Sarvis sued the school for breach of his employment contract, the court concluded that by not disclosing his history, Sarvis clearly exhibited an intent to deceive and that the school had justifiably relied on his misrepresentations. Therefore, the school could rescind Sarvis's employment contract.[9] ◀

INNOCENT MISREPRESENTATION If a person makes a statement that she or he believes to be true but that actually misrepresents material facts, the person is guilty only of an **innocent misrepresentation**, not of fraud. When an innocent misrepresentation occurs, the aggrieved party can rescind the contract but usually cannot seek damages. ▶ **Example 12.8** Parris tells Roberta that a tract of land contains 250 acres. Parris is mistaken—the tract contains only 215 acres—but Parris had no knowledge of the mistake. Roberta relies on the statement and contracts to buy the land. Even though the misrepresentation is innocent, Roberta can avoid the contract if the misrepresentation is material. ◀

---

8. Pronounced sy-*en*-ter.

9. *Sarvis v. Vermont State Colleges,* 172 Vt. 76, 772 A.2d 494 (2001).

NEGLIGENT MISREPRESENTATION Sometimes, a party will make a misrepresentation through carelessness, believing the statement is true. If the party did not exercise reasonable care in uncovering or disclosing the facts or use the skill and competence that her or his business or profession requires, the misrepresentation may constitute **negligent misrepresentation.** For instance, an operator of a weight scale certifies the weight of Sneed's commodity, even though the scale's accuracy has not been checked for more than three years.

In almost all states, such negligent misrepresentation is equal to *scienter*, or knowingly making a misrepresentation. In effect, negligent misrepresentation is treated as fraudulent misrepresentation, even though the misrepresentation was not purposeful. In negligent misrepresentation, culpable ignorance of the truth supplies the intention to mislead, even if the defendant can claim, "I didn't know."

Reliance on the Misrepresentation

The third element of fraud is reasonably *justifiable reliance* on the misrepresentation of fact. The deceived party must have a justifiable reason for relying on the misrepresentation. Also, the misrepresentation must be an important factor (but not necessarily the sole factor) in inducing the deceived party to enter into the contract.

Reliance is not justified if the innocent party knows the true facts or relies on obviously extravagant statements (such as, "this pickup truck will get fifty miles to the gallon"). ▶ **Example 12.9** Meese, a securities broker, offers to sell BIM stock to Packer. Meese assures Packer that BIM shares are blue chip securities—that is, they are stable, have limited risk, and yield a good return on investment over time. In reality, Meese knows nothing about the quality of BIM stock and does not believe the truth of what he is saying. Thus, Meese's statement is an intentional misrepresentation of a material fact. If Packer is induced by Meese's statement to enter into a contract to buy the stock, he probably can avoid the contract. Packer justifiably relied on his broker's misrepresentation of material fact. ◀

The same rule applies to defects in property sold. If the defects would be obvious on inspection, the buyer cannot justifiably rely on the seller's representations. If the defects are hidden or latent, as previously discussed, the buyer is justified in relying on the seller's statements.

In the following case, the receiver for a car wash assured the buyer that the property would be "appropriately winterized," but it was not. Was the buyer justified in relying on the seller's representations? (A *receiver*, also called a *trustee*, is an independent, impartial party appointed by a bankruptcy court to manage property in bankruptcy and dispose of it in an orderly manner for the benefit of the creditors.)

CASE ANALYSIS

Case 12.2   Cronkelton v. Guaranteed Construction Services, LLC
Court of Appeals of Ohio, Third District, 988 N.E.2d 656 (2013).

IN THE LANGUAGE OF THE COURT
PRESTON, P.J. [Presiding Judge]

* * * *

The case before this Court stems from a real estate transaction for a foreclosed car wash in Bellefontaine, Ohio. [A court had appointed Patrick Shivley to be a receiver for the protection of the property, which was offered

for sale by Huntington Bank. Clifford] Cronkelton filed a complaint against appellants [Guaranteed Construction Services, LLC, and Shivley] in the Logan County Court of Common Pleas following his purchase of the car wash. Cronkelton asserted * * * fraud.

* * * *

* * * The trial court held a jury trial on the fraud claim. The jury returned a verdict for Cronkelton.

* * * The trial court filed its judgment entry recording the jury's verdict for Cronkelton and awarding Cronkelton $43,671 in compensatory damages, $66,000 in punitive damages, and $30,000 for attorney fees. [Guaranteed Construction Services and Shivley filed an appeal.]

* * * *

* * * [At the trial] Cronkelton testified that he first inspected

CASE 12.2 CONTINUES ▶

the foreclosed car wash at the end of November 2009. At that time, Cronkelton tested the equipment and knew that some of the pieces of equipment were fully functioning and some were not. * * * Shortly thereafter, Cronkelton called Shivley to discuss the winterization of the property. Cronkelton testified:

> so I called him, said, hey, it's going to freeze here this week. * * * It's supposed to get down to like ten degrees, have you got it winterized, you know. If it's not winterized, I'm not interested in the property. If it freezes, I'm not interested in the property at all. And he guaranteed me. He said, no, it will be taken care of. We don't have a problem. That's my job as receiver. I'll take care of it.

After the phone call, Shivley sent Cronkelton an e-mail dated December 7, 2009 that stated:

> As per our phone conversation Guaranteed [Construction Services] will winterize the Car Wash with the anticipation of reopening the wash in the near future. Within this Winterization we will put antifreeze and secure floor heating as well as blow water out of all lines in self serve bays as well as empty tanks, etc. We will leave the heat on at a minimal level in the pump room. * * * We will complete all of this on Wednesday, December 9, 2009.

[Guaranteed Construction hired Strayer Company to winterize the property. But on December 10, Strayer's owner sent a memo to Guaranteed Construction and Shivley stating that the building was not designed to be winterized and that the only way to avoid problems was to leave the heat

on. Shivley knew Huntington Bank had shut off the heat because the property was not generating income. In March 2010, Shivley informed Huntington of damage to the property as a result of freezing. Shivley did not share any of this information with Cronkelton.]

Cronkelton testified that they closed on the property in June and he received the keys at that time. Cronkelton testified that he immediately went to the property:

> I opened the door, and the huge canisters that I was telling you about were all busted. The tops had been exploded off the top of them. * * * You could see pipes that were bursted * * * . So it was clear at that time that this whole thing had froze up, and the extent of the damage could not even be, you know, detailed at that point.

* * * *

* * * Appellants argue Cronkelton unjustifiably relied on Shivley's statements about the car wash's condition because Cronkelton had the opportunity to inspect the property prior to closing.

* * * *

* * * Whether or not reliance on a material misrepresentation was justified under the facts of a case is a question for the trier of fact. Consequently, we must determine whether the jury's decision is supported by competent, credible evidence.

In the present case, it is undisputed that the damage caused by freezing was open and obvious upon inspection, that Cronkelton did inspect the property in November

2009, and that he could have inspected the property again before signing the purchase agreement. Cronkelton testified regarding why he did not inspect the property after November 2009:

> * * * [Shivley] wrote me this e-mail, guaranteed me it was taken care of in detail what he was going to do, so I had no reason. And because * * * he was appointed by the Court, I don't know how much more I could have done to know that I could trust him.

* * * The jury found that Cronkelton had reasonably relied on Shivley's representations.

The jury's finding was supported by competent, credible evidence. * * * *When determining whether reliance is justifiable, courts consider the various circumstances involved, such as the nature of the transaction, the form and materiality of the transaction, the form and materiality of the representation, the relationship of the parties, the respective intelligence, experience, age, and mental and physical condition of the parties, and their respective knowledge and means of knowledge.* [Emphasis added.]

Cronkelton relied on representations made by Shivley * * *. As a receiver, Shivley had a fiduciary duty to the assets under his control. Under the circumstances of this case, Cronkelton had a reasonable basis to believe that Shivley, who was acting as an arm of the court, would take the promised steps to winterize the property.

* * * *

* * * We affirm the judgment of the trial court.

LEGAL REASONING QUESTIONS

1. What is a receiver? What are a receiver's duties?

2. In evaluating a claim of fraud, what factors does a court consider in determining whether reliance was justifiable?

3. In this case, what did the jury find with respect to the plaintiff's claim of reliance? What was the appellate court's opinion of this finding?

4. Did Shivley's misrepresentations rise to the level of fraud? Explain.

Injury to the Innocent Party

Most courts do not require a showing of injury when the action is to rescind the contract. These courts hold that because rescission returns the parties to the positions they held before the contract was made, a showing of injury to the innocent party is unnecessary.

In contrast, to recover damages caused by fraud, proof of harm is universally required. The measure of damages is ordinarily equal to the property's value had it been delivered as represented, less the actual price paid for the property. (What if someone pretends to be someone else online? Can the victim of the hoax prove injury sufficient to recover for fraudulent misrepresentation? See this chapter's *Insight into Social Media* feature on the following page for a discussion of this topic.)

Additionally, because fraud actions necessarily involve wrongful conduct, courts may also award *punitive damages,* or *exemplary damages.* As discussed in Chapter 4, punitive damages are intended to punish the defendant and are granted to a plaintiff over and above compensation for the proved, actual loss. Because of the potential for punitive damages, which normally are not available in contract actions, plaintiffs often include a claim for fraudulent misrepresentation in their contract disputes.

SECTION 3
UNDUE INFLUENCE

Undue influence arises from relationships in which one party can greatly influence another party, thus overcoming that party's free will. A contract entered into under excessive or undue influence lacks voluntary consent and is therefore voidable.[10]

One Party Dominates the Other

In various types of relationships, one party may have the opportunity to dominate and unfairly influence another party. Minors and elderly people, for instance, are often under the influence of guardians (persons who are legally responsible for another). If a guardian induces a young or elderly ward (a person whom the guardian looks after) to enter into a contract that benefits the guardian, the guardian may have exerted undue influence. Undue influence can arise from a number of fiduciary relationships, such as physician-patient, parent-child, husband-wife, or guardian-ward situations.

The essential feature of undue influence is that the party being taken advantage of does not, in reality, exercise free will in entering into a contract. It is not enough that a person is elderly or suffers from some physical or mental impairment. There must be clear and convincing evidence that the person did not act out of her or his free will.[11] Similarly, the existence of a fiduciary relationship alone is insufficient to prove undue influence.[12]

A Presumption of Undue Influence in Certain Situations

When the dominant party in a fiduciary relationship (such as the one between an attorney and a client) benefits from that relationship, a presumption of undue influence arises. The dominant party (the attorney) must exercise the utmost good faith in dealing with the other party. When a contract enriches the dominant party, the court will often *presume* that the contract was made under undue influence.

▶ **Example 12.10**   Erik is the guardian for Kinsley, his ward. On her behalf, he enters into a contract from which he benefits financially. If Kinsley challenges the contract, the court will likely presume that the guardian has taken advantage of his ward. To rebut (refute) this presumption, Erik has to show that he made full disclosure to Kinsley and that consideration was present. He must also show that Kinsley received, if available, independent and competent advice before completing the transaction. Unless the presumption can be rebutted, the contract will be rescinded. ◀

SECTION 4
DURESS

Agreement to the terms of a contract is not voluntary if one of the parties is *forced* into the agreement. The use of threats to force a party to enter into a contract is referred to as **duress.** In addition, blackmail or extortion to induce consent to a contract constitutes duress. Duress is both a defense to the enforcement of a contract and a ground for the rescission of a contract.

---

10. *Restatement (Second) of Contracts,* Section 177.

11. See, for example, *Bailey v. Turnbow,* 273 Va. 262, 639 S.E.2d 291 (2007); and *Hooten v. Jensen,* 94 Ark.App. 130, 227 S.W.3d 431 (2006).
12. See, for example, *Landers v. Sgouros,* 224 S.W.3d 651 (Mo.App. 2007); and *Ware v. Ware,* 161 P.3d 1188 (Alaska 2007).

INSIGHT INTO SOCIAL MEDIA
"Catfishing": Is That Online "Friend" Who You Think It Is?

When you are communicating with a person you have met only online, how do you know that person is who she or he purports to be? After all, the person could turn out to be a "catfish." The term comes from *Catfish*, a 2010 film about a fake online persona.

According to a story told in the film, when live cod were shipped long distances, they were inactive and their flesh became mushy. When catfish were added to the tanks, the cod swam around and stayed in good condition. At the end of the film, a character says of the creator of the fake persona, "There are those people who are catfish in life. And they keep you on your toes. They keep you guessing, they keep you thinking, they keep you fresh."

Catfishing Makes National Headlines

Catfishing made headlines in 2012 when a popular Notre Dame football star supposedly fell victim to it. Linebacker Manti Te'o said that his girlfriend Lennay Kekua, a student at Stanford, had died of leukemia after a near-fatal car accident. Although Kekua had Facebook and Twitter accounts and Te'o had communicated with her online and by telephone for several years, reporters could find no evidence of her existence. Te'o later claimed that he had been a victim of a catfishing hoax. Others suggested that his friends created the persona and her tragic death to provide an inspirational story what would increase Te'o's chances of winning the Heisman Trophy.

Is Online Fraudulent Misrepresentation Actionable?

Some victims of catfishing have turned to the courts, but they have had little success. A few have attempted to sue Internet service providers for allowing fake personas, but the courts have generally dismissed these suits.[a] Laws in some states make it a crime to impersonate someone online, but these laws generally do not apply to those who create totally fake personas.

Attempts to recover damages for fraudulent misrepresentation have generally failed to meet the requirement that there must be proof of actual injury. For instance, Paula Bonhomme developed an online romantic relationship with a man called Jesse. Jesse was actually a woman named Janna St. James, who also communicated with Bonhomme using her own name and pretending to be a friend of Jesse's.

St. James created a host of fictional characters, including an ex-wife and a son for Jesse. Bonhomme, in turn, sent gifts totaling more than $10,000 to Jesse and the other characters. After being told by St. James that Jesse had attempted suicide, Bonhomme suffered such emotional distress that she incurred more than $5,000 in bills for a therapist. Eventually, she was told that Jesse had died of liver cancer. When Bonhomme finally learned the truth, she suffered additional emotional distress, resulting in more expenses for a therapist and lost earnings due to her "affected mental state."

Although Bonhomme had incurred considerable expenses, the Illinois Supreme Court ruled that she could not bring a suit for fraudulent misrepresentation. The case involved only a "purely personal relationship" without any "commercial, transactional, or regulatory component." Bonhomme and St. James "were not engaged in any kind of business dealings or bargaining." Therefore, the truth of representations "made in the context of purely private personal relationships is simply not something the state regulates or in which the state possesses any kind of valid public policy interest."[b]

LEGAL CRITICAL THINKING
INSIGHT INTO THE LEGAL ENVIRONMENT

So far, victims of catfishing have had little success in the courts. Under what circumstances might a person be able to collect damages for fraudulent misrepresentation involving online impersonation?

a. See, for example, *Robinson v. Match.com, LLC*, 2012 WL 3263992 (N.D.Tex. 2012).

b. *Bonhomme v. St. James*, 970 N.E.2d 1 (Ill. 2012).

The Threatened Act Must Be Wrongful or Illegal

To establish duress, there must be proof of a threat to do something that the threatening party has no right to do. Generally, for duress to occur, the threatened act must be wrongful or illegal, and it must render the person incapable of exercising free will. A threat to exercise a legal right, such as the right to sue someone, ordinarily does not constitute duress.

▶ **Example 12.11** Joan accidentally drives into Olin's car at a stoplight. Joan has no automobile insurance, but she has substantial assets. At the scene, Olin claims to have suffered whiplash and tells Joan that he will agree not to file a lawsuit against her if she pays him $5,000. Joan initially refuses, but Olin says, "If you don't pay me $5,000 right now, I'm going to sue you for $25,000." Joan then gives Olin a check for $5,000 to avoid the lawsuit. The next day, Joan stops payment on the check. When Olin later sues to enforce their oral settlement agreement for $5,000, Joan claims duress as a defense to its enforcement. In this situation, because Olin had a right to sue Joan, his threat to sue her does not constitute duress. A court normally would not consider the threat of a civil suit to be duress. ◄

Economic Duress

Economic need generally is not sufficient to constitute duress, even when one party exacts a very high price for an item that the other party needs. If the party exacting the price also creates the need, however, *economic duress* may be found.

▶ **Example 12.12** The Internal Revenue Service (IRS) assesses a large tax and penalty against Weller. Weller retains Eyman, the accountant who prepared the tax returns on which the assessment was based, to challenge the assessment. Two days before the deadline for filing a reply with the IRS,

Eyman declines to represent Weller unless he signs a very expensive contingency-fee agreement for the services.

In this situation, a court might find that the agreement was unenforceable because of economic duress. Although Eyman has threatened only to withdraw his services, something that he is legally entitled to do, he is responsible for delaying the withdrawal until two days before the IRS deadline. It would be impossible at that late date to obtain adequate representation elsewhere. Therefore, Weller could argue that he was forced either to sign the contract or to lose his right to challenge the IRS assessment. ◄

See *Concept Summary 12.1* below for a review of all of the factors that may indicate a lack of voluntary consent.

SECTION 5
WRITING REQUIREMENT: THE STATUTE OF FRAUDS

Every state has a statute that stipulates what types of contracts must be in writing. We refer to such a statute as the **Statute of Frauds.** The name derives from an English act passed in 1677. The primary purpose of

---

CONCEPT SUMMARY 12.1
Voluntary Consent

PROBLEMS OF ASSENT	RULE
Mistakes	1. *Unilateral mistake*—Generally, the mistaken party is bound by the contract, unless the other party knows or should have known of the mistake, or the mistake is an inadvertent mathematical error in addition, subtraction, or the like that is committed without gross negligence. 2. *Bilateral (mutual) mistake*—If both parties are mistaken about a material fact, such as the identity of the subject matter, either party can avoid the contract. If the mistake relates to the value or quality of the subject matter, either party can enforce the contract.
Fraudulent Misrepresentation	The elements of fraudulent misrepresentation are: 1. A misrepresentation of a material fact has occurred. 2. There has been an intent to deceive. 3. The innocent party has justifiably relied on the misrepresentation. 4. To collect damages, a party must have been harmed as a result of the misrepresentation.
Undue Influence and Duress	1. *Undue influence*—Arises from special relationships, such as fiduciary relationships, in which one party's free will has been overcome by the undue influence of another. Usually, the contract is voidable. 2. *Duress*—Defined as the use of threats to force a party to enter into a contract out of fear; for example, the threat of violence or economic pressure. The party forced to enter into the contract can rescind the contract.

the statute was to ensure that, for certain types of contracts, there was reliable evidence of the contracts and their terms.

The actual name of the Statute of Frauds is misleading because the statute does not apply to fraud. Rather, it denies enforceability to certain contracts that do not comply with its writing requirements. The statute prevents harm to innocent parties by requiring written evidence of agreements concerning important transactions. A contract that is oral when it is required to be in writing is normally voidable by a party who later does not wish to follow through with the agreement.

The following types of contracts are generally required to be in writing or evidenced by a written memorandum or electronic record:

1. Contracts involving interests in land.
2. Contracts that cannot *by their terms* be performed within one year from the day after the date of formation.
3. Collateral, or secondary, contracts, such as promises to answer for the debt or duty of another and promises by the administrator or executor of an estate to pay a debt of the estate personally—that is, out of her or his own pocket.
4. Promises made in consideration of marriage.
5. Under the Uniform Commercial Code (UCC—see Chapter 15), contracts for the sale of goods priced at $500 or more.

Contracts Involving Interests in Land

A contract calling for the sale of land is not enforceable unless it is in writing or evidenced by a written memorandum. Land is *real property* and includes all physical objects that are permanently attached to the soil, such as buildings, fences, trees, and the soil itself.

The Statute of Frauds operates as a *defense* to the enforcement of an oral contract for the sale of land. ▶ **Example 12.13** Skylar contracts orally to sell his property in Fair Oaks to Beth. If he later decides not to sell, under most circumstances, Beth cannot enforce the contract. ◀

The Statute of Frauds also requires written evidence of contracts for the transfer of other interests in land, such as mortgage agreements and leases. Similarly, an agreement that includes an option to purchase real property must be in writing for the option to be enforced.

The One-Year Rule

Contracts that cannot, *by their own terms,* be performed within one year *from the day after* the contract is formed must be in writing to be enforceable.[13] The reason for this rule is that the parties' memory of their contract's terms is not reliable for longer than a year.

TIME PERIOD STARTS THE DAY AFTER THE CONTRACT IS FORMED The one-year period begins to run *the day after the contract is made.* ▶ **Example 12.14** Superior University forms a contract with Kimi San stating that San will teach three courses in history during the coming academic year (September 15 through June 15). If the contract is formed in March, it must be in writing to be enforceable—because it cannot be performed within one year. If the contract is not formed until July, however, it does not have to be in writing to be enforceable—because it can be performed within one year. ◀

CONTRACT MUST BE OBJECTIVELY IMPOSSIBLE TO PERFORM WITHIN ONE YEAR The test for determining whether an oral contract is enforceable under the one-year rule is whether performance is *possible* within one year. It does not matter whether the agreement is *likely* to be performed during that period.

When performance of a contract is objectively impossible during the one-year period, the oral contract will be unenforceable. ▶ **Example 12.15** A contract to provide five crops of tomatoes to be grown on a specific farm in Illinois would be objectively impossible to perform within one year. No farmer in Illinois can grow five crops of tomatoes in a single year. ◀

If performance is possible within one year under the contract's terms, the contract does not "fall within" or "under" the Statute of Frauds and need not be in writing. ▶ **Example 12.16** Janine enters a contract to provide security services for a warehouse for as long as the warehouse needs them. The contract could be fully performed within a year because the warehouse could go out of business within twelve months. Therefore, the contract need not be in writing to be enforceable. ◀ Similarly, an oral contract for lifetime employment does not fall within the Statute of Frauds because an employee can die within a year, so the contract can be performed within one year.[14]

Exhibit 12–2 on the next page graphically illustrates the one-year rule.

---

13. *Restatement (Second) of Contracts,* Section 130.
14. See, for example, *Gavegnano v. TLT Construction Corp.,* 67 Mass.App. Ct. 1102, 851 N.E.2d 1133 (2006).

EXHIBIT 12-2 The One-Year Rule

Under the Statute of Frauds, contracts that by their terms are impossible to perform within one year from the day after the date of contract formation must be in writing to be enforceable. Put another way, if it is at all possible to perform an oral contract within one year from the day after the contract is made, the contract will fall outside the Statute of Frauds and be enforceable.

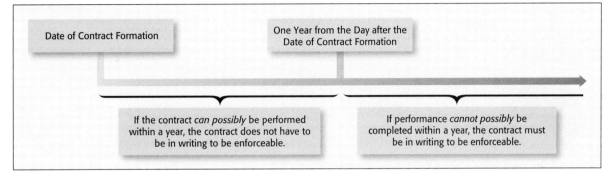

Collateral Promises

A **collateral promise,** or secondary promise, is one that is ancillary (subsidiary) to a principal transaction or primary contractual relationship. In other words, a collateral promise is one made by a third party to assume the debts or obligations of a primary party to a contract if that party does not perform. Any collateral promise of this nature falls under the Statute of Frauds and therefore must be in writing to be enforceable.

To understand this concept, it is important to distinguish between primary and secondary promises and obligations.

PRIMARY OBLIGATIONS A primary obligation is a third party's promise to pay another person's debt (or other obligation) that is not conditioned on the person's failure to pay (or perform). As a general rule, a contract in which a party assumes a primary obligation does not need to be in writing to be enforceable.
▶ **Example 12.17** Nigel tells Leanne Lu, an orthodontist, that he will pay for the services provided for Nigel's niece. Because Nigel has assumed direct financial responsibility for his niece's debt, this is a primary obligation and need not be in writing to be enforceable. ◀

SECONDARY OBLIGATIONS A secondary obligation is a promise to pay another's debt only if that party fails to pay. ▶ **Example 12.18** Kareem's mother borrows $10,000 from the Medford Trust Company on a promissory note payable in six months. Kareem promises

the bank officer handling the loan that he will pay the $10,000 *if his mother does not pay the loan on time.* Kareem, in this situation, becomes what is known as a *guarantor* on the loan. He is guaranteeing to the bank (the creditor) that he will pay the loan if his mother fails to do so. This kind of collateral promise must be in writing to be enforceable. ◀

Exhibit 12–3 on the following page illustrates the concept of a collateral promise. (Notice that the bottom arrow says "Promises to Answer for A's Debt." It does not say "Promises to Pay.")

AN EXCEPTION—THE "MAIN PURPOSE" RULE An oral promise to answer for the debt of another is covered by the Statute of Frauds *unless* the guarantor's main purpose in incurring a secondary obligation is to secure a personal benefit. This type of contract need not be in writing.[15] The assumption is that a court can infer from the circumstances of a particular case whether the "leading objective" of the guarantor was to secure a personal benefit. In this situation, the guarantor is, in effect, answering for (guaranteeing) her or his own debt.

▶ **Example 12.19** Carlie Braswell contracts with Custom Manufacturing Company to have some machines custom-made for her factory. She promises Newform Supply, Custom's supplier, that if Newform continues to deliver the materials to Custom for the production of the custom-made machines, she will guarantee payment. This promise need not be in writing, even though the effect may be to pay the debt of

---

15. *Restatement (Second) of Contracts,* Section 116.

EXHIBIT 12-3 Collateral Promises

A collateral (secondary) promise is one made by a third party (C, in this exhibit) to a creditor (B, in this exhibit) to pay the debt of another (A, in this exhibit), who is primarily obligated to pay the debt. Under the Statute of Frauds, collateral promises must be in writing to be enforceable.

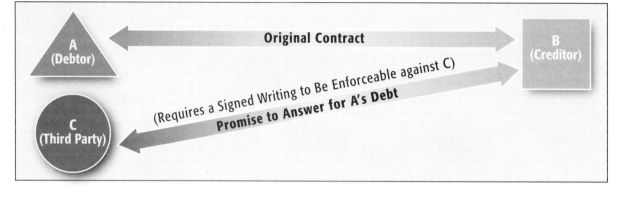

another. This is because Braswell's main purpose in forming the contract is to secure a benefit for herself. ◄

Another typical application of the main purpose rule occurs when one creditor guarantees a debtor's debt to another creditor to forestall litigation. A creditor might do this because it allows the debtor to remain in business long enough to generate profits sufficient to pay *both* creditors. In this situation, the guaranty does not need to be in writing to be enforceable.

Promises Made in Consideration of Marriage

A unilateral promise to make a monetary payment or to give property in consideration of a promise to marry must be in writing. In other words, if a mother promises to pay a man $20,000 if he marries her daughter, that promise must be in writing to be enforceable. ▶ **Example 12.20** Evan promises to buy Celeste a house in Maui if she marries him. Celeste would need written evidence of Evan's promise to enforce it. ◄

The same rule applies to **prenuptial agreements**—agreements made before marriage that define each partner's ownership rights in the other partner's property. Prenuptial agreements must be in writing to be enforceable. ▶ **Example 12.21** Before marrying country singer Keith Urban, actress Nicole Kidman entered into a prenuptial agreement with him. Kidman agreed that if the couple divorced, she would pay Urban $640,000 for every year they had been married, unless Urban had relapsed and used drugs again. In that event, he would receive nothing. ◄

Contracts for the Sale of Goods

The Uniform Commercial Code (UCC) includes Statute of Frauds provisions that require written evidence or an electronic record of a contract for the sale of goods priced at $500 or more. (This low threshold amount may be increased in the future.)

A writing that will satisfy the UCC requirement need only state the quantity term (such as 6,000 boxes of cotton gauze, for instance). The contract will not be enforceable for any quantity greater than that set forth in the writing. Other agreed-on terms can be omitted or even stated imprecisely in the writing, as long as they adequately reflect both parties' intentions.

A written memorandum or series of communications evidencing a contract will suffice, provided that the writing is signed by the party against whom enforcement is sought. The writing normally need not designate the buyer or the seller, the terms of payment, or the price. Requirements of the Statute of Frauds under the UCC will be discussed in more detail in Chapter 15.

Exceptions to the Writing Requirement

Exceptions to the writing requirement are made in certain circumstances. We describe those situations here.

PARTIAL PERFORMANCE When a contract has been partially performed and the parties cannot be returned to their positions prior to the contract, a court may grant *specific performance*. Specific performance is an equitable remedy that requires performance of the contract according to its precise terms (see Chapter 14).

Courts may grant specific performance of an oral contract to transfer an interest in land that has been partially performed. Partial performance can arise when the purchaser has paid part of the price, taken possession of the property, and made permanent improvements to it. Whether a court will enforce an oral contract usually is determined by the degree of harm that would be suffered if the court chose *not* to enforce the oral contract. The parties still must prove that an oral contract existed, however.

In some states, mere reliance on certain types of oral contracts is enough to remove them from the Statute of Frauds.[16] Under the UCC, an oral contract

for the sale of goods is enforceable to the extent that a seller accepts payment or a buyer accepts delivery of the goods.[17] ▶ **Example 12.22** Cooper orders twenty chairs from an online seller. After ten chairs have been delivered and accepted, Cooper repudiates (denies the existence of) the contract. In that situation, the seller can enforce the contract (and obtain payment) to the extent of the ten chairs already accepted by Cooper. ◀

Partial performance is an unmistakable indication that one party believes there is a contract. In the following case, the court considered whether by accepting that performance, the other party indicated that it also understood that a contract was in effect.

---

16. *Restatement (Second) of Contracts,* Section 129.

17. UCC 2–201(3)(c). See Chapter 15.

CASE 12.3

NYKCool A.B. v. Pacific Fruit, Inc.

United States Court of Appeals, Second Circuit, 2013 WL 163621 (2013).

COMPANY PROFILE NYKCool A.B., based in Stockholm, Sweden, provides maritime transportation for hire. It is a subsidiary of NYKReefers Limited, which operates as a subsidiary of Nippon Yusen Kabushiki Kaisha, one of the world's largest shipping companies. NYKCool has a fleet of more than fifty ships and offices in Argentina, Brazil, Chile, Ecuador, Japan, New Zealand, South Africa, the United Kingdom, and the United States. NYKCool focuses on transporting perishables, especially fruit. To reduce the number of empty containers, the firm disperses its large fleet around the globe in cost-efficient patterns and carries other cargoes on its vessels' return trips.

BACKGROUND AND FACTS Pacific Fruit, Inc., exports cargo from Ecuador. NYKCool and Pacific entered into a written contract with a two-year duration, under which NYKCool agreed to transport weekly shipments of bananas from Ecuador to California and Japan. At the end of the period, the parties agreed to extend the deal. Due to a disagreement over one of the terms, a new contract was never signed, but the parties' trade continued. After nearly four more years of performance between 2005 and 2008, a dispute arose over unused cargo capacity and unpaid freight charges. An arbitration panel of the Society of Maritime Arbitrators found that Pacific Fruit was liable to NYKCool for $8,787,157 for breach of contract. NYKCool filed a petition in a federal district court to confirm the award. Pacific Fruit appealed the judgment in NYKCool's favor, contending that the arbitration panel "manifestly disregarded" the law when it concluded that the parties had an enforceable contract.

 IN THE LANGUAGE OF THE COURT
Robert A. *KATZMANN,* Barrington D. *PARKER* and Richard C. *WESLEY,* Circuit Judges.

* * * *

On appeal, Pacific Fruit first contends that the arbitration panel manifestly disregarded the New York contract law by concluding that Pacific Fruit * * * entered into an oral contract with NYKCool, under which NYKCool agreed to transport weekly shipments of [Pacific Fruit's] bananas from Ecuador to California and Japan for the period between 2005 and 2008. In order to vacate an arbitration award for manifest disregard of the law, a court must conclude that the arbitrator knew of the relevant legal principle, appreciated that this principle controlled

CASE 12.3 CONTINUES ▶

CASE 12.3 CONTINUED the outcome of the disputed issue, and nonetheless willfully flouted the governing law by refusing to apply it. This rigorous standard ensures that awards are vacated on grounds of manifest disregard only in those exceedingly rare instances where some egregious [shocking] impropriety on the part of the arbitrator is apparent. As such, the standard essentially bars review of whether an arbitrator misconstrued a contract.

Here, we detect no manifest disregard of the law in the arbitration panel's conclusion that the parties had entered into a binding oral contract for the period between 2005 and 2008. In particular, we agree with the panel's conclusion that *the parties' substantial partial performance on the contract weighs strongly in favor of contract formation.* It is undisputed that in 2005 and 2006 NYKCool transported 30 million boxes of cargo for [Pacific Fruit] on over 100 voyages, for which it received $70 million dollars in payments even though there was no written contract in place. Moreover, *the parties' behavior during 2005 and 2006 strongly suggests that they believed themselves subject to a binding agreement.* Notably, the parties engaged in extensive renegotiation of the terms of the contract when [Pacific Fruit] began facing difficulties meeting its cargo commitments. In these circumstances, the panel cannot be said to have engaged in egregious impropriety in concluding that the parties intended to enter a binding oral agreement. [Emphasis added.]

* * * *

For the foregoing reasons, the Order of the district court confirming the arbitration award is hereby AFFIRMED.

DECISION AND REMEDY *The U.S. Court of Appeals for the Second Circuit affirmed the judgment of the lower court. The appellate court reasoned that "the parties' substantial partial performance on the contract weighs strongly in favor of contract formation."*

THE LEGAL ENVIRONMENT DIMENSION *What circumstance in this case demonstrates most strongly that Pacific did not truly believe that it did not have a contract with NYKCool? Explain.*

THE ECONOMIC DIMENSION *How can a carrier avoid losses under a contract that obligates it only to transport cargo one way and not on the return voyage?*

ADMISSIONS If a party against whom enforcement of an oral contract is sought "admits" under oath that a contract for sale was made, the contract will be enforceable.[18] The party's admission can occur at any stage of the court proceedings, such as during a deposition or other discovery, pleadings, or testimony.

If a party admits a contract subject to the UCC, it is enforceable, but only to the extent of the quantity admitted.[19] ▶ **Example 12.23** Rachel, the president of Bistro Corporation, admits under oath that an oral agreement was made with Commercial Kitchens, Inc., to buy certain equipment for $10,000. A court will enforce the agreement only to the extent admitted ($10,000), even if Commercial Kitchens claims that the agreement involved $20,000 worth of equipment. ◀

PROMISSORY ESTOPPEL An oral contract that would otherwise be unenforceable under the Statute of Frauds may be enforced in some states under the doctrine of promissory estoppel. Recall from Chapter 11

that if a person justifiably relies on another's promise to his or her detriment, a court may *estop* (prevent) the promisor from denying that a contract exists. Section 139 of the *Restatement (Second) of Contracts* provides that in these circumstances, an oral promise can be enforceable notwithstanding the Statute of Frauds.

For the promise to be enforceable, the promisee must have justifiably relied on it to her or his detriment, and the reliance must have been foreseeable to the person making the promise. In addition, there must be no way to avoid injustice except to enforce the promise. (Note the similarities between promissory estoppel and the doctrine of partial performance discussed previously. Both require reasonable reliance and operate to estop a party from claiming that no contract exists.)

SPECIAL EXCEPTIONS UNDER THE UCC Special exceptions to the writing requirement apply to sales contracts. Oral contracts for customized goods may be enforced in certain circumstances. Another exception has to do with oral contracts *between*

---

18. *Restatement (Second) of Contracts,* Section 133.
19. UCC 2–201(3)(b).

merchants that have been confirmed in a written memorandum. We will examine these exceptions in more detail in Chapter 15, when we discuss the UCC's Statute of Frauds provisions.

Exhibit 12–4 below graphically summarizes the types of contracts that fall under the Statute of Frauds and the various exceptions that apply.

Sufficiency of the Writing

A written contract will satisfy the writing requirement, as will a written memorandum or an electronic record that evidences the agreement and is signed by the party against whom enforcement is sought. The signature need not be placed at the end of the document but can be anywhere in the writing. A signature can consist of a typed name (as discussed in Chapter 10) or even just initials rather than the full name.

WHAT CONSTITUTES A WRITING? A writing can consist of any order confirmation, invoice, sales slip, check, fax, or e-mail—or such items in combination. The written contract need not consist of a single document in order to constitute an enforceable contract. One document may incorporate another document by expressly referring to it. Several documents may form a single contract if they are physically attached, such as by staple, paper clip, or glue. Several documents may form a single contract even if they are only placed in the same envelope.

▶ **Example 12.24** Simpson orally agrees to sell some land next to a shopping mall to Terro Properties. Simpson gives Terro an unsigned memo that contains a legal description of the property, and Terro gives Simpson an unsigned first draft of their real estate contract. Simpson sends Terro a signed letter that refers to the memo and to the first and final drafts of the contract. Terro sends Simpson an unsigned copy of the final draft of the contract with a signed check stapled to it. Together, the documents can constitute a writing sufficient to satisfy the writing requirement and bind both parties to the terms of the contract. ◀

WHAT MUST BE CONTAINED IN THE WRITING? A memorandum or note evidencing the oral contract need only contain the essential terms of the contract, not every term. There must, of course, also be some indication that the parties voluntarily agreed to the terms. As mentioned earlier, under the UCC, a writing evidencing a contract for the sale of goods need only state the quantity and be signed by the party against whom enforcement is sought.

Under most state laws, the writing must also name the parties and identify the subject matter, the consideration, and the essential terms with reasonable certainty. In addition, contracts for the sale of land often are required to state the price and describe the property with sufficient clarity to allow them to be determined without reference to outside sources. Note that because only the party against whom enforcement is sought must have signed the writing, a contract may be enforceable by one of its parties but not by the other.

EXHIBIT 12-4 Business Contracts and the Writing Requirement

Business Contracts That Must Be in Writing to Be Enforceable

Contracts for the sale of goods priced at $500 or more	Contracts involving interests in land	Contracts that cannot be performed within one year	Contracts containing collateral promises
EXCEPTIONS • Customized goods • Admissions (quantity) • Partial performance • Merchants confirmed in writing	**EXCEPTIONS** • Partial performance • Admissions[a] • Promissory estoppel[a]	**EXCEPTIONS** • Admissions[a] • Promissory estoppel[a]	**EXCEPTIONS** • Main purpose rule • Admissions[a] • Promissory estoppel[a]

a. Some states follow Section 133 (on admissions) and Section 139 (on promissory estoppel) of the *Restatement (Second) of Contracts.*

SECTION 6
THE PAROL EVIDENCE RULE

Sometimes, a written contract does not include— or contradicts—an oral understanding reached by the parties before or at the time of contracting. For instance, a landlord might tell a person who agrees to rent an apartment that cats are allowed, whereas the lease contract clearly states that no pets are permitted. In deciding such disputes, the courts look to a common law rule governing the admissibility in court of oral evidence, or *parol evidence.*

Under the **parol evidence rule,** if a court finds that a written contract represents the complete and final statement of the parties' agreement, it will not allow either party to present parol evidence. *Parol evidence* is testimony or other evidence of communications between the parties that is not contained in the contract itself. A party normally cannot present evidence of the parties' prior negotiations, prior agreements, or contemporaneous (happening at the same time) oral agreements if that evidence contradicts or varies the terms of the written contract.[20]

▶ **Example 12.25** TKTS, Inc., sends Gwen an offer to sell season tickets to the Dallas Cowboys football games in Cowboys Stadium. Prices and seat locations are indicated in diagrams in a brochure that accompanies the offer. Gwen responds, listing her seat preference. TKTS sends her the tickets, along with a different diagram showing seat locations. Also enclosed is a document that reads, "This is the entire agreement of the parties," which Gwen signs and returns. When Gwen goes to the first game, she discovers that her seat is not where she expected, based on the brochure. Under the parol evidence rule, however, the brochure is not part of the parties' agreement. The document that Gwen signed was identified as the parties' entire contract. Therefore, she cannot introduce in court any evidence of prior negotiations or agreements that contradict or vary the contract's terms. ◀

Exceptions to the Parol Evidence Rule

Because of the rigidity of the parol evidence rule, the courts have created exceptions. These exceptions are discussed next.

CONTRACTS SUBSEQUENTLY MODIFIED Evidence of any subsequent modification (oral or written) of a written contract can be introduced in court. Oral modifications *may* not be enforceable under the Statute of Frauds, however (for instance, a modification that increases the price of the goods being sold to more than $500). Also, oral modifications will not be enforceable if the original contract provides that any modification must be in writing.[21]

VOIDABLE OR VOID CONTRACTS Oral evidence can be introduced in all cases to show that the contract was voidable or void (for example, induced by mistake, fraud, or misrepresentation). The reason is simple: if deception led one of the parties to agree to the terms of a written contract, oral evidence attesting to the fraud should not be excluded. Courts frown on bad faith and are quick to allow such evidence when it establishes fraud.

CONTRACTS CONTAINING AMBIGUOUS TERMS When the terms of a written contract are ambiguous and require interpretation, evidence is admissible to show the meaning of the terms.

▶ **Case in Point 12.26** Pamela Watkins bought a home from Sandra Schexnider. Their agreement stated that Watkins would make payments on the mortgage until the note was paid in full, when "the house" would become hers. The agreement also stipulated that she would pay for insurance on "the property." The home was destroyed in a hurricane, and the insurance proceeds satisfied (paid off) the mortgage. Watkins claimed that she owned the land, but Schexnider argued that she had sold only the house. The court found that because "the house" term in the contract was ambiguous, parol evidence was admissible. The court also concluded that the parties intended to transfer ownership of both the house and the land, and ordered that title to the property be transferred to Watkins.[22] ◀

INCOMPLETE CONTRACTS When the written contract is incomplete in that it lacks one or more of the essential terms, the courts allow additional evidence to "fill in the gaps."

PRIOR DEALING, COURSE OF PERFORMANCE, OR USAGE OF TRADE Under the UCC, evidence can be introduced to explain or supplement a written contract by showing a prior dealing, course of performance, or usage of trade.[23] This is because when

---

20. *Restatement (Second) of Contracts,* Section 213.
21. UCC 2–209(2), (3).
22. *Watkins v. Schexnider,* 31 So.3d 609 (La.App. 3 Cir. 2010).
23. UCC 1–205, 2–202.

buyers and sellers deal with each other over extended periods of time, certain customary practices develop. These practices are often overlooked in writing the contract, so courts allow the introduction of evidence to show how the parties have acted in the past. Usage of trade—practices and customs generally followed in a particular industry—can also shed light on the meaning of certain contract provisions. Thus, evidence of trade usage may be admissible. We will discuss these terms in further detail in Chapter 15, in the context of sales contracts.

CONTRACTS SUBJECT TO AN ORALLY AGREED-ON CONDITION PRECEDENT   As you will read in Chapter 13, sometimes the parties agree that a condition must be fulfilled before a party is required to perform the contract. This is called a *condition precedent.* If the parties have orally agreed on a condition precedent that does not conflict with the terms of their written agreement, a court may allow parol evidence to prove the oral condition. The parol evidence rule does not apply here because the existence of the entire written contract is subject to an orally agreed-on condition. Proof of the condition does not alter or modify the written terms but affects the *enforceability* of the written contract.

CONTRACTS WITH AN OBVIOUS ERROR   When an obvious or gross clerical (or typographic) error exists that clearly would not represent the agreement of the parties, parol evidence is admissible to correct the error. ▶ **Example 12.27**   Davis agrees to lease office space from Stone Enterprises for $3,000 per month. The signed written lease provides for a monthly payment of $300 rather than the $3,000 agreed to by the parties. Because the error is obvious, Stone Enterprises would be allowed to admit parol evidence to correct the mistake. ◀

Integrated Contracts

In determining whether to allow parol evidence, courts consider whether the written contract is intended to be the complete and final statement of the terms of the agreement. If it is, the contract is referred to as an **integrated contract,** and extraneous evidence (evidence from outside the contract) is excluded.

An integrated contract can be either completely or partially integrated. If it contains all of the terms of the parties' agreement, it is completely integrated. If it contains only some of the terms that the parties agreed on and not others, it is partially integrated. If the contract is only partially integrated, evidence of consistent additional terms is admissible to supplement the written agreement.[24] Note that for both completely and partially integrated contracts, courts exclude any evidence that *contradicts* the writing and allow parol evidence only to add to the terms of a partially integrated contract.

Exhibit 12–5 below illustrates the relationship between integrated contracts and the parol evidence rule.

---

24. *Restatement (Second) of Contracts,* Section 216; and UCC 2–202.

EXHIBIT 12-5 The Parol Evidence Rule

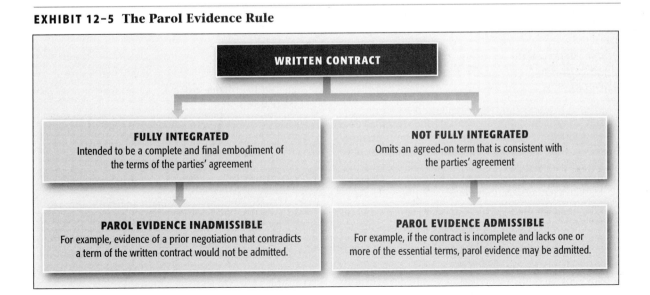

Reviewing: Defenses to Contract Enforceability

Charter Golf, Inc., manufactures and sells golf apparel and supplies. Ken Odin had worked as a Charter sales representative for six months when he was offered a position with a competing firm. Charter's president, Jerry Montieth, offered Odin a 10 percent commission "for the rest of his life" if Ken would turn down the offer and stay with Charter. He also promised that Odin would not be fired unless he was dishonest. Odin turned down the competitor's offer and stayed with Charter. Three years later, Charter fired Odin for no reason. Odin sued, alleging breach of contract. Using the information presented in the chapter, answer the following questions.

1. Would a court likely decide that Odin's employment contract falls within the Statute of Frauds? Why or why not?
2. Assume that the court does find that the contract falls within the Statute of Frauds and that the state in which the court sits recognizes every exception to the Statute of Frauds discussed in the chapter. What exception provides Odin with the best chance of enforcing the oral contract in this situation?
3. Now suppose that Montieth had taken out a pencil, written "10 percent for life" on the back of a register receipt, and handed it to Odin. Would this satisfy the Statute of Frauds? Why or why not?
4. Assume that Odin had signed a written employment contract at the time he was hired to work for Charter, but it was not completely integrated. Would a court allow Odin to present parol evidence of Montieth's subsequent promises?

DEBATE THIS . . . *Many countries have eliminated the Statute of Frauds except for sales of real estate. The United States should do the same.*

Terms and Concepts

collateral promise 247
duress 243
innocent misrepresentation 240
integrated contract 253

latent defects 239
negligent misrepresentation 241
parol evidence rule 252
prenuptial agreement 248

scienter 240
Statute of Frauds 245
undue influence 243
voluntary consent 236

ExamPrep

Issue Spotters

1. GamesCo orders $800 worth of game pieces from Midstate Plastic, Inc. Midstate delivers, and GamesCo pays for $450 worth. GamesCo then says it wants no more pieces from Midstate. GamesCo and Midstate have never dealt with each other before and have nothing in writing. Can Midstate enforce a deal for $350 more? Explain your answer. **(See page 248.)**

2. Elle, an accountant, certifies several audit reports for Flite Corporation, her client, knowing that Flite intends to use the reports to obtain loans from Good Credit Company (GCC). Elle believes that the reports are true and does not intend to deceive GCC, but she does not check the reports before certifying them. Can

Elle be held liable to GCC? Why or why not? **(See page 238.)**

• **Check your answers to the Issue Spotters against the answers provided in Appendix B at the end of this text.**

Before the Test

Go to **www.cengagebrain.com**, enter the ISBN 9781285770192, and click on "Find" to locate this textbook's Web site. Then, click on "Access Now" under "Study Tools," and select Chapter 12 at the top. There, you will find a Practice Quiz that you can take to assess your mastery of the concepts in this chapter, as well as Flashcards and a Glossary of important terms

Business Scenarios

12–1. The One-Year Rule. On May 1, by telephone, Yu offers to hire Benson to perform personal services. On May 5, Benson returns Yu's call and accepts the offer. Discuss fully whether this contract falls under the Statute of Frauds in the following circumstances: **(See page 246.)**

(a) The contract calls for Benson to be employed for one year, with the right to begin performance immediately.

(b) The contract calls for Benson to be employed for nine months, with performance of services to begin on September 1.

(c) The contract calls for Benson to submit a written research report, with a deadline of two years for submission.

12–2. Collateral Promises. Mallory promises a local hardware store that she will pay for a lawn mower that her brother is purchasing on credit if her brother fails to pay the debt. Must this promise be in writing to be enforceable? Why or why not? **(See page 247.)**

12–3. Undue Influence. Juan is an elderly man who lives with his nephew, Samuel. Juan is totally dependent on Samuel's support. Samuel tells Juan that unless he transfers a tract of land he owns to Samuel for a price 35 percent below its market value, Samuel will no longer support and take care of him. Juan enters into the contract. Discuss fully whether Juan can set aside this contract. **(See page 243.)**

Business Case Problems

12–4. The Parol Evidence Rule. Evangel Temple Assembly of God leased a facility from Wood Care Centers, Inc., to house evacuees who had lost their homes in Hurricane Katrina. One clause in the lease contract said that Evangel could terminate the lease at any time by giving Wood Care notice and paying 10 percent of the balance remaining on the lease. Another clause stated that if the facility was not given a property tax exemption (as a church), Evangel had the option to terminate the lease without making the 10 percent payment. Nine months later, the last of the evacuees left the facility, and Evangel notified Wood Care that it would end the lease. Wood Care demanded the 10 percent payment. Is parol evidence admissible to interpret this lease? Why or why not? [*Wood Care Centers, Inc. v. Evangel Temple Assembly of God of Wichita Falls,* 307 S.W.3d 816 (Tex.App.—Fort Worth 2010)] **(See page 252.)**

12–5. Sufficiency of the Writing. Newmark & Co. Real Estate, Inc., contacted 2615 East 17 Street Realty, LLC, to lease certain real property on behalf of a client. Newmark e-mailed the landlord a separate agreement for the payment of Newmark's commission. The landlord e-mailed it back with a separate demand to pay the commission in installments. Newmark revised the agreement and e-mailed a final copy to the landlord. Does the agreement qualify as a writing under the Statute of Frauds? Explain. [*Newmark & Co. Real Estate, Inc. v. 2615 East 17 Street Realty, LLC,* 80 A.D.3d 476, 914 N.Y.S.2d 162 (1 Dept. 2011)] **(See page 251.)**

12–6. BUSINESS CASE PROBLEM WITH SAMPLE ANSWER: Fraudulent Misrepresentation.

 Ricky and Sherry Wilcox hired Esprit Log and Timber Frame Homes to build a log house, which the Wilcoxes intended to sell. They paid Esprit $125,260 for materials and services. They eventually sold the home for $1,620,000 but sued Esprit due to construction delays. The logs were supposed to arrive at the construction site precut and predrilled, but that did not happen. So it took five extra months to build the house while the logs were cut and drilled one by one. The Wilcoxes claimed that the interest they paid on a loan for the extra construction time cost them about $200,000. The jury agreed and awarded them that much in damages, plus $250,000 in punitive damages and $20,000 in attorneys' fees. Esprit appealed, claiming that the evidence did not support the verdict because the Wilcoxes had sold the house for a good price. Is Esprit's argument credible? Why or why not? How should the court rule? [*Esprit Log and Timber Frame Homes, Inc. v. Wilcox,* 302 S.E.2d 550, 691 S.E.2d 344 (2010)] **(See pages 237–241.)**

- For a sample answer to Problem 12–6, go to Appendix C at the end of this text.

12–7. Mutual Mistake. When Steven Simkin divorced Laura Blank, they agreed to split their assets equally. They owned an account with Bernard L. Madoff Investment Securities estimated to be worth $5.4 million. Simkin kept the account and paid Blank more than $6.5 million—including $2.7 million to offset the amount of the funds that they believed were in the account. Later, they learned that the account actually contained no funds due to its manager's fraud. Could their agreement be rescinded on the basis of a mistake? Discuss. [*Simkin v. Blank,* 80 A.D.3d 401, 915 N.Y.S.2d 47 (1 Dept. 2011)] **(See page 237.)**

12–8. Promises Made in Consideration of Marriage. After twenty-nine years of marriage, Robert and Mary Lou Tuttle were divorced. They admitted in court that before they were married, they had signed a prenuptial agreement. They agreed that the agreement had stated that each would keep his or her own property and anything derived from that property. Robert came into the marriage owning farmland while Mary Lou owned no real estate. During the marriage, ten different parcels of land, totaling about six hundred acres, were acquired, and two corporations,

Tuttle Grain, Inc., and Tuttle Farms, Inc., were formed. A copy of the prenuptial agreement could not be found. Can the court enforce the agreement without a writing? Why or why not? [*In re Marriage of Tuttle*, 2013 WL 164035 (Ill. App. 5 Dist. 2013)] **(See page 248.)**

12–9. A QUESTION OF ETHICS: Mistake.

On behalf of BRJM, LLC, Nicolas Kepple offered Howard Engelsen $210,000 for a parcel of land known as lot five on the north side of Barnes Road in Stonington, Connecticut. Engelsen's company, Output Systems, Inc., owned the land. Engelsen had the lot surveyed and obtained an appraisal. The appraiser valued the property at $277,000, after determining that it was 3.0 acres in size and thus could not be subdivided because it did not meet the town's minimum legal requirement of 3.7 acres for subdivision. Engelsen responded to Kepple's offer with a counteroffer of $230,000, which Kepple accepted. On May 3, 2002, the parties signed a contract. When Engelsen refused to go through with the deal, BRJM filed a suit in a Connecticut state court against Output, seeking specific performance and other relief. The defendant asserted the defense of mutual mistake on at least two grounds. [BRJM, LLC v. Output Systems, Inc., 100 Conn.App. 153, 917 A.2d 605 (2007)] **(See pages 236 and 237.)**

(a) In the counteroffer, Engelsen asked Kepple to remove from their contract a clause requiring written confirmation of the availability of a "free split," which meant that the property could be subdivided without the town's prior approval. Kepple agreed. After signing the contract, Kepple learned that the property was *not* entitled to a free split. Would this circumstance qualify as a mistake on which the defendant could avoid the contract? Discuss.

(b) After signing the contract, Engelsen obtained a second appraisal that established the size of lot five as 3.71 acres, which meant that it could be subdivided, and valued the property at $490,000. Can the defendant avoid the contract on the basis of a mistake in the first appraisal? Explain.

Legal Reasoning Group Activity

12–10. The Writing Requirement. Jason Novell, doing business as Novell Associates, hired Barbara Meade to work for him. The parties orally agreed on the terms of employment, including payment of a share of the company's income to Meade, but they did not put anything in writing. Two years later, Meade quit. Novell then told Meade that she was entitled to $9,602—25 percent of the difference between the accounts receivable and the accounts payable as of Meade's last day of work. Meade disagreed and demanded more than $63,500—25 percent of the revenue from all invoices, less the cost of materials and outside processing, for each of the years that she had worked for Novell. Meade filed a lawsuit against Novell for breach of contract. **(See pages 245–248.)**

(a) The first group should decide whether the parties had an enforceable contract.

(b) The second group should decide whether the parties' oral agreement falls within any exception to the Statute of Frauds.

(c) The third group should discuss how the lawsuit would be affected if Novell admitted that the parties had an oral contract under which Meade was entitled to 25 percent of the difference between accounts receivable and payable as of the day Meade quit.

CHAPTER 13

THIRD PARTY RIGHTS AND DISCHARGE

Once it has been determined that a valid and legally enforceable contract exists, attention can turn to the rights and duties of the parties to the contract. A contract is a private agreement between the parties who have entered into it, and traditionally these parties alone have rights and liabilities under the contract. This principle is referred to as **privity of contract**. A *third party*—one who is not a direct party to a particular contract—normally does not have rights under that contract.

There are exceptions to the rule of privity of contract. One exception allows a party to a contract to transfer the rights or duties arising from the contract to another person through an *assignment* (of rights) or a *delegation* (of duties). Another exception involves a *third party beneficiary contract*—a contract in which the parties to the contract intend that the contract benefit a third party. We examine these exceptions in the following pages.

We also examine how contractual obligations can be *discharged*. Normally, contract discharge is accomplished by both parties performing the acts promised in the contract. Sometimes, however, the duty to perform under the contract is conditioned on a certain event, such as when an agreement to buy a house is conditioned on obtaining financing.

In this chapter, we look at the effect of conditions, consider the degree of performance required to discharge a contractual obligation, and discuss some other ways in which contract discharge can occur.

ASSIGNMENTS AND DELEGATIONS

In a bilateral contract, the two parties have corresponding rights and duties. One party has a *right* to require the other to perform some task, and the other has a *duty* to perform it. The transfer of contractual *rights* to a third party is known as an **assignment.** The transfer of contractual *duties* to a third party is known as a **delegation.** An assignment or a delegation occurs *after* the original contract was made.

Assignments

Assignments are important because they are used in many types of business financing. Banks, for instance, frequently assign their rights to receive payments under their loan contracts to other firms, which pay for those rights. ▶ **Example 13.1** If Tia obtains a loan from a bank, she may later receive a notice from the bank stating that it has transferred (assigned) its rights to receive payments on the loan to another firm. When it is time to repay the loan, Tia must make the payments to that other firm. ◀

Financial institutions that make *mortgage* loans (loans to enable prospective home buyers to purchase land or a home) often assign their rights to collect the mortgage payments to a third party, such as PNC Mortgage. Following the assignment, the home buyers are notified that they must make future payments not to the bank that loaned them the funds but to the third party. Billions of dollars change hands daily in the business world in the form of assignments of rights in contracts. If it were not possible to transfer contractual rights, many businesses could not continue to operate.

THE EFFECT OF AN ASSIGNMENT In an assignment, the party assigning the rights to a third party is known as the **assignor,**[1] and the party receiving the rights is the **assignee.**[2] Other traditional terms used to describe the parties in assignment relationships are **obligee** (the person to whom a duty, or obligation, is owed) and **obligor** (the person who is obligated to perform the duty).

---
1. Pronounced uh-*sye*-nore.
2. Pronounced uh-*sye*-nee.

Extinguishes the Rights of the Assignor. When rights under a contract are assigned unconditionally, the rights of the assignor are extinguished.[3] The third party (the assignee) has a right to demand performance from the other original party to the contract. The assignee takes only those rights that the assignor originally had, however.

▶ **Example 13.2** Brower is obligated by contract to pay Horton $1,000. Brower is the obligor because she owes an obligation, or duty, to Horton. Horton is the obligee, the one to whom the obligation, or duty, is owed. If Horton then assigns his right to receive the $1,000 to Kuhn, Horton is the assignor and Kuhn is the assignee. Kuhn now becomes the obligee because Brower owes Kuhn the $1,000. Here, a valid assignment of a debt exists. Kuhn (the assignee-obligee) is entitled to enforce payment in court if Brower (the obligor) does not pay him the $1,000. ◀ These concepts are illustrated in Exhibit 13–1 on the following page.

In the following case, a lender assigned its rights to loan payments from a borrower. The court had to decide whether the borrower owed the payments to the assignee.

---

3. *Restatement (Second) of Contracts,* Section 317.

CASE 13.1

Hosch v. Colonial Pacific Leasing Corp.

Court of Appeals of Georgia, 113 Ga.App. 873, 722 S.E.2d 778 (2012).

BACKGROUND AND FACTS Edward Hosch entered into four loan agreements with Citicapital Commercial Corporation to finance the purchase of heavy construction equipment. A few months later, Citicapital merged into Citicorp Leasing, Inc., which was then renamed GE Capital Commercial, Inc. One year later, GE Capital assigned the loans to Colonial Pacific Leasing Corporation. When Hosch defaulted on the loans, Colonial provided a notice of default and demanded payment. Hosch failed to repay the loans, so Colonial sued to collect the amount due. The trial court granted summary judgment to Colonial and entered final judgment against Hosch. On appeal, Hosch argued that there was insufficient evidence that the loans had been assigned to Colonial.

IN THE LANGUAGE OF THE COURT
McFADDEN, Judge.

* * * *

Hosch contends that the trial court erred in granting Colonial's motion for summary judgment because there is no evidence that the contracts were assigned to Colonial. However, the contention is refuted by the record, which includes affidavits of a GE litigation specialist, a written assignment and other documents establishing that Hosch's four loans were assigned to Colonial. Hosch has presented no contradictory evidence showing that the loans were not assigned to Colonial, and instead submitted his own affidavit stating that he had not been notified of any such assignment. However, the loan agreements expressly provide that the lender may transfer or assign any or all of its rights under the agreements without notice to or the consent of Hosch.

"A party may assign to another a contractual right to collect payment, including the right to sue to enforce the right. But an assignment must be in writing in order for the contractual right to be enforceable by the assignee." Because the record, as noted above, contains a written assignment of the loans to Colonial, as well as other evidence of the assignment, the trial court did not err in granting summary judgment to Colonial. [Emphasis added.]

DECISION AND REMEDY *The Georgia appellate court found sufficient evidence that GE Capital had assigned the loans to Colonial. It therefore affirmed the trial court's judgment for Colonial.*

THE LEGAL ENVIRONMENT DIMENSION *Do borrowers benefit from the fact that lenders may freely assign their rights under loan agreements? If so, how?*

WHAT IF THE FACTS WERE DIFFERENT? *Suppose that Hosch had sold the equipment financed by the loans from Citicapital to a third party. Would Hosch still have been liable to Colonial Pacific? Why or why not?*

EXHIBIT 13-1 Assignment Relationships

In the assignment relationship illustrated here, Horton assigns his *rights* under a contract that he made with Brower to a third party, Kuhn. Horton thus becomes the *assignor* and Kuhn the *assignee* of the contractual rights. Brower, the *obligor*, now owes performance to Kuhn instead of Horton. Horton's original contract rights are extinguished after assignment.

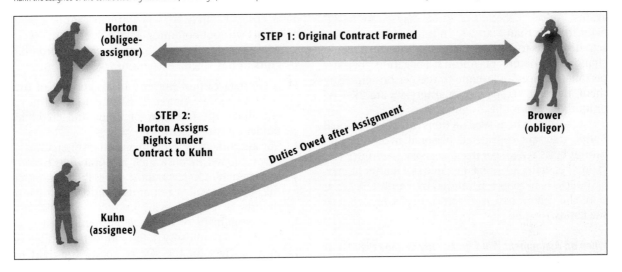

Assignee's Rights Are Subject to the Same Defenses. The assignee's rights are subject to the defenses that the obligor has against the assignor. In other words, the assignee obtains only those rights that the assignor originally had.

▶ **Example 13.3** In *Example 13.2,* Brower owes Horton the $1,000 under a contract in which Brower agreed to buy Horton's 15-inch MacBook Pro laptop. When Brower decided to purchase the laptop, she relied on Horton's fraudulent misrepresentation that the MacBook had retina display. When Brower discovers that it does not have this feature, she tells Horton that she is going to return the laptop to him and cancel the contract. Even though Horton has assigned his "right" to receive the $1,000 to Kuhn, Brower need not pay Kuhn the $1,000. Brower can raise the defense of Horton's fraudulent misrepresentation to avoid payment. ◀

Form of the Assignment. In general, an assignment can take any form, oral or written. Naturally, it is more difficult to prove that an oral assignment occurred, so it is advisable to put all assignments in writing. Of course, assignments covered by the Statute of Frauds—such as an assignment of an interest in land—must be in writing to be enforceable. In addition, most states require contracts for the assignment of wages to be in writing.[4]

---

4. See, for example, California Labor Code Section 300. There are other assignments that must be in writing as well.

RIGHTS THAT CANNOT BE ASSIGNED As a general rule, all rights can be assigned. Exceptions are made, however, under certain circumstances. Some of these exceptions are listed below and described in more detail in the following subsections:

1. The assignment is prohibited by statute.
2. The contract is personal.
3. The assignment significantly changes the risk or duties of the obligor.
4. The contract prohibits assignment.

When a Statute Prohibits Assignment. When a statute expressly prohibits assignment of a particular right, that right cannot be assigned. ▶ **Example 13.4** Quincy is an employee of Specialty Travel, Inc. Specialty is an employer bound by workers' compensation statutes in this state, and thus Quincy is a covered employee. Quincy is injured on the job and begins to collect monthly workers' compensation checks. In need of a loan, Quincy borrows from Draper, assigning to Draper all of her future workers' compensation benefits. A state statute prohibits the assignment of *future* workers' compensation benefits, and thus such rights cannot be assigned. ◀

When a Contract Is Personal in Nature. If a contract is for personal services, the rights under the contract normally cannot be assigned unless all that remains is a monetary payment.[5] ▶ **Example 13.5** Anton signs a contract to be a tutor for Marisa's children. Marisa then attempts to assign to Roberto her right to Anton's services. Roberto cannot enforce the contract against Anton. Roberto's children may be more difficult to tutor than Marisa's. Thus, if Marisa could assign her rights to Anton's services to Roberto, it would change the nature of Anton's obligation. Because personal services are unique to the person rendering them, rights to receive personal services are likewise unique and cannot be assigned. ◀

Note that when legal actions involve personal rights, they are considered personal in nature and cannot be assigned. For instance, personal-injury tort claims generally are nonassignable as a matter of public policy. If Elizabeth is injured by Randy's defamation, she cannot assign to someone else her right to sue Randy for damages.

When an Assignment Will Significantly Change the Risk or Duties of the Obligor.

A right cannot be assigned if the assignment will significantly increase or alter the risks to or the duties of the obligor (the party owing performance under the contract).[6] ▶ **Example 13.6** Larson owns a hotel. To insure it, he takes out a policy with Southeast Insurance. The policy insures against fire, theft, floods, and vandalism. Larson attempts to assign the insurance policy to Hewitt, who also owns a hotel.

The assignment is ineffective because it substantially alters Southeast Insurance's *duty of performance.* An insurance company evaluates the particular risk of a certain party and tailors its policy to fit that risk. If the policy is assigned to a third party, the insurance risk is materially altered because the insurance company may have no information on the third party. Therefore, the assignment will not operate to give Hewitt any rights against Southeast Insurance. ◀

When the Contract Prohibits Assignment.

When a contract specifically stipulates that a right cannot be assigned, then *ordinarily* it cannot be assigned. Note that restraints on the power to assign operate only against the parties themselves. They do not prohibit an assignment by operation of law, such as an assignment pursuant to bankruptcy or death.

Whether an *antiassignment clause* is effective depends, in part, on how it is phrased. A contract that states that *any* assignment is void effectively prohibits any assignment. ▶ **Example 13.7** Ramirez agrees

to build a house for Carmen. Their contract states "This contract cannot be assigned by Carmen without Ramirez's consent. Any assignment without such consent renders the contract void." This antiassignment clause is effective, and Carmen cannot assign her rights without obtaining Ramirez's consent. ◀

The general rule that a contract can prohibit assignment has several exceptions:

1. A contract cannot prevent an assignment of the right to receive funds. This exception exists to encourage the free flow of funds and credit in modern business settings.
2. The assignment of rights in real estate often cannot be prohibited because such a prohibition is contrary to public policy in most states. Prohibitions of this kind are called restraints against **alienation** (transfer of land ownership).
3. The assignment of *negotiable instruments* (such as checks and promissory notes) cannot be prohibited.
4. In a contract for the sale of goods, the right to receive damages for breach of contract or payment of an account owed may be assigned even though the sales contract prohibits such an assignment.[7]

NOTICE OF ASSIGNMENT Once a valid assignment of rights has been made, the assignee (the third party to whom the rights have been assigned) should notify the obligor (the one owing performance) of the assignment. For instance, in *Example 13.2* on page 258, when Horton assigns to Kuhn his right to receive the $1,000 from Brower, Kuhn should notify Brower, the obligor, of the assignment.

Giving notice is not legally necessary to establish the validity of the assignment: an assignment is effective immediately, whether or not notice is given. Two major problems arise, however, when notice of the assignment is not given to the obligor:

1. *Priority issues.* If the assignor assigns the same right to two different persons, the question arises as to which one has priority—that is, which one has the right to the performance by the obligor. The rule most often observed in the United States is that the first assignment in time is the first in right. Nevertheless, some states follow the English rule, which basically gives priority to the first assignee who gives notice. ▶ **Example 13.8** Jason owes Alexis $5,000 under a contract. Alexis first assigns the claim to Carmen, who does not give notice to Jason, and then assigns it to Dorman, who notifies

---

5. *Restatement (Second) of Contracts,* Sections 317 and 318.
6. Section 2–210(2) of the Uniform Commercial Code (UCC).

7. UCC 2–210(2).

Jason. In most states, Carmen would have priority because the assignment to her was first in time. In some states, however, Dorman would have priority because he gave first notice. ◀

2. *Potential for discharge by performance to the wrong party.* Until the obligor has notice of an assignment, the obligor can discharge his or her obligation by performance to the assignor (the obligee). Performance by the obligor to the assignor (obligee) constitutes a discharge to the assignee. Once the obligor receives proper notice, however, only performance to the assignee can discharge the obligor's obligations.

▶ **Example 13.9** Recall that Alexis, the obligee in *Example 13.8*, assigned to Carmen her right

to collect $5,000 from Jason, and Carmen did not give notice to Jason. Jason subsequently pays Alexis the $5,000. Although the assignment was valid, Jason's payment to Alexis is a discharge of the debt. Carmen's failure to notify Jason of the assignment causes her to lose the right to collect the $5,000 from Jason. (Note that Carmen still has a claim against Alexis for the $5,000.) If Carmen had given Jason notice of the assignment, however, Jason's payment to Alexis would not have discharged the debt. ◀

In the following *Spotlight Case,* the parties disputed whether the right to buy advertising space in publications at a steep discount was validly assigned from the original owner to companies that he later formed.

SP☉TLIGHT on *PC Magazine*

Case 13.2   Gold v. Ziff Communications Co.
Appellate Court of Illinois, First District, 322 Ill.App.3d 32, 748 N.E.2d 198, 254 Ill.Dec. 752 (2001).

BACKGROUND AND FACTS Ziff Communications Company, a publisher of specialty magazines, bought *PC Magazine* from its founder, Anthony Gold, for more than $10 million. As part of the deal, Ziff gave Gold or a company that he owned and controlled "ad/list rights"—rights to advertise at an 80 percent discount on a limited number of pages in Ziff publications and free use of Ziff's subscriber lists. In 1983, Gold formed Software Communications, Inc. (SCI), a mail-order software business that he wholly owned, to use the ad/list rights. In 1987 and 1988, he formed two new mail-order companies, Hanson & Connors, Inc., and PC Brand, Inc. Gold told Ziff that he was allocating his ad/list rights to Hanson & Connors, which took over most of SCI's business, and to PC Brand, of which Gold owned 90 percent. Ziff's other advertisers complained about this "allocation."

Ziff refused to run large ads for Hanson & Connors or to release its subscriber lists to the company. Ziff also declared PC Brand ineligible for the ad discount because it "was not controlled by Gold." Gold and his companies filed a suit in an Illinois state court against Ziff, alleging breach of contract. The court ordered Ziff to pay the plaintiffs more than $88 million in damages and interest. Ziff appealed to an intermediate state appellate court, arguing, in part, that Gold had not properly assigned the ad/list rights to Hanson & Connors and PC Brand.

IN THE LANGUAGE OF THE COURT
Justice *COUSINS* delivered the opinion of the court.

* * * *

Ziff * * * argues that Gold never properly reassigned his rights under the amended ad/list agreement from SCI to PC Brand and Hanson. We agree with plaintiffs that assignments can be implied from circumstances. *No particular mode or form * * * is necessary to effect a valid assignment, and any acts or words are sufficient which show an intention of transferring or appropriating the owner's interest.* [Emphasis added.]

In the instant case, it is undisputed that Gold owned 100% of SCI. In a letter dated May 13, 1988, Gold, as president of SCI, instructed Ziff that he was allocating the ad/list rights to Hanson and PC Brand. Additionally, SCI stopped using the ad/list rights when PC Brand and

CASE 13.2 CONTINUES ▶

CASE 13.2 CONTINUED   Hanson were formed. * * * Gold's behavior toward his companies and his conduct toward the obligor, Ziff, implied that the ad/list rights were assigned to PC Brand and Hanson.

DECISION AND REMEDY *The state intermediate appellate court affirmed the lower court's decision that the rights had been properly assigned. The appellate court remanded the case for a new trial on the amount of the damages, however.*

THE SOCIAL DIMENSION *Would the assignments in this case have been valid if Gold had not notified Ziff? Why or why not?*

THE ECONOMIC DIMENSION *How might Ziff have effectively avoided both this dispute with Gold and complaints from its other advertisers?*

Delegations

Just as a party can transfer rights through an assignment, a party can also transfer duties. Duties are not assigned, however, they are *delegated*. The party delegating the duties is the **delegator,** and the party to whom the duties are delegated is the **delegatee.** Normally, a delegation of duties does not relieve the delegator of the obligation to perform in the event that the delegatee fails to do so.

No special form is required to create a valid delegation of duties. As long as the delegator expresses an intention to make the delegation, it is effective. The delegator need not even use the word *delegate*. Exhibit 13–2 below illustrates delegation relationships.

DUTIES THAT CANNOT BE DELEGATED As a general rule, any duty can be delegated. There are, however, some exceptions to this rule. Delegation is prohibited in the circumstances discussed next.

When the Duties Are Personal in Nature. When special trust has been placed in the obligor or when performance depends on the personal skill or talents of the obligor, contractual duties cannot be delegated. ▶ **Example 13.10** O'Brien, who is impressed with

EXHIBIT 13–2 Delegation Relationships

In the delegation relationship illustrated here, Brower delegates her *duties* under a contract that she made with Horton to a third party, Kuhn. Brower thus becomes the *delegator* and Kuhn the *delegatee* of the contractual duties. Kuhn now owes performance of the contractual duties to Horton. Note that a delegation of duties normally does not relieve the delegator (Brower) of liability if the delegatee (Kuhn) fails to perform the contractual duties.

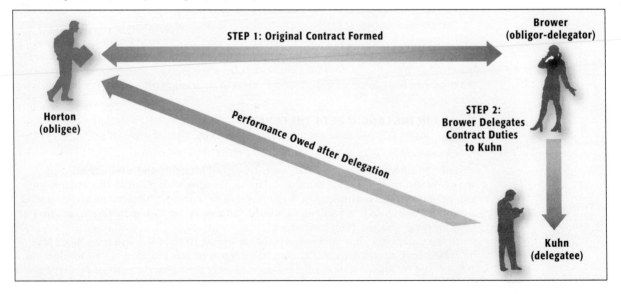

STEP 1: Original Contract Formed

Brower (obligor-delegator)

Horton (obligee)

Performance Owed after Delegation

STEP 2: Brower Delegates Contract Duties to Kuhn

Kuhn (delegatee)

Brodie's ability to perform veterinary surgery, contracts with Brodie to have her perform surgery on O'Brien's prize-winning stallion in July. Brodie later decides that she would rather spend the summer at the beach, so she delegates her duties under the contract to Lopez, who is also a competent veterinary surgeon. The delegation is not effective without O'Brien's consent, no matter how competent Lopez is, because the contract is for *personal* performance.

In contrast, nonpersonal duties may be delegated. Assume that Brodie contracts with O'Brien to pick up and deliver a large horse trailer to O'Brien's property. Brodie delegates this duty to Lopez, who owns a towing business. This delegation is effective because the performance required is of a *routine* and *nonpersonal* nature. ◄

When Performance by a Third Party Will Vary Materially from That Expected by the Obligee. When performance by a third party will vary materially from that expected by the obligee under the contract, contractual duties cannot be delegated. ▶ **Example 13.11** Jared, a wealthy investor, established the company Heaven Sent to provide grants of capital to struggling but potentially successful businesses. Jared contracted with Merilyn, whose judgment Jared trusted, to select the recipients of the grants. Later, Merilyn delegated this duty to Donald. Jared did not trust Donald's ability to select worthy recipients. This delegation is not effective because it materially alters Jared's expectations under the contract with Merilyn. ◄

When the Contract Prohibits Delegation. When the contract expressly prohibits delegation by including an *antidelegation clause*, the duties cannot be delegated. ▶ **Example 13.12** Stark, Ltd., contracts with Belisario, a certified public accountant, to perform its annual audits for five years. The contract prohibits delegation. Belisario cannot delegate the duty to perform the audit to another accountant—not even an accountant at the same firm. ◄

EFFECT OF A DELEGATION If a delegation of duties is enforceable, the obligee must accept performance from the delegatee. ▶ **Example 13.13** Bryan has a duty to pick up and deliver metal fabrication equipment to Alicia's property. Bryan delegates his duty to Liam. In this situation, Alicia (the obligee) must accept performance from Liam (the delegatee) because the delegation is effective. ◄ The obligee can legally refuse performance from the delegatee only if the duty is one that cannot be delegated.

As noted, a valid delegation of duties does not relieve the delegator of obligations under the contract. Although there are many exceptions, the general rule today is that the obligee can sue both the delegatee and the delegator. ▶ **Example 13.14** In *Example 13.13,* if Liam (the delegatee) fails to perform, Bryan (the delegator) is still liable to Alicia (the obligee to whom performance is owed). The obligee can also hold the delegatee liable if the delegatee made a promise of performance that will directly benefit the obligee. For instance, if Liam promised Bryan in a contract to deliver the equipment to Alicia's property but fails to do so, Alicia can sue Bryan, Liam, or both. ◄

Concept Summary 13.1 on the following page outlines the basic principles of the laws governing assignments and delegations.

Assignment of "All Rights"

When a contract provides for an "assignment of all rights," this wording may create both an assignment of rights and a delegation of duties.[8] Typically, this occurs when general words are used, such as "I assign the contract" or "I assign all my rights under the contract." A court normally will construe such words as implying both an assignment of rights and a delegation of any duties of performance. Thus, the assignor remains liable if the assignee fails to perform the contractual obligations.

SECTION 2
THIRD PARTY BENEFICIARIES

Another exception to the doctrine of privity of contract arises when the contract is intended to benefit a third party. When the original parties to the contract agree that the contract performance should be rendered to or directly benefit a third person, the third person becomes an *intended* **third party beneficiary** of the contract. As the **intended beneficiary** of the contract, the third party has legal rights and can sue the promisor directly for breach of the contract.

Who Is the Promisor?

Who, though, is the promisor? In a bilateral contract, both parties to the contract make promises that can be enforced, so the court has to determine which party

---

8. *Restatement (Second) of Contracts,* Section 328; UCC 2–210(3), (4).

CONCEPT SUMMARY 13.1
Assignments and Delegations

Which Rights Can Be Assigned, and Which Duties Can Be Delegated?	All rights can be assigned *unless:* 1. A statute expressly prohibits assignment. 2. The contract is for personal services. 3. The assignment will materially alter the obligor's risk or duties. 4. The contract prohibits assignment.	All duties can be delegated *unless:* 1. Performance depends on the obligor's personal skills or talents or special trust has been placed in the obligor. 2. Performance by a third party will materially vary from that expected by the obligee. 3. The contract prohibits delegation.
What If the Contract Prohibits Assignment or Delegation?	No rights can be assigned *except:* 1. Rights to receive funds. 2. Ownership rights in real estate. 3. Rights to negotiable instruments. 4. Rights to damages for breach of a sales contract or payments under a sales contract.	No duties can be delegated.
What Is the Effect on the Original Party's Rights?	On a valid assignment, effective immediately, the original party (assignor) no longer has any rights under the contract.	On a valid delegation, if the delegatee fails to perform, the original party (delegator) is liable to the obligee (who may also hold the delegatee liable).

made the promise that benefits the third party. That person is the promisor. In effect, allowing a third party to sue the promisor directly circumvents the "middle person" (the promisee) and thus reduces the burden on the courts. Otherwise, the third party would sue the promisee, who would then sue the promisor.

▶ **Case in Point 13.15** The classic case that gave third party beneficiaries the right to bring a suit directly against a promisor was decided in 1859. The case involved three parties—Holly, Lawrence, and Fox. Holly had borrowed $300 from Lawrence. Shortly thereafter, Holly loaned $300 to Fox, who in return promised Holly that he would pay Holly's debt to Lawrence on the following day. When Lawrence failed to obtain the $300 from Fox, he sued Fox to recover the funds. The court had to decide whether Lawrence could sue Fox directly (rather than suing Holly). The court held that when "a promise [is] made for the benefit of another, he for whose benefit it is made may bring an action for its breach."[9] ◀

Types of Intended Beneficiaries

The law distinguishes between *intended* beneficiaries and *incidental* beneficiaries. Only intended beneficiaries acquire legal rights in a contract.

CREDITOR BENEFICIARY One type of intended beneficiary is a *creditor beneficiary*. Like the plaintiff in *Case in Point 13.15*, a creditor beneficiary benefits from a contract in which one party (the promisor) promises another party (the promisee) to pay a debt that the promisee owes to a third party (the creditor beneficiary).

▶ **Case in Point 13.16** Autumn Allan owned a condominium unit in a Texas complex located directly beneath a condo unit owned by Aslan Koraev. Over the course of two years, Allan's unit suffered eight incidents of water and sewage incursion as a result of plumbing problems and misuse of appliances in Koraev's unit. Allan sued Koraev for breach of contract and won.

Koraev appealed, arguing that he had no contractual duty to Allan. The court found that Allan was an intended third party beneficiary of the contract between Koraev and the condominium owners' association. Because the governing documents stated that each owner had to comply strictly with their provisions, failure to comply created grounds for an action by the condominium association or an aggrieved (wronged) owner. Here, Allan was clearly an aggrieved owner and could sue Koraev directly for his failure to perform his contract duties to the condominium association.[10] ◀

9. *Lawrence v. Fox*, 20 N.Y. 268 (1859).

10. *Allan v. Nersesova*, 307 S.W.3d 564 (Tx.App.—Dallas 2010).

DONEE BENEFICIARY Another type of intended beneficiary is a *donee beneficiary.* When a contract is made for the express purpose of giving a *gift* to a third party, the third party (the donee beneficiary) can sue the promisor directly to enforce the promise.[11]

The most common donee beneficiary contract is a life insurance contract. ▶ **Example 13.17** Ang (the promisee) pays premiums to Standard Life, a life insurance company. Standard Life (the promisor) promises to pay a certain amount upon Ang's death to anyone Ang designates as a beneficiary. The designated beneficiary is a donee beneficiary under the life insurance policy and can enforce the promise made by the insurance company to pay her or him on Ang's death. ◀

Most third party beneficiaries do not fit neatly into either the creditor beneficiary or the donee beneficiary category. Thus, the modern view adopted by the *Restatement (Second) of Contracts* does not draw clear lines between the types of intended beneficiaries. Today, courts frequently distinguish only between *intended beneficiaries* (who can sue to enforce contracts made for their benefit) and *incidental beneficiaries* (who cannot sue, as will be discussed shortly).

When the Rights of an Intended Beneficiary Vest

An intended third party beneficiary cannot enforce a contract against the original parties until the rights of the third party have *vested,* which means the rights have taken effect and cannot be taken away. Until these rights have vested, the original parties to the contract—the promisor and the promisee—can modify or rescind the contract without the consent of the third party.

When do the rights of third parties vest? The majority of courts hold that the rights vest when any of the following occurs:

1. The third party materially changes his or her position in justifiable reliance on the promise.
2. The third party brings a lawsuit on the promise.
3. The third party demonstrates her or his consent to the promise at the request of the promisor or promisee, such as by sending a letter or e-mail indicating that she or he is aware of and consents to a contract formed for her or his benefit.[12]

If the contract expressly reserves to the contracting parties the right to cancel, rescind, or modify the contract, the rights of the third party beneficiary are subject to any changes that result. If the original contract reserves the right to revoke the promise or change the beneficiary, the vesting of the third party's rights does not terminate that power.[13] In most life insurance contracts, for instance, the policyholder reserves the right to change the designated beneficiary.

Incidental Beneficiaries

Sometimes, a third person receives a benefit from a contract even though that person's benefit is not the reason the contract was made. Such a person is known as an **incidental beneficiary.** Because the benefit is *unintentional,* an incidental beneficiary cannot sue to enforce the contract.

▶ **Case in Point 13.18** Spectators at the infamous boxing match in which Mike Tyson was disqualified for biting his opponent's ear sued Tyson and the fight's promoters for a refund on the basis of breach of contract. The spectators claimed that they were third party beneficiaries of the contract between Tyson and the fight's promoters. The court, however, held that the spectators could not sue because they were not in contractual privity with the defendants. Any benefits they received from the contract were incidental to the contract, and according to the court, the spectators got what they paid for: "the right to view whatever event transpired."[14] ◀

Intended versus Incidental Beneficiaries

In determining whether a third party beneficiary is an intended or an incidental beneficiary, the courts focus on intent, as expressed in the contract language and implied by the surrounding circumstances. Any beneficiary who is not deemed an intended beneficiary is considered incidental. Exhibit 13–3 on the following page illustrates the distinction between intended beneficiaries and incidental beneficiaries.

Although no single test can embrace all possible situations, courts often apply the *reasonable person* test: Would a reasonable person in the position of the beneficiary believe that the promisee intended to confer on the beneficiary the right to enforce the contract? In addition, the presence of one or more of

11. This principle was first enunciated in *Seaver v. Ransom,* 224 N.Y. 233, 120 N.E. 639 (1918).
12. *Restatement (Second) of Contracts,* Section 311.
13. Defenses against third party beneficiaries are given in the *Restatement (Second) of Contracts,* Section 309.
14. *Castillo v. Tyson,* 268 A.D.2d 336, 701 N.Y.S.2d 423 (Sup.Ct.App.Div. 2000).

EXHIBIT 13-3 Third Party Beneficiaries

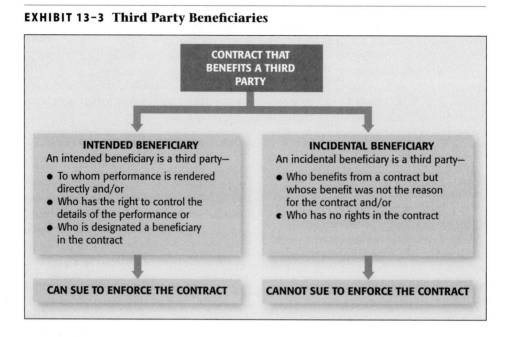

the following factors strongly indicates that the third party is an intended beneficiary to the contract:

1. Performance is rendered directly to the third party.
2. The third party has the right to control the details of performance.
3. The third party is expressly designated as a beneficiary in the contract.

SECTION 3
CONTRACT DISCHARGE

The legal environment of business requires the identification of some point at which the parties can reasonably know that their duties have ended. The most common way to **discharge,** or terminate, one's contractual duties is by the **performance** of those duties. ▶ **Example 13.19** Trey and Claris enter into an agreement via e-mail for the sale of a 2014 Lexus for $42,000. This contract will be discharged by performance when Trey, the buyer, pays $42,000 to Claris, the seller, and Claris transfers possession of the Lexus to Trey. ◀

The duty to perform under any contract (including e-contracts) may be *conditioned* on the occurrence or nonoccurrence of a certain event, or the duty may be *absolute,* as will be discussed next.

Conditions of Performance

In most contracts, promises of performance are not expressly conditioned or qualified. Instead, they are *absolute promises*. They must be performed, or the parties promising the acts will be in breach of contract. ▶ **Example 13.20** Paloma Enterprises contracts to sell a truckload of organic produce to Tran for $10,000. The parties' promises are unconditional: Paloma will deliver the produce to Tran, and Tran will pay $10,000 to Paloma. The payment does not have to be made if the produce is not delivered. ◀

In some situations, however, performance is contingent on the occurrence or nonoccurrence of a certain event. A **condition** is a qualification in a contract based on a possible future event. The occurrence or nonoccurrence of the event will trigger the performance of a legal obligation or terminate an existing obligation under a contract.[15] If the condition is not satisfied, the obligations of the parties are discharged.

---

15. The *Restatement (Second) of Contracts,* Section 224, defines a condition as "an event, not certain to occur, which must occur, unless its nonoccurrence is excused, before performance under a contract becomes due."

Three types of conditions can be present in contracts: conditions *precedent,* conditions *subsequent,* and *concurrent* conditions. Conditions are also classified as *express* or *implied.*

CONDITIONS PRECEDENT A condition that must be fulfilled before a party's performance can be required is called a **condition precedent.** The condition precedes the absolute duty to perform. Life insurance contracts frequently specify that certain conditions, such as passing a physical examination, must be met before the insurance company will be obligated to perform under the contract.

In addition, many contracts are conditioned on an independent appraisal of value. ▶ **Example 13.21** Restoration Motors offers to buy Charlie's 1960 Cadillac limousine only if an expert appraiser estimates that it can be restored for less than a certain price. Thus, the parties' obligations are conditioned on the outcome of the appraisal. If the condition is not satisfied—that is, if the appraiser deems the cost to be above that price—their obligations are discharged. ◀

CONDITIONS SUBSEQUENT When a condition operates to terminate a party's absolute promise to perform, it is called a **condition subsequent.** The condition follows, or is subsequent to, the time that the absolute duty to perform arose. If the condition occurs, the party's duty to perform is discharged. ▶ **Example 13.22** A law firm hires Julie Mendez, a recent law school graduate. Their contract provides that the firm's obligation to continue employing Mendez is discharged if Mendez fails to pass the bar exam by her second attempt. This is a condition subsequent because a failure to pass the exam—and thus to obtain a license to practice law—would discharge a duty (employment) that has already arisen. ◀

Generally, conditions precedent are common, and conditions subsequent are rare. The *Restatement (Second) of Contracts* does not use the terms *condition subsequent* and *condition precedent* but refers to both simply as conditions.[16]

CONCURRENT CONDITIONS When each party's performance is conditioned on the other party's performance or tender of performance (offer to perform), **concurrent conditions** are present. These conditions exist only when the contract expressly or impliedly calls for the parties to perform their respective duties *simultaneously.*

▶ **Example 13.23** If Janet Feibush promises to pay for goods when Hewlett-Packard delivers them, the parties' promises to perform are mutually dependent. Feibush's duty to pay for the goods does not become absolute until Hewlett-Packard either delivers or tenders the goods. Likewise, Hewlett-Packard's duty to deliver the goods does not become absolute until Feibush tenders or actually makes payment. Therefore, neither can recover from the other for breach without first tendering performance. ◀

EXPRESS AND IMPLIED CONDITIONS Conditions can also be classified as express or implied in fact. *Express conditions* are provided for by the parties' agreement. Although no particular words are necessary, express conditions are normally prefaced by the words *if, provided, after,* or *when.*

▶ **Case in Point 13.24** Alejandro Alvarado's automobile insurance policy stated that, if he was involved in an accident, he must cooperate with the insurance company in the defense of any claim or lawsuit. Alvarado was involved in an accident and was sued for negligence. He notified the insurance company, but then failed to cooperate in his defense and did not appear in court for the trial. Although Alvarado was found to have been negligent, the insurance company was not liable for the damages awarded. The court found that the cooperation clause was a condition precedent to coverage under the policy. Therefore, because Alvarado did not cooperate with the insurer, the accident was not covered by the policy.[17] ◀

Implied conditions are understood to be part of the agreement, but they are not found in the express language of the agreement. Courts may imply conditions from the purpose of the contract or from the intent of the parties. Conditions are often implied when they are necessarily inherent in the actual performance of the contract.

Discharge by Performance

The great majority of contracts are discharged by performance. The contract comes to an end when both parties fulfill their respective duties by performing the acts they have promised.

16. *Restatement (Second) of Contracts,* Section 224.

17. *Progressive County Mutual Insurance Co. v. Trevino,* 202 S.W.3d 811 (Tex.App.—San Antonio 2006).

Performance can also be accomplished by *tender.* **Tender** is an unconditional offer to perform by a person who is ready, willing, and able to do so. Therefore, a seller who places goods at the disposal of a buyer has tendered delivery and can demand payment. A buyer who offers to pay for goods has tendered payment and can demand delivery of the goods.

Once performance has been tendered, the party making the tender has done everything possible to carry out the terms of the contract. If the other party then refuses to perform, the party making the tender can sue for breach of contract. There are two basic types of performance—*complete performance* and *substantial performance.*

COMPLETE PERFORMANCE When a party performs exactly as agreed, there is no question as to whether the contract has been performed. When a party's performance is perfect, it is said to be complete. Normally, conditions expressly stated in a contract must fully occur in all respects for complete performance (strict performance) of the contract to take place. Any deviation breaches the contract and discharges the other party's obligations to perform.

Most construction contracts, for instance, require the builder to meet certain specifications. If the specifications are conditions, complete performance is required to avoid material breach (*material breach* will be discussed shortly). If the conditions are met, the other party to the contract must then fulfill her or his obligation to pay the builder.

If the parties to the contract did not expressly make the specifications a condition, however, and the builder fails to meet the specifications, performance is not complete. What effect does such a failure have on the other party's obligation to pay? The answer is part of the doctrine of *substantial performance.*

SUBSTANTIAL PERFORMANCE A party who in good faith performs substantially all of the terms of a contract can enforce the contract against the other party under the doctrine of substantial performance. The basic requirements for performance to qualify as substantial performance are as follows:

1. The party must have performed in good faith. Intentional failure to comply with the contract terms is a breach of the contract.
2. The performance must not vary greatly from the performance promised in the contract. An omission, variance, or defect in performance is

considered minor if it can easily be remedied by compensation (monetary damages).
3. The performance must create substantially the same benefits as those promised in the contract.

Courts decide whether the performance was substantial on a case-by-case basis, examining all of the facts of the particular situation. ▶ **Case in Point 13.25** Wisconsin Electric Power Company (WEPCO) contracted with Union Pacific Railroad to transport coal to WEPCO from mines in Colorado. The contract required WEPCO to notify Union Pacific monthly of how many tons of coal (below a specified maximum) it wanted to have shipped the next month. Union Pacific was to make "good faith reasonable efforts" to meet the schedule.

The contract also required WEPCO to supply the railcars. When WEPCO did not supply the railcars, Union Pacific used its own railcars and delivered 84 percent of the requested coal. In this situation, a federal court held that the delivery of 84 percent of the contracted amount constituted substantial performance.[18] ◀

Effect on Duty to Perform. If performance is substantial, the other party's duty to perform remains absolute (except that the party can sue for damages due to the minor deviations). In other words, the parties must continue performing under the contract (for instance, making payment to the party who substantially performed). If performance is not substantial, there is a *material breach* (to be discussed shortly), and the non-breaching party is excused from further performance.

Measure of Damages. Because substantial performance is not perfect, the other party is entitled to damages to compensate for the failure to comply with the contract. The measure of the damages is the cost to bring the object of the contract into compliance with its terms, if that cost is reasonable under the circumstances.

If the cost is unreasonable, the measure of damages is the difference in value between the performance that was rendered and the performance that would have been rendered if the contract had been performed completely.

PERFORMANCE TO THE SATISFACTION OF ANOTHER Contracts often state that completed work must per-

---

18. *Wisconsin Electric Power Co. v. Union Pacific Railroad Co.,* 557 F.3d 504 (7th Cir. 2009).

sonally satisfy one of the parties or a third person. The question then is whether this satisfaction becomes a condition precedent, requiring actual personal satisfaction or approval for discharge, or whether the performance need only satisfy a *reasonable person* (substantial performance).

When the Contract Is Personal. When the subject matter of the contract is *personal,* the obligation is conditional, and performance must actually satisfy the party specified in the contract. For instance, contracts for portraits, works of art, and tailoring are considered personal because they involve matters of personal taste. Therefore, only the personal satisfaction of the party fulfills the condition—unless a court finds that the party is expressing dissatisfaction simply to avoid payment or otherwise is not acting in good faith.

Reasonable Person Standard. Most other contracts need to be performed only to the satisfaction of a reasonable person unless they *expressly state otherwise.* When the subject matter of the contract is mechanical, courts are more likely to find that the performing party has performed satisfactorily if a reasonable person would be satisfied with what was done. ▶ **Example 13.26** Mason signs a contract with Jen to mount a new heat pump on a concrete platform to her satisfaction. Such a contract normally need only be performed to the satisfaction of a reasonable person. ◀

When contracts require performance to the satisfaction of a third party with superior knowledge or training in the subject matter—such as a supervising engineer—the courts are divided. A majority of courts require the work to be satisfactory to a reasonable person, but some courts require the personal satisfaction of the third party designated in the contract. (Again, the personal judgment must be made honestly, or the condition will be excused.)

MATERIAL BREACH OF CONTRACT A **breach of contract** is the nonperformance of a contractual duty. The breach is *material* when performance is not at least substantial.[19] As mentioned earlier, when there is a material breach, the nonbreaching party is excused from the performance of contractual duties. That party can also sue the breaching party for damages resulting from the breach.

▶ **Example 13.27** When country singer Garth Brooks's mother died, he donated $500,000 to a hospital in his hometown to build a new women's health center named after his mother. After several years passed and the health center was not built, Brooks demanded a refund. The hospital refused, claiming that while it had promised to honor his mother in some way, it did not promise to build a women's health center. Brooks sued for breach of contract. A jury determined that the hospital's failure to build a women's health center and name it after Brooks's mother was a material breach of the contract. The jury awarded Brooks $500,000 in actual damages for the contract breach—plus another $500,000 because it found the hospital guilty of reckless disregard and intentionally acting with malice toward others. ◀

Material versus Minor Breach. If the breach is *minor* (not material), the nonbreaching party's duty to perform can sometimes be suspended until the breach has been remedied, but the duty to perform is not entirely excused. Once the minor breach has been cured, the nonbreaching party must resume performance of the contractual obligations.

Both parties in the following case were arguably in breach of their contract. The court had to determine which party's breach was material.

---

19. *Restatement (Second) of Contracts,* Section 241.

CASE ANALYSIS

Case 13.3   Kohel v. Bergen Auto Enterprises, LLC
Superior Court of New Jersey, Appellate Division, 2013 WL 439970 (2013).

IN THE LANGUAGE OF THE COURT
PER CURIAM. [By the Whole Court]
* * * *

On May 24, 2010, plaintiffs Marc and Bree Kohel entered into a sales contract with defendant Bergen Auto Enterprises, L.L.C. d/b/a Wayne Mazda

Inc. (Wayne Mazda), for the purchase of a used 2009 Mazda. Plaintiffs agreed to pay $26,430.22 for the Mazda and were credited $7,000 as a trade-in, for

CASE 13.3 CONTINUES ▶

their 2005 Nissan Altima. As plaintiffs still owed $8,118.28 on the Nissan, Wayne Mazda assessed plaintiffs a net pay-off of this amount and agreed to remit the balance due to satisfy the outstanding lien.

Plaintiffs took possession of the Mazda with temporary plates and left the Nissan with defendant. A few days later, a representative of defendant advised plaintiffs that the Nissan's vehicle identification tag (VIN tag) was missing. The representative claimed it was unable to sell the car and offered to rescind the transaction. Plaintiffs refused.

When the temporary plates on the Mazda expired on June 24, 2010, defendant refused to provide plaintiffs with the permanent plates they had paid for. In addition, defendant refused to pay off plaintiffs' outstanding loan on the Nissan, as they had agreed. As a result, plaintiffs were required to continue to make monthly payments on both the Nissan and the Mazda.

On July 28, 2010, plaintiffs filed a complaint in [a New Jersey state court] against Wayne Mazda * * * . Plaintiffs alleged breach of contract.

* * * *

On February 2, 2012, the court rendered an oral decision finding that there was a breach of contract by Wayne Mazda * * * . On February 17, 2012, the court entered judgment in the amount of $5,405.17 in favor of plaintiffs against Wayne Mazda. [The defendant appealed to a state intermediate appellate court.]

* * * *

Defendant argues that plaintiffs' delivery of the Nissan without a VIN tag was, itself, a breach of the contract of sale and precludes a finding that defendant breached the contract. However, the trial court found that plaintiffs were not aware that the Nissan lacked a VIN tag when they offered it in trade. Moreover, defendant's representatives examined the car twice before accepting it in trade and did not notice the missing VIN until they took the car to an auction where they tried to sell it. *There is a material distinction in plaintiffs' conduct, which the court found unintentional, and defendant's refusal to release the permanent plates for which the plaintiffs had paid, an action the court concluded was done to maintain "leverage."* [Emphasis added.]

* * * The evidence * * * indicated that * * * the problem with the missing VIN tag could be rectified. Marc Kohel applied and paid for a replacement VIN tag at Meadowlands [Nissan for $35.31]. While he initially made some calls to Meadowlands, he did not follow up in obtaining the VIN tag after the personnel at Wayne Mazda began refusing to take his calls.

* * * The court concluded that "Wayne Mazda didn't handle this as—as adroitly [skillfully] as they could * * * ." Kevin DiPiano, identified in the complaint as the owner and/or CEO of Wayne Mazda, would not even take [the plaintiffs'] calls to discuss this matter. The court found:

> Mr. DiPiano could have been a better businessman, could have been a little bit more compassionate or at least responsive, you know? He was not. He acted like he didn't care. That obviously went a long way to infuriate the plaintiffs. I don't blame them for being infuriated.

* * * *

* * * Here, plaintiffs attempted to remedy the VIN tag issue but this resolution was frustrated by defendant's unreasonable conduct. We thus reject defendant's argument that plaintiffs' failure to obtain the replacement VIN tag amounted to a repudiation of the contract.

* * * *

Affirmed.

LEGAL REASONING QUESTIONS

1. What is a *material* breach of contract? When a material breach occurs, what are the nonbreaching party's options?

2. What is a *minor* breach of contract? When a minor breach occurs, is the nonbreaching party excused from performance? Explain.

3. In this case, what were the defendant's main arguments that the plaintiffs should not have been granted relief for Wayne Mazda's breach?

4. Was there a difference in the degree to which the plaintiffs and the defendant failed to perform the contract? Explain. Which party was in material breach?

Discharges Nonbreaching Party from Further Performance. Any breach entitles the nonbreaching party to sue for damages, but only a material breach discharges the nonbreaching party from the contract. The policy underlying these rules allows a contract to go forward when only minor problems occur but allows it to be terminated if major difficulties arise.

▶ **Case in Point 13.28** Su Yong Kim sold an apartment building with substandard plumbing that violated the city's housing code. The contract stated that

Kim would have the plumbing fixed (brought up to code) within eight months. A year later, Kim still had not made the necessary repairs, so the buyers stopped making the payments due under the contract. A court found that Kim's failure to make the required repairs was a material breach because it defeated the purpose of the contract—to lease the building to tenants. Because Kim's breach was material, the buyers were no longer obligated to continue making payments under the contract.[20] ◀

ANTICIPATORY REPUDIATION Before either party to a contract has a duty to perform, one of the parties may refuse to carry out his or her contractual obligations. This is called **anticipatory repudiation**[21] of the contract.

Repudiation Is a Material Breach. When an anticipatory repudiation occurs, it is treated as a material breach of the contract, and the nonbreaching party is permitted to bring an action for damages immediately. The nonbreaching party can file suit even though the scheduled time for performance under the contract may still be in the future. Until the nonbreaching party treats an early repudiation as a breach, however, the repudiating party can retract her or his anticipatory repudiation by proper notice and restore the parties to their original obligations.[22]

An anticipatory repudiation is treated as a present, material breach for two reasons. First, the nonbreaching party should not be required to remain ready and willing to perform when the other party has already repudiated the contract. Second, the nonbreaching party should have the opportunity to seek a similar contract elsewhere and may have a duty to do so to minimize his or her loss.[23]

Anticipatory Repudiation and Market Prices. Quite often, anticipatory repudiation occurs when performance of the contract would be extremely unfavorable to one of the parties because of a sharp fluctuation in market prices.
▶ **Example 13.29** Mobile X enters into an e-contract to manufacture and sell 100,000 cell phones to Best Com, a global telecommunications company.

Delivery is to be made two months from the date of the contract. One month later, three inventory suppliers raise their prices to Mobile X. Because of these higher prices, Mobile X stands to lose $500,000 if it sells the cell phones to Best Com at the contract price. Mobile X immediately sends an e-mail to Best Com, stating that it cannot deliver the 100,000 cell phones at the contract price. Even though you may sympathize with Mobile X, its e-mail is an anticipatory repudiation of the contract. Best Com can treat the repudiation as a material breach and immediately pursue remedies, even though the contract delivery date is still a month away. ◀

TIME FOR PERFORMANCE If no time for performance is stated in the contract, a *reasonable time* is implied.[24] If a specific time is stated, the parties must usually perform by that time. Unless time is expressly stated to be vital, though, a delay in performance will not destroy the performing party's right to payment.[25]

When time is expressly stated to be "of the essence" or vital, the parties normally must perform within the stated time period because the time element becomes a condition. Even when the contract states that time is of the essence, a court may find that a party who fails to complain about the other party's delay has waived the breach of the time provision.

Discharge by Agreement

Any contract can be discharged by agreement of the parties. The agreement can be contained in the original contract, or the parties can form a new contract for the express purpose of discharging the original contract.

DISCHARGE BY MUTUAL RESCISSION As mentioned in previous chapters, *rescission* is the process by which a contract is canceled or terminated and the parties are returned to the positions they occupied prior to forming it. For **mutual rescission** to take place, the parties must make another agreement that also satisfies the legal requirements for a contract. There must be an *offer,* an *acceptance,* and *consideration.* Ordinarily, if the parties agree to rescind the original contract, their promises not to perform the acts stipulated in the original contract will be legal consideration for the second contract (the rescission).

Agreements to rescind most executory contracts (in which neither party has performed) are enforceable,

20. *Kim v. Park,* 192 Or.App. 365, 86 P.3d 63 (2004).
21. *Restatement (Second) of Contracts,* Section 253; Section 2–610 of the Uniform Commercial Code (UCC).
22. See UCC 2–611.
23. The doctrine of anticipatory repudiation first arose in the landmark case of *Hochster v. De La Tour,* 2 Ellis and Blackburn Reports 678 (1853). An English court recognized the delay and expense inherent in a rule requiring a nonbreaching party to wait until the time of performance before suing on an anticipatory repudiation.
24. See UCC 2–204.
25. See, for example, *Manganaro Corp. v. Hitt Contracting, Inc.,* 193 F.Supp.2d 88 (D.D.C. 2002).

even if the agreement is made orally and even if the original agreement was in writing. Under the Uniform Commercial Code (UCC), however, agreements to rescind a sales contract must be in writing (or contained in an electronic record) when the contract requires a written rescission.[26] Agreements to rescind contracts involving transfers of realty also must be evidenced by a writing or record.

When one party has fully performed, an agreement to cancel the original contract normally will *not* be enforceable unless there is additional consideration. Because the performing party has received no consideration for the promise to call off the original bargain, additional consideration is necessary to support a rescission contract.

DISCHARGE BY NOVATION A contractual obligation may also be discharged through novation. A **novation** occurs when both of the parties to a contract agree to substitute a third party for one of the original parties. The requirements of a novation are as follows:

1. A previous valid obligation.
2. An agreement by all parties to a new contract.
3. The extinguishing of the old obligation (discharge of the prior party).
4. A new contract that is valid.

▶ **Example 13.30** Union Corporation contracts to sell its pharmaceutical division to British Pharmaceuticals, Ltd. Before the transfer is completed, Union, British Pharmaceuticals, and a third company, Otis Chemicals, execute a new agreement to transfer all of British Pharmaceuticals' rights and duties in the transaction to Otis Chemicals. As long as the new contract is supported by consideration, the novation will discharge the original contract (between Union and British Pharmaceuticals) and replace it with the new contract (between Union and Otis Chemicals). ◀

A novation expressly or impliedly revokes and discharges a prior contract. The parties involved may expressly state in the new contract that the old contract is now discharged. If the parties do not expressly discharge the old contract, it will be impliedly discharged if the new contract's terms are inconsistent with the old contract's terms. It is this immediate discharge of the prior contract that distinguishes a novation from both an accord and satisfaction, which will be discussed shortly, and an assignment of all rights, discussed earlier in this chapter.

DISCHARGE BY SETTLEMENT AGREEMENT A compromise, or settlement agreement, that arises out of a genuine dispute over the obligations under an existing contract will be recognized at law. The agreement will be substituted as a new contract and will either expressly or impliedly revoke and discharge the obligations under the prior contract. In contrast to a novation, a substituted agreement does not involve a third party. Rather, the two original parties to the contract form a different agreement to substitute for the original one.

DISCHARGE BY ACCORD AND SATISFACTION As discussed in Chapter 11, in an accord and satisfaction, the parties agree to accept performance that is different from the performance originally promised. An *accord* is a contract to perform some act to satisfy an existing contractual duty that is not yet discharged.[27] A *satisfaction* is the performance of the accord agreement. An accord and its satisfaction discharge the original contractual obligation.

Once the accord has been made, the original obligation is merely suspended until the accord agreement is fully performed. If it is not performed, the obligee (the one to whom performance is owed) can file a lawsuit based on the original obligation or the accord. ▶ **Example 13.31** Fahreed has a judgment against Ling for $8,000. Later, both parties agree that the judgment can be satisfied by Ling's transfer of his automobile to Fahreed. This agreement to accept the auto in lieu of $8,000 in cash is the accord. If Ling transfers the car to Fahreed, the accord is fully performed, and the debt is discharged. If Ling refuses to transfer the car, the accord is breached. Because the original obligation was merely suspended, Fahreed can sue Ling to enforce the original judgment for $8,000 in cash or bring an action for breach of the accord. ◀

Discharge by Operation of Law

Under specified circumstances, contractual duties may be discharged by operation of law. These circumstances include material alteration of the contract, the running of the statute of limitations, bankruptcy, and the impossibility or impracticability of performance.

MATERIAL ALTERATION OF THE CONTRACT To discourage parties from altering written contracts, the law allows an innocent party to be discharged when the other party has materially altered a written con-

---

26. UCC 2–209(2), (4).

27. *Restatement (Second) of Contracts*, Section 281.

tract without consent. For instance, a party alters a material term of a contract, such as the stated quantity or price, without the knowledge or consent of the other party. In this situation, the party who was unaware of the alteration can treat the contract as discharged or terminated.

STATUTES OF LIMITATIONS As mentioned earlier in this text, statutes of limitations restrict the period during which a party can sue on a particular cause of action. After the applicable limitations period has passed, a suit can no longer be brought. The limitations period for bringing suits for breach of oral contracts usually is two to three years, and for written or otherwise recorded contracts, four to five years. Parties generally have ten to twenty years to file for recovery of amounts awarded in judgments, depending on state law.

Lawsuits for breach of a contract for the sale of goods generally must be brought within four years after the cause of action has accrued.[28] By their original agreement, the parties can reduce this four-year period to not less than one year, but they cannot agree to extend it.

BANKRUPTCY A proceeding in bankruptcy attempts to allocate the debtor's assets to the creditors in a fair and equitable fashion. Once the assets have been allocated, the debtor receives a **discharge in bankruptcy.** A discharge in bankruptcy ordinarily prevents the creditors from enforcing most of the debtor's contracts. Partial payment of a debt *after* discharge in bankruptcy will not revive the debt.

IMPOSSIBILITY OF PERFORMANCE After a contract has been made, supervening events (such as a fire) may make performance impossible in an objective sense. This is known as **impossibility of performance** and can discharge a contract.[29] The doctrine of impossibility of performance applies only when the parties could not have reasonably foreseen, at the time the contract was formed, the event that rendered performance impossible. Performance may also become so difficult or costly due to some unforeseen event that a court will consider it commercially unfeasible, or impracticable, as will be discussed later in the chapter.

---

28. Section 2–725 of the UCC contains this four-year limitation period. A cause of action for a sales contract generally accrues when the breach occurs, even if the aggrieved party is not aware of the breach. A breach of warranty normally occurs when the seller delivers the goods to the buyer.
29. *Restatement (Second) of Contracts,* Section 261.

Objective impossibility ("It can't be done") must be distinguished from *subjective impossibility* ("I'm sorry, I simply can't do it"). An example of subjective impossibility occurs when a party cannot deliver goods on time because of freight car shortages or cannot make payment on time because the bank is closed. In effect, in each of these situations the party is saying, "It is impossible for *me* to perform," not "It is impossible for *anyone* to perform." Accordingly, such excuses do not discharge a contract, and the nonperforming party is normally held in breach of contract.

When Performance Is Impossible. Three basic types of situations may qualify as grounds for the discharge of contractual obligations based on impossibility of performance:[30]

1. *When one of the parties to a personal contract dies or becomes incapacitated prior to performance.*
   ▶ **Example 13.32** Frederic, a famous dancer, contracts with Ethereal Dancing Guild to play a leading role in its new ballet. Before the ballet can be performed, Frederic becomes ill and dies. His personal performance was essential to the completion of the contract. Thus, his death discharges the contract and his estate's liability for his nonperformance. ◀

2. *When the specific subject matter of the contract is destroyed.*
   ▶ **Example 13.33** A-1 Farm Equipment agrees to sell Gunther the green tractor on its lot and promises to have the tractor ready for Gunther to pick up on Saturday. On Friday night, however, a truck veers off the nearby highway and smashes into the tractor, destroying it beyond repair. Because the contract was for this specific tractor, A-1's performance is rendered impossible owing to the accident. ◀

3. *When a change in law renders performance illegal.*
   ▶ **Example 13.34** Hopper contracts with Playlist, Inc., to create a Web site through which users can post and share movies, music, and other forms of digital entertainment. Hopper goes to work. Before the site is operational, however, Congress passes the No Online Piracy in Entertainment (NOPE) Act. The NOPE Act makes it illegal to operate a Web site on which copyrighted works are posted without the copyright owners' consent. In this situation, the contract is discharged by

---

30. *Restatement (Second) of Contracts,* Sections 262–266; UCC 2–615.

operation of law. The purpose of the contract has been rendered illegal, and contract performance is objectively impossible. ◀

Temporary Impossibility. An occurrence or event that makes performance temporarily impossible operates to suspend performance until the impossibility ceases. Once the temporary event ends, the parties ordinarily must perform the contract as originally planned.

▶ **Case in Point 13.35** Keefe Hurwitz contracted to sell his home in Louisiana to Wesley and Gwendolyn Payne for $241,500. Four days later, Hurricane Katrina made landfall and caused extensive damage to the house. Hurwitz refused to pay the cost ($60,000) for the necessary repairs before the deal closed. The Paynes filed a lawsuit to enforce the contract at the agreed-on price. Hurwitz argued that Hurricane Katrina had made it impossible for him to perform and had discharged his duties under the contract. The court, however, ruled that Hurricane Katrina had caused only a temporary impossibility. Hurwitz was required to pay for the necessary repairs and to perform the contract as written. He could not obtain a higher purchase price to offset the cost of the repairs.[31] ◀

Sometimes, the lapse of time and the change in circumstances surrounding the contract make it sub-

stantially more burdensome for the parties to perform the promised acts. In that situation, the contract is discharged. ▶ **Case in Point 13.36** In 1942, actor Gene Autry was drafted into the U.S. Army. Being drafted rendered his contract with a Hollywood movie company temporarily impossible to perform, and it was suspended until the end of World War II in 1945. When Autry got out of the army, the purchasing power of the dollar had declined so much that performance of the contract would have been substantially burdensome to him. Therefore, the contract was discharged.[32] ◀

It can be difficult to predict how a court will—or should—rule on whether performance is impossible in a particular situation, as discussed in this chapter's *Insight into Ethics* feature below.

COMMERCIAL IMPRACTICABILITY Courts may also excuse parties from their performance when it becomes much more difficult or expensive than the parties originally contemplated at the time the contract was formed. For someone to invoke the doctrine of **commercial impracticability** successfully, however, the anticipated performance must become *significantly* difficult or costly.[33]

The added burden of performing not only must be extreme but also *must not have been known by the*

---

31. *Payne v. Hurwitz,* 978 So.2d 1000 (La.App. 1st Cir. 2008).

32. *Autry v. Republic Productions,* 30 Cal.2d 144, 180 P.2d 888 (1947).
33. *Restatement (Second) of Contracts,* Section 264.

INSIGHT INTO ETHICS
When Is Impossibility of Performance a Valid Defense?

The doctrine of impossibility of performance is applied only when the parties could not have reasonably foreseen, at the time the contract was formed, the event or events that rendered performance impossible. In some cases, the courts may seem to go too far in holding that the parties should have foreseen certain events or conditions. Thus, the parties cannot avoid their contractual obligations under the doctrine of impossibility of performance.

Actually, courts today are more likely to allow parties to raise this defense than courts were in the past, which rarely excused parties from performance under the impossibility doctrine. Indeed, until the latter part of the nineteenth century, courts were reluctant to discharge a contract even when performance appeared to be

impossible. Generally, the courts must balance the freedom of parties to contract (and thereby assume the risks involved) against the injustice that may result when certain contractual obligations are enforced. If the courts allowed parties to raise impossibility of performance as a defense to contractual obligations more often, freedom of contract would suffer.

LEGAL CRITICAL THINKING
INSIGHT INTO THE SOCIAL ENVIRONMENT

Why might those entering into contracts be worse off in the long run if the courts increasingly accept impossibility of performance as a defense?

EXHIBIT 13–4 Contract Discharge

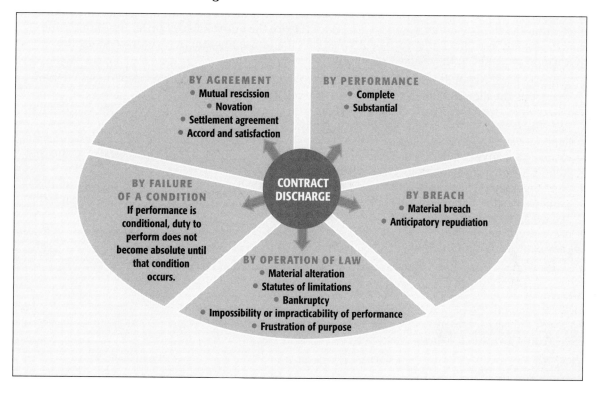

parties when the contract was made. In one classic case, for example, a court held that a contract could be discharged because a party would otherwise have to pay ten times more than the original estimate to excavate a certain amount of gravel.[34]

FRUSTRATION OF PURPOSE Closely allied with the doctrine of commercial impracticability is the doctrine of **frustration of purpose.** In principle, a contract will be discharged if supervening circumstances make it impossible to attain the purpose both parties had in mind when they made the contract. As with commer-

cial impracticability and impossibility, the supervening event must not have been reasonably foreseeable at the time the contract was formed.

There are some differences between the doctrines, however. Commercial impracticability usually involves an event that increases the cost or difficulty of performance. In contrast, frustration of purpose typically involves an event that decreases the value of what a party receives under the contract.[35]

See Exhibit 13–4 above for a summary of the ways in which a contract can be discharged.

---

34. *Mineral Park Land Co. v. Howard,* 172 Cal. 289, 156 P. 458 (1916).

35. See, for example, *East Capitol View Community Development Corp. v. Robinson,* 941 A.2d 1036 (D.C.App. 2008).

Reviewing: Third Party Rights and Discharge

Val's Foods signs a contract to buy 1,500 pounds of basil from Sun Farms, a small organic herb grower, as long as an independent organization inspects the crop and certifies that it contains no pesticide or herbicide residue. Val's has a contract with several restaurant chains to supply pesto and intends to use

Continued

Sun Farms' basil in the pesto to fulfill these contracts. While Sun Farms is preparing to harvest the basil, an unexpected hailstorm destroys half the crop. Sun Farms attempts to purchase additional basil from other farms, but it is late in the season and the price is twice the normal market price. Sun Farms is too small to absorb this cost and immediately notifies Val's that it will not fulfill the contract. Using the information presented in the chapter, answer the following questions.

1. Suppose that the basil does not pass the chemical-residue inspection. Which concept discussed in the chapter might allow Val's to refuse to perform the contract in this situation?
2. Under which legal theory or theories might Sun Farms claim that its obligation under the contract has been discharged by operation of law? Discuss fully.
3. Suppose that Sun Farms contacts every basil grower in the country and buys the last remaining chemical-free basil anywhere. Nevertheless, Sun Farms is able to ship only 1,475 pounds to Val's. Would this fulfill Sun Farms' obligations to Val's? Why or why not?
4. Now suppose that Sun Farms sells its operations to Happy Valley Farms. As a part of the sale, all three parties agree that Happy Valley will provide the basil as stated under the original contract. What is this type of agreement called?

DEBATE THIS . . . *The doctrine of commercial impracticability should be abolished.*

Terms and Concepts

alienation 260
anticipatory repudiation 271
assignee 257
assignment 257
assignor 257
breach of contract 269
commercial impracticability 274
concurrent conditions 267
condition 266
condition precedent 267

condition subsequent 267
delegatee 262
delegation 257
delegator 262
discharge 266
discharge in bankruptcy 273
frustration of purpose 275
impossibility of performance 273
incidental beneficiary 265
intended beneficiary 263

mutual rescission 271
novation 272
obligee 257
obligor 257
performance 266
privity of contract 257
tender 268
third party beneficiary 263

ExamPrep

Issue Spotters

1. C&D Services contracts with Ace Concessions, Inc., to service Ace's vending machines. Later, C&D wants Dean Vending Services to assume the duties under a new contract. Ace consents. What type of agreement is this? Are Ace's obligations discharged? Why or why not? **(See page 272.)**
2. Brian owes Jeff $100. Ed tells Brian to give him the $100 and he will pay Jeff. Brian gives Ed the $100. Ed never pays Jeff. Can Jeff successfully sue Ed for the $100? Why or why not? **(See pages 263–265.)**

• Check your answers to the Issue Spotters against the answers provided in Appendix B at the end of this text.

Before the Test

Go to **www.cengagebrain.com**, enter the ISBN 9781285770192, and click on "Find" to locate this textbook's Web site. Then, click on "Access Now" under "Study Tools," and select Chapter 13 at the top. There, you will find a Practice Quiz that you can take to assess your mastery of the concepts in this chapter, as well as Flashcards and a Glossary of important terms.

Business Scenarios

13–1. Discharge by Agreement. Junior owes creditor Iba $1,000, which is due and payable on June 1. Junior has been in a car accident, has missed a great deal of work, and consequently will not have the funds on June 1. Junior's father, Fred, offers to pay Iba $1,100 in four equal installments if Iba will discharge Junior from any further liability on the debt. Iba accepts. Is this transaction a novation or an accord and satisfaction? Explain. **(See page 271.)**

13–2. Assignment. Five years ago, Hensley purchased a house. At that time, being unable to pay the full purchase price, she borrowed funds from Thrift Savings and Loan, which in turn took a mortgage at 6.5 percent interest on the house. The mortgage contract did not prohibit the assignment of the mortgage. Then Hensley secured a new job in another city and sold the house to Sylvia. The purchase price included payment to Hensley of the value of her equity and the assumption of the mortgage debt still owed to Thrift. At the time the contract between Hensley and Sylvia was made, Thrift did not know about or consent to the sale. On the basis of these facts, if Sylvia defaults in making the mortgage payments to Thrift, what are Thrift's rights? Discuss. **(See page 257.)**

13–3. Impossibility of Performance. In the following situations, certain events take place after the contracts are formed. Discuss which of these contracts are discharged because the events render the contracts impossible to perform. **(See page 273.)**

(a) Jimenez, a famous singer, contracts to perform in your nightclub. He dies prior to performance.

(b) Raglione contracts to sell you her land. Just before title is to be transferred, she dies.

(c) Oppenheim contracts to sell you one thousand bushels of apples from her orchard in the state of Washington. Because of a severe frost, she is unable to deliver the apples.

(d) Maxwell contracts to lease a service station for ten years. His principal income is from the sale of gasoline. Because of an oil embargo by foreign oil-producing nations, gasoline is rationed, cutting sharply into Maxwell's gasoline sales. He cannot make his lease payments.

13–4. Delegation. Inez has a specific set of plans to build a sailboat. The plans are detailed, and any boatbuilder can construct the boat. Inez secures bids, and the low bid is made by the Whale of a Boat Corp. Inez contracts with Whale to build the boat for $4,000. Whale then receives unexpected business from elsewhere. To meet the delivery date in the contract with Inez, Whale delegates its obligation to build the boat, without Inez's consent, to Quick Brothers, a reputable boatbuilder. When the boat is ready for delivery, Inez learns of the delegation and refuses to accept delivery, even though the boat is built to her specifications. Discuss fully whether Inez is obligated to accept and pay for the boat. Would your answer be any different if Inez had not had a specific set of plans but had instead contracted with Whale to design and build a sailboat for $4,000? Explain. **(See page 262.)**

Business Case Problems

13–5. Spotlight on Drug Testing—Third Party Beneficiary. Bath Iron Works (BIW) offered a job to Thomas Devine, contingent on Devine's passing a drug test. The testing was conducted by NorDx, a subcontractor of Roche Biomedical Laboratories. When NorDx found that Devine's urinalysis showed the presence of opiates, a result confirmed by Roche, BIW refused to offer Devine permanent employment. Devine sued Roche, claiming that the ingestion of poppy seeds can yield a positive result and that he tested positive only because of his daily consumption of poppy seed muffins. Devine argued that he was a third party beneficiary of the contract between his prospective employer (BIW) and NorDx (Roche). Is Devine an intended third party beneficiary of the BIW–NorDx contract? Why or why not? Do drug-testing labs have a duty to the persons being tested to exercise reasonable care in conducting the tests? Explain. [*Devine v. Roche Biomedical Laboratories*, 659 A.2d 868 (Me. 1995)] **(See page 263.)**

13–6. Condition Precedent. Just Homes, LLC (JH), hired Mike Building & Contracting, Inc., to do $1.35 million worth of renovation work on three homes. Community Preservation Corporation (CPC) supervised Mike's work on behalf of JH. The contract stated that in the event of a dispute, JH would have to obtain the project architect's certification to justify terminating Mike. As construction progressed, relations between Mike and CPC worsened. At a certain point in the project, Mike requested partial payment, and CPC recommended that JH not make it. Mike refused to continue work without further payment. JH evicted Mike from the project. Mike sued for breach of contract. JH contended that it had the right to terminate the contract due to CPC's negative reports and Mike's failure to agree with the project's engineer. Mike moved for summary judgment for the amounts owed for work performed. Mike claimed that JH had not fulfilled the condition precedent—JH never obtained the project architect's certification for Mike's termination. Which of the two parties involved breached the contract? Explain your answer. [*Mike Building & Contracting, Inc. v. Just Homes, LLC*, 27 Misc.3d 833, 901 N.Y.S.2d 458 (2010)] **(See page 267.)**

13–7. BUSINESS CASE PROBLEM
WITH SAMPLE ANSWER: Conditions of Performance.

James Maciel leased an apartment in Regent Village, a university-owned housing facility for Regent University (RU) students in Virginia Beach, Virginia. The lease ran until the end of the fall semester. Maciel had an option to renew the lease semester by semester as long as he maintained his status as an RU student. When Maciel completed his coursework for the spring semester, he told RU that he intended to withdraw. The university told him that he could stay in the apartment until May 31, the final day of the spring semester. Maciel asked for two additional weeks, but the university denied the request. On June 1, RU changed the locks on the apartment. Maciel entered through a window and e-mailed the university that he planned to stay "for another one or two weeks." When he was charged with trespassing, Maciel argued that he had "legal authority" to occupy the apartment. Was Maciel correct? Explain. [*Maciel v. Commonwealth*, __ S.E.2d __ (Va.App. 2011)] **(See pages 266 and 267.)**

• **For a sample answer to Problem 13–7, go to Appendix C at the end of this text.**

13–8. Third Party Beneficiary.
David and Sandra Dess contracted with Sirva Relocation, LLC, to assist in selling their home. In their contract, the Desses agreed to disclose all information about the property on which Sirva "and other prospective buyers may rely in deciding whether and on what terms to purchase the Property." The Kincaids contracted with Sirva to buy the house. After the closing, they discovered dampness in the walls, defective and rotten windows, mold, and other undisclosed problems. Can the Kincaids bring an action against the Desses for breach of their contract with Sirva? Why or why not? [*Kincaid v. Dess*, 298 P.3d 358 (2013)] **(See page 263.)**

13–9. A QUESTION OF ETHICS: Assignment and Delegation.

*Premier Building & Development, Inc., entered a listing agreement giving Sunset Gold Realty, LLC, the exclusive right to find a tenant for some commercial property. The terms of the listing agree-*ment stated that it was binding on both parties and "their . . . assigns." Premier Building did not own the property at the time, but had the option to purchase it. To secure financing for the project, Premier Building established a new company called Cobblestone Associates. Premier Building then bought the property and conveyed it to Cobblestone the same day. Meanwhile, Sunset Gold found a tenant for the property, and Cobblestone became the landlord. Cobblestone acknowledged its obligation to pay Sunset Gold for finding a tenant, but it later refused to pay Sunset Gold's commission. Sunset Gold then sued Premier Building and Cobblestone for breach of the listing agreement. [*Sunset Gold Realty, LLC v. Premier Building & Development, Inc.*, 36 A.3d 243 (Conn.App.Ct. 2012)] **(See pages 257–263.)**

(a) Is Premier Building relieved of its contractual duties if it assigned the contract to Cobblestone? Why or why not?

(b) Given that Sunset Gold performed its obligations under the listing agreement, did Cobblestone behave unethically in refusing to pay Sunset Gold's commission? Why or why not?

13–10. SPECIAL CASE ANALYSIS: Material Breach.

Go to Case Analysis Case 13.3, *Kohel v. Bergen Auto Enterprises, LLC*, on pages 269 and 270. Read the excerpt and answer the following questions.

(a) **Issue:** This case involved allegations of breach of contract involving which parties and for what actions?

(b) **Rule of Law:** What is the difference between a *material* breach and a *minor* breach of contract?

(c) **Applying the Rule of Law:** How did the court determine which party was in material breach of the contract in this case?

(d) **Conclusion:** Was the defendant liable for breach? Why or why not?

Legal Reasoning Group Activity

13–11. Anticipatory Repudiation. ABC Clothiers, Inc., has a contract with Taylor & Sons, a retailer, to deliver one thousand summer suits to Taylor's place of business on or before May 1. On April 1, Taylor receives a letter from ABC informing him that ABC will not be able to make the delivery as scheduled. Taylor is very upset, as he had planned a big ad campaign. **(See page 271.)**

(a) The first group will discuss whether Taylor can immediately sue ABC for breach of contract (on April 2).

(b) Now suppose that Taylor's son, Tom, tells his father that they cannot file a lawsuit until ABC actually fails to deliver the suits on May 1. The second group will decide who is correct, Taylor senior or Tom.

(c) Assume that Taylor & Sons can either file immediately or wait until ABC fails to deliver the goods. The third group will evaluate which course of action is better, given the circumstances.

CHAPTER 14

BREACH OF CONTRACT AND REMEDIES

When one party breaches a contract, the other party—the nonbreaching party—can choose one or more of several remedies. (Does changing terms of service on a social networking site constitute a breach of contract? See this chapter's *Insight into Social Media* feature on page 281 for a look at this issue.) A *remedy* is the relief provided for an innocent party when the other party has breached the contract. It is the means employed to enforce a right or to redress an injury.

The most common remedies available to a nonbreaching party include damages, *rescission* and *restitution, specific performance,* and *reformation.* As discussed in Chapter 1, a distinction is made between *remedies at law* and *remedies in equity.* Today, the remedy at law normally is monetary damages, which are discussed in the first part of this chapter. Equitable remedies include rescission and restitution, specific performance, and reformation, all of which will be examined later in the chapter. Usually, a court will not award an equitable remedy unless the remedy at law is inadequate.

SECTION 1
DAMAGES

A breach of contract entitles the nonbreaching party to sue for monetary damages. As discussed in Chapter 4, tort law damages are designed to compensate a party for harm suffered as a result of another's wrongful act. In the context of contract law, damages compensate the nonbreaching party for the loss of the bargain. Often, courts say that innocent parties are to be placed in the position they would have occupied had the contract been fully performed.[1]

Realize at the outset, though, that collecting damages through a court judgment requires litigation, which can be expensive and time consuming. Also keep in mind that court judgments are often difficult to enforce, particularly if the breaching party does not have sufficient assets to pay the damages awarded. For these reasons, most parties settle their lawsuits for damages (or other remedies) prior to trial.

Types of Damages

There are four broad categories of damages:

1. Compensatory (to cover direct losses and costs).

2. Consequential (to cover indirect and foreseeable losses).
3. Punitive (to punish and deter wrongdoing).
4. Nominal (to recognize wrongdoing when no monetary loss is shown).

Compensatory and punitive damages were discussed in Chapter 4 in the context of tort law. Here, we look at these types of damages, as well as consequential and nominal damages, in the context of contract law.

COMPENSATORY DAMAGES Damages that compensate the nonbreaching party for the *loss of the bargain* are known as *compensatory damages.* These damages compensate the injured party only for damages actually sustained and proved to have arisen directly from the loss of the bargain caused by the breach of contract. They simply replace what was lost because of the wrong or damage and, for this reason, are often said to "make the person whole."

Can an award of damages for a breach of contract elevate the nonbreaching party to a better position than he or she would have been in if the contract had not been breached? That was the question in the following case.

---

1. *Restatement (Second) of Contracts,* Section 347.

279

CASE ANALYSIS

Case 14.1 Hallmark Cards, Inc. v. Murley

United States Court of Appeals, Eighth Circuit, 703 F.3d 456 (2013).

IN THE LANGUAGE OF THE COURT

BYE, Circuit Judge.

* * * *

[Janet] Murley served as [Hallmark Cards, Inc.'s] vice-president of marketing from 1999 to 2002. In this capacity, she was responsible for product and business development, advertising, and research, and had access to confidential information including Hallmark's business plans, market research, and financial information. In 2002, Hallmark eliminated Murley's position as part of a corporate restructuring. Murley and Hallmark entered into a negotiated separation agreement which laid out the terms of Murley's departure. Pursuant to the agreement, Murley agreed not to work in the greeting card or gift industry for a period of eighteen months, solicit Hallmark employees, disclose or use any proprietary or confidential information, or retain any business records or documents relating to Hallmark. She also agreed to release Hallmark from any claims arising from her termination. In exchange, Hallmark offered Murley a $735,000 severance payment, eighteen months of paid COBRA benefits, executive outplacement services, and paid tax preparation for two years.

In 2006, after the expiration of her non-compete agreement, Murley accepted a consulting assignment with Recycled Paper Greetings ("RPG") for $125,000. Murley admits that in the course of that assignment, she disclosed to RPG confidential Hallmark information including

slides from Hallmark's business model redesign, information regarding Hallmark's consumer buying process, and long-term industry analysis gathered from Hallmark's market research. Hallmark was unaware of Murley's disclosures until 2009, when RPG was purchased by American Greetings. Prior to the closing of that sale, American Greetings contacted Hallmark to arrange a third-party review of RPG's records to ensure none of Hallmark's confidential information was contained therein. The third-party reviewer uncovered a number of Hallmark's documents in the records and alerted Hallmark to its findings.

On May 14, 2009, Hallmark filed suit [in a federal district court] against Murley, alleging breach of contract.

Hallmark sought damages of $860,000, consisting of the $735,000 severance payment it made to Hurley under the parties' 2002 agreement and the $125,000 Murley received from RPG in exchange for her consulting services. * * * The jury returned a verdict in Hallmark's favor and awarded it exactly $860,000 in damages.

* * * This appeal followed.

* * * *

With respect to the $735,000, Murley contends Hallmark was not entitled to a return of its full payment under the parties' separation agreement because Murley fulfilled several material terms of that agreement (e.g., the release of liability and non-compete provisions). Under the circumstances, we cannot characterize the jury's reimbursement of Hallmark's original payment under the separation agreement as grossly excessive or glar-

ingly unwarranted by the evidence. Hallmark's terms under the separation agreement clearly indicated its priority in preserving confidentiality. At trial, Hallmark presented ample evidence that Murley not only retained but disclosed Hallmark's confidential materials to a competitor in violation of the terms and primary purpose of that agreement. Thus, the jury's determination that Hallmark was entitled to a full refund of its $735,000 is not against the weight of the evidence.

With respect to the remaining $125,000 of the jury award, Murley argues Hallmark can claim no entitlement to her compensation by RPG for consulting services unrelated to Hallmark. We agree. *In an action for breach of contract, a plaintiff may recover the benefit of his or her bargain as well as damages naturally and proximately caused by the breach and damages that could have been reasonably contemplated by the defendant at the time of the agreement.* Moreover, the law cannot elevate the non-breaching party to a better position than she would have enjoyed had the contract been completed on both sides. By awarding Hallmark more than its $735,000 severance payment, the jury award placed Hallmark in a better position than it would find itself had Murley not breached the agreement. The jury's award of the $125,000 payment by RPG was, therefore, improper. We vacate the award and remand for the district court to reduce the fee award appropriately. [Emphasis added.]

* * * *

* * * So modified, the judgment will stand affirmed.

LEGAL REASONING QUESTIONS

1. What are compensatory damages? What is the standard measure of compensatory damages?

2. In this case, what was the basis for Hallmark's suit against Murley? How much did Hallmark seek to recover in the form of damages?

CASE 14.1 CONTINUED

3. What were Murley's arguments against the amount of damages that Hallmark requested?

4. Did the court award Hallmark the amount that it sought in damages? Why or why not?

Standard Measure. The standard measure of compensatory damages is the difference between the value of the breaching party's promised performance under the contract and the value of her or his actual performance. This amount is reduced by any loss that the injured party has avoided, however.

INSIGHT INTO SOCIAL MEDIA
Was Instagram's Revision of Its Terms of Service a Breach of Contract?

In 2012, Facebook acquired the social networking site Instagram for $715 million. Instagram is a photo-sharing service that also allows users to add filters and effects to the photos.

The Terms of Service Are a Contract

When you use social media or other services on the Internet or download an app for your mobile devices, you normally have to indicate that you accept the terms of service associated with that service or app. Of course, users rarely, if ever, actually read those terms. They simply click on "accept" and start using the service. By clicking on "accept," however, those users are entering into a contract.

Instagram Changes Its Terms of Service

In 2013, to the consternation of a number of users, Instagram changed its terms of service to give it the right and ability to transfer and otherwise use user content on the site, apparently without compensation. The new terms also limited users' ability to bring class-action lawsuits against Instagram, limited the damages they could recover to $100, and required arbitration of any disputes.

Lucy Funes, an Instagram user in California, filed a class-action lawsuit on behalf of herself and other users, claiming breach of contract and breach of the covenant of good faith and fair dealing that a contract implies.[a] Although Instagram subsequently modified the language that appeared to give it the right to use users' photos without compensation, it retained other controversial terms, including the mandatory arbitration clause and a provision allowing it to place ads in conjunction with user content.

Instagram Seeks Dismissal of the Lawsuit

While Funes is contending that Instagram breached their contract by changing its terms of service, Instagram argues that Funes cannot claim breach of contract. The reason is that she—and other users—were given thirty days' notice before the new terms of service took effect. Because Funes continued to use her account after that thirty-day period, Instagram maintains that, in effect, she agreed to the new terms.

Behind the Change in Terms of Service

In revising its terms of service, Instagram, or rather its new owner Facebook, was trying to monetize, or find a way to make revenue, from the many users of its site. A challenge for Facebook is how to translate its billions of users into profits. This challenge has become particularly acute for Facebook since its initial public offering in 2012. Now that it is a public company, Facebook must answer to its shareholders.

Facebook has faced a number of class-action lawsuits, including an ongoing suit for $15 billion from users who claim that Facebook has been "improperly tracking the Internet use of its members even after they have logged out of their accounts." As Facebook tries to increase its profits to please its shareholders, it is likely to face even more lawsuits from users who resent the company's efforts to monetize the content on its site.

LEGAL CRITICAL THINKING

INSIGHT INTO THE ETHICAL ENVIRONMENT

Within Instagram's current terms of service there is a statement, "We may not always identify paid services, sponsored content, or commercial communications as such." Is it ethical for Instagram to act this way? Discuss.

---

a. *Funes v. Instagram, Inc.,* 3:12-CV06482-WHA (N.D.Cal. 2012).

▶ **Example 14.1** Randall contracts to perform certain services exclusively for Hernandez during the month of March for $4,000. Hernandez cancels the contract and is in breach. Randall is able to find another job during March but can earn only $3,000. He can sue Hernandez for breach and recover $1,000 as compensatory damages. Randall can also recover from Hernandez the amount that he spent to find the other job. ◀

Expenses that are caused directly by a breach of contract—such as those incurred to obtain performance from another source—are known as **incidental damages.** Note that the measure of compensatory damages often varies by type of contract. Certain types of contracts deserve special mention.

Sale of Goods. In a contract for the sale of goods, the usual measure of compensatory damages is an amount equal to the difference between the contract price and the market price.[2] ▶ **Example 14.2** Medik Laboratories contracts to buy ten model UTS network servers from Cal Industries for $4,000 each. Cal Industries, however, fails to deliver the ten servers to Medik. The market price of the servers at the time Medik learns of the breach is $4,500. Therefore, Medik's measure of damages is $5,000 (10 × $500), plus any incidental damages (expenses) caused by the breach. ◀

When the buyer breaches and the seller has not yet produced the goods, compensatory damages normally equal lost profits on the sale, not the difference between the contract price and the market price.

Sale of Land. Ordinarily, because each parcel of land is unique, the remedy for a seller's breach of a contract for a sale of real estate is specific performance. The buyer is awarded the parcel of property for which she or he bargained (*specific performance* will be discussed more fully later in this chapter). When the buyer is the party in breach, the measure of damages is typically the difference between the contract price and the market price of the land. The same measure is used when specific performance is not available (because the seller has sold the property to someone else, for example). The majority of states follow this rule.

A minority of states follow a different rule when the seller breaches the contract and the breach is not deliberate (intentional).[3] These states limit the prospective buyer's damages to a refund of any down payment made plus any expenses incurred (such as fees for title searches, attorneys, and escrows). Thus, the minority rule effectively returns purchasers to the positions they occupied prior to the sale, rather than giving them the benefit of the bargain.

Construction Contracts. The measure of damages in a building or construction contract varies depending on which party breaches and when the breach occurs.

1. *Breach by owner.* The owner may breach at three different stages—before performance has begun, during performance, or after performance has been completed. If the owner breaches *before performance has begun,* the contractor can recover only the profits that would have been made on the contract (that is, the total contract price less the cost of materials and labor).

   If the owner breaches *during performance,* the contractor can recover the profits plus the costs incurred in partially constructing the building. If the owner breaches *after the construction has been completed,* the contractor can recover the entire contract price, plus interest.

2. *Breach by contractor.* When the construction contractor breaches the contract—either by failing to begin construction or by stopping work partway through the project—the measure of damages is the cost of completion. The cost of completion includes reasonable compensation for any delay in performance. If the contractor finishes late, the measure of damages is the loss of use.

3. *Breach by both owner and contractor.* When the performance of both parties—the construction contractor and the owner—falls short of what their contract required, the courts attempt to strike a fair balance in awarding damages.

   ▶ **Case in Point 14.3** Jamison Well Drilling, Inc., contracted to drill a well for Ed Pfeifer for $4,130. Jamison drilled the well and installed a storage tank. The well did not comply with state health department requirements, however, and failed repeated tests for bacteria. The health department ordered the well to be abandoned and sealed. Pfeifer used the storage tank but paid Jamison nothing. Jamison filed a suit to

---

2. More specifically, the amount is the difference between the contract price and the market price at the time and place at which the goods were to be delivered or tendered. See Sections 2–708 and 2–713 of the Uniform Commercial Code (UCC).

3. "Deliberate" breaches include the seller's failure to convey (transfer title to) the land because the market price has gone up. "Nondeliberate" breaches include the seller's failure to convey the land because of a problem with the title, such as the discovery of an unknown *easement* that gives another party a right of use over the property.

EXHIBIT 14-1 Measurement of Damages—Breach of Construction Contracts

Party in Breach	Time of Breach	Measurement of Damages
Owner	Before construction has begun.	Profits (contract price less cost of materials and labor).
Owner	During construction.	Profits, plus costs incurred up to time of breach.
Owner	After construction is completed.	Full contract price, plus interest.
Contractor	Before construction has begun.	Cost in excess of contract price to complete work.
Contractor	Before construction is completed.	Generally, all costs incurred by owner to complete.

recover. The court held that Jamison was entitled to $970 for the storage tank but was not entitled to the full contract price because the well was not usable.[4] ◄

The rules concerning the measurement of damages in breached construction contracts are summarized in Exhibit 14–1 above.

Construction Contracts and Economic Waste. If the contractor substantially performs, a court may use the cost-of-completion formula, but only if requiring completion will not entail unreasonable economic waste. *Economic waste* occurs when the cost of repairing or completing the performance as required by the contract greatly outweighs the benefit to the owner.

▶ **Example 14.4** Halverson Contracting discovers that it will cost $20,000 to move a large coral rock eleven inches as specified in the contract. Changing the rock's position will alter the appearance of the project only slightly. In this situation, a court would likely conclude that full completion would involve economic waste. Thus, the contractor will not be required to incur addition $20,000 in expenses to complete performance. ◄

CONSEQUENTIAL DAMAGES Foreseeable damages that result from a party's breach of contract are called **consequential damages,** or *special damages*. They

---
4. *Jamison Well Drilling, Inc. v. Pfeifer,* 2011 Ohio 521 (2011).

differ from compensatory damages in that they are caused by special circumstances beyond the contract itself. They flow from the consequences, or results, of a breach. When a seller fails to deliver goods, knowing that the buyer is planning to use or resell those goods immediately, a court may award consequential damages for the loss of profits from the planned resale.

▶ **Example 14.5** Marty contracts to buy a certain quantity of Quench, a specialty sports drink, from Nathan. Nathan knows that Marty has contracted with Ruthie to resell and ship the Quench within hours of its receipt. The beverage will then be sold to fans attending the Super Bowl. Nathan fails to timely deliver the Quench. Marty can recover the consequential damages—the loss of profits from the planned resale to Ruthie—caused by the nondelivery. (If Marty purchases Quench from another vender, he can also recover compensatory damages for the difference between the contract price and the market price.) ◄

For the nonbreaching party to recover consequential damages, the breaching party must have known (or had reason to know) that special circumstances would cause the nonbreaching party to suffer an additional loss. This rule was enunciated in the following *Classic Case.* In reading this decision, it is helpful to understand that in the mid-nineteenth century, large flour mills customarily kept more than one main crankshaft on hand in the event that one broke and had to be repaired.

CLASSIC CASE 14.2

Hadley v. Baxendale
Court of Exchequer, 156 Eng.Rep. 145 (1854).

BACKGROUND AND FACTS The Hadleys (the plaintiffs) ran a flour mill in Gloucester, England. The main crankshaft attached to the steam engine in the mill broke, causing the mill to shut down. The crankshaft had to be sent to a foundry located in Greenwich so that a new shaft could be made to fit the other parts of the engine. Baxendale, the defendant, was a common carrier that transported the shaft from

CASE 14.2 CONTINUES ▶

CASE 14.2 CONTINUED Gloucester to Greenwich. The freight charges were collected in advance, and Baxendale promised to deliver the shaft the following day. It was not delivered for a number of days, however. As a consequence, the mill was closed for several days. The Hadleys sued to recover the profits lost during that time. Baxendale contended that the loss of profits was "too remote" to be recoverable. The court held for the plaintiffs, and the jury was allowed to take into consideration the lost profits. The defendant appealed.

IN THE LANGUAGE OF THE COURT
ALDERSON, J. [Judge]

* * * *

* * * Where two parties have made a contract which one of them has broken, the damages which the other party ought to receive in respect of such breach of contract should be such as may fairly and reasonably be considered either arising naturally, [that is,] according to the usual course of things, from such breach of contract itself, or such as may reasonably be supposed to have been in the contemplation of both parties, at the time they made the contract, as the probable result of the breach of it. Now, if the special circumstances under which the contract was actually made were communicated by the plaintiffs to the defendants, and thus known to both parties, the damages resulting from the breach of such a contract, *which they would reasonably contemplate,* would be the amount of injury which would ordinarily follow from a breach of contract under these special circumstances so known and communicated. * * * Now, in the present case, if we are to apply the principles above laid down, we find that the only circumstances here communicated by the plaintiffs to the defendants at the time the contract was made, were, that the article to be carried was the broken shaft of a mill, and that the plaintiffs were the millers of that mill. * * * Special circumstances were here never communicated by the plaintiffs to the defendants. It follows, therefore, that the loss of profits here cannot reasonably be considered such a consequence of the breach of contract as could have been fairly and reasonably contemplated by both the parties when they made this contract. [Emphasis added.]

DECISION AND REMEDY *The Court of Exchequer ordered a new trial. According to the court, to collect consequential damages, the plaintiffs would have to have given express notice of the special circumstances that caused the loss of profits.*

THE E-COMMERCE DIMENSION *If a Web merchant loses business due to a computer system's failure that can be attributed to malfunctioning software, can the merchant recover the lost profits from the software maker? Explain.*

IMPACT OF THIS CASE ON TODAY'S LAW *This case established the rule that consequential damages are awarded only for injuries that the defendant could reasonably have foreseen as a probable result of the usual course of events following a breach. Today, the rule enunciated by the court in this case still applies. To recover consequential damages, the plaintiff must show that the defendant had reason to know or foresee that a particular loss or injury would occur.*

PUNITIVE DAMAGES Punitive damages generally are not awarded in lawsuits for breach of contract. Because punitive damages are designed to punish a wrongdoer and set an example to deter similar conduct in the future, they have no legitimate place in contract law. A contract is simply a civil relationship between the parties. The law may compensate one party for the loss of the bargain—no more and no less. When a person's actions cause both a breach of contract and a tort (such as fraud), punitive damages may be available. Overall, though, punitive damages are almost never available in contract disputes.

NOMINAL DAMAGES When no actual damage or financial loss results from a breach of contract and only a technical injury is involved, the court may award **nominal damages** to the innocent party. Awards of nominal damages are often small, such as one dollar, but they do establish that the defendant acted wrongfully. Most lawsuits for nominal damages are brought as a matter of principle under the theory that a breach has occurred and some damages must be imposed regardless of actual loss.

▶ **Example 14.6**   Jackson contracts to buy potatoes from Stanley at fifty cents a pound. Stanley breaches the contract and does not deliver the potatoes. In the meantime, the price of potatoes has fallen. Jackson is able to buy them in the open market at half the price he contracted for with Stanley. He is clearly better off because of Stanley's breach. Thus, because Jackson sustained only a technical injury and suffered no monetary loss, he is likely to be awarded only nominal damages if he brings a suit for breach of contract. ◀

Mitigation of Damages

In most situations, when a breach of contract occurs, the innocent injured party is held to a duty to mitigate, or reduce, the damages that he or she suffers. Under this doctrine of **mitigation of damages,** the duty owed depends on the nature of the contract.

RENTAL AGREEMENTS   Some states require a landlord to use reasonable means to find a new tenant if a tenant abandons the premises and fails to pay rent. If an acceptable tenant is found, the landlord is required to lease the premises to this tenant to mitigate the damages recoverable from the former tenant.

The former tenant is still liable for the difference between the amount of the rent under the original lease and the rent received from the new tenant. If the landlord has not taken reasonable steps to find a new tenant, a court will likely reduce any award made by the amount of rent the landlord could have received had he or she done so.

EMPLOYMENT CONTRACTS   In the majority of states, a person whose employment has been wrongfully terminated owes a duty to mitigate the damages suffered because of the employer's breach of the employment contract. In other words, a wrongfully terminated employee has a duty to take a similar job if one is available. If the employee fails to do this, the damages awarded will be equivalent to the person's former salary less the income he or she would have received in a similar job obtained by reasonable means.

The employer has the burden of proving that such a job existed and that the employee could have been hired. Normally, the employee is under no duty to take a job of a different type and rank.

Liquidated Damages versus Penalties

A **liquidated damages** provision in a contract specifies that a certain dollar amount is to be paid in the event of a *future* default or breach of contract. (*Liquidated* means determined, settled, or fixed.)

Liquidated damages differ from penalties. Although a **penalty** also specifies a certain amount to be paid in the event of a default or breach of contract, it is designed to penalize the breaching party, not to make the innocent party whole. Liquidated damages provisions usually are enforceable. In contrast, if a court finds that a provision calls for a penalty, the agreement as to the amount will not be enforced, and recovery will be limited to actual damages.

ENFORCEABILITY   To determine if a particular provision is for liquidated damages or for a penalty, a court must answer two questions:

1. When the contract was entered into, was it apparent that damages would be difficult to estimate in the event of a breach?
2. Was the amount set as damages a reasonable estimate and not excessive?[5]

If the answers to both questions are yes, the provision normally will be enforced. If either answer is no, the provision usually will not be enforced.

▶ **Case in Point 14.7**   James Haber contracted with B-Sharp Musical Productions, Inc., to provide a particular band to perform at his son's bar mitzvah for $30,000. The contract contained a liquidated damages clause under which if Haber canceled within ninety days of the date of the bar mitzvah, he would still owe $30,000 to B-Sharp. If he canceled more than ninety days beforehand, Haber would owe B-Sharp half of that amount ($15,000).

Haber canceled less than ninety days before the bar mitzvah and refused to pay B-Sharp the $25,000 balance due under the contract. B-Sharp sued. The court held that the liquidated damages clause was enforceable. The court reasoned that the expense and possibility of rebooking a canceled performance could not be determined at the time of contracting and that the clause provided a reasonable amount of damages.[6] ◀

---

5. *Restatement (Second) of Contracts,* Section 356(1).
6. *B-Sharp Musical Productions, Inc. v. Haber,* 27 Misc.3d 41, 899 N.Y.S.2d 792 (2010).

LIQUIDATED DAMAGES COMMON IN CERTAIN CONTRACTS Liquidated damages provisions are frequently used in construction contracts. For instance, a provision requiring a construction contractor to pay $300 for every day he or she is late in completing the project is a liquidated damages provision.

Such provisions are also common in contracts for the sale of goods.[7] In addition, contracts with entertainers and professional athletes often include liquidated damages provisions. ▶ **Example 14.8**   A television network settled its contract dispute with *Tonight Show* host Conan O'Brien for $33 million. The amount of the settlement was somewhat less than the $40 million O'Brien could have received under a liquidated damages clause in his contract. ◀

SECTION 2
EQUITABLE REMEDIES

Sometimes, damages are an inadequate remedy for a breach of contract. In these situations, the nonbreaching party may ask the court for an equitable remedy. Equitable remedies include rescission and restitution, specific performance, and reformation.

Rescission and Restitution

As discussed in Chapter 13, *rescission* is essentially an action to undo, or terminate, a contract—to return the contracting parties to the positions they occupied prior to the transaction.[8] When fraud, a mistake, duress, undue influence, misrepresentation, or lack of capacity to contract is present, unilateral rescission is available. Rescission may also be available by statute.[9] The failure of one party to perform entitles the other party to rescind the contract. The rescinding party must give prompt notice to the breaching party.

RESTITUTION Generally, to rescind a contract, both parties must make **restitution** to each other by returning goods, property, or funds previously conveyed.[10] If the property or goods can be returned, they must be. If the goods or property have been consumed, restitution must be made in an equivalent dollar amount.

Essentially, restitution involves the plaintiff's recapture of a benefit conferred on the defendant that has unjustly enriched her or him. ▶ **Example 14.9**   Katie contracts with Mikhail to design a house for her. Katie pays Mikhail $9,000 and agrees to make two more payments of $9,000 (for a total of $27,000) as the design progresses. The next day, Mikhail calls Katie and tells her that he has taken a position with a large architectural firm in another state and cannot design the house. Katie decides to hire another architect that afternoon. Katie can obtain restitution of the $9,000. ◀

RESTITUTION IS NOT LIMITED TO RESCISSION CASES Restitution may be appropriate when a contract is rescinded, but the right to restitution is not limited to rescission cases. Because an award of restitution basically returns something to its rightful owner, a party can seek restitution in actions for breach of contract, tort actions, and other types of actions.

Restitution can be obtained when funds or property have been transferred by mistake or because of fraud or incapacity. Similarly, restitution might be available when there has been misconduct by a party in a confidential or other special relationship. Even in criminal cases, a court can order restitution of funds or property obtained through embezzlement, conversion, theft, or copyright infringement.

Specific Performance

The equitable remedy of **specific performance** calls for the performance of the act promised in the contract. This remedy is attractive to a nonbreaching party because it provides the exact bargain promised in the contract. It also avoids some of the problems inherent in a suit for damages, such as collecting a judgment and arranging another contract. In addition, the actual performance may be more valuable than the monetary damages.

Normally, however, specific performance will not be granted unless the party's legal remedy (monetary damages) is inadequate.[11] For this reason, contracts for the sale of goods rarely qualify for specific performance. The legal remedy—monetary damages—is ordinarily

---

7. Section 2–718(1) of the UCC specifically authorizes the use of liquidated damages provisions.

8. The rescission discussed here is *unilateral* rescission, in which only one party wants to undo the contract. In mutual rescission, which was discussed in Chapter 13, both parties agree to undo the contract. Mutual rescission discharges the contract. Unilateral rescission generally is available as a remedy for breach of contract.

9. Many states have statutes allowing individuals who enter "home solicitation contracts" to rescind those contracts within three business days for any reason. See, for example, California Civil Code Section 1689.5.

10. *Restatement (Second) of Contracts*, Section 370.

11. *Restatement (Second) of Contracts*, Section 359.

adequate in such situations because substantially identical goods can be bought or sold in the market. Only if the goods are unique will a court grant specific performance. For instance, paintings, sculptures, or rare books or coins are so unique that monetary damages will not enable a buyer to obtain substantially identical substitutes in the market.

SALE OF LAND A court may grant specific performance to a buyer in an action for a breach of contract involving the sale of land. In this situation, the legal remedy of monetary damages may not compensate the buyer adequately because every parcel of land is unique: the same land in the same location obviously cannot be obtained elsewhere. Only when specific performance is unavailable (such as when the seller has sold the property to someone else) will monetary damages be awarded instead.

▶ **Case in Point 14.10**   Howard Stainbrook entered into a contract to sell Trent Low forty acres of mostly timbered land for $45,000. Low agreed to pay for a survey of the property and other costs in addition to the price. He gave Stainbrook a check for $1,000 to show his intent to fulfill the contract. One month later, Stainbrook died. His son David became the executor of the estate. After he discovered that the timber on the property was worth more than $100,000, David asked Low to withdraw his offer to buy the forty acres. Low refused and filed a suit against David seeking specific performance of the contract. The court found that because Low had substantially performed his obligations under the contract and offered to perform the rest, he was entitled to specific performance.[12] ◀

CONTRACTS FOR PERSONAL SERVICES Contracts for personal services require one party to work personally for another party. Courts generally refuse to grant specific performance of personal-service contracts because to order a party to perform personal services against his or her will amounts to a type of involuntary servitude.[13]

Moreover, the courts do not want to monitor contracts for personal services, which usually require the exercise of personal judgment or talent. ▶ **Example 14.11**   Nicole contracts with a surgeon to perform surgery to remove a tumor on her brain. If he refuses, the court would not compel (nor would Nicole want) the surgeon to perform under those circumstances. A court cannot ensure meaningful performance in such a situation.[14] ◀

If a contract is not deemed personal, the remedy at law of monetary damages may be adequate if substantially identical service (such as lawn mowing) is available from other persons.

Reformation

Reformation is an equitable remedy used when the parties have *imperfectly* expressed their agreement in writing. Reformation allows a court to rewrite the contract to reflect the parties' true intentions.

Exhibit 14–2 on the following page graphically summarizes the remedies, including reformation, that are available to the nonbreaching party.

WHEN FRAUD OR MUTUAL MISTAKE IS PRESENT Courts order reformation most often when fraud or mutual mistake (for example, a clerical error) is present. Typically, a party seeks reformation so that some other remedy may then be pursued.

▶ **Example 14.12**   If Carson contracts to buy a forklift from Yoshie but their contract mistakenly refers to a crane, a mutual mistake has occurred (see Chapter 12). Accordingly, a court can reform the contract so that it conforms to the parties' intentions and accurately refers to the forklift being sold. ◀

WRITTEN CONTRACT INCORRECTLY STATES THE PARTIES' ORAL AGREEMENT A court will also reform a contract when two parties enter into a binding oral contract but later make an error when they attempt to put the terms into writing. Normally, a court will allow into evidence the correct terms of the oral contract, thereby reforming the written contract.

COVENANTS NOT TO COMPETE Courts also may reform contracts when the parties have executed a written covenant not to compete (discussed in Chapter 11). If the covenant is for a valid and legitimate purpose (such as the sale of a business) but the area or time restraints of the covenant are unreasonable, reformation may occur. Some courts will reform the restraints by making them reasonable and then

---

12. *Stainbrook v. Low,* 842 N.E.2d 386 (Ind.App. 2006).
13. Involuntary servitude, or slavery, is contrary to the public policy expressed in the Thirteenth Amendment to the U.S. Constitution. A court can, however, enter an order (injunction) prohibiting a person who breached a personal-service contract from engaging in similar contracts for a period of time in the future.

14. Similarly, courts often refuse to order specific performance of construction contracts because courts are not set up to operate as construction supervisors or engineers.

EXHIBIT 14-2 Remedies for Breach of Contract

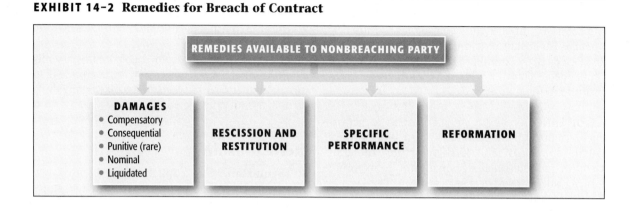

will enforce the entire contract as reformed. Other courts, however, will throw out the entire restrictive covenant as illegal.

In the following case, a physician claimed that the covenant not to compete he signed was unreasonable and should therefore be declared illegal.

CASE 14.3

Emerick v. Cardiac Study Center, Inc.
Court of Appeals of Washington, 166 Wash.App. 1039 (2012).

BACKGROUND AND FACTS Cardiac Study Center is a medical practice group of approximately fifteen cardiologists. In 2002, Cardiac hired Dr. Robert Emerick as an employee. In 2004, Emerick became a shareholder of Cardiac. He signed a shareholder agreement and an employment contract that included a covenant not to compete. Under the covenant, any physician who left the group would have to promise not to practice competitively in the surrounding area for a period of five years. In 2005, patients and other medical providers began to complain to Cardiac about Emerick's conduct. Some physicians stopped referring patients to Cardiac as a result. Finally, Cardiac terminated Emerick's employment in 2009. Emerick sued Cardiac seeking a declaration that the covenant not to compete was unenforceable. He prevailed at trial, and Cardiac appealed.

 IN THE LANGUAGE OF THE COURT
ARMSTRONG, P.J. [Presiding Judge]

* * * *

* * * *Courts will enforce a covenant not to compete if it is reasonable and lawful.* We test reasonableness by asking (1) whether the restraint is necessary to protect the employer's business or goodwill, (2) whether it imposes on the employee any greater restraint than is reasonably necessary to secure the employer's business or goodwill, and (3) whether enforcing the covenant would injure the public through loss of the employee's service and skill to the extent that the court should not enforce the covenant, [that is,] whether it violates public policy. [Emphasis added.]

* * * Specifically, an employer has a "legitimate interest in protecting its existing client base" and in prohibiting the employee from taking its clients.

* * * Cardiac provided Emerick with an immediate client base and established referral sources when he moved to the area. Moreover, Emerick had access to Cardiac's business model and goodwill. These are all protectable business interests that the trial court should have considered in assessing the covenant's enforceability.

CASE 14.3 CONTINUED

DECISION AND REMEDY *The state appellate court ruled in favor of Cardiac Study Center. The court reversed and remanded the trial court's decision and held that the covenant not to compete was reasonable.*

THE GLOBAL DIMENSION *Should an employer be able to restrict a former employee from engaging in a competing business on a global level? Why or why not?*

WHAT IF THE FACTS WERE DIFFERENT? *Suppose that Emerick had authored a nationally published book,* How to Avoid Cardiac Surgery through Diet and Exercise. *Could Cardiac have blocked the book's distribution in Cardiac's area based on the covenant not to compete?*

SECTION 3
RECOVERY BASED ON QUASI CONTRACT

In some situations, when no actual contract exists, a court may step in to prevent one party from being unjustly enriched at the expense of another party. As discussed in Chapter 9, quasi contract is a legal theory under which an obligation is imposed in the absence of an agreement.

The legal obligation arises because the law considers that the party accepting the benefits has made an implied promise to pay for them. Generally, when one party has conferred a benefit on another party, justice requires that the party receiving the benefit pay the reasonable value for it. The party conferring the benefit can recover in *quantum meruit,* which means "as much as he or she deserves."

When Quasi Contract Is Used

Quasi contract allows a court to act as if a contract exists when there is no actual contract or agreement between the parties. A court can also use this theory when the parties entered into a contract, but it is unenforceable for some reason.

Quasi-contractual recovery is often granted when one party has partially performed under a contract that is unenforceable. It provides an alternative to suing for damages and allows the party to recover the reasonable value of the partial performance. Depending on the case, the amount of the recovery may be measured either by the benefit received or by the detriment suffered.

▶ **Example 14.13** Ericson contracts to build two oil derricks for Petro Industries. The derricks are to be built over a period of three years, but the parties do not make a written contract. Thus, the writing requirement will bar enforcement of the contract.[15] After Ericson completes one derrick, Petro Industries informs him that it will not pay for the derrick. Ericson can sue Petro Industries under the theory of quasi contract. ◀

The Requirements of Quasi Contract

To recover under the theory of quasi contract, the party seeking recovery must show the following:

1. The party has conferred a benefit on the other party.
2. The party conferred the benefit with the reasonable expectation of being paid.
3. The party did not act as a volunteer in conferring the benefit.
4. The party receiving the benefit would be unjustly enriched if allowed to retain the benefit without paying for it.

Applying these requirements to *Example 14.13,* Ericson can sue in quasi contract because all of the conditions for quasi-contractual recovery have been fulfilled. Ericson conferred a benefit on Petro Industries by building the oil derrick. Ericson built the derrick with the reasonable expectation of being paid. He was not intending to act as a volunteer. The derrick conferred an obvious benefit on Petro Industries. Petro Industries would be unjustly enriched if it was allowed to keep the derrick without paying Ericson for the work. Therefore, Ericson should be able to recover in *quantum meruit* the reasonable value of the oil derrick that was built, which is ordinarily equal to its fair market value.

Concept Summary 14.1 on the following page reviews all of the equitable remedies, including quasi

---

15. Contracts that by their terms cannot be performed within one year must be in writing to be enforceable (see Chapter 12).

CONCEPT SUMMARY 14.1
Equitable Remedies

REMEDY	DESCRIPTION
Rescission and Restitution	1. *Rescission*—A remedy whereby a contract is canceled and the parties are restored to the original positions that they occupied prior to the transaction. 2. *Restitution*—When a contract is rescinded, both parties must make restitution to each other by returning the goods, property, or funds previously conveyed.
Specific Performance	An equitable remedy calling for the performance of the act promised in the contract. Only available when monetary damages would be inadequate—such as in contracts for the sale of land or unique goods—and never available in personal-service contracts.
Reformation	An equitable remedy allowing a contract to be reformed, or rewritten, to reflect the parties' true intentions. Available when an agreement is imperfectly expressed in writing, such as when a mutual mistake has occurred.
Recovery Based on Quasi Contract	An equitable theory under which a party who confers a benefit on another with the reasonable expectation of being paid can seek a court order for the fair market value of the benefit conferred.

contract, that may be available in the event that a contract is breached.

SECTION 4
WAIVER OF BREACH

Under certain circumstances, a nonbreaching party may be willing to accept a defective performance of the contract. This knowing relinquishment of a legal right (that is, the right to require satisfactory and full performance) is called a **waiver.**

Consequences of a Waiver of Breach

When a waiver of a breach of contract occurs, the party waiving the breach cannot take any later action on it. In effect, the waiver erases the past breach, and the contract continues as if the breach had never occurred. Of course, the waiver of breach of contract extends only to the matter waived and not to the whole contract.

Reasons for Waiving a Breach

Businesspersons often waive breaches of contract to obtain whatever benefit is still possible out of the contract. For instance, a seller contracts with a buyer to deliver to the buyer ten thousand tons of coal on or before November 1. The contract calls for the buyer to pay by November 10 for coal delivered. Because of a coal miners' strike, coal is hard to find. The seller breaches the contract by not tendering delivery until November 5. The buyer will likely choose to waive the seller's breach, accept delivery of the coal, and pay as contracted.

Waiver of Breach and Subsequent Breaches

Ordinarily, a waiver by a contracting party will not operate to waive subsequent, additional, or future breaches of contract. This is always true when the subsequent breaches are unrelated to the first breach. ▶ **Example 14.14** Ashton owns a multimillion-dollar apartment complex that is under construction. Ashton allows the contractor to complete a stage of construction late. By doing so, Ashton waives his right to sue for the delay. Ashton does not, however, waive the right to sue for failure to comply with engineering specifications on the same job. ◀

PATTERN-OF-CONDUCT EXCEPTION A waiver can extend to subsequent defective performance if a reasonable person would conclude that similar defective performance in the future will be acceptable. Therefore, a *pattern of conduct* that waives a number of successive breaches will operate as a continued waiver. To change this result, the nonbreaching party should give notice to the breaching party that full performance will be required in the future.

EFFECT ON THE CONTRACT The party who has rendered defective or less-than-full performance remains liable for the damages caused by the breach of contract. In effect, the waiver operates to keep the contract going. The waiver prevents the nonbreaching party from declaring the contract at an end or rescinding the contract. The contract continues, but the nonbreaching party can recover damages caused by the defective or less-than-full performance.

SECTION 5
CONTRACT PROVISIONS LIMITING REMEDIES

A contract may include provisions stating that no damages can be recovered for certain types of breaches or that damages will be limited to a maximum amount. The contract may also provide that the only remedy for breach is replacement, repair, or refund of the purchase price. The contract may also provide that one party can seek injunctive relief if the other party breaches the contract. Provisions stating that no damages can be recovered are called *exculpatory clauses* (see Chapter 11). Provisions that affect the availability of certain remedies are called *limitation-of-liability clauses*.

The UCC Allows Sales Contracts to Limit Remedies

The Uniform Commercial Code (UCC) provides that in a contract for the sale of goods, remedies can be limited. We will examine the UCC provisions on limited remedies in Chapter 16, in the context of the remedies available on the breach of a contract for the sale or lease of goods.[16]

Enforceability of Limitation-of-Liability Clauses

Whether a limitation-of-liability clause in a contract will be enforced depends on the type of breach that is excused by the provision. Normally, a provision excluding liability for fraudulent or intentional injury will not be enforced. Likewise, a clause excluding liability for illegal acts, acts that are contrary to public policy, or violations of law will not be enforced. A clause that excludes liability for negligence may be enforced in some situations when the parties have roughly equal bargaining positions.

▶ **Case in Point 14.15** Engineering Consulting Services, Ltd. (ECS), contracted with RSN Properties, Inc, a real estate developer. ECS was to perform soil studies for $2,200 and render an opinion on the use of septic systems in a particular subdivision being developed. A clause in the contract limited ECS's liability to RSN to the value of the engineering services or the sum of $50,000, whichever was greater.

ECS concluded that most of the lots were suitable for septic systems, so RSN proceeded with the development. RSN constructed the roads and water lines to the subdivision in reliance on ECS's conclusions, which turned out to be incorrect. RSN sued ECS for breach of contract and argued that the limitation of liability was against public policy and unenforceable. The court, however, enforced the limitation-of-liability clause as "a reasonable allocation of risks in an arm's-length business transaction."[17] ◀

---

16. See UCC 2–719(1).
17. *RSN Properties, Inc. v. Engineering Consulting Services, Ltd.*, 301 Ga.App. 52, 686 S.E.2d 853 (2009).

Reviewing: Breach of Contract and Remedies

Kyle Bruno enters a contract with X Entertainment to be a stuntman in a movie. Bruno is widely known as the best motorcycle stuntman in the business, and the movie to be produced, *Xtreme Riders*, has numerous scenes involving high-speed freestyle street-bike stunts. Filming is set to begin August 1 and end by December 1 so that the film can be released the following summer. Both parties to the contract have stipulated that the filming must end on time to capture the profits from the summer movie market. The contract states that Bruno will be paid 10 percent of the net proceeds from the movie for his stunts.

The contract also includes a liquidated damages provision, which specifies that if Bruno breaches the contract, he will owe X Entertainment $1 million. In addition, the contract includes a limitation-of-liability clause stating that if Bruno is injured during filming, X Entertainment's liability is limited to nominal damages. Using the information presented in the chapter, answer the following questions.

1. One day, while Bruno is preparing for a difficult stunt, he gets into an argument with the director and refuses to perform any stunts at all. Can X Entertainment seek specific performance of the contract? Why or why not?

2. Suppose that while performing a high-speed wheelie on a motorcycle, Bruno is injured by the intentionally reckless act of an X Entertainment employee. Will a court be likely to enforce the limitation-of-liability clause? Why or why not?

3. What factors would a court consider to determine whether the $1 million liquidated damages provision constitutes valid damages or is a penalty?

4. Suppose that there was no liquidated damages provision (or the court refused to enforce it) and X Entertainment breached the contract. The breach caused the release of the film to be delayed until after summer. Could Bruno seek consequential (special) damages for lost profits from the summer movie market in that situation? Explain.

DEBATE THIS ... *Courts should always uphold limitation-of-liability clauses, whether or not the two parties to the contract had equal bargaining power.*

Terms and Concepts

consequential damages 283

incidental damages 282

liquidated damages 285

mitigation of damages 285

nominal damages 284

penalty 285

reformation 287

restitution 286

specific performance 286

waiver 290

ExamPrep

Issue Spotters

1. Greg contracts to build a storage shed for Haney, who pays Greg in advance, but Greg completes only half the work. Haney pays Ipswich $500 to finish the shed. If Haney sues Greg, what would be the measure of recovery? **(See pages 279–282.)**

2. Lyle contracts to sell his ranch to Marley, who is to take possession on June 1. Lyle delays the transfer until August 1. Marley incurs expenses in providing for cattle that he bought for the ranch. When they made the contract, Lyle had no reason to know of the cattle. Is Lyle liable for Marley's expenses in providing for the cattle? Why or why not? **(See page 283.)**

• Check your answers to the Issue Spotters against the answers provided in Appendix B at the end of this text.

Before the Test

Go to **www.cengagebrain.com**, enter the ISBN 9781285770192, and click on "Find" to locate this textbook's Web site. Then, click on "Access Now" under "Study Tools," and select Chapter 14 at the top. There, you will find a Practice Quiz that you can take to assess your mastery of the concepts in this chapter, as well as Flashcards and a Glossary of important terms.

Business Scenarios

14–1. Liquidated Damages. Cohen contracts to sell his house and lot to Windsor for $100,000. The terms of the contract call for Windsor to pay 10 percent of the purchase price as a deposit toward the purchase price, or a down payment. The terms further stipulate that if the buyer breaches the contract, Cohen will retain the deposit as liquidated damages.

Windsor pays the deposit, but because her expected financing of the $90,000 balance falls through, she breaches the contract. Two weeks later Cohen sells the house and lot to Ballard for $105,000. Windsor demands her $10,000 back, but Cohen refuses, claiming that Windsor's breach and the contract terms entitle him to keep the deposit. Discuss who is correct. **(See page 285.)**

14-2. Specific Performance. In which of the following situations would specific performance be an appropriate remedy? Discuss fully. **(See page 286.)**

(a) Thompson contracts to sell her house and lot to Cousteau. Then, on finding another buyer willing to pay a higher purchase price, she refuses to deed the property to Cousteau.

(b) Amy contracts to sing and dance in Fred's nightclub for one month, beginning May 1. She then refuses to perform.

(c) Hoffman contracts to purchase a rare coin owned by Erikson, who is breaking up his coin collection. At the last minute, Erikson decides to keep his coin collection intact and refuses to deliver the coin to Hoffman.

(d) ABC Corp. has three shareholders: Panozzo, who owns 48 percent of the stock; Chang, who owns another 48 percent; and Ryan, who owns 4 percent. Ryan contracts to sell her 4 percent to Chang. Later, Ryan refuses to transfer the shares to Chang.

Business Case Problems

14-3. Quasi Contract. Middleton Motors, Inc., a struggling Ford dealership in Madison, Wisconsin, sought managerial and financial assistance from Lindquist Ford, Inc., a successful Ford dealership in Bettendorf, Iowa. While the two dealerships negotiated the terms for the services and a cash infusion, Lindquist sent Craig Miller, its general manager, to assume control of Middleton. After about a year, the parties had not agreed on the terms, Lindquist had not invested any funds, Middleton had not made a profit, and Miller was fired without being paid. Lindquist and Miller filed a suit in a federal district court against Middleton based on quasi contract, seeking to recover Miller's pay for his time. What are the requirements to recover on a theory of quasi contract? Which of these requirements is most likely to be disputed in this case? Why? [*Lindquist Ford, Inc. v. Middleton Motors, Inc.*, 557 F.3d 469 (7th Cir. 2009)] **(See page 289.)**

14-4. Liquidated Damages and Penalties. Planned Pethood Plus, Inc., is a veterinarian-owned clinic. It borrowed $389,000 from KeyBank at an interest rate of 9.3 percent per year for ten years. The loan had a "prepayment penalty" clause that clearly stated that if the loan was repaid early, a specific formula would be used to assess a lump-sum payment to extinguish the obligation. The sooner the loan was paid off, the higher the prepayment penalty. After a year, the veterinarians decided to pay off the loan. KeyBank invoked a prepayment penalty of $40,525.92, which was equal to 10.7 percent of the balance due. The veterinarians sued, contending that the prepayment requirement was unenforceable because it was a penalty. The bank countered that the amount was not a penalty but liquidated damages and that the sum was reasonable. The trial court agreed with the bank, and the veterinarians appealed. Was the loan's prepayment charge reasonable, and should it have been enforced? Why or why not? [*Planned Pethood Plus, Inc. v. KeyCorp, Inc.*, 228 P.3d 262 (Colo.App. 2010)] **(See page 285.)**

14-5. Measure of Damages. Before buying a house, Dean and Donna Testa hired Ground Systems, Inc. (GSI), to inspect the sewage and water disposal system. GSI reported a split system with a watertight septic tank, a wastewater tank, a distribution box, and a leach field. The Testas bought the house. Later, Dean saw that the system was not as GSI described—there was no distribution box or leach field, and there was only one tank, which was not watertight. The Testas arranged for the installation of a new system and sold the house. Assuming that GSI is liable for breach of contract, what is the measure of damages? [*Testa v. Ground Systems, Inc.*, 206 N.J. 330, 20 A.3d 435 (App.Div. 2011)] **(See pages 279–281.)**

14-6. BUSINESS CASE PROBLEM WITH SAMPLE ANSWER: Consequential Damages.

 After submitting the high bid at a foreclosure sale, David Simard entered into a contract to purchase real property in Maryland for $192,000. Simard defaulted (failed to pay) on the contract. A state court ordered the property to be resold at Simard's expense, as required by state law. The property was then resold for $163,000, but the second purchaser also defaulted on his contract. The court then ordered a second resale, resulting in a final price of $130,000. Assuming that Simard is liable for consequential damages, what is the extent of his liability? Is he liable for losses and expenses related to the first resale? If so, is he also liable for losses and expenses related to the second resale? Why or why not? [Burson v. Simard, 35 A.3d 1154 (Md. 2012)] **(See page 283.)**

- For a sample answer to Problem 14-6, go to Appendix C at the end of this text.

14-7. Liquidated Damages. Cuesport Properties, LLC, sold a condominium in Anne Arundel County, Maryland, to Critical Developments, LLC. As part of the sale, Cuesport agreed to build a wall between Critical Developments' unit and an adjacent unit within thirty days of closing. If Cuesport failed to do so, it was to pay $126 per day until completion. This was an estimate of the amount of rent that Critical Developments would lose until the wall was finished and the unit could be rented. Actual damages were otherwise difficult to estimate at the time of the contract. The wall was built on time, but without a county permit, and it did not comply with the county building code. Critical Developments did not modify the wall to comply with the code until 260 days after the date of the contract deadline for completion of the wall. Does Cuesport have to pay Critical Developments $126 for each of the 260 days? Explain. [*Cuesport Properties, LLC v. Critical Developments, LLC*, 209 Md.App. 607, 61 A.3d 91 (2013)] **(See page 285.)**

14–8. A QUESTION OF ETHICS: Remedies.

On a weekday, Tamara Cohen, a real estate broker, showed a townhouse owned by Ray and Harriet Mayer to Jessica Seinfeld, the wife of comedian Jerry Seinfeld. On the weekend, when Cohen was unavailable because her religious beliefs prevented her from working, the Seinfelds revisited the townhouse on their own and agreed to buy it. The contract stated that the "buyers will pay buyer's real estate broker's fees." [Cohen v. Seinfeld, 15 Misc.3d 1118(A), 839 N.Y.S.2d 432 (Sup. 2007)] **(See page 286.)**

(a) Is Cohen entitled to payment even though she was not available to show the townhouse to the Seinfelds on the weekend? Explain.

(b) What obligation do parties involved in business deals owe to each other with respect to their religious beliefs? How might the situation in this case have been avoided?

Legal Reasoning Group Activity

14–9. Breach and Remedies. Frances Morelli agreed to sell Judith Bucklin a house in Rhode Island for $177,000. The sale was supposed to be closed by September 1, when the parties were to exchange the deed for the price. The contract included a provision that "if Seller is unable to convey good, clear, insurable, and marketable title, Buyer shall have the option to: (a) accept such title as Seller is able to convey without reduction of the Purchase Price, or (b) cancel this Agreement and receive a return of all Deposits."

An examination of the public records revealed that the house did not have marketable title. Bucklin offered Morelli additional time to resolve the problem, and the closing did not occur as scheduled. Morelli decided "the deal is over" and offered to return the deposit. Bucklin refused and, in mid-October, decided to exercise her option to accept the house without marketable title. She notified Morelli, who did not respond. She then filed a lawsuit against Morelli in a state court.

(a) One group will discuss whether Morelli breached the contract and will decide in whose favor the court should rule.

(b) A second group will assume that Morelli did breach the contract and will determine what the appropriate remedy is in this situation.

AN ACCELERATED COURSE

MILLER

UNIT THREE

COMMERCIAL TRANSACTIONS

Contents

CHAPTER 15

THE FORMATION OF SALES AND LEASE CONTRACTS

When we turn to contracts for the sale and lease of goods, we move away from common law principles and into the area of statutory law. State statutory law governing sales and lease transactions is based on the uniform Commercial code (UCC), which, as mentioned in Chapter 1, has been adopted as law by all of the states.[1] Of all the attempts to produce a uniform body of laws relating to commercial transactions in the United States, none has been as successful as the UCC.

1. Louisiana has not adopted Articles 2 and 2A, however.

We open this chapter with a discussion of the UCC's Article 2 (on sales) and Article 2A (on leases) as a background to the topic of this chapter, which is the formation of contracts for the sale and lease of goods. (Article 2 of the UCC is available for review in Appendix A at the end of this text.)

The goal of the UCC is to simplify and to streamline commercial transactions. The UCC allows parties to form sales and lease contracts, including those entered into online, without observing the same degree of formality used in forming other types of contracts. (We look at the important issue

of whether online sales can be taxed in this chapter's *Insight into E-Commerce* feature on page 301.)

Today, businesses often engage in sales and lease transactions on a global scale. Because international sales transactions are increasingly commonplace, we conclude the chapter with an examination of the United Nations Convention on Contracts for the International Sale of Goods (CISG), which governs international sales contracts. The CISG is a model uniform law that applies only when a nation has adopted it, just as the UCC applies only to the extent that it has been adopted by a state.

SECTION 1

THE UNIFORM COMMERCIAL CODE

In the early years of this nation, sales law varied from state to state, and this lack of uniformity complicated the formation of multistate sales contracts. The problems became especially troublesome in the late nineteenth century as multistate contracts became the norm. For this reason, numerous attempts were made to produce a uniform body of laws relating to commercial transactions. The National Conference of Commissioners on Uniform State Laws (NCCUSL) drafted two uniform ("model") acts that were widely adopted by the states: the Uniform Negotiable Instruments Law (1896) and the Uniform Sales Act (1906). Several other proposed uniform acts followed, although most were not as widely adopted.

In the 1940s, the NCCUSL recognized the need to integrate the half dozen or so uniform acts covering commercial transactions into a single, comprehensive body of statutory law. The NCCUSL developed the Uniform Commercial Code (UCC) to serve that purpose. First issued in 1949, the UCC facilitates commercial transactions by making the laws governing sales and lease contracts clearer, simpler, and more readily applicable to the numerous difficulties that can arise during such transactions.

Comprehensive Coverage of the UCC

The UCC is the single most comprehensive codification of the broad spectrum of laws involved in a total commercial transaction. The UCC views the entire "commercial transaction for the sale of and payment for goods" as a single legal occurrence having numerous facets. The articles and sections of the UCC are periodically revised or supplemented to clarify certain aspects or to establish new rules as needed when the business environment changes.

You can gain an idea of the UCC's comprehensiveness by reviewing the titles of the articles on the first page of Appendix A. As you will note, Article 1 is titled General Provisions. That article sets forth definitions and general principles applicable to commercial transactions. For instance, there is an obligation to perform in "good faith" all contracts falling under the UCC [UCC 1–304]. Article 1 thus provides the basic groundwork for the remaining articles, each of which focuses on a particular aspect of commercial transactions.

Does the duty of good faith and fair dealing apply to contracts other than contracts for sales of goods? That question arose in the following case.

CASE ANALYSIS

Case 15.1   Amaya v. Brater
Court of Appeals of Indiana, 981 N.E.2d 1235 (2013).

IN THE LANGUAGE OF THE COURT
CRONE, Judge.

* * * *

* * * In the spring of 2010, [Peter] Amaya, an Ohio resident, was a third-year medical student at Indiana University School of Medicine [IUSM] located in Indianapolis. He was attending medical school on scholarship. On March 29, 2010, Amaya sat for a combined mini-block examination consisting of Introduction to Clinical Medicine II, Pharmacology, and Pathology. Three professors, Drs. [Joseph] DiMicco, [Klaus] Hilgarth, and [Kathleen] Prag, each observed Amaya during the examination and concluded that he was cheating by looking at the paper of the student to his right. On March 30, 2010, Dr. DiMicco confronted Amaya with his observations, and Amaya denied cheating on the mini-block examination. On April 5, 2010, Dr. Hilgarth confronted Amaya with his observations and explained to Amaya that his behavior of looking into the workspace of the student to his right gave the appearance of cheating. Amaya denied that he cheated or that he engaged in any behavior that gave the appearance of cheating. Amaya maintained that he was merely looking over and up at the clock on the right-hand wall of the testing room.

* * * *

* * * On August 18, 2010, Dean [Craig] Brater advised Amaya that he * * * was dismissed from Indiana University School of Medicine.

* * * Amaya filed a * * * complaint [in an Indiana state court against the dean and IUSM, alleging] breach of contract and * * * breach of good faith and fair dealing.

* * * The trial court * * * granted IUSM's motion for summary judgment.

* * * Amaya now appeals.

* * * *

* * * Amaya raises two separate theories of liability against IUSM: (1) breach of contract, and (2) breach of the duty of good faith and fair dealing. * * * A separate cause of action for alleged breach of duty of good faith and fair dealing is inapposite [unsuitable] here. *The duty of good faith and fair dealing is a concept created by the Uniform Commercial Code and restricted to contracts for the sale of goods * * * .* Accordingly, the sole issue for our determination on appeal is whether the trial court erred when it entered summary judgment on Amaya's claim for breach of contract. [Emphasis added.]

* * * The legal relationship between a student and a university [is] one of implied contract.

* * * The courts' approach has been similar to that used with contracts conditioned upon the satisfaction of one party. The university requires that the student's academic performance be satisfactory to the university in its honest judgment.

* * * *

IUSM's *Student Handbook* provides that the [Student Promotions Committee (SPC)] is appointed by the dean to monitor student academic and professional standards as determined by the faculty. Section V(F), entitled "Dismissal," provides that "a student may be required to meet with the SPC to show cause why he/she should not be dismissed from school when he/she * * * has been cited for lack of acceptable academic ethics or professional behavior." The designated evidence indicates that three faculty members observed Amaya cheating during the mini-block examination. Amaya was informed of these observations and was requested to prepare for a * * * hearing before the SPC. Amaya appeared before the SPC and presented a PowerPoint presentation. He also tendered voluminous written material, including photographs, field studies, experts' reports, timelines, and statistical analysis. Following Amaya's presentation, the SPC tabled its vote in order to further deliberate and thoroughly review Amaya's information. The SPC also asked for written submissions from the three faculty members and from Amaya.

CASE 15.1 CONTINUES ▶

Thereafter, Amaya was informed that a subcommittee of the SPC had conducted field tests to determine the validity of the information he had submitted. Considering the results of those field tests as well as the written responses to additional questions, the SPC determined that the evidence supported the charge of cheating. Amaya was granted his request for a reconsideration hearing as provided by section VI of the *Student Handbook.* When the SPC declined to reverse its decision, Amaya was then afforded the opportunity to meet with the dean for further review as provided for in the *Student Handbook.* After considering all the evidence presented, the Dean determined that dismissal was warranted.

* * * IUSM's conclusion that Amaya failed to maintain acceptable professional standards was a rational determination arrived at after much deliberation and after Amaya had numerous opportunities to be heard.

* * * *

* * * We affirm the trial court's entry of summary judgment.

LEGAL REASONING QUESTIONS

1. What is the duty of good faith and fair dealing (see page 303)?

2. To what type of contracts does the duty apply?

3. What type of contract was at the center of this case?

4. Did the court conclude that the duty of good faith and fair dealing applied in this case? Why or why not?

A Single, Integrated Framework for Commercial Transactions

The UCC attempts to provide a consistent and integrated framework of rules to deal with all the phases *ordinarily arising* in a commercial sales transaction from start to finish. For an example how several articles of the UCC can apply to a single commercial transaction, see Exhibit 15–1 on the following page.

SECTION 2
THE SCOPE OF ARTICLES 2 (SALES) AND 2A (LEASES)

Article 2 of the UCC sets forth the requirements for *sales contracts,* as well as the duties and obligations of the parties involved in the sales contract. Article 2A covers similar issues for *lease contracts.* Bear in mind, however, that the parties to sales or lease contracts are free to agree to terms different from those stated in the UCC.

Article 2—The Sale of Goods

Article 2 of the UCC (as adopted by state statutes) governs **sales contracts,** or contracts for the sale of goods. To facilitate commercial transactions, Article 2

modifies some of the common law contract requirements that were discussed in the previous chapters.

To the extent that it has not been modified by the UCC, however, the common law of contracts also applies to sales contracts. In other words, the common law requirements for a valid contract—agreement, consideration, capacity, and legality—that were discussed in previous chapters are also applicable to sales contracts.

In general, the rule is that whenever a conflict arises between a common law contract rule and the state statutory law based on the UCC, the UCC controls. Thus, when a UCC provision addresses a certain issue, the UCC rule governs. When the UCC is silent, the common law governs.

The relationship between general contract law and the law governing sales of goods is illustrated in Exhibit 15–2 on page 300.

In regard to Article 2, keep two points in mind.

1. Article 2 deals with the sale of *goods.* It does not deal with real property (real estate), services, or intangible property such as stocks and bonds. Thus, if the subject matter of a dispute is goods, the UCC governs. If it is real estate or services, the common law applies.

2. In some situations, the rules can vary depending on whether the buyer or the seller is a *merchant.*

We look now at how the UCC defines a *sale, goods,* and *merchant status.*

EXHIBIT 15-1 How Several Articles of the UCC Can Apply to a Single Transaction

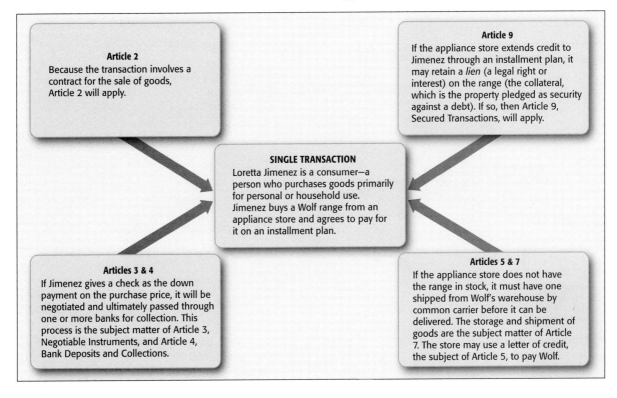

Article 2
Because the transaction involves a contract for the sale of goods, Article 2 will apply.

Article 9
If the appliance store extends credit to Jimenez through an installment plan, it may retain a *lien* (a legal right or interest) on the range (the collateral, which is the property pledged as security against a debt). If so, then Article 9, Secured Transactions, will apply.

SINGLE TRANSACTION
Loretta Jimenez is a consumer—a person who purchases goods primarily for personal or household use. Jimenez buys a Wolf range from an appliance store and agrees to pay for it on an installment plan.

Articles 3 & 4
If Jimenez gives a check as the down payment on the purchase price, it will be negotiated and ultimately passed through one or more banks for collection. This process is the subject matter of Article 3, Negotiable Instruments, and Article 4, Bank Deposits and Collections.

Articles 5 & 7
If the appliance store does not have the range in stock, it must have one shipped from Wolf's warehouse by common carrier before it can be delivered. The storage and shipment of goods are the subject matter of Article 7. The store may use a letter of credit, the subject of Article 5, to pay Wolf.

WHAT IS A SALE? The UCC defines a **sale** as "the passing of title [evidence of ownership rights] from the seller to the buyer for a price" [UCC 2–106(1)]. The price may be payable in cash or in other goods or services.

WHAT ARE GOODS? To be characterized as a *good,* an item of property must be *tangible,* and it must be *movable.* **Tangible property** has physical existence—it can be touched or seen. **Intangible property**—such as corporate stocks and bonds, patents and copyrights, and ordinary contract rights—has only conceptual existence and thus does not come under Article 2. A *movable* item can be carried from place to place. Hence, real estate is excluded from Article 2.

Goods Associated with Real Estate. Goods *associated* with real estate often do fall within the scope of Article 2, however [UCC 2–107]. For instance, a contract for the sale of minerals, oil, or gas is a contract for the sale of goods if *severance, or separation, is to be made by the seller.* Similarly, a contract for the sale of growing crops or timber to be cut is a contract for the sale of goods *regardless of who severs them from the land.*

▶ **Case in Point 15.1** Homeowners in Colorado installed underground radiant heating systems to warm indoor flooring or melt snow and ice under driveways and sidewalks. The systems began to leak as a result of the hardening of a hose called Entran II. The homeowners sued Goodyear Tire and Rubber Company, the maker of the hose, asserting claims under Colorado's version of the UCC. The court held that because the hose was a tangible and movable good at the time the contract was made, it was a "good" under the UCC. Therefore, the UCC applied to the contract even though the hose was later incorporated into real property (under flooring).[2] ◀

Goods and Services Combined. When contracts involve a combination of goods and services, courts generally use the **predominant-factor test** to determine

2. *Loughridge v. Goodyear Tire and Rubber Co.,* 192 F.Supp.2d 1175 (D.Colo. 2002).

EXHIBIT 15-2 The Law Governing Contracts

This exhibit graphically illustrates the relationship between general contract law and statutory law (UCC Articles 2 and 2A) governing contracts for the sale and lease of goods. Sales contracts are not governed exclusively by Article 2 of the UCC but are also governed by general contract law whenever it is relevant and has not been modified by the UCC.

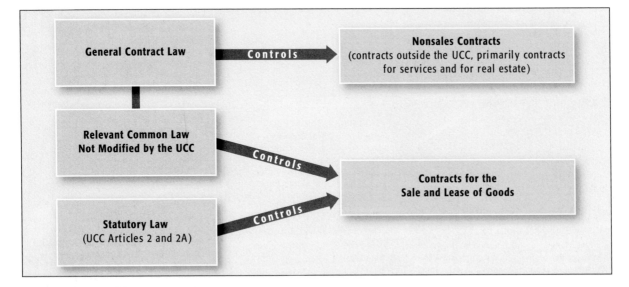

whether a contract is primarily for the sale of goods or the sale of services.[3] If a court decides that a mixed contract is primarily a goods contract, *any* dispute, even a dispute over the services portion, will be decided under the UCC.

▶ **Case in Point 15.2** Gene and Martha Jannusch agreed to sell Festival Foods, a concessions business, to Lindsey and Louann Naffziger for a price of $150,000. The deal included a truck, a trailer, freezers, roasters, chairs, tables, a fountain service, signs, and lighting. The Naffzigers paid $10,000 down with the balance to come from a bank loan. They took possession of the equipment and began to use it immediately in Festival Foods operations at various events.

After six events, the Naffzigers returned the truck and all the equipment, and wanted out of the deal because the business did not generate as much income as they expected. The Jannusches sued the Naffzigers for the balance due on the purchase price, claiming that the Naffzigers could no longer reject the goods under the UCC. The Naffzigers claimed that the UCC did not apply because the deal primarily involved the sale of a business rather than the sale of goods. The court found that the UCC governed under the predominant-factor test. The primary value of the

contract was in the goods, not the value of the business. The parties had agreed on the essential terms of the contract (such as the price). Thus, a contract had been formed, and the Naffzigers had breached it. The Naffzigers took possession and control of all of the physical aspects of the business. Therefore, they had no right to return them.[4] ◀

WHO IS A MERCHANT? Article 2 governs the sale of goods in general. It applies to sales transactions between all buyers and sellers. In a limited number of instances, though, the UCC presumes that special business standards ought to be imposed because of merchants' relatively high degree of commercial expertise.[5] Such standards do not apply to the casual or inexperienced seller or buyer (consumer).

Section 2–104 sets forth three ways in which merchant status can arise:

1. A merchant is a person who *deals in goods of the kind* involved in the sales contract. Thus, a retailer, a wholesaler, or a manufacturer is a merchant of the goods sold in his or her business. A merchant for one type of goods is not necessarily a merchant

---

3. UCC 2–314(1) does stipulate that serving food or drinks is a "sale of goods" for purposes of the implied warranty of merchantability, as will be discussed in Chapter 16. The UCC also specifies that selling unborn animals or rare coins qualifies as a "sale of goods."

4. *Jannusch v. Naffziger*, 379 Ill.App.3d 381, 883 N.E.2d 711 (2008).

5. The provisions that apply only to merchants deal principally with the Statute of Frauds, firm offers, confirmatory memoranda, warranties, and contract modification. These special rules reflect expedient business practices commonly known to merchants in the commercial setting. They will be discussed later in this chapter.

INSIGHT INTO E-COMMERCE
Taxing Web Purchases

In 1992, the United States Supreme Court ruled that an individual state cannot compel an out-of-state business that lacks a substantial physical presence within that state to collect and remit state taxes.[a] Although Congress has the power to pass legislation requiring out-of-state corporations to collect and remit state sales taxes, it has not yet done so. Thus, only online retailers that also have a physical presence within a state must collect state taxes on any Web sales made to residents of that state. (State residents are supposed to self-report their purchases and pay use taxes to the state, which they rarely do.)

Redefining Physical Presence

Several states have found a way to collect taxes on Internet sales made to state residents by out-of-state corporations—by redefining *physical presence*. In 2008, New York changed its tax laws in this manner. Now, an online retailer that pays any party within New York to solicit business for its products is considered a physical presence in the state and must collect state taxes. Since then, at least seventeen other states have made similar changes in their laws in an effort to increase their revenues by collecting sales tax from online retailers.

These new laws, often called the "Amazon tax" because they are largely aimed at Amazon.com, affect all online sellers, including Overstock.com and Drugstore.com. These tax laws especially affect those retailers that pay affiliates to direct traffic to their Web sites. These laws allow states to tax online commerce even though, to date, Congress has explicitly chosen not to tax Internet sales.

Local Governments Sue Online Travel Companies

Travelocity, Priceline.com, Hotels.com, and Orbitx.com are online travel companies (OTCs) that offer, among other things, hotel booking services. By 2013, more than twenty cities, including Atlanta, Charleston, Philadelphia, and San Antonio, had filed suits claiming that the OTCs owed taxes on hotel reservations that they had booked. All of the cities involved in the suits impose a hotel occupancy tax, which is essentially a sales tax.

Initially, some cities won their cases, but more recently, they have been losing in court.[b] As of 2013, the OTCs had prevailed in fifteen of nineteen cases nationwide.

The Market Place Fairness Act

By the time you read this, online sales taxes may have become a reality for every online business that has annual revenues in excess of $1 million. For several years now, legislation called the Market Place Fairness Act has been introduced in the U.S. Senate. The act would allow states to collect sales taxes from online retailers for transactions within the state.

There are several problems with such legislation. The current tax system involves 9,600 taxing jurisdictions. Even one zip code may cover multiple taxing entities such as different cities and counties. Just consider that the Dallas–Fort Worth airport includes six separate taxing jurisdictions. Current software solutions for retailers that allow them to collect and remit sales taxes for different jurisdictions are extremely costly to install and operate. Overstock.com, for example, spent $1.3 million to add just one state to its sales tax collection system.

LEGAL CRITICAL THINKING
INSIGHT INTO ETHICS

Some argue that if online retailers are required to collect and pay sales taxes in jurisdictions in which they have no physical presence, they have no democratic way to fight high taxes in those places. Is this an instance of taxation without representation? Discuss.

---

a. *Quill Corp. v. North Dakota,* 504 U.S. 298, 112 S.Ct. 1904, 119 L.Ed.2d 91 (1992).

b. *Travelscape, LLC v. South Carolina Department of Revenue,* 391 S.C. 89, 705 S.E.2d 28 (2011).

---

for another type. For instance, a sporting goods retailer is a merchant when selling tennis rackets but not when selling a used computer.

2. A merchant is a person who, by occupation, *holds himself or herself out as having knowledge and skill unique to the practices or goods involved in the* transaction. This broad definition may include banks or universities as merchants.

3. A person who *employs a merchant as a broker, agent, or other intermediary* has the status of merchant in that transaction. Hence, if an art collector hires a broker to purchase or sell art for

her, the collector is considered a merchant in the transaction.

In summary, a person is a **merchant** when she or he, acting in a mercantile capacity, possesses or uses an expertise specifically related to the goods being sold. This basic distinction is not always clear-cut. For instance, state courts appear to be split on whether farmers should be considered merchants.

Article 2A—Leases

Leases of personal property (goods such as automobiles and industrial equipment) have become increasingly common. In this context, a lease is a transfer of the right to possess and use goods for a period of time in exchange for payment. Article 2A of the UCC was created to fill the need for uniform guidelines in this area.

Article 2A covers any transaction that creates a lease of goods or a sublease of goods [UCC 2A–102, 2A–103(1)(k)]. Article 2A is essentially a repetition of Article 2, except that it applies to leases of goods rather than sales of goods and thus varies to reflect differences between sales and lease transactions. (Note that Article 2A is not concerned with leases of real property, such as land or buildings.)

DEFINITION OF A LEASE AGREEMENT Article 2A defines a **lease agreement** as a lessor's and lessee's bargain with respect to the lease of goods, as found in their language and as implied by other circumstances [UCC 2A–103(1)(k)]. A **lessor** is one who transfers the right to the possession and use of goods under a lease [UCC 2A–103(1)(p)]. A **lessee** is one who acquires the right to the possession and use of goods under a lease [UCC 2A–103(1)(o)]. In other words, the lessee is the party who is leasing the goods from the lessor.

Article 2A applies to all types of leases of goods. Special rules apply to certain types of leases, however, including consumer leases and finance leases.

CONSUMER LEASES A *consumer lease* involves three elements:

1. A lessor who regularly engages in the business of leasing or selling.
2. A lessee (except an organization) who leases the goods "primarily for a personal, family, or household purpose."

3. Total lease payments that are less than $25,000 [UCC 2A–103(1)(e)].

To ensure special protection for consumers, certain provisions of Article 2A apply only to consumer leases. For instance, one provision states that a consumer may recover attorneys' fees if a court determines that a term in a consumer lease contract is unconscionable [UCC 2A–108(4)(a)].

FINANCE LEASES A *finance lease* involves a lessor, a lessee, and a supplier. The lessor buys or leases goods from the supplier and leases or subleases them to the lessee [UCC 2A–103(1)(g)]. Typically, in a finance lease, the lessor is simply financing the transaction. ▶ **Example 15.3** Marlin Corporation wants to lease a crane for use in its construction business. Marlin's bank agrees to purchase the equipment from Jenco, Inc., and lease the equipment to Marlin. In this situation, the bank is the lessor-financer, Marlin is the lessee, and Jenco is the supplier. ◀

Article 2A, unlike ordinary contract law, makes the lessee's obligations under a finance lease irrevocable and independent from the financer's obligations [UCC 2A–407]. In other words, the lessee must perform and continue to make lease payments even if the leased equipment turns out to be defective. The lessee must look almost entirely to the supplier for any recovery.

▶ **Example 15.4** McKessen Company obtains surgical ophthalmic equipment from a manufacturer and leases it to Vasquez for use at his medical eye center. When the equipment turns out to be defective, Vasquez stops making the lease payments. McKessen sues. Because the lease clearly qualifies as a finance lease under Article 2A, a court would hold in favor of McKessen. Vasquez is obligated to make all payments due under the lease regardless of the condition or performance of the leased equipment. Vasquez can sue the manufacturer of the defective equipment, however. ◀

SECTION 3
THE FORMATION OF SALES AND LEASE CONTRACTS

In regard to the formation of sales and lease contracts, the UCC modifies the common law in several ways. We look here at how Articles 2 and 2A of the UCC modify common law contract rules. Remember, though, that parties to sales and lease contracts are basically free to establish whatever terms they wish.

The UCC comes into play when the parties either fail to provide certain terms in their contract or wish to change the effect of the UCC's terms in the contract's application. The UCC makes this very clear by its repeated use of such phrases as "unless the parties otherwise agree" and "absent a contrary agreement by the parties."

Offer

In general contract law, the moment a definite offer is met by an unqualified acceptance, a binding contract is formed. In commercial sales transactions, the verbal exchanges, correspondence, and actions of the parties may not reveal exactly when a binding contractual obligation arises. The UCC states that an agreement sufficient to constitute a contract can exist even if the moment of its making is undetermined [UCC 2–204(2), 2A–204(2)].

OPEN TERMS According to general contract law, an offer must be definite enough for the parties (and the courts) to ascertain its essential terms when it is accepted. In contrast, the UCC states that a sales or lease contract will not fail for indefiniteness even if one or more terms are left open as long as *both* of the following are true:

1. The parties intended to make a contract.
2. There is a reasonably certain basis for the court to grant an appropriate remedy [UCC 2–204(3), 2A–204(3)].

The UCC provides numerous *open-term* provisions (discussed next) that can be used to fill the gaps in a contract. Thus, if a dispute occurs, all that is necessary to prove the existence of a contract is an indication (such as a purchase order) that there is a contract. Missing terms can be proved by evidence, or a court can presume that the parties intended whatever is reasonable under the circumstances.

Keep in mind, though, that if too many terms are left open, a court may find that the parties did not intend to form a contract. Also, the *quantity* of goods involved usually must be expressly stated in the contract. If the quantity term is left open, the courts will have no basis for determining a remedy.

Open Price Term. If the parties have not agreed on a price, the court will determine a "reasonable price at the time for delivery" [UCC 2–305(1)]. If either the

buyer or the seller is to determine the price, the price is to be decided in good faith [UCC 2–305(2)]. Under the UCC, *good faith* means honesty in fact and the observance of reasonable commercial standards of fair dealing in the trade [UCC 2–103(1)(b)]. The concepts of *good faith* and *commercial reasonableness* permeate the UCC.

Sometimes, the price fails to be set through the fault of one of the parties. In that situation, the other party can treat the contract as canceled or determine a reasonable price. ▶ **Example 15.5** Perez and Merrick enter into a contract for the sale of goods and agree that Perez will determine the price. Perez refuses to specify the price. Merrick can either treat the contract as canceled or set a reasonable price [UCC 2–305(3)]. ◀

Open Payment Term. When the parties do not specify payment terms, payment is due at the time and place at which the buyer is to receive the goods [UCC 2–310(a)]. The buyer can tender payment using any commercially normal or acceptable means, such as a check or credit card. If the seller demands payment in cash, however, the buyer must be given a reasonable time to obtain it [UCC 2–511(2)]. This is especially important when the contract states a definite and final time for performance.

▶ **Case in Point 15.6** Max Alexander agreed to purchase hay from Wagner's farm. Alexander left his truck and trailer at the farm for the seller to load the hay. Nothing was said about when payment was due, and the parties were unaware of the UCC's rules. When Alexander came back to get the hay, a dispute broke out. Alexander claimed that he had been given less hay than he had ordered and argued that he did not have to pay at that time. Wagner refused to release the hay (or the vehicles on which the hay was loaded) until Alexander paid for it. Eventually, Alexander jumped into his truck and drove off without paying for the hay—for which he was later prosecuted for the crime of theft (see Chapter 7). Because the parties had failed to specify when payment was due, UCC 2–310(a) controlled, and payment was due at the time Alexander picked up the hay.[6] ◀

Open Delivery Term. When no delivery terms are specified, the buyer normally takes delivery at the seller's place of business [UCC 2–308(a)]. If the seller has no place of business, the seller's residence is used. When goods are located in some other place and both parties

---

6. *State v. Alexander*, 186 Or.App. 600, 64 P.3d 1148 (2003).

know it, delivery is made there. If the time for shipment or delivery is not clearly specified in the sales contract, then the court will infer a "reasonable" time for performance [UCC 2–309(1)].

Duration of an Ongoing Contract. A single contract might specify successive performances but not indicate how long the parties are required to deal with each other. In this situation, either party may terminate the ongoing contractual relationship. Nevertheless, principles of good faith and sound commercial practice call for reasonable notification before termination so as to give the other party sufficient time to seek a substitute arrangement [UCC 2–309(2), (3)].

Options and Cooperation with Regard to Performance. When the contract contemplates shipment of the goods but does not specify the shipping arrangements, the *seller* has the right to make these arrangements in good faith, using commercial reasonableness in the situation [UCC 2–311].

When a sales contract omits terms relating to the assortment of goods, the *buyer* can specify the assortment. ▶ **Example 15.7** Petry Drugs agrees to purchase one thousand toothbrushes from Marconi's Dental Supply. The toothbrushes come in a variety of colors, but the contract does not specify color. Petry, the buyer, has the right to take six hundred blue toothbrushes and four hundred green ones if it wishes. Petry, however, must exercise good faith and commercial reasonableness in making the selection [UCC 2–311]. ◀

REQUIREMENTS AND OUTPUT CONTRACTS Normally, as mentioned earlier, if the parties do not specify a quantity, no contract is formed. A court will have no basis for determining a remedy because there is almost no way to determine objectively what is a reasonable quantity of goods for someone to buy. (In contrast, a court can objectively determine a reasonable price for particular goods by looking at the market for like goods.) The UCC recognizes two exceptions to this rule in requirements and output contracts [UCC 2–306(1)].

Requirements Contracts. Requirements contracts are common in the business world and normally are enforceable. In a **requirements contract,** the buyer agrees to purchase and the seller agrees to sell all or up to a stated amount of what the buyer requires. ▶ **Example 15.8** Newport Cannery forms a contract with Victor Tu. The cannery agrees to purchase from Tu, and Tu agrees to sell to the cannery, all of the green beans that the cannery requires during the following summer. ◀ There is implicit consideration in a requirements contract because the buyer (the cannery, in *Example 15.8*) gives up the right to buy from any other seller, and this forfeited right creates a legal detriment (consideration).

If, however, the buyer promises to purchase only if he or she *wishes* to do so, the promise is illusory (without consideration) and unenforceable by either party.[7] Similarly, if the buyer reserves the right to buy the goods from someone other than the seller, the promise is unenforceable (illusory) as a requirements contract.

Output Contracts. In an **output contract,** the seller agrees to sell and the buyer agrees to buy all or up to a stated amount of what the seller *produces.* ▶ **Example 15.9** Ruth Sewell has planted two acres of organic tomatoes. Bella Union, a local restaurant, agrees to buy all of the tomatoes that Sewell produces that year to use at the restaurant. ◀ Again, because the seller essentially forfeits the right to sell goods to another buyer, there is implicit consideration in an output contract.

The UCC imposes a *good faith limitation* on requirements and output contracts. The quantity under such contracts is the amount of requirements or the amount of output that occurs during a *normal* production period. The actual quantity purchased or sold cannot be unreasonably disproportionate to normal or comparable prior requirements or output [UCC 2–306(1)].

MERCHANT'S FIRM OFFER Under regular contract principles, an offer can be revoked at any time before acceptance. The major common law exception is an *option contract* (discussed in Chapter 10), in which the offeree pays consideration for the offeror's irrevocable promise to keep the offer open for a stated period. The UCC creates a second exception for *firm offers* made by a merchant concerning the sale or lease of goods (regardless of whether or not the offeree is a merchant).

When a Merchant's Firm Offer Arises. A **firm offer** arises when a merchant-offeror gives *assurances in a signed writing* that the offer will remain open. The merchant's firm offer is irrevocable without the neces-

---

7. See, for example, *In re Anchor Glass Container Corp.*, 345 Bankr. 765 (M.D.Fla. 2006).

sity of consideration[8] for the stated period or, if no definite period is stated, a reasonable period (neither to exceed three months) [UCC 2–205, 2A–205].

▶ **Example 15.10** Osaka, a used-car dealer, e-mails a letter to Gomez on January 1, stating, "I have a used 2013 Toyota RAV4 on the lot that I'll sell you for $22,000 any time between now and January 31." This e-mail creates a firm offer, and Osaka will be liable for breach of contract if he sells the RAV4 to another person before January 31. ◀

Requirements for a Firm Offer. To qualify as a firm offer, the offer must be:

1. *Written* (or electronically recorded, such as in an e-mail).
2. *Signed* by the offeror.[9]

When a firm offer is contained in a form contract prepared by the offeree, the offeror must also sign a separate assurance of the firm offer. The requirement of a separate signature ensures that the offeror will be made aware of the firm offer.

For instance, an offeree might respond to an initial offer by sending its own form contract containing a clause stating that the offer will remain open for three months. If the firm offer is buried amid copious language on the last page of the offeree's form contract, the offeror may inadvertently sign the contract without realizing that it contains a firm offer. This would defeat the purpose of the rule—which is to give effect to a merchant's *deliberate* intent to be bound to a firm offer.

Acceptance

Acceptance of an offer to buy, sell, or lease goods generally may be made in any reasonable manner and by any reasonable means. The UCC permits acceptance of an offer to buy goods "either by a prompt *promise* to ship or by the prompt or current shipment of conforming or nonconforming goods" [UCC 2–206(1)(b)]. *Conforming goods* accord with the contract's terms, whereas *nonconforming goods* do not.

The prompt shipment of nonconforming goods constitutes both an acceptance, which creates a contract, and a breach of that contract. This rule does not apply if the seller **seasonably** (within a reasonable amount of time) notifies the buyer that the nonconforming ship-

ment is offered only as an *accommodation,* or as a favor. The notice of accommodation must clearly indicate to the buyer that the shipment does not constitute an acceptance and that, therefore, no contract has been formed.

▶ **Example 15.11** McFarren Pharmacy orders five cases of Johnson & Johnson 3-by-5-inch gauze pads from H.T. Medical Supply, Inc. If H.T. ships five cases of Xeroform 3-by-5-inch gauze pads instead, the shipment acts as both an acceptance of McFarren's offer and a *breach* of the resulting contract. McFarren may sue H.T. for any appropriate damages. If, however, H.T. notifies McFarren that the Xeroform gauze pads are being shipped *as an accommodation*—because H.T. has only Xeroform pads in stock—the shipment will constitute a counteroffer, not an acceptance. A contract will be formed only if McFarren accepts the Xeroform gauze pads. ◀

COMMUNICATION OF ACCEPTANCE Under the common law, because a unilateral offer invites acceptance by performance, the offeree need not notify the offeror of performance unless the offeror would not otherwise know about it. In other words, a unilateral offer can be accepted by beginning performance.

The UCC is more stringent than the common law in this regard because it requires notification. Under the UCC, if the offeror is not notified within a reasonable time that the offeree has accepted the contract by beginning performance, then the offeror can treat the offer as having lapsed before acceptance [UCC 2–206(2), 2A–206(2)].

ADDITIONAL TERMS Recall from Chapter 10 that under the common law, the mirror image rule requires that the terms of the acceptance exactly match those of the offer. ▶ **Example 15.12** Aldrich e-mails an offer to sell twenty Samsung Galaxy model 7.0 tablets to Beale. If Beale accepts the offer but changes it to require model 8.9 tablets, then there is no contract. ◀

To avoid these problems, the UCC dispenses with the mirror image rule. Under the UCC, a contract is formed if the offeree's response indicates a *definite* acceptance of the offer, *even if the acceptance includes terms additional to or different from those contained in the offer* [UCC 2–207(1)]. Whether the additional terms become part of the contract depends, in part, on whether the parties are nonmerchants or merchants.

Rules When One Party or Both Parties Are Nonmerchants. If one (or both) of the parties is a *nonmerchant,* the contract is formed according to the terms of the original

---

8. If the offeree pays consideration, then an option contract (not a merchant's firm offer) is formed.
9. *Signed* includes any symbol executed or adopted by a party with a present intention to authenticate a writing [UCC 1–201(37)]. A complete signature is not required.

offer and does not include any of the additional terms in the acceptance [UCC 2–207(2)].

▶ **Case in Point 15.13** OfficeSupplyStore.com sells office supplies on the Web. Employees of the Kansas City School District in Missouri ordered $17,642.54 worth of office supplies—without the authority or approval of their employer—from the Web site. The invoices accompanying the goods contained a *forum-selection clause* (see Chapter 10) that required all disputes to be resolved in California.

When the goods were not paid for, Office Supply filed suit in California. The Kansas City School District objected, arguing that the forum-selection clause was not binding. The court held that the forum-selection clause was not part of the parties' contract. The clause was an additional term included in the invoices delivered to a nonmerchant buyer (the school district) with the purchased goods. Therefore, the clause did not become part of the contract unless the buyer expressly agreed, which did not happen in this case.[10] ◀

Rules When Both Parties Are Merchants. The drafters of the UCC created a special rule for merchants to avoid

the "battle of the forms," which occurs when two merchants exchange separate standard forms containing different contract terms.

Under UCC 2–207(2), in contracts *between merchants,* the additional terms *automatically* become part of the contract *unless* one of the following conditions arises:

1. The original offer expressly limited acceptance to its terms.
2. The new or changed terms materially alter the contract.
3. The offeror objects to the new or changed terms within a reasonable period of time.

When determining whether an alteration is material, courts consider several factors. Generally, if the modification does not involve any unreasonable element of surprise or hardship for the offeror, a court will hold that the modification did not materially alter the contract. Courts also consider the parties' prior dealings.

In the following case, a party conditioned its acceptance of an offer on the other parties' agreement to additional terms by a specific date. When the parties agreed to the most important terms after the deadline, the court had to decide if there was an enforceable contract.

---

10. *OfficeSupplyStore.com v. Kansas City School Board,* 334 S.W.3d 574 (Kan. 2011).

CASE 15.2

WPS, Inc. v. Expro Americas, LLC

Court of Appeals of Texas, First District, 369 S.W.3d 384 (2012).

BACKGROUND AND FACTS In April 2006, WPS, Inc., submitted a formal proposal to manufacture equipment for Expro Americas, LLC, and Surface Production Systems, Inc. (SPS). Expro and SPS then submitted two purchase orders. WPS accepted the first purchase order in part, and it accepted the second order conditionally. Among other things, WPS required that, by April 28, 2006, Expro and SPS give their "full release to proceed" and agree to "pay all valid costs associated with any order cancellation." The parties' negotiations continued, and Expro and SPS eventually submitted a third purchase order on May 9, 2006.

The third purchase order did not comply with all of WPS's requirements, but it did give WPS full permission to proceed and agreed that Expro and SPS would pay all cancellation costs. With Expro and SPS's knowledge, WPS then began work under the third purchase order. Expro and SPS soon canceled the order, however, so WPS sent them an invoice charging them for the cancellation costs. At trial, the jury and court concluded that there was a contract and found in WPS's favor. Expro and SPS appealed.

 IN THE LANGUAGE OF THE COURT
Terry *JENNINGS,* Justice.

* * * *

* * * WPS replied with a conditional acceptance of the second purchase order. WPS also stated that its conditional acceptance depended upon the receipt of a revised purchase order by April 28, 2006. Although it is undisputed that Expro * * * and SPS did not issue a revised purchase order by this date, the evidence * * * reveals that the parties continued their discus-

CASE 15.2 CONTINUED sions and negotiations over those matters that had yet to be resolved. * * * *The parties operated as if they had additional time to resolve the outstanding differences.* [Emphasis added.]

Expro * * * and SPS submitted their revised third purchase order on May 9, 2006, agreeing in writing to virtually all the matters that had remained unresolved to that date. * * * Most importantly, Expro * * * and SPS provided * * * a "full release to proceed" and agreed to "pay all valid costs associated with any order cancellation." In his testimony, [SPS's vice president] conceded that *the term "Release to Proceed" "basically means that one party is in agreement," authorizing the other party to go forward.* * * * WPS had previously sought the release to proceed so that it could "diligently" perform its obligations under the contract. The jury could have reasonably concluded that WPS, having now obtained the release * * * and * * * [the] promise to pay cancellation charges * * *, was contractually obligated to perform and meet the delivery date. [Emphasis added.]

DECISION AND REMEDY   *The Texas appellate court found that WPS had a contract with Expro and SPS. It affirmed the lower court's judgment for WPS.*

THE LEGAL ENVIRONMENT DIMENSION   *In allowing a party to condition its acceptance on additional terms, does contract law make negotiations more or less efficient? Explain your answer.*

THE ECONOMIC DIMENSION   *Why would a manufacturer like WPS want its purchase orders to include terms such as those at issue in this case? Why would a buyer like Expro or SPS want to exclude such terms?*

Conditioned on Offeror's Assent. Regardless of merchant status, the UCC provides that the offeree's response cannot be construed as an acceptance if it contains additional or different terms and is expressly *conditioned* on the offeror's assent to those terms [UCC 2–207(1)].

▶ **Example 15.14**   Philips offers to sell Hundert 650 pounds of turkey thighs at a specified price and with specified delivery terms. Hundert responds, "I accept your offer for 650 pounds of turkey thighs *on the condition that you agree to give me ninety days to pay for them.*" Hundert's response will be construed not as an acceptance but as a counteroffer, which Philips may or may not accept. ◀

Additional Terms May Be Stricken. The UCC provides yet another option for dealing with conflicting terms in the parties' writings. Section 2–207(3) states that conduct by both parties that recognizes the existence of a contract is sufficient to establish a contract for sale even though the writings of the parties do not otherwise establish a contract. In this situation, "the terms of the particular contract will consist of those terms on which the writings of the parties agree, together with any supplementary terms incorporated under any other provisions of this Act." In a dispute over contract terms, this provision allows a court simply to strike from the contract those terms on which the parties do not agree.

▶ **Example 15.15**   SMT Marketing orders goods over the phone from Brigg Sales, Inc., which ships the goods to SMT with an acknowledgment form (confirming the order). SMT accepts and pays for the goods. The parties' writings do not establish a contract, but there is no question that a contract exists. If a dispute arises over the terms, such as the extent of any warranties, UCC 2–207(3) provides the governing rule. ◀

As noted previously, the fact that a merchant's acceptance frequently contains terms that add to or even conflict with those of the offer is often referred to as the "battle of the forms." Although the UCC tries to eliminate this battle, the problem of differing contract terms still arises in commercial settings, particularly when standard forms (for placing and confirming orders) are used.

Consideration

The common law rule that a contract requires consideration also applies to sales and lease contracts. Unlike the common law, however, the UCC does not require a contract modification to be supported by new consideration. The UCC states that an agreement modifying a contract for the sale or lease of goods "needs no consideration to be binding" [UCC 2–209(1), 2A–208(1)]. Of course, any contract modification must be made in good faith [UCC 1–304].

In some situations, an agreement to modify a sales or lease contract without consideration must be in writing to be enforceable. For instance, if the contract itself specifies that any changes to the contract must be in a signed writing, only those changes agreed to in a signed writing are enforceable.

Sometimes, when a consumer (nonmerchant) is buying goods from a merchant-seller, the merchant supplies a form that contains a prohibition against oral modification. In those situations, the consumer must sign a separate acknowledgment of the clause for it to be enforceable [UCC 2–209(2), 2A–208(2)]. Also, any modification that makes a sales contract come under Article 2's writing requirement (its Statute of Frauds, discussed next) usually requires a writing (or electronic record) to be enforceable.

The Statute of Frauds

The UCC contains Statute of Frauds provisions covering sales and lease contracts. Under these provisions, sales contracts for goods priced at $500 or more and lease contracts requiring total payments of $1,000 or more must be in writing to be enforceable [UCC 2–201(1), 2A–201(1)]. (These low threshold amounts may eventually be raised.)

SUFFICIENCY OF THE WRITING A writing, e-mail, or other electronic record will be sufficient to satisfy the UCC's Statute of Fraud as long as it:

1. Indicates that the parties intended to form a contract.
2. Is signed by the party (or agent of the party) against whom enforcement is sought. (Remember that a typed name can qualify as a signature on an electronic record, as discussed in Chapter 6.)

The contract normally will not be enforceable beyond the quantity of goods shown in the writing, however. All other terms can be proved in court by oral testimony. For leases, the writing must reasonably identify and describe the goods leased and the lease term.

SPECIAL RULES FOR CONTRACTS BETWEEN MERCHANTS The UCC provides a special rule for merchants in sales transactions (there is no corresponding rule that applies to leases under Article 2A). Merchants can satisfy the Statute of Frauds if, after the parties have agreed orally, one of the merchants sends a signed written (or electronic) confirmation to the other merchant within a reasonable time.

The communication must indicate the terms of the agreement, and the merchant receiving the confirmation must have reason to know of its contents. Unless the merchant who receives the confirmation gives written notice of objection to its contents within ten days after receipt, the writing is sufficient against the receiving merchant, even though she or he has not signed it [UCC 2–201(2)].

▶ **Example 15.16** Alfonso is a merchant-buyer in Cleveland. He contracts over the telephone to purchase $6,000 worth of spare aircraft parts from Goldstein, a merchant-seller in New York City. Two days later, Goldstein e-mails a signed confirmation detailing the terms of the oral contract, and Alfonso subsequently receives it. Alfonso does not notify Goldstein in writing (or e-mail) that he objects to the contents of the confirmation within ten days of receipt. Therefore, Alfonso cannot raise the Statute of Frauds as a defense against the enforcement of the oral contract. ◀

EXCEPTIONS The UCC defines three exceptions to the writing requirements of the Statute of Frauds. An oral contract for the sale of goods priced at $500 or more or the lease of goods involving total payments of $1,000 or more will be enforceable despite the absence of a writing in the circumstances described next [UCC 2–201(3), 2A–201(4)].

Specially Manufactured Goods. An oral contract for the sale or lease of custom-made goods will be enforceable if:

1. The goods are *specially manufactured* for a particular buyer or specially manufactured or obtained for a particular lessee.
2. The goods are *not suitable for resale or lease* to others in the ordinary course of the seller's or lessor's business.
3. The seller or lessor has *substantially started to manufacture* the goods or has made commitments for the manufacture or procurement of the goods.

In these situations, once the seller or lessor has taken action, the buyer or lessee cannot repudiate the agreement claiming the Statute of Frauds as a defense.

▶ **Example 15.17** Womach orders custom window treatments to use at a day spa business for $6,000 from Hunter Douglas. The contract is oral. When Hunter Douglas manufactures the window coverings and tenders delivery to Womach, she refuses to pay for them, even though the job has been completed on time. Womach claims that she is not liable because the contract was oral. If the unique style, size, and color of the window treatments make it improbable that Hunter Douglas can find another buyer, Womach is liable to Hunter Douglas. ◀

Admissions. An oral contract for the sale or lease of goods is enforceable if the party against whom enforcement is sought admits in pleadings, testimony, or other court proceedings that a sales or lease contract was made. In this situation, the contract will be enforceable even though it was oral, but enforceability will be limited to the quantity of goods admitted.

▶ **Case in Point 15.18**   Gerald Lindgren, a farmer, agreed by phone to sell his crops to Glacial Plains Cooperative. The parties reached four oral agreements: two for the delivery of soybeans and two for the delivery of corn. Lindgren made the soybean deliveries and part of the first corn delivery, but he sold the rest of his corn to another dealer. Glacial Plains bought corn elsewhere, paying a higher price, and then sued Lindgren for breach of contract. In papers filed with the court, Lindgren acknowledged his oral agreements with Glacial Plains and admitted that he did not fully perform. The court applied the admissions exception and held that the four agreements were enforceable.[11] ◀

Partial Performance. An oral contract for the sale or lease of goods is enforceable if payment has been made and accepted or goods have been received and accepted. This is the "partial performance" exception. The oral contract will be enforced at least to the extent that performance actually took place.

▶ **Case in Point 15.19**   Quality Pork International formed an oral contract with Rupari Food Services, Inc., which buys food products and sells them to retail operations. Quality was to ship three orders of pork to Star Food Processing, Inc., and Rupari was to pay for the products. Quality shipped the goods to Star and sent invoices to Rupari. Rupari billed Star for all three orders but paid Quality only for the first two. Quality filed a suit against Rupari to recover $44,051.98, the cost of the third order.

Rupari argued that because the parties did not have a written agreement, there was no enforceable contract. The court held that even though Rupari had not signed a written contract or purchase order, it had accepted the goods and partially performed the contract by paying for the first two shipments. Rupari's conduct was sufficient to prove the existence of a con-

tract, and the court required Rupari to pay for the last shipment.[12] ◀

The exceptions just discussed and other ways in which sales law differs from general contract law are summarized in Exhibit 15–3 on the following page.

Parol Evidence

Recall from Chapter 12 that parol evidence consists of evidence outside the contract such as evidence of the parties' prior negotiations, prior agreements, or contemporaneous (simultaneous) oral agreements. When a contract completely sets forth all the terms and conditions agreed to by the parties and is intended as a final statement of their agreement, it is considered fully *integrated* (see Chapter 12). The terms of a **fully integrated contract** cannot be contradicted by evidence of any prior agreements or contemporaneous oral agreements.

If, however, the writing contains some of the terms the parties agreed on but not others, then the contract is not fully integrated. When a court finds that a contract is *not fully integrated,* then the court may allow evidence of *consistent additional terms* to explain or supplement the terms in the contract. The court may also allow the parties to submit evidence of *course of dealing, usage of trade,* or *course of performance* [UCC 2–202, 2A–202].

COURSE OF DEALING AND USAGE OF TRADE   Under the UCC, the meaning of any agreement, evidenced by the language of the parties and by their actions, must be interpreted in light of commercial practices and other surrounding circumstances. In interpreting a commercial agreement, a court will assume that the course of dealing between the parties and the general usage of trade were taken into account when the agreement was phrased.

Course of Dealing. A **course of dealing** is a sequence of actions and communications between the parties to a particular transaction that establishes a common basis for their understanding [UCC 1–303(b)]. A course of dealing is restricted to the sequence of conduct between the parties in their transactions prior to the agreement.

Under the UCC, a course of dealing between the parties is relevant in ascertaining the meaning of the parties' agreement. It "may give particular meaning

11. *Glacial Plains Cooperative v. Lindgren,* 759 N.W.2d 661 (Min.App. 2009).

12. *Quality Pork International v. Rupari Food Services, Inc.,* 267 Neb. 474, 675 N.W.2d 642 (2004).

EXHIBIT 15-3 Major Differences between Contract Law and Sales Law

Topic	Contract Law	Sales Law
Contract Terms	Contract must contain all material terms.	Open terms are acceptable if parties intended to form a contract, but the contract is not enforceable beyond quantity term.
Acceptance	Mirror image rule applies. If additional terms are added in acceptance, a counteroffer is created.	Additional terms will not negate acceptance unless acceptance is expressly conditioned on assent to the additional terms.
Contract Modification	Modification requires consideration.	Modification does not require consideration.
Irrevocable Offers	Option contracts (with consideration).	Merchants' firm offers (without consideration).
Statute of Frauds Requirements	All material terms must be included in the writing.	Writing is required only for sale of goods priced at $500 or more, but the contract is not enforceable beyond the quantity specified. Merchants can satisfy the writing by a confirmation evidencing their agreement. *Exceptions:* 1. Specially manufactured goods. 2. Admissions by party against whom enforcement is sought. 3. Partial performance.

to specific terms of the agreement, and may supplement or qualify the terms of the agreement" [UCC 1–303(d)].

Usage of Trade. Any practice or method of dealing that is so regularly observed in a place, vocation, or trade as to justify an expectation by the parties that it will be observed in their transaction is a **usage of trade** [UCC 1–303(c)].

▶ **Example 15.20** Phat Khat Loans, Inc., hires Fleet Title Review Company to search the public records for prior claims on potential borrrowers' assets. Fleet's invoice states, "Liability limited to amount of fee." In the title search industry, liability limits are common. After conducting many searches for Phat Khat, Fleet reports that there are no claims with respect to Main Street Autos. Phat Khat loans $100,000 to Main, with payment guaranteed by Main's assets. When Main defaults on the loan, Phat Khat learns that another lender has priority to Main's assets under a previous claim. If Phat Khat sues Fleet Title for breach of contract, Fleet's liability will normally be limited to the amount of its fee. The statement in the invoice was part of the contract between Phat Khat and Fleet, according to the usage of trade in the industry and the parties' course of dealing. ◀

COURSE OF PERFORMANCE The conduct that occurs under the terms of a particular agreement is called a **course of performance** [UCC 1–303(a)]. Presumably, the parties themselves know best what they meant by their words. Thus, the course of performance actually carried out under the parties' agreement is the best indication of what they meant [UCC 2–208(1), 2A–207(1)].

▶ **Example 15.21** Janson's Lumber Company contracts with Lopez to sell Lopez a specified number of two-by-fours. The lumber in fact does not measure exactly 2 inches by 4 inches but rather 1⅞ inches by 3¾ inches. Janson's agrees to deliver the lumber in five deliveries, and Lopez, without objection, accepts the lumber in the first three deliveries. On the fourth delivery, however, Lopez objects that the two-by-fours do not measure precisely 2 inches by 4 inches.

The course of performance in this transaction— that is, the fact that Lopez accepted three deliveries without objection under the agreement—is relevant in determining that here a "two-by-four" actually means a "1⅞-by-3¾." Janson's can also prove that two-by-fours need not be exactly 2 inches by 4 inches by applying usage of trade, course of dealing, or both. Janson's can, for example, show that in previous transactions, Lopez took 1⅞-inch-by-3¾-inch lumber without objection. In addition, Janson's can show that in the trade, two-by-fours are commonly 1⅞ inches by 3¾ inches. ◀

RULES OF CONSTRUCTION The UCC provides *rules of construction* for interpreting contracts. Express terms, course of performance, course of dealing, and usage of trade are to be construed to be consistent with each other whenever reasonable. When such a construction is unreasonable, however, the UCC establishes the following order of priority [UCC 1–303(e), 2–208(2), 2A–207(2)]:

1. Express terms.
2. Course of performance.
3. Course of dealing.
4. Usage of trade.

Unconscionability

As discussed in Chapters 11 and 12, an unconscionable contract is one that is so unfair and one sided that it would be unreasonable to enforce it. The UCC allows a court to evaluate a contract or any clause in a contract, and if the court deems it to have been unconscionable *at the time it was made,* the court can do any of the following [UCC 2–302, 2A–108]:

1. Refuse to enforce the contract.
2. Enforce the remainder of the contract without the unconscionable part.
3. Limit the application of the unconscionable term to avoid an unconscionable result.

The following *Classic Case* illustrates an early application of the UCC's unconscionability provisions.

CLASSIC CASE 15.3

Jones v. Star Credit Corp.
Supreme Court of New York, Nassau County, 59 Misc.2d 189, 298 N.Y.S.2d 264 (1969).

BACKGROUND AND FACTS The Joneses agreed to purchase a freezer for $900 as the result of a salesperson's visit to their home. Tax and financing charges raised the total price to $1,234.80. At trial, the freezer was found to have a maximum retail value of approximately $300. The Joneses, who had made payments totaling $619.88, brought a suit in a New York state court to have the purchase contract declared unconscionable under the UCC.

 IN THE LANGUAGE OF THE COURT
Sol M. *WACHTLER,* Justice.

* * * *

* * * [Section 2–302 of the UCC] authorizes the court to find, as a matter of law, that a contract or a clause of a contract was "unconscionable at the time it was made," and upon so finding the court may refuse to enforce the contract, excise the objectionable clause or limit the application of the clause to avoid an unconscionable result.

* * * *

* * * The question which presents itself is whether or not, under the circumstances of this case, the sale of a freezer unit having a retail value of $300 for $900 ($1,439.69 including credit charges and $18 sales tax) is unconscionable as a matter of law.

Concededly, deciding [this case] is substantially easier than explaining it. No doubt, the mathematical disparity between $300, which presumably includes a reasonable profit margin, and $900, which is exorbitant on its face, carries the greatest weight. Credit charges alone exceed by more than $100 the retail value of the freezer. These alone may be sufficient to sustain the decision. Yet, a caveat [warning] is warranted lest we reduce the import of Section 2–302 solely to a mathematical ratio formula. It may, at times, be that; yet it may also be much more. The very limited financial resources of the purchaser, known to the sellers at the time of the sale, is entitled to weight in the balance. Indeed, the value disparity itself leads inevitably to the felt conclusion that knowing advantage was taken of the plaintiffs. In addition, *the meaningfulness of choice essential to the making of a contract can be negated by a gross inequality of bargaining power.* [Emphasis added.]

* * * *

CASE 15.3 CONTINUES ▶

* * * The defendant has already been amply compensated. In accordance with the statute, the application of the payment provision should be limited to amounts already paid by the plaintiffs and the contract be reformed and amended by changing the payments called for therein to equal the amount of payment actually so paid by the plaintiffs.

DECISION AND REMEDY *The court held that the contract was not enforceable and reformed the contract so that no further payments were required.*

THE SOCIAL DIMENSION *Why would the seller's knowledge of the buyers' limited resources support a finding of unconscionability?*

IMPACT OF THIS CASE ON TODAY'S LAW *This early classic case illustrates the approach that many courts take today when deciding whether a sales contract is unconscionable—an approach that focuses on "excessive" price and unequal bargaining power. Most of the litigants who have used UCC 2–302 successfully could demonstrate both an absence of meaningful choice and that the contract terms were unreasonably favorable to the other party.*

Concept Summary 15.1 on the next page reviews the concepts and rules related to the formation of sales and lease contracts.

SECTION 4
CONTRACTS FOR THE INTERNATIONAL SALE OF GOODS

International sales contracts between firms or individuals located in different countries may be governed by the 1980 United Nations Convention on Contracts for the International Sale of Goods (CISG). The CISG governs international contracts only if the countries of the parties to the contract have ratified the CISG and if the parties have not agreed that some other law will govern their contract. As of 2013, the CISG had been adopted by seventy-eight countries, including the United States, Canada, some Central and South American countries, China, most European nations, Japan, and Mexico. That means that the CISG is the uniform international sales law of countries that account for more than two-thirds of all global trade.

Essentially, the CISG is to international sales contracts what Article 2 of the UCC is to domestic sales contracts. In domestic transactions, the UCC applies when the parties to a contract for a sale of goods have failed to specify in writing some important term, such as the price or delivery. Similarly, whenever the parties to international transactions have failed to specify in writing the precise terms of a contract, the CISG will be applied.

Unlike the UCC, *the CISG does not apply to consumer sales.* Neither the UCC nor the CISG applies to contracts for services.

A Comparison of CISG and UCC Provisions

The provisions of the CISG, although similar for the most part to those of the UCC, differ from them in some respects. If the CISG and the UCC conflict, the CISG applies (because it is a treaty of the U.S. national government and therefore is supreme—see the discussion of the supremacy clause in Chapter 2).

The major differences between the CISG and the UCC in regard to contract formation concern the mirror image rule, irrevocable offers, the Statute of Frauds, and the time of contract formation. We discuss these differences in the subsections that follow. CISG provisions relating to risk of loss, performance, remedies, and warranties will be discussed in the following chapters as those topics are examined.

THE MIRROR IMAGE RULE Under the UCC, a definite expression of acceptance that contains additional terms can still result in the formation of a contract, unless the additional terms are conditioned on the assent of the offeror. In other words, the UCC does away with the mirror image rule in domestic sales contracts.

Article 19 of the CISG provides that a contract can be formed even though the acceptance contains additional terms, unless the additional terms materially alter the contract. Under the CISG, however, the definition of a "material alteration" includes almost any

CONCEPT SUMMARY 15.1
The Formation of Sales and Lease Contracts

CONCEPT	DESCRIPTION
Offer and Acceptance	1. *Offer—* a. Not all terms have to be included for a contract to be formed. b. The price does not have to be included for a contract to be formed. c. Particulars of performance can be left open. d. An offer by a merchant in a signed writing with assurances that the offer will not be withdrawn is irrevocable without consideration (for up to three months). 2. *Acceptance—* a. Acceptance may be made by any reasonable means of communication. It is effective when dispatched. b. The acceptance of a unilateral offer can be made by a promise to ship or by the shipment of conforming or nonconforming goods. c. Acceptance by performance requires notice within a reasonable time. Otherwise, the offer can be treated as lapsed. d. A definite expression of acceptance creates a contract even if the terms of the acceptance modify the terms of the offer.
Consideration	A modification of a contract for the sale of goods does not require consideration.
Requirements under the Statute of Frauds	1. All contracts for the sale of goods priced at $500 or more must be in writing. A writing is sufficient as long as it indicates a contract between the parties and is signed by the party against whom enforcement is sought. A contract is not enforceable beyond the quantity shown in the writing. 2. When written confirmation of an oral contract between merchants is not objected to in writing by the receiver within ten days, the oral contract is enforceable. 3. Exceptions to the requirement of a writing exist in the following situations: a. When the oral contract is for specially manufactured or obtained goods not suitable for resale or lease to others and the seller or lessor has made commitments for the manufacture or procurement of the goods. b. If the defendant admits in pleadings, testimony, or other court proceedings that an oral contract for the sale or lease of goods was made, then the contract will be enforceable to the extent of the quantity of goods admitted. c. The oral agreement will be enforceable to the extent that payment has been received and accepted or to the extent that goods have been received and accepted.
Parol Evidence Rule	1. The terms of a clearly and completely worded written contract cannot be contradicted by evidence of prior agreements or contemporaneous oral agreements. 2. Evidence is admissible to clarify the terms of a writing in the following situations: a. If the contract terms are ambiguous. b. If evidence of course of dealing, usage of trade, or course of performance is necessary to learn or to clarify the intentions of the parties to the contract.

change in the terms. If an additional term relates to payment, quality, quantity, price, time and place of delivery, extent of one party's liability to the other, or the settlement of disputes, the CISG considers the added term a material alteration. In effect, then, the CISG requires that the terms of the acceptance mirror those of the offer.

Therefore, as a practical matter, businesspersons undertaking international sales transactions should not use the sale or purchase forms that they customarily use for transactions within the United States. Instead, they should draft specific forms to suit the needs of the particular transaction.

IRREVOCABLE OFFERS UCC 2–205 provides that a merchant's firm offer is irrevocable, even without consideration, if the merchant gives assurances in a signed writing. In contrast, under the CISG, an offer can become irrevocable without a signed writing. Article 16(2) of the CISG provides that an offer will be irrevocable if:

1. The offeror states orally that the offer is irrevocable.
2. The offeree reasonably relies on the offer as being irrevocable.

In both of these situations, the offer will be irrevocable even without a writing and without consideration.

THE WRITING REQUIREMENT As discussed previously, the UCC has a Statute of Frauds provision. UCC 2–201 requires contracts for the sale of goods priced at $500 or more to be evidenced by a written or electronic record signed by the party against whom enforcement is sought.

Article 11 of the CISG, however, states that a contract of sale "need not be concluded in or evidenced by writing and is not subject to any other requirements as to form. It may be proved by any means, including witnesses." Article 11 of the CISG accords with the legal customs of most nations, which no longer require contracts to meet certain formal or writing requirements to be enforceable.

TIME OF CONTRACT FORMATION Under the common law of contracts and the UCC, an acceptance is effective on dispatch, so a contract is created when the acceptance is transmitted. Under the CISG, in contrast, a contract is created not at the time the acceptance is transmitted but only on its *receipt* by the offeror. (The offer becomes *irrevocable,* however, when the acceptance is sent.)

Article 18(2) states that an acceptance by return promise (a unilateral contract—see Chapter 9) "becomes effective at the moment the indication of assent reaches the offeror." Under Article 18(3), the offeree may also bind the offeror by performance even without giving any notice to the offeror. The acceptance becomes effective "at the moment the act is performed." Thus, it is the offeree's reliance, rather than the communication of acceptance to the offeror, that creates the contract.

Special Provisions in International Contracts

Language and legal differences among nations can create various problems for parties to international contracts when disputes arise. It is possible to avoid these problems by including in a contract special provisions relating to choice of language, choice of

forum, choice of law, and the types of events that may excuse the parties from performance.

CHOICE OF LANGUAGE A deal struck between a U.S. company and a company in another country frequently involves two languages. One party may not understand complex contractual terms that are written in the other party's language. Translating the terms poses its own problems, as typically many phrases are not readily translatable into another language.

To make sure that no disputes arise out of this language problem, an international sales contract should include a **choice-of-language clause,** designating the official language by which the contract will be interpreted in the event of disagreement. The clause might also specify that the agreement is to be translated into, say, Spanish, and that the translation is to be approved by both parties so that they can rely on it. If arbitration is anticipated, an additional clause must be added to indicate the official language that will be used at the arbitration proceeding.

CHOICE OF FORUM A *forum-selection clause* designates the forum (place, or court) in which any disputes that arise under the contract will be litigated. Including a forum-selection clause in an international contract is especially important because when several countries are involved, litigation may be sought in courts in different nations. There are no universally accepted rules regarding the jurisdiction of a particular court over subject matter or parties to a dispute, although the adoption of the 2005 Choice of Court Convention helps resolve certain issues.

A forum-selection clause should indicate the specific court that will have jurisdiction. The forum does not necessarily have to be within the geographic boundaries of either party's nation.

Under certain circumstances, a forum-selection clause will not be valid. Specifically, if the clause denies one party an effective remedy, or is the product of fraud or unconscionable conduct, the clause will not be enforced. Similarly, if the designated forum causes substantial inconvenience to one of the parties, or violates public policy, the clause may not be enforced.

CHOICE OF LAW A contractual provision designating the applicable law, called a **choice-of-law clause,** is typically included in every international contract. At common law and in European civil law systems, parties are allowed to choose the law that will govern their contractual relationship.

There must normally be some connection between the chosen law and the contracting parties to show that the parties are not merely trying to avoid the laws of their own jurisdictions. ▶ **Example 15.22** A U.S. automaker contracts with a German company. The parties cannot choose the law of China to govern their agreement if neither the contract nor the parties have anything to do with China. The choice of Chinese law in that situation might reflect an attempt to avoid consumer, environmental, or employment laws that would otherwise apply to the transaction. ◀

Under the UCC, parties may choose the law that will govern the contract as long as the choice is "reasonable." Article 6 of the CISG, however, imposes no limitation on the parties in their choice of what law will govern the contract. The 1986 Hague Convention on the Law Applicable to Contracts for the International Sale of Goods—often referred to as the Choice-of-Law Convention—allows unlimited autonomy in the choice of law. Whenever a choice of law is not specified in a contract, the Hague Convention indicates that the law of the country where the seller's place of business is located will govern.

FORCE MAJEURE CLAUSE Every contract, and particularly those involving international transactions, should have a *force majeure* **clause.** The meaning of the French term *force majeure* is "impossible or irresistible force"—sometimes loosely defined as "an act of God." *Force majeure* clauses commonly stipulate that in addition to acts of God, a number of other eventualities (such as governmental orders or regulations, embargoes, or extreme shortages of materials) may excuse a party from liability for nonperformance.

Reviewing: The Formation of Sales and Lease Contracts

Guy Holcomb owns and operates Oasis Goodtime Emporium, an adult entertainment establishment. Holcomb wanted to create an adult Internet system for Oasis that would offer customers adult theme videos and "live" chat room programs using performers at the club. On May 10, Holcomb signed a work order authorizing Thomas Consulting Group (TCG) "to deliver a working prototype of a customer chat system, demonstrating the integration of live video and chatting in a Web browser." In exchange for creating the prototype, Holcomb agreed to pay TCG $64,697. On May 20, Holcomb signed an additional work order in the amount of $12,943 for TCG to install a customized firewall system. The work orders stated that Holcomb would make monthly installment payments to TCG, and both parties expected the work would be finished by September.

Due to unforeseen problems largely attributable to system configuration and software incompatibility, the project required more time than anticipated. By the end of the summer, the Web site was still not ready, and Holcomb had fallen behind in his payments to TCG. TCG threatened to cease work and file a suit for breach of contract unless the bill was paid. Rather than make further payments, Holcomb wanted to abandon the Web site project. Using the information presented in the chapter, answer the following questions.

1. Would a court be likely to decide that the transaction between Holcomb and TCG was covered by the Uniform Commercial Code (UCC)? Why or why not?
2. Would a court be likely to consider Holcomb a merchant under the UCC? Why or why not?
3. Did the parties have a valid contract under the UCC? Were any terms left open in the contract? If so, which terms? How would a court deal with open terms?
4. Suppose that Holcomb and TCG meet in October in an attempt to resolve their problems. At that time, the parties reach an oral agreement that TCG will continue to work without demanding full payment of the past due amounts and Holcomb will pay TCG $5,000 per week. Assuming the contract falls under the UCC, is the oral agreement enforceable? Why or why not?

DEBATE THIS . . . *The UCC should require the same degree of definiteness of terms, especially with respect to price and quantity, as contract law does.*

Terms and Concepts

choice-of-language clause 314	intangible property 299	requirements contract 304
choice-of-law clause 314	lease agreement 302	sale 299
course of dealing 309	lessee 302	sales contract 298
course of performance 310	lessor 302	seasonably 305
firm offer 304	merchant 302	tangible property 299
force majeure clause 315	output contract 304	usage of trade 310
fully integrated contract 309	predominant-factor test 299	

ExamPrep

Issue Spotters

1. E-Design, Inc., orders 150 computer desks. Fav-O-Rite Supplies, Inc., ships 150 printer stands. Is this an acceptance of the offer or a counteroffer? If it is an acceptance, is it a breach of the contract? Why or why not? What if Fav-O-Rite told E-Design it was sending the printer stands as "an accommodation"? **(See page 305.)**

2. Truck Parts, Inc. (TPI), often sells supplies to United Fix-It Company (UFC), which services trucks. Over the phone, they negotiate for the sale of eighty-four sets of tires. TPI sends a letter to UFC detailing the terms and two weeks later ships the tires. Is there an enforceable contract between them? Why or why not? **(See page 306.)**

• Check your answers to the Issue Spotters against the answers provided in Appendix B at the end of this text.

Before the Test

Go to **www.cengagebrain.com**, enter the ISBN 9781285770192, and click on "Find" to locate this textbook's Web site. Then, click on "Access Now" under "Study Tools," and select Chapter 15 at the top. There, you will find a Practice Quiz that you can take to assess your mastery of the concepts in this chapter, as well as Flashcards and a Glossary of important terms.

Business Scenarios

15–1. The Statute of Frauds. Fresher Foods, Inc., orally agreed to purchase one thousand bushels of corn for $1.25 per bushel from Dale Vernon, a farmer. Fresher Foods paid $125 down and agreed to pay the remainder of the purchase price on delivery, which was scheduled for one week later. When Fresher Foods tendered the balance of $1,125 on the scheduled day of delivery and requested the corn, Vernon refused to deliver it. Fresher Foods sued Vernon for damages, claiming that Vernon had breached their oral contract. Can Fresher Foods recover? If so, to what extent? **(See page 308.)**

15–2. Additional Terms. Strike offers to sell Bailey one thousand shirts for a stated price. The offer declares that shipment will be made by Dependable Truck Line. Bailey replies, "I accept your offer for one thousand shirts at the price quoted. Delivery to be by Yellow Express Truck Line." Both Strike and Bailey are merchants. Three weeks later, Strike ships the shirts by Dependable Truck Line, and Bailey refuses to accept delivery. Strike sues for breach of contract. Bailey claims that there never was a contract because his reply, which included a modification of carriers, did not constitute an acceptance. Bailey further claims that even if there had been a contract, Strike would have been in breach because Strike shipped the shirts by Dependable, contrary to the contract terms. Discuss fully Bailey's claims. **(See pages 305–307.)**

Business Case Problems

15–3. Spotlight on Goods and Services—The Statute of Frauds. Fallsview Glatt Kosher Caterers ran a business that provided travel packages, including food, entertainment, and lectures on religious subjects, to customers during the Passover holiday at a New York resort. Willie Rosenfeld verbally agreed to pay Fallsview $24,050 for the Passover package for himself and his family. Rosenfeld did not appear at the resort and never paid the amount owed. Fallsview sued Rosenfeld for breach of contract. Rosenfeld claimed that the contract was unenforceable because it was not in writing and violated the UCC's Statute of Frauds. Is the contract valid? Explain. [*Fallsview Glatt Kosher Caterers, Inc. v. Rosenfeld*, 794 N.Y.S.2d 790 (N.Y.Super. 2005)] **(See page 308.)**

15–4. BUSINESS CASE PROBLEM
WITH SAMPLE ANSWER: Additional Terms.

B.S. International, Ltd. (BSI), makes costume jewelry. JMAM, LLC, is a wholesaler of costume jewelry. JMAM sent BSI a letter with the terms for orders, including the necessary procedure for obtaining credit for items that customers rejected. The letter stated, "By signing below, you agree to the terms." Steven Baracsi, BSI's owner, signed the letter and returned it. For six years, BSI made jewelry for JMAM, which resold it. Items rejected by customers were sent back to JMAM, but were never returned to BSI. BSI filed a suit against JMAM, claiming $41,294.21 for the unreturned items. BSI showed the court a copy of JMAM's terms. Across the bottom had been typed a "PS" requiring the return of rejected merchandise. Was this "PS" part of the contract? Discuss. [B.S. International, Ltd. v. JMAM, LLC, 13 A.3d 1057 (R.I. 2011)] **(See pages 305–307.)**

- For a sample answer to Problem 15–4, go to Appendix C at the end of this text.

15–5. Partial Performance and the Statute of Frauds. After a series of e-mails, Jorge Bonilla, the sole proprietor of a printing company in Uruguay, agreed to buy a used printer from Crystal Graphics Equipment, Inc., in New York. Crystal Graphics, through its agent, told Bonilla that the printing press was fully operational, contained all of its parts, and was in excellent condition except for some damage to one of the printing towers. Bonilla paid $95,000. Crystal Graphics sent him a signed, stamped invoice reflecting this payment. The invoice was dated six days after Bonilla's conversation with the agent. When the printing press arrived, Bonilla discovered that it was missing parts and was damaged. Crystal Graphics sent replacement parts, but they did not work. Ultimately, Crystal Graphics was never able to make the printer operational. Bonilla sued, alleging breach of contract, breach of the implied covenant of good faith and fair dealing, breach of express warranty, and breach of implied warranty. Crystal Graphics claimed that the contract was not enforceable because it did not satisfy the Statute of Frauds. Can Crystal Graphics prevail on this basis? Why or why not? [*Bonilla v. Crystal Graphics Equipment, Inc.*, 2012 WL 360145 (S.D.Fla. 2012)] **(See page 309.)**

15–6. The Statute of Frauds. Kendall Gardner agreed to buy from B&C Shavings, a specially built shaving mill to pro-

duce wood shavings for poultry processors. B&C faxed an invoice to Gardner reflecting a purchase price of $86,200, with a 30 percent down payment and the "balance due before shipment." Gardner paid the down payment. B&C finished the mill and wrote Gardner a letter telling him to "pay the balance due or you will lose the down payment." By then, Gardner had lost his customers for the wood shavings, could not pay the balance due, and asked for the return of his down payment. Did these parties have an enforceable contract under the Statute of Frauds? Explain. [*Bowen v. Gardner*, 2013 Ark.App. 52 (2013)] **(See page 308.)**

15–7. A QUESTION OF ETHICS: Contract Terms.

Daniel Fox owned Fox & Lamberth Enterprises, Inc., a kitchen and bath remodeling business, in Dayton, Ohio. Fox leased a building from Carl and Bellulah Hussong. Craftsmen Home Improvement, Inc., also remodeled baths and kitchens. When Fox planned to close his business, Craftsmen expressed an interest in buying his showroom assets. Fox set a price of $50,000. Craftsmen's owners agreed and gave Fox a list of the desired items and "A Bill of Sale" that set the terms for payment. The parties did not discuss Fox's arrangement with the Hussongs, but Craftsmen expected to negotiate a new lease and extensively modified the premises, including removing some of the displays to its own showroom. When the Hussongs and Craftsmen could not agree on new terms, Craftsmen told Fox that the deal was off. [Fox & Lamberth Enterprises, Inc. v. Craftsmen Home Improvement, Inc., __ N.E.2d __ (2 Dist. 2006)] **(See pages 299 and 308.)**

(a) In Fox's suit in an Ohio state court for breach of contract, Craftsmen raised the Statute of Frauds as a defense. What are the requirements of the Statute of Frauds? Did the deal between Fox and Craftsmen meet these requirements? Did it fall under one of the exceptions? Explain.

(b) Craftsmen also claimed that the predominant factor of its agreement with Fox was a lease for the Hussongs' building. What is the "predominant-factor" test? Does it apply here? In any event, is it fair to hold a party to a contract to buy a business's assets when the buyer cannot negotiate a favorable lease of the premises on which the assets are located? Discuss.

Legal Reasoning Group Activity

15–8. Parol Evidence. Mountain Stream Trout Co. agreed to buy "market size" trout from trout grower Lake Farms, LLC. Their five- year contract did not define *market size*. At the time, in the trade, *market size* referred to fish of one-pound live weight. After three years, Mountain Stream began taking fewer, smaller deliveries of larger fish, claiming that *market size* varied according to whatever its customers demanded and that its customers now demanded larger fish. Lake Farms filed a suit for breach of contract. **(See page 309.)**

(a) The first group will decide whether parol (outside) evidence is admissible to explain the terms of this contract. Are there any exceptions that could apply?

(b) A second group will determine the impact of course of dealing and usage of trade on the interpretation of contract terms.

(c) A third group will discuss how parties to a commercial contract can avoid the possibility that a court will interpret the contract terms in accordance with trade usage.

CHAPTER 16

PERFORMANCE, BREACH, AND WARRANTIES OF SALES AND LEASE CONTRACTS

The performance that is required of the parties under a sales or lease contract consists of the duties and obligations each party has under the terms of the contract. The basic obligation of the seller or lessor is to transfer and deliver the goods as stated in the contract, and the basic duty of the buyer or lessee is to accept and pay for the goods.

Keep in mind that "duties and obligations" under the terms of the contract include those specified by the agreement, by custom, and by the Uniform Commercial Code (UCC). Thus, parties to a sales or lease contract may be bound not only by terms they expressly agreed on, but also by terms implied by custom, such as a customary method of weighing or measuring particular goods. In addition, the UCC sometimes imposes terms on parties to a sales contract, such as the requirement that a seller find a substitute carrier to deliver goods to the buyer if the agreed-on carrier becomes unavailable.

The UCC also imposes certain warranties of title in all sales and lease contracts, and it identifies several other types of warranties that can arise.

In this chapter, we examine the basic performance obligations of the parties to a sales or lease contract. We also examine the remedies available to one party when the other party breaches the contract. The UCC provides a range of possible remedies, from retaining the goods to requiring the breaching party's performance under the contract. In contrast to the common law of contracts, remedies under the UCC are *cumulative*. In other words, an innocent party to a breached sales or lease contract is not limited to one exclusive remedy. We conclude this chapter with a discussion of the warranties that occur in sales and lease contracts.

PERFORMANCE OBLIGATIONS

As discussed in Chapter 15, the obligations of good faith and commercial reasonableness underlie every sales and lease contract.

The UCC's Good Faith Provision

The UCC's good faith provision, which can never be disclaimed, reads as follows: "Every contract or duty within this Act imposes an obligation of good faith in its performance or enforcement" [UCC 1–304]. *Good faith* means honesty in fact. For a merchant, it means honesty in fact and the observance of reasonable commercial standards of fair dealing in the trade [UCC 2–103(1)(b)]. In other words, merchants are held to a higher standard of performance or duty than are nonmerchants.

Good Faith and Contract Performance

The principle of good faith applies to both parties and provides a framework for the entire agreement. If a sales contract leaves open some particulars of performance, for instance, the parties must exercise good faith and commercial reasonableness when later specifying the details. In performing a sales or lease contract, the basic obligation of the seller or lessor is to *transfer and deliver conforming goods*. The basic obligation of the buyer or lessee is to *accept and pay for conforming goods* in accordance with the contract [UCC 2–301, 2A–516(1)]. Overall performance of a sales or lease contract is controlled by the agreement between the parties. When the contract is unclear and disputes arise, the courts look to the UCC and impose standards of good faith and commercial reasonableness.

Obligations of the Seller or Lessor

As stated, the basic duty of the seller or lessor is to deliver the goods called for under the contract to the buyer or lessee.

TENDER OF DELIVERY Goods that conform to the contract description in every way are called **conforming goods.** To fulfill the contract, the seller or lessor must either deliver or tender delivery of conforming goods to the buyer or lessee. **Tender of delivery** occurs when the seller or lessor makes conforming goods available and gives the buyer or lessee whatever notification is reasonably necessary to enable the buyer or lessee to take delivery [UCC 2–503(1), 2A–508(1)].

Tender must occur at a *reasonable hour* and in a *reasonable manner.* For example, a seller cannot call the buyer at 2:00 A.M. and say, "The goods are ready. I'll give you twenty minutes to get them." Unless the parties have agreed otherwise, the goods must be tendered for delivery at a reasonable hour and kept available for a reasonable time to enable the buyer to take possession [UCC 2–503(1)(a)].

Normally, all goods called for by a contract must be tendered in a single delivery—unless the parties have agreed on delivery in several lots or *installments* (to be discussed shortly) [UCC 2–307, 2–612, 2A–510]. ▶ **Example 16.1** An order for 1,000 Under Armour men's shirts cannot be delivered two shirts at a time. If, however, the parties agree that the shirts will be delivered in four orders of 250 each as they are produced (for summer, fall, winter, and spring inventory), then tender of delivery may occur in this manner. ◀

PLACE OF DELIVERY The buyer and seller (or lessor and lessee) may agree that the goods will be delivered to a particular destination where the buyer or lessee will take possession. If the contract does not indicate where the goods will be delivered, then the place for delivery will be one of the following:

1. The *seller's place of business.*
2. The *seller's residence,* if the seller has no business location [UCC 2–308(a)].
3. The *location of the goods,* if both parties know at the time of contracting that the goods are located somewhere other than the seller's business [UCC 2–308(b)].

▶ **Example 16.2** Li Wan and Boyd both live in San Francisco. In San Francisco, Li Wan contracts to sell Boyd five used trucks, which both parties know are located in a Chicago warehouse. If nothing more is specified in the contract, the place of delivery for the trucks is Chicago. Li Wan may tender delivery by giving Boyd either a negotiable or a nonnegotiable document of title. Alternatively, Li Wan may obtain the bailee's (warehouser's) acknowledgment that Boyd is entitled to possession.[1] ◀

DELIVERY VIA CARRIER In many instances, it is clear from the surrounding circumstances or delivery terms in the contract that the parties intended the goods to be moved by a carrier. In carrier contracts, the seller fulfills the obligation to deliver the goods through either a shipment contract or a destination contract.

Shipment Contracts. A *shipment contract* requires or authorizes the seller to ship goods by a carrier, rather than to deliver them at a particular destination [UCC 2–319, 2–509(1)(a)]. Under a shipment contract, unless otherwise agreed, the seller must do the following:

1. Place the goods into the hands of the carrier.
2. Make a contract for their transportation that is reasonable according to the nature of the goods and their value. (For example, certain types of goods need refrigeration in transit.)
3. Obtain and promptly deliver or tender to the buyer any documents necessary to enable the buyer to obtain possession of the goods from the carrier.
4. Promptly notify the buyer that shipment has been made [UCC 2–504].

If the seller does not make a reasonable contract for transportation or notify the buyer of the shipment, the buyer can reject the goods, but only if a *material loss* or a *significant delay* results. ▶ **Example 16.3** Zigi's Organic Fruits sells strawberries to Lozier under a shipment contract. If Zigi's does not arrange for refrigerated transportation and the berries spoil during transport, a material loss will likely result because Lozier will be unable to sell them. ◀ (Of course, the parties are free to make agreements that alter the UCC's rules and allow the buyer to reject goods for other reasons.)

Destination Contracts. In a *destination contract,* the seller agrees to deliver conforming goods to the buyer

---

1. Unless the buyer objects, the seller may also tender delivery by instructing the bailee in a writing (record) to release the goods to the buyer without the bailee's acknowledgment of the buyer's rights [UCC 2–503(4)]. Risk of loss, however, does not pass until the buyer has had a reasonable amount of time in which to present the document or the instructions.

at a particular destination. The goods must be tendered at a reasonable hour and held at the buyer's disposal for a reasonable length of time. The seller must also give the buyer appropriate notice and any necessary documents to enable the buyer to obtain delivery from the carrier [UCC 2–503].

THE PERFECT TENDER RULE As previously noted, the seller or lessor has an obligation to ship or tender *conforming goods,* which the buyer or lessee is then obligated to accept and pay for according to the terms of the contract [UCC 2–507]. Under the common law,

the seller was obligated to deliver goods that conformed with the terms of the contract in every detail. This is called the **perfect tender rule.**

The UCC preserves the perfect tender doctrine. It states that if goods or tender of delivery fails *in any respect* to conform to the contract, the buyer or lessee may accept the goods, reject the entire shipment, or accept part and reject part [UCC 2–601, 2A–509].

The corollary to this rule is that if the goods conform in every respect, the buyer or lessee does not have a right to reject the goods, as the following case illustrates.

CASE ANALYSIS

Case 16.1   Wilson Sporting Goods Co. v. U.S. Golf and Tennis Centers, Inc.
Court of Appeals of Tennessee, 2012 WL 601804 (2012).

IN THE LANGUAGE OF THE COURT
Charles D. *SUSANO,* Jr., J.
[Judge]

* * * *

[U.S. Golf & Tennis Centers, Inc. (the Company), and its owners, Arthur and Louise Bell, operate] two retail sporting goods stores specializing in the sale of golf and tennis equipment: one in Tennessee and the one in Ohio. * * * The Company agreed to purchase from Wilson [Sporting Goods Company] 4,000 units of second-hand golf balls at a unit price of $5.00—a unit being two dozen golf balls. Thus, the Company purchased 96,000 golf balls for a total price of $20,000. The order was shipped * * * with half of the shipment being received at the Ohio store and the other half being delivered to the Tennessee store. It is undisputed that the shipment conformed in quantity and quality to the specifications of the parties' contract.

When Wilson filed suit in [a Tennessee state court against U.S. Golf] the $20,000 balance on the contract was past due and owing.

The record reflects a series of fax communications between Mr. Bell and Wilson * * * in which Mr. Bell repeatedly sought written confirmation that the Company had received the "lowest price" for the golf balls. In its faxes, Wilson confirmed that the Company received the lowest price "that Wilson offered to any one in the market." The communications ended with Wilson seeking "prompt payment," and with Mr. Bell, apparently unsatisfied with Wilson's responses, seeking authorization to return the shipment to Wilson.

In answer to Wilson's suit, the defendants alleged breach of contract in that Wilson had "misrepresented the price of the goods at issue. * * * Before delivery the defendants heard that in fact Wilson had sold the product for $2.00 per dozen. * * * Accordingly, there was never a meeting of the minds as to the amount that would be charged."

[After a trial, the court entered a judgment in favor of Wilson for $33,099.28, including interest, attorneys' fees, and other expenses. The defendants appealed.]

* * * *

The defendants contend that they were legally entitled to cancel the subject contract and that, therefore, the trial court erred in upholding the contract and awarding Wilson a judgment for $33,099.28.

* * * The defendants point, in particular, to Tennessee Code Section 47–2–601 [Tennessee's version of UCC 2–601] which provides, in relevant part, that *"if the goods or the tender of delivery fail in any respect to conform to the contract,"* the buyer may, among other options, *"reject the whole * * * ."* From the defendants' point of view, the goods in this case failed to conform to the contract because, according to the defendants, Wilson charged the defendants a higher price for the goods than that agreed upon. The defendants assert that Mr. Bell, acting upon behalf of the Company, was thus entitled to and did in fact reject the shipment. The defendants argue that once they rejected the goods, they were entitled to cancel the contract pursuant to Tennessee Code Section 47–2–711 [Tennessee's version of UCC 2–711]. That section provides as follows:

"Where * * * the buyer rightfully rejects * * * , the buyer may cancel." [Emphasis added.]

* * * Wilson responds that the goods in no way failed to conform to the contract, and that there was no rejection * * * of the goods by the Company. Accordingly, Wilson concludes that the Code sections relied upon by the defendants do not apply to permit the defendants to cancel the contract. In a word, Wilson is correct.

Nothing in the evidence before us shows or even suggests that the defendants ever rejected delivery of the shipment of the golf balls or that [they] ever had the right to do so. *The defendants do not dispute that the product received by the Company conformed to the contract with respect to quantity and quality. Their sole contention at trial was that the price charged was not the lowest available price, as contemplated by the contract.* The trial court, however, found that the parties had a contract for an agreed total purchase price of $20,000, and that "the lowest price for the specific goods ordered and received was confirmed." * * * In addition to the fact that the contract's terms regarding price are clear, there is nothing in the record to contradict Wilson's confirmations to Mr. Bell that the defendants did receive the lowest price offered to anyone for the goods received. [Emphasis added.]

In summary, the cited UCC provisions regarding rejection * * * and cancellation do not apply in this case where the trial court properly found that the seller, [that is,] Wilson, fully performed, but the buyer, the Company, failed to make any payments. As discussed, the agreed contract terms, including purchase price, were clear. The trial court did not err in upholding the contract and holding the defendants liable for the goods received.

* * * *

The judgment of the trial court is affirmed.

LEGAL REASONING QUESTIONS

1. What is the perfect tender rule?

2. According to the UCC, what are a buyer's options if the goods do *not* conform to the contract? Does a buyer have those same options if the goods conform in every respect? Explain.

3. In this case, what provision in the parties' contract was at the heart of their dispute?

4. What did the court rule on the dispute between these parties? Why?

EXCEPTIONS TO THE PERFECT TENDER RULE Because of the rigidity of the perfect tender rule, several exceptions to the rule have been created, some of which we discuss here.

Agreement of the Parties. Exceptions to the perfect tender rule may be established by agreement. If the parties have agreed, for instance, that defective goods or parts will not be rejected if the seller or lessor is able to repair or replace them within a reasonable period of time, the perfect tender rule does not apply.

Cure. The UCC does not specifically define the term **cure,** but it refers to the right of the seller or lessor to repair, adjust, or replace defective or nonconforming goods [UCC 2–508, 2A–513].

The seller or lessor has a right to attempt to "cure" a defect when the following are true:

1. A delivery is rejected because the goods were nonconforming.

2. The time for performance has not yet expired.

3. The seller or lessor provides timely notice to the buyer or lessee of the intention to cure.

4. The cure can be made *within the contract time for performance.*

Once the time for performance under the contract has expired, the seller or lessor no longer has a right to cure. Nevertheless, the seller or lessor can still cure if he or she has *reasonable grounds to believe that the nonconforming tender will be acceptable to the buyer or lessee* [UCC 2–508(2), 2A–513(2)].

▶ **Example 16.4** In the past, EZ Office Supply has frequently accepted blue pens when the seller, Baxter's Wholesale, did not have black pens in stock. In this context, Baxter's has reasonable grounds to believe that EZ will again accept such a substitute. Even if EZ rejected the substituted goods on one particular occasion, Baxter's has reasonable grounds to believe that blue pens will be acceptable. Therefore, if EZ indicates that it will not accept blue pens, Baxter's normally will have a reasonable time to obtain and tender black pens. ◀

A seller or lessor will sometimes tender nonconforming goods with some type of price allowance (discount). A discounted price can serve as the "reasonable grounds" to believe that the buyer or lessee will accept the nonconforming tender.

The right to cure substantially restricts the right of the buyer or lessee to reject goods. To reject, the buyer or lessee must inform the seller or lessor of the particular defect. If the defect is not disclosed, the buyer or lessee cannot later assert the defect as a defense if the defect is one that the seller or lessor could have cured. Generally, buyers and lessees must act in good faith and state specific reasons for refusing to accept goods [UCC 2–605, 2A–514].

Substitution of Carriers. Sometimes, an agreed-on manner of delivery (such as the use of a particular carrier to transport the goods) becomes impracticable or unavailable through no fault of either party. In that situation, if a commercially reasonable substitute is available, this substitute performance is sufficient tender to the buyer and must be used [UCC 2–614(1)]. The seller or lessor is required to arrange for a substitute carrier and normally is responsible for any additional shipping costs (unless the contract states otherwise).

▶ **Example 16.5** A sales contract calls for a large generator to be shipped by Mac's Trucking on or before June 1. The contract terms clearly state the importance of the delivery date. The employees of Mac's go on strike. The seller must make a reasonable substitute tender, by another trucking company or perhaps by rail, if it is available. ◀

Installment Contracts. An **installment contract** is a single contract that requires or authorizes delivery in two or more separate lots to be accepted and paid for separately. With an installment contract, a buyer or lessee can reject an installment *only if the nonconformity substantially impairs the value* of the installment and cannot be cured [UCC 2–307, 2–612(2), 2A–510(1)]. If the buyer or lessee fails to notify the seller or lessor of the rejection, however, and subsequently accepts a nonconforming installment, the contract is reinstated [UCC 2–612(3), 2A–510(2)].

Unless the contract provides otherwise, the entire installment contract is breached only when one or more nonconforming installments *substantially* impair the value of the *whole contract*. ▶ **Example 16.6** A contract calls for the parts of a machine to be delivered in installments. The first part is necessary for the

operation of the machine, but when it is delivered, it is irreparably defective. The failure of this first installment will be a breach of the whole contract because the machine will not operate without the first part.

Suppose that, instead, the contract had called for twenty carloads of plywood and only 6 percent of one carload had deviated from the thickness specifications in the contract. It is unlikely that a court would find that a defect in 6 percent of one installment substantially impaired the value of the whole contract. ◀

The point to remember is that the UCC significantly alters the right of the buyer or lessee to reject the entire contract if the contract requires delivery to be made in several installments. The UCC strictly limits rejection to instances of *substantial* nonconformity.

Commercial Impracticability. As discussed in Chapter 13, occurrences unforeseen by either party when a contract was made may make performance commercially impracticable. When this occurs, the perfect tender rule no longer applies. The seller or lessor must, however, notify the buyer or lessee as soon as practicable that there will be a delay or nondelivery.

▶ **Example 16.7** Houston Oil Company, which receives its oil from the Middle East, has a contract to supply Northwest Fuels with one hundred thousand barrels of oil. Because of an oil embargo by the Organization of Petroleum Exporting Countries, Houston is unable to secure oil from the Middle East or any other source to meet the terms of the contract. This situation comes fully under the commercial impracticability exception to the perfect tender doctrine. ◀

The doctrine of commercial impracticability does not extend to problems that could have been foreseen—such as an increase in cost resulting from inflation. The nonoccurrence of the contingency must have been a basic assumption on which the contract was made [UCC 2–615, 2A–405].

Sometimes, the unforeseen event only *partially* affects the capacity of the seller or lessor to perform. Therefore, the seller or lessor can *partially* fulfill the contract but cannot tender total performance. In this event, the seller or lessor is required to distribute any remaining goods or deliveries fairly and reasonably among the parties to whom it is contractually obligated to deliver the goods [UCC 2–615(b), 2A–405(b)]. The buyer or lessee must receive notice of the allocation and has the right to accept or reject it [UCC 2–615(c), 2A–405(c)].

▶ **Example 16.8** A Florida orange grower, Best Citrus, Inc., contracts to sell this season's crop to a number of customers, including Martin's grocery chain. Martin's contracts to purchase two thousand crates of oranges. Best Citrus has sprayed *some* of its orange groves with a chemical called Karmoxin. The U.S. Department of Agriculture discovers that persons who eat products sprayed with Karmoxin may develop cancer and issues an order prohibiting the sale of these products. Best Citrus picks all the oranges not sprayed with Karmoxin, but the quantity is insufficient to meet all the contracted-for deliveries. In this situation, Best Citrus is required to allocate its production. It notifies Martin's that it cannot deliver the full quantity specified in the contract and indicates the amount it will be able to deliver. Martin's can either accept or reject the allocation, but Best Citrus has no further contractual liability. ◀

Destruction of Identified Goods. Sometimes, an unexpected event, such as a fire, totally destroys goods through no fault of either party before risk passes to the buyer or lessee. In such a situation, *if the goods were identified at the time the contract was formed,* the parties are excused from performance [UCC 2–613, 2A–221]. If the goods are only partially destroyed, however, the buyer or lessee can inspect them and either treat the contract as void or accept the damaged goods with a reduction in the contract price.

▶ **Example 16.9** Atlas Sporting Equipment agrees to lease to River Bicycles sixty bicycles of a particular model that has been discontinued. No other bicycles of that model are available. River specifies that it needs the bicycles to rent to tourists. Before Atlas can deliver the bicycles, they are destroyed by a fire. In this situation, Atlas is not liable to River for failing to deliver the bicycles. Through no fault of either party, the goods were destroyed before the risk of loss passed to the lessee. The loss was total, so the contract is avoided. Clearly, Atlas has no obligation to tender the bicycles, and River has no obligation to make the lease payments for them. ◀

Assurance and Cooperation. Two other exceptions to the perfect tender doctrine apply equally to both parties to sales and lease contracts: *the right of assurance* and the *duty of cooperation.*

The UCC provides that if one party has "reasonable grounds" to believe that the other party will not perform, the first party may *in writing* "demand adequate assurance of due performance" from the other

party. Until such assurance is received, the first party may "suspend" further performance without liability. What constitutes "reasonable grounds" is determined by commercial standards. If such assurances are not forthcoming within a reasonable time (not to exceed thirty days), the failure to respond may be treated as a repudiation of the contract [UCC 2–609, 2A–401].

▶ **Case in Point 16.10** Two companies that made road-surfacing materials, Koch Materials and Shore Slurry Seal, Inc., entered into a contract. Koch obtained a license to use Novachip, a special material made by Shore, and Shore agreed to buy all of its asphalt from Koch for the next seven years. A few years into the contract term, Shore notified Koch that it planned to sell its assets to Asphalt Paving Systems, Inc. Koch demanded assurances that Asphalt Paving would continue the deal, but Shore refused to provide assurances. The court held that Koch could treat Shore's failure to give assurances as a repudiation and sue Shore for breach of contract.[2] ◀

Sometimes, the performance of one party depends on the cooperation of the other. The UCC provides that when cooperation is not forthcoming, the other party can suspend performance without liability and hold the uncooperative party in breach or proceed to perform the contract in any reasonable manner [UCC 2–311(3)].

▶ **Example 16.11** Aman is required by contract to deliver 1,200 LG washing machines to various locations in California on or before October 1. Frieda, the buyer, is to specify the locations for delivery. Aman repeatedly requests the delivery locations, but Frieda does not respond. The washing machines are ready for shipment on October 1, but Frieda still refuses to give Aman the delivery locations. If Aman does not ship on October 1, he cannot be held liable. Aman is excused for any resulting delay of performance because of Frieda's failure to cooperate. ◀

Obligations of the Buyer or Lessee

The main obligation of the buyer or lessee under a sales or lease contract is to pay for the goods tendered in accordance with the contract. Once the seller or lessor has adequately tendered delivery, the buyer or lessee is obligated to accept the goods and pay for them according to the terms of the contract.

---

2. *Koch Materials Co. v. Shore Slurry Seal, Inc.,* 205 F.Supp.2d 324 (D.N.J. 2002).

PAYMENT In the absence of any specific agreements, the buyer or lessee must make payment at the time and place the goods are *received* [UCC 2–310(a), 2A–516(1)]. When a sale is made on credit, the buyer is obligated to pay according to the specified credit terms (for example, 60, 90, or 120 days), not when the goods are received. The credit period usually begins on the *date of shipment* [UCC 2–310(d)]. Under a lease contract, a lessee must make the lease payment that was specified in the contract [UCC 2A–516(1)].

Payment can be made by any means agreed on between the parties—cash or any other method generally acceptable in the commercial world. If the seller demands cash, the seller must permit the buyer reasonable time to obtain it [UCC 2–511].

RIGHT OF INSPECTION Unless the parties otherwise agree, or for C.O.D. (collect on delivery) transactions, the buyer or lessee has an absolute right to inspect the goods before making payment. This right allows the buyer or lessee to verify that the goods tendered or delivered conform to the contract. If the goods are not as ordered, the buyer or lessee has no duty to pay. *An opportunity for inspection is therefore a condition precedent to the right of the seller or lessor to enforce payment* [UCC 2–513(1), 2A–515(1)].

Inspection can take place at any reasonable place and time and in any reasonable manner. Generally, what is reasonable is determined by custom of the trade, past practices of the parties, and the like. The buyer bears the costs of inspecting the goods but can recover the costs from the seller if the goods do not conform and are rejected [UCC 2–513(2)].

ACCEPTANCE After having had a reasonable opportunity to inspect the goods, the buyer or lessee can demonstrate acceptance in any of the following ways:

1. The buyer or lessee indicates (by words or conduct) to the seller or lessor that the goods are conforming or that he or she will retain them in spite of their nonconformity [UCC 2–606(1)(a), 2A–515(1)(a)].
2. The buyer or lessee *fails to reject* the goods within a reasonable period of time [UCC 2–602(1), 2–606(1)(b), 2A–515(1)(b)].
3. In sales contracts, the buyer will be deemed to have accepted the goods if he or she *performs any act inconsistent with the seller's ownership.* For instance, any use or resale of the goods—except for the limited purpose of testing or inspecting the goods—generally constitutes an acceptance [UCC 2–606(1)(c)].

PARTIAL ACCEPTANCE If some of the goods delivered do not conform to the contract and the seller or lessor has failed to cure, the buyer or lessee can make a *partial* acceptance [UCC 2–601(c), 2A–509(1)]. The same is true if the nonconformity was not reasonably discoverable before acceptance. (In the latter situation, the buyer or lessee may be able to revoke the acceptance, as will be discussed later in this chapter.)

A buyer or lessee cannot accept less than a single commercial unit, however. The UCC defines a *commercial unit* as a unit of goods that, by commercial usage, is viewed as a "single whole" for purposes of sale and that cannot be divided without materially impairing the character of the unit, its market value, or its use [UCC 2–105(6), 2A–103(1)(c)]. A commercial unit can be a single article (such as a machine), a set of articles (such as a suite of furniture), a quantity (such as a bale, a gross, or a carload), or any other unit treated in the trade as a single whole.

See *Concept Summary 16.1* on the following page for a review of the obligations of both parties to a sales or lease contract.

Anticipatory Repudiation

What if, before the time for contract performance, one party clearly communicates to the other the intention *not* to perform? As discussed in Chapter 13, such an action is a breach of the contract by *anticipatory repudiation.*

When anticipatory repudiation occurs, the nonbreaching party has a choice of two responses:

1. Treat the repudiation as a final breach by pursuing a remedy.
2. Wait to see if the repudiating party will decide to honor the contract despite the avowed intention to renege [UCC 2–610, 2A–402].

In either situation, the nonbreaching party may suspend performance.

The UCC permits the breaching party to "retract" his or her repudiation (subject to some limitations). This can be done by any method that clearly indicates the party's intent to perform. Once retraction is made, the rights of the repudiating party under the contract are reinstated. There can be no retraction, however, if since the time of the repudiation the other party has canceled or materially changed position or otherwise indicated that the repudiation is final [UCC 2–611, 2A–403].

CONCEPT SUMMARY 16.1
Performance of Sales and Lease Contracts

CONCEPT	DESCRIPTION
Obligations of the Seller or Lessor	1. The seller or lessor must tender *conforming* goods to the buyer or lessee at a *reasonable hour* and in a *reasonable manner.* Under the perfect tender doctrine, the seller or lessor must tender goods that conform exactly to the terms of the contract [UCC 2–503(1), 2A–508(1)].
	2. If the seller or lessor tenders nonconforming goods and the buyer or lessee rejects them, the seller or lessor may *cure* (repair or replace the goods) within the contract time for performance [UCC 2–508(1), 2A–513(1)]. Even if the time for performance under the contract has expired, the seller or lessor has a reasonable time to substitute conforming goods without liability if the seller or lessor has reasonable grounds to believe the nonconforming tender will be acceptable to the buyer or lessee [UCC 2–508(2), 2A–513(2)].
	3. If the agreed-on means of delivery becomes impracticable or unavailable, the seller must substitute an alternative means (such as a different carrier) if a reasonable one is available [UCC 2–614(1)].
	4. If a seller or lessor tenders nonconforming goods in any one installment under an installment contract, the buyer or lessee may reject the installment only if the nonconformity substantially impairs its value and cannot be cured. The entire installment contract is breached only when one or more installments *substantially* impair the value of the *whole* contract [UCC 2–612, 2A–510].
	5. When performance becomes commercially impracticable owing to circumstances unforeseen when the contract was formed, the perfect tender rule no longer applies [UCC 2–615, 2A–405].
Obligations of the Buyer or Lessee	1. On tender of delivery by the seller or lessor, the buyer or lessee must pay for the goods at the time and place the goods are *received,* unless the sale is made on credit. Payment can be made by any method generally acceptable in the commercial world, but the seller can demand cash [UCC 2–310, 2–511].
	2. Unless otherwise agreed or in C.O.D. shipments, the buyer or lessee has an absolute right to inspect the goods before acceptance [UCC 2–513(1), 2A–515(1)].
	3. The buyer or lessee can manifest acceptance of delivered goods in words or by conduct, such as by failing to reject the goods after having had a reasonable opportunity to inspect them. A buyer will be deemed to have accepted goods if he or she performs any act inconsistent with the seller's ownership [UCC 2–606(1), 2A–515(1)].

SECTION 2
REMEDIES OF THE SELLER OR LESSOR

When the buyer or lessee is in breach, the seller or lessor has numerous remedies under the UCC. Generally, the remedies available to the seller or lessor depend on the circumstances existing at the time of the breach. The most pertinent considerations are which party has possession of the goods, whether the goods are in transit, and whether the buyer or lessee has rejected or accepted the goods.

When the Goods Are in the Possession of the Seller or Lessor

Under the UCC, if the buyer or lessee breaches the contract before the goods have been delivered, the seller or lessor has the right to pursue the following remedies:

1. Cancel (rescind) the contract.
2. Resell the goods and sue to recover damages.
3. Sue to recover the purchase price or lease payments due.
4. Sue to recover damages for the buyer's nonacceptance of goods.

THE RIGHT TO CANCEL THE CONTRACT If the buyer or lessee breaches the contract, the seller or lessor can choose to simply cancel the contract [UCC 2–703(f), 2A–523(1)(a)]. The seller or lessor must notify the buyer or lessee of the cancellation, and at that point all remaining obligations of the seller or lessor are discharged. The buyer or lessee is not discharged from all remaining obligations, however. She or he is in breach, and the seller or lessor can pursue remedies available under the UCC for breach.

THE RIGHT TO WITHHOLD DELIVERY In general, sellers and lessors can withhold delivery or discontinue performance of their obligations under sales or lease contracts when the buyers or lessees are in breach. This is true whether a buyer or lessee has wrongfully rejected or revoked acceptance of contract goods (discussed later in this chapter), failed to make a payment, or repudiated the contract [UCC 2–703(a), 2A–523(1) (c)]. The seller or lessor can also refuse to deliver the goods to a buyer or lessee who is insolvent (unable to pay debts as they become due) unless the buyer or lessee pays in cash [UCC 2–702(1), 2A–525(1)].

THE RIGHT TO RESELL OR DISPOSE OF THE GOODS When a buyer or lessee breaches or repudiates the contract while the seller or lessor is in possession of the goods, the seller or lessor can resell or dispose of the goods. The seller can retain any profits made as a result of the sale and can hold the buyer or lessee liable for any loss [UCC 2–703(d), 2–706(1), 2A–523(1)(e), 2A–527(1)].

The seller must give the original buyer reasonable notice of the resale, unless the goods are perishable or will rapidly decline in value [UCC 2–706(2), (3)]. The resale can be private or public, and the goods can be sold as a unit or in parcels. A good faith purchaser at the resale takes the goods free of any of the rights of the original buyer [UCC 2–706(5)].

When the Goods Are Unfinished. When the goods contracted for are unfinished at the time of the breach, the seller or lessor can do either of the following:

1. Cease manufacturing the goods and resell them for scrap or salvage value.
2. Complete the manufacture and resell or dispose of the goods, and hold the buyer or lessee liable for any deficiency.

In choosing between these two alternatives, the seller or lessor must exercise reasonable commercial judgment in order to mitigate the loss and obtain maximum value from the unfinished goods [UCC 2–704(2),

2A–524(2)]. Any resale of the goods must be made in good faith and in a commercially reasonable manner.

When the Resale Price Is Insufficient. In sales transactions, the seller can recover any deficiency between the resale price and the contract price. The seller can also recover *incidental damages* (see Chapter 14), defined as the costs to the seller resulting from the breach [UCC 2–706(1), 2–710]. In lease transactions, the lessor may lease the goods to another party and recover damages from the original lessee. Damages include any unpaid lease payments up to the beginning date of the lease term under the new lease. The lessor can also recover any deficiency between the lease payments due under the original lease contract and those under the new lease contract, along with incidental damages [UCC 2A–527(2)].

THE RIGHT TO RECOVER THE PURCHASE PRICE OR LEASE PAYMENTS DUE Under the UCC, an unpaid seller or lessor can bring an action to recover the purchase price or the payments due under the lease contract, plus incidental damages [UCC 2–709(1), 2A–529(1)]. If a seller or lessor is unable to resell or dispose of the goods and sues for the contract price or lease payments due, the goods must be held for the buyer or lessee. The seller or lessor can resell the goods at any time before collecting the judgment from the buyer or lessee. If the goods are resold, the net proceeds from the sale must be credited to the buyer or lessee because of the duty to mitigate damages.

▶ **Example 16.12** Southern Realty contracts with Gem Point, Inc., to purchase one thousand pens with Southern Realty's name inscribed on them. Gem Point tenders delivery of the pens, but Southern Realty wrongfully refuses to accept them. In this situation, Gem Point can bring an action for the purchase price because it delivered conforming goods, and Southern Realty refused to accept or pay for the goods. Gem Point obviously cannot resell the pens inscribed with the buyer's business name, so this situation falls under UCC 2–709. Gem Point is required to make the pens available for Southern Realty, but can resell them (in the event that it can find a buyer) at any time prior to collecting the judgment from Southern Realty. ◀

THE RIGHT TO RECOVER DAMAGES FOR THE BUYER'S NONACCEPTANCE If a buyer or lessee repudiates a contract or wrongfully refuses to accept the goods, a seller or lessor can bring an action to recover the damages sustained. Ordinarily, the amount of damages equals the difference between the contract price or lease payments and the market price or lease payments at the time and place of tender of the goods, plus incidental damages [UCC 2–708(1), 2A–528(1)].

When the ordinary measure of damages is inadequate to put the seller or lessor in as good a position as the buyer's or lessee's performance would have, the UCC provides an alternative. In that situation, the proper measure of damages is the lost profits of the seller or lessor, including a reasonable allowance for overhead and other expenses [UCC 2–708(2), 2A–528(2)].

When the Goods Are in Transit

When the seller or lessor has delivered the goods to a carrier or a bailee but the buyer or lessee has not yet received them, the goods are said to be *in transit*.

EFFECT OF INSOLVENCY AND BREACH If the seller or lessor learns that the buyer or lessee is insolvent, the seller or lessor can stop the delivery of the goods still in transit, regardless of the quantity of goods shipped. A different rule applies if the buyer or lessee is in breach but is not insolvent. In this situation, the seller or lessor can stop the goods in transit only if the quantity shipped is at least a carload, a truckload, a planeload, or a larger shipment [UCC 2–705(1), 2A–526(1)].

▶ **Example 16.13** Arturo Ortega orders a truckload of lumber from Timber Products, Inc., to be shipped to Ortega six weeks later. Ortega, who has not paid Timber Products for a past shipment, promises to pay the debt immediately and to pay for the current shipment as soon as it is received. After the lumber has been shipped, a bankruptcy court judge notifies Timber Products that Ortega has filed a petition in bankruptcy and listed Timber Products as one of his creditors. If the goods are still in transit, Timber Products can stop the carrier from delivering the lumber to Ortega. ◀

REQUIREMENTS FOR STOPPING DELIVERY To stop delivery, the seller or lessor must *timely notify* the carrier or other bailee that the goods are to be returned or held for the seller or lessor. If the carrier has sufficient time to stop delivery, the goods must be held and delivered according to the instructions of the seller or lessor. The seller or lessor is liable to the carrier for any additional costs incurred [UCC 2–705(3), 2A–526(3)].

The seller or lessor has the right to stop delivery of the goods under UCC 2–705(2) and 2A–526(2) until the time when:

1. The buyer or lessee receives the goods.
2. The carrier or the bailee acknowledges the rights of the buyer or lessee in the goods (by reshipping or holding the goods for the buyer or lessee, for example).
3. A negotiable document of title covering the goods has been properly transferred to the buyer in a sales transaction, giving the buyer ownership rights in the goods [UCC 2–705(2)].

Once the seller or lessor reclaims the goods in transit, she or he can pursue the remedies allowed to sellers and lessors when the goods are in their possession.

When the Goods Are in the Possession of the Buyer or Lessee

When the buyer or lessee breaches the contract while the goods are in his or her possession, the seller or lessor can sue. The seller or lessor can recover the purchase price of the goods or the lease payments due, plus incidental damages [UCC 2–709(1), 2A–529(1)].

In some situations, a seller may also have a right to reclaim the goods from the buyer. For instance, in a sales contract, if the buyer has received the goods on credit and the seller discovers that the buyer is insolvent, the seller can demand the return of the goods [UCC 2–702(2)]. Ordinarily, the demand must be made within ten days of the buyer's receipt of the goods.[3] The seller's right to reclaim the goods is subject to the rights of a good faith purchaser or other subsequent buyer in the ordinary course of business who purchases the goods from the buyer before the seller reclaims them.

In regard to lease contracts, if the lessee is in default (fails to make payments that are due, for instance), the lessor may reclaim the leased goods that are in the lessee's possession [UCC 2A–525(2)].

SECTION 3

REMEDIES OF THE BUYER OR LESSEE

When the seller or lessor breaches the contract, the buyer or lessee has numerous remedies available under the UCC. Like the remedies available to sellers and

---

3. The seller can demand and reclaim the goods at any time, though, if the buyer misrepresented his or her solvency in writing within three months prior to the delivery of the goods.

lessors, the remedies available to buyers and lessees depend on the circumstances existing at the time of the breach. Relevant factors include whether the seller has refused to deliver conforming goods or delivered nonconforming goods.

When the Seller or Lessor Refuses to Deliver the Goods

If the seller or lessor refuses to deliver the goods to the buyer or lessee, the basic remedies available to the buyer or lessee include the right to:

1. Cancel (rescind) the contract.
2. Obtain goods that have been paid for if the seller or lessor is insolvent.
3. Sue to obtain specific performance if the goods are unique or if damages are an inadequate remedy.
4. Buy other goods (obtain *cover*—defined on this page) and recover damages from the seller.
5. Sue to obtain identified goods held by a third party (*replevy* goods—defined on page 329).
6. Sue to obtain damages.

THE RIGHT TO CANCEL THE CONTRACT When a seller or lessor fails to make proper delivery or repudiates the contract, the buyer or lessee can cancel, or rescind, the contract. The buyer or lessee is relieved of any further obligations under the contract but retains all rights to other remedies against the seller or lessor [UCC 2–711(1), 2A–508(1)(a)]. (The right to cancel the contract is also available to a buyer or lessee who has rightfully rejected goods or revoked acceptance, as will be discussed shortly.)

THE RIGHT TO OBTAIN THE GOODS UPON INSOLVENCY If a buyer or lessee has partially or fully paid for goods that are in the possession of a seller or lessor who becomes insolvent, the buyer or lessee can obtain the goods. The seller or lessor must have become insolvent within ten days after receiving the first payment, and the goods must be identified to the contract. To exercise this right, the buyer or lessee must pay the seller or lessor any unpaid balance of the purchase price or lease payments [UCC 2–502, 2A–522].

THE RIGHT TO OBTAIN SPECIFIC PERFORMANCE A buyer or lessee can obtain specific performance if the goods are unique or the remedy at law (monetary damages) is inadequate [UCC 2–716(1), 2A–521(1)]. Ordinarily, an award of damages is sufficient to place

a buyer or lessee in the position she or he would have occupied if the seller or lessor had fully performed.

When the contract is for the purchase of a particular work of art or a similarly unique item, however, damages may not be sufficient. Under these circumstances, equity requires that the seller or lessor perform exactly by delivering the particular goods identified to the contract (the remedy of specific performance).

▶ **Case in Point 16.14** Together, Doreen Houseman and Eric Dare bought a house and a pedigreed dog. When the couple separated, they agreed that Dare would keep the house (and pay Houseman for her interest in it) and that Houseman would keep the dog. Houseman allowed Dare to take the dog for visits, but after one visit, Dare kept the dog. Houseman filed a lawsuit seeking specific performance of their agreement. The court found that because pets have special subjective value to their owners, a dog can be considered a unique good. Thus, an award of specific performance was appropriate.[4] ◀

THE RIGHT OF COVER In certain situations, buyers and lessees can protect themselves by obtaining **cover**— that is, by buying or leasing substitute goods for those that were due under the contract. This option is available when the seller or lessor repudiates the contract or fails to deliver the goods, or when a buyer or lessee has rightfully rejected goods or revoked acceptance.

In purchasing or leasing substitute goods, the buyer or lessee must act in good faith and without unreasonable delay [UCC 2–712, 2A–518]. The buyer or lessee can recover from the seller or lessor:

1. The difference between the cost of cover and the contract price (or lease payments).
2. Incidental damages that resulted from the breach.
3. Consequential damages to compensate for indirect losses (such as lost profits) resulting from the breach that were reasonably foreseeable at the time of contract formation. The amount of consequential damages is reduced by any amount the buyer or lessee saved as a result of the breach (such as when a buyer obtains cover without having to pay delivery charges that were part of the original sales contract).

Buyers and lessees are not required to cover, and failure to do so will not bar them from using any other remedies available under the UCC. A buyer or lessee who fails to cover, however, risks collecting a lower amount of consequential damages. A court may

---

4. *Houseman v. Dare,* 405 N.J.Super. 538, 966 A.2d 24 (2009).

reduce the consequential damages by the amount of the loss that could have been avoided had the buyer or lessee purchased or leased substitute goods.

THE RIGHT TO REPLEVY GOODS Buyers and lessees also have the right to replevy goods. **Replevin**[5] is an action to recover identified goods in the hands of a party who is unlawfully withholding them. Under the UCC, a buyer or lessee can replevy goods identified to the contract if the seller or lessor has repudiated or breached the contract. To maintain an action to replevy goods, buyers and lessees must usually show that they were unable to cover for the goods after making a reasonable effort [UCC 2–716(3), 2A–521(3)].

THE RIGHT TO RECOVER DAMAGES If a seller or lessor repudiates the contract or fails to deliver the goods, the buyer or lessee can sue for damages. For the buyer, the measure of recovery is the difference between the contract price and the market price of the goods at the time the buyer *learned* of the breach. For the lessee, the measure is the difference between the lease payments and the lease payments that could be obtained for the goods at the time the lessee learned of the breach.

The market price or market lease payments are determined at the place where the seller or lessor was supposed to deliver the goods. The buyer or lessee can also recover incidental and consequential damages less the expenses that were saved as a result of the breach [UCC 2–713, 2A–519].

▶ **Case in Point 16.15** Les Entreprises Jacques Defour & Fils, Inc., contracted to buy a thirty-thousand-gallon industrial tank from Dinsick Equipment Corporation for $70,000. Les Entreprises hired Xaak Transport, Inc., to pick up the tank, but when Xaak arrived at the pickup location, there was no tank. Les Entreprises paid Xaak $7,459 for its services and filed a suit against Dinsick. The court awarded compensatory damages of $70,000 for the tank and incidental damages of $7,459 for the transport. To establish a breach of contract requires an enforceable contract, substantial performance by the nonbreaching party, a breach by the other party, and damages. In this case, Les Entreprises agreed to buy a tank and paid the price. Dinsick failed to tender or deliver the tank, or to refund the price. The shipping costs were a necessary part of performance, so this was a reasonable expense.[6] ◀

When the Seller or Lessor Delivers Nonconforming Goods

When the seller or lessor delivers nonconforming goods, the buyer or lessee has several remedies available under the UCC.

THE RIGHT TO REJECT THE GOODS If either the goods or their tender fails to conform to the contract in any respect, the buyer or lessee can reject all of the goods or any commercial unit of the goods [UCC 2–601, 2A–509]. On rejecting the goods, the buyer or lessee may obtain cover or cancel the contract, and may seek damages just as if the seller or lessor had refused to deliver the goods. (See the earlier discussion of these remedies.)

▶ **Case in Point 16.16** Jorge Jauregui contracted to buy a new Kawai RX5 piano for $24,282 from Bobb's Piano Sales & Service, Inc. When the piano was delivered with "unacceptable damage," Jauregui rejected it and filed a lawsuit for breach of contract. The court ruled that Bobb's had breached the contract by delivering nonconforming goods. Jauregui was entitled to damages equal to the contract price with interest, plus the sales tax, delivery charge, and attorneys' fees.[7] ◀

Timeliness and Reason for Rejection Are Required. The buyer or lessee must reject the goods within a reasonable amount of time after delivery or tender of delivery and must seasonably (timely) notify the seller or lessor [UCC 2–602(1), 2A–509(2)]. If the buyer or lessee fails to reject the goods within a reasonable amount of time, acceptance will be presumed.

When rejecting goods, the buyer or lessee must also designate defects that are ascertainable by reasonable inspection. Failure to do so precludes the buyer or lessee from using such defects to justify rejection or to establish breach when the seller or lessor could have cured the defects if they had been disclosed seasonably [UCC 2–605, 2A–514].

Duties of Merchant-Buyers and Lessees When Goods Are Rejected. Sometimes, a *merchant-buyer or lessee* rightfully rejects goods, and the seller or lessor has no agent or business at the place of rejection. In that situation, the merchant-buyer or lessee has a good faith obligation to follow any reasonable instructions received from the seller or lessor with respect to the

---

5. Pronounced ruh-*pleh*-vun, derived from the Old French word *plevir*, meaning "to pledge."
6. *Les Enterprises Jacques Defour & Fils, Inc. v. Dinsick Equipment Corp.*, 2011 WL 307501(N.D.Ill. 2011).
7. *Jauregui v. Bobb's Piano Sales & Service, Inc.*, 922 So.2d 303 (Fla.App. 2006).

goods [UCC 2–603, 2A–511]. The buyer or lessee is entitled to be reimbursed for the care and cost entailed in following the instructions. The same requirements apply if the buyer or lessee rightfully revokes her or his acceptance of the goods at some later time [UCC 2–608(3), 2A–517(5)]. (Revocation of acceptance will be discussed shortly.)

If no instructions are forthcoming and the goods are perishable or threaten to decline in value quickly, the buyer or lessee can resell the goods. The buyer or lessee must exercise good faith and can take appropriate reimbursement and a selling commission (not to exceed 10 percent of the gross proceeds) from the proceeds [UCC 2–603(1), (2); 2A–511(1)]. If the goods are not perishable, the buyer or lessee may store them for the seller or lessor or reship them to the seller or lessor [UCC 2–604, 2A–512].

REVOCATION OF ACCEPTANCE Acceptance of the goods precludes the buyer or lessee from exercising the right of rejection, but it does not necessarily prevent the buyer or lessee from pursuing other remedies. In certain circumstances, a buyer or lessee is permitted to *revoke* his or her acceptance of the goods.

Acceptance of a lot or a commercial unit can be revoked if the nonconformity *substantially* impairs the value of the lot or unit *and* if one of the following factors is present:

1. Acceptance was based on the reasonable assumption that the nonconformity would be cured, and it has not been cured within a reasonable period of time [UCC 2–608(1)(a), 2A–517(1)(a)].
2. The failure of the buyer or lessee to discover the nonconformity was reasonably induced by either the difficulty of discovery before acceptance or by assurances made by the seller or lessor [UCC 2–608(1)(b), 2A–517(1)(b)].

Revocation of acceptance is not effective until notice is given to the seller or lessor. Notice must occur within a reasonable time after the buyer or lessee either discovers or *should have discovered* the grounds for revocation. Additionally, revocation must occur before the goods have undergone any substantial change (such as spoilage) not caused by their own defects [UCC 2–608(2), 2A–517(4)]. Once acceptance is revoked, the buyer or lessee can pursue remedies, just as if the goods had been rejected.

THE RIGHT TO RECOVER DAMAGES FOR ACCEPTED GOODS A buyer or lessee who has accepted nonconforming goods may also keep the goods and recover damages [UCC 2–714(1), 2A–519(3)]. To do so, the buyer or lessee must notify the seller or lessor of the breach within a reasonable time after the defect was or should have been discovered. Failure to give notice of the defects (breach) to the seller or lessor bars the buyer or lessee from pursuing any remedy [UCC 2–607(3), 2A–516(3)]. In addition, the parties to a sales or lease contract can insert into the contract a provision requiring the buyer or lessee to give notice of any defects in the goods within a prescribed period.

When the goods delivered are not as promised, the measure of damages equals the difference between the value of the goods as accepted and their value if they had been delivered as warranted, unless special circumstances show proximately caused damages of a different amount [UCC 2–714(2), 2A–519(4)]. The buyer or lessee is also entitled to incidental and consequential damages when appropriate [UCC 2–714(3), 2A–519]. With proper notice to the seller or lessor, the buyer or lessee can also deduct all or any part of the damages from the price or lease payments still due under the contract [UCC 2–717, 2A–516(1)].

Is two years after a sale of goods a reasonable time period in which to discover a defect in those goods and notify the seller of a breach? That was the question in the following *Spotlight Case.*

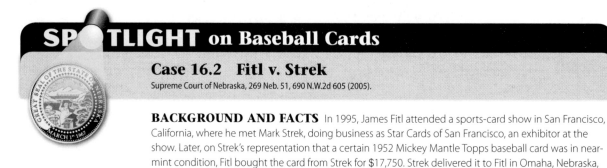

SPOTLIGHT on Baseball Cards

Case 16.2   Fitl v. Strek
Supreme Court of Nebraska, 269 Neb. 51, 690 N.W.2d 605 (2005).

BACKGROUND AND FACTS In 1995, James Fitl attended a sports-card show in San Francisco, California, where he met Mark Strek, doing business as Star Cards of San Francisco, an exhibitor at the show. Later, on Strek's representation that a certain 1952 Mickey Mantle Topps baseball card was in near-mint condition, Fitl bought the card from Strek for $17,750. Strek delivered it to Fitl in Omaha, Nebraska, and Fitl placed it in a safe-deposit box.

CASE 16.2 CONTINUED

In May 1997, Fitl sent the card to Professional Sports Authenticators (PSA), a sports-card grading service. PSA told Fitl that the card was ungradable because it had been discolored and doctored. Fitl complained to Strek, who replied that Fitl should have initiated a return of the card within "a typical grace period for the unconditional return of a card, . . . 7 days to 1 month" of its receipt. In August, Fitl sent the card to ASA Accugrade, Inc. (ASA), another grading service, for a second opinion of the value. ASA also concluded that the card had been refinished and trimmed. Fitl filed a suit in a Nebraska state court against Strek, seeking damages. The court awarded Fitl $17,750, plus his court costs. Strek appealed to the Nebraska Supreme Court.

 IN THE LANGUAGE OF THE COURT
WRIGHT, J. [Judge]

* * * *

Strek claims that the [trial] court erred in determining that notification of the defective condition of the baseball card 2 years after the date of purchase was timely pursuant to [UCC] 2–607(3)(a).

* * * The [trial] court found that Fitl had notified Strek within a reasonable time after discovery of the breach. Therefore, our review is whether the [trial] court's finding as to the reasonableness of the notice was clearly erroneous.

Section 2–607(3)(a) states: "Where a tender has been accepted * * * the buyer must within a reasonable time after he discovers or should have discovered any breach notify the seller of breach or be barred from any remedy." [Under UCC 1–204(2)] *"what is a reasonable time for taking any action depends on the nature, purpose and circumstances of such action."* [Emphasis added.]

The notice requirement set forth in Section 2–607(3)(a) serves three purposes.

* * * The most important one is to enable the seller to make efforts to cure the breach by making adjustments or replacements in order to minimize the buyer's damages and the seller's liability. A second policy is to provide the seller a reasonable opportunity to learn the facts so that he may adequately prepare for negotiation and defend himself in a suit. A third policy * * * is the same as the policy behind statutes of limitation: to provide a seller with a terminal point in time for liability.

* * * *A party is justified in relying upon a representation made to the party as a positive statement of fact when an investigation would be required to ascertain its falsity.* In order for Fitl to have determined that the baseball card had been altered, he would have been required to conduct an investigation. We find that he was not required to do so. Once Fitl learned that the baseball card had been altered, he gave notice to Strek. [Emphasis added.]

* * * One of the most important policies behind the notice requirement * * * is to allow the seller to cure the breach by making adjustments or replacements to minimize the buyer's damages and the seller's liability. However, even if Fitl had learned immediately upon taking possession of the baseball card that it was not authentic and had notified Strek at that time, there is no evidence that Strek could have made any adjustment or taken any action that would have minimized his liability. In its altered condition, the baseball card was worthless.

* * * Earlier notification would not have helped Strek prepare for negotiation or defend himself in a suit because the damage to Fitl could not be repaired. Thus, the policies behind the notice requirement, to allow the seller to correct a defect, to prepare for negotiation and litigation, and to protect against stale claims at a time beyond which an investigation can be completed, were not unfairly prejudiced by the lack of an earlier notice to Strek. Any problem Strek may have had with the party from whom he obtained the baseball card was a separate matter from his transaction with Fitl, and an investigation into the source of the altered card would not have minimized Fitl's damages.

DECISION AND REMEDY *The state supreme court affirmed the decision of the lower court. Under the circumstances, notice of a defect in the card two years after its purchase was reasonable. The buyer had reasonably relied on the seller's representation that the card was "authentic" (which it was not), and when the defects were discovered, the buyer had given timely notice.*

CASE 16.2 CONTINUES ▶

WHAT IF THE FACTS WERE DIFFERENT? *Suppose that Fitl and Strek had included in their deal a written clause requiring Fitl to give notice of any defect in the card within "7 days to 1 month" of its receipt. Would the result have been different? Why or why not?*

THE LEGAL ENVIRONMENT DIMENSION *What might a court award to a buyer who prevails in a dispute such as the one in this case?*

Additional Provisions Affecting Remedies

The parties to a sales or lease contract can vary their respective rights and obligations by contractual agreement. For instance, a seller and buyer can expressly provide for remedies in addition to those provided in the UCC. They can also specify remedies in lieu of those provided in the UCC (including liquidated damages clauses—see Chapter 14), or they can change the measure of damages. A seller can provide that the buyer's only remedy on the seller's breach will be repair or replacement of the item. Alternatively, the seller can limit the buyer's remedy to return of the goods and refund of the purchase price.

In sales and lease contracts, an agreed-on remedy is in addition to those provided in the UCC unless the parties expressly agree that the remedy is exclusive of all others [UCC 2–719(1), 2A–503(1),(2)].

EXCLUSIVE REMEDIES If the parties state that a remedy is *exclusive,* then it is the sole (only) remedy. ▶ **Example 16.17** Standard Tool Company agrees to sell a pipe-cutting machine to United Pipe & Tubing Corporation. The contract limits United's remedy exclusively to repair or replacement of any defective parts. Thus, repair or replacement of defective parts is the buyer's only remedy under this contract. ◀

When circumstances cause an exclusive remedy to fail in its essential purpose, however, it is no longer exclusive, and the buyer or lessee may pursue other remedies available under the UCC [UCC 2–719(2), 2A–503(2)]. In *Example 16.17,* suppose that Standard Tool Company was unable to repair a defective part, and no replacement parts were available. In this situation, because the exclusive remedy failed in its essential purpose (to provide recovery), the buyer could pursue other remedies available under the UCC. (See the *Managerial Strategy* feature on the following page for guidelines on what to do when a contract is breached.)

CONSEQUENTIAL DAMAGES As discussed in this chapter, and in Chapter 14, *consequential damages* are spe-

cial damages that compensate for indirect losses (such as lost profits) resulting from a breach of contract that were reasonably foreseeable. Under the UCC, parties to a contract can limit or exclude consequential damages, provided the limitation is not unconscionable.

When the buyer or lessee is a consumer, any limitation of consequential damages for personal injuries resulting from consumer goods is *prima facie* (presumed to be) unconscionable. The limitation of consequential damages is not necessarily unconscionable when the loss is commercial in nature—for example, lost profits and property damage [UCC 2–719(3), 2A–503(3)].

STATUTE OF LIMITATIONS An action for breach of contract under the UCC must be commenced *within four years after the cause of action accrues* [UCC 2–725(1)]. This means that a buyer or lessee must file the lawsuit within four years after the breach occurs.[8] The parties can agree in their contract to reduce this period to not less than one year, but cannot extend it beyond four years [UCC 2–725(1), 2A–506(1)].

If a buyer or lessee has accepted nonconforming goods, that party has a reasonable time to notify the seller or lessor of the breach. Failure to provide notice will bar the buyer or lessee from pursuing any remedy [UCC 2–607(3) (a), 2A–516(3)].

SECTION 4

SALES AND LEASE WARRANTIES

Most goods are covered by some type of warranty designed to protect buyers. In sales and lease law, a warranty is an assurance or guarantee by the seller or lessor about the quality and features of the goods being sold or leased. The Uniform Commercial Code (UCC) has numerous rules governing product warranties as they occur in sales and lease contracts.

---

8. For breach of warranty, to be discussed shortly, the cause of action arises when the seller or lessor delivers the contracted goods [UCC 2–725(2), 2A–506(2)]. Thus, the buyer or lessee has four years from the delivery date to file a suit for breach of warranty.

MANAGERIAL STRATEGY

Facing a Breach of Contract

A contract for the sale of goods has been breached. Can the dispute be settled without a trip to court? The answer, of course, depends on the willingness of the parties to agree on an appropriate remedy.

A Store Policy against Refunds

As the manager of a retail outlet, you may wish to establish a policy of not providing refunds. Instead, you will offer only to repair or replace items that are defective. Does this mean that you will never have to provide a refund if a customer purchases a good (or service) that turns out to be defective and cannot be repaired? That was the question facing a court in New York when a store cited its no-refund policy in declining to provide a dissatisfied customer with a full refund.

Sarah Milligan purchased a wig from Shuly Wigs, Inc., but discovered that the wig was defective. Shuly twice tried to repair the wig, but both attempts failed. Milligan purchased another wig and asked Shuly for a refund. When Shuly refused, Milligan sued. A small claims court ruled in Milligan's favor. On appeal, the reviewing court affirmed the ruling. The court observed that when "a vendor prohibits refunds and limits the purchaser's remedies to repair or replacement of its goods, the remedy fails of its essential purpose if a delay or failure adequately to repair or replace the goods in a reasonable time deprives the plaintiff of a substantial benefit of her bargain."[a]

Contractual Clauses Concerning Applicable Remedies

Often, the parties to sales and lease contracts agree in advance in their contracts on what remedies will be applicable in the event of a breach. This may take the form of a contract provision restricting or expanding remedies available under Section 2–719 of the Uniform Commercial Code (UCC). Such clauses help to reduce uncertainty and the necessity for costly litigation.

When the Contract Is Silent on Applicable Remedies

If your agreement does not cover a breach and you are the nonbreaching party, the UCC gives you a variety of alternatives. You need to determine the available remedies, analyze them, rank them in order of priority, and then predict how successful you might be in pursuing each remedy if you decide to go to court. Before going to court, however, consider the position of the breaching party to determine if you can negotiate a settlement.

For example, when defective goods are delivered and accepted, usually it is preferable for the buyer and seller to reach an agreement on a reduced purchase price. Practically speaking, though, the buyer may be unable to obtain a partial refund from the seller. In this situation, UCC 2–717 allows the buyer to give notice of the intention to deduct the damages from any part of the purchase price not yet paid. If you are a buyer who has accepted defective goods and has not yet paid in full, you may wish to exercise your rights under UCC 2–717 and deduct appropriate damages from your final payment. Remember that most breaches of contract do not end up in court—they are settled beforehand.

MANAGERIAL IMPLICATIONS

Of course, the best way to avoid having to go to court to settle a dispute about a breached contract is to specify in the contract itself what remedies will be available to each party in the event of a breach. Nothing in the UCC prevents parties from expanding the remedies available under it, as UCC 2–719 points out. In general, the more clearly remedies for breach are outlined in a sales contract, the less chance there will be a lawsuit.

BUSINESS QUESTIONS

1. *Under what circumstances is a negotiated settlement for a breach preferable to litigation?*

2. *Assume that you are in a dispute over a breach of contract and you discover that the contract does not explicitly mention any remedies. What do you do now?*

a. *Milligan v. Shuly Wigs, Inc.,* 34 Misc.3d. 128(A), 941 N.Y.S.2d 539 (2011).

Because a warranty imposes a duty on the seller or lessor, a breach of warranty is a breach of the seller's or lessor's promise. Assuming that the parties have not agreed to limit or modify the remedies available, if the seller or lessor breaches a warranty, the buyer or lessee can sue to recover damages from the seller or lessor. Under some circumstances, a breach of warranty can allow the buyer or lessee to rescind (cancel) the agreement.

Warranties of Title

Under the UCC, three types of title warranties—*good title, no liens,* and *no infringements*—can automatically arise in sales and lease contracts [UCC 2–312, 2A–211]. Normally, a seller or lessor can disclaim or modify these title warranties only by including *specific language* in the contract. For example, sellers may assert that they are transferring only such rights, title, and interest as they have in the goods.

GOOD TITLE In most sales, sellers warrant that they have good and valid title to the goods sold and that the transfer of the title is rightful [UCC 2–312(1)(a)]. If the buyer subsequently learns that the seller did not have valid title to the goods that were purchased, the buyer can sue the seller for breach of this warranty.

▶ **Example 16.18** Alexis steals two iPads from Camden and sells them to Emma, who does not know that they are stolen. If Camden discovers that Emma has the iPads, then he has the right to reclaim them from her. When Alexis sold Emma the iPads, Alexis *automatically* warranted to Emma that the title conveyed was valid and that its transfer was rightful. Because a thief has no title to stolen goods, Alexis breached the warranty of title imposed by UCC 2–312(1)(a) and became liable to Emma for appropriate damages. ◀

NO LIENS A second warranty of title protects buyers and lessees who are *unaware* of any encumbrances (claims, charges, or liabilities—usually called *liens*[9]) against goods at the time the contract is made [UCC 2–312(1)(b), 2A–211(1)].

This warranty protects buyers who, for instance, unknowingly purchase goods that are subject to a creditor's security interest. (A *security interest* in this context is an interest in the goods that secures payment or performance of an obligation.) If a creditor legally repossesses the goods from a buyer *who had no actual knowledge of the security interest,* the buyer can recover from the seller for breach of warranty. (In contrast, a buyer who has *actual knowledge of a security interest* has no recourse against a seller.)

▶ **Example 16.19** Henderson buys a used boat from Loring for cash. A month later, Barish proves that she has a valid security interest in the boat and that Loring, who has missed five payments, is in default. Barish then repossesses the boat from Henderson. Henderson demands his cash back from Loring. Under Section 2–312(1)(b), Henderson has legal grounds to recover from Loring because the seller of goods warrants that the goods are delivered free from any security interest or other lien of which the buyer has no knowledge. ◀

Article 2A affords similar protection for lessees. Section 2A–211(1) provides that during the term of the lease, no claim of any third party will interfere with the lessee's enjoyment of the leasehold interest.

NO INFRINGEMENTS A third type of warranty of title arises automatically when the seller or lessor is a merchant. A merchant-seller or lessor warrants that the buyer or lessee takes the goods *free of infringements* from any copyright, trademark, or patent claims of a third person[10] [UCC 2–312(3), 2A–211(2)].

Notice Required in Sales Contracts. If the buyer is subsequently sued by a third party holding copyright, trademark, or patent rights in the goods, then this warranty is breached. The buyer *must notify the seller* of the litigation within a reasonable time to enable the seller to decide whether to defend the lawsuit. The seller then decides whether to defend the buyer and bear all expenses in the action.

If the seller agrees in a writing (or record) to defend and to pay the expenses, then the buyer must turn over control of the litigation to the seller. Otherwise, the buyer is barred from any remedy against the seller for liability established by the litigation [UCC 2–607(3)(b), 2–607(5)(b)]. Thus, if a buyer wins at trial but did not notify the seller of the litigation, the buyer cannot sue the seller to recover the expenses of the lawsuit.

Notice in Lease Contracts. In situations that involve leases rather than sales, Article 2A provides for the same notice of infringement litigation [UCC 2A–516(3)(b), 2A–516(4)(b)]. After being notified of the lawsuit, the lessor (or supplier, in a finance lease) who agrees to pay all expenses can demand that the lessee turn over the control of the litigation. Failure to provide notice normally bars any subsequent remedy against the lessor for liability established by the litigation.

---

9. Pronounced *leens.*

10. Recall from Chapter 15 that a *merchant* is defined in UCC 2–104(1) as a person who deals in goods of the kind involved in the sales contract or who, by occupation, presents himself or herself as having knowledge or skill peculiar to the goods involved in the transaction.

There is an exception for leases to individual consumers for personal, family, or household purposes. A consumer who fails to notify the lessor within a reasonable time does not lose his or her remedy against the lessor for whatever liability is established in the litigation [UCC 2A–516(3)(b)].

Express Warranties

A seller or lessor can create an **express warranty** by making representations concerning the quality, condition, description, or performance potential of the goods.

Under UCC 2–313 and 2A–210, express warranties arise when a seller or lessor indicates any of the following:

1. That the goods conform to any *affirmation* (declaration that something is true) *of fact* or *promise* that the seller or lessor makes to the buyer or lessee about the goods. Such affirmations or promises are usually made during the bargaining process. ▶ **Example 16.20** D. J. Vladick, a salesperson at Home Depot, tells a customer, "These drill bits will *easily* penetrate stainless steel—and without dulling." Vladick's statement is an express warranty. ◀
2. That the goods conform to any *description* of them. ▶ **Example 16.21** A label reads "Crate contains one Kawasaki 750 4X4 ATV," and a contract calls for the delivery of a "wool coat." Both statements create express warranties that the content of the goods sold conforms to the description. ◀
3. That the goods conform to any *sample or model* of the goods shown to the buyer or lessee. ▶ **Example 16.22** Melissa Faught orders a stainless steel 5500 Super Angel juicer for $1,100 after seeing a dealer demonstrate its use at a raw foods health fair. The Super Angel is shipped to her. When the juicer arrives, it is an older model, not the 5500 model. This is a breach of an express warranty because the dealer warranted that the juicer would be the same model used in the demonstration. ◀

Express warranties can be found in a seller's or lessor's advertisement, brochure, or promotional materials, in addition to being made orally or in an express warranty provision in a sales or lease contract.

BASIS OF THE BARGAIN To create an express warranty, a seller or lessor does not have to use formal words such as *warrant* or *guarantee*. It is only necessary that a reasonable buyer or lessee would regard the representation as being part of the basis of the bargain [UCC 2–313(2), 2A–210(2)].

The UCC does not explicitly define the phrase "basis of the bargain." Generally, it means that the buyer or lessee must have relied on the representation at the time of entering into the agreement. Therefore, a court must determine in each case whether a representation was made at such a time and in such a way that it induced the buyer or lessee to enter into the contract.

STATEMENTS OF OPINION AND VALUE Only statements of fact create express warranties. A seller or lessor who makes a statement that merely relates to the value or worth of the goods, or states an opinion about or recommends the goods, does not create an express warranty [UCC 2–313(2), 2A–210(2)].
▶ **Example 16.23** A car salesperson claims that "this is the best used car to come along in years. It has four new tires and a 250-horsepower engine just rebuilt this year." The seller has made several *affirmations of fact* that can create a warranty. The automobile has an engine. It is a 250-horsepower engine and was rebuilt this year. There are four tires on the car and the tires are new. The seller's *opinion* that the vehicle is "the best used car to come along in years," however, is known as "puffery" and creates no warranty. (*Puffery* is an expression of opinion by a seller or lessor that is not made as a representation of fact.) ◀

A statement about the value of the goods, such as "this is worth a fortune" or "anywhere else you'd pay $10,000 for it," usually does not create a warranty. Ordinarily, statements of opinion do not create warranties. If the seller or lessor is an expert, however, and gives an opinion as an expert to a layperson, then a warranty may be created. It is not always easy to determine whether a statement constitutes an express warranty or puffery. The reasonableness of the buyer's or lessee's reliance appears to be the controlling criterion in many cases. Additionally, the context in which a statement is made may be relevant in determining the reasonableness of a buyer's or lessee's reliance. A reasonable person is more likely to rely on a written statement made in an advertisement than on a statement made orally by a salesperson.
▶ **Case in Point 16.24** A tobacco farmer read an advertisement for Chlor-O-Pic, a chemical fumigant. The ad stated that, if applied as directed, Chlor-O-Pic would give "season-long control with application in fall, winter, or spring" against black shank disease, a fungal disease that destroys tobacco crops. The farmer bought Chlor-O-Pic and applied it as directed to his tobacco crop. Nonetheless, the crop developed black

shank disease. The farmer sued the manufacturer of Chlor-O-Pic, arguing that he had purchased the product in reliance on a "strong promise" of "season-long control." The court found that the manufacturer's strong promise had created an express warranty and that the farmer was entitled to the value of the damaged crop.[11] ◄

Implied Warranties

An **implied warranty** is one that *the law derives* by inference from the nature of the transaction or the relative situations or circumstances of the parties. Under the UCC, merchants impliedly warrant that the goods they sell or lease are merchantable and, in certain circumstances, fit for a particular purpose. In addition, an implied warranty may arise from a course of dealing or usage of trade. We examine these three types of implied warranties in the following subsections.

IMPLIED WARRANTY OF MERCHANTABILITY Every sale or lease of goods made by a merchant who deals in goods of the kind sold or leased automatically gives rise to an **implied warranty of merchantability** [UCC 2–314, 2A–212]. Thus, a merchant who is in the business of selling ski equipment makes an implied warranty of merchantability every time he sells a pair of skis. A neighbor selling her skis at a garage sale does not (because she is not in the business of selling goods of this type).

Merchantable Goods. To be *merchantable*, goods must be "reasonably fit for the ordinary purposes for which such goods are used." They must be of at least average, fair, or medium-grade quality. The quality must be comparable to quality that will pass without objection in the trade or market for goods of the same description.

To be merchantable, the goods must also be adequately packaged and labeled, and they must conform to the promises or affirmations of fact made on the container or label, if any. Of course, merchants are not absolute insurers against *all* accidents arising in connection with the goods. A bar of soap is not unmerchantable merely because a user could slip and fall by stepping on it.

The warranty of merchantability may be breached even though the merchant did not know or could not have discovered that a product was defective (not merchantable). ▶ **Example 16.25** Christine contracts to purchase a log home package from Milde, a log home dealer. The dealer provides the logs and other materials and constructs the home. Immediately after Christine moves into the house, she finds that when it rains, water seeps through the exterior walls, staining and discoloring the interior walls. The problem occurs because a defective waterproofing product was used on the logs. Even though Milde did not know that the product was defective, he can be held liable because the waterproofing product was not reasonably fit for its ordinary purpose—that is, making the house waterproof. ◄

Merchantable Food. The serving of food or drink to be consumed on or off the premises is also treated as a sale of goods and subject to the implied warranty of merchantability [UCC 2–314(1)]. "Merchantable" food is food that is fit to eat.

Courts generally determine whether food is fit to eat on the basis of consumer expectations. Consumers should reasonably expect to find on occasion bones in fish fillets, cherry pits in cherry pie, a nutshell in a package of shelled nuts, and the like—because such substances are natural to the ingredients or the finished food product. In contrast, consumers would not reasonably expect to find an inchworm in a can of peas or a piece of glass in a soft drink—because these substances are *not* natural to the food product.

In the following *Classic Case*, the court had to determine whether one should reasonably expect to find a fish bone in fish chowder.

---

11. *Triple E, Inc. v. Hendrix & Dail, Inc.,* 344 S.C. 186, 543 S.E.2d 245 (2001). See also *Nomo Agroindustrial Sa De CV v. Enza Zaden North America, Inc.,* 492 F.Supp.2d 1175 (D.Ariz. 2007).

CLASSIC CASE 16.3

Webster v. Blue Ship Tea Room, Inc.
Supreme Judicial Court of Massachusetts, 347 Mass. 421 198 N.E.2d 309 (1964).

BACKGROUND AND FACTS Blue Ship Tea Room, Inc., was located in Boston in an old building overlooking the ocean. Priscilla Webster, who had been born and raised in New England, went to the restaurant and ordered fish chowder. The chowder was milky in color. After three or four spoonfuls, she felt

CASE 16.3 CONTINUED   something lodged in her throat. As a result, she underwent two esophagoscopies (procedures in which a telescope-like instrument is used to look into the throat). In the second esophagoscopy, a fish bone was found and removed. Webster filed a suit against the restaurant in a Massachusetts state court for breach of the implied warranty of merchantability. The jury rendered a verdict for Webster, and the restaurant appealed to the state's highest court.

IN THE LANGUAGE OF THE COURT
REARDON, Justice.

[The plaintiff] ordered a cup of fish chowder. Presently, there was set before her "a small bowl of fish chowder." * * * After 3 or 4 [spoonfuls] she was aware that something had lodged in her throat because she "couldn't swallow and couldn't clear her throat by gulping and she could feel it." This misadventure led to two esophagoscopies at the Massachusetts General Hospital, in the second of which, on April 27, 1959, a fish bone was found and removed. The sequence of events produced injury to the plaintiff which was not insubstantial.

We must decide whether a fish bone lurking in a fish chowder, about the ingredients of which there is no other complaint, constitutes a breach of implied warranty under applicable provisions of the Uniform Commercial Code * * * . As the judge put it in his charge [jury instruction], "Was the fish chowder fit to be eaten and wholesome? * * * Nobody is claiming that the fish itself wasn't wholesome. * * * But the bone of contention here—I don't mean that for a pun—but was this fish bone a foreign substance that made the fish chowder unwholesome or not fit to be eaten?"

* * * *

[We think that it] is not too much to say that a person sitting down in New England to consume a good New England fish chowder embarks on a gustatory [taste-related] adventure which may entail the removal of some fish bones from his bowl as he proceeds. We are not inclined to tamper with age-old recipes by any amendment reflecting the plaintiff's view of the effect of the Uniform Commercial Code upon them. We are aware of the heavy body of case law involving foreign substances in food, but we sense a strong distinction between them and those relative to unwholesomeness of the food itself, [such as] tainted mackerel, and a fish bone in a fish chowder. * * * We consider that the joys of life in New England include the ready availability of fresh fish chowder. We should be prepared to cope with the hazards of fish bones, the occasional presence of which in chowders is, it seems to us, to be anticipated, and which, in the light of a hallowed tradition, do not impair their fitness or merchantability.

DECISION AND REMEDY   *The Supreme Judicial Court of Massachusetts "sympathized with a plaintiff who has suffered a peculiarly New England injury" but entered a judgment for the defendant, Blue Ship Tea Room. A fish bone in fish chowder is not a breach of the implied warranty of merchantability.*

THE E-COMMERCE DIMENSION   *If Webster had made the chowder herself from a recipe that she had found on the Internet, could she have successfully brought an action against its author for a breach of the implied warranty of merchantability? Explain.*

IMPACT OF THIS CASE ON TODAY'S LAW   *This classic case, phrased in memorable language, was an early application of the UCC's implied warranty of merchantability to food products. The case established the rule that consumers should expect to find, on occasion, elements of food products that are natural to the product (such as fish bones in fish chowder). Courts today still apply this rule.*

IMPLIED WARRANTY OF FITNESS FOR A PARTICULAR PURPOSE The **implied warranty of fitness for a particular purpose** arises in the sale or lease of goods when a seller or lessor (merchant or nonmerchant) knows *both* of the following:

1. The particular purpose for which a buyer or lessee will use the goods.
2. That the buyer or lessee is relying on the skill and judgment of the seller or lessor to select suitable goods [UCC 2–315, 2A–213].

Particular versus Ordinary Purpose. A "particular purpose" of the buyer or lessee differs from the "ordinary purpose for which goods are used" (merchantability). Goods can be merchantable but unfit for a particular purpose.

▶ **Example 16.26** Shakira needs a gallon of paint to match the color of her living room walls—a light shade somewhere between coral and peach. She takes a sample to Sherwin-Williams and requests a gallon of paint of that color. Instead, the salesperson gives her a gallon of bright blue paint. Here, the salesperson has not breached any warranty of implied merchantability—the bright blue paint is of high quality and suitable for interior walls. The salesperson has breached an implied warranty of fitness for a particular purpose, though, because the paint is not the right color for Shakira's purpose (to match her living room walls). ◀

Knowledge and Reliance Requirements. A seller or lessor need not have actual knowledge of the buyer's or lessee's particular purpose. It is sufficient if a seller or lessor "has reason to know" the purpose. For an implied warranty to be created, however, the buyer or lessee must have *relied* on the skill or judgment of the seller or lessor in selecting or furnishing suitable goods. Moreover, the seller or lessor must have reason to know that the buyer or lessee is relying on her or his judgment or skill.

▶ **Example 16.27** Carlos Fuentes tells Tyrone, a salesperson at GamerPC, that he is looking to buy a new PC, such as the Cyberpower Black Pearl or Velocity Raptor Signature Edition, to use for gaming. Fuentes's statement implies that he needs a PC with a video card that is capable of running fast-paced video games with detailed graphics. Tyrone recommends and sells Carlos a computer that does not have a video card and is too slow to run such video games. By doing so, Tyrone has breached the implied warranty of fitness for a particular purpose. ◀

WARRANTIES IMPLIED FROM PRIOR DEALINGS OR TRADE CUSTOM Implied warranties can also arise (or be excluded or modified) as a result of course of dealing or usage of trade [UCC 2–314(3), 2A–212(3)]. Without evidence to the contrary, when both parties to a sales or lease contract have knowledge of a well-recognized trade custom, the courts will infer that both parties intended for that custom to apply to their contract.

▶ **Example 16.28** Industry-wide custom is to lubricate a new car before it is delivered. If a dealer fails to lubricate a car, the dealer can be held liable to a buyer for damages resulting from the breach of an implied warranty. (This, of course, would also be negligence on the part of the dealer.) ◀

LEMON LAWS Purchasers of defective automobiles—called "lemons"—may have remedies in addition to those offered by the UCC. All of the states and the District of Columbia have enacted *lemon laws.*

Basically, state lemon laws provide remedies to consumers who buy automobiles that repeatedly fail to meet standards of quality and performance because they are "lemons." Although lemon laws vary by state, typically they apply to automobiles under warranty that are defective in a way that significantly affects the vehicle's value or use. Lemon laws do not necessarily cover used-car purchases (unless the car is covered by a manufacturer's extended warranty) or vehicles that are leased.[12]

Seller Has Had an Opportunity to Remedy Defect. Generally, the seller or manufacturer is given a number of opportunities to remedy the defect (usually four). If the seller fails to cure the problem despite a reasonable number of attempts (as specified by state law), the buyer is entitled to a new car, replacement of defective parts, or return of all consideration paid. Buyers who prevail in a lemon-law dispute may also be entitled to reimbursement of their attorneys' fees.

Arbitration Often Required. In most states, lemon laws require the owner of the vehicle to notify the dealer or manufacturer of the problem and to provide the dealer or manufacturer with an opportunity to solve it. If the problem remains, the owner must then submit complaints to the arbitration program specified in the manufacturer's warranty before taking the case to court.

Decisions by arbitration panels are binding on the manufacturer—that is, cannot be appealed by the manufacturer to the courts—but usually are not binding on the purchaser. Most major automobile companies operate their own arbitration panels. All arbitration boards must meet state and/or federal standards of impartiality, and some states have established mandatory government-sponsored arbitration programs for lemon-law disputes.

MAGNUSON-MOSS WARRANTY ACT The Magnuson-Moss Warranty Act of 1975[13] was designed to prevent deception in warranties by making them easier to understand. The Magnuson-Moss Warranty Act modi-

---

12. Note that in some states, such as California, these laws may extend beyond automobile purchases and apply to other consumer goods.
13. 15 U.S.C. Sections 2301–2312.

fies UCC warranty rules to some extent when *consumer* transactions are involved. The UCC, however, remains the primary codification of warranty rules for commercial transactions.

Under the Magnuson-Moss Act, no seller is *required* to give a written warranty for consumer goods sold. If a seller chooses to make an express written warranty, however, and the cost of the consumer goods is more than $25, the warranty must be labeled as either "full" or "limited."

A *full warranty* requires free repair or replacement of any defective part. If the product cannot be repaired within a reasonable time, the consumer has the choice of a refund or a replacement without charge. A full warranty can be for an unlimited or limited time period, such as a "full twelve-month warranty." A *limited warranty* is one in which the buyer's recourse is limited in some fashion, such as to replacement of an item. The fact that only a limited warranty is being given must be conspicuously stated.

The Magnuson-Moss Act further requires the warrantor to make certain disclosures fully and conspicuously in a single document in "readily understood language." The seller must disclose the name and address of the warrantor, specifically what is warranted, and the procedures for enforcing the warranty. The seller must also clarify that the buyer has legal rights and explain limitations on warranty relief.

See *Concept Summary 16.2* below for a review of the various types of warranties.

CONCEPT SUMMARY 16.2
Types of Warranties

CONCEPT	DESCRIPTION
Warranties of Title	The UCC provides for the following warranties of title [UCC 2–312, 2A–211]: 1. *Good title*—A seller warrants that he or she has the right to pass good and rightful title to the goods. 2. *No liens*—A seller warrants that the goods sold are free of any encumbrances (claims, charges, or liabilities—usually called *liens*). A lessor warrants that the lessee will not be disturbed in her or his possession of the goods by the claims of a third party. 3. *No infringements*—A merchant-seller warrants that the goods are free of infringement claims (claims that a patent, trademark, or copyright has been infringed) by third parties. Lessors make similar warranties.
Express Warranties	An express warranty arises under the UCC when a seller or lessor indicates any of the following as part of the sale or bargain [UCC 2–313, 2A–210]: 1. An affirmation of fact or promise. 2. A description of the goods. 3. A sample or model shown as conforming to the contract goods.
Implied Warranty of Merchantability	When a seller or lessor is a merchant who deals in goods of the kind sold or leased, the seller or lessor warrants that the goods sold or leased are properly packaged and labeled, are of proper quality, and are reasonably fit for the ordinary purposes for which such goods are used [UCC 2–314, 2A–212].
Implied Warranty of Fitness for a Particular Purpose	An implied warranty of fitness for a particular purpose arises when the buyer's or lessee's purpose or use is known by the seller or lessor, and the buyer or lessee purchases or leases the goods in reliance on the seller's or lessor's selection [UCC 2–315, 2A–213].
Other Implied Warranties	Other implied warranties can arise as a result of course of dealing or usage of trade [UCC 2–314(3), 2A–212(3)].
Magnuson-Moss Warranty Act	An express written warranty covering consumer goods priced at more than $25, *if made,* must be labeled as either a full warranty or a limited warranty. A full warranty requires free repair or replacement of defective parts and refund or replacement for goods that cannot be repaired in a reasonable time. A limited warranty is one in which the buyer's recourse is limited in some fashion, such as to replacement of an item. Sellers must make certain disclosures to buyers and must state any limitations on a warranty clearly, conspicuously, and in readily understood language.

Overlapping Warranties

Sometimes, two or more warranties are made in a single transaction. An implied warranty of merchantability, an implied warranty of fitness for a particular purpose, or both can exist in addition to an express warranty. ▶ **Example 16.29**   A sales contract for a new car states that "this car engine is warranted to be free from defects for 36,000 miles or thirty-six months, whichever occurs first." This statement creates an express warranty against all defects, as well as an implied warranty that the car will be fit for normal use. ◀

The rule under the UCC is that express and implied warranties are construed as *cumulative* if they are consistent with one another [UCC 2–317, 2A–215]. In other words, courts interpret two or more warranties as being in agreement with each other unless this construction is unreasonable. If it is unreasonable for the two warranties to be consistent, then the court looks at the intention of the parties to determine which warranty is dominant.

If the warranties are *inconsistent,* the courts usually apply the following rules to interpret which warranty is most important:

1. *Express* warranties displace inconsistent *implied* warranties, except implied warranties of fitness for a particular purpose.
2. Samples take precedence over inconsistent general descriptions.
3. Exact or technical specifications displace inconsistent samples or general descriptions.

▶ **Example 16.30**   Innova, Ltd., leases a high-speed server from Vernon Sources. The contract contains an express warranty concerning the speed of the CPU and the application programs that the server is capable of running. Innova does not realize that the speed expressly warranted in the contract is insufficient for its needs until it tries to run the software and the server slows to a crawl.

Because Innova made it clear that it was leasing the server to perform certain tasks, Innova files an action against Vernon for breach of the implied warranty of fitness for a particular purpose. In this situation, Innova normally will prevail. Although the express warranty on CPU speed takes precedence over the implied warranty of merchantability, it normally does not take precedence over an implied warranty of fitness for a particular purpose. ◀

Warranty Disclaimers and Limitations on Liability

The UCC generally permits warranties to be disclaimed or limited by specific and unambiguous language, provided that this is done in a manner that protects the buyer or lessee from surprise. Because each type of warranty is created in a different way, the manner in which a seller or lessor can disclaim warranties varies with the type of warranty.

EXPRESS WARRANTIES   A seller or lessor can disclaim all oral express warranties by including in the contract a written (or an electronically recorded) disclaimer. The disclaimer must be in language that is clear and conspicuous, and called to a buyer's or lessee's attention [UCC 2–316(1), 2A–214(1)]. This allows the seller or lessor to avoid false allegations that oral warranties were made, and it ensures that only representations made by properly authorized individuals are included in the bargain.

Note, however, that a buyer or lessee must be made aware of any warranty disclaimers or modifications *at the time the contract is formed.* In other words, the seller or lessor cannot modify any warranties or disclaimers made during the bargaining process without the consent of the buyer or lessee.

IMPLIED WARRANTIES   Generally, unless circumstances indicate otherwise, the implied warranties of merchantability and fitness are disclaimed by an expression such as "as is" or "with all faults." Both parties must be able to clearly understand from the language used that there are no implied warranties [UCC 2–316(3)(a), 2A–214(3)(a)]. (Note, however, that some states have passed consumer protection statutes that forbid "as is" sales or make it illegal to disclaim warranties of merchantability on consumer goods.)

▶ **Case in Point 16.31**   Mandy Morningstar advertised a "lovely, eleven-year-old mare" with extensive jumping ability for sale. After examining the horse twice, Sue Hallett contracted to buy the horse. She signed a contract that described the horse as an eleven-year-old mare and as being sold "as is." Shortly after the purchase, a veterinarian determined that the horse was actually sixteen years old and in no condition for jumping. Hallett stopped payment, and Morningstar filed a lawsuit for breach of contract.

The court held that the statement in the contract describing the horse as eleven years old constituted an express warranty, which Morningstar had breached. Although the "as is" clause effectively disclaimed any implied warranties (of merchantability and fitness for a particular purpose, such as jumping), the court ruled that it did not disclaim the express warranty concerning the horse's age.[14] ◀

---

14. *Morningstar v. Hallett,* 858 A.2d 125 (Pa.Super.Ct. 2004).

Disclaimer of the Implied Warranty of Merchantability.
To specifically disclaim an implied warranty of merchantability, a seller or lessor must mention the word *merchantability*. The disclaimer need not be written, but if it is, the writing (or record) must be conspicuous [UCC 2–316(2), 2A–214(4)].

Under the UCC, a term or clause is conspicuous when it is written or displayed in such a way that a reasonable person would notice it. Conspicuous terms include words set in capital letters, in a larger font size, or in a different color so as to be set off from the surrounding text.

Disclaimer of the Implied Warranty of Fitness. To disclaim an implied warranty of fitness for a particular purpose, the disclaimer must be in a writing (or record) and must be conspicuous. The writing does not have to mention the word *fitness*. It is sufficient if, for instance, the disclaimer states, "There are no warranties that extend beyond the description on the face hereof."

BUYER'S OR LESSEE'S EXAMINATION OR REFUSAL TO INSPECT
If a buyer or lessee examines the goods (or a sample or model) as fully as desired, *there is no implied warranty with respect to defects that a reasonable examination would reveal or defects that are found on examination* [UCC 2–316(3)(b), 2A–214(2)(b)]. Also, if a buyer or lessee refuses to examine the goods on the seller's or lessor's request that he or she do so, there is no implied warranty with respect to reasonably evident defects.

▶ **Example 16.32**   Janna buys a table at Gershwin's Home Store. No express warranties are made. Gershwin asks Janna to inspect the table before buying it, but she refuses. Had Janna inspected the table, she would have noticed that one of its legs was obviously cracked, which made it unstable. Janna takes the table home and sets a lamp on it. The table later collapses, and the lamp starts a fire that causes significant damage. Janna normally will not be able to hold Gershwin's liable for breach of the warranty of merchantability because she refused to examine the table as Gershwin requested. Janna therefore assumed the risk that the table was defective. ◀

WARRANTY DISCLAIMERS AND UNCONSCIONABILITY
The UCC sections dealing with warranty disclaimers do not refer specifically to unconscionability as a factor. Ultimately, however, the courts will test warranty disclaimers with reference to the UCC's unconscionability standards [UCC 2–302, 2A–108]. Factors such as lack of bargaining position, "take-it-or-leave-it" choices, and a buyer's or lessee's failure to understand or know of a warranty disclaimer will be relevant to the issue of unconscionability.

STATUTE OF LIMITATIONS
As discussed earlier in this chapter, a cause of action for breach of contract under the UCC must be commenced within four years after the breach occurs (unless the parties agree to a shorter period). An action for breach of warranty accrues when the seller or lessor *tenders* delivery, even if the buyer or lessee is unaware of the breach at that time [UCC 2–725(2), 2A–506(2)]. In addition, the non-breaching party usually must notify the breaching party within a reasonable time after discovering the breach or be barred from pursuing any remedy [UCC 2–607(3)(a), 2A–516(3)].

Reviewing: Performance, Breach, and Warranties of Sales and Lease Contracts

Shalene Kolchek bought a Great Lakes spa from Val Porter, a dealer who was selling spas at the state fair. Porter told Kolchek that Great Lakes spas were "top of the line" and "the Cadillac of spas" and indicated that the spa she was buying was "fully warranted for three years." Kolchek signed an installment contract. Then, Porter handed her the manufacturer's paperwork and arranged for the spa to be delivered and installed for her. Three months later, Kolchek noticed that one corner of the spa was leaking onto her new deck and causing damage. She complained to Porter, but he did nothing about the problem. Kolchek's family continued to use the spa. Using the information presented in the chapter, answer the following questions.

1. Did Porter's statement that the spa was "top of the line" and "the Cadillac of spas" create any type of warranty? Why or why not?

2. If the paperwork provided to Kolchek after her purchase indicated that the spa had no warranty, would this be an effective disclaimer under the Uniform Commercial Code? Explain.

3. Can Kolchek sue Porter for breach of the implied warranty of merchantability because the spa leaked? Explain.

4. Suppose that one year later, Pacific Credit Union contacted Kolchek and claimed that it had a security interest in the spa. Would this be a breach of any of the title warranties discussed in the chapter? Explain.

DEBATE THIS ... *No express warranties should be created by the oral statements made by salespersons about a product.*

Terms and Concepts

conforming goods 319

cover 328

cure 321

express warranty 335

implied warranty 336

implied warranty of fitness for a
  particular purpose 337

implied warranty of
  merchantability 336

installment contract 322

perfect tender rule 320

replevin 329

tender of delivery 319

ExamPrep

Issue Spotters

1. Country Fruit Stand orders eighty cases of peaches from Downey Farms. Without stating a reason, Downey delivers thirty cases instead of eighty at the wrong time. Does Country have the right to reject the shipment? Explain. **(See page 320.)**

2. Stella bought a cup of coffee at the Roasted Bean Drive-Thru. The coffee had been heated to 190 degrees and consequently had dissolved the inside of the cup. When Stella lifted the lid, the cup collapsed, spilling the contents on her lap. To recover for third-degree burns on her thighs, Stella filed a suit against the Roasted Bean. Can Stella recover for breach of the implied warranty of merchantability? Why or why not? **(See page 336.)**

• Check your answers to the Issue Spotters against the answers provided in Appendix B at the end of this text.

Before the Test

Go to **www.cengagebrain.com**, enter the ISBN 9781285770192, and click on "Find" to locate this text-book's Web site. Then, click on "Access Now" under "Study Tools," and select Chapter 16 at the top. There, you will find a Practice Quiz that you can take to assess your mastery of the concepts in this chapter, as well as Flashcards and a Glossary of important terms.

Business Scenarios

16–1. Implied Warranties. Moon, a farmer, needs to install a two-thousand-pound piece of equipment in his barn. This will require lifting the equipment thirty feet up into a hayloft. Moon goes to Davidson Hardware and tells Davidson that he needs some heavy-duty rope to be used on his farm. Davidson recommends a one-inch-thick nylon rope, and Moon purchases two hundred feet of it. Moon ties the rope around the piece of equipment; puts the rope through a pulley; and, with a tractor, lifts the equipment off the ground. Suddenly, the rope breaks. The equipment crashes to the ground and is severely damaged. Moon files a suit against Davidson for breach of the implied warranty of fitness for a particular purpose. Discuss how successful Moon will be in his suit. **(See pages 336 and 337.)**

16–2. Remedies of the Buyer or Lessee. Lehor collects antique cars. He contracts to purchase spare parts for a 1938 engine from Beem. These parts are not made anymore and are scarce. To obtain the contract with Beem, Lehor agrees to pay 50 percent of the purchase price in advance. Lehor sends the payment on May 1, and Beem receives it on May 2. On May 3, Beem, having found another buyer willing to pay substantially more for the parts, informs Lehor that he will not deliver as contracted. That same day, Lehor learns that Beem is insolvent. Discuss fully any possible remedies available to Lehor to enable him to take possession of these parts. **(See pages 327–328.)**

16–3. Right of Inspection. Jessie Romero offered to deliver two trade-in vehicles—a 2003 Mitsubishi Montero SP and a 2002 Chevrolet Silverado pickup—to Scoggin-Dickey Chevrolet Buick, Inc., in exchange for a 2006 Silverado pickup. Scoggin-Dickey agreed. The parties negotiated a price, including a value for the trade-in vehicles, plus cash. Romero paid the cash and took the new Silverado. On inspecting the trade-in vehicles, however, Scoggin-Dickey found that they had little value. The dealer repossessed the Silverado. Did the dealership have the right to inspect the goods and reject them when it did? Why or why not? [*Romero v. Scoggin-Dickey Chevrolet Buick, Inc.*, __ S.W.3d __ (Tex.Civ.App.—Amarillo 2010)] **(See page 320.)**

16–4. Spotlight on Apple—Implied Warranties. Alan Vitt pur-

chased an iBook G4 laptop computer from Apple, Inc. Shortly after the one-year warranty expired, the laptop failed to work due to a weakness in the product manufacture. Vitt sued Apple, arguing that the laptop should have lasted "at least a couple of years," which Vitt believed was a reasonable consumer expectation for a laptop. Vitt claimed that Apple's descriptions of the laptop as "durable," "rugged," "reliable," and "high performance" were affirmative statements concerning the quality and performance of the laptop, which Apple did not meet. How should the court rule? Why? [*Vitt v. Apple Computer, Inc.*, 2012 WL 627702 (9th Cir. 2011)] **(See page 336.)**

**16–5. BUSINESS CASE PROBLEM
WITH SAMPLE ANSWER: Nonconforming Goods.**

Padma Paper Mills, Ltd., converts waste paper into usable paper. In 2007, Padma entered into a contract with Universal Exports, Inc., under which Universal Exports certified that it would ship white envelope cuttings, and Padma paid $131,000 for the paper. When the shipment arrived, however, Padma discovered that Universal Exports had sent multicolored paper plates and other brightly colored paper products. Padma accepted the goods but notified Universal Exports that they did not conform to the con-

tract. Can Padma recover even though it accepted the goods knowing that they were nonconforming? If so, how? [Padma Paper Mills, Ltd. v. Universal Exports, Inc., *34 Misc.3d 1236(A) (N.Y.Sup. 2012)*] **(See page 329.)**

• **For a sample answer for Problem 16–5, go to Appendix C at the end of this text.**

16–6. Implied Warranties. Bariven, S.A., agreed to buy 26,000 metric tons of powdered milk for $123.5 million from Absolute Trading Corp. to be delivered in shipments from China to Venezuela. After the first three shipments, China halted dairy exports due to the presence of melamine in some products. Absolute assured Bariven that its milk was safe, and when China resumed dairy exports, Absolute delivered sixteen more shipments. Tests of samples of the milk revealed that it contained dangerous levels of melamine. Did Absolute breach any implied warranties? Discuss. [*Absolute Trading Corp. v. Bariven S.A.*, 2013 WL 49735 (11th Cir. 2013)] **(See page 336.)**

16–7. A QUESTION OF ETHICS: Lemon Laws.

Randal Schweiger bought a 2008 Kia Spectra EX from Kia Motors America, Inc., for his stepdaughter, April Kirichkow. The cost was $17,231, plus sales tax, fees, and other items. April had trouble starting the car. The Kia dealership replaced different parts of the motor several times, but was unable to fix the problem. Schweiger sought a refund under the state's lemon law. When they could not agree on the amount, Schweiger filed a suit in a Wisconsin state court against Kia. From a judgment in Schweiger's favor, Kia appealed. [Schweiger v. Kia Motors America, Inc., *347 Wis.2d 550, 830 N.W.2d 723 (Wis.App. 2013)*] **(See page 338.)**

(a) Kia offered a refund of $3,306.24. Should this offer bar Schweiger's claim for a refund? Why or why not?

(b) Schweiger claimed that Kia's offer did not include the $1,301 cost of a service contract. Kia argued that the "payoff to the lender" of $13,060.16, which Schweiger agreed was the correct amount, "would by definition refund the cost of the service contract." The court found "no logical basis" for this argument. Is it ethical for a party to argue a position for which there is no logical basis? Discuss.

Legal Reasoning Group Activity

16–8. Warranties. Milan purchased saffron extract, marketed as "America's Hottest New Way to a Flat Belly," online from Dr. Chen. The Web site stated that recently published studies showed a significant weight loss (more than 25 percent) for people who used pure saffron extract as a supplement *without diet and exercise.* Dr. Chen said that the saffron suppresses appetite by increasing levels of serotonin, which reduces emotional eating. Milan took the extract as directed without any resulting weight loss. **(See pages 332–338.)**

(a) The first group will determine whether Dr. Chen's Web site made any express warranty on the saffron extract or its effectiveness in causing weight loss.

(b) The second group will discuss whether the implied warranty of merchantability applies to the purchase of weight-loss supplements.

(c) The third group will decide if Dr. Chen's sale of saffron extract breached the implied warranty of fitness for a particular purpose.

AN ACCELERATED COURSE

MILLER

UNIT FOUR

AGENCY AND BUSINESS FORMS

CONTENTS

CHAPTER 17

AGENCY RELATIONSHIPS IN BUSINESS

One of the most common, important, and pervasive legal relationships is that of **agency.** In an agency relationship involving two parties, one of the parties, called the **agent,** agrees to represent or act for the other, called the *principal*. The **principal** has the right to control the agent's conduct in matters entrusted to the agent. By using agents, a principal can conduct multiple business operations simultaneously in various locations. Thus, for example, contracts that bind the principal can be made at different places with different persons at the same time.

A familiar example of an agent is a corporate officer who serves in a representative capacity for the owners of the corporation. In this capacity, the officer has the authority to bind the principal (the corporation) to a contract. In fact, agency law is essential to the existence and operation of a corporate entity because only through its agents can a corporation function and enter into contracts.

Most employees are also considered to be agents of their employers. Indeed, agency relationships permeate the business world. For that reason, an understanding of the law of agency is crucial to understanding business law.

SECTION 1
AGENCY RELATIONSHIPS

Section 1(1) of the *Restatement (Third) of Agency*[1] defines *agency* as "the fiduciary relation [that] results from the manifestation of consent by one person to another that the other shall act in his [or her] behalf and subject to his [or her] control, and consent by the other so to act." In other words, in a principal-agent relationship, the parties have agreed that the agent will act *on behalf and instead of* the principal in negotiating and transacting business with third parties.

The term **fiduciary** is at the heart of agency law. This term can be used both as a noun and as an adjective. When used as a noun, it refers to a person having a duty created by his or her undertaking to act primarily for another's benefit in matters connected with the undertaking. When used as an adjective, as in the phrase *fiduciary relationship,* it means that the relationship involves trust and confidence.

Agency relationships commonly exist between employers and employees. Agency relationships may sometimes also exist between employers and independent contractors who are hired to perform special tasks or services.

Employer-Employee Relationships

Normally, all employees who deal with third parties are deemed to be agents. A salesperson in a department store, for instance, is an agent of the store's owner (the principal) and acts on the owner's behalf. Any sale of goods made by the salesperson to a customer is binding on the principal. Similarly, most representations of fact made by the salesperson with respect to the goods sold are binding on the principal.

Because employees who deal with third parties generally are deemed to be agents of their employers, agency law and employment law overlap considerably. Agency relationships, though, as will become apparent, can exist outside an employer-employee relationship, and thus agency law has a broader reach than employment law does.

Employment laws (state and federal) apply only to the employer-employee relationship. Thus, statutes that govern Social Security, withholding taxes, workers' compensation, unemployment compensation, and workplace safety apply only when an employer-

---

1. The *Restatement (Third) of Agency* is an authoritative summary of the law of agency and is often referred to by judges in their decisions and opinions.

employee relationship exists. Similarly, laws that prohibit employment discrimination apply only to employers and employees. *These laws do not apply to an independent contractor.*

Employer–Independent Contractor Relationships

Independent contractors are not employees because, by definition, those who hire them have no control over the details of their work performance. Section 2 of the *Restatement (Third) of Agency* defines an **independent contractor** as follows:

> [An independent contractor is] a person who contracts with another to do something for him [or her] but who is not controlled by the other nor subject to the other's right to control with respect to his [or her] physical conduct in the performance of the undertaking. He [or she] may or may not be an agent.

Building contractors and subcontractors are independent contractors. A property owner who hires a contractor and subcontractors to complete a project does not control the details of the way they perform their work. Truck drivers who own their vehicles and hire out on a per-job basis are independent contractors, but truck drivers who drive company trucks on a regular basis usually are employees.

The relationship between a principal and an independent contractor may or may not involve an agency relationship. To illustrate: A homeowner who hires a real estate broker to sell her house has not only contracted with an independent contractor (the broker) but also established an agency relationship for the specific purpose of selling the property. Another example is an insurance agent, who is both an independent contractor and an agent of the insurance company for which he sells policies. (Note that an insurance *broker,* in contrast, normally is an agent of the person obtaining insurance and not of the insurance company.)

Determination of Employee Status

The courts are frequently asked to determine whether a particular worker is an employee or an independent contractor. How a court decides this issue can have a significant effect on the rights and liabilities of the parties. For instance, employers are required to pay certain taxes, such as Social Security and unemployment taxes, for employees but not for independent contractors.

CRITERIA USED BY THE COURTS In deciding whether a worker is categorized as an employee or an independent contractor, courts often consider the following questions:

1. *How much control does the employer exercise over the details of the work?* If the employer exercises considerable control over the details of the work and the day-to-day activities of the worker, this indicates employee status. This is perhaps the most important factor weighed by the courts in determining employee status.

2. *Is the worker engaged in an occupation or business distinct from that of the employer?* If so, this points to independent-contractor, not employee, status.

3. *Is the work usually done under the employer's direction or by a specialist without supervision?* If the work is usually done under the employer's direction, this indicates employee status.

4. *Does the employer supply the tools at the place of work?* If so, this indicates employee status.

5. *For how long is the person employed?* If the person is employed for a long period of time, this indicates employee status.

6. *What is the method of payment—by time period or at the completion of the job?* Payment by time period, such as once every two weeks or once a month, indicates employee status.

7. *What degree of skill is required of the worker?* If a great degree of skill is required, this may indicate that the person is an independent contractor hired for a specialized job and not an employee.

Disputes Involving Employment Law. Sometimes, workers may benefit from having employee status—for tax purposes and to be protected under certain employment laws, for example. As mentioned earlier, federal statutes governing employment discrimination apply only when an employer-employee relationship exists. Protection under employment-discrimination statutes provides a significant incentive for workers to claim that they are employees rather than independent contractors.

▶ **Case in Point 17.1** A Puerto Rican television station, WIPR, contracted with Victoria Alberty-Vélez to cohost a television show. Alberty signed a new contract for each episode and was committed to work for WIPR only during the filming of the episodes. WIPR paid her a lump sum for each contract and did not withhold any taxes. When Alberty became pregnant, WIPR stopped contracting with her. She filed a lawsuit claiming that WIPR was discriminating against her in violation of federal antidiscrimination laws, but the court found in favor of WIPR. Because the parties had used repeated fixed-length contracts and had described Alberty as an independent contractor on tax documents, she could not maintain an employment-discrimination suit.[2] ◀

---
2. *Alberty-Vélez v. Corporación de Puerto Rico para la Difusión Pública,* 361 F.3d 1 (1st Cir. 2004).

Disputes Involving Tort Liability. Whether a worker is an employee or an independent contractor can also affect the employer's liability for the worker's actions.

In the following case, the court had to determine the status of an auto service company and its tow truck driver who assaulted the passenger of a vehicle the company had been hired to tow.

CASE 17.1

Coker v. Pershad

Superior Court of New Jersey, Appellate Division, 2013 WL 1296271 (2013).

BACKGROUND AND FACTS AAA North Jersey, Inc., contracted with Five Star Auto Service to perform towing and auto repair services for AAA. Terence Pershad, the driver of a tow truck for Five Star, responded to a call to AAA for assistance by the driver of a car involved in an accident in Hoboken, New Jersey. Pershad got into a fight with Nicholas Coker, a passenger in the car, and assaulted Coker with a knife. Coker filed a suit in a New Jersey state court against Pershad, Five Star, and AAA. The court determined that Pershad was Five Star's employee and that Five Star was an independent contractor, not AAA's employee. Thus, AAA was "not responsible for the alleged negligence of its independent contractor, defendant Five Star, in hiring Mr. Pershad." Five Star entered into a settlement with Coker. Coker appealed the ruling in AAA's favor.

  IN THE LANGUAGE OF THE COURT
PER CURIAM. [By the Whole Court]

* * * *

The important difference between an employee and an independent contractor is that one who hires an independent contractor has no right of control over the manner in which the work is to be done. [Emphasis added.]

* * * *

* * * Plaintiff [Coker] argues AAA controlled the means and method of the work performed by Five Star. * * * Factors * * * [that] determine whether a principal maintains the right of control over an individual or a corporation claimed to be an independent contractor [include]:

(a) the extent of control which, by the agreement, the master may exercise over the details of the work;
(b) whether or not the one employed is engaged in a distinct occupation or business;
(c) the kind of occupation, with reference to whether, in the locality, the work is usually done under the direction of the employer or by a specialist without supervision;
(d) the skill required in the particular occupation;
(e) whether the employer or the workman supplies the * * * tools * * * ;
(f) the length of time for which the person is employed * * * .

Applying these factors to the facts of this case, it is clear AAA did not control the manner and means of Five Star's work. The Agreement specifically stated Five Star was an independent contractor. Five Star purchased its own trucks and any other necessary equipment. AAA assigned jobs to Five Star and Five Star completed the work without any further supervision by AAA. Five Star chose the employees to send on towing calls and the trucks and equipment the employees would use.

Five Star was also in business for itself and performed auto repair services for principals and customers other than AAA. Five Star hired and fired its own employees * * * .

* * * *

Plaintiff also argues Five Star should be considered to be controlled by AAA because "providing towing and other roadside assistance is arguably the focus of the regular business

CASE 17.1 CONTINUED

of AAA." * * * [But] AAA is an automobile club that provides a wide variety of services to its members. It contracts with numerous service providers, such as gas stations, motels and other businesses, to provide these services. Thus, AAA is not solely in the towing business.

* * * AAA had used Five Star to provide towing services for approximately eight years and there is nothing in the record to demonstrate it lacked the skill needed to provide these services.

DECISION AND REMEDY *A state intermediate appellate court affirmed the lower court's ruling. AAA could not be held liable for the actions of Five Star, its independent contractor, because "AAA did not control the manner and means of Five Star's work."*

THE LEGAL ENVIRONMENT DIMENSION *Five Star's contract with AAA required Five Star to be available to provide service for AAA members. Does this support Coker's argument that Five Star was AAA's employee? Why or why not?*

MANAGERIAL IMPLICATIONS *When an employment contract clearly designates one party as an independent contractor, the relationship between the parties is presumed to be that of employer and independent contractor. But this is only a presumption. Evidence can be introduced to show that the employer exercised sufficient control to establish the other party as an employee. The Internal Revenue Service is increasingly pursuing employers that it claims have wrongly classified employees as independent contractors. Thus, from a tax perspective, business managers need to ensure that all independent contractors fully control their own work.*

CRITERIA USED BY THE IRS The Internal Revenue Service (IRS) has established its own criteria for determining whether a worker is an independent contractor or an employee. The most important factor is the degree of control the business exercises over the worker.

The IRS tends to closely scrutinize a firm's classification of its workers because, as mentioned, employers can avoid certain tax liabilities by hiring independent contractors instead of employees. Even when a firm has classified a worker as an independent contractor, the IRS may decide that the worker is actually an employee. If the IRS decides that an employee is misclassified, the employer will be responsible for paying any applicable Social Security, withholding, and unemployment taxes.

EMPLOYEE STATUS AND "WORKS FOR HIRE" Under the Copyright Act, any copyrighted work created by an employee within the scope of her or his employment at the request of the employer is a "work for hire." The employer owns the copyright to the work. In contrast, when an employer hires an independent contractor—a freelance artist, writer, or computer programmer, for example—the independent contractor normally owns the copyright. An exception is made if the parties agree in writing that the work is a "work for hire" and the work falls into one of nine specific categories, including audiovisual and other works.

▶ **Case in Point 17.2** Artisan House, Inc., hired a professional photographer, Steven H. Lindner, owner of SHL Imaging, Inc., to take pictures of its products for the creation of color slides to be used by Artisan's sales force. Lindner controlled his own work and carefully chose the lighting and angles used in the photographs. When Artisan published the photographs in a catalogue and brochures without Lindner's permission, SHL filed a lawsuit for copyright infringement. Artisan claimed that its publication of the photographs was authorized because they were works for hire. The court, however, decided that SHL was an independent contractor and owned the copyright to the photographs. Because SHL had not given Artisan permission (a license) to reproduce the photographs in other publications, Artisan was liable for copyright infringement.[3] ◀

SECTION 2

FORMATION OF THE AGENCY RELATIONSHIP

Agency relationships normally are *consensual*—that is, they come about by voluntary consent and agreement between the parties. Generally, the agreement need not be in writing and consideration is not required.

---
3. *SHL Imaging, Inc. v. Artisan House, Inc.*, 117 F.Supp.2d 301 (S.D.N.Y. 2000).

There are two main exceptions to the statement that agency agreements need not be in writing: (1) under the *equal dignity rule* (see page 354), an agreement must be in writing if it empowers the agent to enter into a contract that the Statute of Frauds requires to be in writing. (2) An agreement that gives an agent power of attorney must also be in writing.

A person must have contractual capacity to be a principal.[4] Those who cannot legally enter into contracts directly should not be allowed to do so indirectly through an agent. Any person can be an agent, however, regardless of whether he or she has the capacity to contract (including minors).

An agency relationship can be created for any legal purpose. An agency relationship created for a purpose that is illegal or contrary to public policy is unenforceable. ▶ **Example 17.3** Archer (as principal) contracts with Burke (as agent) to sell illegal narcotics. The agency relationship is unenforceable because selling illegal narcotics is a felony and is contrary to public policy. If Burke sells the narcotics and keeps the profits, Archer cannot sue to enforce the agency agreement. ◀

An agency relationship can arise in four ways: by *agreement of the parties*, by *ratification*, by *estoppel*, and by *operation of law*.

Agency by Agreement of the Parties

Most agency relationships are based on an express or implied agreement that the agent will act for the principal and that the principal agrees to have the agent so act. An agency agreement can take the form of an express written contract or be created by an oral agreement. ▶ **Example 17.4** Rees asks Grace, a gardener, to contract with others for the care of his lawn on a regular basis. If Grace agrees, an agency relationship exists between Reese and Grace for the lawn care. ◀

An agency agreement can also be implied by conduct. ▶ **Example 17.5** A hotel expressly allows only Boris Renke to park cars, but Renke has no employment contract there. The hotel's manager tells Renke when to work, as well as where and how to park the cars. The hotel's conduct manifests a willingness to have Renke park its customers' cars, and Renke can infer from the hotel's conduct that he has authority to act as a parking valet. Thus, there is an implied

agreement that Renke is an agent of the hotel and provides valet parking services for hotel guests. ◀

Agency by Ratification

On occasion, a person who is in fact not an agent (or who is an agent acting outside the scope of her or his authority) may make a contract on behalf of another (a principal). If the principal approves or affirms that contract by word or by action, an agency relationship is created by *ratification*. Ratification involves a question of intent, and intent can be expressed by either words or conduct. The basic requirements for ratification will be discussed later on page 358.

Agency by Estoppel

Sometimes, a principal causes a third person to believe that another person is the principal's agent, and the third person acts to his or her detriment in reasonable reliance on that belief. When this occurs, the principal is "estopped to deny" (prevented from denying) the agency relationship. An agency by estoppel arises when the principal's actions have created the *appearance* of an agency that does not in fact exist.

THE THIRD PARTY'S RELIANCE MUST BE REASONABLE
The third person must prove that he or she *reasonably* believed that an agency relationship existed, however.[5] Facts and circumstances must show that an ordinary, prudent person familiar with business practice and custom would have been justified in concluding that the agent had authority.
▶ **Case in Point 17.6** Marsha and Jerry Wiedmaier owned Wiedmaier, Inc., a corporation that operated a truck stop. Their son, Michael, did not own any interest in the corporation but had worked at the truck stop as a fuel operator. Michael decided to form his own business called Extreme Diecast, LLC. To obtain a line of credit with Motorsport Marketing, Inc., which sells racing memorabilia, Michael asked his mother to sign the credit application form.

After Marsha had signed as "Secretary-Owner" of Wiedmaier, Inc., Michael added his name to the list of corporate owners and faxed the form to Motorsport. Later, when Michael stopped making payments on the merchandise he had ordered, Motorsport sued Wiedmaier, Inc., for the unpaid balance. The court ruled that Michael was an apparent

---

4. Note that some states allow a minor to be a principal. When a minor is permitted to be a principal, any resulting contracts will be voidable by the minor principal but *not* by the adult third party.

5. These concepts also apply when a person who is in fact an agent undertakes an action that is beyond the scope of her or his authority, as will be discussed later in this chapter.

agent of Wiedmaier, Inc., because the credit application had caused Motorsport to reasonably believe that Michael was acting as Wiedmaier's agent in ordering merchandise.[6] ◄

CREATED BY THE PRINCIPAL'S CONDUCT Note that the acts or declarations of a purported *agent* in and of themselves do not create an agency by estoppel. Rather, it is the deeds or statements of the *principal* that create an agency by estoppel. Thus, in *Case in Point 17.6*, if Marsha Wiedmaier had not signed the credit application on behalf of the principal-corporation, then Motorsport would not have been justified in believing that Michael was Wiedmaier's agent.

Agency by Operation of Law

The courts may find an agency relationship in the absence of a formal agreement in other situations as well. This may occur in family relationships, such as when one spouse purchases certain basic necessaries and charges them to the other spouse's account. The courts often rule that a spouse is liable for payment for the necessaries because of either a social policy or a legal duty to supply necessaries to family members.

Agency by operation of law may also occur in emergency situations. If an agent cannot contact the principal and failure to act would cause the principal substantial loss, the agent may take steps beyond

---

6. *Motorsport Marketing, Inc. v. Wiedmaier, Inc.,* 195 S.W.3d 492 (Mo.App. 2006).

the scope of her or his authority. For example, a railroad engineer may contract on behalf of his or her employer for medical care for an injured motorist hit by the train.

Concept Summary 17.1 below reviews the various ways that agencies are formed.

SECTION 3
DUTIES AND RIGHTS OF AGENTS AND PRINCIPALS

Once the principal-agent relationship has been created, both parties have duties that govern their conduct. As discussed previously, the principal-agent relationship is *fiduciary*—based on trust. In a fiduciary relationship, each party owes the other the duty to act with the utmost good faith. In this section, we examine the various duties of agents and principals.

Agent's Duties to the Principal

Generally, the agent owes the principal five duties—performance, notification, loyalty, obedience, and accounting.

PERFORMANCE An implied condition in every agency contract is the agent's agreement to use reasonable diligence and skill in performing the work. When an agent fails to perform his or her duties, liability for breach of contract may result.

CONCEPT SUMMARY 17.1
Formation of the Agency Relationship

METHOD OF FORMATION	DESCRIPTION
By Agreement	The agency relationship is formed through express consent (oral or written) or implied by conduct between the agent and the principal.
By Ratification	The principal either by act or by agreement ratifies the conduct of a person who is not in fact an agent.
By Estoppel	The principal causes a third person to believe that another person is the principal's agent, and the third person acts to his or her detriment in reasonable reliance on that belief.
By Operation of Law	The agency relationship is based on a social or legal duty (such as the need to support family members) or formed in emergency situations when the agent is unable to contact the principal and failure to act outside the scope of the agent's authority would cause the principal substantial loss.

Standard of Care. The degree of skill or care required of an agent is usually that expected of a reasonable person under similar circumstances. Generally, this is interpreted to mean ordinary care. If an agent has represented herself or himself as possessing special skills, however, the agent is expected to exercise the degree of skill claimed. Failure to do so constitutes a breach of the agent's duty.

Gratuitous Agents. Not all agency relationships are based on contract. In some situations, an agent acts gratuitously—that is, without payment. A gratuitous agent cannot be liable for breach of contract because there is no contract. He or she is subject only to tort liability. Once a gratuitous agent has begun to act in an agency capacity, he or she has the duty to continue to perform in that capacity. A gratuitous agent must perform in an acceptable manner and is subject to the same standards of care and duty to perform as other agents.

▶ **Example 17.7** Bower's friend Alcott is a real estate broker. Alcott offers to sell Bower's vacation home at no charge. If Alcott never attempts to sell the home, Bower has no legal cause of action to force her to do so. If Alcott does attempt to sell the home to Friedman, but then performs so negligently that the sale falls through, Bower can sue Alcott for negligence. ◀

NOTIFICATION An agent is required to notify the principal of all matters that come to her or his attention concerning the subject matter of the agency. This is the *duty of notification,* or the duty to inform.

▶ **Example 17.8** Perez, an artist, is about to negotiate a contract to sell a series of paintings to Barber's Art Gallery for $25,000. Perez's agent learns that Barber is insolvent and will be unable to pay for the paintings. The agent has a duty to inform Perez of Barber's insolvency because it is relevant to the subject matter of the agency, which is the sale of Perez's paintings. ◀

Generally, the law assumes that the principal is aware of any information acquired by the agent that is relevant to the agency—regardless of whether the agent actually passes on this information to the principal. It is a basic tenet of agency law that notice to the agent is notice to the principal.

LOYALTY Loyalty is one of the most fundamental duties in a fiduciary relationship. Basically, the agent has the duty to act *solely for the benefit of his or her principal* and not in the interest of the agent or a third party. For instance, an agent cannot represent two principals in the same transaction unless both know of the dual capacity and consent to it.

Maintain Confidentiality. The duty of loyalty also means that any information or knowledge acquired through the agency relationship is confidential. It is a breach of loyalty to disclose such information either during the agency relationship or after its termination. Typical examples of confidential information are trade secrets and customer lists compiled by the principal.

Actions Must Benefit the Principal. The agent's loyalty must be undivided. The agent's actions must be strictly for the benefit of the principal and must not result in any secret profit for the agent.

▶ **Case in Point 17.9** Don Cousins contracted with Leo Hodgins, a real estate agent, to negotiate the purchase of an office building. While working for Cousins, Hodgins discovered that the property owner would sell the building only as a package deal with another parcel. Hodgins therefore bought the two properties intending to resell the building to Cousins. When Cousins found out, he sued.

The court held that Hodgins had breached his fiduciary duties. As a real estate agent, Hodgins had a duty to communicate all offers to his principal and not to secretly purchase the property and then resell it to his principal. Hodgins was required to act in Cousins's best interests and could only become the purchaser in this situation with Cousins's knowledge and approval.[7] ◀

OBEDIENCE When acting on behalf of the principal, an agent has a duty to follow all lawful and clearly stated instructions of the principal. Any deviation from such instructions is a violation of this duty.

During emergency situations, however, when the principal cannot be consulted, the agent may deviate from the instructions without violating this duty. Whenever instructions are not clearly stated, the agent can fulfill the duty of obedience by acting in good faith and in a manner reasonable under the circumstances.

ACCOUNTING Unless the agent and principal agree otherwise, the agent must keep and make available to the principal an account of all property and funds received and paid out on the principal's behalf. This includes gifts from third parties in connection with

---

7. *Cousins v. Realty Ventures, Inc.,* 844 So.2d 860 (La.App. 5 Cir. 2003).

the agency. For instance, a gift from a customer to a salesperson for prompt deliveries made by the salesperson's firm, in the absence of a company policy to the contrary, belongs to the firm.

The agent has a duty to maintain a separate account for the principal's funds and must not intermingle these funds with the agent's personal funds. If a licensed professional (such as an attorney) violates this duty, he or she may be subject to disciplinary proceedings carried out by the appropriate regulatory institution (such as the state bar association). Of course, the professional will also be liable to the principal (the professional's client) for failure to account.

Principal's Duties to the Agent

The principal also has certain duties to the agent. These duties relate to compensation, reimbursement and indemnification, cooperation, and safe working conditions.

COMPENSATION In general, when a principal requests certain services from an agent, the agent reasonably expects payment. The principal therefore has a duty to pay the agent for services rendered. For instance, when an accountant or an attorney is asked to act as an agent, an agreement to compensate the agent for this service is implied.

The principal also has a duty to pay that compensation in a timely manner. Unless the agency relationship is gratuitous and the agent does not act in exchange for payment, the principal must pay the agreed-on value for the agent's services. If no amount has been expressly agreed on, then the principal owes the agent the customary compensation for such services.

REIMBURSEMENT AND INDEMNIFICATION The principal has a duty to reimburse the agent for any funds disbursed at the principal's request. The principal must also reimburse the agent for any necessary expenses incurred in the course of the reasonable performance of her or his agency duties.[8] Agents cannot recover for expenses incurred as a result of their own misconduct or negligence, though.

Subject to the terms of the agency agreement, the principal has the duty to *indemnify* (compensate) an agent for liabilities incurred because of authorized and lawful acts and transactions. For instance, if the agent, on the principal's behalf, forms a contract with a third party, and the principal fails to perform the contract, the third party may sue the agent for damages. In this situation, the principal is obligated to compensate the agent for any costs incurred by the agent as a result of the principal's failure to perform the contract.

Additionally, the principal must indemnify the agent for the value of benefits that the agent confers on the principal. The amount of indemnification usually is specified in the agency contract. If it is not, the courts will look to the nature of the business and the type of loss to determine the amount. Note that this rule applies to acts by gratuitous agents as well.

COOPERATION A principal has a duty to cooperate with the agent and to assist the agent in performing his or her duties. The principal must do nothing to prevent that performance.

For instance, when a principal grants an agent an exclusive territory, the principal creates an **exclusive agency,** in which the principal cannot compete with the agent or appoint or allow another agent to compete. If the principal does so, he or she violates the exclusive agency and is exposed to liability for the agent's lost profits.

▶ **Example 17.10** River City Times Company (the principal) grants Emir (the agent) the right to sell its newspapers at a busy downtown intersection to the exclusion of all other vendors. This creates an exclusive territory within which only Emir has the right to sell those newspapers. If River City Times allows another vendor to sell its papers in that area, Emir can sue for lost profits. ◀

SAFE WORKING CONDITIONS The common law requires the principal to provide safe working premises, equipment, and conditions for all agents and employees. The principal has a duty to inspect working areas and to warn agents and employees about any unsafe situations. When the agent is an employee, the employer's liability is frequently covered by state workers' compensation insurance.

Rights and Remedies of Agents and Principals

In general, for every duty of the principal, the agent has a corresponding right, and vice versa. When one party to the agency relationship violates his or her duty to the other party, the remedies available to the

---

8. This principle applies to acts by gratuitous agents as well. If a finder of a dog that becomes sick takes the dog to a veterinarian and pays the veterinarian's fees, the gratuitous agent is entitled to be reimbursed by the dog's owner.

nonbreaching party arise out of contract and tort law. These remedies include monetary damages, termination of the agency relationship, an *injunction,* and required accountings.

S E C T I O N 4
SCOPE OF AGENT'S AUTHORITY

The liability of a principal to third parties with whom an agent contracts depends on whether the agent had the authority to enter into legally binding contracts on the principal's behalf. An agent's authority can be either *actual* (express or implied) or *apparent.* If an agent contracts outside the scope of his or her authority, the principal may still become liable by ratifying the contract.

Express Authority

Express authority is authority declared in clear, direct, and definite terms. Express authority can be given orally or in writing.

THE EQUAL DIGNITY RULE In most states, the **equal dignity rule** requires that if the contract being executed is or must be in writing, then the agent's authority must also be in writing. Failure to comply with the equal dignity rule can make a contract voidable *at the option of the principal.* The law regards the contract at that point as a mere offer. If the principal decides to accept the offer, the acceptance must be ratified, or affirmed, in writing (or in an electronic record).

▶ **Example 17.11** Paloma (the principal) orally asks Austin (the agent) to sell a ranch that Paloma owns. Austin finds a buyer and signs a sales contract (a contract for an interest in realty must be in writing) on behalf of Paloma to sell the ranch. The buyer cannot enforce the contract unless Paloma subsequently ratifies Austin's agency status *in writing.* Once the sales contract is ratified, either party can enforce rights under the contract. ◀

Modern business practice allows several exceptions to the equal dignity rule:

1. An executive officer of a corporation normally can conduct *ordinary* business transactions without obtaining written authority from the *corporation* (see Chapter 19).
2. When the agent acts in the presence of the principal, the rule does not apply.

3. When the agent's act of signing is merely a formality, then the agent does not need written authority to sign. ▶ **Example 17.12** Sandra Healy (the principal) negotiates a contract but is called out of town the day it is to be signed. If Healy orally authorizes Santini to sign, the oral authorization is sufficient. ◀

POWER OF ATTORNEY Giving an agent a **power of attorney** confers express authority.[9] The power of attorney is a written document and is usually notarized. (A document is notarized when a **notary public**—a public official authorized to attest to the authenticity of signatures—signs and dates the document and imprints it with her or his seal of authority.) Most states have statutory provisions for creating a power of attorney.

A power of attorney can be *special* (permitting the agent to perform specified acts only), or it can be *general* (permitting the agent to transact all business for the principal). Because of the extensive authority granted to an agent by a general power of attorney (see Exhibit 17–1 on the next page), it should be used with great caution and usually only in exceptional circumstances. Ordinarily, a power of attorney terminates on the incapacity or death of the person giving the power.[10]

Implied Authority

An agent has the **implied authority** to do what is reasonably necessary to carry out express authority and accomplish the objectives of the agency. Authority can also be implied by custom or inferred from the position the agent occupies. (For a discussion of what happens when an employee-agent makes unauthorized use of the employer's computer data, see this chapter's *Insight into Ethics* feature on page 356.)

▶ **Example 17.13** Archer is employed by Packard Grocery to manage one of its stores. Packard has not expressly stated that Archer has authority to contract with third persons. Nevertheless, authority to manage a business implies authority to do what is rea-

---

9. An agent who holds a power of attorney is called an *attorney-in-fact* for the principal. The holder does not have to be an attorney-at-law (and often is not).

10. A *durable* power of attorney, however, continues to be effective despite the principal's incapacity. An elderly person, for example, might grant a durable power of attorney to provide for the handling of property and investments or specific health-care needs should he or she become incompetent.

EXHIBIT 17-1 A Sample General Power of Attorney

GENERAL POWER OF ATTORNEY

Know All Men by These Presents:

That I, _____ , hereinafter referred to as PRINCIPAL, in the County of _____
State of _____ , do(es) appoint _____ as my true and lawful attorney.

In principal's name, and for principal's use and benefit, said attorney is authorized hereby;

(1) To demand, sue for, collect, and receive all money, debts, accounts, legacies, bequests, interest, dividends, annuities, and demands as are now or shall hereafter become due, payable, or belonging to principal, and take all lawful means, for the recovery thereof and to compromise the same and give discharges for the same;
(2) To buy and sell land, make contracts of every kind relative to land, any interest therein or the possession thereof, and to take possession and exercise control over the use thereof;
(3) To buy, sell, mortgage, hypothecate, assign, transfer, and in any manner deal with goods, wares and merchandise, choses in action, certificates or shares of capital stock, and other property in possession or in action, and to make, do, and transact all and every kind of business of whatever nature;
(4) To execute, acknowledge, and deliver contracts of sale, escrow instructions, deeds, leases including leases for minerals and hydrocarbon substances and assignments of leases, covenants, agreements and assignments of agreements, mortgages and assignments of mortgages, conveyances in trust, to secure indebtedness or other obligations, and assign the beneficial interest thereunder, subordinations of liens or encumbrances, bills of lading, receipts, evidences of debt, releases, bonds, notes, bills, requests to reconvey deeds of trust, partial or full judgments, satisfactions of mortgages, and other debts, and other written instruments of whatever kind and nature, all upon such terms and conditions as said attorney shall approve.

GIVING AND GRANTING to said attorney full power and authority to do all and every act and thing whatsoever requisite and necessary to be done relative to any of the foregoing as fully to all intents and purposes as principal might or could do if personally present.

All that said attorney shall lawfully do or cause to be done under the authority of this power of attorney is expressly approved.

Dated: _____   /s/_____

State of _____ ⎫ SS.
    County of _____ ⎭
On _____ , before me, the undersigned, a Notary Public in and for said
State, personally appeared _____

known to me to be the person _____ whose name _____ subscribed
to the within instrument and acknowledged that _____ executed the same.

Witness my hand and official seal.   (Seal) _____
                                        Notary Public in and for said State.

---

sonably required (as is customary or can be inferred from a manager's position) to operate the business. This includes forming contracts to hire employees, to buy merchandise and equipment, and to advertise the products sold in the store. ◄

Note, however, that an agent's implied authority cannot contradict his or her express authority. Thus, if a principal has limited an agent's express authority, then the fact that the agent customarily would have such authority is irrelevant. ▶ **Example 17.14** Juanita Alvarez is the owner of six Baja Tacos restaurants. Alvarez (the principal) strictly forbids the managers (agents) of her taco shops from entering into contracts to hire additional workers. Therefore, the fact that

INSIGHT INTO ETHICS
The Ethical and Legal Implications of Breaching Company Policy on the Use of Electronic Data

Suppose that an employee-agent who is authorized to access company trade secrets contained in computer files takes those secrets to a competitor for whom the employee is about to begin working. Clearly, the agent has violated the ethical—and legal—duty of loyalty to the principal. Does this breach of loyalty mean that the employee's act of accessing the trade secrets was unauthorized?

The question has significant implications for both parties. If the act was unauthorized, the employee will be subject to state and federal laws prohibiting unauthorized access to computer information and data, including the Computer Fraud and Abuse Act (CFAA, discussed in Chapter 7). If the act was authorized, these laws will not apply.

Does Exceeding Authorized Access to a Company's Database Violate the Law?

David Nosal once worked for Korn/Ferry and had access to the company's confidential database. When he left, he encouraged several former colleagues who still worked there to join him in starting a competing firm. He asked them to access Korn/Ferry's database and download source lists, names, and client contact information before they quit. The employees had authority to access the database, but Korn/Ferry's policy forbade disclosure of confidential information.

The government filed charges against Nosal and his colleagues for violating the CFAA, among other things.

A Court Rules That Violating an Employer's Use Restrictions Is Not a Crime

The U.S. Court of Appeals for the Ninth Circuit refused to find that the defendants had violated the CFAA. The court ruled that the phrase "exceed authorized access" in the CFAA refers to restrictions on access, not restrictions on use. The court reasoned that Congress's intent in enacting the CFAA was to prohibit people from hacking into computers without authorization.

The court also stated that the CFAA should not be used to criminally prosecute persons who use data in an unauthorized or unethical way. The court pointed out that "adopting the government's interpretation would turn vast numbers of teens and pre-teens into juvenile delinquents—and their parents and teachers into delinquency contributors." Furthermore, "the effect this broad construction of the CFAA has on workplace conduct pales by comparison with its effect on everyone else who uses a computer, smart-phone, iPad, Kindle, Nook, X-box, Blu-Ray player or any other Internet-enabled device."[a]

LEGAL CRITICAL THINKING
INSIGHT INTO THE LEGAL ENVIRONMENT

If an employee accesses Facebook at work even though personal use of a workplace computer is against the employer's stated policies, can the employee be criminally prosecuted? Why or why not?

a. *United States. v. Nosal,* 675 F.3d 854 (9th Cir. 2012).

---

managers customarily would have authority to hire employees is immaterial. ◄

Apparent Authority

Actual authority (express or implied) arises from what the principal makes clear *to the agent.* Apparent authority, in contrast, arises from what the principal causes a third party to believe. An agent has **apparent authority** when the principal, by either word or action, causes a *third party* reasonably to believe that the agent has authority to act, even though the agent has no express or implied authority.

A PATTERN OF CONDUCT Apparent authority usually comes into existence through a principal's pattern of conduct over time. ► **Example 17.15**   Bailey is a traveling salesperson with the authority to solicit orders for the goods of Carlon Industries (the principal). Because she does not carry any goods with her, she normally would not have the implied authority to collect payments from customers on Carlon's behalf.

Suppose that Bailey does accept payments from Jayco Enterprises, however, and submits them to Carlon's accounting department for processing. If Carlon does nothing to stop Bailey from continuing this practice, a pattern develops over time. Thus, the principal confers apparent authority on Bailey to accept payments from Jayco. ◀

At issue in the following *Spotlight Case* was whether the manager of a horse breeding operation had the authority to bind the farm's owner in a contract guaranteeing breeding rights.

SP TLIGHT on Apparent Authority

Case 17.2 Lundberg v. Church Farm, Inc.
Court of Appeals of Illinois, 151 Ill.App.3d 452, 502 N.E.2d 806 (1986).

BACKGROUND AND FACTS Gilbert Church owned a horse breeding farm managed by Herb Bagley. Advertisements for the breeding rights to one of Church Farm's stallions, Imperial Guard, directed all inquiries to "Herb Bagley, Manager." Vern and Gail Lundberg bred Thoroughbred horses. The Lundbergs contacted Bagley and executed a preprinted contract giving them breeding rights to Imperial Guard "at Imperial Guard's location," subject to approval of the mares by Church. Bagley handwrote a statement on the contract that guaranteed the Lundbergs "six live foals in the first two years." He then signed it "Gilbert G. Church by H. Bagley."

The Lundbergs bred four mares, which resulted in one live foal. Church then moved Imperial Guard from Illinois to Oklahoma. The Lundbergs sued Church for breaching the contract by moving the horse. Church claimed that Bagley was not authorized to sign contracts for Church or to change or add terms, but only to present preprinted contracts to potential buyers. Church testified that although Bagley was his farm manager and the contact person for breeding rights, Bagley had never before modified the preprinted forms or signed Church's name on these contracts. The jury found in favor of the Lundbergs and awarded $147,000 in damages. Church appealed.

 IN THE LANGUAGE OF THE COURT
Justice *UNVERZAGT* delivered the opinion of the court.

* * * *

* * * Defendant contends that plaintiffs have failed to establish that Bagley had apparent authority to negotiate and sign the Lundberg contract for Church Farm * * *.

*The party asserting an agency has the burden of proving its existence * * * but may do so by inference and circumstantial evidence. * * * Additionally, an agent may bind his principal by acts which the principal has not given him actual authority to perform, but which he appears authorized to perform.* * * * An agent's apparent authority is that authority which "the principal knowingly permits the agent to assume or which he holds his agent out as possessing. It is the authority that a reasonably prudent man, exercising diligence and discretion, in view of the principal's conduct, would naturally suppose the agent to possess." [Emphasis added.]

Plaintiffs produced evidence at trial that Gil Church approved the Imperial Guard advertisement listing Herb Bagley as Church Farm's manager, and directing all inquiries to him. Church also permitted Bagley to live on the farm and to handle its daily operations. Bagley was the only person available to visitors to the farm. Bagley answered Church Farm's phone calls, and there was a preprinted signature line for him on the breeding rights package.

The conclusion is inescapable that Gil Church affirmatively placed Bagley in a managerial position giving him complete control of Church Farm and its dealings with the public. We believe that this is just the sort of "holding out" of an agent by a principal that justifies a third person's reliance on the agent's authority.

We cannot accept defendant's contention that the Lundbergs were affirmatively obligated to seek out Church to ascertain the actual extent of Bagley's authority. Where an agent has apparent authority to act, the principal will be liable in spite of any undisclosed limitations the principal has placed on that authority.

CASE 17.2 CONTINUES ➡

DECISION AND REMEDY *The state appellate court affirmed the lower court's judgment in favor of the Lundbergs for $147,000. Because Church allowed circumstances to lead the Lundbergs to believe Bagley had the authority, Church was bound by Bagley's actions.*

THE LEGAL ENVIRONMENT DIMENSION *The court held that Church had allowed the Lundbergs to believe that Bagley was his agent. What steps could Church have taken to protect himself against a finding of apparent authority?*

THE ETHICAL DIMENSION *Does a principal have an ethical responsibility to inform an unaware third party that an apparent agent does not in fact have the authority to act on the principal's behalf?*

APPARENT AUTHORITY AND ESTOPPEL A court can apply the doctrine of agency by estoppel (see page 350) when a principal has given a third party reason to believe that an agent has authority to act. If the third party honestly relies on the principal's representations to his or her detriment, the principal may be *estopped* (prevented) from denying that the agent had authority.

▶ **Case in Point 17.16** Francis Azur was president and chief executive officer of ATM Corporation of America. Michelle Vanek, Azur's personal assistant at ATM, reviewed his credit-card statements, among other duties. For seven years, Vanek took unauthorized cash advances from Azur's credit-card account with Chase Bank. The charges appeared on at least sixty-five monthly statements. When Azur discovered Vanek's fraud, he fired her and closed the account. He filed a suit against Chase, arguing that the bank should not have allowed Vanek to take cash advances. The court concluded that Azur (the principal) had given the bank reason to believe that Vanek (the agent) had authority. Therefore, Azur was estopped (prevented) from denying Vanek's authority.[11] ◀

Emergency Powers

When an unforeseen emergency demands action by the agent to protect or preserve the property and rights of the principal, but the agent is unable to communicate with the principal, the agent has emergency power.

▶ **Example 17.17** Rob Fulsom is an engineer for Pacific Drilling Company. While Fulsom is acting within the scope of his employment, he is severely injured in an accident at an oil rig many miles from home.

Acosta, the rig supervisor, directs Thompson, a physician, to give medical aid to Fulsom and to charge Pacific for the medical services. Acosta, an agent, has no express or implied authority to bind the princi-

pal, Pacific Drilling, for Thompson's medical services. Because of the emergency situation, however, the law recognizes Acosta as having authority to act appropriately under the circumstances. ◀

Ratification

Ratification occurs when the principal affirms, or accepts responsibility for, an agent's *unauthorized* act. When ratification occurs, the principal is bound to the agent's act, and the act is treated as if it had been authorized by the principal *from the outset*. Ratification can be either express or implied.

If the principal does not ratify the contract, the principal is not bound, and the third party's agreement with the agent is viewed as merely an unaccepted offer. Because the third party's agreement is an unaccepted offer, the third party can revoke it at any time, without liability, before the principal ratifies the contract. The agent, however, may be liable to the third party for misrepresenting her or his authority.

The requirements for ratification can be summarized as follows:

1. The agent must have acted on behalf of an identified principal who subsequently ratifies the action.
2. The principal must know all of the material facts involved in the transaction. If a principal ratifies a contract without knowing all of the facts, the principal can rescind (cancel) the contract.[12]
3. The principal must affirm the agent's act in its entirety.
4. The principal must have the legal capacity to authorize the transaction at the time the agent engages in the act and at the time the principal ratifies. The third party must also have the legal capacity to engage in the transaction.

---

11. *Azur v. Chase Bank, USA, N.A.*, 601 F.3d 212 (3d Cir. 2010).

12. If the third party has changed position in reliance on the apparent contract, however, the principal can rescind but must reimburse the third party for any costs.

5. The principal's affirmation (ratification) must occur before the third party withdraws from the transaction.

6. The principal must observe the same formalities when ratifying the act as would have been required to authorize it initially.

Concept Summary 17.2 below summarizes the rules concerning an agent's authority to bind the principal and a third party.

SECTION 5
LIABILITY FOR CONTRACTS

Liability for contracts formed by an agent depends on how the principal is classified and on whether the actions of the agent were authorized or unauthorized. Principals are classified as disclosed, partially disclosed, or undisclosed.[13]

1. A **disclosed principal** is a principal whose identity is known by the third party at the time the contract is made by the agent.

2. A **partially disclosed principal** is a principal whose identity is not known by the third party. Nevertheless, the third party knows that the agent is or *may* be acting for a principal at the time the contract is made. ▶ **Example 17.18** Eileen has

---
13. *Restatement (Third) of Agency,* Section 1.04(2).

contracted with a real estate agent to sell certain property. She wishes to keep her identity a secret, but the agent makes it clear to potential buyers of the property that the agent is acting in an agency capacity. In this situation, Eileen is a partially disclosed principal. ◀

3. An **undisclosed principal** is a principal whose identity is totally unknown by the third party. In addition, the third party has no knowledge that the agent is acting in an agency capacity at the time the contract is made.

Authorized Acts

If an agent acts within the scope of her or his authority, normally the principal is obligated to perform the contract regardless of whether the principal was disclosed, partially disclosed, or undisclosed.

Whether the *agent may also be held liable* under the contract, however, depends on the disclosed, partially disclosed, or undisclosed status of the principal.

DISCLOSED OR PARTIALLY DISCLOSED PRINCIPAL A disclosed or partially disclosed principal is liable to a third party for a contract made by the agent. If the principal is disclosed, the agent has no contractual liability for the nonperformance of the principal or the third party. If the principal is partially disclosed, in most states the agent is also treated as a party to the

CONCEPT SUMMARY 17.2
Authority of an Agent to Bind the Principal and a Third Party

AUTHORITY OF AGENT	DEFINITION	EFFECT ON PRINCIPAL AND THIRD PARTY
Express Authority	Authority expressly given by the principal to the agent.	Principal and third party are bound in contract.
Implied Authority	Authority implied (1) by custom, (2) from the position in which the principal has placed the agent, or (3) because such authority is necessary if the agent is to carry out expressly authorized duties and responsibilities.	Principal and third party are bound in contract.
Apparent Authority	Authority created when the conduct of the principal leads a third party to believe that the principal's agent has authority.	Principal and third party are bound in contract.
Unauthorized Acts	Acts committed by an agent that are outside the scope of his or her express, implied, or apparent authority.	Principal and third party are not bound in contract—*unless* the principal ratifies prior to the third party's withdrawal.

contract, and the third party can hold the agent liable for contractual nonperformance.[14]

▶ **Case in Point 17.19** Walgreens leased commercial property at a mall owned by Kedzie Plaza Associates. Kedzie used Taxman Corporation, a property management company. Taxman signed the lease with Walgreens on behalf of the principal, Kedzie. The lease required the landlord to keep the sidewalks free of snow and ice. Therefore, Taxman, on behalf of Kedzie, contracted with another company to remove ice and snow from the sidewalks surrounding the Walgreens store.

When a Walgreens employee slipped on ice outside the store and was injured, she sued Taxman, among others, for negligence. Because the identity of the principal (Kedzie) was fully disclosed in the snow-removal contract, however, the court ruled that the agent, Taxman, could not be held liable. Taxman did not assume a contractual obligation to remove the snow but merely retained a contractor to do so on behalf of the owner.[15] ◀

UNDISCLOSED PRINCIPAL When neither the fact of an agency relationship nor the identity of the principal is disclosed, the undisclosed principal is bound to perform just as if the principal had been fully disclosed at the time the contract was made.

When a principal's identity is undisclosed and the agent is forced to pay the third party, the agent is entitled to be *indemnified* (compensated) by the principal. The principal had a duty to perform, even though his or her identity was undisclosed,[16] and failure to do so will make the principal ultimately liable. Once the undisclosed principal's identity is revealed, the third party generally can elect to hold either the principal or the agent liable on the contract.

Conversely, the undisclosed principal can require the third party to fulfill the contract, *unless* one of the following is true:

1. The undisclosed principal was expressly excluded as a party in the written contract.
2. The contract is a negotiable instrument signed by the agent with no indication of signing in a representative capacity.[17]

3. The performance of the agent is personal to the contract, thus allowing the third party to refuse the principal's performance.

▶ **Case in Point 17.20** Bobby Williams bought a car at Sherman Henderson's auto repair business in Monroe, Louisiana, for $3,000. Henderson negotiated and made the sale for the car's owner, Joe Pike, whose name was not disclosed. Williams drove the car to Memphis, Tennessee, where his daughter was a student. Three days after the sale, the car erupted in flames. Williams extinguished the blaze and contacted Henderson. The vehicle was soon stolen, which prevented Williams from returning it to Henderson. Williams later filed suits against both Pike and Henderson. The court noted that the state had issued Pike a permit to sell the car. The car was displayed for sale at Henderson's business, and Henderson actually sold it. This made Pike the principal and Henderson his agent. The fact that their agency relationship was not made clear to Williams made Pike an undisclosed principal. Williams could thus hold both Pike and Henderson liable for the condition of the car.[18] ◀

Unauthorized Acts

If an agent has no authority but nevertheless contracts with a third party, the *principal* cannot be held liable on the contract. It does not matter whether the principal was disclosed, partially disclosed, or undisclosed. The *agent* is liable, however.

▶ **Example 17.21** Chu signs a contract for the purchase of a truck, purportedly acting as an agent under authority granted by Navarro. In fact, Navarro has not given Chu any such authority. Navarro refuses to pay for the truck, claiming that Chu had no authority to purchase it. The seller of the truck is entitled to hold Chu liable for payment. ◀

IMPLIED WARRANTY If the principal is disclosed or partially disclosed, and the agent contracts with a third party without authorization, the agent is liable to the third party who relied on the agency status. The agent's liability here is based on his or her breach of the *implied warranty of authority,* not on the breach of the contract itself.[19] An agent impliedly warrants that he or she has the authority to enter a contract on behalf of the principal.

---

14. *Restatement (Third) of Agency,* Section 6.02.
15. *McBride v. Taxman Corp.,* 327 Ill.App.3d 992, 765 N.E.2d 51 (2002).
16. If the agent is a gratuitous agent, and the principal accepts the benefits of the agent's contract with a third party, then the principal will be liable to the agent on the theory of *quasi contract* (see Chapter 9).
17. Under the Uniform Commercial Code (UCC), only the agent is liable if the instrument neither names the principal nor shows that the agent signed in a representative capacity [UCC 3–402(b)(2)].

18. *Williams v. Pike,* 58 So.3d 525 (La.App. 2011).
19. The agent is not liable on the contract because the agent was never intended personally to be a party to the contract.

▶ **Example 17.22** Pinnell, a reclusive artist, hires Auber to solicit offers for particular paintings from various galleries, but does not authorize her to enter into sales agreements. Olaf, a gallery owner, offers to buy two of Pinnell's paintings for an upcoming show. If Auber draws up a sales contract with Olaf, she impliedly warrants that she has the authority to enter into sales contracts on behalf of Pinnell. If Pinnell does not agree to ratify Auber's sales contract, Olaf cannot hold Pinnell liable, but he can hold Auber liable for breaching the implied warranty of authority. ◀

THIRD PARTY'S KNOWLEDGE Note that if the third party knows at the time the contract is made that the agent does not have authority, then the agent is not liable. Similarly, if the agent expressed to the third party *uncertainty* as to the extent of her or his authority, the agent is not personally liable.

Actions by E-Agents

Although in the past standard agency principles applied only to *human* agents, today these same agency principles also apply to e-agents. An electronic agent, or **e-agent,** is a semiautonomous computer program that is capable of executing specific tasks. For instance, software that can search through many databases and retrieve only relevant information for the user is an e-agent.

The Uniform Electronic Transactions Act (UETA), which was discussed in Chapter 10, sets forth provisions relating to the principal's liability for the actions of e-agents. According to Section 15 of the UETA, e-agents can enter into binding agreements on behalf of their principals—at least, in those states that have adopted the act. Thus, if consumers place an order over the Internet, and the company (principal) takes the order via an e-agent, the company cannot later claim that it did not receive the order.

The UETA also stipulates that if an e-agent does not provide an opportunity to prevent errors at the time of the transaction, the other party to the transaction can avoid the transaction. Therefore, if an e-agent fails to provide an on-screen confirmation of a purchase or sale, the other party can avoid the effect of any errors. ▶ **Example 17.23** Bigelow wants to purchase three copies of three different books (a total of nine items). The e-agent mistakenly records an order for thirty-three of a single book and does not provide an on-screen verification of the order. If thirty-three books are then sent to Bigelow, he can avoid the contract to purchase them. ◀

LIABILITY FOR TORTS AND CRIMES

Obviously, any person, including an agent, is liable for his or her own torts and crimes. Whether a principal can also be held liable for an agent's torts and crimes depends on several factors, which we examine here. In some situations, a principal may be held liable not only for the torts of an agent but also for torts committed by an independent contractor.

Principal's Tortious Conduct

A principal who acts through an agent may be liable for harm resulting from the principal's own negligence or recklessness. Thus, a principal may be liable if he or she gives improper instructions, authorizes the use of improper materials or tools, or establishes improper rules that result in the agent's committing a tort.

▶ **Example 17.24** Parker knows that Audrey's driver's license has been suspended but nevertheless tells her to use the company truck to deliver some equipment to a customer. If someone is injured as a result, Parker will be liable for his own negligence in instructing Audrey to drive without a valid license. ◀

Principal's Authorization of Agent's Tortious Conduct

Similarly, a principal who authorizes an agent to commit a tort may be liable to persons or property injured thereby, because the act is considered to be the principal's. ▶ **Example 17.25** Pedro directs his agent, Andy, to cut the corn on specific acreage, which neither of them has the right to do. The harvest is therefore a trespass (a tort), and Pedro is liable to the owner of the corn. ◀

Note that an agent acting at the principal's direction can be liable as a *tortfeasor* (one who commits a wrong, or tort), along with the principal, for committing the tortious act even if the agent was unaware that the act was wrong. Assume in *Example 17.25* that Andy, the agent, did not know that Pedro lacked the right to harvest the corn. Andy can still be held liable to the owner of the field for damages, along with Pedro, the principal.

Liability for Agent's Misrepresentation

A principal is exposed to tort liability whenever a third person sustains a loss due to the agent's misrepresentation. The principal's liability depends on whether the agent was actually or apparently authorized to make representations and whether the representations were made within the scope of the agency. The principal is always directly responsible for an agent's misrepresentation made within the scope of the agent's authority.

▶ **Example 17.26** Ainsley is a demonstrator for Pavlovich's products. Pavlovich sends Ainsley to a home show to demonstrate the products and to answer questions from consumers. Pavlovich has given Ainsley authority to make statements about the products. If Ainsley makes only true representations, all is fine. But if he makes false claims, Pavlovich will be liable for any injuries or damages sustained by third parties in reliance on Ainsley's false representations. ◀

APPARENT IMPLIED AUTHORITY When a principal has placed an agent in a position of apparent authority—making it possible for the agent to defraud a third party—the principal may also be liable for the agent's fraudulent acts. For instance, partners in a partnership generally have the apparent implied authority to act as agents of the firm, as will be discussed in Chapter 18. Thus, if one of the partners commits a tort or a crime, the partnership itself—and often the other partners personally—can be held liable for the loss.

▶ **Case in Point 17.27** Selheimer & Company, a securities broker-dealer that operated as a partnership, provided various financial services. The managing partner, Perry Selheimer, embezzled funds that clients had turned over to the firm for investment. After Selheimer was convicted, other partners in the firm claimed that they were not liable for losses resulting from his illegal activities. The court, however, held that Selheimer had apparent implied authority to act in the ordinary course of the partnership's business. Thus, the firm, as principal, was liable, and under the law of partnerships the personal assets of the individual partners could be used to cover the firm's liability.[20] ◀

INNOCENT MISREPRESENTATION Tort liability based on fraud requires proof that a material misstatement was made knowingly and with the intent to deceive. An agent's *innocent* misstatements in a contract or warranty transaction can also provide grounds for the third party's rescission of the contract and the award of damages. Justice dictates that when a principal knows that an agent is not accurately advised of facts but does not correct either the agent's or the third party's impressions, the principal is responsible. The point is that the principal is always directly responsible for an agent's misrepresentation made within the scope of authority.

Liability for Agent's Negligence

Under the doctrine of ***respondeat superior*** (a Latin term meaning "let the master respond),"[21] a principal may also be liable for harm that his or her agent causes to a third party. This doctrine imposes **vicarious liability,** or indirect liability, on an employer regardless of fault. Under this doctrine, the employer is liable for torts committed by an employee acting within the course or scope of employment. (Of course, the employee is also liable for any torts that she or he commits.)

Third parties injured through the negligence of an employee can sue either that employee or the employer, if the employee's negligent conduct occurred while the employee was acting within the scope of employment.

▶ **Case in Point 17.28** Aegis Communications hired Southwest Desert Images (SDI) to provide landscaping services for its property. An herbicide sprayed by SDI employee David Hoggatt entered the Aegis building through the air-conditioning system and caused Catherine Warner, an Aegis employee, to suffer a heart attack. Warner sued SDI and Hoggatt for negligence, but the lower court dismissed the suit against Hoggatt. On appeal, the court found that Hoggatt was also liable. An agent is not excused from responsibility for tortious conduct just because he is working for a principal. Both the agent and the principal are liable.[22] ◀

THE DOCTRINE OF *RESPONDEAT SUPERIOR* At early common law, a servant (employee) was viewed as the master's (employer's) property. The master was deemed to have absolute control over the servant's acts and was held strictly liable for them, no mat-

---

20. *In re Selheimer & Co.,* 319 Bankr. 395 (E.D.Pa. 2005).

21. Pronounced ree-*spahn*-dee-uht soo-*peer*-ee-your. The doctrine of *respondeat superior* applies not only to employer-employee relationships but also to other principal-agent relationships in which the principal has the right of control over the agent.

22. *Warner v. Southwest Desert Images, LLC,* 218 Ariz. 121, 180 P.3d 986 (2008).

ter how carefully the master supervised the servant. Although employers today are not masters of their employees, control is still a central concept to liability.

Underlying Rationale. The rationale for the doctrine of *respondeat superior* is based on the social duty that requires every person to manage his or her affairs so as not to injure another. This duty applies even when a person acts through an agent (controls the conduct of another).

Public Policy. Generally, public policy requires that an injured person be afforded effective relief, and a business enterprise is usually better able to provide that relief than is an individual employee. Employers normally carry liability insurance to cover any damages awarded as a result of such lawsuits. They are also able to spread the cost of risk over the entire business enterprise.

The courts have applied the doctrine of *respondeat superior* for nearly two centuries. It continues to have practical implications in all situations involving principal-agent (employer-employee) relationships. Today, the small-town grocer with one clerk and the multinational corporation with thousands of employees are equally subject to the doctrine.

THE SCOPE OF EMPLOYMENT The key to determining whether a principal may be liable for the torts of an agent under the doctrine of *respondeat superior* is whether the torts are committed within the scope of the agency or employment. Courts may consider the following factors in determining whether a particular act occurred within the course and scope of employment:

1. Whether the employee's act was authorized by the employer.
2. The time, place, and purpose of the act.
3. Whether the act was one commonly performed by employees on behalf of their employers.
4. The extent to which the employer's interest was advanced by the act.
5. The extent to which the private interests of the employee were involved.
6. Whether the employer furnished the means or instrumentality (for example, a truck or a machine) by which an injury was inflicted.
7. Whether the employer had reason to know that the employee would perform the act in question and whether the employee had done it before.
8. Whether the act involved the commission of a serious crime.

Whether a salesperson's actions in connection with certain real estate transactions fell within the salesperson's scope of employment was at issue in the following case.

CASE ANALYSIS

Case 17.3   Auer v. Paliath

Court of Appeals of Ohio, Second District, 986 N.E.2d 1052 (2013).

IN THE LANGUAGE OF THE COURT
FROELICH, J. [Judge]
* * * *

Torri Auer [a California resident] brought suit [in an Ohio state court] against real estate salesperson Jamie Paliath, real estate broker Keller Williams Home Town Realty, and others based on alleged fraud by Paliath in the sale of several rental properties [in Dayton, Ohio] to Auer * * * . After a jury trial * * * , Paliath was found liable to Torri Auer in the amount of $135,200 for fraud in the inducement of Auer's purchases of the properties. * * * The jury also awarded $135,200 to Auer from Home Town Realty, based on the broker's vicarious liability for Paliath's actions in connection with Auer's purchases of the properties.

Home Town Realty appeals from the trial court's judgment.
* * * *

* * * Under [Ohio Revised Code (R.C.) Section 4735.01] the term "real estate broker" includes "any person, partnership, association, limited liability company, limited liability partnership, or corporation * * * who for another * * * and who for a fee,

commission, or other valuable consideration" engages in various activities regarding real estate, including selling, purchasing, leasing, renting, listing, auctioning, buying, managing, and advertising real estate. A real estate salesperson generally means "any person associated with a licensed real estate broker to do or to deal with any acts or transactions set out or comprehended by the definition of a real estate broker, for compensation or otherwise."

Under R.C. Section 4735.21, no real estate salesperson may collect

CASE 17.3 CONTINUES ▶

any money in connection with any real estate transaction, except as in the name of and with the consent of the licensed real estate broker under whom the salesperson is licensed.

* * * *

* * * A real estate broker will be held vicariously liable for intentional torts committed by salesmen acting within the scope of their authority. Vicarious liability is appropriate because a real estate salesman has no independent status or right to conclude a sale and can only function through the broker with whom he is associated. A salesman is required to be under the supervision of a licensed broker in all of his activities related to real estate transactions. [Emphasis added.]

* * * *

* * * When a real estate salesperson acts in the name of a real estate broker in connection with the type of real estate transaction for which he or she was hired and the broker collects a commission for the transaction, the salesperson's actions in connection with that real estate transaction are within the scope of the salesperson's employment, as a matter of law.

In this case, Paliath contracted with Home Town Realty as a real estate salesperson to assist clients with the purchase and sale of real estate. Paliath advised and assisted Auer in the purchase of the * * * properties, and her fraudulent conduct involved misrepresentations regarding those properties.

Reviewing the properties separately, the evidence at trial established that Home Town Realty was listed as the real estate broker on the purchase contract, the agency disclosure statement, and the settlement statement for the Belton Street sale. Home Town Realty received a commission check of $180 from the title company that conducted the closing. Based on this evidence, it was established, as a mat-

ter of law, that Paliath acted within the scope of her employment as a real estate salesperson with Home Town Realty in relation to Auer's purchase of the Belton property.

Similarly, Paliath's actions with respect to the 1111–1115 Richmond Avenue properties were taken as a real estate salesperson assisting Auer with the purchase of the properties. Home Town was listed as a broker on the purchase contract, the agency disclosure statement, and the settlement statement for 1111 Richmond Avenue, and it received a commission of $2,400 following the closing. * * * The evidence thus demonstrated, as a matter of law, that Paliath was acting in the scope of her employment regarding the sale of 1111 Richmond Avenue.

* * * *

* * * The trial court's judgment will be affirmed.

LEGAL REASONING QUESTIONS

1. What conduct was at the center of the dispute in this case?
2. Who did the plaintiff allege was liable for this conduct? Which of these parties was the principal, and which was the agent?
3. What factors did the court apply to determine liability in this case?
4. How did the court rule on the question of vicarious liability?

A "DETOUR" AND A "FROLIC" A useful insight into the concept of "scope of employment" may be gained from Judge Baron Parke's classic distinction between a "detour" and a "frolic" in the case of *Joel v. Morison*.[23] In this case, the English court held that if a servant merely took a detour from his master's business, the master will be responsible. If, however, the servant was on a "frolic of his own" and not in any way "on his master's business," the master will not be liable.

▶ **Example 17.29** Mandel, a traveling salesperson, while driving his employer's vehicle to call on a customer, decides to stop at the post office—which is one block off his route—to mail a personal letter.

As Mandel approaches the post office, he negligently runs into a parked vehicle owned by Chan. In this situation, because Mandel's detour from the employer's business is not substantial, he is still acting within the scope of employment, and the employer is liable.

The result would be different, though, if Mandel had decided to pick up a few friends for drinks in another city and in the process had negligently run his vehicle into Chan's. In that circumstance, the departure from the employer's business would be substantial, and the employer normally would not be liable to Chan for damages. Mandel would be considered to have been on a "frolic" of his own. ◀

EMPLOYEE TRAVEL TIME An employee going to and from work or to and from meals usually is considered

---

23. 6 Car. & P. 501, 172 Eng.Rep. 1338 (1834).

to be outside the scope of employment. In contrast, all travel time of traveling salespersons or others whose jobs require travel is normally considered to be within the scope of employment for the duration of the business trip, including the return trip home.

NOTICE OF DANGEROUS CONDITIONS The employer is charged with knowledge of any dangerous conditions discovered by an employee and pertinent to the employment situation.

▶ **Example 17.30** Brad, a maintenance employee in an apartment building, notices a lead pipe protruding from the ground in the building's courtyard. Brad neglects either to fix the pipe or to inform his employer of the danger. John trips on the pipe and is injured. The employer is charged with knowledge of the dangerous condition regardless of whether Brad actually informed the employer. That knowledge is imputed to the employer by virtue of the employment relationship. ◀

Liability for Agent's Intentional Torts

Most intentional torts that individuals commit have no relation to their employment, and their employers will not be held liable. Nevertheless, under the doctrine of *respondeat superior,* the employer can be liable for intentional torts that an employee commits within the course and scope of employment. For instance, an employer is liable when an employee (such as a "bouncer" at a nightclub or a security guard at a department store) commits the tort of assault and battery or false imprisonment while acting within the scope of employment.

In addition, an employer who knows or should know that an employee has a propensity for committing tortious acts is liable for the employee's acts even if they would not ordinarily be considered within the scope of employment. ▶ **Example 17.31** Chaz, the owner of the Comedy Club, hires Alec as a bouncer for the club even though he knows that Alec has a history of arrests for criminal assault and battery. In this situation, Chaz may be liable if Alec viciously attacks a customer in the parking lot after hours. ◀

An employer is also liable for permitting an employee to engage in reckless actions that can injure others. ▶ **Example 17.32** The owner of Bates Trucking observes an employee smoking while filling containerized trucks with highly flammable liquids. Failure to stop the employee will cause the employer to be liable for any injuries that result if a truck explodes. ◀

Liability for Independent Contractor's Torts

Generally, an employer is not liable for physical harm caused to a third person by the negligent act of an independent contractor in the performance of the contract. This is because the employer does not have *the right to control* the details of an independent contractor's performance. Courts make an exception to this rule when the contract involves unusually hazardous activities, such as blasting operations, the transportation of highly volatile chemicals, or the use of poisonous gases. In these situations, an employer cannot be shielded from liability merely by using an independent contractor.

Liability for Agent's Crimes

An agent is liable for his or her own crimes. A principal or employer normally is *not* liable for an agent's crime even if the crime was committed within the scope of authority or employment. An exception to this rule is made when the principal or employer participated in the crime by conspiracy or other action.

Also, in some jurisdictions, a principal may be liable under specific statutes if an agent, in the course and scope of employment, violates certain regulations. For instance, a principal might be liable for an agent's violation of sanitation rules or regulations governing prices, weights, and the sale of liquor.

SECTION 7
TERMINATION OF AN AGENCY

Agency law is similar to contract law in that both an agency and a contract may be terminated *by an act of the parties or by operation of law.* Once the relationship between the principal and the agent has ended, the agent no longer has the right (*actual* authority) to bind the principal. For an agent's *apparent* authority to be terminated, though, third persons may also need to be notified that the agency has been terminated.

Termination by Act of the Parties

An agency relationship may be terminated by act of the parties in any of the following ways:

1. *Lapse of time.* When an agency agreement specifies the time period during which the agency

relationship will exist, the agency ends when that time period expires. If no definite time is stated, then the agency continues for a reasonable time and can be terminated at will by either party. What constitutes a reasonable time depends on the circumstances and the nature of the agency relationship.

2. *Purpose achieved.* If an agent is employed to accomplish a particular objective, such as the purchase of breeding stock for a cattle rancher, the agency automatically ends after the cattle have been purchased. If more than one agent is employed to accomplish the same purpose, such as the sale of real estate, the first agent to complete the sale automatically terminates the agency relationship for all the others.

3. *Occurrence of a specific event.* When an agency relationship is to terminate on the happening of a certain event, the agency automatically ends when the event occurs. ▶ **Example 17.33** If Posner appoints Rubik to handle her business affairs while she is away, the agency automatically terminates when Posner returns. ◀

4. *Mutual agreement.* The parties to an agency can cancel (rescind) their contract by mutually agreeing to terminate the agency relationship, even if it was for a specific (longer) duration.

5. *Termination by one party.* As a general rule, either party can terminate the agency relationship. The act of termination is called *revocation* if done by the principal and *renunciation* if done by the agent. Although both parties may have the *power* to terminate the agency, they may not possess the right and therefore may be liable for breach of contract or *wrongful termination.*

WRONGFUL TERMINATION Wrongful termination can subject the canceling party to a lawsuit for breach of contract. ▶ **Example 17.34** Rawlins has a one-year employment contract with Munro to act as agent in return for $65,000. Although Munro has the *power* to discharge Rawlins before the contract period expires, if he does so, he can be sued for breaching the contract because he had no *right* to terminate the agency. ◀

Even in an agency at will—in which either party may terminate at any time—the principal who wishes to terminate must give the agent *reasonable* notice. The notice must be at least sufficient to allow the agent to recoup his or her expenses and, in some situations, to make a normal profit.

AGENCY COUPLED WITH AN INTEREST A special rule applies to an *agency coupled with an interest.* In an **agency coupled with an interest,** the agent has some legal right to (an interest in) the property that is the subject of the agency. For instance, a principal might provide inventory for the agent to sell and then to keep the profits. Because the agent has an additional interest in the property beyond the normal commission for selling it, the agent's position cannot be terminated until the agent's interest ends.

This type of agency is not an agency in the usual sense because it is created for the agent's benefit instead of for the principal's benefit. ▶ **Example 17.35** Julie borrows $5,000 from Rob, giving Rob some of her jewelry and signing a letter authorizing him to sell the jewelry as her agent if she fails to repay the loan. After Julie receives the $5,000 from Rob, she attempts to revoke his authority to sell the jewelry as her agent. Julie will not succeed in this attempt because a principal cannot revoke an agency created for the agent's benefit. ◀

An agency coupled with an interest should not be confused with a situation in which the agent merely derives proceeds or profits from the sale of the subject matter. Many agents are paid a commission for their services, but the agency relationship involved does not constitute an agency coupled with an interest. For instance, a real estate agent who merely receives a commission from the sale of real property does not have a beneficial interest in the property itself.

NOTICE OF TERMINATION When the parties terminate an agency, it is the principal's duty to inform any third parties who know of the existence of the agency that it has been terminated. No particular form is required for notice of termination of the principal-agent relationship to be effective. The principal can personally notify the agent, or the agent can learn of the termination through some other means.

Although an agent's actual authority ends when the agency is terminated, an agent's *apparent authority* continues until the third party receives notice (from any source) that such authority has been terminated. ▶ **Example 17.36** Manning bids on a shipment of steel, and Stone is hired as an agent to arrange transportation for the shipment. When Stone learns that Manning has lost the bid, Stone's authority to make the transportation arrangement terminates. ◀

If the principal knows that a third party has dealt with the agent, the principal is expected to notify that person *directly*. For third parties who have heard about the agency but have not yet dealt with the agent, *constructive notice* is sufficient.[24] If the agent's authority is written, however, normally it must be revoked in writing (unless the written document contained an expiration date).

Termination by Operation of Law

Certain events terminate agency authority automatically because their occurrence makes it impossible for the agent to perform or improbable that the principal would continue to want performance. We look at these events next. Note that when an agency terminates by operation of law, there is no duty to notify third persons—unless the agent's authority is coupled with an interest.

DEATH OR INSANITY The general rule is that the death or insanity of either the principal or the agent automatically and immediately terminates an ordinary agency relationship. Knowledge of the death or insanity is not required.

▶ **Example 17.37** Grey sends Bosley to Japan to purchase a rare book. Before Bosley makes the purchase, Grey dies. Bosley's agent status is terminated at the moment of Grey's death, even though Bosley does not know that Grey has died. ◀ (Some states, however, have enacted statutes that change the common law rule to require an agent's knowledge of the principal's death before termination.)

---

24. With *constructive notice* of a fact, knowledge of the fact is imputed by law to a person if he or she could have discovered the fact by proper diligence. Constructive notice is often accomplished by publication in a newspaper.

IMPOSSIBILITY When the specific subject matter of an agency is destroyed or lost, the agency terminates. ▶ **Example 17.38** Tsang employs Arnez to sell Tsang's house. Prior to any sale, the house is destroyed by fire. Arnez's agency and authority to sell the house terminate. ◀ Similarly, when it is impossible for the agent to perform the agency lawfully because of a change in the law, the agency terminates.

CHANGED CIRCUMSTANCES Sometimes, an event occurs that has such an unusual effect on the subject matter of the agency that the agent can reasonably infer that the principal will not want the agency to continue. In such situations, the agency terminates.

▶ **Example 17.39** Baird hires Joslen to sell a tract of land for $40,000. Subsequently, Joslen learns that there is oil under the land and that the land is therefore worth $1 million. The agency and Joslen's authority to sell the land for $40,000 are terminated. ◀

BANKRUPTCY If either the principal or the agent petitions for bankruptcy, the agency is *usually* terminated. In certain circumstances, such as when the agent's financial status is irrelevant to the purpose of the agency, the agency relationship may continue. *Insolvency* (the inability to pay debts when they come due or when liabilities exceed assets), as distinguished from bankruptcy, does not necessarily terminate the relationship.

WAR When the principal's country and the agent's country are at war with each other, the agency is terminated. In this situation, the agency is automatically suspended or terminated because there is no way to enforce the legal rights and obligations of the parties.

See *Concept Summary 17.3* on the following page for a synopsis of the rules governing the termination of an agency.

CONCEPT SUMMARY 17.3
Termination of an Agency

METHOD OF TERMINATION	RULES	TERMINATION OF AGENT'S AUTHORITY
Act of the Parties		
1. Lapse of time.	Automatic at end of the stated time.	
2. Purpose achieved.	Automatic on the completion of the purpose.	
3. Occurrence of a specific event.	Normally automatic on the happening of the event.	**Notice to Third Parties Required—** 1. Direct to those who have dealt with agency. 2. Constructive to all others.
4. Mutual agreement.	Mutual consent required.	
5. At the option of one party (revocation, if by principal, renunciation, if by agent).	Either party normally has a right to terminate the agency but may lack the power to do so, which can lead to liability for breach of contract.	
Operation of Law		
1. Death or insanity.	Automatic on the death or insanity of either the principal or the agent (except when the agency is coupled with an interest).	
2. Impossibility— destruction of the specific subject matter.	Applies any time the agency cannot be performed because of an event beyond the parties' control.	
3. Changed circumstances.	Events so unusual that it would be inequitable to allow the agency to continue to exist.	**No Notice Required—** Automatic on the happening of the event.
4. Bankruptcy.	Bankruptcy petition (not mere insolvency) usually terminates the agency.	
5. War between principal's country and agent's country.	Automatically suspends or terminates agency—no way to enforce legal rights.	

Reviewing: Agency Relationships in Business

Lynne Meyer, on her way to a business meeting and in a hurry, stopped at a Buy-Mart store for a new car charger for her smartphone. There was a long line at one of the checkout counters, but a cashier, Valerie Watts, opened another counter and began loading the cash drawer. Meyer told Watts that she was in a hurry and asked Watts to work faster. Instead, Watts slowed her pace. At this point, Meyer hit Watts.

It is not clear whether Meyer hit Watts intentionally or, in an attempt to retrieve the car charger, hit her inadvertently. In response, Watts grabbed Meyer by the hair and hit her repeatedly in the back of the head, while Meyer screamed for help. Management personnel separated the two women and questioned them about the incident. Watts was immediately fired for violating the store's no-fighting policy. Meyer subsequently sued Buy-Mart, alleging that the store was liable for the tort (assault and battery) committed by its employee. Using the information presented in the chapter, answer the following questions.

1. Under what doctrine discussed in this chapter might Buy-Mart be held liable for the tort committed by Watts?
2. What is the key factor in determining whether Buy-Mart is liable under this doctrine?
3. How is Buy-Mart's potential liability affected by whether Watts's behavior constituted an intentional tort or a tort of negligence?
4. Suppose that when Watts applied for the job at Buy-Mart, she disclosed in her application that she had previously been convicted of felony assault and battery. Nevertheless, Buy-Mart hired Watts as a cashier. How might this fact affect Buy-Mart's liability for Watts's actions?

DEBATE THIS . . . *The doctrine of* respondeat superior *should be modified to make agents solely liable for their tortious (wrongful) acts committed within the scope of employment.*

Terms and Concepts

agency 346
agency coupled with an interest 366
agent 346
apparent authority 356
disclosed principal 359
e-agent 361
equal dignity rule 354

exclusive agency 353
express authority 354
fiduciary 346
implied authority 354
independent contractor 347
notary public 354
partially disclosed principal 359

power of attorney 354
principal 346
ratification 358
respondeat superior 362
undisclosed principal 359
vicarious liability 362

ExamPrep

Issue Spotters

1. Winona contracted with XtremeCast, a broadcast media firm, to cohost an Internet-streaming sports program. Winona and XtremeCast signed a new contract for each episode. In each contract, Winona agreed to work a certain number of days for a certain salary. During each broadcast, Winona was free to improvise her performance. She had no other obligation to work for XtremeCast. Was Winona an independent contractor? Explain. **(See page 347.)**

2. Vivian, owner of Wonder Goods Company, employs Xena as an administrative assistant. In Vivian's absence, and without authority, Xena represents herself as Vivian and signs a promissory note in Vivian's

name. In what circumstance is Vivian liable on the note? **(See pages 358–360.)**

• **Check your answers to the Issue Spotters against the answers provided in Appendix B at the end of this text.**

Before the Test

Go to **www.cengagebrain.com**, enter the ISBN 9781285770192, and click on "Find" to locate this textbook's Web site. Then, click on "Access Now" under "Study Tools," and select Chapter 17 at the top. There, you will find a Practice Quiz that you can take to assess your mastery of the concepts in this chapter, as well as Flashcards and a Glossary of important terms.

Business Scenarios

17–1. Unauthorized Acts. Janell Arden is a purchasing agent-employee for the A&B Coal Supply partnership. Arden has authority to purchase the coal needed by A&B to satisfy the needs of its customers. While Arden is leaving a coal

mine from which she has just purchased a large quantity of coal, her car breaks down. She walks into a small roadside grocery store for help. While there, she encounters Will Wilson, who owns 360 acres back in the mountains with all mineral rights. Wilson, in need of cash, offers to sell Arden the property for $1,500 per acre.

On inspection of the property, Arden forms the opinion that the subsurface contains valuable coal deposits. Arden contracts to purchase the property for A&B Coal Supply, signing the contract "A&B Coal Supply, Janell Arden, agent." The closing date is August 1. Arden takes the contract to the partnership. The managing partner is furious, as A&B is not in the property business. Later, just before closing, both Wilson and the partnership learn that the value of the land is at least $15,000 per acre. Discuss the rights of A&B and Wilson concerning the land contract. **(See pages 360 and 361.)**

17–2. Duty of Loyalty. Peter hires Alice as an agent to sell a piece of property he owns. The price is to be at least $30,000. Alice discovers that the fair market value of Peter's property is actually at least $45,000 and could be higher because a shopping mall is going to be built nearby. Alice forms a real estate partnership with her cousin Carl. Then she prepares for Peter's signature a contract for the sale of the property to Carl for $32,000. Peter signs the contract. Just before closing and passage of title, Peter learns about the shopping mall and the increased fair market value of his property. Peter refuses to deed the property to Carl.

Carl claims that Alice, as Peter's agent, solicited a price above that agreed on when the agency was created and that the contract is therefore binding and enforceable. Discuss fully whether Peter is bound to this contract. **(See page 352.)**

17–3. *Respondeat Superior.* ABC Tire Corp. hires Arnez as a traveling salesperson and assigns him a geographic area and time schedule in which to solicit orders and service customers. Arnez is given a company car to use in covering the territory. One day, Arnez decides to take his personal car to cover part of his territory. It is 11:00 A.M., and Arnez has just finished calling on all customers in the city of Tarrytown. His next appointment is at 2:00 P.M. in the city of Austex, twenty miles down the road. Arnez starts out for Austex, but halfway there he decides to visit a former college roommate who runs a farm ten miles off the main highway. Arnez is enjoying his visit with his former roommate when he realizes that it is 1:45 P.M. and that he will be late for the appointment in Austex. Driving at a high speed down the country road to reach the main highway, Arnez crashes his car into a tractor, severely injuring Thomas, the driver of the tractor. Thomas claims that he can hold ABC Tire Corp. liable for his injuries. Discuss fully ABC's liability in this situation. **(See page 362.)**

Business Case Problems

17–4. Spotlight on Agency—Independent Contractors. Frank

Frausto delivered newspapers under a renewable six-month contract called a "Delivery Agent Agreement." The agreement identified Frausto as an independent contractor. The company collected payment from customers and took complaints about delivery. Frausto was given the route for his paper delivery and was required to deliver the paper within a certain time period each day. Frausto delivered the papers using his own vehicle and had to provide proof of insurance to the company. The company provided health and disability insurance but did not withhold taxes from Frausto's weekly income. One morning, Frausto was delivering papers and collided with Santiago on his motorcycle. Santiago filed a negligence action against Frausto and the newspaper company. The newspaper company argued that it should not be liable because Frausto was an independent contractor. What was the result? Why? [*Santiago v. Phoenix Newspapers, Inc.*, 794 P.2d 138 (Ariz. 1990)] **(See page 347.)**

17–5. Disclosed Principal. To display desserts in restaurants, Mario Sclafani ordered refrigeration units from Felix Storch, Inc. Felix faxed a credit application to Sclafani. The application was faxed back with a signature that appeared to be Sclafani's. Felix delivered the units. When they were not paid for, Felix filed a suit against Sclafani to collect. Sclafani denied that he had seen the application or signed

it. He testified that he referred all credit questions to "the girl in the office." Who was the principal? Who was the agent? Who is liable on the contract? Explain. [*Felix Storch, Inc. v. Martinucci Desserts USA, Inc.*, 30 Misc.2d 1217, 924 N.Y.S.2d 308 (Suffolk Co. 2011)] **(See page 359.)**

17–6. BUSINESS CASE PROBLEM
WITH SAMPLE ANSWER: Liability for Contracts.

Thomas Huskin and his wife entered into a contract to have their home remodeled by House Medic Handyman Service. Todd Hall signed the contract as an authorized representative of House Medic. It turned out that House Medic was a fictitious name for Hall Hauling, Ltd. The contract did not indicate this, however, and Hall did not inform the Huskins about Hall Hauling. When a contract dispute later arose, the Huskins sued Todd Hall personally for breach of contract. Can Hall be held personally liable? Why or why not? [Huskin v. Hall, 2012 WL 553136 (Ohio Ct.App. 2012)] **(See page 359.)**

- **For a sample answer to Problem 17–6, go to Appendix C at the end of this text.**

17–7. Agent's Duties to Principal. William and Maxine Miller were shareholders of Claimsco International, Inc. They filed a suit against the other shareholders, Michael Harris and Kenneth Hoxie, and the accountant who worked for all of them—John Verchota. The Millers alleged that Verchota had breached a duty that he owed them. They claimed that at Harris's instruction, Verchota had adjusted Claimsco's books to maximize the Millers' financial liabilities, falsely reflect income to them without actually transferring that income, and unfairly disadvantage them compared to the other shareholders. Which duty are the Millers referring to? If the allegations can be proved, did Verchota breach this duty? Explain. [*Miller v. Harris*, 985 N.E.2d 671 (Ill. App. 2 Dist. 2013)] **(See page 351.)**

17–8. Agent's Authority. Basic Research, LLC, advertised its products on television networks owned by Rainbow Media Holdings, Inc., through an ad agency, Icebox Advertising, Inc. As Basic's agent, Icebox had the express authority to buy ads from Rainbow on Basic's behalf, but the authority was limited to buying ads with cash in advance. Despite this limit, Rainbow sold ads to Basic through Icebox on credit. Basic paid Icebox for the ads, but Icebox did not pass all of the payments on to Rainbow. Icebox filed for bankruptcy. Can Rainbow recoup the unpaid amounts from Basic? Explain. [*American Movie Classics v. Rainbow Media Holdings*, 2013 WL 323229 (10th Cir. 2013)] **(See page 354.)**

17–9. A QUESTION OF ETHICS: Agency Formation and Duties.

 Western Fire Truck, Inc., contracted with Emergency One, Inc. (EO), to be its exclusive dealer in Colorado and Wyoming through December 2003. James Costello, a Western salesperson, was authorized to order EO vehicles for his customers. Without informing Western, Costello e-mailed EO about Western's difficulties in obtaining cash to fund its operations. He asked about the viability of Western's contract and his possible employment with EO. On EO's request, and in disregard of Western's instructions, Costello sent some payments for EO vehicles directly to EO. In addition, Costello, with EO's help, sent a competing bid to a potential Western customer. EO's representative e-mailed Costello, "You have my permission to kick [Western's] ass." In April 2002, EO terminated its contract with Western, and, after reviewing Costello's e-mail, fired Costello. Western filed a suit in a Colorado state court, alleging that Costello breached his duty as an agent and that EO aided and abetted the breach. [Western Fire Truck, Inc. v. Emergency One, Inc., 134 P.3d 570 (Colo. App. 2006)] **(See pages 349–351.)**

(a) Was there an agency relationship between Western and Costello? Western required monthly reports from its sales staff, but Costello did not report regularly. Does this indicate that Costello was not Western's agent? In determining whether an agency relationship exists, is the right to control or the fact of control more important? Explain.

(b) Did Costello owe Western a duty? If so, what was the duty? Did Costello breach it? If so, how?

(c) A Colorado state statute allows a court to award punitive damages in "circumstances of fraud, malice, or willful and wanton conduct." Did any of these circumstances exist in this case? Should punitive damages be assessed against either defendant? Why or why not?

Legal Reasoning Group Activity

17–10. Liability for Independent Contractor's Torts. Dean Brothers Corp. owns and operates a steel drum manufacturing plant. Lowell Wyden, the plant superintendent, hired Best Security Patrol, Inc. (BSP), a security company, to guard Dean property and "deter thieves and vandals." Some BSP security guards, as Wyden knew, carried firearms. Pete Sidell, a BSP security guard, was not certified as an armed guard but nevertheless came to work with his gun (in a briefcase).

While working at the Dean plant on October 31, 2014, Sidell fired his gun at Tyrone Gaines, in the belief that Gaines was an intruder. The bullet struck and killed Gaines. Gaines's mother filed a lawsuit claiming that her son's death was the result of BSP's negligence, for which Dean was responsible. **(See pages 361–365.)**

(a) The first group will determine what the plaintiff's best argument is to establish that Dean is responsible for BSP's actions.

(b) The second group will discuss Dean's best defense and formulate arguments in support of it.

CHAPTER 18

SOLE PROPRIETORSHIPS, PARTNERSHIPS, AND LIMITED LIABILITY COMPANIES

Anyone who starts a business must first decide which form of business organization will be most appropriate for the new endeavor. In making this decision, the **entrepreneur** (an individual who initiates and assumes the financial risk of a new enterprise) needs to consider a number of factors. In particular, an entrepreneur needs to consider (1) the ease of creation, (2) the liability of the owners, (3) the tax consequences, and (4) the ability to raise capital. Keep these factors in mind as you read about the various business organizational forms available to entrepreneurs. You may also find it helpful to refer to Exhibit 19–3 on pages 420 and 421, which compares the major business forms in use today with respect to these and other factors.

Traditionally, entrepreneurs have relied on three major business forms—the sole proprietorship, the partnership, and the corporation. In this chapter, we look at two of these—the sole proprietorship and the partnership forms of business. We also examine the limited liability company (LLC), a relatively new and increasingly popular form of business enterprise. The third major traditional form—the corporation—will be discussed in detail in Chapter 19.

SOLE PROPRIETORSHIPS

The simplest form of business organization is a **sole proprietorship.** In this form, the owner is the business. Thus, anyone who does business without creating a separate business organization has a sole proprietorship. More than two-thirds of all U.S. businesses are sole proprietorships. They are usually small enterprises—about 99 percent of the sole proprietorships in the United States have revenues of less than $1 million per year. Sole proprietors can own and manage any type of business from an informal home-office or Web-based undertaking to a large restaurant or construction firm.

Advantages of the Sole Proprietorship

A major advantage of the sole proprietorship is that the proprietor owns the entire business and receives all of the profits (because she or he assumes all of the risk). In addition, starting a sole proprietorship is often easier and less costly than starting any other kind of business, as few legal formalities are required.

Generally, no documents need to be filed with the government to start a sole proprietorship.[1]

FLEXIBILITY This form of business organization also offers more flexibility than does a partnership or a corporation. The sole proprietor is free to make any decision he or she wishes concerning the business—such as whom to hire, when to take a vacation, and what kind of business to pursue.

The sole proprietor can sell or transfer all or part of the business to another party at any time and does not need approval from anyone else. (In contrast, approval is typically required from partners in a partnership and from shareholders in a corporation.)

Sometimes, a sole proprietor can even benefit in a lawsuit from the fact that the business is indistinguishable from the owner. ▶ **Case in Point 18.1** James Ferguson operated "Jim's 11-E Auto Sales" as a sole proprietorship and obtained insurance from Consumers Insurance Company. The policy was issued to "Jim Ferguson, Jim's 11-E Auto Sales." Later,

---

1. Although starting a sole proprietorship involves fewer legal formalities than other business organizational forms, even a small sole proprietorship may need to comply with zoning requirements, obtain a state business license, and the like.

Ferguson bought a motorcycle in his own name, intending to repair and sell it through his dealership. One day when he was riding the motorcycle, he was struck by a car and seriously injured.

When Ferguson sued Consumers Insurance, the insurer argued that because Ferguson bought the motorcycle in his own name and was riding it at the time of the accident, it was his personal vehicle and was not covered under the dealership's policy. The court, however, held that the policy covered Ferguson's injuries. "Because the business is operated as a sole proprietorship, Jim Ferguson and 'Jim's 11-E Auto Sales' are one and the same."[2] ◀

TAXES A sole proprietor pays only personal income taxes (including Social Security and Medicare taxes) on the business's profits, which are reported as per-

sonal income on the proprietor's personal income tax return. Sole proprietors are also allowed to establish certain retirement accounts that are tax-exempt until the funds are withdrawn.

Disadvantages of the Sole Proprietorship

The major disadvantage of the sole proprietorship is that the proprietor alone bears the burden of any losses or liabilities incurred by the business enterprise. In other words, the sole proprietor has unlimited liability, or legal responsibility, for all obligations that arise in doing business. Any lawsuit against the business or its employees can lead to unlimited personal liability for the owner of a sole proprietorship.

The personal liability of the owner of a sole proprietorship was at issue in the following case.

---

2. *Ferguson v. Jenkins,* 204 S.W.3d 779 (Tenn.App. 2006).

CASE 18.1

Quality Car & Truck Leasing, Inc. v. Sark

Court of Appeals of Ohio, Fourth District, 2013-Ohio-44, 2013 WL 139359 (2013).

BACKGROUND AND FACTS Michael Sark operated a logging business as a sole proprietorship. To acquire equipment for the business, Sark and his wife, Paula, borrowed funds from Quality Car & Truck Leasing, Inc. When his business encountered financial difficulties, Sark became unable to pay his creditors, including Quality. The Sarks sold their house (valued at $203,500) to their son, Michael, Jr., for one dollar, but they continued to live in it. Three months later, Quality obtained a judgment in an Ohio state court against the Sarks for $150,481.85 and then filed a claim to set aside the transfer of the house to Michael, Jr., as a fraudulent conveyance. From a decision in Quality's favor, the Sarks appealed, arguing that they did not intend to defraud Quality and that they were not actually Quality's debtors.

 IN THE LANGUAGE OF THE COURT
KLINE, J. [Judge]

＊ ＊ ＊ ＊

The trial court found that summary judgment was proper under [Ohio Revised Code (R.C.) Section] 1336.04(A)(2)(a). That statute provides as follows:

> A transfer made or an obligation incurred by a debtor is fraudulent as to a creditor, whether the claim of the creditor arose before or after the transfer was made or the obligation was incurred, if the debtor made the transfer or incurred the obligation ＊ ＊ ＊ without receiving a reasonably equivalent value in exchange for the transfer or obligation, and ＊ ＊ ＊ the debtor was engaged or was about to engage in a business or a transaction for which the remaining assets of the debtor were unreasonably small in relation to the business or transaction.

The trial court found "that Michael Senior and Paula made a transfer without the exchange of reasonably equivalent value and that the debtor was engaged or was about to engage in a business ＊ ＊ ＊ transaction for which the remaining assets of the debtor were unreasonably small in relation to the business or transaction."

＊ ＊ ＊ The Sarks argue that summary judgment was not proper because there is a genuine issue of material fact regarding whether they intended to defraud Quality Leasing. The Sarks'

CASE 18.1 CONTINUES ▶

CASE 18.1 CONTINUED argument fails because intent is not relevant to an analysis under R.C. Section 1336.04(A)(2)(a). *A creditor does not need to show that a transfer was made with intent to defraud in order to prevail under R.C. Section 1336.04(A)(2)(a). Thus, the Sarks cannot defeat summary judgment by showing that they did not act with fraudulent intent when Michael Senior and Paula transferred the Property to Michael Junior.* [Emphasis added.]

The Sarks also claim that summary judgment was improper because there is an issue of fact regarding whether Michael Senior and Paula are actually Quality Leasing's debtors. Michael Senior apparently returned the equipment that secured the debts owed to Quality Leasing. According to the Sarks, Quality Leasing's appraisals of the equipment showed that the value of the equipment would be enough to satisfy the debts.

The Sarks' argument, however, does not address the fact that they are clearly judgment debtors to Quality Leasing and that the judgment has not been satisfied. * * * The Sarks have not challenged the validity of the judgment against them nor have they shown that the judgment has been satisfied. Thus, there is no genuine issue of material fact regarding whether Paula and Michael Senior are debtors to Quality Leasing.

In conclusion, there is no genuine issue as to any material fact. Quality Leasing is entitled to judgment as a matter of law.

DECISION AND REMEDY *A state intermediate appellate court affirmed the lower court's judgment in Quality's favor. "Reasonable minds can come to only one conclusion, and that conclusion is adverse to the Sarks," said the court. The Sarks "are clearly judgment debtors to Quality Leasing and . . . the judgment has not been satisfied."*

THE ECONOMIC DIMENSION *What might the Sarks have done to avoid this dispute, as well as the loss of their home and their apparently declining business?*

THE ETHICAL DIMENSION *Why did the Sarks take the unethical step of fraudulently conveying their home to their son? What should they have done instead?*

PERSONAL ASSETS AT RISK Creditors can pursue the owner's personal assets to satisfy any business debts. Although sole proprietors may obtain insurance to protect the business, liability can easily exceed policy limits. This unlimited liability is a major factor to be considered in choosing a business form.

▶ **Example 18.2** Sheila Fowler operates a golf shop near a world-class golf course as a sole proprietorship. One of Fowler's employees fails to secure a display of golf clubs. They fall on Dean Maheesh, a professional golfer, and seriously injure him. If Maheesh sues Fowler's shop and wins, Fowler's personal liability could easily exceed the limits of her insurance policy. Fowler could lose not only her business, but also her house, car, and any other personal assets that can be attached to pay the judgment. ◀

LACK OF CONTINUITY The sole proprietorship also has the disadvantage of lacking continuity after the death of the proprietor. When the owner dies, so does the business—it is automatically dissolved. Another disadvantage is that in raising capital, the proprietor

is limited to his or her personal funds and funds from any loans that he or she can obtain for the business.

SECTION 2
PARTNERSHIPS

Partnerships are governed both by common law concepts—in particular, those relating to agency—and by statutory law. As in so many other areas of business law, the National Conference of Commissioners on Uniform State Laws has drafted uniform laws for partnerships, and these have been widely adopted by the states.

Agency Concepts and Partnership Law

When two or more persons agree to do business as partners, they enter into a special relationship with one another. To an extent, their relationship is similar to an agency relationship because each partner is deemed to be the agent of the other partners and of the partnership. The agency concepts that were discussed in Chapter 17 thus apply—specifically, the imputation of knowledge of, and responsibility for, acts carried out within the scope of the partnership relationship. In their relationships with one another, partners, like agents, are bound by fiduciary ties.

In one important way, however, partnership law differs from agency law. The partners in a partnership agree to commit funds or other assets, labor, and skills to the business with the understanding that profits and losses will be shared. Thus, each partner has an *ownership interest* in the firm. In a nonpartnership agency relationship, the agent usually does not have an ownership interest in the business and is not obligated to bear a portion of ordinary business losses.

The Uniform Partnership Act

The Uniform Partnership Act (UPA) governs the operation of partnerships *in the absence of express agreement* and has done much to reduce controversies in the law relating to partnerships. A majority of the states have enacted the most recent version of the UPA (as amended in 1997) to provide limited liability for partners in a limited liability partnership.[3] We therefore base our discussion of the UPA in this chapter on the 1997 version of the act and refer to older versions of the UPA in footnotes when appropriate.

Definition of a Partnership

The UPA defines a **partnership** as "an association of two or more persons to carry on as co-owners a business for profit" [UPA 101(6)]. Note that the UPA's definition of *person* includes corporations, so a corporation can be a partner in a partnership [UPA 101(10)]. The *intent* to associate is a key element of a partnership, and one cannot join a partnership unless all other partners consent [UPA 401(i)].

Elements of a Partnership

Conflicts sometimes arise over whether a business enterprise is a legal partnership, especially when there is no formal, written partnership agreement. To determine whether a partnership exists, courts usually look

for the following three essential elements, which are implicit in the UPA's definition:

1. A sharing of profits or losses.
2. A joint ownership of the business.
3. An equal right to be involved in the management of the business.

If the evidence in a particular case is insufficient to establish all three factors, the UPA provides a set of guidelines to be used.

THE SHARING OF PROFITS AND LOSSES The sharing of both profits and losses from a business creates a presumption (legal inference) that a partnership exists. ▶ **Example 18.3** Syd and Drake start a business that sells fruit smoothies near a college campus. They open a joint bank account from which they pay for supplies and expenses, and they share the proceeds (and losses) that the smoothie stand generates. If a conflict arises as to their business relationship, a court will assume that a partnership exists unless the parties prove otherwise. ◀

A court will not presume that a partnership exists, however, if shared profits were received as payment of any of the following [UPA 202(c)(3)]:

1. A debt by installments or interest on a loan.
2. Wages of an employee or for the services of an independent contractor.
3. Rent to a landlord.
4. An annuity to a surviving spouse or representative of a deceased partner.
5. A sale of the **goodwill** (the valuable reputation of a business viewed as an intangible asset) of a business or property.

▶ **Example 18.4** Mason Snopel owes a creditor, Alice Burns, $5,000 on an unsecured debt. They agree that Mason will pay 10 percent of his monthly business profits to Alice until the loan with interest has been repaid. Although Mason and Alice are sharing profits from the business, they are not presumed to be partners. ◀

JOINT PROPERTY OWNERSHIP Joint ownership of property does not in and of itself create a partnership [UPA 202(c)(1) and (2)]. The parties' intentions are key. ▶ **Example 18.5** Chiang and Burke jointly own farmland and lease it to a farmer for a share of the profits from the farming operation in lieu of fixed rental payments. This arrangement normally would not make Chiang, Burke, and the farmer partners. ◀

---

3. At the time this book went to press, more than two-thirds of the states, as well as the District of Columbia, Puerto Rico, and the U.S. Virgin Islands, had adopted the UPA with the 1997 amendments.

Entity versus Aggregate

At common law, a partnership was treated only as an aggregate of individuals and never as a separate legal entity. Thus, at common law a lawsuit could never be brought by or against the firm in its own name. Each individual partner had to sue or be sued.

Today, in contrast, a majority of the states follow the UPA and treat a partnership as an entity for most purposes. For instance, a partnership usually can sue or be sued, collect judgments, and have all accounting performed in the name of the partnership entity [UPA 201, 307(a)].

As an entity, a partnership may hold the title to real or personal property in its name rather than in the names of the individual partners. Additionally, federal procedural laws permit the partnership to be treated as an entity in suits in federal courts and bankruptcy proceedings.

Tax Treatment of Partnerships

Modern law does treat a partnership as an aggregate of the individual partners rather than a separate legal entity in one situation—for federal income tax purposes. The partnership is a pass-through entity and not a taxpaying entity. A **pass-through entity** is a business entity that has no tax liability—the entity's income is passed through to the owners of the entity, who pay income taxes on it.

Thus, the income or losses the partnership incurs are "passed through" the entity framework and attributed to the partners on their individual tax returns. The partnership itself pays no taxes and is responsible only for filing an **information return** with the Internal Revenue Service.

A partner's profit from the partnership (whether distributed or not) is taxed as individual income to the individual partner. Similarly, partners can deduct a share of the partnership's losses on their individual tax returns (in proportion to their partnership interests).

Partnership Formation

As a general rule, agreements to form a partnership can be *oral, written,* or *implied by conduct.* Some partnership agreements, however, such as one authorizing partners to transfer interests in real property, must be in writing (or in an electronic record) to be legally enforceable (see Chapter 12).

THE PARTNERSHIP AGREEMENT A partnership agreement, also known as **articles of partnership,** can include almost any terms that the parties wish, unless they are illegal or contrary to public policy or statute [UPA 103]. The terms commonly included in a partnership agreement are listed in Exhibit 18–1 on the facing page.

The rights and duties of partners are governed largely by the specific terms of their partnership agreement. In the absence of provisions to the contrary in the partnership agreement, the law imposes certain rights and duties, as discussed in the following subsections. The character and nature of the partnership business generally influence the application of these rights and duties.

The partnership agreement can specify the duration of the partnership by stating that it will continue until a designated date or until the completion of a particular project. This is called a *partnership for a term.* Generally, withdrawal from a partnership for a term prematurely (before the expiration date) constitutes a breach of the agreement, and the responsible partner can be held liable for any resulting losses [UPA 602(b)(2)]. If no fixed duration is specified, the partnership is a *partnership at will,* which means that the partnership can be dissolved at any time.

PARTNERSHIP BY ESTOPPEL Occasionally, persons who are not partners nevertheless hold themselves out as partners and make representations that third parties rely on in dealing with them. When a third person has reasonably and detrimentally relied on the representation that a nonpartner was part of a partnership, a court may conclude that a **partnership by estoppel** exists and impose liability—but not partnership *rights*—on the alleged partner.

Similarly, a partnership by estoppel may be imposed when a partner represents, expressly or impliedly, that a nonpartner is a member of the firm. When a partnership by estoppel is deemed to exist, the nonpartner is regarded as an agent whose acts are binding on the partnership [UPA 308].

▶ **Case in Point 18.6** Jackson Paper Manufacturing Company makes paper that is used by Stonewall Packaging, LLC. Jackson and Stonewall have officers and directors in common, and they share employees, property, and equipment. In reliance on Jackson's business reputation, Best Cartage, Inc., agreed to provide transportation services for Stonewall and bought thirty-seven tractor-trailers to use in fulfilling the contract. Best provided the services until Stonewall terminated the agreement.

EXHIBIT 18-1 Common Terms Included in a Partnership Agreement

Term	Description
Basic Structure	1. Name of the partnership. 2. Names of the partners. 3. Location of the business and the state law under which the partnership is organized. 4. Purpose of the partnership. 5. Duration of the partnership.
Capital Contributions	1. Amount of capital that each partner is contributing. 2. The agreed-on value of any real or personal property that is contributed instead of cash. 3. How losses and gains on contributed capital will be allocated, and whether contributions will earn interest.
Sharing of Profits and Losses	1. Percentage of the profits and losses of the business that each partner will receive. 2. When distributions of profit will be made and how net profit will be calculated.
Management and Control	1. How management responsibilities will be divided among the partners. 2. Name(s) of the managing partner or partners, and whether other partners have voting rights.
Accounting and Partnership Records	1. Name of the bank in which the partnership will maintain its business and checking accounts. 2. Statement that an accounting of partnership records will be maintained and that any partner or her or his agent can review these records at any time. 3. The dates of the partnership's fiscal year (if used) and when the annual audit of the books will take place.
Dissociation and Dissolution	1. Events that will cause the dissociation of a partner or dissolve the partnership, such as the retirement, death, or incapacity of any partner. 2. How partnership property will be valued and apportioned on dissociation and dissolution. 3. Whether an arbitrator will determine the value of partnership property on dissociation and dissolution and whether that determination will be binding.
Arbitration	1. Whether arbitration is required for any dispute relating to the partnership agreement.

Best filed a suit for breach of contract against Stonewall and Jackson, seeking $500,678 in unpaid invoices and consequential damages of $1,315,336 for the tractor-trailers it had purchased. Best argued that Stonewall and Jackson had a partnership by estoppel. The court agreed, finding that "defendants combined labor, skills, and property to advance their alleged business partnership." Jackson had negotiated the agreement on Stonewall's behalf, and a news release stated that Jackson had sought tax incentives for Stonewall. Jackson also had bought real estate, equipment, and general supplies for Stonewall with no expectation of payment from Stonewell to Jackson. This was sufficient to prove a partnership by estoppel.[4] ◀

Rights of Partners

The rights of partners in a partnership relate to the following areas: management, interest in the partnership, compensation, inspection of books, accounting, and property.

MANAGEMENT RIGHTS In a general partnership, all partners have equal rights in managing the partnership [UPA 401(f)]. Unless the partners agree otherwise, each partner has one vote in management matters *regardless of the proportional size of his or her interest in the firm*. In a large partnership, partners often agree to delegate daily management responsibilities to a management committee made up of one or more of the partners.

The majority rule controls decisions on ordinary matters connected with partnership business, unless otherwise specified in the agreement. Decisions that significantly affect the nature of the partnership or that are outside the ordinary course of the partnership business, however, require the *unanimous* consent of the partners [UPA 301(2), 401(i), 401(j)].

Unanimous consent is likely to be required for any decision to:

1. Alter the essential nature of the firm's business as expressed in the partnership agreement.

4. *Best Cartage, Inc. v. Stonewall Packaging, LLC*, 727 S.E.2d 291 (N.C.App. 2012).

2. Change the capital structure of the partnership.
3. Amend the terms of the partnership agreement.
4. Admit a new partner.
5. Engage in a completely new business.
6. Assign partnership property to a trust for the benefit of creditors, or allow a creditor to enter a judgment against the partnership, for an agreed sum, without the use of legal proceedings.
7. Dispose of the partnership's *goodwill* (defined on page 375).
8. Submit partnership claims to arbitration.
9. Undertake any act that would make further conduct of the partnership business impossible.

INTEREST IN THE PARTNERSHIP Each partner is entitled to the proportion of business profits and losses that is specified in the partnership agreement. If the agreement does not apportion profits (indicate how the profits will be shared), the UPA provides that profits will be shared equally. If the agreement does not apportion losses, losses will be shared in the same ratio as profits [UPA 401(b)].

▶ **Example 18.7** Rimi and Brett form a partnership. The partnership agreement provides for capital contributions of $60,000 from Rimi and $40,000 from Brett, but it is silent as to how they will share profits or losses. In this situation, they will share both profits and losses equally. If their partnership agreement had provided that they would share profits in the same ratio as capital contributions, however, 60 percent of the profits would go to Rimi, and 40 percent would go to Brett. If the agreement was silent as to losses, losses would be shared in the same ratio as profits (60 percent and 40 percent, respectively). ◀

COMPENSATION Devoting time, skill, and energy to partnership business is a partner's duty and generally is not a compensable service. Rather, as mentioned, a partner's income from the partnership takes the form of a distribution of profits according to the partner's share in the business. Partners can, of course, agree otherwise. For instance, the managing partner of a law firm often receives a salary—in addition to her or his share of profits—for performing special administrative or managerial duties.

INSPECTION OF THE BOOKS Partnership books and records must be kept accessible to all partners. Each partner has the right to receive (and the corresponding duty to produce) full and complete information concerning the conduct of all aspects of partnership business [UPA 403]. Each firm retains books for recording and securing such information. Partners contribute the information, and a bookkeeper typically has the duty to preserve it.

The partnership books must be kept at the firm's principal business office (unless the partners agree otherwise). Every partner is entitled to inspect all books and records on demand and can make copies of the materials. The personal representative of a deceased partner's estate has the same right of access to partnership books and records that the decedent would have had [UPA 403].

ACCOUNTING OF PARTNERSHIP ASSETS OR PROFITS
An accounting of partnership assets or profits is required to determine the value of each partner's share in the partnership. An accounting can be performed voluntarily, or it can be compelled by court order. Under UPA 405(b), a partner has the right to bring an action for an accounting during the term of the partnership, as well as on the partnership's dissolution and winding up.

PROPERTY RIGHTS Property acquired *by* a partnership is the property of the partnership and not of the partners individually [UPA 203]. Partnership property includes all property that was originally contributed to the partnership and anything later purchased by the partnership or in the partnership's name (except in rare circumstances) [UPA 204].

A partner may use or possess partnership property only on behalf of the partnership [UPA 401(g)]. A partner is *not* a co-owner of partnership property and has no right to sell, mortgage, or transfer partnership property to another [UPA 501].[5]

In other words, partnership property is owned by the partnership as an entity and not by the individual partners. Thus, partnership property cannot be used to satisfy the personal debt of an individual partner. That partner's creditor, however, can petition a court for a **charging order** to attach the partner's *interest* in the partnership to satisfy the partner's obligation [UPA 502]. A partner's interest in the partnership includes her or his proportionate share of the profits and losses and the right to receive distributions. (A partner can also assign her or his right to a share of the partnership profits to another to satisfy a debt.)

---

5. Under the previous version of the UPA, partners were *tenants in partnership*. This meant that every partner was a co-owner with all other partners of the partnership property. The current UPA does not recognize this concept.

Duties and Liabilities of Partners

The duties and liabilities of partners are derived from agency law. Each partner is an agent of every other partner and acts as both a principal and an agent in any business transaction within the scope of the partnership agreement.

Each partner is also a general agent of the partnership in carrying out the usual business of the firm "or business of the kind carried on by the partnership" [UPA 301(1)]. Thus, every act of a partner concerning partnership business and "business of the kind" and every contract signed in the partnership's name bind the firm.

FIDUCIARY DUTIES The fiduciary duties that a partner owes to the partnership and the other partners are the duty of care and the duty of loyalty [UPA 404(a)]. Under the UPA, a partner's *duty of care* is limited to refraining from "grossly negligent or reckless conduct, intentional misconduct, or a knowing violation of law" [UPA 404(c)].[6] A partner is not liable to the partnership for simple negligence or honest errors in judgment in conducting partnership business.

The *duty of loyalty* requires a partner to account to the partnership for "any property, profit, or benefit" derived by the partner in the conduct of the partnership's business or from the use of its property. A partner must also refrain from competing with the partnership in business or dealing with the firm as an adverse party [UPA 404(b)].

BREACH AND WAIVER OF FIDUCIARY DUTIES A partner's fiduciary duties may not be waived or eliminated in the partnership agreement. In fulfilling them, each partner must act consistently with the obligation of good faith and fair dealing [UPA 103(b), 404(d)]. The agreement can specify acts that the partners agree will violate a fiduciary duty.

Note that a partner may pursue his or her own interests without automatically violating these duties [UPA 404(e)]. The key is whether the partner has disclosed the interest to the other partners. ▶ **Example 18.8** Jayne Trell, a partner at Jacoby & Meyers, owns a shopping mall. Trell may vote against a partnership proposal to open a competing mall, provided that she has fully disclosed her interest in the existing shopping mall to the other partners at the firm. ◀ A partner cannot make secret profits or put self-interest before his or her duty to the interest of the partnership, however.

AUTHORITY OF PARTNERS The UPA affirms general principles of agency law that pertain to a partner's authority to bind a partnership in contract. A partner may also subject the partnership to tort liability under agency principles. When a partner is carrying on partnership business with third parties in the usual way, apparent authority exists, and both the partner and the firm share liability.

If a partner acts within the scope of her or his authority, the partnership is legally bound to honor the partner's commitments to third parties. The partnership will not be liable, however, if the third parties *know* that the partner has no such authority.

Limitations on Authority. A partnership may limit a partner's capacity to act as the firm's agent or transfer property on its behalf by filing a "statement of partnership authority" in a designated state office [UPA 105, 303]. Such limits on a partner's authority normally are effective only with respect to third parties who are notified of the limitation.

The Scope of Implied Powers. The agency concepts relating to apparent authority, actual authority, and ratification that were discussed in Chapter 17 also apply to partnerships. The extent of *implied authority generally is broader for partners than for ordinary agents,* however.

In an ordinary partnership, the partners can exercise all implied powers reasonably necessary and customary to carry on that particular business. Some customarily implied powers include the authority to make warranties on goods in the sales business and the power to enter into contracts consistent with the firm's regular course of business.

▶ **Example 18.9** Jamie Schwab is a partner in a firm that operates a retail tire store. He regularly promises that "each tire will be warranted for normal wear for 40,000 miles." Because Schwab has authority to make warranties, the partnership is bound to honor the warranty. Schwab would not, however, have the authority to sell the partnership's office equipment or other property without the consent of all of the other partners. ◀

LIABILITY OF PARTNERS One significant disadvantage associated with a traditional partnership is that the partners are *personally* liable for the debts of the partnership. Moreover, in most states, the liability is essentially unlimited because the acts of one partner in the ordinary course of business subject the other partners to personal liability [UPA 305].

---

6. The previous version of the UPA touched only briefly on the duty of loyalty and left the details of the partners' fiduciary duties to be developed under the law of agency (see Chapter 17).

Joint Liability. At one time, each partner in a partnership generally was jointly liable for the partnership's obligations. **Joint liability** means that a third party must sue all of the partners as a group, but each partner can be held liable for the full amount.[7]

If, for instance, a third party sued one partner on a partnership contract, that partner has the right to demand that the other partners be sued with her or him. In fact, if the third party does not name all of the partners in the lawsuit, the assets of the partnership cannot be used to satisfy the judgment. With joint liability, the partnership's assets must be exhausted before creditors can reach the partners' individual assets.[8]

Joint and Several Liability. In the majority of the states, under UPA 306(a), partners are both jointly and severally (separately, or individually) liable for all partnership obligations, including contracts, torts, and breaches of trust. **Joint and several liability** means that a third party has the option of suing all of the partners together (jointly) or one or more of the partners separately (severally).

All partners in a partnership can be held liable even if a particular partner did not participate in, know about, or ratify the conduct that gave rise to the cause of action. Normally, though, the partnership's assets must be exhausted before a creditor can enforce a judgment against a partner's separate assets [UPA 307(d)].

A judgment against one partner severally (separately) does not extinguish the others' liability. (Similarly, a release of one partner does not discharge the partners' several liability.) Those not sued in the first action normally may be sued subsequently, unless the court in the first action held that the partnership was in no way liable. If a plaintiff is successful in a suit against a partner or partners, he or she may collect on the judgment only against the assets of those partners named as defendants.

Indemnification. With joint and several liability, a partner who commits a tort can be required to indemnify (reimburse) the partnership for any damages it pays. Indemnification will typically be granted *unless* the tort was committed in the ordinary course of the partnership's business.

▶ **Case in Point 18.10** Nicole Moren was a partner in Jax Restaurant. After work one day, Moren was called back to the restaurant to help in the kitchen. She brought her two-year-old son, Remington, and placed him on the kitchen counter. While she was making pizzas, Remington reached into the dough press. His hand was crushed, causing permanent injuries. Through his father, Remington filed a suit against the partnership for negligence.

The partnership filed a complaint against Moren, arguing that it was entitled to indemnification from her for her negligence. The court held in favor of Moren and ordered the partnership to pay damages to Remington. Moren was not required to indemnify the partnership because her negligence occurred in the ordinary course of the partnership's business.[9] ◀

Liability of Incoming Partners. A partner newly admitted to an existing partnership is not personally liable for any partnership obligations incurred before the person became a partner [UPA 306(b)]. In other words, the new partner's liability to existing creditors of the partnership is limited to her or his capital contribution to the firm.

▶ **Example 18.11** Smartclub, an existing partnership with four members, admits a new partner, Alex Jaff. He contributes $100,000 to the partnership. Smartclub has debts amounting to $600,000 at the time Jaff joins the firm. Although Jaff's capital contribution of $100,000 can be used to satisfy Smartclub's obligations, Jaff is not personally liable for partnership debts incurred before he became a partner. Thus, his personal assets cannot be used to satisfy the partnership's preexisting debt. If, however, the partnership incurs additional debts after Jaff becomes a partner, he will be personally liable for those amounts, along with all the other partners. ◀

Dissociation of a Partner

Dissociation occurs when a partner ceases to be associated in the carrying on of the partnership business. Although a partner always has the *power* to dissociate from the firm, he or she may not have the *right* to dissociate.

Dissociation normally entitles the partner to have his or her interest purchased by the partnership. It also terminates the partner's actual authority to act for the partnership and to participate in running its

---

7. Under the prior version of the UPA, which is still in effect in a few states, partners were subject to joint liability on partnership debts and contracts, but not on partnership debts arising from torts.
8. For a case applying joint liability to a partnership, see *Shar's Cars, LLC v. Elder*, 97 P.3d 724 (Utah App. 2004).

9. *Moren v. Jax Restaurant*, 679 N.W.2d 165 (Minn.App. 2004).

business. The partnership may continue to do business without the dissociated partner.[10]

EVENTS THAT CAUSE DISSOCIATION Under UPA 601, a partner can be dissociated from a partnership in any of the following ways:

1. By the partner's voluntarily giving notice of an "express will to withdraw." (When a partner gives notice of intent to withdraw, the remaining partners must decide whether to continue the partnership business. If they decide not to continue, the voluntary dissociation of a partner will dissolve the firm [UPA 801(1)].)
2. By the occurrence of an event specified in the partnership agreement.
3. By a unanimous vote of the other partners under certain circumstances, such as when a partner transfers substantially all of her or his interest in the partnership, or when it becomes unlawful to carry on partnership business with that partner.
4. By order of a court or arbitrator if the partner has engaged in wrongful conduct that affects the partnership business. The court may order dissociation if a partner breached the partnership agreement, violated a duty owed to the partnership or the other partners, or engaged in conduct that makes it "not reasonably practicable to carry on the business in partnership with the partner" [UPA 601(5)].
5. By the partner's declaring bankruptcy, assigning his or her interest in the partnership for the benefit of creditors, or becoming physically or mentally incapacitated, or by the partner's death.

WRONGFUL DISSOCIATION As mentioned, a partner has the power to dissociate from a partnership at any time, but if she or he lacks the right to dissociate, then the dissociation is considered wrongful under the law [UPA 602]. When a partner's dissociation breaches a partnership agreement, for instance, it is wrongful.
▶ **Example 18.12** Jenkins & Whalen's partnership agreement states that it is a breach of the agreement for any partner to assign partnership property to a creditor without the consent of the other partners. If Kenzie, a partner, makes such an assignment, she has not only breached the agreement but has also wrongfully dissociated from the partnership. ◀

A partner who wrongfully dissociates is liable to the partnership and to the other partners for damages caused by the dissociation. This liability is in addition to any other obligation of the partner to the partnership or to the other partners.

EFFECTS OF DISSOCIATION Dissociation (rightful or wrongful) terminates some of the rights of the dissociated partner, requires that the partnership purchase his or her interest, and alters the liability of the parties to third parties.

Rights and Duties. On a partner's dissociation, his or her right to participate in the management and conduct of the partnership business terminates [UPA 603]. The partner's duty of loyalty also ends. A partner's duty of care continues only with respect to events that occurred before dissociation, unless the partner participates in winding up the partnership's business (discussed shortly).
▶ **Example 18.13** Debbie Pearson, a partner who leaves the accounting firm Bubb & Flint, can immediately compete with that firm for new clients. She must exercise care in completing ongoing client transactions, however. Pearson must also account to Bubb & Flint for any fees received from the old clients based on those transactions. ◀

Buyouts. After a partner's dissociation, his or her interest in the partnership must be purchased according to the rules in UPA 701. The **buyout price** is based on the amount that would have been distributed to the partner if the partnership had been wound up on the date of dissociation. Offset against the price are amounts owed by the partner to the partnership, including damages for wrongful dissociation.
▶ **Case in Point 18.14** Wilbur and Dee Warnick and their son Randall bought a ranch for $335,000 and formed a partnership to operate it. The partners' initial capital contributions totaled $60,000, of which Randall paid 34 percent. Over the next twenty years, each partner contributed funds to the operation and received cash distributions from the partnership. In 1999, Randall dissociated from the partnership.

When the parties could not agree on a buyout price, Randall filed a lawsuit. The court awarded Randall $115,783.13—the amount of his cash contributions, plus 34 percent of the increase in the value of the partnership's assets above all partners' cash contributions. Randall's parents appealed, arguing that $50,000 should be deducted from the appraised value of the assets for the estimated expenses of selling

---

10. Under the previous version of the UPA, when a partner withdrew from a partnership, the partnership was considered dissolved, and the business had to end. The new UPA dramatically changed the law governing partnership breakups by no longer requiring that a partnership end if one partner dissociates.

them. The court affirmed the buyout price, however, because "purely hypothetical costs of sale are not a required deduction in valuing partnership assets" to determine a buyout price.[11] ◀

Liability to Third Parties. For two years after a partner dissociates from a continuing partnership, the partnership may be bound by the acts of the dissociated partner based on apparent authority [UPA 702]. In other words, if a third party reasonably believed at the time of a transaction that the dissociated partner was still a partner, the partnership may be liable. Also, a dissociated partner may be liable for partnership obligations entered into during a two-year period following dissociation [UPA 703].

To avoid this possible liability, a partnership should notify its creditors, customers, and clients of a partner's dissociation. In addition, either the partnership or the dissociated partner can file a statement of dissociation in the appropriate state office to limit the dissociated partner's authority to ninety days after the filing [UPA 704]. Filing this statement helps to minimize the firm's potential liability for the former partner and vice versa.

Partnership Termination

The same events that cause dissociation can result in the end of the partnership if the remaining partners no longer wish to (or are unable to) continue the partnership business. Only certain departures of a partner will end the partnership, though, and generally the partnership can continue if the remaining partners consent [UPA 801].

The termination of a partnership is referred to as **dissolution,** which essentially means the commencement of the winding up process. **Winding up** is the actual process of collecting, liquidating, and distributing the partnership assets.

DISSOLUTION Dissolution of a partnership generally can be brought about by acts of the partners, by operation of law, or by judicial decree [UPA 801]. Any partnership (including one for a fixed term) can be dissolved by the partners' agreement.

If the partnership agreement states that it will dissolve on a certain event, such as a partner's death or bankruptcy, then the occurrence of that event will dissolve the partnership. A partnership for a fixed term or a particular undertaking is dissolved by operation of law at the expiration of the term or on the completion of the undertaking.

Illegality or Impracticality. Any event that makes it unlawful for the partnership to continue its business will result in dissolution [UPA 801(4)]. Under the UPA, a court may order dissolution when it becomes obviously impractical for the firm to continue—for instance, if the business can only be operated at a loss [UPA 801(5)]. Even when one partner has brought a court action seeking to dissolve a partnership, the partnership continues to exist until it is legally dissolved by the court or by the parties' agreement.[12]

Good Faith. Each partner must exercise good faith when dissolving a partnership. Some state statutes allow partners injured by another partner's bad faith to file a tort claim for wrongful dissolution of a partnership.

▶ **Case in Point 18.15** Attorneys Randall Jordan and Mary Helen Moses formed a two-member partnership. Although the partnership was for an indefinite term, Jordan ended the partnership three years later and asked the court for declarations concerning the partners' financial obligations. Moses, who had objected to ending the partnership, filed a claim against Jordan for wrongful dissolution and for appropriating $180,000 in fees that should have gone to the partnership. Ultimately, the court held in favor of Moses.

A claim for wrongful dissolution of a partnership may be based on the excluded partner's loss of "an existing, or continuing, business opportunity" or of income and material assets. Because Jordan had attempted to appropriate partnership assets through dissolution, Moses could sue for wrongful dissolution.[13] ◀

WINDING UP AND DISTRIBUTION OF ASSETS After dissolution, the partnership continues for the limited purpose of winding up the business. The partners cannot create new obligations on behalf of the partnership. They have authority only to complete transactions begun but not finished at the time of dissolution and to wind up the business of the partnership [UPA 803, 804(1)].

Duties and Compensation. *Winding up* includes collecting and preserving partnership assets, discharging lia-

---

11. *Warnick v. Warnick,* 2006 WY 58, 133 P.3d 997 (2006).

12. See, for example, *Curley v. Kaiser,* 112 Conn.App. 213, 962 A.2d 167 (2009).

13. *Jordan v. Moses,* 291 Ga. 39, 727 S.E.2d 469 (2012).

bilities (paying debts), and accounting to each partner for the value of his or her interest in the partnership. Partners continue to have fiduciary duties to one another and to the firm during this process.

UPA 401(h) provides that a partner is entitled to compensation for services in winding up partnership affairs above and apart from his or her share in the partnership profits. A partner may also receive reimbursement for expenses incurred in the process.

Creditors' Claims. Both creditors of the partnership and creditors of the individual partners can make claims on the partnership's assets. In general, partnership creditors share proportionately with the partners' individual creditors in the partners' assets, which include their interests in the partnership. A partnership's assets are distributed according to the following priorities [UPA 807]:

1. Payment of debts, including those owed to partner and nonpartner creditors.
2. Return of capital contributions and distribution of profits to partners.[14]

If the partnership's liabilities are greater than its assets, the partners bear the losses—in the absence of a contrary agreement—in the same proportion in which they shared the profits (rather than, for exam-

---

14. Under the previous version of the UPA, creditors of the partnership had priority over creditors of the individual partners. Also, in distributing partnership assets, third party creditors were paid before partner creditors, and capital contributions were returned before profits.

ple, in proportion to their contributions to the partnership's capital).

PARTNERSHIP BUY-SELL AGREEMENTS Before entering into a partnership, partners should agree on how the assets will be valued and divided in the event that the partnership dissolves. A **buy-sell agreement,** sometimes called simply a *buyout agreement,* provides for one or more partners to buy out the other or others, should the situation warrant.

Agreeing beforehand on who buys what, under what circumstances, and, if possible, at what price may eliminate costly negotiations or litigation later. Alternatively, the agreement may specify that one or more partners will determine the value of the interest being sold and that the other or others will decide whether to buy or sell.

Under UPA 701(a), if a partner's dissociation does not result in a dissolution of the partnership, a buyout of the partner's interest is mandatory. The UPA contains an extensive set of buyout rules that apply when the partners do not have a buyout agreement. Basically, a withdrawing partner receives the same amount through a buyout that he or she would receive if the business were winding up [UPA 701(b)].

In the following case, one of the three partners in an agricultural partnership died. Despite provisions in the partnership agreement that required its dissolution on a certain date or on a partner's death, whichever came first, the remaining partners did not dissolve the firm and did not liquidate the assets.

CASE ANALYSIS

Case 18.2   Estate of Webster v. Thomas

Appellate Court of Illinois, Fifth District, 2013 WL 164041 (2013).

IN THE LANGUAGE OF THE COURT

Justice *WEXSTTEN* delivered the opinion of the court:

* * * *

Clyde L. Webster, Jr., who formed T&T Agri-Partners Company with partners [James] Theis and [Larry] Thomas, died September 18, 2002. The T&T Agri-Partners Company owns approximately 180 acres of farmland

in Christian County [Illinois] subject to mortgage liability to the Rochester State Bank and/or Farm Credit Services of Central Illinois. This farmland constitutes T&T Agri-Partners Company's only asset.

The September 1, 1997, partnership agreement executed by Clyde, Theis, and Thomas * * * issued 180 partnership units, with Thomas holding 40 (22.2%), Theis holding

80 (44.5%), and Clyde holding 60 (33.3%). The partnership agreement further provided as follows: * * *

> Unless extended by the written consent of those Partners whose combined ownership interest equals at least one hundred twenty (120) Partnership units, the Partnership shall continue until the first to occur of January 31, 2010 A.D., or the earlier dissolution of the Partnership.

CASE 18.2 CONTINUES ➡

* * * *

* * * If a Partner dies, the Partnership will be dissolved, unless those Partners owning at least one hundred twenty (120) Partnership units including the personal representative of the deceased Partner's estate * * * vote to continue the Partnership within one hundred twenty (120) days of the date of the deceased Partner's death.

Upon dissolution, the assets of the Partnership shall be liquidated and distributed. * * *

Any Partner who shall violate any of the terms of this Agreement * * * shall indemnify and hold harmless the Partnership, and all other Partners from any and all * * * losses, * * * including but not limited to attorneys' fees.

On October 14, 2008, [the Estate of Webster through its personal representative Joseph Webster (the plaintiff)] filed its complaint [in an Illinois state circuit court] against [Theis, Thomas, and the partnership (the defendants)]. The plaintiff's complaint sought a declaratory judgment ordering the partnership assets to be distributed based upon the then-current value of the acreage.

* * * *

On December 9, 2009, the circuit court entered an order granting summary judgment on * * * the plaintiff's complaint. [But the defendants did not liquidate the partnership, and the case went to trial.]

* * * *

On September 2, 2011, after the * * * trial, the circuit court entered its order, finding that the partnership expired by its terms on January 31, 2010, and despite demand by the plaintiff, the partnership had failed and refused to liquidate the assets and disburse funds to the plaintiff according to * * * the partnership agreement. The circuit court thereby ordered the defendants to liquidate the partnership.

* * * *

The circuit court further * * * ordered [the defendants to pay] reasonable attorney fees and costs incurred by the plaintiff.

* * * On March 8, 2012, the defendants filed a notice of appeal [arguing that the circuit court erred in ordering them to pay the plaintiff's attorney fees].

* * * *

The partnership agreement clearly provided that upon Clyde's death and the

partners' failure to vote to continue the partnership, the partnership dissolved. Pursuant to the plain language of the partnership agreement, the assets upon dissolution were to be liquidated and distributed by paying the partners in proportion to their capital accounts. Yet, the defendants failed to do so. [Emphasis added.]

On December 9, 2009, seven years after Clyde's death, the circuit court entered summary judgment on * * * the plaintiff's complaint and construed the partnership agreement by determining that upon dissolution, which occurred at Clyde's death on September 18, 2002, and as a result of the remaining partners not agreeing to continue partnership, the assets of the partnership were to be liquidated and distributed * * * . Again, however, despite the agreement's language and despite the circuit court's order, the defendants failed to liquidate the partnership assets. In failing to do so, they violated the partnership agreement and were liable for the plaintiff's attorney fees pursuant to the same agreement.

* * * *

* * * The judgment of the * * * court of Christian County is affirmed.

LEGAL REASONING QUESTIONS

1. What did the partnership agreement at the center of this case require on the death of a partner and the dissolution of the firm?

2. What conduct by which parties triggered this litigation?

3. On what did the court base its order regarding attorneys' fees?

4. What might the defendants have done to avoid the dispute that arose from the circumstances of this case?

SECTION 3
THE LIMITED LIABILITY COMPANY

A **limited liability company (LLC)** is a hybrid that combines the limited liability aspects of a corporation and the tax advantages of a partnership. The LLC has been available for only a few decades, but it has become the preferred structure for many small businesses.

LLCs are governed by state statutes, which vary from state to state. In an attempt to create more uniformity, the National Conference of Commissioners on Uniform State Laws issued the Uniform Limited Liability Company Act (ULLCA). Less than one-fifth of the states have adopted it, though. Thus, the law governing LLCs remains far from uniform.

Some provisions are common to most state statutes, however, and we base our discussion of LLCs in this section on these common elements.

The Nature of the LLC

LLCs share many characteristics with corporations. Like corporations, LLCs must be formed and operated in compliance with state law. Like the shareholders of a corporation, the owners of an LLC, who are called **members,** enjoy limited liability [ULLCA 303].[15]

Members of LLCs are shielded from personal liability in many situations, even sometimes when sued by employees of the firm. ▶ **Case in Point 18.16** Penny McFarland was the activities director at a retirement community in Virginia that was owned by an LLC. Her supervisor told her to take the residents outside for a walk when the temperature was 95 degrees. McFarland complained to the state health department and was fired from her job. She sued a number of managers and members of the LLC for wrongful discharge.

The court held that under Virginia state law, members, managers, and agents of an LLC are not responsible for its liabilities "solely" by virtue of their status. Only those who "have played a key role in contributing to the company's tortious conduct" can be part of a wrongful discharge claim. The court therefore dismissed the action against all but one defendant.[16] ◀

Another similarity between corporations and LLCs is that LLCs are legal entities apart from their owners. As a legal person, the LLC can sue or be sued, enter into contracts, and hold title to property [ULLCA 201]. The terminology used to describe LLCs formed in other states or nations is also similar to that used in corporate law. For instance, an LLC formed in one state but doing business in another state is referred to in the second state as a *foreign LLC.*

The Formation of the LLC

LLCs are creatures of statute and thus must follow state statutory requirements. To form an LLC, **articles of organization** must be filed with a central state agency—usually the secretary of state's office [ULLCA 202].[17]

CONTENTS OF THE ARTICLES Typically, the articles of organization must include the name of the business, its principal address, the name and address of a registered agent, the members' names, and how the LLC will be managed [ULLCA 203]. The business's name must include the words *Limited Liability Company* or the initials *LLC* [ULLCA 105(a)]. Although a majority of the states permit one-member LLCs, some states require at least two members.

PREFORMATION CONTRACTS Businesspersons sometimes enter into contracts on behalf of a business organization that is not yet formed. As you will read in Chapter 19, persons who are forming a corporation may enter into contracts during the process of incorporation but before the corporation becomes a legal entity. These contracts are referred to as *preincorporation contracts.* Once the corporation is formed and adopts the preincorporation contracts (by means of a *novation,* discussed in Chapter 13), it can enforce the contract terms.

In dealing with the preorganization contracts of LLCs, courts may apply the well-established principles of corporate law relating to preincorporation contracts. ▶ **Case in Point 18.17** 607 South Park, LLC, entered into an agreement to sell a hotel to 607 Park View Associates, Ltd., which then assigned the rights to the purchase to another company, 02 Development, LLC. At the time, 02 Development did not yet exist—it was legally created several months later. 607 South Park subsequently refused to sell the hotel to 02 Development, and 02 Development sued for breach of the purchase agreement.

A California appellate court ruled that LLCs should be treated the same as corporations with respect to preorganization contracts. Although 02 Development did not exist when the agreement was executed, once it came into existence, it could enforce any preorganization contract made on its behalf.[18] ◀

Jurisdictional Requirements

As we have seen, LLCs and corporations share several characteristics, but a significant difference between these organizational forms involves federal

---

15. Members of an LLC can also bring derivative actions, which you will read about in Chapter 19, on behalf of the LLC [ULLCA 101]. As with a corporate shareholder's derivative suit, any damages recovered go to the LLC, not to the members personally.

16. *McFarland v. Virginia Retirement Services of Chesterfield, LLC,* 477 F.Supp.2d 727 (2007).

17. In addition to requiring articles of organization to be filed, a few states require that a notice of the intention to form an LLC be published in a local newspaper.

18. *02 Development, LLC v. 607 South Park, LLC,* 159 Cal.App.4th 609, 71 Cal.Rptr.3d 608 (2008).

jurisdictional requirements. Under the federal juris-diction statute, a corporation is deemed to be a citizen of the state where it is incorporated and maintains its principal place of business. The statute does not mention the state citizenship of partnerships, LLCs, and other unincorporated associations, but the courts have tended to regard these entities as citizens of every state of which their members are citizens.

The state citizenship of an LLC may come into play when a party sues the LLC based on diversity of citizenship. Remember from Chapter 3 that when parties to a lawsuit are from different states and the amount in controversy exceeds $75,000, a federal court can exercise diversity jurisdiction. *Total* diversity of citizenship must exist, however.

▶ **Example 18.18**   Jen Fong, a citizen of New York, wishes to bring a suit against Skycel, an LLC formed under the laws of Connecticut. One of Skycel's members also lives in New York. Fong will not be able to bring a suit against Skycel in federal court on the basis of diversity jurisdiction because the defendant LLC is also a citizen of New York. The same would be true if Fong was bringing a suit against multiple defendants and one of the defendants lived in New York. ◀

Advantages of the LLC

The LLC offers many advantages to businesspersons, which is why this form of business organization has become increasingly popular.

LIMITED LIABILITY   A key advantage of the LLC is that the liability of members is limited to the amount of their investments. Although the LLC as an entity can be held liable for any loss or injury caused by the wrongful acts or omissions of its members, the members themselves generally are not personally liable.

FLEXIBILITY IN TAXATION   Another advantage of the LLC is its flexibility in regard to taxation. An LLC that has *two or more members* can choose to be taxed as either a partnership or a corporation. As will be discussed in Chapter 19, a corporate entity must pay income taxes on its profits, and the shareholders pay personal income taxes on profits distributed as dividends. An LLC that wants to distribute profits to its members may prefer to be taxed as a partnership to avoid the "double taxation" that is characteristic of the corporate entity.

Unless an LLC indicates that it wishes to be taxed as a corporation, the Internal Revenue Service (IRS)

automatically taxes it as a partnership. This means that the LLC, as an entity, pays no taxes. Rather, as in a partnership, profits are "passed through" the LLC to the members, who then personally pay taxes on the profits. If an LLC's members want to reinvest profits in the business rather than distribute the profits to members, however, they may prefer to be taxed as a corporation. Corporate income tax rates may be lower than personal tax rates. Part of the attractiveness of the LLC is this flexibility with respect to taxation.

An LLC that has only *one member* cannot be taxed as a partnership. For federal income tax purposes, one-member LLCs are automatically taxed as sole proprietorships unless they indicate that they wish to be taxed as corporations. With respect to state taxes, most states follow the IRS rules.

MANAGEMENT AND FOREIGN INVESTORS   Another advantage of the LLC for businesspersons is the flexibility it offers in terms of business operations and management—as will be discussed shortly. Foreign investors are allowed to become LLC members, so organizing as an LLC can enable a business to attract investors from other countries.

Disadvantages of the LLC

The main disadvantage of the LLC is that state LLC statutes are not uniform. Therefore, businesses that operate in more than one state may not receive consistent treatment in these states. Generally, most states apply to a foreign LLC (an LLC formed in another state) the law of the state where the LLC was formed. Difficulties can arise, though, when one state's court must interpret and apply another state's laws.

Management of the LLC

Basically, LLC members have two options for managing the firm. It can be either a "member-managed" LLC or a "manager-managed" LLC. Most state LLC statutes and the ULLCA provide that unless the articles of organization specify otherwise, an LLC is assumed to be member managed [ULLCA 203(a)(6)].

In a *member-managed* LLC, all of the members participate in management, and decisions are made by majority vote [ULLCA 404(a)]. In a *manager-managed* LLC, the members designate a group of persons to manage the firm. The management group may consist of only members, both members and nonmembers, or only nonmembers.

FIDUCIARY DUTIES Under the ULLCA, managers in a manager-managed LLC owe fiduciary duties (the duty of loyalty and the duty of care) to the LLC and its members [ULLCA 409(a), 409(h)]. (As you will read in Chapter 19, this same rule applies in corporate law—corporate directors and officers owe fiduciary duties to the corporation and its shareholders.) Because not all states have adopted the ULLCA, though, some state statutes provide that managers owe fiduciary duties only to the LLC and not to the LLC's members. Although to whom the duty is owed may seem insignificant at first glance, it can have a dramatic effect on the outcome of litigation.

▶ **Case in Point 18.19**   Leslie Polk and his children, Yurii and Dusty Polk and Lezanne Proctor, formed Polk Plumbing, LLC. Dusty and Lezanne were managers of the LLC. The operating agreement provided that the managers served until replaced or recalled by a vote of the majority of the members. After a couple of years, Leslie "fired" Dusty and Lezanne. He denied them access to the firm's books and offices but continued to operate the business. The court explained that Dusty and Lezanne were managers of Polk Plumbing. Under the operating agreement, they could only be replaced or recalled by a vote of a majority of the members. Because no vote was taken to recall or replace them, their father (Leslie) did not have the authority to terminate their employment. His attempted "firing" of them violated the *operating agreement.*[19] ◀

THE OPERATING AGREEMENT The members of an LLC can decide how to operate the various aspects of the business by forming an **operating agreement** [ULLCA 103(a)]. In many states, an operating agreement is not required for an LLC to exist, and if there is one, it need not be in writing. Generally, though, LLC members should protect their interests by creating a written operating agreement.

Operating agreements typically contain provisions relating to the following areas:

1. Management and how future managers will be chosen or removed. (Although most LLC statutes are silent on this issue, the ULLCA provides that members may choose and remove managers by majority vote [ULLCA 404(b)(3)].)
2. How profits will be divided.
3. How membership interests may be transferred.
4. Whether the dissociation of a member, such as by death or departure, will trigger dissolution of the LLC.

5. Whether formal members' meetings will be held.
6. How voting rights will be apportioned. (If the agreement does not cover voting, LLC statutes in most states provide that voting rights are apportioned according to each member's capital contributions.[20] Some states provide that, in the absence of an agreement to the contrary, each member has one vote.)

State Statutes Fill in Gaps. If the agreement does not cover a topic, such as how profits will be divided, the state LLC statute will govern. Most LLC statutes provide that if the members have not specified how profits will be divided, they will be divided equally among the members.

Partnership Law May Apply. If a dispute arises and the state's LLC statute does not cover the issue, courts sometimes apply the principles of partnership law. ▶ **Case in Point 18.20**   Clifford Kuhn, Jr., and Joseph Tumminelli formed Touch of Class Limousine Service as an LLC. They did not create a written operating agreement but orally agreed that Kuhn would provide the financial backing and that Tumminelli would manage the day-to-day operations. Tumminelli embezzled $283,000 from the company after cashing customers' checks at Quick Cash, Inc., a local check-cashing service.

Kuhn sued Tumminelli and Quick Cash to recover the embezzled funds. He argued that Quick Cash was liable because Tumminelli did not have the authority to cash the company's checks. The court, however, held that in the absence of a written operating agreement to the contrary, a member of an LLC, like a partner in a partnership, has the authority to cash a firm's checks. Therefore, Kuhn's claim against Quick Cash was dismissed.[21] ◀

Dissociation of the LLC

Recall earlier from this chapter that in a partnership, *dissociation* occurs when a partner ceases to be associated in the carrying on of the partnership business. The same concept applies to LLCs. A member of an LLC has the *power* to dissociate from the LLC at any time, but he or she may not have the *right* to dissociate.

Under the ULLCA, the events that trigger a member's dissociation from an LLC are similar to the events

---

19. *Polk v. Polk,* 70 So.3d 363 (Ala.Civ.App. 2010).

20. In contrast, partners in a partnership generally have equal rights in management and equal voting rights unless they specify otherwise in their partnership agreement.

21. *Kuhn v. Tumminelli,* 366 N.J.Super. 431, 841 A.2d 496 (2004).

causing a partner to be dissociated under the Uniform Partnership Act (UPA). These include voluntary withdrawal, expulsion by other members or by court order, incompetence, and death. Generally, if a member dies or otherwise dissociates from an LLC, the other members may continue to carry on the LLC business, unless the operating agreement provides otherwise.

When a member dissociates from an LLC, he or she loses the right to participate in management and the right to act as an agent for the LLC. The member's duty of loyalty to the LLC also terminates, and the duty of care continues only with respect to events that occurred before dissociation. Generally, the dissociated member also has a right to have his or her interest in the LLC bought out by the other members. The LLC's operating agreement may contain provisions establishing a buyout price, but if it does not, the member's interest is usually purchased at a fair value. In states that have adopted the ULLCA, the LLC must purchase the interest at fair value within 120 days after the dissociation.

If the member's dissociation violates the LLC's operating agreement, it is considered legally wrongful, and the dissociated member can be held liable for damages caused by the dissociation. ▶ **Example 18.21** Chadwick and Barrow are members in an LLC. Chadwick manages the accounts, and Barrow, who has many connections in the community and is a skilled investor, brings in the business. If Barrow wrongfully dissociates from the LLC, the LLC's business will suffer, and Chadwick can hold Barrow liable for the loss of business resulting from her withdrawal. ◀

Dissolution of the LLC

Regardless of whether a member's dissociation was wrongful or rightful, normally the dissociated member has no right to force the LLC to dissolve. The remaining members can opt either to continue or to dissolve the business.

Members can also stipulate in their operating agreement that certain events will cause dissolution, or they can agree that they have the power to dissolve the LLC by vote. As with partnerships, a court can order an LLC to be dissolved in certain circumstances. For instance, a court might order dissolution when the members have engaged in illegal or oppressive conduct, or when it is no longer feasible to carry on the business.

In the following case, the court had to decide whether an LLC could be dissolved because continuing the business was impracticable.

CASE 18.3

Venture Sales, LLC v. Perkins
Supreme Court of Mississippi, 86 So.3d 910 (2012).

BACKGROUND AND FACTS Walter Perkins, Gary Fordham, and David Thompson formed Venture Sales, LLC, to develop a subdivision in Petal, Mississippi. All three members contributed land and funds to Venture Sales, resulting in total holdings of 466 acres of land and about $158,000 in cash.

Perkins was an assistant coach for the Cleveland Browns, so he trusted Fordham and Thompson to develop the property. Over a decade later, however, Fordham and Thompson still had not done anything with the property, although they had developed at least two other subdivisions in the area. Fordham and Thompson said that they did not know when they could develop the property and that they had been unable to get the additional $8 million they needed to proceed. Fordham and Thompson suggested selling the property, but Perkins did not agree with the proposed listing price of $3.5 million. Perkins then sought a judicial dissolution of Venture Sales in Mississippi state court. The trial court ordered the company dissolved. Fordham, Thompson, and Venture Sales appealed.

 IN THE LANGUAGE OF THE COURT
WALLER, Chief Justice, for the Court.

* * * *

* * * [Under the Mississippi Code, an LLC may be dissolved if it] is not reasonably practicable to carry on the business in conformity with the certificate of formation or the limited liability company agreement * * *.

* * * *

While no definitive, widely accepted test or standard exists for determining "reasonable practicability," it is clear that *when a limited liability company is not meeting the economic purpose for which it was established, dissolution is appropriate. In making this determination, we must first look to the company's operating agreement to determine the purpose for which the company was formed.* [Emphasis added.]

Venture Sales' operating agreement states that the company's purpose is "to initially acquire, *develop and sale* [sic] *commercial and residential properties* near Petal, Forrest County, Mississippi." At trial, Fordham admitted that the company was formed for the purpose of acquiring and developing property. Yet, more than ten years after Venture Sales was formed with Perkins as a member, the property remains completely undeveloped. Fordham and Thompson have offered a number of reasons why development has been delayed to this point. [Emphasis in original.]

* * * *

Despite [the] alleged hindrances, Fordham and Thompson have, during this ten-year period, successfully formed two other LLCs and have developed at least two other subdivisions with around 200 houses, collectively, within twenty-five miles of the subject property. More importantly, though, Fordham and Thompson presented no evidence that Venture Sales would be able to develop the land as intended within the foreseeable future. When asked by the trial court when Venture Sales might be able to begin developing as it had planned, Fordham could not say. Fordham and Thompson admitted that it would take around $8 million to "kick off" construction of the subdivision as planned, and the [trial court] found that Venture Sales was currently unable to get additional bank loans or other funding needed to begin development.

* * * *

Fordham and Thompson claim that Perkins has blocked Venture Sales from taking advantage of certain "business opportunities," such as selling the property at a reduced price of $3.5 million * * * . However, these "business opportunities" were merely ideas from Fordham about how to make use of the property. * * * As discussed above, they presented no evidence that Venture Sales could develop the property, which is the purpose for which the company was formed.

DECISION AND REMEDY *The Mississippi Supreme Court held that Venture Sales could be judicially dissolved. It therefore affirmed the decision of the trial court.*

THE LEGAL ENVIRONMENT DIMENSION *Would dissolution be appropriate if the parties had formed a partnership rather than an LLC? Explain your answer.*

MANAGERIAL IMPLICATIONS *To avoid the type of dispute in which the members of Venture Sales became embroiled, the managers of an LLC or other business organization should take care to act on the firm's "economic purpose" within a reasonable time. To ensure that they will be able to do so, the managers should draw up plans and determine the full cost of the project. They should also ascertain how the needed funds will be obtained. If bank loans or other funding will not be available, as occurred in this case, the LLC should require a higher level of contributions from its members to ensure that there will be sufficient funds to complete the project successfully.*

Reviewing: Sole Proprietorships, Partnerships, and Limited Liability Companies

Grace Tarnavsky and her sons, Manny and Jason, bought a ranch known as the Cowboy Palace in March 2010, and the three verbally agreed to share the business for five years. Grace contributed 50 percent of the investment, and each son contributed 25 percent. Manny agreed to handle the livestock, and Jason

Continued

agreed to handle the bookkeeping. The Tarnavskys took out joint loans and opened a joint bank account into which they deposited the ranch's proceeds and from which they made payments toward property, cattle, equipment, and supplies. In September 2012, Manny severely injured his back while baling hay and became permanently unable to handle livestock. Manny therefore hired additional laborers to tend the livestock, causing the Cowboy Palace to incur significant debt. In September 2013, Al's Feed Barn filed a lawsuit against Jason to collect $32,400 in unpaid debts. Using the information presented in the chapter, answer the following questions.

1. Was this relationship a partnership for a term or a partnership at will?
2. Did Manny have the authority to hire additional laborers to work at the ranch after his injury? Why or why not?
3. Under the current UPA, can Al's Feed Barn bring an action against Jason individually for the Cowboy Palace's debt? Why or why not?
4. Suppose that after his back injury in 2012, Manny sent his mother and brother a notice indicating his intent to withdraw from the partnership. Can he still be held liable for the debt to Al's Feed Barn? Why or why not?

DEBATE THIS . . . *Because LLCs are essentially just partnerships with limited liability for members, all partnership laws should apply.*

Terms and Concepts

articles of organization 385
articles of partnership 376
buyout price 381
buy-sell agreement 383
charging order 378
dissociation 380
dissolution 382

entrepreneur 372
goodwill 375
information return 376
joint and several liability 380
joint liability 380
limited liability company (LLC) 384
member 385

operating agreement 387
partnership 375
partnership by estoppel 376
pass-through entity 376
sole proprietorship 372
winding up 382

ExamPrep

Issue Spotters

1. Frank plans to open a sporting goods store and to hire Gogi and Hap. Frank will invest only his own funds. He expects that he will not make a profit for at least eighteen months and will make only a small profit in the three years after that. He hopes to expand eventually. Would a sole proprietorship be an appropriate form for Frank's business? Why or why not? **(See page 372.)**

2. Finian and Gloria are partners in F&G Delivery Service. When business is slow, without Gloria's knowledge, Finian leases the delivery vehicles as moving vans. Because the vehicles would otherwise be sitting idle in a parking lot, can Finian keep the income re-

sulting from the leasing of the delivery vehicles? Explain your answer. **(See page 379.)**

- **Check your answers to the Issue Spotters against the answers provided in Appendix B at the end of this text.**

Before the Test

Go to **www.cengagebrain.com**, enter the ISBN 9781285770192, and click on "Find" to locate this textbook's Web site. Then, click on "Access Now" under "Study Tools," and select Chapter 18 at the top. There, you will find a Practice Quiz that you can take to assess your mastery of the concepts in this chapter, as well as Flashcards and a Glossary of important terms.

Business Scenarios

18–1. Limited Liability Companies. John, Lesa, and Tabir form a limited liability company. John contributes 60 percent of the capital, and Lesa and Tabir each contribute 20 percent. Nothing is decided about how profits will be divided. John assumes that he will be entitled to 60 percent of the profits, in accordance with his contribution. Lesa and Tabir, however, assume that the profits will be divided equally. A dispute over the profits arises, and ultimately a court has to decide the issue. What law will the court apply? In most states, what will result? How could this dispute have been avoided in the first place? Discuss fully. **(See page 384.)**

18–2. Partnership Formation. Daniel is the owner of a chain of shoe stores. He hires Rubya to be the manager of a new store, which is to open in Grand Rapids, Michigan. Daniel, by written contract, agrees to pay Rubya a monthly salary and 20 percent of the profits. Without Daniel's knowledge, Rubya represents himself to Classen as Daniel's partner and shows Classen the agreement to share profits. Classen extends credit to Rubya. Rubya defaults. Discuss whether Classen can hold Daniel liable as a partner. **(See page 376.)**

Business Case Problems

18–3. Limited Liability Companies. Coco Investments, LLC, and other investors participated in a condominium conversion project to be managed by Zamir Manager River Terrace, LLC. The participants entered into a new LLC agreement for the project. The investors subsequently complained that Zamir had failed to disclose its plans for dramatic changes involving higher-than-expected construction costs and delays, had failed to provide financial information, and had restructured loans in a manner that allowed Zamir representatives to avoid personal liability. The investors sued Zamir on various grounds, including breach of contract and breach of fiduciary duty. Zamir moved for summary judgment. How should the court rule? Explain. [*Coco Investments, LLC v. Zamir Manager River Terrace, LLC,* 26 Misc.3d 1231 (N.Y.Sup. 2010)] **(See page 387.)**

18–4. LLC Dissolution. Walter Van Houten and John King formed 1545 Ocean Avenue, LLC, with each managing 50 percent of the business. Its purpose was to renovate an existing building and construct a new commercial building. Van Houten and King quarreled over many aspects of the work on the properties. King claimed that Van Houten paid the contractors too much for the work performed. As the projects neared completion, King demanded that the LLC be dissolved and that Van Houten agree to a buyout. Because the parties could not agree on a buyout, King sued for dissolution. The trial court enjoined (prevented) further work on the projects until the dispute was settled. As the ground for dissolution, King cited the fights over management decisions. There was no claim of fraud or frustration of purpose. The trial court ordered that the LLC be dissolved, and Van Houten appealed. Should either of the owners be forced to dissolve the LLC before the completion of its purpose—that is, before the building projects are finished? Explain. [*In re 1545 Ocean Avenue, LLC,* 893 N.Y.S.2d 590 (N.Y.A.D. 2 Dept. 2010)] **(See page 388.)**

18–5. Jurisdictional Requirements. Fadal Machining Centers, LLC, and MAG Industrial Automation Centers, LLC, sued a New Jersey–based corporation, Mid-Atlantic CNC, Inc., in federal district court. Ten percent of MAG was owned by SP MAG Holdings, a Delaware LLC. SP MAG had six members, including a Delaware limited partnership called Silver Point Capital Fund and a Delaware LLC called SPCP Group III. In turn, Silver Point and SPCP Group had a com- mon member, Robert O'Shea, who was a New Jersey citizen. Assuming that the amount in controversy exceeds $75,000, does the district court have diversity jurisdiction? Why or why not? [*Fadal Machining Centers, LLC v. Mid-Atlantic CNC, Inc.,* 2012 WL 8669 (9th Cir. 2012)] **(See pages 385–386.)**

18–6. Fiduciary Duties of Partners. Karl Horvath, Hein Rüsen, and Carl Thomas formed a partnership, HRT Enterprises, to buy a manufacturing plant. Rüsen and Thomas leased the plant to their own company, Merkur Steel. Merkur then sublet the premises to other companies owned by Rüsen and Thomas. The rent that these companies paid to Merkur was higher than the rent that Merkur paid to HRT. Rüsen and Thomas did not tell Horvath about the subleases. Did Rüsen and Thomas breach their fiduciary duties to HRT and Horvath? Discuss. [*Horvath v. HRT Enterprises,* 489 Mich.App. 992, 800 N.W.2d 595 (2011)] **(See page 379.)**

**18–7. BUSINESS CASE PROBLEM
WITH SAMPLE ANSWER: Partnership Formation.**

Patricia Garcia and Bernardo Lucero were in a romantic relationship. While they were seeing each other, Garcia and Lucero acquired an electronics service center, paying $30,000 apiece. Two years later, they purchased an apartment complex. The property was deeded to Lucero, but neither Garcia nor Lucero made a down payment. The couple considered both properties to be owned "50/50," and they agreed to share profits, losses, and management rights. When the couple's romantic relationship ended, Garcia asked a court to declare that she had a partnership with Lucero. In court, Lucero argued that the couple did not have a written partnership agreement. Did they have a partnership?

Why or why not? [Garcia v. Lucero, *366 S.W.3d 275 (Tex. App. 2012)]* **(See page 376.)**

- For a sample answer to Problem 18–7, go to Appendix C at the end of this text.

18–8. Winding Up and Distribution of Assets. Dan and Lori Cole operated a Curves franchise exercise facility in Angola, Indiana, as a partnership. The firm leased commercial space from Flying Cat, LLC, for a renewable three-year term and renewed the lease for a second three-year term. But two years after the renewal, the Coles divorced. By the end of the second term, Flying Cat was owed more than $21,000 on the lease. Without telling the landlord about the divorce, Lori signed another extension. More rent went unpaid. Flying Cat obtained a judgment in an Indiana state court against the partnership for almost $50,000. Can Dan be held liable? Why or why not? [*Curves for Women Angola v. Flying Cat, LLC,* 983 N.E.2d 629 (Ind. App. 2013)] **(See pages 382–383.)**

18–9. A QUESTION OF ETHICS: Sole Proprietorship.

 In August 2004, Ralph Vilardo contacted Travel Center, Inc., in Cincinnati, Ohio, to buy a trip to Florida in December for his family to celebrate his fiftieth wedding anniversary. Vilardo paid $6,900 to David Sheets, the sole proprietor of Travel Center. Vilardo also paid $195 to Sheets for a separate trip to Florida in February 2005. Sheets assured Vilardo that everything was set, but in fact no arrangements were made. Later, two unauthorized charges for travel services totaling $1,182.35 appeared on Vilardo's credit-card statement. Vilardo filed a suit in an Ohio state court against Sheets and his business, alleging, among other things, fraud and violations of the state consumer protection law. Vilardo served Sheets and Travel Center with copies of the complaint, the summons, a request for admissions, and other documents filed with the court, including a motion for summary judgment. Each of these filings asked for a response within a certain time period. Sheets responded once on his own behalf with a denial of all of Vilardo's claims. Travel Center did not respond. [*Vilardo v. Sheets,* 2006 WL 1843585 (12 Dist. 2006)] **(See page 372.)**

(a) Almost four months after Vilardo filed his complaint, Sheets decided that he was unable to adequately represent himself and retained an attorney, who asked the court for more time. Should the court grant this request? Why or why not? Ultimately, what should the court rule?

(b) Sheets admitted that Travel Center, Inc., was a sole proprietorship. He also argued that liability might be imposed on his business but not on himself. How would you rule with respect to this argument? Why? Would there be anything unethical about allowing Sheets to avoid liability on this basis? Explain.

Legal Reasoning Group Activity

18–10. Fiduciary Duties in LLCs. Newbury Properties Group owns, manages, and develops real property. Jerry Stoker and the Stoker Group, Inc. (the Stokers), also develop real property. Newbury entered into agreements with the Stokers concerning a large tract of property in Georgia. The parties formed Bellemare, LLC, to develop various parcels of the tract for residential purposes. The operating agreement of Bellemare indicated that "no Member shall be accountable to the LLC or to any other Member with respect to any other business or activity even if the business or activity competes with the LLC's business." Later, when the Newbury group contracted with other parties to develop parcels within the tract in competition with Bellemare, LLC, the Stokers sued, alleging breach of fiduciary duty. **(See page 387.)**

(a) The first group will discuss and outline the fiduciary duties that the members of an LLC owe to each other.

(b) The second group will determine whether the terms of an operating agreement can alter these fiduciary duties.

(c) The last group will decide in whose favor the court should rule in this situation.

CHAPTER 19

CORPORATIONS

The corporation is a creature of statute. A corporation is an artificial being, existing only in law and neither tangible nor visible. Its existence generally depends on state law, although some corporations, especially public organizations, are created under federal law. Each state has its own body of corporate law, and these laws are not entirely uniform.

The Model Business Corporation Act (MBCA) is a codification of modern corporation law that has been influential in shaping state corporation statutes. Today, the majority of state statutes are guided by the most recent version of the MBCA, often referred to as the Revised Model Business Corporation Act (RMBCA).

Keep in mind, however, that there is considerable variation among the laws of states that have used the MBCA or the RMBCA as a basis for their statutes. In addition, several states do not follow either act. Consequently, individual state corporation laws should be relied on to determine corporate law rather than the MBCA or RMBCA.

In this chapter, we examine the nature of the corporate form of business enterprise and the various classifications of corporations. We then discuss the formation of today's corporation and its powers. We also consider the roles of corporate directors, officers, and shareholders.

SECTION 1

THE NATURE AND CLASSIFICATION OF CORPORATIONS

A corporation is a legal entity created and recognized by state law. This business entity can have one or more owners (called shareholders), and it operates under a name distinct from the names of its owners. The owners may be individuals, or *natural persons* (as opposed to the artificial *legal person* of the corporation), or other businesses. Although the corporation substitutes itself for its shareholders when conducting corporate business and incurring liability, its authority to act and the liability for its actions are separate and apart from the individuals who own it.

A corporation is recognized as a "person," and it enjoys many of the same rights and privileges under state and federal law that U.S. citizens enjoy. For instance, corporations possess the same right of access to the courts as citizens and can sue or be sued. The constitutional guarantees of due process, free speech, and freedom from unreasonable searches and seizures also apply to corporations.

Corporate Personnel

In a corporation, the responsibility for the overall management of the firm is entrusted to a *board of directors,* whose members are elected by the shareholders. The board of directors makes the policy decisions and hires *corporate officers* and other employees to run the daily business operations of the corporation.

When an individual purchases a share of stock in a corporation, that person becomes a shareholder and an owner of the corporation. Unlike the partners in a partnership, the body of shareholders can change constantly without affecting the continued existence of the corporation. A shareholder can sue the corporation, and the corporation can sue a shareholder. Additionally, under certain circumstances, a shareholder can sue on behalf of a corporation.

The Limited Liability of Shareholders

One of the key advantages of the corporate form is the limited liability of its owners. Normally, corporate shareholders are not personally liable for the obligations of the corporation beyond the extent of their investments.

In certain limited situations, however, a court can *pierce the corporate veil* (see page 403) and impose liability on shareholders for the corporation's obligations. Additionally, creditors often will not extend credit to small companies unless the shareholders assume personal liability, as guarantors, for corporate obligations.

Corporate Earnings and Taxation

When a corporation earns profits, it can either pass them on to shareholders in the form of **dividends** or retain them as profits. These **retained earnings,** if invested properly, will yield higher corporate profits in the future and thus cause the price of the company's stock to rise. Individual shareholders can then reap the benefits of these retained earnings in the capital gains that they receive when they sell their stock.

CORPORATE TAXATION Whether a corporation retains its profits or passes them on to the shareholders as dividends, those profits are subject to income tax by various levels of government. Failure to pay taxes can lead to severe consequences. The state can suspend the entity's corporate status until the taxes are paid or even dissolve the corporation for failing to pay taxes. (Businesses today, including corporations, may also be required to collect state sales taxes on goods or services sold via the Internet, as discussed in the *Insight into E-Commerce* feature in Chapter 15.)

Another important aspect of corporate taxation is that corporate profits can be subject to *double taxation.* The company pays tax on its profits. Then, if the profits are passed on to the shareholders as dividends, the shareholders must also pay income tax on them (unless the dividends represent distributions of capital). The corporation normally does not receive a tax deduction for dividends it distributes. This double-taxation feature is one of the major disadvantages of the corporate form.

HOLDING COMPANIES Some U.S. corporations use holding companies to reduce or defer their U.S. income taxes. At its simplest, a **holding company** (sometimes referred to as a *parent company*) is a company whose business activity consists of holding shares in another company. Typically, the holding company is established in a low-tax or no-tax offshore jurisdiction, such as the Cayman Islands, Dubai, Hong Kong, Luxembourg, Monaco, or Panama.

Sometimes, a U.S. corporation sets up a holding company in a low-tax offshore environment and then transfers its cash, bonds, stocks, and other investments to the holding company. In general, any profits received by the holding company on these investments are taxed at the rate of the offshore jurisdiction where the company is registered. In other words, holding company profits are not taxed at the rates applicable to the parent company or its shareholders in their country of residence. Thus, deposits of cash, for instance, may earn interest that is taxed at only a minimal rate.

Once the profits are brought "onshore," though, they are taxed at the federal corporate income tax rate, and any payments received by the shareholders are also taxable at the full U.S. rates.

Tort Liability

A corporation is liable for the torts committed by its agents or officers within the course and scope of their employment. This principle applies to a corporation exactly as it applies to the ordinary agency relationships discussed in Chapter 17. It follows the doctrine of *respondeat superior.*

In the following case, the court had to determine whether the corporate employer of an officer could be liable for his actions.

CASE ANALYSIS

Case 19.1 Belmont v. MB Investment Partners, Inc.

United States Court of Appeals, Third Circuit, 708 F.3d 470 (2013).

IN THE LANGUAGE OF THE COURT
JORDAN, Circuit Judge.
* * * *

[Mark] Bloom formed North Hills [L.P.] in 1997, as an enhanced stock index fund based on various stock indices. Bloom was the sole principal and managing member of North Hills Management, LLC, the general partner of North Hills, and he had sole authority over the selection of the fund's investments. * * * Between 2001 and 2007, Bloom raised approximately $30 million from 40 to 50 investors for the North Hills fund. He claimed that North Hills consistently generated investment returns of 10–15 percent per year without significant risk.

In fact, however, North Hills was a Ponzi scheme that Bloom used to finance his lavish personal lifestyle, and, over time, he diverted at least $20 million from North Hills for his own personal use. Bloom used those funds to acquire multiple apartments and homes, furnishings, luxury cars and boats, and jewelry, and to fund parties and travel.

* * * *

Bloom operated North Hills the entire time that he was an executive of [MB Investment Partners, Inc.] He made no attempt, while working at MB, to conceal his activities related to North Hills. Investments in North Hills were administered by Bloom and other MB personnel, using MB's offices, computers, filing facilities, and office equipment. MB support staff sometimes carried out tasks related to North Hills.

MB officers and directors were aware that Bloom was operating North Hills while he was also working as an investment adviser at MB.

* * * During the period of the North Hills fraud, MB did not have in place basic compliance procedures employed throughout the investment advising industry to identify and prevent fraud and self-dealing by MB employees and affiliates. Compliance weaknesses permitted Bloom to avoid required disclosures to MB about North Hills as a personal investment vehicle. *MB officers and directors failed to make basic inquiries about Bloom's operation of North Hills, and did not collect any information on North Hills or monitor sales of investments in North Hills to MB's own customers.* [Emphasis added.]

* * * *

* * * In 2008, * * * two large investors in North Hills requested a full redemption of their investments. By that time, most of the money that had been invested in North Hills was gone * * * . [Bloom] was arrested on February 25, 2009, and he was terminated by MB that same day.

* * * *

The Investors filed their * * * Complaint in this action on October 28, 2009 * * * , alleging * * * fraud * * * on the part of Bloom * * * and MB.

* * * *

* * * On January 5, 2012, the District Court granted summary judgment to [MB]. * * * On February 17, 2012, the Court entered a default judgment against Bloom and in favor of the Investors in the amount of approximately $5.7 million.

* * * This timely appeal followed.

* * * *

* * * Bloom's violations * * * are beyond dispute, and the Investors argue that those violations may be imputed to MB as his employer.

* * * *The fraud of an officer of a corporation is imputed to the corporation when the officer's fraudulent contact was (1) in the course of his employment, and (2) for the benefit of the corporation.* This is true even if the officer's conduct was unauthorized, effected for his own benefit but clothed with apparent authority of the corporation, or contrary to instructions. The underlying reason is that a corporation can speak and act only through its agents and so must be accountable for any acts committed by one of its agents within his actual or apparent scope of authority and while transacting corporate business. [Emphasis added.]

* * * *

* * * We therefore conclude that imputation may be appropriate in this case, if the Investors can prove that the manner in which Bloom marketed North Hills to them while he was working for MB, and the apparent benefit to MB, made it appear that he marketed North Hills within the scope of his authority as a senior executive of MB.

* * * *

For the foregoing reasons, we * * * will vacate the grant of summary judgment to MB * * * , and we will remand this case for a trial with respect to those claims against MB.

LEGAL REASONING QUESTIONS

1. What is the imputation doctrine? What public-policy reasons support imputing the fraud of a corporate officer to the corporation?

2. What circumstances in this case suggest that MB should be held liable for Bloom's fraud?

3. What conditions did the court place on the application of the imputation doctrine in this case?

4. MB, which was already in financial distress, had to cease operations as a result of Bloom's fraud. How might MB have discovered the fraud before it grew so large as to have such dire effects?

Criminal Acts

Under modern criminal law (see Chapter 7), a corporation may also be held liable for the criminal acts of its agents and employees, provided the punishment is one that can be applied to the corporation. Although corporations cannot be imprisoned, they can be fined. (Of course, corporate directors and officers can be imprisoned, and some have been in recent years.) In addition, under sentencing guidelines for crimes committed by corporate employees (white-collar crimes), corporate lawbreakers can face fines amounting to hundreds of millions of dollars.[1]

▶ **Case in Point 19.1** Brian Gauthier drove a dump truck for Angelo Todesca Corporation. The truck was missing its back-up alarm, but Angelo allowed Gauthier to continue driving it. At a worksite, Gauthier backed up to dump a load and struck and killed a police officer who was directing traffic. The state charged Angelo and Gauthier with the crime of vehicular homicide.

Angelo argued that a corporation could not be guilty of vehicular homicide because it cannot operate a vehicle. The court ruled that if an employee commits a crime "while engaged in corporate business that the employee has been authorized to conduct," the corporation can be held liable for the crime. Hence, the court held that Angelo Todesca Corporation was liable for Gauthier's negligent operation of its truck, which resulted in a person's death.[2] ◀

Classification of Corporations

Corporations can be classified in several ways. The classification of a corporation normally depends on its location, purpose, and ownership characteristics, as described in the following subsections.

DOMESTIC, FOREIGN, AND ALIEN CORPORATIONS A corporation is referred to as a **domestic corporation** by its home state (the state in which it incorporates). A corporation formed in one state but doing business in another is referred to in the second state as a **foreign corporation.** A corporation formed in another country (say, Mexico) but doing business in the United States is referred to in the United States as an **alien corporation.**

A corporation does not have an automatic right to do business in a state other than its state of incorporation. In some instances, it must obtain a *certificate of authority* in any state in which it plans to do business. Once the certificate has been issued, the corporation generally can exercise in that state all of the powers conferred on it by its home state. If a foreign corporation does business in a state without obtaining a certificate of authority, the state can impose substantial fines and sanctions on that corporation.

Note that most state statutes specify certain activities, such as soliciting orders via the Internet, that are not considered "doing business" within the state. Thus, a foreign corporation normally does not need a certificate of authority to sell goods or services via the Internet or by mail.

PUBLIC AND PRIVATE CORPORATIONS A **public corporation** is a corporation formed by the government to meet some political or governmental purpose. Cities and towns that incorporate are common examples. In addition, many federal government organizations, such as the U.S. Postal Service, the Tennessee Valley Authority, and AMTRAK, are public corporations.

Note that a public corporation is not the same as a *publicly held* corporation. A **publicly held corporation** (often called a *public company*) is any corporation whose shares are publicly traded in a securities market, such as the New York Stock Exchange or the NASDAQ (an electronic stock exchange founded by the National Association of Securities Dealers).

In contrast to public corporations (*not* public companies), private corporations are created either wholly or in part for private benefit—that is, for profit. Most corporations are private. Although they may serve a public purpose, as a public electric or gas utility does, they are owned by private persons rather than by a government.[3]

NONPROFIT CORPORATIONS Corporations formed for purposes other than making a profit are called *nonprofit* or *not-for-profit* corporations. Private hospitals, educational institutions, charities, and religious organizations, for example, are frequently organized as nonprofit corporations. The nonprofit corporation is a convenient form of organization that allows various groups to own property and to form contracts without exposing the individual members to personal liability.

CLOSE CORPORATIONS Most corporate enterprises in the United States fall into the category of close corporations. A **close corporation** is one whose shares are held by members of a family or by relatively few persons. Close corporations are also referred to as *closely held, family,* or *privately held* corporations. Usually, the members of the small group constituting the shareholders of a close corporation are personally known to each other. Because the number of shareholders is so small, there is no trading market for the shares.

---

1. Note that the Sarbanes-Oxley Act of 2002 (see Chapter 8) stiffened the penalties for certain types of corporate crime and ordered the U.S. Sentencing Commission to revise the sentencing guidelines accordingly.
2. *Commonwealth v. Angelo Todesca Corp.*, 446 Mass. 128, 842 N.E.2d 930 (2006).
3. The United States Supreme Court first recognized the property rights of private corporations and clarified the distinction between public and private corporations in the landmark case *Trustees of Dartmouth College v. Woodward*, 17 U.S. (4 Wheaton) 518, 4 L.Ed. 629 (1819).

In practice, a close corporation is often operated like a partnership. Some states have enacted special statutory provisions that apply to these corporations and allow them to depart significantly from certain formalities required by traditional corporation law.[4]

Additionally, the RMBCA gives a close corporation considerable flexibility in determining its rules of operation [RMBCA 7.32]. If all of a corporation's shareholders agree in writing, the corporation can operate without directors and bylaws. In addition, the corporation can operate without annual or special shareholders' or directors' meetings, stock certificates, or formal records of shareholders' or directors' decisions.[5]

Management of Close Corporations.

Management of a close corporation resembles that of a sole proprietorship or a partnership, in that a single shareholder or a tightly knit group of shareholders usually hold the positions of directors and officers. As a corporation, however, the firm must meet all specific legal requirements set forth in state statutes.

To prevent a majority shareholder from dominating the company, a close corporation may require that more than a simple majority of the directors approve any action taken by the board. Typically, this would apply only to extraordinary actions, such as changing the amount of dividends or dismissing an employee-shareholder, and not to ordinary business decisions.

Transfer of Shares in Close Corporations.

By definition, a close corporation has a small number of shareholders. Thus, the transfer of one shareholder's shares to someone else can cause serious management problems. The other shareholders may find themselves required to share control with someone they do not know or like.

▶ **Example 19.2** Three brothers, Terry, Damon, and Henry Johnson, are the only shareholders of Johnson's Car Wash, Inc. Terry and Damon do not want Henry to sell his shares to an unknown third person. To avoid this situation, the corporation could restrict the transferability of shares to outside persons. Shareholders could be required to offer their shares to the corporation or the other shareholders before selling them to an outside purchaser. ◀

In fact, a few states have statutes that prohibit the transfer of close corporation shares unless certain persons—including shareholders, family members, and the corporation—are first given the opportunity to purchase the shares for the same price.

Control of a close corporation can also be stabilized through the use of a *shareholder agreement*. A shareholder agreement can provide for proportional control when one of the original shareholders dies. The decedent's shares of stock in the corporation would be divided in such a way that the proportionate holdings of the survivors, and thus their proportionate control, would be maintained.

Agreements between shareholders can also restrict the transfer of a close corporation's stock in other ways. For instance, shareholders might agree that existing shareholders will have an option to purchase stock before it is sold or transferred to an outside party.

Misappropriation of Close Corporation Funds.

Sometimes, a majority shareholder in a close corporation takes advantage of his or her position and misappropriates company funds. In such situations, the normal remedy for the injured minority shareholders is to have their shares appraised and to be paid the fair market value for them.

▶ **Case in Point 19.3** John Murray, Stephen Hopkins, and Paul Ryan were officers, directors, employees, and majority shareholders of Olympic Adhesives, Inc. Merek Rubin was a minority shareholder. Murray, Hopkins, and Ryan were paid salaries. Twice a year, Murray, Hopkins, and Ryan paid themselves additional compensation—between 75 and 98 percent of Olympic's net profits. Rubin filed a suit against the majority shareholders, alleging that their compensation deprived him of his share of Olympic's profits. The court explained that a salary should reasonably relate to a corporate officer's ability and the quantity and quality of his or her services. Profits resulting from an officer's performance may also affect the amount of compensation. In this case, the court found that a reasonable amount of compensation would have been 10 percent of Olympic's average annual net sales. This was comparable to the average compensation for officers in similar firms.[6] ◀

S CORPORATIONS

A close corporation that meets the qualifying requirements specified in Subchapter S of the Internal Revenue Code can choose to operate as an **S corporation.** (A corporation will automatically be taxed under Subchapter C unless it elects S corporation status.) If a corporation has S corporation status, it can avoid the imposition of income taxes at the

---

4. For example, in some states (such as Maryland), a close corporation need not have a board of directors.

5. Shareholders cannot agree, however, to eliminate certain rights of shareholders, such as the right to inspect corporate books and records or the right to bring *derivative actions* (see page 417).

6. *Rubin v. Murray*, 79 Mass.App.Ct. 64, 943 N.E.2d 949 (2011).

corporate level while retaining many of the advantages of a corporation, particularly limited liability.

Important Requirements. Among the numerous requirements for S corporation status, the following are the most important:

1. The corporation must be a domestic corporation.
2. The corporation must not be a member of an affiliated group of corporations.
3. The shareholders of the corporation must be individuals, estates, or certain trusts and tax-exempt organizations.
4. The corporation must have no more than one hundred shareholders.
5. The corporation must have only one class of stock, although all shareholders do not need to have the same voting rights.
6. No shareholder of the corporation may be a non-resident alien.

Effect of S Election. An S corporation is treated differently than a regular corporation for tax purposes. An S corporation is taxed like a partnership, so the corporate income passes through to the shareholders, who pay personal income tax on it. This treatment enables the S corporation to avoid the double taxation imposed on regular corporations.

In addition, the shareholders' tax brackets may be lower than the tax bracket that the corporation would have been in if the tax had been imposed at the corporate level. The resulting tax saving is particularly attractive when the corporation wants to accumulate earnings for some future business purpose. If the corporation has losses, the S election allows the shareholders to use the losses to offset other income. Nevertheless, because the limited liability company (see Chapter 18) offers similar tax advantages and greater flexibility, the S corporation has lost much of its appeal.

PROFESSIONAL CORPORATIONS Professionals such as physicians, lawyers, dentists, and accountants can incorporate. Professional corporations are typically identified by the letters *P.C.* (professional corporation), *S.C.* (service corporation), or *P.A.* (professional association).

In general, the laws governing the formation and operation of professional corporations are similar to those governing ordinary business corporations. There are some differences in terms of liability, however, because the shareholder-owners are professionals who are held to a higher standard of conduct.

For liability purposes, some courts treat a professional corporation somewhat like a partnership and hold each professional liable for any malpractice committed within the scope of the business by the others in the firm. With the exception of malpractice or a breach of duty to clients or patients, a shareholder in a professional corporation generally cannot be held liable for the torts committed by other professionals at the firm.

BENEFIT CORPORATIONS A growing number of states have enacted legislation that creates a new corporate form called a *benefit corporation*. A **benefit corporation** is a for-profit corporation that seeks to have a material positive impact on society and the environment. Benefit corporations differ from traditional corporations in the following three ways:

1. *Purpose.* Although the corporation is designed to make a profit, its purpose is to benefit the public as a whole (rather than just to provide long-term shareholder value, as in ordinary corporations). The directors of a benefit corporation must, during the decision-making process, consider the impact of their decisions on society and the environment.
2. *Accountability.* Shareholders of a benefit corporation determine whether the company has achieved a material positive impact. Shareholders also have a right of private action, called a *benefit enforcement proceeding*, enabling them to sue the corporation if it fails to pursue or create public benefit.
3. *Transparency.* A benefit corporation must issue an annual benefit report on its overall social and environmental performance that uses a recognized third-party standard to assess its performance. The report must be delivered to the shareholders and posted on a public Web site.

SECTION 2
CORPORATE FORMATION AND POWERS

Many Fortune 500 companies started as sole proprietorships or partnerships and then converted to corporate entities as the businesses grew and needed to obtain additional capital by issuing shares of stock. Incorporating a business is much simpler today than it was twenty years ago, and many states allow businesses to incorporate via the Internet. Here, we examine the process by which a corporation comes into existence.

Promotional Activities

In the past, preliminary steps were taken to organize and promote the business prior to incorporating. Contracts were made with investors and others on behalf of the future corporation. Today, due to the relative ease of forming a corporation in most states, persons incorporating their business rarely, if ever, engage in preliminary promotional activities.

Nevertheless, it is important for businesspersons to understand that they are personally liable for all preincorporation contracts made with investors, accountants, or others on behalf of the future corporation. Personal liability continues until the newly formed corporation assumes liability for the preincorporation contracts through a *novation* (see Chapter 13).

▶ **Example 19.4** Jade Sorrel contracts with an accountant, Ray Cooper, to provide tax advice for a proposed corporation, Blackstone, Inc. Cooper provides the services to Sorrel, knowing that the corporation has not yet been formed. Once Blackstone, Inc., is formed, Cooper sends an invoice to the corporation and to Sorrel personally, but the bill is not paid. Because Sorrel is personally liable for the preincorporation contract, Cooper can sue Sorrel for breach of the contract. Cooper cannot seek to hold Blackstone, Inc., liable unless he has entered into a contract with the corporation through a novation. ◀

Incorporation Procedures

Exact procedures for incorporation differ among states, but the basic steps are as follows: (1) select a state of incorporation, (2) secure the corporate name, (3) prepare the articles of incorporation, and (4) file the articles of incorporation with the secretary of state. These steps are discussed in more detail in the following subsections.

SELECT THE STATE OF INCORPORATION The first step in the incorporation process is to select a state in which to incorporate. Because state laws differ, individuals may look for the states that offer the most advantageous tax or incorporation provisions. Another consideration is the fee that a particular state charges to incorporate, as well as the annual fees and the fees for specific transactions (such as stock transfers).

Delaware has historically had the least restrictive laws and provisions that favor corporate management. Consequently, many corporations, including a number of the largest, have incorporated there. Delaware's statutes permit firms to incorporate in that state and conduct business and locate their operating headquarters elsewhere. Most other states now permit this as well.

Note, though, that close corporations, particularly those of a professional nature, generally incorporate in the state where their principal shareholders live and work. For reasons of convenience and cost, businesses often choose to incorporate in the state in which most of the corporation's business will be conducted.

SECURE THE CORPORATE NAME The choice of a corporate name is subject to state approval to ensure against duplication or deception. State statutes usually require that the secretary of state run a check on the proposed name in the state of incorporation.

Some states require that the persons incorporating a firm run a check on the proposed name at their own expense. A check can often be made via the Internet. If a firm is likely to do business in other states—or over the Internet—the incorporators should check existing corporate names in those states as well.

Once cleared, a name can be reserved for a short time, for a fee, pending the completion of the articles of incorporation. All states require the corporation's name to include the word *Corporation (Corp.)*, *Incorporated (Inc.)*, *Company (Co.)*, or *Limited (Ltd.)*.[7]

First Check Available Domain Names. All corporations need to have an online presence to compete effectively in today's business climate. The corporate name should be one that can be used as the business's Internet domain name. Therefore, it is advisable to check what domain names are available *before* securing a corporate name with the state.

Incorporators can do this by going to one of the many companies that issue domain names, such as Network Solutions (**www.whois.com/whois**), and finding out if the preferred name is available. If another business is using that name, the incorporators can select an alternative name that can be used as the business's URL, and then seek approval from the state for the name.

---

7. Failure to use one of these abbreviations to disclose corporate status may be grounds for holding an individual incorporator liable for corporate contracts under agency law (see Chapter 17).

Trade Name Disputes. A new corporation's name cannot be the same as (or deceptively similar to) the name of an existing corporation doing business within the same state. If a firm does business under a name that is the same as or deceptively similar to an existing company's name, it may be liable for trade name infringement (see Chapter 5).

▶ **Example 19.5** An existing corporation is named Digital Synergy, Inc. The state is not likely to allow a new corporation to use the name Digital Synergy Company. That name is deceptively similar to the first and could cause confusion. The use of too similar a name could also transfer part of the goodwill established by the first corporate user to the second, thus infringing on the first company's trademark rights. ◀

PREPARE THE ARTICLES OF INCORPORATION The primary document needed to incorporate a business is the **articles of incorporation.** The articles include basic information about the corporation and serve as a primary source of authority for its future organization and business functions. The person or persons who execute (sign) the articles are the *incorporators*.

Generally, the articles of incorporation *must* include the following information [RMBCA 2.02].

1. The name of the corporation.
2. The number of shares the corporation is authorized to issue.
3. The name and street address of the corporation's initial registered agent and registered office.
4. The name and address of each incorporator.

In addition, the articles *may* set forth other information, such as the names and addresses of the initial members of the board of directors, and the duration and purpose of the corporation.

Articles of incorporation vary widely depending on the jurisdiction and the size and type of the corporation. Frequently, the articles do not provide much detail about the firm's operations, which are spelled out in the company's **bylaws** (internal rules of management adopted by the corporation at its first organizational meeting).

Shares of the Corporation. The articles must specify the number of shares of stock the corporation is authorized to issue [RMBCA 2.02(a)]. For instance, a company might state that the aggregate number of shares that the corporation has the authority to is-

sue is five thousand. Large corporations often state a par value for each share, such as $.20 per share, and specify the various types or classes of stock authorized for issuance.

Sometimes, the articles set forth the capital structure of the corporation and other relevant information. To allow for the raising of additional capital in the future, the articles of incorporation often authorize many more shares of stock than will initially be issued.

Registered Office and Agent. The corporation must indicate the location and street address of its registered office within the state. Usually, the registered office is also the principal office of the corporation.

The corporation must also give the name and address of a specific person who has been designated as an *agent*. The registered agent is the person who can receive legal documents (such as orders to appear in court) on behalf of the corporation.

Incorporators. Each incorporator must be listed by name and address. The incorporators need not have any interest at all in the corporation, and sometimes signing the articles is their only duty. Many states do not have residency or age requirements for incorporators. It can be as few as one or as many as three. Incorporators frequently participate in the first organizational meeting of the corporation.

Duration and Purpose. A corporation has perpetual existence unless the articles state otherwise. The RMBCA does not require a specific statement of purpose to be included in the articles. A corporation can be formed for any lawful purpose.

Some incorporators choose to specify the intended business activities (such as "to engage in the production and sale of agricultural products"). It is increasingly common, though, for the articles to include only a general statement of purpose. The articles may indicate that the corporation is organized for "any legal business." By not mentioning specifics, the corporation avoids the need for future amendments to the corporate articles [RMBCA 2.02(b)(2)(i), 3.01].

Internal Organization. The articles can describe the corporation's internal management structure, although this usually is included in the bylaws adopted after the corporation is formed. The articles of incorporation commence the corporation, whereas the bylaws are formed after commencement by the board of directors.

Bylaws cannot conflict with the incorporation statute or the articles of incorporation [RMBCA 2.06].

Under the RMBCA, shareholders may amend or repeal the bylaws. The board of directors may also amend or repeal the bylaws unless the articles of incorporation or state statutory provisions reserve this power to the shareholders exclusively [RMBCA 10.20].

The bylaws typically describe such matters as voting requirements for shareholders, the election of the board of directors, and the methods of replacing directors. Bylaws also frequently outline the manner and time of holding shareholders' and board meetings.

FILE THE ARTICLES WITH THE STATE Once the articles of incorporation have been prepared and signed, they are sent to the appropriate state official, usually the secretary of state, along with the required filing fee. In most states, the secretary of state then stamps the articles "Filed" and returns a copy of the articles to the incorporators. Once this occurs, the corporation officially exists.

First Organizational Meeting to Adopt Bylaws

After incorporation, the first organizational meeting must be held. Usually, the most important function of this meeting is the adoption of bylaws, which, as mentioned, are the internal rules of management for the corporation. If the articles of incorporation named the initial board of directors, then the directors, by majority vote, call the meeting to adopt the bylaws and complete the company's organization.

If the articles did not name the directors (as is typical), then the incorporators hold the meeting to elect the directors and adopt bylaws. The incorporators may also complete the routine business of incorporation (such as authorizing the issuance of shares and hiring employees) at this meeting. The business transacted depends on the requirements of the state's corporation statute, the nature of the corporation, the provisions made in the articles, and the desires of the incorporators.

Improper Incorporation

The procedures for incorporation are very specific. If they are not followed precisely, others may be able to challenge the existence of the corporation. Errors in incorporation procedures can become important when, for instance, a third party who is attempting to enforce a contract or bring a suit for a tort injury learns of them.

DE JURE CORPORATIONS If a corporation has substantially complied with all conditions precedent to incorporation, the corporation is said to have _de jure_ (rightful and lawful) existence. In most states and under RMBCA 2.03(b), the secretary of state's filing of the articles of incorporation is conclusive proof that all mandatory statutory provisions have been met [RMBCA 2.03(b)].

Sometimes, the incorporators fail to comply with all statutory mandates. If the defect is minor, such as an incorrect address listed on the articles of incorporation, most courts will overlook the defect and find that a corporation (_de jure_) exists.

DE FACTO CORPORATIONS If the defect in formation is substantial, however, such as a corporation's failure to hold an organizational meeting to adopt bylaws, the outcome will vary depending on the jurisdiction. Some states, including Mississippi, New York, Ohio, and Oklahoma, still recognize the common law doctrine of _de facto_ corporation.[8] In those states, the courts will treat a corporation as a legal corporation despite the defect in its formation if the following three requirements are met:

1. A state statute exists under which the corporation can be validly incorporated.
2. The parties have made a good faith attempt to comply with the statute.
3. The parties have already undertaken to do business as a corporation.

Many state courts, however, have interpreted their states' version of the RMBCA as abolishing the common law doctrine of _de facto_ corporations. These states include Alaska, Arizona, Minnesota, New Mexico, Oregon, South Dakota, Tennessee, Utah, and Washington, as well as the District of Columbia. In those jurisdictions, if there is a substantial defect in complying with the incorporation statute, the corporation does not legally exist, and the incorporators are personally liable.

Corporation by Estoppel

Sometimes, a business association holds itself out to others as being a corporation when it has made no attempt to incorporate. In those situations, the firm

---

8. See, for example, _In re Hausman,_ 13 N.Y.3d 408, 921 N.E.2d 191, 893 N.Y.S.2d 499 (2009).

normally will be estopped (prevented) from denying corporate status in a lawsuit by a third party. The estoppel doctrine most commonly applies when a third party contracts with an entity that claims to be a corporation but has not filed articles of incorporation. It may also apply when a third party contracts with a person claiming to be an agent of a corporation that does not in fact exist.

When justice requires, courts in some states will treat an alleged corporation as if it were an actual corporation for the purpose of determining the rights and liabilities in particular circumstances.[9] Recognition of corporate status does not extend beyond the resolution of the problem at hand.

▶ **Case in Point 19.6** W.P. Media, Inc., and Alabama MBA, Inc., agreed to form a wireless Internet services company. W.P. Media was to create a wireless network, and Alabama MBA was to contribute the capital. Hugh Brown signed the parties' contract on behalf of Alabama MBA as the chair of its board. At the time, however, Alabama MBA's articles of incorporation had not yet been filed. Brown filed the articles of incorporation the following year. Later, Brown and Alabama MBA filed a suit alleging that W.P. Media had breached their contract by not building the wireless network. The Supreme Court of Alabama held that because W.P. Media had treated Alabama MBA as a corporation, W.P. Media was estopped from denying Alabama MBA's corporate existence.[10] ◀

Corporate Powers

Under modern law, a corporation generally can engage in any act and enter into any contract available to a natural person in order to accomplish the purposes for which it was formed. When a corporation is created, the express and implied powers necessary to achieve its purpose also come into existence.

EXPRESS POWERS The express powers of a corporation are found in its articles of incorporation, in the law of the state of incorporation, and in the state and federal constitutions. Corporate bylaws and the resolutions of the corporation's board of directors also establish the express powers of the corporation. Because state corporation statutes frequently provide

default rules that apply if the company's bylaws are silent on an issue, it is important that the bylaws set forth the specific operating rules of the corporation. In addition, after the bylaws are adopted, the corporation's board of directors will pass resolutions that also grant or restrict corporate powers.

The following order of priority is used if a conflict arises among the various documents involving a corporation:

1. The U.S. Constitution.
2. State constitutions.
3. State statutes.
4. The articles of incorporation.
5. Bylaws.
6. Resolutions of the board of directors.

IMPLIED POWERS When a corporation is created, certain implied powers arise. In the absence of express constitutional, statutory, or other prohibitions, the corporation has the implied power to perform all acts reasonably necessary to accomplish its corporate purposes. For this reason, a corporation has the implied power to borrow funds within certain limits, lend funds, and extend credit to those with whom it has a legal or contractual relationship.

To borrow funds, the corporation acts through its board of directors to authorize the loan. Most often, the president or chief executive officer of the corporation will execute the necessary documents on behalf of the corporation. Corporate officers such as these have the implied power to bind the corporation in matters directly connected with the *ordinary* business affairs of the enterprise.

There is a limit to what a corporate officer can do, though. A corporate officer does not have the authority to bind the corporation to an action that will greatly affect the corporate purpose or undertaking, such as the sale of substantial corporate assets.

THE *ULTRA VIRES* DOCTRINE The term ***ultra vires*** means "beyond the power." In corporate law, acts of a corporation that are beyond its express or implied powers are *ultra vires* acts.

When a Corporation's Actions Exceed Its Stated Purpose. In the past, most cases dealing with *ultra vires* acts involved contracts made for unauthorized purposes. Now, however, most private corporations are organized for "any legal business" and do not state a specific purpose, so the *ultra vires* doctrine has declined in importance.

---

9. Some states have expressly rejected the common law theory of corporation by estoppel, finding that it is inconsistent with their statutory law. Other states have abolished only the doctrines of *de facto* and *de jure* corporations. See, for example, *Stone v. Jetmar Properties, LLC*, 733 N.W.2d 480 (Minn.App. 2007).
10. *Brown v. W.P. Media, Inc.*, 17 So.3d 1167 (2009).

Today, cases that allege *ultra vires* acts usually involve nonprofit corporations or municipal (public) corporations. ▶ **Case in Point 19.7** Four men formed a nonprofit corporation to create the Armenian Genocide Museum & Memorial (AGM&M). The bylaws appointed them as trustees (similar to corporate directors) for life. One of the trustees, Gerard L. Cafesjian, became the chair and president of AGM&M. Eventually, the relationship among the trustees deteriorated, and Cafesjian resigned.

The corporation then brought a suit claiming that Cafesjian had engaged in numerous *ultra vires* acts, self-dealing, and mismanagement. Although the bylaws required an 80 percent affirmative vote of the trustees to take action, Cafesjian had taken many actions without the board's approval. He had also entered into contracts for real estate transactions in which he had a personal interest. Because Cafesjian had taken actions that exceeded his authority and had failed to follow the rules set forth in the bylaws for board meetings, the court ruled that the corporation could go forward with its suit.[11] ◀

Remedies for Ultra Vires Acts. Under Section 3.04 of the RMBCA, the shareholders can seek an injunction from a court to prevent (or stop) the corporation from engaging in *ultra vires* acts. The attorney general in the state of incorporation can also bring an action to obtain an injunction against the *ultra vires* transactions or to seek dissolution of the corporation. The corporation or its shareholders (on behalf of the corporation) can seek damages from the officers and directors who were responsible for the *ultra vires* acts.

SECTION 3
PIERCING THE CORPORATE VEIL

Occasionally, the owners use a corporate entity to perpetrate a fraud, circumvent the law, or in some other way accomplish an illegitimate objective. In these situations, the courts will ignore the corporate structure and **pierce the corporate veil**, exposing the shareholders to personal liability [RMBCA 2.04].

Generally, courts pierce the veil when the corporate privilege is abused for personal benefit or

when the corporate business is treated so carelessly that it is indistinguishable from that of a controlling shareholder. When the facts show that great injustice would result from the use of a corporation to avoid individual responsibility, a court will look behind the corporate structure to the individual shareholders.

Factors That Lead Courts to Pierce the Corporate Veil

The following are some of the factors that frequently cause the courts to pierce the corporate veil:

1. A party is tricked or misled into dealing with the corporation rather than the individual.
2. The corporation is set up never to make a profit or always to be insolvent, or it is too "thinly" capitalized. That is, it has insufficient capital at the time it is formed to meet its prospective debts or potential liabilities.
3. The corporation is formed to evade an existing legal obligation.
4. Statutory corporate formalities, such as holding required corporation meetings, are not followed.
5. Personal and corporate interests are mixed together, or **commingled,** to such an extent that the corporation has no separate identity.

Although state corporation codes usually do not prohibit a shareholder from lending funds to her or his corporation, courts will scrutinize the transaction closely if the loan comes from an officer, director, or majority shareholder. Loans from persons who control the corporation must be made in good faith and for fair value.

A Potential Problem for Close Corporations

The potential for corporate assets to be used for personal benefit is especially great in a close corporation, in which the shares are held by a single person or by only a few individuals, usually family members. In such a situation, the separate status of the corporate entity and the sole shareholder (or family-member shareholders) must be carefully preserved.

Certain practices invite trouble for the one-person or family-owned (close) corporation, including any of the following:

1. The commingling of corporate and personal funds.

11. *Armenian Assembly of America, Inc. v. Cafesjian,* 692 F.Supp.2d 20 (D.C. 2010).

2. The failure to hold board of directors' meetings and record the minutes.
3. The shareholders' continuous personal use of corporate property (for instance, company-owned vehicles).

The Alter-Ego Theory

Sometimes, courts pierce the corporate veil under the theory that the corporation was not operated as a separate entity, but was just another side (or alter ego) of the individual or group that actually controlled the corporation. This is called the *alter-ego theory.* The alter-ego theory is applied when a corporation is so dominated and controlled by an individual or group that the separate identities of the person (or group) and the corporation are no longer distinct. Courts use the alter-ego theory to avoid injustice or fraud that would result if wrongdoers were allowed to hide behind the protection of limited liability.

▶ **Case in Point 19.8** Harvey and Barbara Jacobson owned Aqua Clear Technologies, Inc., which installed and serviced home water-softening systems. The Jacobsons consistently took funds out of the business for their personal expenses, including payments for their home, cars, health-insurance premiums, and credit cards. Three weeks after Aqua filed a bankruptcy petition, Harvey formed another corporation called Discount Water Services, Inc. Discount appropriated Aqua's equipment and inventory (without buying it) and continued to service water-softening systems for Aqua's customers, even using the same phone number. The trustee appointed to Aqua's bankruptcy case sought to recover Aqua's assets on the ground that Discount was Aqua's alter ego. The court ruled that Discount was simply a continuation of Aqua's business (its alter ego) under a new name, and therefore held Discount liable for the claims asserted against Aqua in bankruptcy (totaling $108,732.64).[12] ◀

SECTION 4
DIRECTORS AND OFFICERS

Corporate directors, officers, and shareholders all play different roles within the corporate entity. Sometimes, actions that may benefit the corporation as a whole do not coincide with the separate interests of the individuals making up the corporation. In such situ-

ations, it is important to know the rights and duties of all participants in the corporate enterprise. This section focuses on these rights and duties of directors and officers, as well as the ways in which conflicts among corporate participants are resolved.

The Role of Directors

The board of directors is the ultimate authority in every corporation. Directors have responsibility for all policymaking decisions necessary to the management of all corporate affairs. Additionally, the directors must act as a body in carrying out routine corporate business. The board selects and removes the corporate officers, determines the capital structure of the corporation, and declares dividends. Each director has one vote, and customarily the majority rules. The general areas of responsibility of the board of directors are shown in Exhibit 19–1 on the following page.

Directors are sometimes inappropriately characterized as *agents* because they act on behalf of the corporation. No individual director, however, can act as an agent to bind the corporation. As a group, directors collectively control the corporation in a way that no agent is able to control a principal. In addition, although directors occupy positions of trust and control over the corporation, they are not *trustees* because they do not hold title to property for the use and benefit of others.

Few qualifications are required for directors. Only a handful of states impose minimum age and residency requirements. A director may be a shareholder, but that is not necessary (unless the articles of incorporation or bylaws require ownership interest).

ELECTION OF DIRECTORS Subject to statutory limitations, the number of directors is set forth in the corporation's articles or bylaws. Historically, the minimum number of directors has been three, but today many states permit fewer. Normally, the incorporators appoint the first board of directors at the time the corporation is created, or the directors are named in the articles of incorporation. The initial board serves until the first annual shareholders' meeting. Subsequent directors are elected by a majority vote of the shareholders.

A director usually serves for a term of one year—from annual meeting to annual meeting. Most state statutes permit longer and staggered terms. A common practice is to elect one-third of the board members each year for a three-year term. In this way, there is greater management continuity.

---

12. *In re Aqua Clear Technologies, Inc.,* 361 Bankr. 567 (S.D.Fla. 2007).

EXHIBIT 19-1   Directors' Management Responsibilities

Authorize Major Corporate Policy Decisions	Select and Remove Corporate Officers and Other Managerial Employees, and Determine Their Compensation	Make Financial Decisions
Examples:	*Examples:*	*Examples:*
• Oversee major contract negotiations and management-labor negotiations. • Initiate negotiations on the sale or lease of corporate assets outside the regular course of business. • Decide whether to pursue new product lines or business opportunities.	• Search for and hire corporate executives and determine the elements of their compensation packages, including stock options. • Supervise managerial employees and make decisions regarding their termination.	• Make decisions regarding the issuance of authorized shares and bonds. • Decide when to declare dividends to be paid to shareholders.

Removal of Directors. A director can be removed *for cause*—that is, for failing to perform a required duty—either as specified in the articles or bylaws or by shareholder action. The board of directors may also have the power to remove a director for cause, subject to shareholder review. In most states, a director cannot be removed without cause unless the shareholders have reserved the right to do so at the time of election.

Vacancies on the Board. Vacancies occur on the board if a director dies or resigns or when a new position is created through amendment of the articles or bylaws. In these situations, either the shareholders or the board itself can fill the vacant position, depending on state law or on the provisions of the bylaws.

Note, however, that even when an election appears to be authorized by the bylaws, a court can invalidate the results if the directors were attempting to manipulate the election in order to reduce the shareholders' influence. ▶ **Case in Point 19.9** The bylaws of Liquid Audio, Inc., authorized a board of five directors. Two directors were elected each year. Another company offered to buy all of Liquid Audio's stock, but the board rejected this offer.

To prevent the shareholders from electing new directors who would allow the sale, the directors amended the bylaws. The amendment increased the number of directors to seven, thereby diminishing the shareholders' influence in the upcoming election. The shareholders filed an action challenging the election. The court ruled that the directors' action was illegal because they had attempted to diminish the shareholders' right to vote effectively in an election of directors.[13] ◀

13. *MM Companies, Inc. v. Liquid Audio, Inc.,* 813 A.2d 1118 (Del.Sup.Ct. 2003).

COMPENSATION OF DIRECTORS In the past, corporate directors were rarely compensated. Today, directors are often paid at least nominal sums and may receive more substantial compensation in large corporations because of the time, work, effort, and especially risk involved.

Most states permit the corporate articles or bylaws to authorize compensation for directors. In fact, the Revised Model Business Corporation Act (RMBCA) states that unless the articles or bylaws provide otherwise, the board itself may set the directors' compensation [RMBCA 8.11]. Directors also receive indirect benefits, such as business contacts and prestige, and other rewards, such as stock options.

In many corporations, directors are also chief corporate officers (president or chief executive officer, for example) and receive compensation in their managerial positions. A director who is also an officer of the corporation is referred to as an **inside director**, whereas a director who does not hold a management position is an **outside director.** Typically, a corporation's board of directors includes both inside and outside directors.

BOARD OF DIRECTORS' MEETINGS The board of directors conducts business by holding formal meetings with recorded minutes. The dates of regular meetings are usually established in the articles or bylaws or by board resolution, and ordinarily no further notice is required.

Special meetings can be called, with notice sent to all directors. Most states today allow directors to participate in board of directors' meetings from remote locations via telephone, Web conferencing, or Skype, provided that all the directors can simultaneously hear each other during the meeting [RMBCA 8.20].

Quorum. Unless the articles of incorporation or by-laws specify a greater number, a majority of the board of directors normally constitutes a *quorum* [RMBCA 8.24]. (A **quorum** is the minimum number of members of a body of officials or other group that must be present for business to be validly transacted.) Some state statutes specifically allow corporations to set a quorum at less than a majority but not less than one-third of the directors.[14]

Voting. Once a quorum is present, the directors transact business and vote on issues affecting the corporation. Each director present at the meeting has one vote.[15] Ordinary matters generally require a simple majority vote, but certain extraordinary issues may require a greater-than-majority vote.

COMMITTEES OF THE BOARD OF DIRECTORS When a board of directors has a large number of members and must deal with myriad complex business issues, meetings can become unwieldy. Therefore, the boards of large, publicly held corporations typically create committees of directors and delegate certain tasks to these committees. By focusing on specific subjects, committees can increase the efficiency of the board.

Two common types of committees are the *executive committee* and the *audit committee*. An executive committee handles interim management decisions between board meetings. It is limited to dealing with ordinary business matters, though, and does not have the power to declare dividends, amend the bylaws, or authorize the issuance of stock. The Sarbanes-Oxley Act requires all publicly held corporations to have an audit committee. The audit committee is responsible for the selection, compensation, and oversight of the independent public accountants that audit the firm's financial records.

RIGHTS OF DIRECTORS A corporate director must have certain rights to function properly in that position.

Right to Participation. The *right to participation* means that directors are entitled to participate in all board of directors' meetings and have a right to be notified of these meetings. Because the dates of regular board meetings are usually specified in the bylaws, no notice of these meetings is required. If special meetings are called, however, notice is required unless waived by the director [RMBCA 8.23].

Right of Inspection. A director also has a *right of inspection,* which means that each director can access the corporation's books and records, facilities, and premises. Inspection rights are essential for directors to make informed decisions and to exercise the necessary supervision over corporate officers and employees. This right of inspection is almost absolute and cannot be restricted (by the articles, bylaws, or any act of the board of directors).

Right to Indemnification. When a director becomes involved in litigation by virtue of her or his position or actions, the director may also have a *right to indemnification* (reimbursement) for the legal costs, fees, and damages incurred. Most states allow corporations to indemnify and purchase liability insurance for corporate directors [RMBCA 8.51].

The Role of Corporate Officers

Corporate officers and other executive employees are hired by the board of directors. At a minimum, most corporations have a president, one or more vice presidents, a secretary, and a treasurer. In most states, an individual can hold more than one office, such as president and secretary, and can be both an officer and a director of the corporation.

In addition to carrying out the duties articulated in the bylaws, corporate and managerial officers act as agents of the corporation. Therefore, the ordinary rules of agency (discussed in Chapter 17) normally apply to their employment.

Corporate officers and other high-level managers are employees of the company, so their rights are defined by employment contracts. Nevertheless, the board of directors normally can remove a corporate officer at any time with or without cause. If the directors remove an officer in violation of the terms of an employment contract, however, the corporation may be liable for breach of contract.

For a synopsis of the roles of directors and officers, see *Concept Summary 19.1* on the facing page.

The Duties and Liabilities of Directors and Officers

The duties of corporate directors and officers are similar because both groups are involved in decision making and are in positions of control. Directors and

14. See, for example, Delaware Code Annotated Title 8, Section 141(b); and New York Business Corporation Law Section 707.
15. Except in Louisiana, which allows a director to vote by proxy under certain circumstances.

CONCEPT SUMMARY 19.1
Roles of Directors and Officers

ASPECT	DESCRIPTION
Election of Directors	The incorporators usually appoint the first board of directors. Thereafter, shareholders elect the directors. Directors usually serve a one-year term, although the term can be longer. Few qualifications are required. A director can be a shareholder but is not required to be. Compensation usually is specified in the corporate articles or bylaws.
Board of Directors' Meetings	The board of directors conducts business by holding formal meetings with recorded minutes. The dates of regular meetings are usually established in the corporate articles or bylaws. Special meetings can be called, with notice sent to all directors. Usually, a quorum is a majority of the corporate directors. Once a quorum is present, each director has one vote, and the majority normally rules in ordinary matters.
Rights of Directors	Directors' rights include the rights of participation, inspection, compensation, and indemnification.
Board of Directors' Committees	Directors may appoint committees and delegate some of their responsibilities to the committees and to corporate officers and executives. For example, directors commonly appoint an *executive committee,* which handles ordinary, interim management decisions between board of directors' meetings. Directors may also appoint an *audit committee* to hire and supervise the independent public accountants who audit the corporation's financial records.
Role of Corporate Officers and Executives	The board of directors normally hires the corporate officers and other executive employees. In most states, a person can hold more than one office and can be both an officer and a director of a corporation. The rights of corporate officers and executives are defined by employment contracts.

officers are considered to be fiduciaries of the corporation because their relationship with the corporation and its shareholders is one of trust and confidence. As fiduciaries, directors and officers owe ethical—and legal—duties to the corporation and the shareholders as a whole. These fiduciary duties include the duty of care and the duty of loyalty.

DUTY OF CARE Directors and officers must exercise due care in performing their duties. The standard of *due care* has been variously described in judicial decisions and codified in many state corporation codes. Generally, it requires a director or officer to:

1. Act in good faith (honestly).
2. Exercise the care that an ordinarily prudent (careful) person would exercise in similar circumstances.
3. Do what she or he believes is in the best interests of the corporation [RMBCA 8.30(a), 8.42(a)].

If directors or officers fail to exercise due care and the corporation or its shareholders suffer harm as a result, the directors or officers can be held liable for negligence (unless the *business judgment rule* applies, as will be discussed shortly).

Duty to Make Informed Decisions. Directors and officers are expected to be informed on corporate matters and to conduct a reasonable investigation of the situation before making a decision. This means that they must do what is necessary to be adequately informed: attend meetings and presentations, ask for information from those who have it, read reports, and review other written materials. In other words, directors and officers must investigate, study, and discuss matters and evaluate alternatives before making a decision. They cannot decide on the spur of the moment without adequate research.

Although directors and officers are expected to act in accordance with their own knowledge and training, they are also normally entitled to rely on information given to them by certain other persons. Under the laws of most states and Section 8.30(b) of the RMBCA, such persons include competent officers or employees, professionals such as attorneys and accountants, and committees of the board of directors (on which the director does not serve). The reliance must be in good faith to insulate a director from liability if the information later proves to be inaccurate or unreliable.

Duty to Exercise Reasonable Supervision. Directors are also expected to exercise a reasonable amount of supervision when they delegate work to corporate officers and employees. ▶ **Example 19.10** Dale, a corporate bank director, fails to attend any board of directors' meetings for five years. In addition, Dale never inspects any of the corporate books or records and generally fails to supervise the activities of the bank president and the loan committee. Meanwhile, Brennan, the bank president, who is a corporate officer, makes various improper loans and permits large overdrafts. In this situation, Dale (the corporate director) can be held liable to the corporation for losses resulting from the unsupervised actions of the bank president and the loan committee. ◀

Dissenting Directors. Directors are expected to attend board of directors' meetings, and their votes should be entered into the minutes. Sometimes, an individual director disagrees with the majority's vote (which becomes an act of the board of directors). Unless a dissent is entered in the minutes, the director is presumed to have assented. If the directors are later held liable for mismanagement as a result of a decision, dissenting directors are rarely held individually liable to the corporation. For this reason, a director who is absent from a given meeting sometimes registers a dissent with the secretary of the board regarding actions taken at the meeting.

THE BUSINESS JUDGMENT RULE Directors and officers are expected to exercise due care and to use their best judgment in guiding corporate management, but they are not insurers of business success. Under the **business judgment rule**, a corporate director or officer will not be liable to the corporation or to its shareholders for honest mistakes of judgment and bad business decisions.

Courts give significant deference to the decisions of corporate directors and officers, and consider the reasonableness of a decision at the time it was made, without the benefit of hindsight. Thus, corporate decision makers are not subjected to second-guessing by shareholders or others in the corporation.

Application. The business judgment rule will apply as long as the director or officer:

1. Took reasonable steps to become informed about the matter.
2. Had a rational basis for her or his decision.

3. Did not have a conflict of interest between her or his personal interest and that of the corporation.

Protections. The business judgment rule provides broad protections to corporate decision makers. In fact, unless there is evidence of bad faith, fraud, or a clear breach of fiduciary duties, most courts will apply the rule and protect directors and officers who make bad business decisions from liability for those choices.

▶ **Case in Point 19.11** After a foreign firm announced its intention to acquire Lyondell Chemical Company, Lyondell's directors did nothing to prepare for a possible merger. They failed to research Lyondell's market value and made no attempt to seek out other potential buyers. The $13 billion cash merger was negotiated and finalized in less than a week—and the directors met for only seven hours to discuss it. Shareholders sued, claiming that the directors had breached their fiduciary duties by failing to maximize the sale price of the corporation. The Delaware Supreme Court ruled that the directors were protected by the business judgment rule.[16] ◀

DUTY OF LOYALTY *Loyalty* can be defined as faithfulness to one's obligations and duties. In the corporate context, the duty of loyalty requires directors and officers to subordinate their personal interests to the welfare of the corporation. For instance, a director should not oppose a transaction that is in the corporation's best interest simply because pursuing it may cost the director his or her position.

Directors cannot use corporate funds or confidential corporate information for personal advantage and must refrain from self-dealing. Cases dealing with the duty of loyalty typically involve one or more of the following:

1. Competing with the corporation.
2. Usurping (taking personal advantage of) a corporate opportunity.
3. Pursuing an interest that conflicts with that of the corporation.
4. Using information that is not available to the public to make a profit trading securities (this is called *insider trading*).
5. Authorizing a corporate transaction that is detrimental to minority shareholders.
6. Selling control over the corporation.

The following *Classic Case* illustrates the conflict that can arise between a corporate official's personal interest and his or her duty of loyalty.

---

16. *Lyondell Chemical Co. v. Ryan,* 970 A.2d 235 (Del.Sup. 2009).

CLASSIC CASE 19.2

Guth v. Loft, Inc.
Supreme Court of Delaware, 23 Del.Ch. 255, 5 A.2d 503 (1939).

BACKGROUND AND FACTS   In 1930, Charles Guth became the president of Loft, Inc., a candy-and-restaurant chain. Guth and his family also owned Grace Company, which made syrups for soft drinks. Coca-Cola Company supplied Loft with cola syrup. Unhappy with what he felt was Coca-Cola's high price, Guth entered into an agreement with Roy Megargel to acquire the trademark and formula for Pepsi-Cola and form Pepsi-Cola Corporation. Neither Guth nor Megargel could finance the new venture, however, and Grace Company was insolvent.

Without the knowledge of Loft's board, Guth used Loft's capital, credit, facilities, and employees to further the Pepsi enterprise. At Guth's direction, a Loft employee made the concentrate for the syrup, which was sent to Grace to add sugar and water. Loft charged Grace for the concentrate but allowed forty months' credit. Grace charged Pepsi for the syrup but also granted substantial credit. Grace sold the syrup to Pepsi's customers, including Loft, which paid on delivery or within thirty days. Loft also paid for Pepsi's advertising. Finally, with profits declining as a result of switching from Coca-Cola, Loft filed a suit in a Delaware state court against Guth, Grace, and Pepsi, seeking their Pepsi stock and an accounting. The court entered a judgment in the plaintiff's favor. The defendants appealed to the Delaware Supreme Court.

IN THE LANGUAGE OF THE COURT
LAYTON, Chief Justice, delivering the opinion of the court:

* * * *

Corporate officers and directors are not permitted to use their position of trust and confidence to further their private interests. * * * They stand in a fiduciary relation to the corporation and its stockholders. A public policy, existing through the years, and derived from a profound knowledge of human characteristics and motives, has established *a rule that demands of a corporate officer or director, peremptorily [not open for debate] and inexorably [unavoidably], the most scrupulous observance of his duty, not only affirmatively to protect the interests of the corporation committed to his charge, but also to refrain from doing anything that would work injury to the corporation * * * .* The rule that requires an undivided and unselfish loyalty to the corporation demands that there shall be no conflict between duty and self-interest. [Emphasis added.]

* * * *

* * * *If there is presented to a corporate officer or director a business opportunity which the corporation is financially able to undertake [that] is * * * in the line of the corporation's business and is of practical advantage to it * * * and, by embracing the opportunity, the self-interest of the officer or director will be brought into conflict with that of his corporation, the law will not permit him to seize the opportunity for himself. * * * In such circumstances, * * * the corporation may elect to claim* all of the benefits of the transaction for itself, and the law will impress a trust in favor of the corporation upon the property, interests and profits so acquired. [Emphasis added.]

* * * *

* * * The appellants contend that no conflict of interest between Guth and Loft resulted from his acquirement and exploitation of the Pepsi-Cola opportunity [and] that the acquisition did not place Guth in competition with Loft * * * . [In this case, however,] Guth was Loft, and Guth was Pepsi. He absolutely controlled Loft. His authority over Pepsi was supreme. As Pepsi, he created and controlled the supply of Pepsi-Cola syrup, and he determined the price and the terms. What he offered, as Pepsi, he had the power, as Loft, to accept. Upon any consideration of human characteristics and motives, he created a conflict between self-interest and duty. He made himself the judge in his own cause. * * * Moreover, a reasonable probability of injury to Loft resulted from the situation forced upon it. Guth was in the same position to impose his terms upon Loft as had been the Coca-Cola Company.

* * * The facts and circumstances demonstrate that Guth's appropriation of the Pepsi-Cola opportunity to himself placed him in a competitive position with Loft with respect to

CASE 19.2 CONTINUES ➡

CASE 19.2 CONTINUED a commodity essential to it, thereby rendering his personal interests incompatible with the superior interests of his corporation; and this situation was accomplished, not openly and with his own resources, but secretly and with the money and facilities of the corporation which was committed to his protection.

DECISION AND REMEDY *The Delaware Supreme Court upheld the judgment of the lower court. The state supreme court was "convinced that the opportunity to acquire the Pepsi-Cola trademark and formula, goodwill and business belonged to [Loft], and that Guth, as its President, had no right to appropriate the opportunity to himself."*

WHAT IF THE FACTS WERE DIFFERENT? *Suppose that Loft's board of directors had approved Pepsi-Cola's use of its personnel and equipment. Would the court's decision have been different? Discuss.*

IMPACT OF THIS CASE ON TODAY'S LAW *This early Delaware decision was one of the first to set forth a test for determining when a corporate officer or director has breached the duty of loyalty. The test has two basic parts: Was the opportunity reasonably related to the corporation's line of business, and was the corporation financially able to undertake the opportunity? The court also considered whether the corporation had an interest or expectancy in the opportunity and recognized that when the corporation had "no interest or expectancy, the officer or director is entitled to treat the opportunity as his own."*

CONFLICTS OF INTEREST Corporate directors often have many business affiliations, and a director may sit on the board of more than one corporation. Of course, directors are precluded from entering into or supporting businesses that operate in direct competition with corporations on whose boards they serve. Their fiduciary duty requires them to make a full disclosure of any potential conflicts of interest that might arise in any corporate transaction [RMBCA 8.60].

Sometimes, a corporation enters into a contract or engages in a transaction in which an officer or director has a personal interest. The director or officer must make a *full disclosure* of the nature of the conflicting interest and all facts pertinent to the transaction, and must abstain from voting on the proposed transaction. Otherwise, directors would be prevented from ever having financial dealings with the corporations they serve.

▶ **Example 19.12** Ballo Corporation needs office space. Stephanie Colson, one of its five directors, owns the building adjoining the corporation's headquarters. Colson can negotiate a lease for the space to Ballo if she fully discloses her conflicting interest and any facts known to her about the proposed transaction to Ballo and the other four directors. If the lease arrangement is fair and reasonable, Colson abstains from voting on it, and the other members of the corporation's board of directors unanimously approve it, the contract is valid. ◀

LIABILITY OF DIRECTORS AND OFFICERS Directors and officers are exposed to liability on many fronts. They can be held liable for negligence in certain circumstances, as previously discussed. They may also be held liable for the crimes and torts committed by themselves or by corporate employees under their supervision, as discussed in Chapters 7 and 17. (See this chapter's *Insight into Ethics* on the facing page for a discussion of how one federal statute makes lying a crime.)

Additionally, if shareholders perceive that the corporate directors are not acting in the best interests of the corporation, they may sue the directors, in what is called a *shareholder's derivative suit*, on behalf of the corporation. (This type of action will be discussed later in this chapter, in the context of shareholders' rights.) Directors and officers can also be held personally liable under a number of statutes, such as statutes enacted to protect consumers or the environment.

See *Concept Summary 19.2* on page 412 for a review of the duties and liabilities of directors and officers.

SECTION 5
SHAREHOLDERS

The acquisition of a share of stock makes a person an owner and a shareholder in a corporation. Shareholders thus own the corporation. Although they have no legal title to corporate property, such as buildings and equipment, they do have an equitable (ownership) interest in the firm.

INSIGHT INTO ETHICS
When Is Lying a Federal Crime?

The federal government defines and prosecutes almost 4,500 crimes. In addition to prosecuting defendants for allegedly committing these crimes, the government can also charge them with lying about their actions. Under Section 1001 of Title 18 of the *United States Code,* any person convicted of knowingly and willfully making "any material false, fictitious or fraudulent statements or misrepresentations" can be fined or imprisoned or both. When prosecutors do not have enough evidence to charge someone with the underlying crime, they may still bring charges under Section 1001 if the person made any false statements in interviews.

A Costly Phone Interview

In 2004, attorney Melissa Ann Mahler was interviewed by phone by an official at the Securities and Exchange Commission. She made a false statement about a securities transaction in her personal brokerage account. Ultimately, a court determined that she had violated Section 1001. The court suspended Mahler's attorney's license, sentenced her to two years on probation, fined her $2,500, and ordered her to perform a hundred hours of community service.[a]

Whistling at a Whale Can Be Dangerous

Nancy Black, a marine biologist who operates a whale-watching boat company in California, also ran afoul of Section 1001. When a humpback whale appeared near one of her boats, the captain of the boat whistled at the whale, hoping that the sound would intrigue the whale and cause it to come closer. Regulators investigated whether the whistling constituted harassment of a whale, which is a federal crime.

Prosecutors have not charged Black with whale harassment. Instead, she has been charged with lying about the incident by supplying the regulators with a video that had been edited to delete material that Black thought was not relevant. In an interview, she commented, "I wasn't charged with anything about the dealings with the humpback. So why would they charge me with lying about it? It makes no sense."[b]

What Constitutes a Lie under Section 1001?

The courts have interpreted Section 1001 as encompassing almost any statement made to a federal official. The statement may be oral or in writing. The person making it need not be under oath, and the government does not have to have warned the person that any falsehood could have very serious consequences.

Although the lie has to be "material," any statement that has a "natural tendency to influence, or [is] capable of influencing, the decision of the decision-making body to which it is addressed" is considered material.[c] In other words, the federal government does not have to show that the falsehood actually influenced or misled anyone.

Consider a not-too-far-fetched example. Suppose that you fill out your time sheets at work inaccurately by listing more hours than you actually worked and occasionally complete a time sheet for a day that you did not work. If your employer has to submit employees' time sheets to a federal regulatory agency, you could ultimately be held criminally liable for lying.

LEGAL CRITICAL THINKING

INSIGHT INTO THE SOCIAL ENVIRONMENT
Many businesspersons believe that the federal government's power under Section 1001 is almost without limits. What ethical issues are at stake here?

---

a. *Matter of Mahler,* 94 A.D.3d 114, 939 N.Y.S.2d 900 (2012). See also *In re Simels,* 94 A.D.3d 108, 940 N.Y.S. 2d 577 (2012).

b. " 'Lying' Is a Handy Charge for the U.S. Government," *Wall Street Journal,* April 11, 2012.

c. *United States v. Gaudin,* 515 U.S. 506,115 S.Ct. 2310, 132 L.Ed.2d 444 (1995).

As a general rule, shareholders have no responsibility for the daily management of the corporation, although they are ultimately responsible for choosing the board of directors, which does have such control. Ordinarily, corporate officers and other employees owe no direct duty to individual shareholders (unless some contract or special relationship exists between them in addition to the corporate relationship).

The duty of officers and directors is to act in the best interests of the corporation and its shareholder-owners *as a whole.* In turn, as you will read later in this chapter, controlling shareholders owe a fiduciary duty to minority shareholders.

CONCEPT SUMMARY 19.2
Duties and Liabilities of Directors and Officers

ASPECT	DESCRIPTION
Duties of Directors and Officers	1. *Duty of care*—Directors and officers are obligated to act in good faith, to use prudent business judgment in the conduct of corporate affairs, and to act in the corporation's best interests. If a director or officer fails to exercise this duty of care, he or she may be answerable to the corporation and to the shareholders for breaching the duty. The *business judgment rule* immunizes a director from liability for a corporate decision as long as it was within the power of the corporation and the authority of the director to make and was an informed, reasonable, and loyal decision. 2. *Duty of loyalty*—Directors and officers have a fiduciary duty to subordinate their own interests to those of the corporation in matters relating to the corporation. 3. *Conflicts of interest*—To fulfill their duty of loyalty, directors and officers must make a full disclosure of any potential conflicts between their personal interests and those of the corporation.
Liability of Directors and Officers	Corporate directors and officers are personally liable for their own torts and crimes (when not protected under the business judgment rule). Additionally, they may be held personally liable for the torts and crimes committed by corporate personnel under their direct supervision (see Chapters 4, 7, 17, and 19). They may also be held personally liable for violating certain statutes, such as environmental and consumer protection laws, and can sometimes be sued by shareholders for mismanaging the corporation.

Shareholders' Powers

Shareholders must approve fundamental changes affecting the corporation before the changes can be implemented. Hence, shareholder approval normally is required to amend the articles of incorporation or bylaws, to conduct a merger or dissolve the corporation, and to sell all or substantially all of the corporation's assets. Some of these powers are subject to prior board approval. Shareholder approval may also be requested (though it is not required) for certain other actions, such as to approve an independent auditor.

Shareholders also have the power to vote to elect or remove members of the board of directors. As described earlier, the first board of directors is either named in the articles of incorporation or chosen by the incorporators to serve until the first shareholders' meeting. From that time on, selection and retention of directors are exclusively shareholder functions.

Directors usually serve their full terms. If the shareholders judge them unsatisfactory, they are simply not reelected. Shareholders have the inherent power, however, to remove a director from office *for cause* (breach of duty or misconduct) by a majority vote.[17] As noted earlier in this chapter, some state statutes (and some articles of incorporation) permit removal of directors without cause by the vote of a majority of the shareholders entitled to vote.[18]

Shareholders' Meetings

Shareholders' meetings must occur at least annually. In addition, special meetings can be called to deal with urgent matters.

NOTICE OF MEETINGS   A corporation must notify its shareholders of the date, time, and place of an annual or special shareholders' meeting at least ten days, but not more than sixty days, before the meeting date [RMBCA 7.05].[19] (The date and time of the annual meeting can be specified in the bylaws.) Notice of a special meeting must include a statement of the purpose of the meeting, and business transacted at the meeting is limited to that purpose.

The RMBCA does not specify how the notice must be given (such as by mail, e-mail, or social media), but

---

17. A director can often demand court review of removal for cause, however.

18. Most states allow *cumulative voting* for directors (described later in the chapter). If cumulative voting is authorized, a director may not be removed if the number of votes against removal would be sufficient to elect a director under cumulative voting. See, for example, California Corporations Code Section 303A. See also Section 8.08(c) of the RMBCA.

19. The shareholder can waive the requirement of notice by signing a waiver form [RMBCA 7.06]. A shareholder who does not receive notice but who learns of the meeting and attends without protesting the lack of notice is said to have waived notice by such conduct.

most corporations specify in their bylaws the acceptable methods of notifying shareholders about meetings. Also, some states' incorporation statutes outline the means of notice that a corporation can use in that jurisdiction. For instance, in Alaska, notice may be given in person, by mail, or by fax, e-mail, blog, or Web post—as long as the shareholder has agreed to that electronic method.[20]

PROXIES   It usually is not practical for owners of only a few shares of stock of publicly traded corporations to attend a shareholders' meeting. Therefore, the law allows stockholders to appoint another person as their agent to vote their shares at the meeting. The signed appointment form or electronic transmission authorizing an agent to vote the shares is called a **proxy** (from the Latin *procurare,* meaning "to manage or take care of").

Management often solicits proxies, but any person can do so to concentrate voting power. Groups of shareholders have used proxies as a device for taking over a corporation. Proxies normally are revocable (can be withdrawn), unless they are specifically designated as irrevocable and coupled with an interest. A proxy is coupled with an interest when, for instance, the person receiving the proxies from shareholders has agreed to buy their shares. Under RMBCA 7.22(c), proxies are valid for eleven months, unless the proxy agreement mandates a longer period.

SHAREHOLDER PROPOSALS   When shareholders want to change a company policy, they can put their ideas up for a shareholder vote. They do this by submitting a shareholder proposal to the board of directors and asking the board to include the proposal in the proxy materials that are sent to all shareholders before meetings.

The Securities and Exchange Commission (SEC) regulates the purchase and sale of securities. The SEC has special provisions relating to proxies and shareholder proposals. SEC Rule 14a-8 provides that all shareholders who own stock worth at least $1,000 are eligible to submit proposals for inclusion in corporate proxy materials. The corporation is required to include information on whatever proposals will be considered at the shareholders' meeting along with proxy materials. Only those proposals that relate to significant policy considerations, not ordinary business operations, must be included.

ELECTRONIC PROXY MATERIALS   In the past, corporations had to send large packets of paper documents to shareholders, but today, the SEC requires all publicly held companies to distribute electronic proxy (e-proxy) materials.[21] Although the law requires proxy materials to be posted online, public companies may still choose among several options—including paper documents or a DVD sent by mail—for actually delivering the materials to shareholders.

If a company wishes to distribute proxy materials only via the Internet, it can choose the notice-and-access delivery option. Under this model, the corporation posts the proxy materials on a Web site and notifies the shareholders that the proxy materials are available online. If a shareholder requests paper proxy materials, the company must send them within three business days. Shareholders can permanently elect to receive all future proxy materials on paper or by e-mail with electronic links.

Shareholder Voting

Shareholders exercise ownership control through the power of their votes. Corporate business matters are presented in the form of resolutions, which shareholders vote to approve or disapprove. Unless there is a provision to the contrary, each common shareholder is entitled to one vote per share, although the voting techniques discussed next enhance the power of the shareholder's vote.

The articles of incorporation can exclude or limit voting rights, particularly for certain classes of shares. For instance, owners of preferred shares are usually denied the right to vote [RMBCA 7.21]. If a state statute requires specific voting procedures, the corporation's articles or bylaws must be consistent with the statute.

QUORUM REQUIREMENTS   For shareholders to act during a meeting, a quorum must be present. Generally, a quorum exists when shareholders holding more than 50 percent of the outstanding shares are present, but state laws often permit the articles of incorporation to set higher or lower quorum requirements. In some states, obtaining the unanimous written consent of shareholders is a permissible alternative to holding a shareholders' meeting [RMBCA 7.25].

Once a quorum is present, voting can proceed. A straight majority vote of the shares represented at the meeting is usually required to pass resolutions.
▶ **Example 19.13**   Novo Pictures, Inc., has 10,000

---

20. Alaska Statutes Section 10.06.410 Notice of Shareholders' Meetings.

21. 17 C.F.R. Parts 240, 249, and 274.

outstanding shares of voting stock. Its articles of incorporation set the quorum at 50 percent of outstanding shares and provide that a majority vote of the shares present is necessary to pass ordinary matters. Therefore, for this firm, a quorum of stockholders representing 5,000 outstanding shares must be present to conduct business at the shareholders' meeting. If exactly 5,000 shares are represented at the meeting, a vote of at least 2,501 of those shares is needed to pass a resolution. If 6,000 shares are represented, a vote of 3,001 will be necessary. ◄

At times, more than a simple majority vote will be required either by statute or by the articles of incorporation. Extraordinary corporate matters, such as a merger, a consolidation, or dissolution of the corporation, require a higher percentage (more than a majority) of all corporate shares entitled to vote [RMBCA 7.27].

VOTING LISTS The corporation prepares the voting list before each shareholders' meeting. Ordinarily, only persons whose names appear on the corporation's stockholder records as owners are entitled to vote.[22]

The voting list contains the name and address of each shareholder as shown on the corporate records on a given cutoff date, or *record date*. (Under RMBCA 7.07, the bylaws or board of directors may fix a record date that is as much as seventy days before the meeting.) The voting list also includes the number of voting shares held by each owner. The list is usually kept at the corporate headquarters and must be made available for shareholder inspection [RMBCA 7.20].

CUMULATIVE VOTING Most states permit, and many require, shareholders to elect directors by *cumulative voting,* a voting method designed to allow minority shareholders to be represented on the board of directors.[23]

Formula. With cumulative voting, each shareholder is entitled to a total number of votes equal to the number of board members to be elected multiplied by the number of voting shares that the shareholder owns. The shareholder can cast all of these votes for one candidate or split them among several nominees for director. All nominees stand for election at the same time. When cumulative voting is not required by statute or under the articles, the entire board can be elected by a majority of shares at a shareholders' meeting.

How Cumulative Voting Works. Cumulative voting can best be understood by example. ▶ **Example 19.14** A corporation has 10,000 shares issued and outstanding. The minority shareholders hold 3,000 shares, and the majority shareholders hold the other 7,000 shares. Three members of the board are to be elected. The majority shareholders' nominees are Alvarez, Beasley, and Caravel. The minority shareholders' nominee is Dovrik. Can Dovrik be elected to the board by the minority shareholders?

If cumulative voting is allowed, the answer is yes. The minority shareholders have 9,000 votes among them (the number of directors to be elected times the number of shares, or $3 \times 3,000 = 9,000$ votes). All of these votes can be cast to elect Dovrik. The majority shareholders have 21,000 votes ($3 \times 7,000 = 21,000$ votes), but these votes must be distributed among their three nominees.

The principle of cumulative voting is that no matter how the majority shareholders cast their 21,000 votes, they will not be able to elect all three directors if the minority shareholders cast all of their 9,000 votes for Dovrik, as illustrated in Exhibit 19–2 on the facing page. ◄

SHAREHOLDER VOTING AGREEMENTS Before a shareholders' meeting, a group of shareholders can create a *shareholder voting agreement* by agreeing in writing to vote their shares together in a specified manner. Such agreements usually are held to be valid and enforceable. Nevertheless, corporate managers must be careful that such agreements do not constitute a breach of their fiduciary duties.

▶ **Case in Point 19.15** Several shareholders of Cryo-Cell International, Inc., mounted a proxy contest in an effort to replace the board of directors. Another stockholder, Andrew Filipowski, agreed to support management in exchange for being included in management's slate of directors. The company's chief executive officer, Mercedes Walton, secretly promised Filipowski that if management's slate won, the board of directors would add another board seat to be filled by a Filipowski designee.

After management won the election, Walton prepared to add Filipowski's designee to the board. When the dissident shareholders challenged the elec-

---

22. When the legal owner is deceased, bankrupt, mentally incompetent, or in some other way under a legal disability, his or her vote can be cast by a person designated by law to control and manage that owner's property.

23. See, for example, California Corporations Code Section 708. Some states, such as Nebraska, require cumulative voting in their state constitutions. Under RMBCA 7.28, no cumulative voting rights exist unless the articles of incorporation so provide.

EXHIBIT 19-2 Results of Cumulative Voting

Ballot	Majority Shareholder Votes			Minority Shareholder Votes	Directors Elected
	Alvarez	*Beasley*	*Caravel*	*Dovrik*	
1	10,000	10,000	1,000	9,000	Alvarez, Beasley, Dovrik
2	9,001	9,000	2,999	9,000	Alvarez, Beasley, Dovrik
3	6,000	7,000	8,000	9,000	Beasley, Caravel, Dovrik

tion results, the court held that the board's actions and Walton's secret agreement constituted serious breaches of fiduciary duty that tainted the election. The court therefore ordered a new election to be held.[24] ◀

VOTING TRUST Another voting technique is for shareholders to enter into a *voting trust*. (A shareholder can also appoint a voting agent and vote by proxy, as mentioned previously.) A **voting trust** is an agreement (a trust contract) under which a shareholder assigns the right to vote his or her shares to a trustee, usually for a specified period of time. The trustee is then responsible for voting the shares on behalf of all the shareholders in the trust. The shareholder retains all rights of ownership (for example, the right to receive dividend payments) except the power to vote the shares [RMBCA 7.30].

Rights of Shareholders

Shareholders possess numerous rights. A significant right—the right to vote their shares—has already been discussed. We look at some additional rights of shareholders in the following subsections.

STOCK CERTIFICATES In the past, corporations commonly issued **stock certificates** that evidenced ownership of a specified number of shares in the corporation. Only a few jurisdictions still require physical stock certificates, and shareholders there have the right to demand that the corporation issue certificates (or replace those that were lost or destroyed). Stock is intangible personal property, however, and the ownership right exists independently of the certificate itself.

In most states and under RMBCA 6.26, a board of directors may provide that shares of stock will be uncertificated, or "paperless"—that is, no actual,

---
24. *Portnoy v. Cryo-Cell International, Inc.*, 940 A.2d 43 (Del.Ch. 2008).

physical stock certificates will be issued. When shares are uncertificated, the corporation may be required to send each shareholder a letter or some other form of notice that contains the same information that traditionally appeared on the face of stock certificates. Notice of shareholders' meetings, dividends, and operational and financial reports are all distributed according to the recorded ownership listed in the corporation's books.

PREEMPTIVE RIGHTS Sometimes, the articles of incorporation grant preemptive rights to shareholders. With **preemptive rights,** a shareholder receives a preference over all other purchasers to subscribe to or purchase a prorated share of a new issue of stock. In other words, the shareholder can purchase a percentage of the new shares that is equal to his or her current percentage of ownership in the corporation.

Under RMBCA 6.30, preemptive rights do not exist unless provided for in the articles of incorporation. Generally, preemptive rights apply only to additional, newly issued stock sold for cash, and the preemptive rights must be exercised within a specific time period, which is usually thirty days.

Allow a Shareholder to Maintain Proportionate Interest. Preemptive rights allow each shareholder to maintain her or his proportionate control, voting power, or financial interest in the corporation. ▶ **Example 19.16** Tron Corporation authorizes and issues 1,000 shares of stock, and Omar Loren purchases 100 shares, making him the owner of 10 percent of the company's stock. Subsequently, Tron, by vote of its shareholders, authorizes the issuance of another 1,000 shares (by amending the articles of incorporation). This increases its capital stock to a total of 2,000 shares.

If preemptive rights have been provided, Loren can purchase one additional share of the new stock being issued for each share he already owns—or 100 additional shares. Thus, he will own 200 of the 2,000 shares outstanding, and his relative position as a shareholder will be maintained. If preemptive rights are not provided, his proportionate control and voting power will be diluted from that of a 10 percent shareholder to that of a 5 percent shareholder because the additional 1,000 shares were issued. ◄

Important in Close Corporations. Preemptive rights are most important in close corporations because each shareholder owns a relatively small number of shares but controls a substantial interest in the corporation. Without preemptive rights, it would be possible for a shareholder to lose his or her proportionate control over the firm. Nevertheless, preemptive rights can hinder a corporation from raising capital from new, outside investors who can provide needed expertise as well as capital.

STOCK WARRANTS **Stock warrants** are rights to buy stock at a stated price by a specified date that are given by the company. Usually, when preemptive rights exist and a corporation is issuing additional shares, it gives its shareholders stock warrants. Warrants are often publicly traded on securities exchanges.

DIVIDENDS A **dividend** is a distribution of corporate profits or income *ordered by the directors* and paid to the shareholders in proportion to their respective shares in the corporation. Dividends can be paid in cash, property, stock of the corporation that is paying the dividends, or stock of other corporations.[25]

State laws vary, but each state determines the general circumstances and legal requirements under which dividends are paid. State laws also control the sources of revenue to be used. Only certain funds are legally available for paying dividends. Depending on state law, dividends may be paid from the following sources:

1. *Retained earnings.* All states allow dividends to be paid from the undistributed net profits earned by the corporation, including capital gains from the sale of fixed assets. The undistributed net profits are called *retained earnings.*
2. *Net profits.* A few states allow dividends to be issued from current net profits without regard to deficits in prior years.
3. *Surplus.* A number of states allow dividends to be paid out of any kind of surplus. For instance, earned

surplus is the sum of a company's net profits over a period of time. It increases by the amount of each year's net income after dividend payments. Earned surplus is not extra cash, but shareholder equity. A company's board of directors may choose to pay dividends from the surplus or to use it for some other corporate purpose (such as for acquisitions).

Illegal Dividends. Sometimes, dividends are improperly paid from an unauthorized account, or their payment causes the corporation to become insolvent. Generally, shareholders must return illegal dividends only if they knew that the dividends were illegal when the payment was received (or if the dividends were paid when the corporation was insolvent). Whenever dividends are illegal or improper, the board of directors can be held personally liable for the amount of the payment.

The Directors' Failure to Declare a Dividend. When directors fail to declare a dividend, shareholders can ask a court to compel the directors to meet and declare a dividend. To succeed, the shareholders must show that the directors have acted so unreasonably in withholding the dividend that their conduct is an abuse of their discretion.

Often, a corporation accumulates large cash reserves for a legitimate corporate purpose, such as expansion or research. The mere fact that the firm has sufficient earnings or surplus available to pay a dividend normally is not enough to compel the directors to distribute funds that, in the board's opinion, should not be distributed.[26] The courts are reluctant to interfere with corporate operations and will not compel directors to declare dividends unless abuse of discretion is clearly shown.

INSPECTION RIGHTS Shareholders in a corporation enjoy both common law and statutory inspection rights. The RMBCA provides that every shareholder is entitled to examine specified corporate records, including voting lists [RMBCA 7.20, 16.02]. The shareholder may inspect in person, or an attorney, accountant, or other authorized assistant can do so as the shareholder's agent.

---

25. On one occasion, a distillery declared and paid a dividend in bonded whiskey.

26. A striking exception to this rule was made in *Dodge v. Ford Motor Co.,* 204 Mich. 459, 170 N.W. 668 (1919), when Henry Ford, the president and major stockholder of Ford Motor Company, refused to declare a dividend notwithstanding the firm's large capital surplus. The court, holding that Ford had abused his discretion, ordered the company to declare a dividend.

Proper Purpose. A shareholder only has a right to inspect and copy corporate books and records for a *proper purpose,* however, and the request to inspect must be made in advance. A shareholder who is denied the right of inspection can seek a court order to compel the inspection.

Potential for Abuse. The power of inspection is fraught with potential abuses, and the corporation is allowed to protect itself from them. For instance, a shareholder can properly be denied access to corporate records to prevent harassment or to protect trade secrets or other confidential corporate information.[27] In some states, a shareholder must have held her or his shares for a minimum period of time immediately preceding the demand to inspect or must hold a certain percentage of outstanding shares.

TRANSFER OF SHARES Corporate stock represents an ownership right in intangible personal property. The law generally recognizes the right of an owner to transfer property to another person unless there are valid restrictions on its transferability. Restrictions on the transfer of shares in a close corporation usually are valid.

When shares are transferred, a new entry is made in the corporate stock book to indicate the new owner. Until the corporation is notified and the entry is complete, all rights—including voting rights, notice of shareholders' meetings, and the right to dividend distributions—remain with the current record owner.

RIGHTS ON DISSOLUTION When a corporation is dissolved and its outstanding debts and the claims of its creditors have been satisfied, there may be assets remaining. The remaining assets are distributed to the shareholders in proportion to the percentage of shares owned by each shareholder. The articles of incorporation may provide that certain classes of preferred stock will be given priority. If no class of stock has been given preference in the distribution of assets, all of the stockholders share the remaining assets.

THE SHAREHOLDER'S DERIVATIVE SUIT When the corporation is harmed by the actions of a third party, the directors can bring a lawsuit in the name of the corporation against that party. If the corporate directors fail to bring a lawsuit, shareholders can do so "derivatively" in what is known as a **shareholder's derivative suit.**

Before shareholders can bring a derivative suit, they must submit a written demand to the corporation, asking the board of directors to take appropriate action [RMBCA 7.40]. The directors then have ninety days in which to act. Only if they refuse to do so can the derivative suit go forward.

The right of shareholders to bring a derivative action is especially important when the wrong suffered by the corporation results from the actions of the corporate directors and officers. For obvious reasons, the directors and officers would probably be unwilling to take any action against themselves.

Nevertheless, a court will dismiss a derivative suit if a majority of the directors or an independent panel determines in good faith that the lawsuit is not in the best interests of the corporation [RMBCA 7.44].

When shareholders bring a derivative suit, they are not pursuing rights or benefits for themselves personally but are acting as guardians of the corporate entity. Therefore, if the suit is successful, any damages recovered normally go into the corporation's treasury, not to the shareholders personally.[28]

In the following case, the court had to decide whether the shareholder could bring an individual claim rather than a derivative suit.

---

27. See, for example, *Disney v. Walt Disney Co.,* 857 A.2d 444 (Del.Ch. 2004).

28. The shareholders may be entitled to reimbursement for reasonable expenses of the derivative lawsuit, including attorneys' fees.

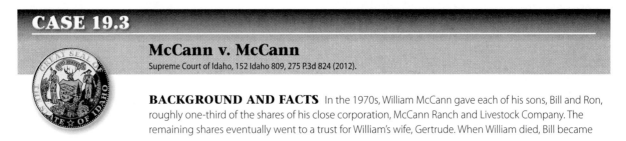

CASE 19.3

McCann v. McCann
Supreme Court of Idaho, 152 Idaho 809, 275 P.3d 824 (2012).

BACKGROUND AND FACTS In the 1970s, William McCann gave each of his sons, Bill and Ron, roughly one-third of the shares of his close corporation, McCann Ranch and Livestock Company. The remaining shares eventually went to a trust for William's wife, Gertrude. When William died, Bill became

CASE 19.3 CONTINUES ▶

CASE 19.3 CONTINUED the corporation's president and chief executive officer. McCann Ranch went to great lengths to provide for Gertrude, giving her about 75 percent of its net income. Bill also received a raise, and soon afterward he began making payments to Gertrude's account. In 2008, Ron filed a direct (nonderivative) lawsuit alleging that the corporation's directors had breached the fiduciary duty they owed him as a minority shareholder. According to the complaint, the directors subjected Ron to a "squeeze-out" designed to deprive him of the benefits of being a shareholder. Ron claimed that the directors refused to give him a corporate job or board membership, failed to pay him dividends, and deprived him of other income through a series of business decisions that benefited only Bill and Gertrude. The district court granted judgment for the defendants, finding that Ron had essentially filed a derivative suit without making a written demand on the corporation. Ron appealed.

IN THE LANGUAGE OF THE COURT
BURDICK, Chief Justice.

* * * *

* * * "In Idaho a director has a fiduciary responsibility to both the corporation and to shareholders." * * *

* * * *

"A well-recognized exception to the rule that a shareholder must bring a derivative action for claims alleging injury to the corporation is that in a [close] corporation a minority shareholder may bring a direct action, rather than a derivative action, if the shareholder alleges harm to himself distinct from that suffered by other shareholders of the corporation or breach of a special duty owed by the defendant to the shareholder." [Emphasis added.]

* * * *

* * * Ron alleges that the Respondents engaged in a squeeze-out by: (1) not paying dividends despite sufficient cash flow; (2) not providing corporate employment to Ron; (3) not providing board membership to Ron; (4) authorizing phony transactions to Gertrude to avoid any benefit to Ron; (5) frustrating the intent of the founder of the Corporation to provide an actual financial benefit to Ron; and (6) making management decisions that allow all of the cash flow to be obtained solely for the benefit of Bill and Gertrude at the expense of Ron.

* * * *

Many of the actions undertaken by the Corporation, in and of themselves, are legitimate uses of corporate power and discretion. Regardless of his ownership interest, Ron is not entitled to a seat on the board of directors. Nor is he entitled to corporate employment. Nor is there evidence he is entitled to a dividend. By themselves, any payments from the Corporation do not harm Ron any more than they harm the other shareholders. However, they may be used as facts to support a squeeze-out.

* * * *

In this light, the actions of the Corporation and its directors have an effect on Ron above and beyond the effect of every other shareholder. Each of these transactions hurts Ron specifically.

The Corporation went to great lengths to provide Gertrude with the money she needed. However, because the Corporation did not use an alternate and less harmful means of providing for Gertrude, it may be argued that the transactions were not made in good faith. The Corporation could have issued a dividend that would benefit all shareholders. Instead, Ron lost his voice in corporate decisions, his corporate employment, and received no meaningful benefit from his ownership stake.

DECISION AND REMEDY *The Idaho Supreme Court held that Ron could bring a direct suit alleging that the corporation's directors had breached their fiduciary duty. It therefore reversed the district court's decision, granting judgment to the defendants.*

THE ETHICAL DIMENSION *If this case proceeds to trial, how might the directors try to defend their decisions? What rule concerning director liability might protect them? Explain your answer.*

THE LEGAL ENVIRONMENT DIMENSION *Can Ron initiate an action to dissolve the McCann Ranch corporation? Why or why not?*

Liabilities of Shareholders

One of the hallmarks of the corporate form of organization is that shareholders are not personally liable for the debts of the corporation. If the corporation fails, the shareholders can lose their investments, but that generally is the limit of their liability. As discussed earlier in this chapter, in certain instances of fraud, undercapitalization, or careless observance of corporate formalities, a court will pierce the corporate veil (disregard the corporate entity) and hold the shareholders individually liable. But these situations are the exception, not the rule.

A shareholder can also be personally liable in certain other rare instances. One relates to illegal dividends, which were discussed previously. Another relates to *watered stock*. Still another concerns the duties majority shareholders owe to minority shareholders.

WATERED STOCK When a corporation issues shares for less than their fair market value, the shares are referred to as **watered stock**.[29] Usually, the shareholder who receives watered stock must pay the difference to the corporation (the shareholder is personally liable). In some states, the shareholder who receives watered stock may be liable to creditors of the corporation for unpaid corporate debts.

▶ **Example 19.17** During the formation of a corporation, Gomez, one of the incorporators, transfers his property, Sunset Beach, to the corporation for 10,000 shares of stock at a par value of $100 per share for a total price of $1 million. After the property is transferred and the shares are issued, Sunset Beach is carried on the corporate books at a value of $1 million.

On appraisal, it is discovered that the market value of the property at the time of transfer was only $500,000. The shares issued to Gomez are therefore watered stock, and he is liable to the corporation for the difference between the value of the shares and the value of the property. ◀

MAJORITY SHAREHOLDERS In some instances, a majority shareholder is regarded as having a fiduciary duty to the corporation and to the minority shareholders. This duty occurs when a single shareholder (or a few shareholders acting in concert) owns a suf-

ficient number of shares to exercise *de facto* (actual) control over the corporation. In these situations, the majority shareholder owes a fiduciary duty to the minority shareholders.

When a majority shareholder breaches her or his fiduciary duty to a minority shareholder, the minority shareholder can sue for damages. A breach of fiduciary duties by those who control a close corporation normally constitutes what is known as *oppressive conduct*. A common example of a breach of fiduciary duty occurs when the majority shareholders "freeze out" the minority shareholders and exclude them from certain benefits of participating in the firm.

▶ **Case in Point 19.18** Brodie, Jordan, and Barbuto formed a close corporation to operate a machine shop. Each owned one-third of the shares in the company, and all three were directors. Brodie served as the corporate president for twelve years but thereafter met with the other shareholders only a few times a year. After disagreements arose, Brodie asked the company to purchase his shares, but his requests were refused. A few years later, Brodie died, and his wife inherited his shares in the company. Jordan and Barbuto refused to perform a valuation of the company, denied her access to the corporate information she requested, did not declare any dividends, and refused to elect her as a director. In this situation, a court found that the majority shareholders had violated their fiduciary duty to Brodie's wife.[30] ◀

S E C T I O N 6

MAJOR BUSINESS FORMS COMPARED

As mentioned in Chapter 18, when deciding which form of business organization to choose, businesspersons normally consider several factors, including ease of creation, the liability of the owners, tax considerations, and the ability to raise capital. Each major form of business organization offers distinct advantages and disadvantages with respect to these and other factors.

Exhibit 19–3 on the following pages summarizes the essential advantages and disadvantages of each of the forms of business organization discussed in Unit Four.

---

29. The phrase *watered stock* was originally used to describe cattle that were kept thirsty during a long drive and then were allowed to drink large quantities of water just before their sale. The increased weight of the watered stock allowed the seller to reap a higher profit.

30. *Brodie v. Jordan,* 447 Mass. 866, 857 N.E.2d 1076 (2006).

EXHIBIT 19–3 **Major Forms of Business Compared**

Characteristic	Sole Proprietorship	Partnership	Corporation
Method of Creation	Created at will by owner.	Created by agreement of the parties.	Authorized by the state under the state's corporation law.
Legal Position	Not a separate entity; owner is the business.	A general partnership is a separate legal entity in most states.	Always a legal entity separate and distinct from its owners—a legal fiction for the purposes of owning property and being a party to litigation.
Liability	Unlimited liability.	Unlimited liability.	Limited liability of shareholders—shareholders are not liable for the debts of the corporation.
Duration	Determined by owner; automatically dissolved on owner's death.	Terminated by agreement of the partners, but can continue to do business even when a partner dissociates from the partnership.	Can have perpetual existence.
Transferability of Interest	Interest can be transferred, but individual's proprietorship then ends.	Although partnership interest can be assigned, assignee does not have full rights of a partner.	Shares of stock can be transferred.
Management	Completely at owner's discretion.	Each partner has a direct and equal voice in management unless expressly agreed otherwise in the partnership agreement.	Shareholders elect directors, who set policy and appoint officers.
Taxation	Owner pays personal taxes on business income.	Each partner pays pro rata share of income taxes on net profits, whether or not they are distributed.	Double taxation—corporation pays income tax on net profits, with no deduction for dividends, and shareholders pay income tax on disbursed dividends they receive.
Organizational Fees, Annual License Fees, and Annual Reports	None or minimal.	None or minimal.	All required.
Transaction of Business in Other States	Generally no limitation.	Generally no limitation.[a]	Normally must qualify to do business and obtain certificate of authority.

a. A few states have enacted statutes requiring that foreign partnerships qualify to do business there.

EXHIBIT 19-3 Major Forms of Business Compared—Continued

Charactistic	Limited Partnership	Limited Liability Company	Limited Liability Partnership
Method of Creation	Created by agreement to carry on a business for profit. At least one party must be a general partner and the other(s) limited partner(s). Certificate of limited partnership is filed. Charter must be issued by the state.	Created by an agreement of the member-owners of the company. Articles of organization are filed. Charter must be issued by the state.	Created by agreement of the partners. A statement of qualification for the limited liability partnership is filed.
Legal Position	Treated as a legal entity.	Treated as a legal entity.	Generally, treated same as a general partnership.
Liability	Unlimited liability of all general partners. Limited partners are liable only to the extent of capital contributions.	Member-owners' liability is limited to the amount of capital contributions or investments.	Varies, but under the Uniform Partnership Act, liability of a partner for acts committed by other partners is limited.
Duration	By agreement in certificate, or by termination of the last general partner (retirement, death, and the like) or last limited partner.	Unless a single-member LLC, can have perpetual existence (same as a corporation).	Remains in existence until cancellation or revocation.
Transferability of Interest	Interest can be assigned (same as a general partnership), but if assignee becomes a member with consent of other partners, certificate must be amended.	Member interests are freely transferable.	Interest can be assigned same as in a general partnership.
Management	General partners have equal voice or by agreement. Limited partners may not retain limited liability if they actively participate in management.	Member-owners can fully participate in management or can designate a group of persons to manage on behalf of the members.	Same as a general partnership.
Taxation	Generally taxed as a partnership.	LLC is not taxed, and members are taxed personally on profits "passed through" the LLC.	Same as a general partnership.
Organizational Fees, Annual License Fees, and Annual Reports	Organizational fee required; usually not others.	Organizational fee required. Others vary with states.	Fees are set by each state for filing statements of qualification, statements of foreign qualification, and annual reports.
Transaction of Business in Other States	Generally no limitations.	Generally no limitations, but may vary depending on state.	Must file a statement of foreign qualification before doing business in another state.

Reviewing: Corporations

David Brock is on the board of directors of Firm Body Fitness, Inc., which owns a string of fitness clubs in New Mexico. Brock owns 15 percent of the Firm Body stock and is also employed as a tanning technician at one of the fitness clubs. After the January financial report showed that Firm Body's tanning division was operating at a substantial net loss, the board of directors, led by Marty Levinson, discussed the possibility of terminating the tanning operations. Brock successfully convinced a majority of the board that the tanning division was necessary to market the clubs' overall fitness package. By April, the tanning division's financial losses had risen. The board hired a business analyst, who conducted surveys and determined that the tanning operations did not significantly increase membership.

A shareholder, Diego Peñada, discovered that Brock owned stock in Sunglow, Inc., the company from which Firm Body purchased its tanning equipment. Peñada notified Levinson, who privately reprimanded Brock. Shortly thereafter, Brock and Mandy Vail, who owned 37 percent of the Firm Body stock and also held shares of Sunglow, voted to replace Levinson on the board of directors. Using the information presented in the chapter, answer the following questions.

1. What duties did Brock, as a director, owe to Firm Body?
2. Does the fact that Brock owned shares in Sunglow establish a conflict of interest? Why or why not?
3. Suppose that Firm Body brought an action against Brock claiming that he had breached the duty of loyalty by not disclosing his interest in Sunglow to the other directors. What theory might Brock use in his defense?
4. Now suppose that Firm Body did not bring an action against Brock. What type of lawsuit might Peñada be able to bring based on these facts?

DEBATE THIS . . . *Because most shareholders never bother to vote for directors, shareholders have no real control over corporations.*

Terms and Concepts

alien corporation 396	foreign corporation 396	quorum 406
articles of incorporation 400	holding company 394	retained earnings 394
benefit corporation 398	inside director 405	S corporation 397
business judgment rule 408	outside director 405	shareholder's derivative suit 417
bylaws 400	pierce the corporate veil 403	stock certificate 415
close corporation 396	preemptive rights 415	stock warrant 416
commingle 403	proxy 413	*ultra vires* 402
dividends 394	public corporation 396	voting trust 415
domestic corporation 396	publicly held corporation 396	watered stock 419

ExamPrep

Issue Spotters

1. Northwest Brands, Inc., is a small business incorporated in Minnesota. Its one class of stock is owned by twelve members of a single family. Ordinarily, corporate income is taxed at the corporate and shareholder levels. Is there a way for Northwest Brands to avoid this double taxation? Explain your answer. **(See page 398.)**

2. Nico is Omega Corporation's majority shareholder. He owns enough stock in Omega that if he were to sell it, the sale would be a transfer of control of the firm. Discuss whether Nico owes a duty to Omega or the minority shareholders in selling his shares. **(See page 419.)**

• **Check your answers to the Issue Spotters against the answers provided in Appendix B at the end of this text.**

Before the Test

Go to **www.cengagebrain.com**, enter the ISBN 9781285770192, and click on "Find" to locate this textbook's Web site. Then, click on "Access Now" under "Study Tools," and select Chapter 19 at the top. There, you will find a Practice Quiz that you can take to assess your mastery of the concepts in this chapter, as well as Flashcards and a Glossary of important terms.

Business Scenarios

19–1. Conflicts of Interest. Oxy Corp. is negotiating with Wick Construction Co. for the renovation of Oxy's corporate headquarters. Wick, the owner of Wick Construction Co., is also one of the five members of Oxy's board of directors. The contract terms are standard for this type of contract. Wick has previously informed two of the other directors of his interest in the construction company. Oxy's board approves the contract by a three-to-two vote, with Wick voting with the majority. Discuss whether this contract is binding on the corporation. **(See page 410.)**

19–2. Liability of Directors. AstroStar, Inc., has approximately five hundred shareholders. Its board of directors consists of three members—Eckhart, Dolan, and Macero. At a regular board meeting, the board selects Galiard as president of the corporation by a two-to-one vote, with Eckhart dissenting. The minutes of the meeting do not register Eckhart's dissenting vote. Later, an audit reveals that Galiard is a former convict and has embezzled $500,000 from the corporation that is not covered by insurance. Can the corporation hold directors Eckhart, Dolan, and Macero personally liable? Discuss. **(See page 410.)**

19–3. Corporate Powers. Oya Paka and two business associates formed a corporation called Paka Corp. for the purpose of selling computer services. Oya, who owned 50 percent of the corporate shares, served as the corporation's president. Oya wished to obtain a personal loan from her bank for $250,000, but the bank required the note to be cosigned by a third party. Oya cosigned the note in the name of the corporation. Later, Oya defaulted on the note, and the bank sued the corporation for payment. The corporation asserted, as a defense, that Oya had exceeded her authority when she cosigned the note on behalf of the corporation. Had she? Explain. **(See page 402.)**

Business Case Problems

19–4. Spotlight on Inventions—Piercing the Corporate Veil. Thomas Persson and Jon Nokes founded Smart Inventions, Inc., to market household consumer products. The success of their first product, the Smart Mop, continued with later products, which were sold through infomercials and other means. Persson and Nokes were the firm's officers and equal shareholders. Persson was responsible for product development, and Nokes was in charge of day-to-day operations. By 1998, they had become dissatisfied with each other's efforts. Nokes represented the firm as financially "dying," "in a grim state, . . . worse than ever," and offered to buy all of Persson's shares for $1.6 million. Persson accepted. On the day that they signed the agreement to transfer the shares, Smart Inventions began marketing a new product—the Tap Light. It was an instant success, generating millions of dollars in revenues. In negotiating with Persson, Nokes had intentionally kept the Tap Light a secret. Persson sued Smart Inventions, asserting fraud and other claims. Under what principle might Smart Inventions be liable for Nokes's fraud? Is Smart Inventions liable? Explain. [*Persson v. Smart Inventions, Inc.*, 125 Cal.App.4th 1141, 23 Cal.Rptr.3d 335 (2 Dist. 2005)] **(See page 403.)**

19–5. Rights of Shareholders. Stanka Woods is the sole member of Hair Ventures, LLC. Hair Ventures owns 3 million shares of stock in Biolustré Inc. For several years, Woods and other Biolustré shareholders did not receive notice of shareholders' meetings or financial reports. On learning that Biolustré planned to issue more stock, Woods, through Hair Ventures, demanded to see Biolustré's books and records. Biolustré asserted that the request was not for a proper purpose. Does Woods have a right to inspect Biolustré's books and records? If so, what are the limits? Do any of those limits apply in this case? Explain. [*Biolustré Inc. v. Hair Ventures, LLC*, 2011 WL 540054 (Tex.App.—San Antonio 2011)] **(See page 415.)**

19–6. BUSINESS CASE PROBLEM WITH SAMPLE ANSWER: Close Corporations.
Mark Burnett and Kamran Pourgol were the only shareholders in a corporation that built and sold a house. When the buyers discovered that the house exceeded the amount of square footage allowed by the building permit, Pourgol agreed to renovate the house to conform to the permit. No work was done, however, and Burnett filed a suit against Pourgol. Burnett claimed that, without his knowledge, Pourgol had submitted incorrect plans to obtain the building permit, misrepresented the extent of the renovation, and failed to fix the house. Was Pourgol guilty of misconduct? If so, how might it have been avoided? Discuss. [*Burnett v. Pourgol, 83 A.D.3d 756, 921 N.Y.S.2d 280 (2 Dept. 2011)] **(See page 396.)**

• **For a sample answer to Problem 19–6, go to Appendix C at the end of this text.**

19–7. Duty of Loyalty. Kids International Corp. produced children's wear for Wal-Mart and other retailers. Gila Dweck was a Kids director and its chief executive officer.

Because she felt that she was not paid enough for the company's success, she started Success Apparel to compete with Kids. Success operated out of Kids' premises, used its employees, borrowed on its credit, took advantage of its business opportunities, and capitalized on its customer relationships. As an "administrative fee," Dweck paid Kids 1 percent of Success's total sales. Did Dweck breach any fiduciary duties? Explain. [*Dweck v. Nasser*, 2012 WL 3194069 (Del.Ch. 2012)] **(See page 408.)**

19–8. Piercing the Corporate Veil. In 1997, Leon Greenblatt, Andrew Jahelka, and Richard Nichols incorporated Loop Corp. with only $1,000 of capital. Three years later, Banco Panamericano, Inc., which was run entirely by Greenblatt and owned by a Greenblatt family trust, extended a large line of credit to Loop. Loop's subsidiaries then participated in the credit, giving $3 million to Loop while acquiring a security interest in Loop itself. Loop then opened an account with Wachovia Securities, LLC, to buy stock shares using credit provided by Wachovia. When the stock values plummeted, Loop owed Wachovia $1.89 million. Loop also defaulted on its loan from Banco, but Banco agreed to lend Loop millions of dollars more. Rather than repay Wachovia with the influx of funds, Loop gave the funds to closely related entities and "compensated" Nichols and Jahelka without issuing any W-2 forms (forms reporting compensation to the Internal Revenue Service). The evidence also showed that Loop made loans to other related entities and shared office space, equipment, and telephone and fax numbers with related entities. Loop also moved employees among related entities, failed to file its tax returns on time (or sometimes at all), and failed to follow its own bylaws. In a lawsuit brought by Wachovia, can the court hold Greenblatt, Jahelka, and Nichols personally liable by piercing the corporate veil? Why or why not? [*Wachovia Securities, LLC v. Banco Panamericano, Inc.*, 674 F.3d 743 (9th Cir. 2012)] **(See page 403.)**

19–9. A QUESTION OF ETHICS: Improper Incorporation.

 Mike Lyons incorporated Lyons Concrete, Inc., in Montana, but did not file its first annual report, so the state involuntarily dissolved the firm in 1996. Unaware of the dissolution, Lyons continued to do

business as Lyons Concrete. In 2003, he signed a written contract with William Weimar to form and pour a certain amount of concrete on Weimar's property in Lake County for $19,810. Weimar was in a rush to complete the entire project, and he and Lyons orally agreed to additional work on a time-and-materials basis. When scheduling conflicts arose, Weimar had his own employees set some of the forms, which proved deficient. Weimar also directed Lyons to pour concrete in the rain, which undercut its quality. In mid-project, Lyons submitted an invoice for $14,389, which Weimar paid. After the work was complete, Lyons sent Weimar an invoice for $25,731, but he refused to pay, claiming that the $14,389 covered everything. To recover the unpaid amount, Lyons filed a mechanic's lien as "Mike Lyons d/b/a Lyons Concrete, Inc." against Weimar's property. Weimar filed a suit in a Montana state court to strike the lien, and Lyons filed a counterclaim to reassert it. [Weimar v. Lyons, 338 Mont. 242, 164 P.3d 922 (2007)] (See page 401.)

(a) Before the trial, Weimar asked for a change of venue on the ground that a sign on the courthouse lawn advertised "Lyons Concrete." How might the sign affect a trial on the parties' dispute? Should the court grant this request? Why or why not?

(b) Weimar asked the court to dismiss the counterclaim on the ground that the state had dissolved Lyons Concrete in 1996. Lyons immediately filed new articles of incorporation for "Lyons Concrete, Inc." Under what doctrine might the court rule that Weimar could not deny the existence of Lyons Concrete? What ethical values underlie this doctrine? Should the court make this ruling? Explain.

(c) At the trial, Weimar argued, in part, that there was no "fixed price" contract between the parties and that even if there were, the poor quality of the work, which required repairs, amounted to a breach, excusing Weimar's further performance. Should the court rule in Weimar's favor on this basis? Why or why not?

Legal Reasoning Group Activity

19–10. Shareholders' Duties. Milena Weintraub and Larry Griffith were shareholders in Grand Casino, Inc., which operated a casino in South Dakota. Griffith owned 51 percent of the stock and Weintraub 49 percent. Weintraub managed the casino, which Griffith typically visited once a week. At the end of 2012, an accounting audit showed that the cash on hand was less than the amount posted in the casino's books. Later, more shortfalls were discovered. In October 2014, Griffith did a complete audit. Weintraub was unable to account for $200,500 in missing cash. Griffith then kept all of the casino's most recent profits, including Weintraub's $90,447.20 share, and, without telling Weintraub, sold the casino for $400,000 and kept

all of the proceeds. Weintraub filed a suit against Griffith, asserting a breach of fiduciary duty. Griffith countered with evidence of Weintraub's misappropriation of corporate cash. **(See page 419.)**

(a) The first group will discuss the duties that these parties owed to each other, and determine whether Weintraub or Griffith, or both, breached those duties.

(b) The second group will decide how this dispute should be resolved and who should pay what to whom to reconcile the finances.

(c) A third group will discuss whether Weintraub or Griffin violated any ethical duties to each other or to the corporation.

(Adopted in fifty-two jurisdictions—all fifty States, although Louisiana has adopted only Articles 1, 3, 4, 7, 8, and 9; the District of Columbia; and the Virgin Islands.) The Uniform Commercial Code consists of the following articles; however, this appendix only features Articles 2 & 2A.

Art.

1. General Provisions
2. Sales
2A. Leases
3. Negotiable Instruments
4. Bank Deposits and Collections
4A. Funds Transfers
5. Letters of Credit
6. Repealer of Article 6—Bulk Transfers and [Revised] Article 6—Bulk Sales
7. Warehouse Receipts, Bills of Lading and Other Documents of Title
8. Investment Securities
9. Secured Transactions
10. Effective Date and Repealer
11. Effective and Transition Provisions

Article 2—Sales

Part 1   Short Title, General Construction and Subject Matter

§ 2-101.   Short Title.

This Article shall be known and may be cited as Uniform Commercial Code—Sales.

§ 2-102.   Scope; Certain Security and Other Transactions Excluded From This Article.

Unless the context otherwise requires, this Article applies to transactions in goods; it does not apply to any transaction which although in the form of an unconditional contract to sell or present sale is intended to operate only as a security transaction nor does this Article impair or repeal any statute regulating sales to consumers, farmers or other specified classes of buyers.

§ 2-103.   Definitions and Index of Definitions.

(1) In this Article unless the context otherwise requires

(a) "Buyer" means a person who buys or contracts to buy goods.

(b) "Good faith" in the case of a merchant means honesty in fact and the observance of reasonable commercial standards of fair dealing in the trade.

(c) "Receipt" of goods means taking physical possession of them.

(d) "Seller" means a person who sells or contracts to sell goods.

(2) Other definitions applying to this Article or to specified Parts thereof, and the sections in which they appear are:

"Acceptance". Section 2–606.
"Banker's credit". Section 2–325.
"Between merchants". Section 2–104.
"Cancellation". Section 2–106(4).
"Commercial unit". Section 2–105.
"Confirmed credit". Section 2–325.
"Conforming to contract". Section 2–106.
"Contract for sale". Section 2–106.
"Cover". Section 2–712.
"Entrusting". Section 2–403.
"Financing agency". Section 2–104.
"Future goods". Section 2–105.
"Goods". Section 2–105.
"Identification". Section 2–501.
"Installment contract". Section 2–612.
"Letter of Credit". Section 2–325.
"Lot". Section 2–105.
"Merchant". Section 2–104.
"Overseas". Section 2–323.
"Person in position of seller". Section 2–707.
"Present sale". Section 2–106.
"Sale". Section 2–106.
"Sale on approval". Section 2–326.
"Sale or return". Section 2–326.
"Termination". Section 2–106.

(3) The following definitions in other Articles apply to this Article:

"Check". Section 3–104.
"Consignee". Section 7–102.
"Consignor". Section 7–102.
"Consumer goods". Section 9–109.
"Dishonor". Section 3–507.
"Draft". Section 3–104.

(4) In addition Article 1 contains general definitions and principles of construction and interpretation applicable throughout this Article.

As amended in 1994 and 1999.

§ 2-104.   Definitions: "Merchant"; "Between Merchants"; "Financing Agency".

(1) "Merchant" means a person who deals in goods of the kind or otherwise by his occupation holds himself out as having knowledge or skill peculiar to the practices or goods involved in the transaction or to whom such knowledge or skill may be attributed by his employment of an agent or broker or other

intermediary who by his occupation holds himself out as having such knowledge or skill.

(2) "Financing agency" means a bank, finance company or other person who in the ordinary course of business makes advances against goods or documents of title or who by arrangement with either the seller or the buyer intervenes in ordinary course to make or collect payment due or claimed under the contract for sale, as by purchasing or paying the seller's draft or making advances against it or by merely taking it for collection whether or not documents of title accompany the draft. "Financing agency" includes also a bank or other person who similarly intervenes between persons who are in the position of seller and buyer in respect to the goods (Section 2–707).

(3) "Between merchants" means in any transaction with respect to which both parties are chargeable with the knowledge or skill of merchants.

§ 2–105.   Definitions: Transferability; "Goods"; "Future" Goods; "Lot"; "Commercial Unit".

(1) "Goods" means all things (including specially manufactured goods) which are movable at the time of identification to the contract for sale other than the money in which the price is to be paid, investment securities (Article 8) and things in action. "Goods" also includes the unborn young of animals and growing crops and other identified things attached to realty as described in the section on goods to be severed from realty (Section 2–107).

(2) Goods must be both existing and identified before any interest in them can pass. Goods which are not both existing and identified are "future" goods. A purported present sale of future goods or of any interest therein operates as a contract to sell.

(3) There may be a sale of a part interest in existing identified goods.

(4) An undivided share in an identified bulk of fungible goods is sufficiently identified to be sold although the quantity of the bulk is not determined. Any agreed proportion of such a bulk or any quantity thereof agreed upon by number, weight or other measure may to the extent of the seller's interest in the bulk be sold to the buyer who then becomes an owner in common.

(5) "Lot" means a parcel or a single article which is the subject matter of a separate sale or delivery, whether or not it is sufficient to perform the contract.

(6) "Commercial unit" means such a unit of goods as by commercial usage is a single whole for purposes of sale and division of which materially impairs its character or value on the market or in use. A commercial unit may be a single article (as a machine) or a set of articles (as a suite of furniture or an assortment of sizes) or a quantity (as a bale, gross, or carload) or any other unit treated in use or in the relevant market as a single whole.

§ 2–106.   Definitions: "Contract"; "Agreement"; "Contract for Sale"; "Sale"; "Present Sale"; "Conforming" to Contract; "Termination"; "Cancellation".

(1) In this Article unless the context otherwise requires "contract" and "agreement" are limited to those relating to the present or future sale of goods. "Contract for sale" includes both a present sale of goods and a contract to sell goods at a future time. A "sale" consists in the passing of title from the seller to the buyer for a price (Section 2–401). A "present sale" means a sale which is accomplished by the making of the contract.

(2) Goods or conduct including any part of a performance are "conforming" or conform to the contract when they are in accordance with the obligations under the contract.

(3) "Termination" occurs when either party pursuant to a power created by agreement or law puts an end to the contract otherwise than for its breach. On "termination" all obligations which are still executory on both sides are discharged but any right based on prior breach or performance survives.

(4) "Cancellation" occurs when either party puts an end to the contract for breach by the other and its effect is the same as that of "termination" except that the cancelling party also retains any remedy for breach of the whole contract or any unperformed balance.

§ 2–107.   Goods to Be Severed From Realty: Recording.

(1) A contract for the sale of minerals or the like (including oil and gas) or a structure or its materials to be removed from realty is a contract for the sale of goods within this Article if they are to be severed by the seller but until severance a purported present sale thereof which is not effective as a transfer of an interest in land is effective only as a contract to sell.

(2) A contract for the sale apart from the land of growing crops or other things attached to realty and capable of severance without material harm thereto but not described in subsection (1) or of timber to be cut is a contract for the sale of goods within this Article whether the subject matter is to be severed by the buyer or by the seller even though it forms part of the realty at the time of contracting, and the parties can by identification effect a present sale before severance.

(3) The provisions of this section are subject to any third party rights provided by the law relating to realty records, and the contract for sale may be executed and recorded as a document transferring an interest in land and shall then constitute notice to third parties of the buyer's rights under the contract for sale.

As amended in 1972.

Part 2   Form, Formation and Readjustment of Contract

§ 2–201.   Formal Requirements; Statute of Frauds.

(1) Except as otherwise provided in this section a contract for the sale of goods for the price of $500 or more is not enforceable by way of action or defense unless there is some writing sufficient to indicate that a contract for sale has been made between the parties and signed by the party against whom enforcement is sought or by his authorized agent or broker. A writing is not insufficient because it omits or incorrectly states a term agreed upon but the contract is not enforceable under this paragraph beyond the quantity of goods shown in such writing.

(2) Between merchants if within a reasonable time a writing in confirmation of the contract and sufficient against the sender is received and the party receiving it has reason to know its contents, its satisfies the requirements of subsection (1) against such party unless written notice of objection to its contents is given within ten days after it is received.

(3) A contract which does not satisfy the requirements of sub-section (1) but which is valid in other respects is enforceable

(a) if the goods are to be specially manufactured for the buyer and are not suitable for sale to others in the ordinary course of the seller's business and the seller, before notice of repudiation is received and under circumstances which reasonably indicate that the goods are for the buyer, has made either a substantial beginning of their manufacture or commitments for their procurement; or

(b) if the party against whom enforcement is sought admits in his pleading, testimony or otherwise in court that a contract for sale was made, but the contract is not enforceable under this provision beyond the quantity of goods admitted; or

(c) with respect to goods for which payment has been made and accepted or which have been received and accepted (Sec. 2–606).

§ 2–202. Final Written Expression: Parol or Extrinsic Evidence.

Terms with respect to which the confirmatory memoranda of the parties agree or which are otherwise set forth in a writing intended by the parties as a final expression of their agreement with respect to such terms as are included therein may not be contradicted by evidence of any prior agreement or of a contemporaneous oral agreement but may be explained or supplemented

(a) by course of dealing or usage of trade (Section 1–205) or by course of performance (Section 2–208); and

(b) by evidence of consistent additional terms unless the court finds the writing to have been intended also as a complete and exclusive statement of the terms of the agreement.

§ 2–203. Seals Inoperative.

The affixing of a seal to a writing evidencing a contract for sale or an offer to buy or sell goods does not constitute the writing a sealed instrument and the law with respect to sealed instruments does not apply to such a contract or offer.

§ 2–204. Formation in General.

(1) A contract for sale of goods may be made in any manner sufficient to show agreement, including conduct by both parties which recognizes the existence of such a contract.

(2) An agreement sufficient to constitute a contract for sale may be found even though the moment of its making is undetermined.

(3) Even though one or more terms are left open a contract for sale does not fail for indefiniteness if the parties have intended to make a contract and there is a reasonably certain basis for giving an appropriate remedy.

§ 2–205. Firm Offers.

An offer by a merchant to buy or sell goods in a signed writing which by its terms gives assurance that it will be held open is not revocable, for lack of consideration, during the time stated or if no time is stated for a reasonable time, but in no event may such period of irrevocability exceed three months; but any such term of assurance on a form supplied by the offeree must be separately signed by the offeror.

§ 2–206. Offer and Acceptance in Formation of Contract.

(1) Unless other unambiguously indicated by the language or circumstances

(a) an offer to make a contract shall be construed as inviting acceptance in any manner and by any medium reasonable in the circumstances;

(b) an order or other offer to buy goods for prompt or current shipment shall be construed as inviting acceptance either by a prompt promise to ship or by the prompt or current shipment of conforming or nonconforming goods, but such a shipment of non-conforming goods does not constitute an acceptance if the seller seasonably notifies the buyer that the shipment is offered only as an accommodation to the buyer.

(2) Where the beginning of a requested performance is a reasonable mode of acceptance an offeror who is not notified of acceptance within a reasonable time may treat the offer as having lapsed before acceptance.

§ 2–207. Additional Terms in Acceptance or Confirmation.

(1) A definite and seasonable expression of acceptance or a written confirmation which is sent within a reasonable time operates as an acceptance even though it states terms additional to or different from those offered or agreed upon, unless acceptance is expressly made conditional on assent to the additional or different terms.

(2) The additional terms are to be construed as proposals for addition to the contract. Between merchants such terms become part of the contract unless:

(a) the offer expressly limits acceptance to the terms of the offer;

(b) they materially alter it; or

(c) notification of objection to them has already been given or is given within a reasonable time after notice of them is received.

(3) Conduct by both parties which recognizes the existence of a contract is sufficient to establish a contract for sale although the writings of the parties do not otherwise establish a contract. In such case the terms of the particular contract consist of those terms on which the writings of the parties agree, together with any supplementary terms incorporated under any other provisions of this Act.

§ 2–208. Course of Performance or Practical Construction.

(1) Where the contract for sale involves repeated occasions for performance by either party with knowledge of the nature of the performance and opportunity for objection to it by the other, any course of performance accepted or acquiesced in without objection shall be relevant to determine the meaning of the agreement.

(2) The express terms of the agreement and any such course of performance, as well as any course of dealing and usage of trade, shall be construed whenever reasonable as consistent with each other; but when such construction is unreasonable, express terms shall control course of performance and course of

performance shall control both course of dealing and usage of trade (Section 1–303).

(3) Subject to the provisions of the next section on modification and waiver, such course of performance shall be relevant to show a waiver or modification of any term inconsistent with such course of performance.

§ 2–209.   Modification, Rescission and Waiver.

(1) An agreement modifying a contract within this Article needs no consideration to be binding.

(2) A signed agreement which excludes modification or rescission except by a signed writing cannot be otherwise modified or rescinded, but except as between merchants such a requirement on a form supplied by the merchant must be separately signed by the other party.

(3) The requirements of the statute of frauds section of this Article (Section 2–201) must be satisfied if the contract as modified is within its provisions.

(4) Although an attempt at modification or rescission does not satisfy the requirements of subsection (2) or (3) it can operate as a waiver.

(5) A party who has made a waiver affecting an executory portion of the contract may retract the waiver by reasonable notification received by the other party that strict performance will be required of any term waived, unless the retraction would be unjust in view of a material change of position in reliance on the waiver.

§ 2–210.   Delegation of Performance; Assignment of Rights.

(1) A party may perform his duty through a delegate unless otherwise agreed or unless the other party has a substantial interest in having his original promisor perform or control the acts required by the contract. No delegation of performance relieves the party delegating of any duty to perform or any liability for breach.

(2) Except as otherwise provided in Section 9–406, unless otherwise agreed, all rights of either seller or buyer can be assigned except where the assignment would materially change the duty of the other party, or increase materially the burden or risk imposed on him by his contract, or impair materially his chance of obtaining return performance. A right to damages for breach of the whole contract or a right arising out of the assignor's due performance of his entire obligation can be assigned despite agreement otherwise.

(3) The creation, attachment, perfection, or enforcement of a security interest in the seller's interest under a contract is not a transfer that materially changes the duty of or increases materially the burden or risk imposed on the buyer or impairs materially the buyer's chance of obtaining return performance within the purview of subsection (2) unless, and then only to the extent that, enforcement actually results in a delegation of material performance of the seller. Even in that event, the creation, attachment, perfection, and enforcement of the security interest remain effective, but (i) the seller is liable to the buyer for damages caused by the delegation to the extent that the damages could not reasonably by prevented by the buyer, and (ii) a court having jurisdiction may grant other appropriate relief, including cancellation of the contract for sale or an injunction against enforcement of the security interest or consummation of the enforcement.

(4) Unless the circumstances indicate the contrary a prohibition of assignment of "the contract" is to be construed as barring only the delegation to the assignee of the assignor's performance.

(5) An assignment of "the contract" or of "all my rights under the contract" or an assignment in similar general terms is an assignment of rights and unless the language or the circumstances (as in an assignment for security) indicate the contrary, it is a delegation of performance of the duties of the assignor and its acceptance by the assignee constitutes a promise by him to perform those duties. This promise is enforceable by either the assignor or the other party to the original contract.

(6) The other party may treat any assignment which delegates performance as creating reasonable grounds for insecurity and may without prejudice to his rights against the assignor demand assurances from the assignee (Section 2–609).

As amended in 1999.

Part 3   General Obligation and Construction of Contract

§ 2–301.   General Obligations of Parties.

The obligation of the seller is to transfer and deliver and that of the buyer is to accept and pay in accordance with the contract.

§ 2–302.   Unconscionable Contract or Clause.

(1) If the court as a matter of law finds the contract or any clause of the contract to have been unconscionable at the time it was made the court may refuse to enforce the contract, or it may enforce the remainder of the contract without the unconscionable clause, or it may so limit the application of any unconscionable clause as to avoid any unconscionable result.

(2) When it is claimed or appears to the court that the contract or any clause thereof may be unconscionable the parties shall be afforded a reasonable opportunity to present evidence as to its commercial setting, purpose and effect to aid the court in making the determination.

§ 2–303.   Allocations or Division of Risks.

Where this Article allocates a risk or a burden as between the parties "unless otherwise agreed", the agreement may not only shift the allocation but may also divide the risk or burden.

§ 2–304.   Price Payable in Money, Goods, Realty, or Otherwise.

(1) The price can be made payable in money or otherwise. If it is payable in whole or in part in goods each party is a seller of the goods which he is to transfer.

(2) Even though all or part of the price is payable in an interest in realty the transfer of the goods and the seller's obligations with reference to them are subject to this Article, but not the transfer of the interest in realty or the transferor's obligations in connection therewith.

§ 2–305.   Open Price Term.

(1) The parties if they so intend can conclude a contract for sale even though the price is not settled. In such a case the price is a reasonable price at the time for delivery if

   (a) nothing is said as to price; or

(b) the price is left to be agreed by the parties and they fail to agree; or

(c) the price is to be fixed in terms of some agreed market or other standard as set or recorded by a third person or agency and it is not so set or recorded.

(2) A price to be fixed by the seller or by the buyer means a price for him to fix in good faith.

(3) When a price left to be fixed otherwise than by agreement of the parties fails to be fixed through fault of one party the other may at his option treat the contract as cancelled or himself fix a reasonable price.

(4) Where, however, the parties intend not to be bound unless the price be fixed or agreed and it is not fixed or agreed there is no contract. In such a case the buyer must return any goods already received or if unable so to do must pay their reasonable value at the time of delivery and the seller must return any portion of the price paid on account.

§ 2–306. Output, Requirements and Exclusive Dealings.

(1) A term which measures the quantity by the output of the seller or the requirements of the buyer means such actual output or requirements as may occur in good faith, except that no quantity unreasonably disproportionate to any stated estimate or in the absence of a stated estimate to any normal or otherwise comparable prior output or requirements may be tendered or demanded.

(2) A lawful agreement by either the seller or the buyer for exclusive dealing in the kind of goods concerned imposes unless otherwise agreed an obligation by the seller to use best efforts to supply the goods and by the buyer to use best efforts to promote their sale.

§ 2–307. Delivery in Single Lot or Several Lots.

Unless otherwise agreed all goods called for by a contract for sale must be tendered in a single delivery and payment is due only on such tender but where the circumstances give either party the right to make or demand delivery in lots the price if it can be apportioned may be demanded for each lot.

§ 2–308. Absence of Specified Place for Delivery.

Unless otherwise agreed

(a) the place for delivery of goods is the seller's place of business or if he has none his residence; but

(b) in a contract for sale of identified goods which to the knowledge of the parties at the time of contracting are in some other place, that place is the place for their delivery; and

(c) documents of title may be delivered through customary banking channels.

§ 2–309. Absence of Specific Time Provisions; Notice of Termination.

(1) The time for shipment or delivery or any other action under a contract if not provided in this Article or agreed upon shall be a reasonable time.

(2) Where the contract provides for successive performances but is indefinite in duration it is valid for a reasonable time but unless otherwise agreed may be terminated at any time by either party.

(3) Termination of a contract by one party except on the happening of an agreed event requires that reasonable notification be received by the other party and an agreement dispensing with notification is invalid if its operation would be unconscionable.

§ 2–310. Open Time for Payment or Running of Credit; Authority to Ship Under Reservation.

Unless otherwise agreed

(a) payment is due at the time and place at which the buyer is to receive the goods even though the place of shipment is the place of delivery; and

(b) if the seller is authorized to send the goods he may ship them under reservation, and may tender the documents of title, but the buyer may inspect the goods after their arrival before payment is due unless such inspection is inconsistent with the terms of the contract (Section 2–513); and

(c) if delivery is authorized and made by way of documents of title otherwise than by subsection (b) then payment is due at the time and place at which the buyer is to receive the documents regardless of where the goods are to be received; and

(d) where the seller is required or authorized to ship the goods on credit the credit period runs from the time of shipment but post-dating the invoice or delaying its dispatch will correspondingly delay the starting of the credit period.

§ 2–311. Options and Cooperation Respecting Performance.

(1) An agreement for sale which is otherwise sufficiently definite (subsection (3) of Section 2–204) to be a contract is not made invalid by the fact that it leaves particulars of performance to be specified by one of the parties. Any such specification must be made in good faith and within limits set by commercial reasonableness.

(2) Unless otherwise agreed specifications relating to assortment of the goods are at the buyer's option and except as otherwise provided in subsections (1)(c) and (3) of Section 2–319 specifications or arrangements relating to shipment are at the seller's option.

(3) Where such specification would materially affect the other party's performance but is not seasonably made or where one party's cooperation is necessary to the agreed performance of the other but is not seasonably forthcoming, the other party in addition to all other remedies

(a) is excused for any resulting delay in his own performance; and

(b) may also either proceed to perform in any reasonable manner or after the time for a material part of his own performance treat the failure to specify or to cooperate as a breach by failure to deliver or accept the goods.

§ 2–312. Warranty of Title and Against Infringement; Buyer's Obligation Against Infringement.

(1) Subject to subsection (2) there is in a contract for sale a warranty by the seller that

(a) the title conveyed shall be good, and its transfer rightful; and

(b) the goods shall be delivered free from any security interest or other lien or encumbrance of which the buyer at the time of contracting has no knowledge.

(2) A warranty under subsection (1) will be excluded or modified only by specific language or by circumstances which give the buyer reason to know that the person selling does not claim title in himself or that he is purporting to sell only such right or title as he or a third person may have.

(3) Unless otherwise agreed a seller who is a merchant regularly dealing in goods of the kind warrants that the goods shall be delivered free of the rightful claim of any third person by way of infringement or the like but a buyer who furnishes specifications to the seller must hold the seller harmless against any such claim which arises out of compliance with the specifications.

§ 2–313. Express Warranties by Affirmation, Promise, Description, Sample.

(1) Express warranties by the seller are created as follows:

(a) Any affirmation of fact or promise made by the seller to the buyer which relates to the goods and becomes part of the basis of the bargain creates an express warranty that the goods shall conform to the affirmation or promise.

(b) Any description of the goods which is made part of the basis of the bargain creates an express warranty that the goods shall conform to the description.

(c) Any sample or model which is made part of the basis of the bargain creates an express warranty that the whole of the goods shall conform to the sample or model.

(2) It is not necessary to the creation of an express warranty that the seller use formal words such as "warrant" or "guarantee" or that he have a specific intention to make a warranty, but an affirmation merely of the value of the goods or a statement purporting to be merely the seller's opinion or commendation of the goods does not create a warranty.

§ 2–314. Implied Warranty: Merchantability; Usage of Trade.

(1) Unless excluded or modified (Section 2–316), a warranty that the goods shall be merchantable is implied in a contract for their sale if the seller is a merchant with respect to goods of that kind. Under this section the serving for value of food or drink to be consumed either on the premises or elsewhere is a sale.

(2) Goods to be merchantable must be at least such as

(a) pass without objection in the trade under the contract description; and

(b) in the case of fungible goods, are of fair average quality within the description; and

(c) are fit for the ordinary purposes for which such goods are used; and

(d) run, within the variations permitted by the agreement, of even kind, quality and quantity within each unit and among all units involved; and

(e) are adequately contained, packaged, and labeled as the agreement may require; and

(f) conform to the promises or affirmations of fact made on the container or label if any.

(3) Unless excluded or modified (Section 2–316) other implied warranties may arise from course of dealing or usage of trade.

§ 2–315. Implied Warranty: Fitness for Particular Purpose.

Where the seller at the time of contracting has reason to know any particular purpose for which the goods are required and that the buyer is relying on the seller's skill or judgment to select or furnish suitable goods, there is unless excluded or modified under the next section an implied warranty that the goods shall be fit for such purpose.

§ 2–316. Exclusion or Modification of Warranties.

(1) Words or conduct relevant to the creation of an express warranty and words or conduct tending to negate or limit warranty shall be construed wherever reasonable as consistent with each other; but subject to the provisions of this Article on parol or extrinsic evidence (Section 2–202) negation or limitation is inoperative to the extent that such construction is unreasonable.

(2) Subject to subsection (3), to exclude or modify the implied warranty of merchantability or any part of it the language must mention merchantability and in case of a writing must be conspicuous, and to exclude or modify any implied warranty of fitness the exclusion must be by a writing and conspicuous. Language to exclude all implied warranties of fitness is sufficient if it states, for example, that "There are no warranties which extend beyond the description on the face hereof."

(3) Notwithstanding subsection (2)

(a) unless the circumstances indicate otherwise, all implied warranties are excluded by expressions like "as is", "with all faults" or other language which in common understanding calls the buyer's attention to the exclusion of warranties and makes plain that there is no implied warranty; and

(b) when the buyer before entering into the contract has examined the goods or the sample or model as fully as he desired or has refused to examine the goods there is no implied warranty with regard to defects which an examination ought in the circumstances to have revealed to him; and

(c) an implied warranty can also be excluded or modified by course of dealing or course of performance or usage of trade.

(4) Remedies for breach of warranty can be limited in accordance with the provisions of this Article on liquidation or limitation of damages and on contractual modification of remedy (Sections 2–718 and 2–719).

§ 2–317. Cumulation and Conflict of Warranties Express or Implied.

Warranties whether express or implied shall be construed as consistent with each other and as cumulative, but if such construction is unreasonable the intention of the parties shall determine which warranty is dominant. In ascertaining that intention the following rules apply:

(a) Exact or technical specifications displace an inconsistent sample or model or general language of description.

(b) A sample from an existing bulk displaces inconsistent general language of description.

(c) Express warranties displace inconsistent implied warranties other than an implied warranty of fitness for a particular purpose.

§ 2–318. Third Party Beneficiaries of Warranties Express or Implied.

Note: If this Act is introduced in the Congress of the United States this section should be omitted. (States to select one alternative.)

Alternative A

A seller's warranty whether express or implied extends to any natural person who is in the family or household of his buyer or who is a guest in his home if it is reasonable to expect that such person may use, consume or be affected by the goods and who is injured in person by breach of the warranty. A seller may not exclude or limit the operation of this section.

Alternative B

A seller's warranty whether express or implied extends to any natural person who may reasonably be expected to use, consume or be affected by the goods and who is injured in person by breach of the warranty. A seller may not exclude or limit the operation of this section.

Alternative C

A seller's warranty whether express or implied extends to any person who may reasonably be expected to use, consume or be affected by the goods and who is injured by breach of the warranty. A seller may not exclude or limit the operation of this section with respect to injury to the person of an individual to whom the warranty extends.

As amended 1966.

§ 2–319. F.O.B. and F.A.S. Terms.

(1) Unless otherwise agreed the term F.O.B. (which means "free on board") at a named place, even though used only in connection with the stated price, is a delivery term under which

(a) when the term is F.O.B. the place of shipment, the seller must at that place ship the goods in the manner provided in this Article (Section 2–504) and bear the expense and risk of putting them into the possession of the carrier; or

(b) when the term is F.O.B. the place of destination, the seller must at his own expense and risk transport the goods to that place and there tender delivery of them in the manner provided in this Article (Section 2–503);

(c) when under either (a) or (b) the term is also F.O.B. vessel, car or other vehicle, the seller must in addition at his own expense and risk load the goods on board. If the term is F.O.B. vessel the buyer must name the vessel and in an appropriate case the seller must comply with the provisions of this Article on the form of bill of lading (Section 2–323).

(2) Unless otherwise agreed the term F.A.S. vessel (which means "free alongside") at a named port, even though used only in connection with the stated price, is a delivery term under which the seller must

(a) at his own expense and risk deliver the goods alongside the vessel in the manner usual in that port or on a dock designated and provided by the buyer; and

(b) obtain and tender a receipt for the goods in exchange for which the carrier is under a duty to issue a bill of lading.

(3) Unless otherwise agreed in any case falling within subsection (1)(a) or (c) or subsection (2) the buyer must seasonably give any needed instructions for making delivery, including when the term is F.A.S. or F.O.B. the loading berth of the vessel and in an appropriate case its name and sailing date. The seller may treat the failure of needed instructions as a failure of cooperation under this Article (Section 2–311). He may also at his option move the goods in any reasonable manner preparatory to delivery or shipment.

(4) Under the term F.O.B. vessel or F.A.S. unless otherwise agreed the buyer must make payment against tender of the required documents and the seller may not tender nor the buyer demand delivery of the goods in substitution for the documents.

§ 2–320. C.I.F. and C. & F. Terms.

(1) The term C.I.F. means that the price includes in a lump sum the cost of the goods and the insurance and freight to the named destination. The term C. & F. or C.F. means that the price so includes cost and freight to the named destination.

(2) Unless otherwise agreed and even though used only in connection with the stated price and destination, the term C.I.F. destination or its equivalent requires the seller at his own expense and risk to

(a) put the goods into the possession of a carrier at the port for shipment and obtain a negotiable bill or bills of lading covering the entire transportation to the named destination; and

(b) load the goods and obtain a receipt from the carrier (which may be contained in the bill of lading) showing that the freight has been paid or provided for; and

(c) obtain a policy or certificate of insurance, including any war risk insurance, of a kind and on terms then current at the port of shipment in the usual amount, in the currency of the contract, shown to cover the same goods covered by the bill of lading and providing for payment of loss to the order of the buyer or for the account of whom it may concern; but the seller may add to the price the amount of the premium for any such war risk insurance; and

(d) prepare an invoice of the goods and procure any other documents required to effect shipment or to comply with the contract; and

(e) forward and tender with commercial promptness all the documents in due form and with any indorsement necessary to perfect the buyer's rights.

(3) Unless otherwise agreed the term C. & F. or its equivalent has the same effect and imposes upon the seller the same obligations and risks as a C.I.F. term except the obligation as to insurance.

(4) Under the term C.I.F. or C. & F. unless otherwise agreed the buyer must make payment against tender of the required documents and the seller may not tender nor the buyer demand delivery of the goods in substitution for the documents.

§ 2–321. C.I.F. or C. & F.: "Net Landed Weights"; "Payment on Arrival"; Warranty of Condition on Arrival.

Under a contract containing a term C.I.F. or C. & F.

(1) Where the price is based on or is to be adjusted according to "net landed weights", "delivered weights", "out turn" quantity or quality or the like, unless otherwise agreed the seller must reasonably estimate the price. The payment due on tender of the documents called for by the contract is the amount so estimated, but after final adjustment of the price a settlement must be made with commercial promptness.

(2) An agreement described in subsection (1) or any warranty of quality or condition of the goods on arrival places upon the seller the risk of ordinary deterioration, shrinkage and the like in transportation but has no effect on the place or time of identification to the contract for sale or delivery or on the passing of the risk of loss.

(3) Unless otherwise agreed where the contract provides for payment on or after arrival of the goods the seller must before payment allow such preliminary inspection as is feasible; but if the goods are lost delivery of the documents and payment are due when the goods should have arrived.

§ 2–322. Delivery "Ex-Ship".

(1) Unless otherwise agreed a term for delivery of goods "ex-ship" (which means from the carrying vessel) or in equivalent language is not restricted to a particular ship and requires delivery from a ship which has reached a place at the named port of destination where goods of the kind are usually discharged.

(2) Under such a term unless otherwise agreed

(a) the seller must discharge all liens arising out of the carriage and furnish the buyer with a direction which puts the carrier under a duty to deliver the goods; and

(b) the risk of loss does not pass to the buyer until the goods leave the ship's tackle or are otherwise properly unloaded.

§ 2–323. Form of Bill of Lading Required in Overseas Shipment; "Overseas".

(1) Where the contract contemplates overseas shipment and contains a term C.I.F. or C. & F. or F.O.B. vessel, the seller unless otherwise agreed must obtain a negotiable bill of lading stating that the goods have been loaded on board or, in the case of a term C.I.F. or C. & F., received for shipment.

(2) Where in a case within subsection (1) a bill of lading has been issued in a set of parts, unless otherwise agreed if the documents are not to be sent from abroad the buyer may demand tender of the full set; otherwise only one part of the bill of lading need be tendered. Even if the agreement expressly requires a full set

(a) due tender of a single part is acceptable within the provisions of this Article on cure of improper delivery (subsection (1) of Section 2–508); and

(b) even though the full set is demanded, if the documents are sent from abroad the person tendering an incomplete set may nevertheless require payment upon furnishing an indemnity which the buyer in good faith deems adequate.

(3) A shipment by water or by air or a contract contemplating such shipment is "overseas" insofar as by usage of trade or

agreement it is subject to the commercial, financing or shipping practices characteristic of international deep water commerce.

§ 2–324. "No Arrival, No Sale" Term.

Under a term "no arrival, no sale" or terms of like meaning, unless otherwise agreed,

(a) the seller must properly ship conforming goods and if they arrive by any means he must tender them on arrival but he assumes no obligation that the goods will arrive unless he has caused the non-arrival; and

(b) where without fault of the seller the goods are in part lost or have so deteriorated as no longer to conform to the contract or arrive after the contract time, the buyer may proceed as if there had been casualty to identified goods (Section 2–613).

§ 2–325. "Letter of Credit" Term; "Confirmed Credit".

(1) Failure of the buyer seasonably to furnish an agreed letter of credit is a breach of the contract for sale.

(2) The delivery to seller of a proper letter of credit suspends the buyer's obligation to pay. If the letter of credit is dishonored, the seller may on seasonable notification to the buyer require payment directly from him.

(3) Unless otherwise agreed the term "letter of credit" or "banker's credit" in a contract for sale means an irrevocable credit issued by a financing agency of good repute and, where the shipment is overseas, of good international repute. The term "confirmed credit" means that the credit must also carry the direct obligation of such an agency which does business in the seller's financial market.

§ 2–326. Sale on Approval and Sale or Return; Rights of Creditors.

(1) Unless otherwise agreed, if delivered goods may be returned by the buyer even though they conform to the contract, the transaction is

(a) a "sale on approval" if the goods are delivered primarily for use, and

(b) a "sale or return" if the goods are delivered primarily for resale.

(2) Goods held on approval are not subject to the claims of the buyer's creditors until acceptance; goods held on sale or return are subject to such claims while in the buyer's possession.

(3) Any "or return" term of a contract for sale is to be treated as a separate contract for sale within the statute of frauds section of this Article (Section 2–201) and as contradicting the sale aspect of the contract within the provisions of this Article or on parol or extrinsic evidence (Section 2–202).

As amended in 1999.

§ 2–327. Special Incidents of Sale on Approval and Sale or Return.

(1) Under a sale on approval unless otherwise agreed

(a) although the goods are identified to the contract the risk of loss and the title do not pass to the buyer until acceptance; and

(b) use of the goods consistent with the purpose of trial is not acceptance but failure seasonably to notify the seller of election to return the goods is acceptance, and if the goods conform to the contract acceptance of any part is acceptance of the whole; and

(c) after due notification of election to return, the return is at the seller's risk and expense but a merchant buyer must follow any reasonable instructions.

(2) Under a sale or return unless otherwise agreed

(a) the option to return extends to the whole or any commercial unit of the goods while in substantially their original condition, but must be exercised seasonably; and

(b) the return is at the buyer's risk and expense.

§ 2–328. Sale by Auction.

(1) In a sale by auction if goods are put up in lots each lot is the subject of a separate sale.

(2) A sale by auction is complete when the auctioneer so announces by the fall of the hammer or in other customary manner. Where a bid is made while the hammer is falling in acceptance of a prior bid the auctioneer may in his discretion reopen the bidding or declare the goods sold under the bid on which the hammer was falling.

(3) Such a sale is with reserve unless the goods are in explicit terms put up without reserve. In an auction with reserve the auctioneer may withdraw the goods at any time until he announces completion of the sale. In an auction without reserve, after the auctioneer calls for bids on an article or lot, that article or lot cannot be withdrawn unless no bid is made within a reasonable time. In either case a bidder may retract his bid until the auctioneer's announcement of completion of the sale, but a bidder's retraction does not revive any previous bid.

(4) If the auctioneer knowingly receives a bid on the seller's behalf or the seller makes or procures such as bid, and notice has not been given that liberty for such bidding is reserved, the buyer may at his option avoid the sale or take the goods at the price of the last good faith bid prior to the completion of the sale. This subsection shall not apply to any bid at a forced sale.

Part 4 Title, Creditors and Good Faith Purchasers

§ 2–401. Passing of Title; Reservation for Security; Limited Application of This Section.

Each provision of this Article with regard to the rights, obligations and remedies of the seller, the buyer, purchasers or other third parties applies irrespective of title to the goods except where the provision refers to such title. Insofar as situations are not covered by the other provisions of this Article and matters concerning title became material the following rules apply:

(1) Title to goods cannot pass under a contract for sale prior to their identification to the contract (Section 2–501), and unless otherwise explicitly agreed the buyer acquires by their identification a special property as limited by this Act. Any retention or reservation by the seller of the title (property) in goods shipped or delivered to the buyer is limited in effect to a reservation of a security interest. Subject to these provisions and to the provisions of the Article on Secured Transactions (Article 9), title to goods passes from the seller to the buyer in any manner and on any conditions explicitly agreed on by the parties.

(2) Unless otherwise explicitly agreed title passes to the buyer at the time and place at which the seller completes his per-formance with reference to the physical delivery of the goods, despite any reservation of a security interest and even though a document of title is to be delivered at a different time or place; and in particular and despite any reservation of a security interest by the bill of lading

(a) if the contract requires or authorizes the seller to send the goods to the buyer but does not require him to deliver them at destination, title passes to the buyer at the time and place of shipment; but

(b) if the contract requires delivery at destination, title passes on tender there.

(3) Unless otherwise explicitly agreed where delivery is to be made without moving the goods,

(a) if the seller is to deliver a document of title, title passes at the time when and the place where he delivers such documents; or

(b) if the goods are at the time of contracting already identified and no documents are to be delivered, title passes at the time and place of contracting.

(4) A rejection or other refusal by the buyer to receive or retain the goods, whether or not justified, or a justified revocation of acceptance revests title to the goods in the seller. Such revesting occurs by operation of law and is not a "sale".

§ 2–402. Rights of Seller's Creditors Against Sold Goods.

(1) Except as provided in subsections (2) and (3), rights of unsecured creditors of the seller with respect to goods which have been identified to a contract for sale are subject to the buyer's rights to recover the goods under this Article (Sections 2–502 and 2–716).

(2) A creditor of the seller may treat a sale or an identification of goods to a contract for sale as void if as against him a retention of possession by the seller is fraudulent under any rule of law of the state where the goods are situated, except that retention of possession in good faith and current course of trade by a merchant-seller for a commercially reasonable time after a sale or identification is not fraudulent.

(3) Nothing in this Article shall be deemed to impair the rights of creditors of the seller

(a) under the provisions of the Article on Secured Transactions (Article 9); or

(b) where identification to the contract or delivery is made not in current course of trade but in satisfaction of or as security for a pre-existing claim for money, security or the like and is made under circumstances which under any rule of law of the state where the goods are situated would apart from this Article constitute the transaction a fraudulent transfer or voidable preference.

§ 2–403. Power to Transfer; Good Faith Purchase of Goods; "Entrusting".

(1) A purchaser of goods acquires all title which his transferor had or had power to transfer except that a purchaser of a limited interest acquires rights only to the extent of the interest purchased. A person with voidable title has power to transfer a good title to a good faith purchaser for value. When goods have been delivered under a transaction of purchase the purchaser has such power even though

(a) the transferor was deceived as to the identity of the purchaser, or

(b) the delivery was in exchange for a check which is later dishonored, or

(c) it was agreed that the transaction was to be a "cash sale", or

(d) the delivery was procured through fraud punishable as larcenous under the criminal law.

(2) Any entrusting of possession of goods to a merchant who deals in goods of that kind gives him power to transfer all rights of the entruster to a buyer in ordinary course of business.

(3) "Entrusting" includes any delivery and any acquiescence in retention of possession regardless of any condition expressed between the parties to the delivery or acquiescence and regardless of whether the procurement of the entrusting or the possessor's disposition of the goods have been such as to be larcenous under the criminal law.

(4) The rights of other purchasers of goods and of lien creditors are governed by the Articles on Secured Transactions (Article 9), Bulk Transfers (Article 6) and Documents of Title (Article 7).

As amended in 1988.

Part 5   Performance

§ 2–501.   Insurable Interest in Goods; Manner of Identification of Goods.

(1) The buyer obtains a special property and an insurable interest in goods by identification of existing goods as goods to which the contract refers even though the goods so identified are non-conforming and he has an option to return or reject them. Such identification can be made at any time and in any manner explicitly agreed to by the parties. In the absence of explicit agreement identification occurs

(a) when the contract is made if it is for the sale of goods already existing and identified;

(b) if the contract is for the sale of future goods other than those described in paragraph (c), when goods are shipped, marked or otherwise designated by the seller as goods to which the contract refers;

(c) when the crops are planted or otherwise become growing crops or the young are conceived if the contract is for the sale of unborn young to be born within twelve months after contracting or for the sale of crops to be harvested within twelve months or the next normal harvest season after contracting whichever is longer.

(2) The seller retains an insurable interest in goods so long as title to or any security interest in the goods remains in him and where the identification is by the seller alone he may until default or insolvency or notification to the buyer that the identification is final substitute other goods for those identified.

(3) Nothing in this section impairs any insurable interest recognized under any other statute or rule of law.

§ 2–502.   Buyer's Right to Goods on Seller's Insolvency.

(1) Subject to subsections (2) and (3) and even though the goods have not been shipped a buyer who has paid a part or all of the price of goods in which he has a special property under the provisions of the immediately preceding section may on making and keeping good a tender of any unpaid portion of their price recover them from the seller if:

(a) in the case of goods bought for personal, family, or household purposes, the seller repudiates or fails to deliver as required by the contract; or

(b) in all cases, the seller becomes insolvent within ten days after receipt of the first installment on their price.

(2) The buyer's right to recover the goods under subsection (1) (a) vests upon acquisition of a special property, even if the seller had not then repudiated or failed to deliver.

(3) If the identification creating his special property has been made by the buyer he acquires the right to recover the goods only if they conform to the contract for sale.

As amended in 1999.

§ 2–503.   Manner of Seller's Tender of Delivery.

(1) Tender of delivery requires that the seller put and hold conforming goods at the buyer's disposition and give the buyer any notification reasonably necessary to enable him to take delivery. The manner, time and place for tender are determined by the agreement and this Article, and in particular

(a) tender must be at a reasonable hour, and if it is of goods they must be kept available for the period reasonably necessary to enable the buyer to take possession; but

(b) unless otherwise agreed the buyer must furnish facilities reasonably suited to the receipt of the goods.

(2) Where the case is within the next section respecting shipment tender requires that the seller comply with its provisions.

(3) Where the seller is required to deliver at a particular destination tender requires that he comply with subsection (1) and also in any appropriate case tender documents as described in subsections (4) and (5) of this section.

(4) Where goods are in the possession of a bailee and are to be delivered without being moved

(a) tender requires that the seller either tender a negotiable document of title covering such goods or procure acknowledgment by the bailee of the buyer's right to possession of the goods; but

(b) tender to the buyer of a non-negotiable document of title or of a written direction to the bailee to deliver is sufficient tender unless the buyer seasonably objects, and receipt by the bailee of notification of the buyer's rights fixes those rights as against the bailee and all third persons; but risk of loss of the goods and of any failure by the bailee to honor the non-negotiable document of title or to obey the direction remains on the seller until the buyer has had a reasonable time to present the document or direction, and a refusal by the bailee to honor the document or to obey the direction defeats the tender.

(5) Where the contract requires the seller to deliver documents

(a) he must tender all such documents in correct form, except as provided in this Article with respect to bills of lading in a set (subsection (2) of Section 2–323); and

(b) tender through customary banking channels is sufficient and dishonor of a draft accompanying the documents constitutes non-acceptance or rejection.

§ 2–504. Shipment by Seller.

Where the seller is required or authorized to send the goods to the buyer and the contract does not require him to deliver them at a particular destination, then unless otherwise agreed he must

(a) put the goods in the possession of such a carrier and make such a contract for their transportation as may be reasonable having regard to the nature of the goods and other circumstances of the case; and

(b) obtain and promptly deliver or tender in due form any document necessary to enable the buyer to obtain possession of the goods or otherwise required by the agreement or by usage of trade; and

(c) promptly notify the buyer of the shipment.

Failure to notify the buyer under paragraph (c) or to make a proper contract under paragraph (a) is a ground for rejection only if material delay or loss ensues.

§ 2–505. Seller's Shipment under Reservation.

(1) Where the seller has identified goods to the contract by or before shipment:

(a) his procurement of a negotiable bill of lading to his own order or otherwise reserves in him a security interest in the goods. His procurement of the bill to the order of a financing agency or of the buyer indicates in addition only the seller's expectation of transferring that interest to the person named.

(b) a non-negotiable bill of lading to himself or his nominee reserves possession of the goods as security but except in a case of conditional delivery (subsection (2) of Section 2–507) a non-negotiable bill of lading naming the buyer as consignee reserves no security interest even though the seller retains possession of the bill of lading.

(2) When shipment by the seller with reservation of a security interest is in violation of the contract for sale it constitutes an improper contract for transportation within the preceding section but impairs neither the rights given to the buyer by shipment and identification of the goods to the contract nor the seller's powers as a holder of a negotiable document.

§ 2–506. Rights of Financing Agency.

(1) A financing agency by paying or purchasing for value a draft which relates to a shipment of goods acquires to the extent of the payment or purchase and in addition to its own rights under the draft and any document of title securing it any rights of the shipper in the goods including the right to stop delivery and the shipper's right to have the draft honored by the buyer.

(2) The right to reimbursement of a financing agency which has in good faith honored or purchased the draft under commitment to or authority from the buyer is not impaired by subsequent discovery of defects with reference to any relevant document which was apparently regular on its face.

§ 2–507. Effect of Seller's Tender; Delivery on Condition.

(1) Tender of delivery is a condition to the buyer's duty to accept the goods and, unless otherwise agreed, to his duty to pay for them. Tender entitles the seller to acceptance of the goods and to payment according to the contract.

(2) Where payment is due and demanded on the delivery to the buyer of goods or documents of title, his right as against the seller to retain or dispose of them is conditional upon his making the payment due.

§ 2–508. Cure by Seller of Improper Tender or Delivery; Replacement.

(1) Where any tender or delivery by the seller is rejected because non-conforming and the time for performance has not yet expired, the seller may seasonably notify the buyer of his intention to cure and may then within the contract time make a conforming delivery.

(2) Where the buyer rejects a non-conforming tender which the seller had reasonable grounds to believe would be acceptable with or without money allowance the seller may if he seasonably notifies the buyer have a further reasonable time to substitute a conforming tender.

§ 2–509. Risk of Loss in the Absence of Breach.

(1) Where the contract requires or authorizes the seller to ship the goods by carrier

(a) if it does not require him to deliver them at a particular destination, the risk of loss passes to the buyer when the goods are duly delivered to the carrier even though the shipment is under reservation (Section 2–505); but

(b) if it does require him to deliver them at a particular destination and the goods are there duly tendered while in the possession of the carrier, the risk of loss passes to the buyer when the goods are there duly so tendered as to enable the buyer to take delivery.

(2) Where the goods are held by a bailee to be delivered without being moved, the risk of loss passes to the buyer

(a) on his receipt of a negotiable document of title covering the goods; or

(b) on acknowledgment by the bailee of the buyer's right to possession of the goods; or

(c) after his receipt of a non-negotiable document of title or other written direction to deliver, as provided in subsection (4)(b) of Section 2–503.

(3) In any case not within subsection (1) or (2), the risk of loss passes to the buyer on his receipt of the goods if the seller is a merchant; otherwise the risk passes to the buyer on tender of delivery.

(4) The provisions of this section are subject to contrary agreement of the parties and to the provisions of this Article on sale on approval (Section 2–327) and on effect of breach on risk of loss (Section 2–510).

§ 2–510. Effect of Breach on Risk of Loss.

(1) Where a tender or delivery of goods so fails to conform to the contract as to give a right of rejection the risk of their loss remains on the seller until cure or acceptance.

(2) Where the buyer rightfully revokes acceptance he may to the extent of any deficiency in his effective insurance coverage treat the risk of loss as having rested on the seller from the beginning.

(3) Where the buyer as to conforming goods already identified to the contract for sale repudiates or is otherwise in breach

before risk of their loss has passed to him, the seller may to the extent of any deficiency in his effective insurance coverage treat the risk of loss as resting on the buyer for a commercially reasonable time.

§ 2–511. Tender of Payment by Buyer; Payment by Check.

(1) Unless otherwise agreed tender of payment is a condition to the seller's duty to tender and complete any delivery.

(2) Tender of payment is sufficient when made by any means or in any manner current in the ordinary course of business unless the seller demands payment in legal tender and gives any extension of time reasonably necessary to procure it.

(3) Subject to the provisions of this Act on the effect of an instrument on an obligation (Section 3–310), payment by check is conditional and is defeated as between the parties by dishonor of the check on due presentment.

As amended in 1994.

§ 2–512. Payment by Buyer Before Inspection.

(1) Where the contract requires payment before inspection non-conformity of the goods does not excuse the buyer from so making payment unless

    (a) the non-conformity appears without inspection; or

    (b) despite tender of the required documents the circumstances would justify injunction against honor under this Act (Section 5–109(b)).

(2) Payment pursuant to subsection (1) does not constitute an acceptance of goods or impair the buyer's right to inspect or any of his remedies.

As amended in 1995.

§ 2–513. Buyer's Right to Inspection of Goods.

(1) Unless otherwise agreed and subject to subsection (3), where goods are tendered or delivered or identified to the contract for sale, the buyer has a right before payment or acceptance to inspect them at any reasonable place and time and in any reasonable manner. When the seller is required or authorized to send the goods to the buyer, the inspection may be after their arrival.

(2) Expenses of inspection must be borne by the buyer but may be recovered from the seller if the goods do not conform and are rejected.

(3) Unless otherwise agreed and subject to the provisions of this Article on C.I.F. contracts (subsection (3) of Section 2–321), the buyer is not entitled to inspect the goods before payment of the price when the contract provides

    (a) for delivery "C.O.D." or on other like terms; or

    (b) for payment against documents of title, except where such payment is due only after the goods are to become available for inspection.

(4) A place or method of inspection fixed by the parties is presumed to be exclusive but unless otherwise expressly agreed it does not postpone identification or shift the place for delivery or for passing the risk of loss. If compliance becomes impossible, inspection shall be as provided in this section unless the place or method fixed was clearly intended as an indispensable condition failure of which avoids the contract.

§ 2–514. When Documents Deliverable on Acceptance; When on Payment.

Unless otherwise agreed documents against which a draft is drawn are to be delivered to the drawee on acceptance of the draft if it is payable more than three days after presentment; otherwise, only on payment.

§ 2–515. Preserving Evidence of Goods in Dispute.

In furtherance of the adjustment of any claim or dispute

    (a) either party on reasonable notification to the other and for the purpose of ascertaining the facts and preserving evidence has the right to inspect, test and sample the goods including such of them as may be in the possession or control of the other; and

    (b) the parties may agree to a third party inspection or survey to determine the conformity or condition of the goods and may agree that the findings shall be binding upon them in any subsequent litigation or adjustment.

Part 6   Breach, Repudiation and Excuse

§ 2–601. Buyer's Rights on Improper Delivery.

Subject to the provisions of this Article on breach in installment contracts (Section 2–612) and unless otherwise agreed under the sections on contractual limitations of remedy (Sections 2–718 and 2–719), if the goods or the tender of delivery fail in any respect to conform to the contract, the buyer may

    (a) reject the whole; or

    (b) accept the whole; or

    (c) accept any commercial unit or units and reject the rest.

§ 2–602. Manner and Effect of Rightful Rejection.

(1) Rejection of goods must be within a reasonable time after their delivery or tender. It is ineffective unless the buyer seasonably notifies the seller.

(2) Subject to the provisions of the two following sections on rejected goods (Sections 2–603 and 2–604),

    (a) after rejection any exercise of ownership by the buyer with respect to any commercial unit is wrongful as against the seller; and

    (b) if the buyer has before rejection taken physical possession of goods in which he does not have a security interest under the provisions of this Article (subsection (3) of Section 2–711), he is under a duty after rejection to hold them with reasonable care at the seller's disposition for a time sufficient to permit the seller to remove them; but

    (c) the buyer has no further obligations with regard to goods rightfully rejected.

(3) The seller's rights with respect to goods wrongfully rejected are governed by the provisions of this Article on Seller's remedies in general (Section 2–703).

§ 2–603. Merchant Buyer's Duties as to Rightfully Rejected Goods.

(1) Subject to any security interest in the buyer (subsection (3) of Section 2–711), when the seller has no agent or place of business at the market of rejection a merchant buyer is under a duty after rejection of goods in his possession or control to follow any reasonable instructions received from the seller with

respect to the goods and in the absence of such instructions to make reasonable efforts to sell them for the seller's account if they are perishable or threaten to decline in value speedily. Instructions are not reasonable if on demand indemnity for expenses is not forthcoming.

(2) When the buyer sells goods under subsection (1), he is entitled to reimbursement from the seller or out of the proceeds for reasonable expenses of caring for and selling them, and if the expenses include no selling commission then to such commission as is usual in the trade or if there is none to a reasonable sum not exceeding ten per cent on the gross proceeds.

(3) In complying with this section the buyer is held only to good faith and good faith conduct hereunder is neither acceptance nor conversion nor the basis of an action for damages.

§ 2–604.   Buyer's Options as to Salvage of Rightfully Rejected Goods.

Subject to the provisions of the immediately preceding section on perishables if the seller gives no instructions within a reasonable time after notification of rejection the buyer may store the rejected goods for the seller's account or reship them to him or resell them for the seller's account with reimbursement as provided in the preceding section. Such action is not acceptance or conversion.

§ 2–605.   Waiver of Buyer's Objections by Failure to Particularize.

(1) The buyer's failure to state in connection with rejection a particular defect which is ascertainable by reasonable inspection precludes him from relying on the unstated defect to justify rejection or to establish breach

    (a) where the seller could have cured it if stated seasonably; or

    (b) between merchants when the seller has after rejection made a request in writing for a full and final written statement of all defects on which the buyer proposes to rely.

(2) Payment against documents made without reservation of rights precludes recovery of the payment for defects apparent on the face of the documents.

§ 2–606.   What Constitutes Acceptance of Goods.

(1) Acceptance of goods occurs when the buyer

    (a) after a reasonable opportunity to inspect the goods signifies to the seller that the goods are conforming or that he will take or retain them in spite of their nonconformity; or

    (b) fails to make an effective rejection (subsection (1) of Section 2–602), but such acceptance does not occur until the buyer has had a reasonable opportunity to inspect them; or

    (c) does any act inconsistent with the seller's ownership; but if such act is wrongful as against the seller it is an acceptance only if ratified by him.

(2) Acceptance of a part of any commercial unit is acceptance of that entire unit.

§ 2–607.   Effect of Acceptance; Notice of Breach; Burden of Establishing Breach After Acceptance; Notice of Claim or Litigation to Person Answerable Over.

(1) The buyer must pay at the contract rate for any goods accepted.

(2) Acceptance of goods by the buyer precludes rejection of the goods accepted and if made with knowledge of a non-conformity cannot be revoked because of it unless the acceptance was on the reasonable assumption that the non-conformity would be seasonably cured but acceptance does not of itself impair any other remedy provided by this Article for non-conformity.

(3) Where a tender has been accepted

    (a) the buyer must within a reasonable time after he discovers or should have discovered any breach notify the seller of breach or be barred from any remedy; and

    (b) if the claim is one for infringement or the like (subsection (3) of Section 2–312) and the buyer is sued as a result of such a breach he must so notify the seller within a reasonable time after he receives notice of the litigation or be barred from any remedy over for liability established by the litigation.

(4) The burden is on the buyer to establish any breach with respect to the goods accepted.

(5) Where the buyer is sued for breach of a warranty or other obligation for which his seller is answerable over

    (a) he may give his seller written notice of the litigation. If the notice states that the seller may come in and defend and that if the seller does not do so he will be bound in any action against him by his buyer by any determination of fact common to the two litigations, then unless the seller after seasonable receipt of the notice does come in and defend he is so bound.

    (b) if the claim is one for infringement or the like (subsection (3) of Section 2–312) the original seller may demand in writing that his buyer turn over to him control of the litigation including settlement or else be barred from any remedy over and if he also agrees to bear all expense and to satisfy any adverse judgment, then unless the buyer after seasonable receipt of the demand does turn over control the buyer is so barred.

(6) The provisions of subsections (3), (4) and (5) apply to any obligation of a buyer to hold the seller harmless against infringement or the like (subsection (3) of Section 2–312).

§ 2–608.   Revocation of Acceptance in Whole or in Part.

(1) The buyer may revoke his acceptance of a lot or commercial unit whose non-conformity substantially impairs its value to him if he has accepted it

    (a) on the reasonable assumption that its nonconformity would be cured and it has not been seasonably cured; or

    (b) without discovery of such non-conformity if his acceptance was reasonably induced either by the difficulty of discovery before acceptance or by the seller's assurances.

(2) Revocation of acceptance must occur within a reasonable time after the buyer discovers or should have discovered the ground for it and before any substantial change in condition of the goods which is not caused by their own defects. It is not effective until the buyer notifies the seller of it.

(3) A buyer who so revokes has the same rights and duties with regard to the goods involved as if he had rejected them.

§ 2–609.   Right to Adequate Assurance of Performance.

(1) A contract for sale imposes an obligation on each party that the other's expectation of receiving due performance will not

be impaired. When reasonable grounds for insecurity arise with respect to the performance of either party the other may in writing demand adequate assurance of due performance and until he receives such assurance may if commercially reasonable suspend any performance for which he has not already received the agreed return.

(2) Between merchants the reasonableness of grounds for insecurity and the adequacy of any assurance offered shall be determined according to commercial standards.

(3) Acceptance of any improper delivery or payment does not prejudice the party's right to demand adequate assurance of future performance.

(4) After receipt of a justified demand failure to provide within a reasonable time not exceeding thirty days such assurance of due performance as is adequate under the circumstances of the particular case is a repudiation of the contract.

§ 2–610. Anticipatory Repudiation.

When either party repudiates the contract with respect to a performance not yet due the loss of which will substantially impair the value of the contract to the other, the aggrieved party may

(a) for a commercially reasonable time await performance by the repudiating party; or

(b) resort to any remedy for breach (Section 2–703 or Section 2–711), even though he has notified the repudiating party that he would await the latter's performance and has urged retraction; and

(c) in either case suspend his own performance or proceed in accordance with the provisions of this Article on the seller's right to identify goods to the contract notwithstanding breach or to salvage unfinished goods (Section 2–704).

§ 2–611. Retraction of Anticipatory Repudiation.

(1) Until the repudiating party's next performance is due he can retract his repudiation unless the aggrieved party has since the repudiation cancelled or materially changed his position or otherwise indicated that he considers the repudiation final.

(2) Retraction may be by any method which clearly indicates to the aggrieved party that the repudiating party intends to perform, but must include any assurance justifiably demanded under the provisions of this Article (Section 2–609).

(3) Retraction reinstates the repudiating party's rights under the contract with due excuse and allowance to the aggrieved party for any delay occasioned by the repudiation.

§ 2–612. "Installment Contract"; Breach.

(1) An "installment contract" is one which requires or authorizes the delivery of goods in separate lots to be separately accepted, even though the contract contains a clause "each delivery is a separate contract" or its equivalent.

(2) The buyer may reject any installment which is non-conforming if the non-conformity substantially impairs the value of that installment and cannot be cured or if the non-conformity is a defect in the required documents; but if the non-conformity does not fall within subsection (3) and the seller gives adequate assurance of its cure the buyer must accept that installment.

(3) Whenever non-conformity or default with respect to one or more installments substantially impairs the value of the whole contract there is a breach of the whole. But the aggrieved party reinstates the contract if he accepts a non-conforming installment without seasonably notifying of cancellation or if he brings an action with respect only to past installments or demands performance as to future installments.

§ 2–613. Casualty to Identified Goods.

Where the contract requires for its performance goods identified when the contract is made, and the goods suffer casualty without fault of either party before the risk of loss passes to the buyer, or in a proper case under a "no arrival, no sale" term (Section 2–324) then

(a) if the loss is total the contract is avoided; and

(b) if the loss is partial or the goods have so deteriorated as no longer to conform to the contract the buyer may nevertheless demand inspection and at his option either treat the contract as voided or accept the goods with due allowance from the contract price for the deterioration or the deficiency in quantity but without further right against the seller.

§ 2–614. Substituted Performance.

(1) Where without fault of either party the agreed berthing, loading, or unloading facilities fail or an agreed type of carrier becomes unavailable or the agreed manner of delivery otherwise becomes commercially impracticable but a commercially reasonable substitute is available, such substitute performance must be tendered and accepted.

(2) If the agreed means or manner of payment fails because of domestic or foreign governmental regulation, the seller may withhold or stop delivery unless the buyer provides a means or manner of payment which is commercially a substantial equivalent. If delivery has already been taken, payment by the means or in the manner provided by the regulation discharges the buyer's obligation unless the regulation is discriminatory, oppressive or predatory.

§ 2–615. Excuse by Failure of Presupposed Conditions.

Except so far as a seller may have assumed a greater obligation and subject to the preceding section on substituted performance:

(a) Delay in delivery or non-delivery in whole or in part by a seller who complies with paragraphs (b) and (c) is not a breach of his duty under a contract for sale if performance as agreed has been made impracticable by the occurrence of a contingency the nonoccurrence of which was a basic assumption on which the contract was made or by compliance in good faith with any applicable foreign or domestic governmental regulation or order whether or not it later proves to be invalid.

(b) Where the causes mentioned in paragraph (a) affect only a part of the seller's capacity to perform, he must allocate production and deliveries among his customers but may at his option include regular customers not then under contract as well as his own requirements for further manufacture. He may so allocate in any manner which is fair and reasonable.

(c) The seller must notify the buyer seasonably that there will be delay or non-delivery and, when allocation is required under paragraph (b), of the estimated quota thus made available for the buyer.

§ 2–616. Procedure on Notice Claiming Excuse.

(1) Where the buyer receives notification of a material or indefinite delay or an allocation justified under the preceding section he may by written notification to the seller as to any delivery concerned, and where the prospective deficiency substantially impairs the value of the whole contract under the provisions of this Article relating to breach of installment contracts (Section 2–612), then also as to the whole,

(a) terminate and thereby discharge any unexecuted portion of the contract; or

(b) modify the contract by agreeing to take his available quota in substitution.

(2) If after receipt of such notification from the seller the buyer fails so to modify the contract within a reasonable time not exceeding thirty days the contract lapses with respect to any deliveries affected.

(3) The provisions of this section may not be negated by agreement except in so far as the seller has assumed a greater obligation under the preceding section.

Part 7 Remedies

§ 2–701. Remedies for Breach of Collateral Contracts Not Impaired.

Remedies for breach of any obligation or promise collateral or ancillary to a contract for sale are not impaired by the provisions of this Article.

§ 2–702. Seller's Remedies on Discovery of Buyer's Insolvency.

(1) Where the seller discovers the buyer to be insolvent he may refuse delivery except for cash including payment for all goods theretofore delivered under the contract, and stop delivery under this Article (Section 2–705).

(2) Where the seller discovers that the buyer has received goods on credit while insolvent he may reclaim the goods upon demand made within ten days after the receipt, but if misrepresentation of solvency has been made to the particular seller in writing within three months before delivery the ten day limitation does not apply. Except as provided in this subsection the seller may not base a right to reclaim goods on the buyer's fraudulent or innocent misrepresentation of solvency or of intent to pay.

(3) The seller's right to reclaim under subsection (2) is subject to the rights of a buyer in ordinary course or other good faith purchaser under this Article (Section 2–403). Successful reclamation of goods excludes all other remedies with respect to them.

§ 2–703. Seller's Remedies in General.

Where the buyer wrongfully rejects or revokes acceptance of goods or fails to make a payment due on or before delivery or repudiates with respect to a part or the whole, then with respect to any goods directly affected and, if the breach is of the whole contract (Section 2–612), then also with respect to the whole undelivered balance, the aggrieved seller may

(a) withhold delivery of such goods;

(b) stop delivery by any bailee as hereafter provided (Section 2–705);

(c) proceed under the next section respecting goods still unidentified to the contract;

(d) resell and recover damages as hereafter provided (Section 2–706);

(e) recover damages for non-acceptance (Section 2–708) or in a proper case the price (Section 2–709);

(f) cancel.

§ 2–704. Seller's Right to Identify Goods to the Contract Notwithstanding Breach or to Salvage Unfinished Goods.

(1) An aggrieved seller under the preceding section may

(a) identify to the contract conforming goods not already identified if at the time he learned of the breach they are in his possession or control;

(b) treat as the subject of resale goods which have demonstrably been intended for the particular contract even though those goods are unfinished.

(2) Where the goods are unfinished an aggrieved seller may in the exercise of reasonable commercial judgment for the purposes of avoiding loss and of effective realization either complete the manufacture and wholly identify the goods to the contract or cease manufacture and resell for scrap or salvage value or proceed in any other reasonable manner.

§ 2–705. Seller's Stoppage of Delivery in Transit or Otherwise.

(1) The seller may stop delivery of goods in the possession of a carrier or other bailee when he discovers the buyer to be insolvent (Section 2–702) and may stop delivery of carload, truckload, planeload or larger shipments of express or freight when the buyer repudiates or fails to make a payment due before delivery or if for any other reason the seller has a right to withhold or reclaim the goods.

(2) As against such buyer the seller may stop delivery until

(a) receipt of the goods by the buyer; or

(b) acknowledgment to the buyer by any bailee of the goods except a carrier that the bailee holds the goods for the buyer; or

(c) such acknowledgment to the buyer by a carrier by reshipment or as warehouseman; or

(d) negotiation to the buyer of any negotiable document of title covering the goods.

(3) (a) To stop delivery the seller must so notify as to enable the bailee by reasonable diligence to prevent delivery of the goods.

(b) After such notification the bailee must hold and deliver the goods according to the directions of the seller but the seller is liable to the bailee for any ensuing charges or damages.

(c) If a negotiable document of title has been issued for goods the bailee is not obliged to obey a notification to stop until surrender of the document.

(d) A carrier who has issued a non-negotiable bill of lading is not obliged to obey a notification to stop received from a person other than the consignor.

§ 2–706. Seller's Resale Including Contract for Resale.

(1) Under the conditions stated in Section 2–703 on seller's remedies, the seller may resell the goods concerned or the undelivered balance thereof. Where the resale is made in good faith and in a commercially reasonable manner the seller may recover the difference between the resale price and the contract price together with any incidental damages allowed under the provisions of this Article (Section 2–710), but less expenses saved in consequence of the buyer's breach.

(2) Except as otherwise provided in subsection (3) or unless otherwise agreed resale may be at public or private sale including sale by way of one or more contracts to sell or of identification to an existing contract of the seller. Sale may be as a unit or in parcels and at any time and place and on any terms but every aspect of the sale including the method, manner, time, place and terms must be commercially reasonable. The resale must be reasonably identified as referring to the broken contract, but it is not necessary that the goods be in existence or that any or all of them have been identified to the contract before the breach.

(3) Where the resale is at private sale the seller must give the buyer reasonable notification of his intention to resell.

(4) Where the resale is at public sale

    (a) only identified goods can be sold except where there is a recognized market for a public sale of futures in goods of the kind; and

    (b) it must be made at a usual place or market for public sale if one is reasonably available and except in the case of goods which are perishable or threaten to decline in value speedily the seller must give the buyer reasonable notice of the time and place of the resale; and

    (c) if the goods are not to be within the view of those attending the sale the notification of sale must state the place where the goods are located and provide for their reasonable inspection by prospective bidders; and

    (d) the seller may buy.

(5) A purchaser who buys in good faith at a resale takes the goods free of any rights of the original buyer even though the seller fails to comply with one or more of the requirements of this section.

(6) The seller is not accountable to the buyer for any profit made on any resale. A person in the position of a seller (Section 2–707) or a buyer who has rightfully rejected or justifiably revoked acceptance must account for any excess over the amount of his security interest, as hereinafter defined (subsection (3) of Section 2–711).

§ 2–707. "Person in the Position of a Seller".

(1) A "person in the position of a seller" includes as against a principal an agent who has paid or become responsible for the price of goods on behalf of his principal or anyone who otherwise holds a security interest or other right in goods similar to that of a seller.

(2) A person in the position of a seller may as provided in this Article withhold or stop delivery (Section 2–705) and resell (Section 2–706) and recover incidental damages (Section 2–710).

§ 2–708. Seller's Damages for Non-Acceptance or Repudiation.

(1) Subject to subsection (2) and to the provisions of this Article with respect to proof of market price (Section 2–723), the measure of damages for non-acceptance or repudiation by the buyer is the difference between the market price at the time and place for tender and the unpaid contract price together with any incidental damages provided in this Article (Section 2–710), but less expenses saved in consequence of the buyer's breach.

(2) If the measure of damages provided in subsection (1) is inadequate to put the seller in as good a position as performance would have done then the measure of damages is the profit (including reasonable overhead) which the seller would have made from full performance by the buyer, together with any incidental damages provided in this Article (Section 2–710), due allowance for costs reasonably incurred and due credit for payments or proceeds of resale.

§ 2–709. Action for the Price.

(1) When the buyer fails to pay the price as it becomes due the seller may recover, together with any incidental damages under the next section, the price

    (a) of goods accepted or of conforming goods lost or damaged within a commercially reasonable time after risk of their loss has passed to the buyer; and

    (b) of goods identified to the contract if the seller is unable after reasonable effort to resell them at a reasonable price or the circumstances reasonably indicate that such effort will be unavailing.

(2) Where the seller sues for the price he must hold for the buyer any goods which have been identified to the contract and are still in his control except that if resale becomes possible he may resell them at any time prior to the collection of the judgment. The net proceeds of any such resale must be credited to the buyer and payment of the judgment entitles him to any goods not resold.

(3) After the buyer has wrongfully rejected or revoked acceptance of the goods or has failed to make a payment due or has repudiated (Section 2–610), a seller who is held not entitled to the price under this section shall nevertheless be awarded damages for non-acceptance under the preceding section.

§ 2–710. Seller's Incidental Damages.

Incidental damages to an aggrieved seller include any commercially reasonable charges, expenses or commissions incurred in stopping delivery, in the transportation, care and custody of goods after the buyer's breach, in connection with return or resale of the goods or otherwise resulting from the breach.

§ 2–711. Buyer's Remedies in General; Buyer's Security Interest in Rejected Goods.

(1) Where the seller fails to make delivery or repudiates or the buyer rightfully rejects or justifiably revokes acceptance then with respect to any goods involved, and with respect to the whole if the breach goes to the whole contract (Section 2–612), the buyer may cancel and whether or not he has done so may in addition to recovering so much of the price as has been paid

    (a) "cover" and have damages under the next section as to all the goods affected whether or not they have been identified to the contract; or

(b) recover damages for non-delivery as provided in this Article (Section 2–713).

(2) Where the seller fails to deliver or repudiates the buyer may also

(a) if the goods have been identified recover them as provided in this Article (Section 2–502); or

(b) in a proper case obtain specific performance or replevy the goods as provided in this Article (Section 2–716).

(3) On rightful rejection or justifiable revocation of acceptance a buyer has a security interest in goods in his possession or control for any payments made on their price and any expenses reasonably incurred in their inspection, receipt, transportation, care and custody and may hold such goods and resell them in like manner as an aggrieved seller (Section 2–706).

§ 2–712. "Cover"; Buyer's Procurement of Substitute Goods.

(1) After a breach within the preceding section the buyer may "cover" by making in good faith and without unreasonable delay any reasonable purchase of or contract to purchase goods in substitution for those due from the seller.

(2) The buyer may recover from the seller as damages the difference between the cost of cover and the contract price together with any incidental or consequential damages as hereinafter defined (Section 2–715), but less expenses saved in consequence of the seller's breach.

(3) Failure of the buyer to effect cover within this section does not bar him from any other remedy.

§ 2–713. Buyer's Damages for Non-Delivery or Repudiation.

(1) Subject to the provisions of this Article with respect to proof of market price (Section 2–723), the measure of damages for non-delivery or repudiation by the seller is the difference between the market price at the time when the buyer learned of the breach and the contract price together with any incidental and consequential damages provided in this Article (Section 2–715), but less expenses saved in consequence of the seller's breach.

(2) Market price is to be determined as of the place for tender or, in cases of rejection after arrival or revocation of acceptance, as of the place of arrival.

§ 2–714. Buyer's Damages for Breach in Regard to Accepted Goods.

(1) Where the buyer has accepted goods and given notification (subsection (3) of Section 2–607) he may recover as damages for any non-conformity of tender the loss resulting in the ordinary course of events from the seller's breach as determined in any manner which is reasonable.

(2) The measure of damages for breach of warranty is the difference at the time and place of acceptance between the value of the goods accepted and the value they would have had if they had been as warranted, unless special circumstances show proximate damages of a different amount.

(3) In a proper case any incidental and consequential damages under the next section may also be recovered.

§ 2–715. Buyer's Incidental and Consequential Damages.

(1) Incidental damages resulting from the seller's breach include expenses reasonably incurred in inspection, receipt, transpor-

tation and care and custody of goods rightfully rejected, any commercially reasonable charges, expenses or commissions in connection with effecting cover and any other reasonable expense incident to the delay or other breach.

(2) Consequential damages resulting from the seller's breach include

(a) any loss resulting from general or particular requirements and needs of which the seller at the time of contracting had reason to know and which could not reasonably be prevented by cover or otherwise; and

(b) injury to person or property proximately resulting from any breach of warranty.

§ 2–716. Buyer's Right to Specific Performance or Replevin.

(1) Specific performance may be decreed where the goods are unique or in other proper circumstances.

(2) The decree for specific performance may include such terms and conditions as to payment of the price, damages, or other relief as the court may deem just.

(3) The buyer has a right of replevin for goods identified to the contract if after reasonable effort he is unable to effect cover for such goods or the circumstances reasonably indicate that such effort will be unavailing or if the goods have been shipped under reservation and satisfaction of the security interest in them has been made or tendered. In the case of goods bought for personal, family, or household purposes, the buyer's right of replevin vests upon acquisition of a special property, even if the seller had not then repudiated or failed to deliver.

As amended in 1999.

§ 2–717. Deduction of Damages From the Price.

The buyer on notifying the seller of his intention to do so may deduct all or any part of the damages resulting from any breach of the contract from any part of the price still due under the same contract.

§ 2–718. Liquidation or Limitation of Damages; Deposits.

(1) Damages for breach by either party may be liquidated in the agreement but only at an amount which is reasonable in the light of the anticipated or actual harm caused by the breach, the difficulties of proof of loss, and the inconvenience or nonfeasibility of otherwise obtaining an adequate remedy. A term fixing unreasonably large liquidated damages is void as a penalty.

(2) Where the seller justifiably withholds delivery of goods because of the buyer's breach, the buyer is entitled to restitution of any amount by which the sum of his payments exceeds

(a) the amount to which the seller is entitled by virtue of terms liquidating the seller's damages in accordance with subsection (1), or

(b) in the absence of such terms, twenty per cent of the value of the total performance for which the buyer is obligated under the contract or $500, whichever is smaller.

(3) The buyer's right to restitution under subsection (2) is subject to offset to the extent that the seller establishes

(a) a right to recover damages under the provisions of this Article other than subsection (1), and

(b) the amount or value of any benefits received by the buyer directly or indirectly by reason of the contract.

(4) Where a seller has received payment in goods their reasonable value or the proceeds of their resale shall be treated as payments for the purposes of subsection (2); but if the seller has notice of the buyer's breach before reselling goods received in part performance, his resale is subject to the conditions laid down in this Article on resale by an aggrieved seller (Section 2–706).

§ 2–719. Contractual Modification or Limitation of Remedy.

(1) Subject to the provisions of subsections (2) and (3) of this section and of the preceding section on liquidation and limitation of damages,

(a) the agreement may provide for remedies in addition to or in substitution for those provided in this Article and may limit or alter the measure of damages recoverable under this Article, as by limiting the buyer's remedies to return of the goods and repayment of the price or to repair and replacement of nonconforming goods or parts; and

(b) resort to a remedy as provided is optional unless the remedy is expressly agreed to be exclusive, in which case it is the sole remedy.

(2) Where circumstances cause an exclusive or limited remedy to fail of its essential purpose, remedy may be had as provided in this Act.

(3) Consequential damages may be limited or excluded unless the limitation or exclusion is unconscionable. Limitation of consequential damages for injury to the person in the case of consumer goods is prima facie unconscionable but limitation of damages where the loss is commercial is not.

§ 2–720. Effect of "Cancellation" or "Rescission" on Claims for Antecedent Breach.

Unless the contrary intention clearly appears, expressions of "cancellation" or "rescission" of the contract or the like shall not be construed as a renunciation or discharge of any claim in damages for an antecedent breach.

§ 2–721. Remedies for Fraud.

Remedies for material misrepresentation or fraud include all remedies available under this Article for non-fraudulent breach. Neither rescission or a claim for rescission of the contract for sale nor rejection or return of the goods shall bar or be deemed inconsistent with a claim for damages or other remedy.

§ 2–722. Who Can Sue Third Parties for Injury to Goods.

Where a third party so deals with goods which have been identified to a contract for sale as to cause actionable injury to a party to that contract

(a) a right of action against the third party is in either party to the contract for sale who has title to or a security interest or a special property or an insurable interest in the goods; and if the goods have been destroyed or converted a right of action is also in the party who either bore the risk of loss under the contract for sale or has since the injury assumed that risk as against the other;

(b) if at the time of the injury the party plaintiff did not bear the risk of loss as against the other party to the contract for sale and there is no arrangement between them for disposition of the recovery, his suit or settlement is, subject to his own interest, as a fiduciary for the other party to the contract;

(c) either party may with the consent of the other sue for the benefit of whom it may concern.

§ 2–723. Proof of Market Price: Time and Place.

(1) If an action based on anticipatory repudiation comes to trial before the time for performance with respect to some or all of the goods, any damages based on market price (Section 2–708 or Section 2–713) shall be determined according to the price of such goods prevailing at the time when the aggrieved party learned of the repudiation.

(2) If evidence of a price prevailing at the times or places described in this Article is not readily available the price prevailing within any reasonable time before or after the time described or at any other place which in commercial judgment or under usage of trade would serve as a reasonable substitute for the one described may be used, making any proper allowance for the cost of transporting the goods to or from such other place.

(3) Evidence of a relevant price prevailing at a time or place other than the one described in this Article offered by one party is not admissible unless and until he has given the other party such notice as the court finds sufficient to prevent unfair surprise.

§ 2–724. Admissibility of Market Quotations.

Whenever the prevailing price or value of any goods regularly bought and sold in any established commodity market is in issue, reports in official publications or trade journals or in newspapers or periodicals of general circulation published as the reports of such market shall be admissible in evidence. The circumstances of the preparation of such a report may be shown to affect its weight but not its admissibility.

§ 2–725. Statute of Limitations in Contracts for Sale.

(1) An action for breach of any contract for sale must be commenced within four years after the cause of action has accrued. By the original agreement the parties may reduce the period of limitation to not less than one year but may not extend it.

(2) A cause of action accrues when the breach occurs, regardless of the aggrieved party's lack of knowledge of the breach. A breach of warranty occurs when tender of delivery is made, except that where a warranty explicitly extends to future performance of the goods and discovery of the breach must await the time of such performance the cause of action accrues when the breach is or should have been discovered.

(3) Where an action commenced within the time limited by subsection (1) is so terminated as to leave available a remedy by another action for the same breach such other action may be commenced after the expiration of the time limited and within six months after the termination of the first action unless the termination resulted from voluntary discontinuance or from dismissal for failure or neglect to prosecute.

(4) This section does not alter the law on tolling of the statute of limitations nor does it apply to causes of action which have accrued before this Act becomes effective.

CHAPTER 1

1. *Under what circumstances might a judge rely on case law to determine the intent and purpose of a statute?* Case law includes courts' interpretations of statutes, as well as constitutional provisions and administrative rules. Statutes often codify common law rules. For these reasons, a judge might rely on the common law as a guide to the intent and purpose of a statute.

2. *Assuming that these convicted war criminals had not disobeyed any law of their country and had merely been following their government's orders, what law had they violated? Explain.* At the time of the Nuremberg trials, "crimes against humanity" were new international crimes. The laws criminalized such acts as murder, extermination, enslavement, deportation, and other inhumane acts committed against any civilian population. These international laws derived their legitimacy from "natural law."

Natural law, which is the oldest and one of the most significant schools of jurisprudence, holds that governments and legal systems should reflect the moral and ethical ideals that are inherent in human nature. Because natural law is universal and discoverable by reason, its adherents believe that all other law is derived from natural law. Natural law therefore supersedes laws created by humans (national, or "positive," law), and in a conflict between the two, national or positive law loses its legitimacy.

The Nuremberg defendants asserted that they had been acting in accordance with German law. The judges dismissed these claims, reasoning that the defendants' acts were commonly regarded as crimes and that the accused must have known that the acts would be considered criminal. The judges clearly believed the tenets of natural law and expected that the defendants, too, should have been able to realize that their acts ran afoul of it. The fact that the "positivist law" of Germany at the time required them to commit these acts is irrelevant. Under natural law theory, the international court was justified in finding the defendants guilty of crimes against humanity.

CHAPTER 2

1. *Can a state, in the interest of energy conservation, ban all advertising by power utilities if conservation could be accomplished by less restrictive means? Why or why not?* No. Even if commercial speech is not related to illegal activities nor misleading, it may be restricted if a state has a substantial interest that cannot be achieved by less restrictive means. In this case, the interest in energy conservation is substantial, but it could be achieved by less restrictive means. That would be the utilities' defense against the enforcement of this state law.

2. *Is this a violation of equal protection if the only reason for the tax is to protect the local firms from out-of-state competition? Explain.* Yes. The tax would limit the liberty of some persons (out of state businesses), so it is subject to a review under the equal protection clause. Protecting local businesses from out-of-state competition is not a legitimate government objective. Thus, such a tax would violate the equal protection clause.

CHAPTER 3

1. *Does the court in Sue's state have jurisdiction over Tipton? What factors will the court consider?* A corporation normally is subject to personal jurisdiction in the state in which it is incorporated, has its principal office, and/or is doing business. Under the authority of a state long arm statute, a court can exercise personal jurisdiction over certain out-of-state defendants based on activities that took place within the state. Before a court can exercise jurisdiction, though, it must be demonstrated that the defendant had minimum contacts with the state to justify the jurisdiction.

The minimum-contacts requirement is usually met if the corporation advertises or sells its products within the state, or places its goods into the "stream of commerce" with the intent that the goods be sold in the state. Therefore, a court will consider whether Tipton advertised or sold its product within Sue's state. The court may also look at whether the contract between Sue and Tipton was negotiated or signed within the state.

2. *If the dispute is not resolved, or if either party disagrees with the decision of the mediator or arbitrator, will a court hear the case? Explain.* Yes. Submission of the dispute to mediation or nonbinding arbitration is mandatory, but compliance with a decision of the mediator or arbitrator is voluntary.

CHAPTER 4

1. *Can Lou recover from Jana? Why or why not?* Probably. To recover on the basis of negligence, the injured party as a plaintiff must show that the truck's owner owed the plaintiff a duty of care, that the owner breached that duty, that the plaintiff was injured, and that the breach caused the injury.

In this situation, the owner's actions breached the duty of reasonable care. The billboard falling on the plaintiff was the direct cause of the injury, not the plaintiff's own negligence. Thus, liability turns on whether the plaintiff can connect the breach of duty to the injury. This involves the test of proximate cause—the question of foreseeability. The consequences to the injured party must have been a foreseeable result of the owner's carelessness.

2. *What might the firm successfully claim in defense?* The company might defend against this electrician's claim by asserting that the electrician should have known of the risk and, therefore, the company had no duty to warn. According to the problem, the danger is common knowledge in the electrician's field and should have been apparent to this electrician, given his years of training and experience. In other words, the company most likely had no need to warn the electrician of the risk.

The firm could also raise comparative negligence. Both parties' negligence, if any, could be weighed and the liability distributed proportionally. The defendant could also assert assumption of risk, claiming that the electrician voluntarily entered into a dangerous situation, knowing the risk involved.

CHAPTER 5

1. *Has Roslyn violated any of the intellectual property rights discussed in this chapter? Explain.* Yes. Roslyn has committed theft of trade secrets. Lists of suppliers and customers cannot be patented, copyrighted, or trademarked, but the information they contain is protected against appropriation by others as trade secrets. And most likely, Roslyn signed a contract, agreeing not to use this information outside her employment by Organic. But even without this contract, Organic could have made a convincing case against its ex-employee for a theft of trade secrets.

2. *Is this patent infringement? If so, how might Global save the cost of suing World for infringement and at the same time profit from World's sales?* This is patent infringement. A software maker in this situation might best protect its product, save litigation costs, and profit from its patent by the use of a license. In the context of this problem, a license would grant permission to sell a patented item. (A license can be limited to certain purposes and to the licensee only.)

CHAPTER 6

1. *Has Karl done anything wrong? Explain.* Karl may have committed trademark infringement. Search engines compile their results by looking through Web sites' key-word fields. Key words, or meta tags, increase the likelihood that a site will be included in search engine results, even if the words have no connection to the site.

A site that appropriates the key words of other sites with more frequent hits will appear in the same search engine results as the more popular sites. But using another's trademark as a key word without the owner's permission normally constitutes trademark infringement. Of course, some uses of another's trademark as a meta tag may be permissible if the use is reasonably necessary and does not suggest that the owner authorized or sponsored the use.

2. *Can Eagle Corporation stop this use of eagle? If so, what must the company show?* Yes. This may be an instance of trademark dilution. Dilution occurs when a trademark is used, without permission, in a way that diminishes the distinctive quality of the mark. Dilution does not require proof that consumers are likely to be confused by the use of the unauthorized mark. The products involved do not have to be similar. Dilution does require, however, that a mark be famous when the dilution occurs.

CHAPTER 7

1. *With respect to the gas station, has she committed a crime? If so, what is it?* Yes. With respect to the gas station, she has obtained goods by false pretenses. She might also be charged with larceny and forgery, and most states have special statutes covering illegal use of credit cards.

2. *Has Ben committed a crime? If so, what is it?* Yes. The Counterfeit Access Device and Computer Fraud and Abuse Act provides that a person who accesses a computer online, without permission, to obtain classified data—such as consumer credit files in a credit agency's database—is subject to criminal prosecution. The crime has two elements: accessing the computer without permission and taking data. It is a felony if done for private financial gain. Penalties include fines and imprisonment for up to twenty years. The victim of the theft can also bring a civil suit against the criminal to obtain damages and other relief.

CHAPTER 8

1. *Are there ethical concerns about putting traumatized children on the news immediately after an event like this? Why or why not?* In determining whether it is ethical to interview these children soon after a tragic event, it is important to analyze the competing interests and reasons behind the interviews. The interviews may generate more viewers, which may lead to higher ratings and more advertising revenue for the company and its shareholders. Alternatively, the value of the interview to the public or to any investigation may be minimal. The children may not have accurate information and may be further traumatized by the interview process.

2. *Is it ethical for Johnny to take a performance-enhancing drug that has not been banned? Why or why not?* Maybe. Individuals and businesses often face ethical dilemmas when the letter of the law seems clear but alternatives exist that may violate what is known as the spirit of the law or the purpose for the law. In this case, the restrictions exist to stop athletes from performing better than they would naturally because of a foreign substance. The list of banned substances may not be able to keep up with the advances in technology and science in developing performance-enhancing drugs.

Some might argue that it is ethical for him to take anything that is not formally banned and that all competitors have the same ability to access and take those substances and therefore any advantage is eliminated. Because there seems to be no unfair advantage, the purpose of the restriction is not frustrated. There is an implicit assumption, however, that all performers have the connections and the resources to obtain the non-banned substance. Because this assumption is not necessarily true, it is more likely an ethical violation to take the non-banned performance enhancing drugs, even if it is not technically against the rules.

CHAPTER 9

1. What standard determines whether these parties have a contract? Under the objective theory of contracts, if a reasonable person would have thought that Joli had accepted Kerin's offer when she signed and returned the letter, then a contract was made, and Joli is obligated to buy the book. This depends, in part, on what was said in the letter and what was said in response. For instance, did the letter contain a valid offer, and did the response constitute a valid acceptance? Under any circumstances, the issue is not whether either party subjectively believed that they did, or did not, have a contract.

2. Can Ed recover? Why or why not? No. This contract, although not fully executed, is for an illegal purpose and therefore is void. A void contract gives rise to no legal obligation on the part of any party. A contract that is void is no contract. There is nothing to enforce.

CHAPTER 10

1. Do Fidelity and Ron have a contract? Why or why not? No. Revocation of an offer may be implied by conduct inconsistent with the offer. When the corporation hired someone else, and the offeree learned of the hiring, the offer was revoked. The acceptance was too late.

2. Under the Uniform Electronic Transactions Act, what determines the effect of the electronic documents evidencing the parties' deal? Is a party's "signature" necessary? Explain. First, it might be noted that the UETA does not apply unless the parties to a contract agree to use e-commerce in their transaction. In this deal, of course, the parties used e-commerce. The UETA removes barriers to e-commerce by giving the same legal effect to e-records and e-signatures as to paper documents and signatures. The UETA it does not include rules for those transactions, however.

CHAPTER 11

1. Can Kenwood enforce the lease against Joan? Why or why not? No. Joan is a minor and may disaffirm this contract. Because the apartment was a necessary, however, she remains liable for the reasonable value of her occupancy of the apartment.

2. Is the new contract binding? Explain. Yes. The original contract was executory. The parties rescinded it and agreed to a new contract. If Sharyn had broken the contract to accept a contract with another employer, she might have been held liable for damages for the breach.

CHAPTER 12

1. Can Midstate enforce a deal for $350 more? Explain your answer. No. Under the UCC, a contract for a sale of goods priced at $500 or more must be in writing to be enforceable. In this case, the contract is not enforceable beyond the quantity already delivered and paid for.

2. Can Elle be held liable to GCC? Why or why not? Yes. The accountant may be liable on the ground of negligent misrepresentation. A misrepresentation is negligent if a person fails to exercise reasonable care in disclosing material facts or does not use the skill and competence required by his or her business or profession.

CHAPTER 13

1. What type of agreement is this? Are Ace's obligations discharged? Why or why not? This is a novation because it substitutes a new party for an original party, by agreement of all the parties. The requirements are a previous valid obligation, an agreement of all the parties to a new contract, extinguishment of the old obligation, and a new, valid contract. Ace's obligations are discharged.

2. Can Jeff successfully sue Ed for the $100? Why or why not? Yes. When one person makes a promise with the intention of benefiting a third person, the third person can sue to enforce it. This is a third party beneficiary contract. The third party in this problem is an intended beneficiary.

CHAPTER 14

1. If Haney sues Greg, what would be the measure of recovery? A nonbreaching party is entitled to his or her benefit of the bargain under the contract. Here, the innocent party is entitled to be put in the position she would have been in if the contract had been fully performed. The measure of the benefit is the cost to complete the work ($500). These are compensatory damages.

2. Is Lyle liable for Marley's expenses in providing for the cattle? Why or why not? No. To recover damages that flow from the consequences of a breach but that are caused by circumstances beyond the contract (consequential damages), the breaching party must know, or have reason to know, that special circumstances will cause the nonbreaching party to suffer the additional loss. That was not the circumstance in this problem.

CHAPTER 15

1. Is this an acceptance of the offer or a counteroffer? If it is an acceptance, is it a breach of the contract? What if Fav-O-Rite told E-Design it was sending the printer stands as "an accommodation"? A shipment of nonconforming goods constitutes an acceptance of the offer and a breach, unless the seller seasonably notifies the buyer that the nonconforming shipment does not constitute an acceptance and is offered only as an accommodation. Thus, since there was no notification here, the shipment was both an acceptance and a breach. If, however, Fav-O-Rite had notified E-Design that it was sending the printer stands as an accommodation, the shipment would not constitute an acceptance and Fav-O-Rite would not be in breach.

2. Is there an enforceable contract between them? Why or why not? Yes. In a transaction between merchants, the requirement of a writing is satisfied if one of them sends to the other a signed written confirmation that indicates the terms of the agreement, and the merchant receiving it has reason to know of its contents. If the merchant who receives the confirmation does not object in writing within ten days after receipt, the writing will be enforceable against him or her even though he or she has not signed anything.

CHAPTER 16

1. *Does Country have the right to reject the shipment? Explain.* Yes. A seller is obligated to deliver goods in conformity with a contract in every detail. This is the perfect tender rule. The exception of the seller's right to cure does not apply here, because the seller delivered too little too late to take advantage of this exception.

2. *Can Stella recover for breach of the implied warranty of merchantability? Why or why not?* Yes. Stella can recover from Roasted Bean for breach of the implied warranty of merchantability. An implied warranty of merchantability arises in every sale of goods sold by a merchant who deals in goods of the kind. Goods that are merchantable are fit for the ordinary purposes for which such goods are used. A sale of food or drink is a sale of goods. Merchantable food is food that is fit to eat or drink on the basis of consumer expectations. A consumer should reasonably expect hot coffee to be hot, but not to be so scalding that it causes third-degree burns.

CHAPTER 17

1. *Was Winona an independent contractor? Explain.* Yes. An independent contractor is a person who contracts with another—the principal—to do something but who is neither controlled by the other nor subject to the other's right to control with respect to the performance. Independent contractors are not employees, because those who hire them have no control over the details of their performance.

2. *In what circumstance is Vivian liable on the note?* When a person enters into a contract on another's behalf without the authority to do so, the other may be liable on the contract if he or she approves or affirms that contract. In other words, the employer-principal would be liable for the note in this problem on ratifying it. Whether the employer-principal ratifies the note or not, the unauthorized agent is most likely also liable for it.

CHAPTER 18

1. *Would a sole proprietorship be an appropriate form for Frank's business? Why or why not?* Yes. When a business is relatively small and is not diversified, employs relatively few people, has modest profits, and is not likely to expand significantly or require extensive financing in the immediate future, the most appropriate form for doing business may be a sole proprietorship.

2. *Because the vehicles would otherwise be sitting idle in a parking lot, can Finian keep the income resulting from the leasing of the delivery vehicles? Explain your answer.* No. Under the partners' fiduciary duty, a partner must account to the partnership for any personal profits or benefits derived without the consent of all the partners in connection with the use of any partnership property. Here, the leasing partner may not keep the money.

CHAPTER 19

1. *Is there a way for Northwest Brands to avoid this double taxation? Explain your answer.* Yes. Small businesses that meet certain requirements can qualify as S corporations, created specifically to permit small businesses to avoid double taxation. The six requirements of an S corporation are (1) the firm must be a domestic corporation, (2) the firm must not be a member of an affiliated group of corporations, (3) the firm must have less than a certain number of shareholders, (4) the shareholders must be individuals, estates, or qualified trusts (or corporations in some cases), (5) there can be only one class of stock, and (6) no shareholder can be a nonresident alien.

2. *Discuss whether Nico owes a duty to Omega or the minority shareholders in selling his shares.* A single shareholder—or a few shareholders acting together—who owns enough stock to exercise *de facto* control over a corporation owes the corporation and minority shareholders a fiduciary duty when transferring those shares.

PROBLEM 1–6. *Reading Citations.* The court's opinion in this case—*United States v. Yi,* 704 F.3d 800 (9th Cir. 2013)—can be found in volume 704 of West's *Federal Reporter,* Third Series, on page 800. The United States Court of Appeals for the Ninth Circuit issued this opinion in 2013.

PROBLEM 2–6. *Establishment Clause.* The establishment clause prohibits the government from passing laws or taking actions that promote religion or show a preference for one religion over another. In assessing a government action, the courts look at the predominant purpose of the action and ask whether the action has the effect of endorsing religion.

Although here DeWeese claimed to have a nonreligious purpose for displaying the poster of the Ten Commandments in a courtroom, his own statements showed a religious purpose. These statements reflected his views about "warring" legal philosophies and his belief that "our legal system is based on moral absolutes from divine law handed down by God through the Ten Commandments." This plainly constitutes a religious purpose that violates the establishment clause because it has the effect of endorsing Judaism or Christianity over other religions. In the case on which this problem is based, the court ruled in favor of the American Civil Liberties Union.

PROBLEM 3–3. *Arbitration Clause.* Based on a recent holding by the Washington state supreme court, the federal appeals court held that the arbitration provision was unconscionable and therefore invalid. Because it was invalid, the restriction on class-action suits was also invalid.

The state court held that placing class action restrictions in arbitrations agreements with consumers improperly stripped consumers of rights they would normally have to attack certain industry practices. Class-action suits are often brought in cases alleging deceptive or unfair industry practices when the losses suffered by the individual consumer are too small to warrant the consumer bringing suit. In other words, the supposed added cell phone fees were so small that no individual consumer would be likely to litigate or arbitrate the matter due to the expenses involved. Therefore, the clause in the arbitration agreement preventing consumers from joining together in a class-action suit violates public policy and is void and unenforceable.

PROBLEM 4–8. *Negligence.* Negligence requires proof that (a) the defendant owed a duty of care to the plaintiff, (b) the defendant breached that duty, (c) the defendant's breach caused the plaintiff's injury, and (d) the plaintiff suffered a legally recognizable injury. With respect to the duty of care, a business owner has a duty to use reasonable care to protect business invitees. This duty includes an obligation to discover and correct or warn of unreasonably dangerous conditions that the owner of the premises should reasonably foresee might endanger an invitee. Some risks are so obvious that an owner need not warn of them. But even if a risk is obvious, a business owner may not be excused from the duty to protect its customers from foreseeable harm.

Because Lucario was the Weatherford's business invitee, the hotel owed her a duty of reasonable care to make its premises safe for her use. The balcony ran nearly the entire width of the window in Lucario's room. She could have reasonably believed that the window was a means of access to the balcony. The window/balcony configuration was dangerous, however, because the window opened wide enough for an adult to climb out, but the twelve-inch gap between one side of the window and the balcony was unprotected. This unprotected gap opened to a drop of more than three stories to a concrete surface below.

Should the hotel have anticipated the potential harm to a guest opening the window in Room 59 and attempting to access the balcony? The hotel encouraged guests to "step out onto the balcony" to smoke. The dangerous window /balcony configuration could have been remedied at a minimal cost. These circumstances could be perceived as creating an "unreasonably dangerous" condition. And it could be concluded that the hotel created or knew of the condition and failed to take reasonable steps to warn of it or correct it. Of course, the Weatherford might argue that the window/ balcony configuration was so obvious that the hotel was not liable for Lucario's fall.

In the actual case on which this problem is based, the court concluded that the Weatherford did not breach its duty of care to Lucario. On McMurtry's appeal, a state intermediate appellate court held that this conclusion was in error, vacated the lower court's judgment in favor of the hotel on this issue, and remanded the case.

PROBLEM 5–5. *Trade Secrets.* Some business information that cannot be protected by trademark, patent, or copyright law is protected against appropriation by competitors as trade secrets. Trade secrets consist of anything that makes a company unique and that would have value to a competitor—customer lists, plans, research and development, pricing information, marketing techniques, and production techniques, for example. Theft of trade secrets is a federal crime.

In this problem, the documents in the boxes in the car could constitute trade secrets. But a number of factors suggest that a finding of theft and imposition of liability would not be appropriate. The boxes were not marked in any way that would indicate they contained confidential information. The boxes were stored in an employee's car. The alleged thief was the employee's spouse, not a CPR competitor, and she apparently had no idea what was in the boxes. Leaving trade secrets so accessible does not show an effort to protect the information.

In the case on which this problem is based, the court dismissed Jones's claim, in part on the reasoning stated above.

PROBLEM 6–6. *Privacy.* No, Rolfe did not have a privacy interest in the information obtained by the subpoenas issued to Midcontinent Communications. The courts have held that the right to privacy is guaranteed by the U.S. Constitution's Bill of Rights, and some state constitutions contain an explicit guarantee of the right. A person must have a reasonable expectation of privacy, though, to maintain a suit or to assert a successful defense for an invasion of privacy.

People clearly have a reasonable expectation of privacy when they enter their personal banking or credit-card information online. They also have a reasonable expectation that online companies will follow their own privacy policies. But people do not a reasonable expectation of privacy in statements made on Twitter and other data that they publicly disseminate. In other words, there is no violation of a subscriber's right to privacy when a third party Internet service provider receives a subpoena and discloses the subscriber's information.

Here, Rolfe supplied his e-mail address and other personal information, including his Internet protocol address, to Midcontinent. In other words, Rolfe publicly disseminated this information. Law enforcement officers obtained this information from Midcontinent through the subpoenas issued by the South Dakota state court. Rolfe provided his information to Midcontinent—he has no legitimate expectation of privacy in that information.

In the actual case on which this problem is based, Rolfe was charged with, and convicted of, possessing, manufacturing, and distributing child pornography, as well as other crimes. As part of the proceedings, the court found that Rolfe had no expectation of privacy in the information that he made available to Midcontinent. On appeal, the South Dakota Supreme Court upheld the conviction.

PROBLEM 7–8. *Criminal Liability.* Yes, Green exhibited the required mental state to establish criminal liability. A wrongful mental state *(mens rea)* is one of the elements typically required to establish criminal liability. The required mental state, or intent, is indicated in an applicable statute or law. For example, for murder, the required mental state is the intent to take another's life. A court can also find that the required mental state is present when a defendant's acts are reckless or criminally negligent. A defendant is criminally reckless if he or she consciously disregards a substantial and unjustifiable risk.

In this problem, Green was clearly aware of the danger to which he was exposing people on the street below, but he did not indicate that he specifically intended to harm anyone. The risk of death created by his conduct, however, was obvious. He must have known what was likely to happen if a bottle or plate thrown from the height of twenty-six stories hit a pedestrian or the windshield of an occupied motor vehicle on the street below. Despite his claim that he was intoxicated, he was sufficiently aware to stop throwing things from the balcony when he saw police in the area, and he later recalled what he had done and what had happened.

In the actual case on which this problem is based, after a jury trial, Green was convicted of reckless endangerment. On appeal, a state intermediate appellate court affirmed the conviction, based in part on the reasoning stated above.

PROBLEM 8–5. *Online Privacy.* Facebook created a program that makes decisions for users. Many believe that privacy is an extremely important right that should be fiercely protected. Thus, using duty-based ethics, any program that has a default setting of giving out information is unethical. Facebook should create the program as an opt-in program.

In addition, under the Kantian categorical imperative, if every company used opt-out programs that allowed the disclosure of potentially personal information, privacy might become merely theoretical. If privacy were reduced or eliminated, the world might not be a better place. From a utilitarian or outcome-based approach, an opt-out program might offer the benefits of being easy to created and start, as well as making it easy to recruit partner programs. On the negative side, the program would eliminate users' ability to chose whether to disclose information about themselves. An opt-in program would maintain that user control but might entail higher start-up costs because it would require more marketing to users up front to persuade them to opt in.

PROBLEM 9–7. *Quasi Contract.* Gutkowski does not have a valid claim for payment, nor should he recover on the basis of a quasi contract. Courts impose quasi contracts on parties in the interest of fairness and justice.

Usually, a quasi contract is imposed to avoid the unjust enrichment of one party at the expense of another. Here, Gutkowski was compensated as a consultant. To establish a claim that he is due more compensation based on unjust enrichment, he must have proof. As it is, he has only his claim that there were discussions about him being a part owner of YES. Discussions and negotiations are not a basis for recovery on a quasi contract.

In the actual case on which this problem is based, the court dismissed Gutkowski's claim for payment.

PROBLEM 10–5. *Offer and Acceptance.* No, a contract was not formed in this case. As the Iowa Supreme Court pointed out, the parties must voluntarily agree to enter into a contract. Courts determine whether an offer has been made objectively—not subjectively.

Under the *Restatement of Contracts (Second)*, "the test for an offer is whether it induces a reasonable belief in the recipient that [the recipient] can, by accepting, bind the sender." The offeror may decide to whom to extend the offer. According to the *Restatement,* an offer may create a power of acceptance in a specified person or in one or more of a specified group or class of persons, acting separately or together.

The court hearing this case explained: "In this situation, Prairie Meadows is the offeror. It makes an offer to its patrons that, if accepted by wagering an amount and the patron wins, it will pay off the wager. Simply stated, the issue is whether Prairie Meadows made an offer to Blackford. Because Prairie Meadows has the ability to determine the class of individuals to whom the offer is made, it may also exclude certain individuals. Blackford had been banned for life from the casino.

. . . Under an objective test, unless the ban had been lifted, Blackford could not have reasonably believed he was among the class of individuals invited to accept Prairie Meadows's offer."

In the actual case on which this problem is based, the jury found that the ban against Blackford had not been lifted and, therefore, Prairie Meadows had not extended him an offer to wager. Because there was no offer to him, no contract could result. The state supreme court therefore reversed the decision of the state appellate court and affirmed the trial court's judgment.

PROBLEM 11–5. *Unconscionable Contracts or Clauses.* In this case, the agreement restricted the buyer's options for resolution of a dispute to arbitration and limited the amount of damages. This agreement was both procedurally and substantively unconscionable. Procedural unconscionability concerns the manner in which the parties enter into a contract. Substantive unconscionability can occur when a contract leaves one party to the agreement without a remedy for the nonperformance of the other.

Here, GeoEx told customers that the arbitration terms in its release form were nonnegotiable and that climbers would encounter the same requirements with any other travel company. This amounted to procedural unconscionability, underscoring the customers' lack of bargaining power. The imbalance resulted in oppressive terms, with no real negotiation and an absence of meaningful choice. Furthermore, the restriction on forum (San Francisco) and the limitation on damages (the cost of the trip)—with no limitation on GeoEx's damages—amounted to substantive unconscionability.

In the actual case on which this problem is based, the court ruled that the agreement was unconscionable.

PROBLEM 12–6. *Fraudulent Misrepresentation.* Esprit's argument is not credible because the fact that the house was later sold for a good price had nothing to do with the extra costs incurred by the Wilcoxes. The Wilcoxes had borrowed about a million dollars to finance the project, and Esprit knew that. The court determined that "a promise made without a present intent to perform is a misrepresentation of a material fact and is sufficient to support a cause of action for fraud."

Esprit had promised to deliver precut and predrilled logs that could be assembled quickly. It knew the delivery of unfinished logs would cause problems. "After the logs arrived at the home, Esprit further misrepresented that there would be only a two- or three-day delay while the logs where cut and drilled on site. The jury could conclude that Esprit's actions amounted to fraud or such indifference to negative consequences for the buyers as to support an award for punitive damages." The judgment of the lower court was affirmed.

PROBLEM 13–7. *Conditions of Performance.* Maciel was not correct. In this problem, the performance of a legal obligation under the parties' contract was contingent on a condition—the occurrence of a certain event. If the condition was not satisfied, the obligations of the parties were discharged. Here, Regent University promised to provide an apartment in its housing facility to Maciel as long as he maintained his status as a Regent

student. Maintaining student status was the condition for the university's provision of an apartment. On the termination of that status, Regent was entitled to require Maciel to vacate the apartment.

Maciel chose to withdraw from the university at the end of the spring semester, which rendered him ineligible to remain in the apartment. In other words, this decision resulted in noncompliance with the condition for the university's provision of an apartment, and the university was thus no longer bound to perform. Contrary to Maciel's argument in court, he did not have the "legal authority" to continue to occupy the apartment.

In the actual case on which this problem is based, the court convicted Maciel of trespassing. In response to Maciel's argument, a state intermediate appellate court applied the reasoning set out above to affirm the conviction.

PROBLEM 14–6. *Consequential Damages.* Simard is liable only for the losses and expenses related to the first resale. Simard could reasonably anticipate that his breach would require another sale and that the sales price might be less than what he agreed to pay. Therefore, he should be liable for the difference between his sales price and the first resale price ($29,000), plus any expenses arising from the first resale. Simard is not liable, however, for any expenses and losses related to the second resale. After all, Simard did not cause the second purchaser's default, and he could not reasonably foresee that default as a probable result of his breach.

PROBLEM 15–4. *Additional Terms.* No. The Uniform Commercial Code (UCC) dispenses with the common law mirror image rule, which requires that the terms of an acceptance exactly mirror the terms of the offer. Under the UCC, a contract is formed if the offeree makes a definite expression of acceptance even though the terms of the acceptance modify or add to the terms of the offer.

When both parties to the contract are merchants, the additional terms become part of their contract *unless* (a) the original offer expressly required acceptance of its terms, (b) the new or changed terms materially alter the contract, or (c) the offeror rejects the new or changed terms within a reasonable time.

In this problem, the UCC applies because the transactions involve sales of goods. The original offer stated, "By signing below, you agree to the terms." This statement could be construed to expressly require acceptance of the terms to make the offer a binding contract (exception a above).

The contract stated that JMAM was to receive credit for any rejected merchandise. Nothing indicated that the merchandise would be returned to BSI. Baracsi, BSI's owner (the offeree), signed JMAM's (the offeror's) letter in the appropriate location, thereby indicating BSI's agreement to the terms. Thus, BSI made a definite expression of acceptance. The practice of the parties—for six years rejected items were not returned—further supports the conclusion that their contract did not contemplate the return of those items. The "PS" could be interpreted as materially altering the contract (exception b above).

In the actual case on which this problem is based, the court dismissed BSI's complaint.

PROBLEM 16–5. *Nonconforming Goods.* Padma Paper Mills notified Universal Exports about its breach, so Padma has two ways to recover even though it accepted the goods.

Padma's first option is to argue that it revoked its acceptance, giving it the right to reject the goods. To revoke acceptance, Padma would have to show that (a) the nonconformity substantially impaired the value of the shipment, (b) it predicated its acceptance on a reasonable assumption that Universal Exports would cure the nonconformity, and (c) Universal Exports did not cure the nonconformity within a reasonable time.

Padma's second option is to keep the goods and recover for the damages caused by Universal Exports' breach. Under this option, Padma could recover at least the difference between the value of the goods as promised and their value as accepted.

PROBLEM 17–6. *Liability for Contracts.* Hall may be held personally liable. Hall could not be an agent for House Medic because it was a fictitious name and not a real entity. Moreover, when the contract was formed, Hall did not disclose his true principal, which was Hall Hauling, Ltd. Thus, Hall may be held personally liable as a party to the contract.

PROBLEM 18–7. *Partnership Formation.* Garcia and Lucero probably satisfied all three requirements for forming a partnership. They owned the two properties equally, agreed to share both profits and losses, and enjoyed equal management rights. Moreover, it is immaterial that they lacked a written partnership agreement. The writing requirement (Statute of Frauds) does not apply to these facts, and a partnership agreement can be oral or implied by the parties' conduct.

PROBLEM 19–6. *Close Corporations.* Yes, Pourgol's acts may likely have constituted misconduct. In this problem, Burnett charged Pourgol with the submission of incorrect plans to obtain the building permit, misrepresentation of the extent of the renovations, and failure to fix the house. The submission of incorrect plans might arguably have been a mistake, and the misrepresentation might have been a misstatement in good faith. But these acts may instead have been intentional and fraudulent. Assuming the charges are true and all of the acts were wrongful, including the misrepresentation and failure to fix the house, they certainly form the basis for a finding of misconduct.

A close corporation is a private corporation with a small number of shareholders. Close corporations are often managed by their shareholders. To prevent such situations as the one that arose in this problem, shareholders must take an active role in the governance of a corporation. The corporate articles or bylaws might be amended to, for example, require more than a single shareholder or a simple majority to approve an action. A minority shareholder, or a dominated shareholder, or a formerly disinterested shareholder may also pursue a remedy through a direct or derivative (on behalf of the corporation) suit.

Here, the facts do not state which shareholder, if either, held a majority of the shares. But Burnett might have taken any of the steps mentioned above to prevent misconduct. In the problem, Burnett has taken the step of filing a suit against Pourgol. In the actual case on which this problem is based, the court denied Pourgol's motion to dismiss Burnett's complaint.

GLOSSARY

A

Acceptance In contract law, the offeree's notification to the offeror that the offeree agrees to be bound by the terms of the offeror's proposal. Although historically the terms of acceptance had to be the mirror image of the terms of the offer, the Uniform Commercial Code provides that even modified terms of the offer in a definite expression of acceptance constitute a contract.

Accord and satisfaction An agreement for payment (or other performance) between two parties, one of whom has a right of action against the other. After the payment has been accepted or other performance has been made, the "accord and satisfaction" is complete and the obligation is discharged.

Acquittal A certification or declaration following a trial that the individual accused of a crime is innocent, or free from guilt, and is thus absolved of the charges.

Actionable Capable of serving as the basis of a lawsuit.

Actual authority Authority of an agent that is express or implied.

Actual malice A condition that exists when a person makes a statement with either knowledge of its falsity or a reckless disregard for the truth. In a defamation suit, a statement made about a public figure normally must be made with actual malice for liability to be incurred.

Actus reus (pronounced *ak*-tus *ray*-uhs) A guilty (prohibited) act. The commission of a prohibited act is one of the two essential elements required for criminal liability, the other element being the intent to commit a crime.

Administrative agency A federal, state, or local government agency established to perform a specific function. Administrative agencies are authorized by legislative acts to make and enforce rules to administer and enforce the acts.

Administrative law The body of law created by administrative agencies (in the form of rules, regulations, orders, and decisions) in order to carry out their duties and responsibilities.

Affirm To validate; to give legal force to. *See also* Ratification

Age of majority The age at which an individual is considered legally capable of conducting himself or herself responsibly. In contract law, the age at which one is no longer an "infant" and can no longer disaffirm a contract.

Agency A relationship between two parties in which one party (the agent) agrees to represent or act for the other (the principal).

Agency by estoppel An agency that arises when a principal negligently allows an agent to exercise powers not granted to the agent, thus justifying others in believing that the agent possesses the requisite agency authority.

Agency coupled with an interest An agency relationship in which the agent has some legal right to (an interest in) the property that is the subject of the agency, and thus the agency is created for the agent's benefit instead of the principal's. Because the agent has an additional interest in the property beyond the normal commission for selling it, the agent's position cannot be terminated until the agent's interest ends.

Agent A person who agrees to represent or act for another, called the principal.

Agreement A meeting of two or more minds in regard to the terms of a contract; usually broken down into two events—an offer by one party to form a contract, and an acceptance of the offer by the person to whom the offer is made.

Alien corporation A designation in the United States for a corporation formed in another country but doing business in the United States.

Alienation In real property law, the voluntary transfer of property from one person to another (as opposed to a transfer by operation of law).

Allege To state, recite, assert, or charge.

Alternative dispute resolution (ADR) The resolution of disputes in ways other than those involved in the traditional judicial process. Negotiation, mediation, and arbitration are forms of ADR.

American Arbitration Association (AAA) The major organization offering arbitration services in the United States.

Anticipatory repudiation An assertion or action by a party indicating that he or she will not perform an obligation that the party is contractually obligated to perform at a future time.

Apparent authority Authority that is only apparent, not real. In agency law, a person may be deemed to have had the power to act as an agent for another party if the other party's manifestations to a third party led the third party to believe that an agency existed when, in fact, it did not.

Appeal Resort to a superior court, such as an appellate court, to review the decision of an inferior court, such as a trial court or an administrative agency.

Appellant The party who takes an appeal from one court to another.

Appellate court A court having appellate jurisdiction. Courts having appellate jurisdiction act as reviewing courts, or appellate courts. Generally, cases can be brought before appellate courts only on appeal from an order or a judgment of a trial court or other lower court.

Appellee The party against whom an appeal is taken—that is, the party who opposes setting aside or reversing the judgment.

Appropriation In tort law, the use by one person of another person's name, likeness, or other identifying characteristic without permission and for the benefit of the user.

Arbitration The settling of a dispute by submitting it to a disinterested third party (other than a court), who renders a decision. The decision may or may not be legally binding.

Arbitration clause A clause in a contract that provides that, in the event of a dispute, the parties will submit the dispute to arbitration rather than litigate the dispute in court.

Arraignment A procedure in which an accused person is brought before the court to answer criminal charges. The charge is read to the person, and he or she is asked to enter a plea—such as "guilty" or "not guilty."

Arson The malicious burning of another's dwelling. Some statutes have expanded this to include any real property regardless of ownership and the destruction of property by other means—for example, by explosion.

Articles of incorporation The document filed with the appropriate governmental agency, usually the secretary of state, when a business is incorporated; state statutes usually prescribe what kind of information must be contained in the articles of incorporation.

Articles of organization The document filed with a designated state official by which a limited liability company is formed.

Articles of partnership A written agreement that sets forth each partner's rights and obligations with respect to the partnership.

Assault Any word or action intended to make another person fearful of immediate physical harm; a reasonably believable threat.

Assignee The person to whom contract rights are assigned.

Assignment The act of transferring to another all or part of one's rights arising under a contract.

Assignor The person who assigns contract rights.

Assumption of risk A defense against negligence that can be used when the plaintiff was aware of a danger and voluntarily assumed the risk of injury from that danger.

Authorized means In contract law, the means of acceptance authorized by the offeror.

Award In the context of litigation, the amount of money awarded to a plaintiff in a civil lawsuit as damages. In the context of arbitration, the arbitrator's decision.

B

Bankruptcy court A federal court of limited jurisdiction that handles only bankruptcy proceedings. Bankruptcy proceedings are governed by federal bankruptcy law.

Battery The unprivileged, intentional touching of another.

Benefit corporation A for-profit corporation that seeks to have a material positive impact on society and the environment. This new business form is available by statute in a growing number of states.

Beyond a reasonable doubt The standard used to determine the guilt or innocence of a person criminally charged. To be guilty of a crime, one must be proved guilty "beyond and to the exclusion of every reasonable doubt." A reasonable doubt is one that would cause a prudent person to hesitate before acting in matters important to him or her.

Bilateral contract A type of contract that arises when a promise is given in exchange for a return promise.

Bill of lading A document that serves both as evidence of the receipt of goods for shipment and as documentary evidence of title to the goods.

Bill of Rights The first ten amendments to the U.S. Constitution.

Binding authority Any source of law that a court must follow when deciding a case. Binding authorities include constitutions, statutes, and regulations that govern the issue being decided, as well as court decisions that are controlling precedents within the jurisdiction.

Bona fide Good faith. A bona fide obligation is one made in good faith—that is, sincerely and honestly.

Bond A certificate that evidences a corporate (or government) debt. It is a security that involves no ownership interest in the issuing entity.

Botnet Short for *robot network*—a group of computers that run an application that is controlled and manipulated only by the software source. Although sometimes a legitimate network, usually this term is reserved for a group of computers that have been infected by malicious robot software. In a botnet, each connected computer becomes a zombie, or drone.

Breach To violate a law, by an act or an omission, or to break a legal obligation that one owes to another person or to society.

Breach of contract The failure, without legal excuse, of a promisor to perform the obligations of a contract.

Bribery The offering, giving, receiving, or soliciting of anything of value with the aim of influencing an official action or an official's discharge of a legal or public duty or (with respect to commercial bribery) a business decision.

Browse-wrap terms Terms and conditions of use that are presented to an Internet user at the time certain products, such as software, are being downloaded but that need not be agreed to (by clicking "I agree," for example) before being able to install or use the product.

Burglary The unlawful entry into a building with the intent to commit a felony. (Some state statutes expand this to include the intent to commit any crime.)

Business ethics Ethics in a business context; a consensus of what constitutes right or wrong behavior in the world of business and the application of moral principles to situations that arise in a business setting.

Business invitees Those people, such as customers or clients, who are invited onto business premises by the owner of those premises for business purposes.

Business judgment rule A rule that immunizes corporate management from liability for actions that result in corporate losses or damages if the actions are undertaken in good faith and are within both the power of the corporation and the authority of management to make.

Business tort Wrongful interference with the business rights of another.

Buyer in the ordinary course of business A buyer who, in good faith and without knowledge that the sale violates the ownership rights or security interest of a third party in the goods, purchases goods in the ordinary course of business from a person in the business of selling goods of that kind.

Buyout price The amount payable to a partner on his or her dissociation from a partnership, based on the amount distributable to that partner if the firm were wound up on that date, and offset by any damages for wrongful dissociation.

Buy-sell agreement In the context of partnerships, an express agreement made at the time of partnership formation for one or more of the partners to buy out the other or others should the situation warrant—and thus provide for the smooth dissolution of the partnership.

Bylaws A set of governing rules adopted by a corporation or other association.

C

Cancellation The act of nullifying, or making void.

Capital Accumulated goods, possessions, and assets used for the production of profits and wealth; the equity of owners in a business.

Carrier An individual or organization engaged in transporting passengers or goods for hire.

Case law The rules of law announced in court decisions. Case law includes the aggregate of reported cases that interpret judicial precedents, statutes, regulations, and constitutional provisions.

Case on point A previous case involving factual circumstances and issues that are similar to those in the case before the court.

Categorical imperative A concept developed by the philosopher Immanuel Kant as an ethical guideline for behavior. In deciding whether an action is right or wrong, or desirable or undesirable, a person should evaluate the action in terms of what would happen if everybody else in the same situation, or category, acted the same way.

Causation in fact An act or omission without ("but for") which an event would not have occurred.

Cause of action A situation or set of facts sufficient to justify a right to sue.

Certification mark A mark used by one or more persons, other than the owner, to certify the region, materials, mode of manufacture, quality, or accuracy of the owner's goods or services. When used by members of a cooperative, association, or other organization, such a mark is referred to as a collective mark. Examples of certification marks include the "Good Housekeeping Seal of Approval" and "UL Tested."

Chancellor An adviser to the king at the time of the early king's courts of England. Individuals petitioned the king for relief when they could not obtain an adequate remedy in a court of law, and these petitions were decided by the chancellor.

Charging order In partnership law, an order granted by a court to a judgment creditor that entitles the creditor to attach profits or assets of a partner on dissolution of the partnership.

Checks and balances The system by which each of the three branches of the national government (executive, legislative, and judicial) exercises checks on the powers of the other branches.

Choice-of-language clause A clause in a contract designating the official language by which the contract will be interpreted in the event of a future disagreement over the contract's terms.

Choice-of-law clause A clause in a contract designating the law (such as the law of a particular state or nation) that will govern the contract.

Citation A reference to a publication in which a legal authority—such as a statute or a court decision—or other source can be found.

Civil law The branch of law dealing with the definition and enforcement of all private or public rights, as opposed to criminal matters.

Claim As a verb, to assert or demand. As a noun, a right to payment.

Click-on agreement An agreement that arises when a buyer, engaging in a transaction on a computer, indicates his or her assent to be bound by the terms of an offer by clicking on a button that says, for example,

"I agree"; sometimes referred to as a click-on license or a click-wrap agreement.

Close corporation A corporation whose shareholders are limited to a small group of persons, often only family members. The rights of shareholders of a close corporation usually are restricted regarding the transfer of shares to others. Also known as a *closely held corporation.*

Cloud computing The delivery to users of on-demand services from third-party servers over a network. Cloud computing is a delivery model. The most widely used cloud computing services are Software as a Service (SaaS), which offers companies a cheaper way to buy and use packaged applications that are no longer run on servers in house.

Collateral promise A secondary promise that is ancillary (subsidiary) to a principal transaction or primary contractual relationship, such as a promise made by one person to pay the debts of another if the latter fails to perform. A collateral promise normally must be in writing to be enforceable.

Collective mark A mark used by members of a cooperative, association, or other organization to certify the region, materials, mode of manufacture, quality, or accuracy of the specific goods or services. Examples of collective marks include the labor union marks found on tags of certain products and the credits of movies, which indicate the various associations and organizations that participated in the making of the movies.

Commerce clause The provision in Article I, Section 8, of the U.S. Constitution that gives Congress the power to regulate interstate commerce.

Commercial impracticability A doctrine under which a seller may be excused from performing a contract when (1) a contingency occurs, (2) the contingency's occurrence makes performance impracticable, and (3) the nonoccurrence of the contingency was a basic assumption on which the contract was made. Despite the fact that UCC 2–615 expressly frees only sellers under this doctrine, courts have not distinguished between buyers and sellers in applying it.

Commingle To put funds or goods together into one mass so that the funds or goods are so mixed that they no longer have separate identities. In corporate law, if personal and corporate interests are commingled to the extent that the corporation has no separate identity, a court may "pierce the corporate veil" and expose the shareholders to personal liability.

Common law That body of law developed from custom or judicial decisions in English and U.S. courts, not attributable to a legislature.

Common stock Shares of ownership in a corporation that give the owner of the stock a proportionate interest in the corporation with regard to control, earnings, and net assets; shares of common stock are lowest in priority with respect to payment of dividends and distribution of the corporation's assets on dissolution.

Comparative negligence A theory in tort law under which the liability for injuries resulting from negligent acts is shared by all parties who were negligent (including the injured party), on the basis of each person's proportionate negligence.

Compelling government interest A test of constitutionality that requires the government to have compelling reasons for passing any law that restricts fundamental rights, such as free speech, or distinguishes between people based on a suspect trait.

Compensatory damages A money award equivalent to the actual value of injuries or damages sustained by the aggrieved party.

Complete performance Performance of a contract strictly in accordance with the contract's terms.

Computer crime Any violation of criminal law that involves knowledge of computer technology for its perpetration, investigation, or prosecution.

Concurrent conditions Conditions in a contract that must occur or be performed at the same time; they are mutually dependent. No obligations arise until these conditions are simultaneously performed.

Concurrent jurisdiction Jurisdiction that exists when two different courts have the power to hear a case. For example, some cases can be heard in either a federal or a state court.

Concurring opinion A written opinion outlining the views of a judge or justice to make or emphasize a point that was not made or emphasized in the majority opinion.

Condition A possible future event, the occurrence or nonoccurrence of which will trigger the performance of a legal obligation or terminate an existing obligation under a contract.

Condition precedent A condition in a contract that must be met before a party's promise becomes absolute.

Condition subsequent A condition in a contract that operates to terminate a party's absolute promise to perform.

Conforming goods Goods that conform to contract specifications.

Consequential damages Special damages that compensate for a loss that is not direct or immediate (for example, lost profits). The special damages must have been reasonably foreseeable at the time the breach or injury occurred in order for the plaintiff to collect them.

Consideration Generally, the value given in return for a promise or a performance. The consideration, which must be present to make the contract legally binding, must be something of legally sufficient value and bargained for.

Constitutional law Law that is based on the U.S. Constitution and the constitutions of the various states.

Constructive condition A condition in a contract that is neither expressed nor implied by the contract but rather is imposed by law for reasons of justice.

Consumer goods Goods that are primarily for personal or household use.

Contingency fee An attorney's fee that is based on a percentage of the final award received by his or her client as a result of litigation.

Contract An agreement that can be enforced in court; formed by two or more parties, each of whom agrees to perform or to refrain from performing some act now or in the future.

Contractual capacity The legal ability to enter into contracts. The threshold mental capacity required by law for a party who enters into a contract to be bound by that contract.

Contributory negligence A theory in tort law under which a complaining party's own negligence contributed to or caused his or her injuries. Contributory negligence is an absolute bar to recovery in a minority of jurisdictions.

Conversion The wrongful taking, using, or retaining possession of personal property that belongs to another.

Conviction The outcome of a criminal trial in which the defendant has been found guilty of the crime.

Cookie Computing a packet of data sent by an Internet server to a browser, which is returned by the browser each time it subsequently accesses the same server. Used to identify the users or track their access to the server.

Copyright The exclusive right of authors to publish, print, or sell an intellectual production for a statutory period of time. A copyright has the same monopolistic nature as a patent or trademark, but it differs in that it applies exclusively to works of art, literature, and other works of authorship, including computer programs.

Corporate social responsibility (CSR) The concept that corporations can and should act ethically and be accountable to society for their actions.

Corporation A legal entity formed in compliance with statutory requirements. The entity is distinct from its shareholders-owners.

Cost-benefit analysis A decision-making technique that involves weighing the costs of a given action against the benefits of the action.

Counteroffer An offeree's response to an offer in which the offeree rejects the original offer and at the same time makes a new offer.

Course of dealing Prior conduct between parties to a contract that establishes a common basis for their understanding.

Course of performance The conduct that occurs under the terms of a particular agreement; such conduct indicates what the parties to an agreement intended it to mean.

Court of equity A court that decides controversies and administers justice according to the rules, principles, and precedents of equity.

Court of law A court in which the only remedies that could be granted were things of value, such as money damages. In the early English king's courts, courts of law were distinct from courts of equity.

Covenant not to compete A contractual promise to refrain from competing with another party for a certain period of time and within a certain geographic area. Although covenants not to compete restrain trade, they are commonly found in partnership agreements, business sale agreements, and employment contracts. If they are ancillary to such agreements, covenants not to compete will normally be enforced by the courts unless the time period or geographic area is deemed unreasonable.

Covenant not to sue An agreement to substitute a contractual obligation for some other type of legal action based on a valid claim.

Cover A buyer or lessee's purchase on the open market of goods to substitute for those promised but never delivered by the seller. Under the Uniform Commercial Code, if the cost of cover exceeds the cost of the contract goods, the buyer or lessee can recover the difference, plus incidental and consequential damages.

Creditor A person to whom a debt is owed by another person (the debtor).

Creditor beneficiary A third party beneficiary who has rights in a contract made by the debtor and a third person. The terms of the contract obligate the third person to pay the debt owed to the creditor. The creditor beneficiary can enforce the debt against either party.

Crime A wrong against society proclaimed in a statute and punishable by society through fines and/or imprisonment—or, in some cases, death.

Criminal law Law that defines and governs actions that constitute crimes. Generally, criminal law has to do with wrongful actions committed against society for which society demands redress.

Cumulative voting A method of shareholder voting designed to allow minority shareholders to be represented on the board of directors. With cumulative voting, the number of members of the board to be elected is multiplied by the total number of voting shares held. The result equals the number of votes a shareholder has, and this total can be cast for one or more nominees for director.

Cure Under the Uniform Commercial Code, the right of a party who tenders nonconforming performance to correct his or her performance within the contract period.

Cyber crime A crime that occurs online, in the virtual community of the Internet, as opposed to the physical world.

Cyber fraud Fraud that involves the online theft of credit card information, banking details, and other information for criminal use.

Cyber mark A trademark in cyberspace.

Cyber tort A tort committed via the Internet.

Cyberlaw An informal term used to refer to all laws governing electronic communications and transactions, particularly those conducted via the Internet.

Cybersquatting The act of registering a domain name that is the same as, or confusingly similar to, the trademark of another and then offering to sell that domain name back to the trademark owner.

Cyberterrorist A hacker whose purpose is to exploit a target computer for a serious impact, such as the corruption of a program to sabotage a business.

D

Damages Money sought as a remedy for a breach of contract or for a tortious act.

Defamation Any published or publicly spoken false statement that causes injury to another's good name, reputation, or character.

Defendant One against whom a lawsuit is brought; the accused person in a criminal proceeding.

Defense Reasons that a defendant offers in an action or suit as to why the plaintiff should not obtain what he or she is seeking.

Delegatee One to whom contract duties are delegated by another, called the delegator.

Delegation The transfer of a contractual duty to a third party. The party delegating the duty (the delegator) to the third party (the delegatee) is still obliged to perform on the contract should the delegatee fail to perform.

Delegator One who delegates his or her duties under a contract to another, called the delegatee.

Delivery In contract law, one party's act of placing the subject matter of the contract within the other party's possession or control.

Delivery order A written order to deliver goods directed to a warehouser, carrier, or other person who, in the ordinary course of business, issues warehouse receipts or bills of lading.

De novo Anew; afresh; a second time. In a hearing *de novo,* an appellate court hears the case as a court of original jurisdiction—that is, as if the case had not previously been tried and a decision rendered.

Destination contract A contract in which the seller is required to ship the goods by carrier and deliver them at a particular destination. The seller assumes liability for any losses or damage to the goods until they are tendered at the destination specified in the contract.

Dilution With respect to trademarks, a doctrine under which distinctive or famous trademarks are protected from certain unauthorized uses of the marks regardless of a showing of competition or a likelihood of confusion. Congress created a federal cause of action for dilution in 1995 with the passage of the Federal Trademark Dilution Act.

Disaffirmance The legal avoidance, or setting aside, of a contractual obligation.

Discharge The termination of an obligation. (1) In contract law, discharge occurs when the parties have fully performed their contractual obligations or when events, conduct of the parties, or operation of the law releases the parties from performance. (2) In bankruptcy proceedings, the extinction of the debtor's dischargeable debts.

Discharge in bankruptcy The release of a debtor from all debts that are provable, except those specifically excepted from discharge by statute.

Disclosed principal A principal whose identity is known to a third party at the time the agent makes a contract with the third party.

Disparagement of property An economically injurious false statement made about another's product or property. A general term for torts that are more specifically referred to as slander of quality or slander of title.

Dissenting opinion A written opinion by a judge or justice who disagrees with the majority opinion.

Dissociation The severance of the relationship between a partner and a partnership when the partner ceases to be associated with the carrying on of the partnership business.

Dissolution The formal disbanding of a partnership or a corporation. It can take place by (1) acts of the partners or, in a corporation, of the shareholders and board of directors; (2) the death of a partner; (3) the expiration of a time period stated in a partnership agreement or a certificate of incorporation; or (4) judicial decree.

Distributed network A network that can be used by persons located (distributed) around the country or the globe to share computer files.

Distributorship A business arrangement that is established when a manufacturer licenses a dealer to sell its product. An example of a distributorship is an automobile dealership.

Diversity of citizenship Under Article III, Section 2, of the Constitution, a basis for federal court jurisdiction over a lawsuit between (1) citizens of different states, (2) a foreign country and citizens of a state or of different states, or (3) citizens of a state and citizens or subjects of a foreign country. The amount in controversy must be more than $75,000 before a federal court can take jurisdiction in such cases.

Dividend A distribution to corporate shareholders of corporate profits or income, disbursed in proportion to the number of shares held.

Docket The list of cases entered on a court's calendar and thus scheduled to be heard by the court.

Document of title Paper exchanged in the regular course of business that evidences the right to possession of goods (for example, a bill of lading or a warehouse receipt).

Domain name The series of letters and symbols used to identify site operators on the Internet. Also referred to as Internet "addresses."

Domestic corporation In a given state, a corporation that does business in, and is organized under the laws of, that state.

Donee beneficiary A third party beneficiary who has rights under a contract as a direct result of the intention of the contract parties to make a gift to the third party.

Double jeopardy A situation occurring when a person is tried twice for the same criminal offense; prohibited by the Fifth Amendment to the Constitution.

Double taxation A feature (and disadvantage) of the corporate form of business. Because a corporation is a separate legal entity, corporate profits are taxed by state and federal governments. Dividends are again taxable as ordinary income to the shareholders receiving them.

Dram shop act A state statute that imposes liability on the owners of bars and taverns, as well as those who serve alcoholic drinks to the public, for injuries resulting from accidents caused by intoxicated persons when the sellers or servers of alcoholic drinks contributed to the intoxication.

Due process clause The provisions of the Fifth and Fourteenth Amendments to the Constitution that guarantee that no person shall be deprived of life, liberty, or property without due process of law. Similar clauses are found in most state constitutions.

Duress Unlawful pressure brought to bear on a person, causing the person to perform an act that he or she would not otherwise perform.

Duty-based ethics An ethical philosophy rooted in the idea that every person has certain duties to others, including both humans and the planet. Those duties may be derived from religious principles or from other philosophical reasoning.

Duty of care The duty of all persons, as established by tort law, to exercise a reasonable amount of care in their dealings with others. Failure to exercise due care, which is normally determined by the "reasonable person standard," constitutes the tort of negligence.

E

E-agent A semiautonomous computer program that is capable of executing specific tasks.

E-commerce Business transacted in cyberspace.

E-contract A contract that is entered into in cyberspace and is evidenced only by electronic impulses (such as those that make up a computer's memory), rather than, for example, a typewritten form.

E-signature As defined by the Uniform Electronic Transactions Act, "an electronic sound, symbol, or process attached to or logically associated with a record and executed or adopted by a person with the intent to sign the record."

Early neutral case evaluation A form of alternative dispute resolution in which a neutral third party evaluates the strengths and weakness of the disputing parties' positions; the evaluator's opinion forms the basis for negotiating a settlement.

Emancipation In regard to minors, the act of being freed from parental control; occurs when a child's parent or legal guardian relinquishes the legal right to exercise control over the child. Normally, a minor who leaves home to support himself or herself is considered emancipated.

Embezzlement The fraudulent appropriation of money or other property by a person to whom the money or property has been entrusted.

Entrapment In criminal law, a defense in which the defendant claims that he or she was induced by a public official—usually an undercover agent or police officer—to commit a crime that he or she would otherwise not have committed.

Entrepreneur One who initiates and assumes the financial risks of a new enterprise and who undertakes to provide or control its management.

Entrustment rule The transfer of goods to a merchant who deals in goods of that kind and who may transfer those goods and all rights to them to a buyer in the ordinary course of business [UCC 2–403(2)].

Equal dignity rule In most states, a rule stating that express authority given to an agent must be in writing if the contract to be made on behalf of the principal is required to be in writing.

Equal protection clause The provision in the Fourteenth Amendment to the Constitution that guarantees that no state will "deny to any person within its jurisdiction the equal protection of the laws." This clause mandates that state governments treat similarly situated individuals in a similar manner.

Equitable maxims General propositions or principles of law that have to do with fairness (equity).

Establishment clause The provision in the First Amendment to the U.S. Constitution that prohibits Congress from creating any law "respecting an establishment of religion."

Estopped Barred, impeded, or precluded.

Estoppel The principle that a party's own acts prevent him or her from claiming a right to the detriment of another who was entitled to and did rely on those acts.

Ethical reasoning A reasoning process in which an individual links his or her moral convictions or ethical standards to the particular situation at hand.

Ethics Moral principles and values applied to social behavior.

Evidence Proof offered at trial—in the form of testimony, documents, records, exhibits, objects, and so on—for the purpose of convincing the court or jury of the truth of a contention.

Exclusionary rule In criminal procedure, a rule under which any evidence that is obtained in violation of the accused's constitutional rights guaranteed by the Fourth, Fifth, and Sixth Amendments, as well as any evidence derived from illegally obtained evidence, will not be admissible in court.

Exclusive agency An agency in which a principal grants an agent an exclusive territory and does not allow another agent to compete in that territory.

Exclusive jurisdiction Jurisdiction that exists when a case can be heard only in a particular court or type of court, such as a federal court or a state court.

Exculpatory clause A clause that releases a contractual party from liability in the event of monetary or physical injury, no matter who is at fault.

Executed contract A contract that has been completely performed by both parties.

Executive agency An administrative agency within the executive branch of government. At the federal level, executive agencies are those within the cabinet departments.

Executory contract A contract that has not as yet been fully performed.

Express authority Authority expressly given by one party to another. In agency law, an agent has express authority to act for a principal if both parties agree, orally or in writing, that an agency relationship exists in which the agent had the power (authority) to act in the place of, and on behalf of, the principal.

Express contract A contract in which the terms of the agreement are fully and explicitly stated in words, oral or written.

Express warranty A seller's or lessor's oral or written promise, ancillary to an underlying sales or lease agreement, as to the quality, description, or performance of the goods being sold or leased.

Extrinsic evidence Evidence that relates to a contract but is not contained within the document itself, such as the testimony of parties and witnesses, or additional agreements or communications. A court may consider extrinsic evidence only when a contract term is ambiguous and the evidence does not contradict the express terms of the contract.

F

Federal form of government A system of government in which the states form a union and the sovereign power is divided between a central government and the member states.

Federal question A question that pertains to the U.S. Constitution, acts of Congress, or treaties. A federal question provides a basis for federal jurisdiction.

Felony A crime—such as arson, murder, rape, or robbery—that carries the most severe sanctions, usually ranging from one year in a state or federal prison to the forfeiture of one's life.

Fiduciary As a noun, a person having a duty created by his or her undertaking to act primarily for another's benefit in matters connected with the undertaking. As an adjective, a relationship founded on trust and confidence.

Fiduciary duty The duty, imposed on a fiduciary by virtue of his or her position, to act primarily for another's benefit.

Filtering software A computer program that includes a pattern through which data are passed. When designed to block access to certain Web sites, the pattern blocks the retrieval of a site whose URL or key words are on a list within the program.

Firm offer An offer (by a merchant) that is irrevocable without consideration for a period of time (not longer than three months). A firm offer by a merchant must be in writing and must be signed by the offeror.

Forbearance The act of refraining from exercising a legal right. An agreement between the lender and the borrower in which the lender agrees to temporarily cease requiring mortgage payments, to delay foreclosure, or to accept smaller payments than previously scheduled.

***Force majeure* clause** (pronounced mah-*zhure*) A provision in a contract stipulating that certain unforeseen events—such as war, political upheavals, acts of God, or other events—will excuse a party from liability for nonperformance of contractual obligations.

Foreign corporation In a given state, a corporation that does business in the state without being incorporated therein.

Foreseeable risk In negligence law, the risk of harm or injury to another that a person of ordinary intelligence and prudence should have reasonably anticipated or foreseen when undertaking an action or refraining from undertaking an action.

Forgery The fraudulent making or altering of any writing in a way that changes the legal rights and liabilities of another.

Formal contract A contract that by law requires a specific form, such as being executed under seal, to be valid.

Forum A jurisdiction, court, or place in which disputes are litigated and legal remedies are sought.

Forum-selection clause A provision in a contract designating the court, jurisdiction, or tribunal that will decide any disputes arising under the contract.

Fraud Any misrepresentation, either by misstatement or omission of a material fact, knowingly made with the intention of deceiving another and on which a reasonable person would and does rely to his or her detriment.

Fraudulent misrepresentation (fraud) Any misrepresentation, either by misstatement or omission of a material fact, knowingly made with the intention of deceiving another and on which a reasonable person would and does rely to his or her detriment.

Free exercise clause The provision in the First Amendment to the U.S. Constitution that prohibits Congress from making any law "prohibiting the free exercise" of religion.

Frustration of purpose A court-created doctrine under which a party to a contract will be relieved of his or her duty to perform when the objective purpose for performance no longer exists (due to reasons beyond that party's control).

Full faith and credit clause A clause in Article IV, Section 1, of the Constitution that provides that "Full Faith and Credit shall be given in each State to the public Acts, Records, and Judicial Proceedings of every other State." The clause ensures that rights established under deeds, wills, contracts, and the like in one state will be honored by the other states and that any judicial decision with respect to such property rights will be honored and enforced in all states.

Full warranty A warranty as to full performance covering generally both labor and materials.

Fully integrated contract A contract that completely sets forth all the terms and conditions agreed to by the parties and is intended as a final statement of their agreement. The terms cannot be contradicted by evidence of any prior agreements or contemporaneous oral agreements.

G

General jurisdiction Exists when a court's subject-matter jurisdiction is not restricted. A court of general jurisdiction normally can hear any type of case.

Good faith Under the Uniform Commercial Code, good faith means honesty in fact; with regard to merchants, good faith means honesty in fact *and* the observance of reasonable commercial standards of fair dealing in the trade.

Good faith purchaser A purchaser who buys without notice of any circumstance that would put a person of ordinary prudence on inquiry as to whether the seller has valid title to the goods being sold.

Good Samaritan statute A state statute that provides that persons who rescue or provide emergency services to others in peril—unless they do so recklessly, thus causing further harm—cannot be sued for negligence.

Goodwill In the business context, the valuable reputation of a business viewed as an intangible asset.

Grand jury A group of citizens called to decide, after hearing the state's evidence, whether a reasonable basis (probable cause) exists for believing that a crime has been committed and whether a trial ought to be held.

H

Hacker A person who uses one computer to break into another. Professional computer programmers refer to such persons as "crackers."

Historical school A school of legal thought that emphasizes the evolutionary process of law and that looks to the past to discover what the principles of contemporary law should be.

Holding company A company whose business activity is holding shares in another company.

I

Identification In a sale of goods, the express designation of the specific goods provided for in the contract.

Identity theft The act of stealing another's identifying information—such as a name, date of birth, or Social Security number—and using that information to access the victim's financial resources.

Illusory promise A promise made without consideration, which renders the promise unenforceable.

Immunity A status of being exempt, or free, from certain duties or requirements. In criminal law, the state may grant an accused person immunity from prosecution—or agree to prosecute for a lesser offense—if the accused person agrees to give the state information that would assist the state in prosecuting other individuals for crimes. In tort law, freedom from liability for defamatory speech.

Implied authority Authority that is created not by an explicit oral or written agreement but by implication. In agency law, implied authority (of the agent) can be conferred by custom, inferred from the position the agent occupies, or implied by virtue of being reasonably necessary to carry out express authority.

Implied contract A contract formed in whole or in part from the conduct of the parties (as opposed to an express contract). Also known as implied-in-fact contract.

Implied warranty A warranty that the law derives by implication or inference from the nature of the transaction or the relative situation or circumstances of the parties.

Implied warranty of fitness for a particular purpose A warranty that goods sold or leased are fit for a particular purpose. The warranty arises when any seller or lessor knows the particular purpose for which a buyer or lessee will use the goods and knows that the buyer or lessee is relying on the skill and judgment of the seller or lessor to select suitable goods.

Implied warranty of merchantability A warranty that goods being sold or leased are reasonably fit for the ordinary purpose for which they are sold or leased, are properly packaged and labeled, and are of fair quality. The warranty automatically arises in every sale or lease of goods made by a merchant who deals in goods of the kind sold or leased.

Impossibility of performance A doctrine under which a party to a contract is relieved of his or her duty to perform when performance becomes impossible or totally impracticable (through no fault of either party).

***In personam* jurisdiction** Court jurisdiction over the "person" involved in a legal action; personal jurisdiction.

***In rem* jurisdiction** Court jurisdiction over a defendant's property.

Incidental beneficiary A third party who incidentally benefits from a contract but whose benefit was not the reason the contract was formed; an incidental beneficiary has no rights in a contract and cannot sue to have the contract enforced.

Incidental damages Expenses that are caused directly by a breach of contract, such as those incurred to obtain performance from another source.

Indemnify To compensate or reimburse another for losses or expenses incurred.

Independent contractor One who works for, and receives payment from, an employer but whose working conditions and methods are not controlled by the employer. An independent contractor is not an employee but may be an agent.

Independent regulatory agency An administrative agency that is not considered part of the government's executive branch and is not subject to the authority of the president. Independent agency officials cannot be removed without cause.

Indictment (pronounced in-*dyte*-ment) A charge by a grand jury that a reasonable basis (probable cause) exists for believing that a crime has been committed and that a trial should be held.

Informal contract A contract that does not require a specified form or formality in order to be valid.

Information A formal accusation or complaint (without an indictment) issued in certain types of actions (usually criminal actions involving lesser crimes) by a law officer, such as a magistrate.

Information return A tax return submitted by a partnership that reports the income earned by the business. The partnership as an entity does not pay taxes on the income received by the partnership. A partner's profit from the partnership (whether distributed or not) is taxed as individual income to the individual partner.

Infringement A violation of another's legally recognized right. The term is commonly used with reference to the invasion by one party of another party's rights in a patent, trademark, or copyright.

Injunction A court decree ordering a person to do or refrain from doing a certain act or activity.

Innocent misrepresentation A false statement of fact or an act made in good faith that deceives and causes harm or injury to another.

Inside director A person on the board of directors who is also an officer of the corporation.

Installment contract Under the Uniform Commercial Code, a contract that requires or authorizes delivery in two or more separate lots to be accepted and paid for separately.

Intangible property Property that is incapable of being apprehended by the senses (such as by sight or touch); intellectual property is an example of intangible property.

Integrated contract A written contract that constitutes the final expression of the parties' agreement. It can be either *fully integrated* or *partially integrated*. If a contract is fully integrated, evidence extraneous to the contract that contradicts or alters the meaning of the contract in any way is inadmissible. If it is partially integrated, such evidence is admissible.

Intellectual property Property resulting from intellectual, creative processes. Patents, trademarks, and copyrights are examples of intellectual property.

Intended beneficiary A third party for whose benefit a contract is formed; an intended beneficiary can sue the promisor if such a contract is breached.

Intentional tort A wrongful act knowingly committed.

Internet service provider (ISP) A business or organization that offers users access to the Internet and related services.

Irrevocable offer An offer that cannot be revoked or recalled by the offeror without liability. A merchant's firm offer is an example of an irrevocable offer.

J

Joint and several liability In partnership law, a doctrine under which a plaintiff may sue, and collect a judgment from, one or more of the partners separately (severally, or individually) or all of the partners together (jointly). This is true even if one of the partners sued did not participate in, ratify, or know about whatever gave rise to the cause of action.

Joint liability Shared liability. In partnership law, partners incur joint liability for partnership obligations and debts. For example, if a third party sues a partner on a partnership debt, the partner has the right to insist that the other partners be sued with him or her.

Judgment The final order or decision resulting from a legal action.

Judgment *n.o.v.* A motion requesting the court to grant judgment in favor of the party making the motion on the ground that the jury verdict against him or her was unreasonable and erroneous.

Judicial process The procedures relating to, or connected with, the administration of justice through the judicial system.

Judicial review The process by which courts decide on the constitutionality of legislative enactments and actions of the executive branch.

Jurisdiction The authority of a court to hear and decide a specific action.

Jurisprudence The science or philosophy of law.

Justiciable controversy A controversy that is not hypothetical or academic but real and substantial. A requirement that must be satisfied before a court will hear a case.

L

Laches The equitable doctrine that bars a party's right to legal action if the party has neglected for an unreasonable length of time to act on his or her rights.

Larceny The wrongful taking and carrying away of another person's personal property with the intent to permanently deprive the owner of the property. Some states classify larceny as either grand or petit, depending on the property's value.

Latent defects A defect that is not obvious or cannot readily be ascertained.

Law A body of enforceable rules governing relationships among individuals and between individuals and their society.

Lawsuit The litigation process.

Lease agreement In regard to the lease of goods, an agreement in which one person (the lessor) agrees to transfer the right to the possession and use of property to another person (the lessee) in exchange for rental payments.

Legal positivism A school of legal thought centered on the assumption that there is no law higher than the laws created by a national government. Laws must be obeyed, even if they are unjust, to prevent anarchy.

Legal realism A school of legal thought that was popular in the 1920s and 1930s and that challenged many existing jurisprudential assumptions, particularly the assumption that subjective elements play no part in judicial reasoning. Legal realists generally advocated a less abstract and more pragmatic approach to the law, an approach that would take into account customary practices and the circumstances in which transactions take place. The school left a lasting imprint on American jurisprudence.

Legal reasoning The process of reasoning by which a judge harmonizes his or her decision with the judicial decisions of previous cases.

Lessee A person who acquires the right to the possession and use of another's goods in exchange for rental payments.

Lessor A person who transfers the right to the possession and use of goods to another in exchange for rental payments.

Liability Any actual or potential legal obligation, duty, debt, or responsibility.

Libel Defamation in writing or other form (such as in a digital recording) having the quality of permanence.

License In the context of intellectual property, a contract permitting the use of a trademark, copyright, patent, or trade secret for certain purposes.

Licensee One who receives a license to use, or enter onto, another's property or to use certain intellectual property rights.

Lien (pronounced *leen*) A claim against specific property to satisfy a debt.

Limited jurisdiction Exists when a court's subject-matter jurisdiction is limited. Bankruptcy courts and probate courts are examples of courts with limited jurisdiction.

Limited liability Exists when the liability of the owners of a business is limited to the amount of their investments in the firm.

Limited liability company (LLC) A hybrid form of business enterprise that offers the limited liability of the corporation but the tax advantages of a partnership.

Liquidated damages An amount, stipulated in the contract, that the parties to a contract believe to be a reasonable estimation of the damages that will occur in the event of a breach.

Liquidated debt A debt that is due and certain in amount.

Litigation The process of resolving a dispute through the court system.

Long arm statute A state statute that permits a state to obtain personal jurisdiction over nonresident defendants. A defendant must have "minimum contacts" with that state for the statute to apply.

M

Mailbox rule A rule providing that an acceptance of an offer becomes effective on dispatch. Acceptance takes effect, thus completing formation of the contract, at the time the offeree sends or delivers the communication via the mode expressly or impliedly authorized by the offeror.

Main purpose rule A rule of contract law under which an exception to the Statute of Frauds is made if the main purpose in accepting secondary liability under a contract is to secure a personal benefit. If this situation exists, the contract need not be in writing to be enforceable.

Majority opinion A court's written opinion, outlining the views of the majority of the judges or justices deciding the case.

Malpractice Professional misconduct or the failure to exercise the requisite degree of skill as a professional. Negligence—the failure to exercise due care—on the part of a professional, such as a physician or an attorney, is commonly referred to as malpractice.

Malware Malicious software programs designed to disrupt or harm a computer, network, smartphone, or other device.

Material fact A fact to which a reasonable person would attach importance in determining his or her course of action. In regard to tender offers, for example, a fact is material if there is a substantial likelihood that a reasonable shareholder would consider it important in deciding how to vote.

Mediation A method of settling disputes outside of court by using the services of a neutral third party, called a mediator. The mediator acts as a communicating agent between the parties and suggests ways in which the parties can resolve their dispute.

Member The term used to designate a person who has an ownership interest in a limited liability company.

Mens rea (pronounced *mehns ray*-uh) Criminal intent. A wrongful mental state, which is as necessary as a wrongful act, to establish criminal liability. What constitutes a guilty mental state varies according to the wrongful action. Thus, for murder, the *mens rea* is the intent to take a life. For theft, the *mens rea* must involve both the knowledge that the property belongs to another and the intent to deprive the owner of it.

Merchant A person who is engaged in the purchase and sale of goods. Under the Uniform Commercial Code, a person who deals in goods of the kind involved in the sales contract.

Meta tags Words inserted into a Web site's key-words field to increase the site's appearance in search engine results.

Minimum-contacts requirement The requirement that before a state court can exercise jurisdiction over a foreign corporation, the foreign corporation must have sufficient contacts with the state. A foreign corporation that has its home office in the state or that has manufacturing plants in the state meets this requirement.

Mini-trial A private proceeding in which each party to a dispute argues its position before the other side and vice versa. A neutral third party may be present and act as an adviser if the parties fail to reach an agreement.

Mirror image rule A common law rule that requires, for a valid contractual agreement, that the terms of the offeree's acceptance adhere exactly to the terms of the offeror's offer.

Misdemeanor A lesser crime than a felony, punishable by a fine or imprisonment for up to one year in other than a state or federal penitentiary.

Misrepresentation A false statement of fact or an action that deceives and causes harm or injury to another. *See also* Fraudulent misrepresentation (fraud); Innocent misrepresentation

Mitigation of damages A rule requiring a plaintiff to have done whatever was reasonable to minimize the damages caused by the defendant.

Money laundering Falsely reporting income that has been obtained through criminal activity as income obtained through a legitimate business enterprise—in effect, "laundering" the "dirty money."

Moral minimum The minimum degree of ethical behavior expected of a business firm, which is usually defined as compliance with the law.

Mutual rescission An agreement between the parties to cancel their contract, releasing the parties from further obligations under the contract. The object of the agreement is to restore the parties to the positions they would have occupied had no contract ever been formed. *See also* Rescission

N

Natural law The belief that government and the legal system should reflect universal moral and ethical principles that are inherent in human nature. The natural law school is the oldest and one of the most significant schools of legal thought.

Necessaries Necessities required for life, such as food, shelter, clothing, and medical attention; may include whatever is believed to be necessary to maintain a person's standard of living or financial and social status.

Necessity In criminal law, a defense against liability; under Section 3.02 of the Model Penal Code, this defense is justifiable if "the harm or evil sought to be avoided" by a given action "is greater than that sought to be prevented by the law defining the offense charged."

Negligence The failure to exercise the standard of care that a reasonable person would exercise in similar circumstances.

Negligence *per se* An act (or failure to act) in violation of a statutory requirement.

Negligent misrepresentation Any manifestation through words or conduct that amounts to an untrue statement of fact made in circumstances in which a reasonable and prudent person would not have done (or failed to do) that which led to the misrepresentation. A representation made with an honest belief in its truth may still be negligent due to (1) a lack of reasonable care in ascertaining the facts, (2) the manner of expression, or (3) the absence of the skill or competence required by a particular business or profession.

Negotiation A process in which parties attempt to settle their dispute without going to court, with or without attorneys to represent them.

Nominal damages A small monetary award (often one dollar) granted to a plaintiff when no actual damage was suffered or when the plaintiff is unable to show such loss with sufficient certainty.

Notary public A public official authorized to attest to the authenticity of signatures.

Novation The substitution, by agreement, of a new contract for an old one, with the rights under the old one being terminated. Typically, there is a substitution of a new person who is responsible for the contract and the removal of an original party's rights and duties under the contract.

O

Objective theory of contracts A theory under which the intent to form a contract will be judged by outward, objective facts (what the party said when entering into the contract, how the party acted or appeared, and the circumstances surrounding the transaction) as interpreted by a reasonable person, rather than by the party's own secret, subjective intentions.

Obligee One to whom an obligation is owed.

Obligor One who owes an obligation to another.

Offer A promise or commitment to perform or refrain from performing some specified act in the future.

Offeree A person to whom an offer is made.

Offeror A person who makes an offer.

Online dispute resolution (ODR) The resolution of disputes with the assistance of organizations that offer dispute-resolution services via the Internet.

Operating agreement In a limited liability company, an agreement in which the members set forth the details of how the business will be managed and operated.

Opinion A statement by the court expressing the reasons for its decision in a case.

Option contract A contract under which the offeror cannot revoke his or her offer for a stipulated time period and the offeree can accept or reject the offer during this period without fear that the offer will be made to another person. The offeree must give consideration for the option (the irrevocable offer) to be enforceable.

Ordinance A law passed by a local governing unit, such as a municipality or a county.

Original jurisdiction Courts having original jurisdiction are courts of the first instance, or trial courts—that is, courts in which lawsuits begin, trials take place, and evidence is presented.

Outcome-based ethics An ethical philosophy that focuses on the impacts of a decision on society or on key stakeholders.

Output contract An agreement in which a seller agrees to sell and a buyer agrees to buy all or up to a stated amount of what the seller produces.

Outside director A person on the board of directors who does not hold a management position at the corporation.

P

Parol evidence A term that originally meant "oral evidence," but that has come to refer to any negotiations or agreements made prior to a contract or any contemporaneous oral agreements made by the parties.

Parol evidence rule A substantive rule of contracts under which a court will not receive into evidence the parties' prior negotiations, prior agreements, or contemporaneous oral agreements if that evidence contradicts or varies the terms of the parties' written contract.

Partially disclosed principal A principal whose identity is unknown by a third person, but the third person knows that the agent is or may be acting for a principal at the time the agent and the third person form a contract.

Partner A co-owner of a partnership.

Partnering agreement An agreement between a seller and a buyer who frequently do business with each other on the terms and conditions that will apply to all subsequently formed electronic contracts.

Partnership An agreement by two or more persons to carry on, as co-owners, a business for profit.

Partnership by estoppel A judicially created partnership that may, at the court's discretion, be imposed for purposes of fairness. The court can prevent those who present themselves as partners (but who are not) from escaping liability if a third person relies on an alleged partnership in good faith and is harmed as a result.

Pass-through entity Any entity that does not have its income taxed at the level of that entity; examples are partnerships, S corporations, and limited liability companies.

Past consideration Something given or some act done in the past, which cannot ordinarily be consideration for a later bargain.

Patent A government grant that gives an inventor the exclusive right or privilege to make, use, or sell his or her invention for a limited time period. The word *patent* usually refers to some invention and designates either the instrument by which patent rights are evidenced or the patent itself.

Peer-to-peer (P2P) networking The sharing of resources (such as files, hard drives, and processing styles) among multiple computers without necessarily requiring a central network server.

Penalty A sum inserted into a contract, not as a measure of compensation for its breach but rather as punishment for a default. The agreement as to the amount will not be enforced, and recovery will be limited to actual damages.

***Per curiam* opinion** By the whole court; a court opinion written by the court as a whole instead of being authored by a judge or justice.

Per se A Latin term meaning "in itself" or "by itself."

Perfect tender rule A common law rule under which a seller was required to deliver to the buyer goods that conformed perfectly to the requirements stipulated in the sales contract. A tender of nonconforming goods would automatically constitute a breach of contract. Under the Uniform Commercial Code, the rule has been greatly modified.

Performance In contract law, the fulfillment of one's duties arising under a contract with another; the normal way of discharging one's contractual obligations.

Persuasive authority Any legal authority or source of law that a court may look to for guidance but need not follow when making its decision.

Petitioner In equity practice, a party that initiates a lawsuit.

Petty offense In criminal law, the least serious kind of criminal offense, such as a traffic or building-code violation.

Phishing Online fraud in which criminals pretend to be legitimate companies by using e-mails or malicious

Web sites that trick individuals and companies into providing useful information, such as bank account numbers, Social Security numbers, and credit card numbers.

Pierce the corporate veil To disregard the corporate entity, which limits the liability of shareholders, and hold the shareholders personally liable for a corporate obligation.

Plaintiff One who initiates a lawsuit.

Plea In criminal law, a defendant's allegation, in response to the charges brought against him or her, of guilt or innocence.

Plea bargaining The process by which a criminal defendant and the prosecutor in a criminal case work out a mutually satisfactory disposition of the case, subject to court approval; usually involves the defendant's pleading guilty to a lesser offense in return for a lighter sentence.

Plurality opinion A court opinion that is joined by the largest number of the judges or justices hearing the case, but less than half of the total number.

Police powers Powers possessed by states as part of their inherent sovereignty. These powers may be exercised to protect or promote the public order, health, safety, morals, and general welfare.

Power of attorney A written document, which is usually notarized, authorizing another to act as one's agent; can be special (permitting the agent to do specified acts only) or general (permitting the agent to transact all business for the principal).

Precedent A court decision that furnishes an example or authority for deciding subsequent cases involving identical or similar facts.

Predominant-factor test A test courts use to determine whether a contract is primarily for the sale of goods or for the sale of services.

Preemption A doctrine under which certain federal laws preempt, or take precedence over, conflicting state or local laws.

Preemptive rights Rights held by shareholders that entitle them to purchase newly issued shares of a corporation's stock, equal in percentage to shares presently held, before the stock is offered to any outside buyers. Preemptive rights enable shareholders to maintain their proportionate ownership and voice in the corporation.

Preferred stock Classes of stock that have priority over common stock as to payment of dividends and distribution of assets on the corporation's dissolution.

Prenuptial agreement An agreement made before marriage that defines each partner's ownership rights in the other partner's property. Prenuptial agreements must be in writing to be enforceable.

Preponderance of the evidence A standard in civil law cases under which the plaintiff must convince the court that, based on the evidence presented by both parties, it is more likely than not that the plaintiff's allegation is true.

Principal In agency law, a person who agrees to have another, called the agent, act on his or her behalf.

Principle of rights The principle that human beings have certain fundamental rights (to life, freedom, and the pursuit of happiness, for example). Those who adhere to this "rights theory" believe that a key factor in determining whether a business decision is ethical is how that decision affects the rights of others. These others include the firm's owners, its employees, the consumers of its products or services, its suppliers, the community in which it does business, and society as a whole.

Privilege In tort law, the ability to act contrary to another person's right without that person's having legal redress for such acts. Privilege may be raised as a defense to defamation.

Privileges and immunities clause Article IV, Section 2, of the Constitution requires states not to discriminate against one another's citizens. A resident of one state cannot be treated as an alien when in another state; he or she may not be denied such privileges and immunities as legal protection, access to courts, travel rights, and property rights.

Privity of contract The relationship that exists between the promisor and the promisee of a contract.

Probable cause Reasonable grounds to believe the existence of facts warranting certain actions, such as the search or arrest of a person.

Probate court A state court of limited jurisdiction that conducts proceedings relating to the settlement of a deceased person's estate.

Procedural due process The requirement that any government decision to take life, liberty, or property must be made fairly. For example, fair procedures must be used in determining whether a person will be subjected to punishment or have some burden imposed on him or her.

Procedural law Rules that define the manner in which the rights and duties of individuals may be enforced.

Procedural unconscionability Occurs when one contractual party lacks knowledge or understanding of the contract terms, often due to inconspicuous print or the lack of an opportunity to read the contract or to ask questions about its meaning. Procedural unconscionability often involves an *adhesion contract,* which is a contract drafted by the dominant party and then presented to the other—the adhering party—on a take-it-or-leave-it basis.

Promise A person's assurance that he or she will or will not do something.

Promisee A person to whom a promise is made.

Promisor A person who makes a promise.

Promissory estoppel A doctrine that applies when a promisor makes a clear and definite promise on which the promisee justifiably relies; such a promise is binding if justice will be better served by the enforcement of the promise. *See also* Estoppel

Promoter A person who takes the preliminary steps in organizing a corporation, including (usually) issuing a prospectus, procuring stock subscriptions, making contract purchases, securing a corporate charter, and the like.

Proximate cause Legal cause; exists when the connection between an act and an injury is strong enough to justify imposing liability.

Proxy In corporation law, a written agreement between a stockholder and another under which the stockholder authorizes the other to vote the stockholder's shares in a certain manner.

Public corporation A corporation owned by a federal, state, or municipal government—not to be confused with a publicly held corporation.

Public figures Individuals who are thrust into the public limelight. Public figures include government officials and politicians, movie stars, well-known businesspersons, and generally anybody who becomes known to the public because of his or her position or activities.

Public policy A government policy based on widely held societal values and (usually) expressed or implied in laws or regulations.

Publicly held corporation A corporation for which shares of stock have been sold to the public.

Puffery A salesperson's exaggerated claims concerning the quality of goods offered for sale. Such claims involve opinions rather than facts and are not considered to be legally binding promises or warranties.

Punitive damages Money damages that may be awarded to a plaintiff to punish the defendant and deter future similar conduct.

Q

Quantum meruit (pronounced *kwahn*-tuhm *mehr*-oo-wuht) Literally, "as much as he deserves"—an expression describing the extent of liability on a contract implied in law (quasi contract). An equitable doctrine based on the concept that one who benefits from another's labor and materials should not be unjustly enriched thereby but should be required to pay a reasonable amount for the benefits received, even absent a contract.

Quasi contract A fictional contract imposed on parties by a court in the interests of fairness and justice; usually, quasi contracts are imposed to avoid the unjust enrichment of one party at the expense of another.

Question of fact In a lawsuit, an issue involving a factual dispute that can only be decided by a judge (or, in a jury trial, a jury).

Question of law In a lawsuit, an issue involving the application or interpretation of a law; therefore, the judge, and not the jury, decides the issue.

Quorum The number of members of a decision-making body that must be present before business may be transacted.

R

Ratification The act of accepting and giving legal force to an obligation that previously was not enforceable.

Reasonable person standard The standard of behavior expected of a hypothetical "reasonable person." The standard against which negligence is measured and that must be observed to avoid liability for negligence.

Record According to the Uniform Electronic Transactions Act, information that is either inscribed on a tangible medium or stored in an electronic or other medium and that is retrievable.

Reformation A court-ordered correction of a written contract so that it reflects the true intentions of the parties.

Release A contract in which one party forfeits the right to pursue a legal claim against the other party.

Remanded Sent back. If an appellate court disagrees with a lower court's judgment, the case may be remanded to the lower court for further proceedings in which the lower court's decision should be consistent with the appellate court's opinion on the matter.

Remedy The relief given to an innocent party to enforce a right or compensate for the violation of a right.

Remedy at law A remedy available in a court of law. Money damages are awarded as a remedy at law.

Remedy in equity A remedy allowed by courts in situations where remedies at law are not appropriate. Remedies in equity are based on settled rules of fairness, justice, and honesty, and include injunction, specific performance, rescission and restitution, and reformation.

Replevin (pronounced rih-*pleh*-vin) An action to recover specific goods in the hands of a party who is wrongfully withholding them from the other party.

Reporter A publication in which court cases are published, or reported.

Repudiation The renunciation of a right or duty; the act of a buyer or seller in rejecting a contract either partially or totally. *See also* Anticipatory repudiation

Requirements contract An agreement in which a buyer agrees to purchase and the seller agrees to sell all or up to a stated amount of what the buyer needs or requires.

Res ipsa loquitur (pronounced *rehs ehp*-suh *low*-quuh-tuhr) A doctrine under which negligence may be inferred simply because an event occurred, if it is the type of event that would not occur in the absence of negligence. Literally, the term means "the facts speak for themselves."

Rescind (pronounced rih-*sihnd*) To cancel. *See also* Rescission

Rescission (pronounced rih-*sih*-zhen) A remedy whereby a contract is canceled and the parties are returned to the positions they occupied before the contract was made; may be effected through the mutual consent of the parties, by their conduct, or by court decree.

Respondeat superior (pronounced ree-*spahn*-dee-uht soo-*peer*-ee-your) In Latin, "Let the master respond." A doctrine under which a principal or an employer is held liable for the wrongful acts committed by agents or employees while acting within the course and scope of their agency or employment.

Respondent In equity practice, the party who answers a bill or other proceeding.

Restitution An equitable remedy under which a person is restored to his or her original position prior to loss or injury, or placed in the position he or she would have been in had the breach not occurred.

Retained earnings The portion of a corporation's profits that has not been paid out as dividends to shareholders.

Reverse To reject or overrule a court's judgment. An appellate court, for example, might reverse a lower court's judgment on an issue if it feels that the lower court committed an error during the trial or that the jury was improperly instructed.

Revocation In contract law, the withdrawal of an offer by an offeror. Unless an offer is irrevocable, it can be revoked at any time prior to acceptance without liability.

Robbery The act of forcefully and unlawfully taking personal property of any value from another; force or intimidation is usually necessary for an act of theft to be considered a robbery.

Rule of four A rule of the United States Supreme Court under which the Court will not issue a writ of *certiorari* unless at least four justices approve of the decision to issue the writ.

S

S corporation A close business corporation that has met certain requirements as set out by the Internal Revenue Code and thus qualifies for special income tax treatment. Essentially, an S corporation is taxed the same as a partnership, but its owners enjoy the privilege of limited liability.

Sale The passing of title (evidence of ownership rights) from the seller to the buyer for a price.

Sales contract A contract for the sale of goods under which the ownership of goods is transferred from a seller to a buyer for a price.

Scienter (pronounced *sy-en*-ter) Knowledge by the misrepresenting party that material facts have been falsely represented or omitted with an intent to deceive.

Search warrant An order granted by a public authority, such as a judge, that authorizes law enforcement personnel to search particular premises or property.

Seasonably Within a specified time period. If no period is specified, within a reasonable time.

Self-defense The legally recognized privilege to protect one's self or property against injury by another. The privilege of self-defense protects only acts that are reasonably necessary to protect one's self or property.

Self-incrimination Giving testimony in a trial or other legal proceeding that could expose the person testifying to criminal prosecution.

Service mark A mark used in the sale or the advertising of services, such as to distinguish the services of one person from the services of others. Titles, character names, and other distinctive features of radio and television programs may be registered as service marks.

Share A unit of stock.

Shareholder One who purchases shares of a corporation's stock, thus acquiring an equity interest in the corporation.

Shareholder's derivative suit A suit brought by a shareholder to enforce a corporate cause of action against a third person.

Sharia Civil law principles of some Middle Eastern countries that are based on the Islamic directives that follow the teachings of the prophet Muhammad.

Shipment contract A contract in which the seller is required to ship the goods by carrier. The buyer assumes liability for any losses or damage to the goods after they are delivered to the carrier. Generally, all contracts are assumed to be shipment contracts if nothing to the contrary is stated in the contract.

Shrink-wrap agreement An agreement whose terms are expressed in a document located inside a box in which goods (usually software) are packaged; sometimes called a *shrink-wrap license.*

Slander Defamation in oral form.

Slander of quality The publication of false information about another's product, alleging that it is not what its seller claims. Also known as *trade libel.*

Slander of title The publication of a statement that denies or casts doubt on another's legal ownership of any property, causing financial loss to that property owner. Also called *trade libel.*

Small claims courts Special courts in which parties may litigate small claims (usually, claims involving $2,500 or less). Attorneys are not required in small claims courts, and in many states attorneys are not allowed to represent the parties.

Social media The means by which people can create, share, and exchange ideas and comments via the Internet.

Sociological school A school of legal thought that views the law as a tool for promoting justice in society.

Sole proprietorship The simplest form of business, in which the owner is the business; the owner reports business income on his or her personal income tax return and is legally responsible for all debts and obligations incurred by the business.

Sovereignty The quality of having independent authority over a geographic area. For instance, state governments have the authority to regulate affairs within their border.

Spam Bulk, unsolicited (junk) e-mail.

Specific performance An equitable remedy requiring the breaching party to perform as promised under the contract; usually granted only when money damages would be an inadequate remedy and the subject matter of the contract is unique (for example, real property).

Stakeholders Groups, other than the company's shareholders, that are affected by corporate decisions. Stakeholders include employees, customers, creditors, suppliers, and the community in which the corporation operates.

Standing to sue The requirement that an individual must have a sufficient stake in a controversy before he or she can bring a lawsuit. The plaintiff must demonstrate that he or she either has been injured or threatened with injury.

Stare decisis (pronounced *ster*-ay dih-*si*-ses) A common law doctrine under which judges are obligated to follow the precedents established in prior decisions.

Statute of Frauds A state statute under which certain types of contracts must be in writing to be enforceable.

Statute of limitations A federal or state statute setting the maximum time period during which a certain action can be brought or certain rights enforced.

Statutory law The body of law enacted by legislative bodies (as opposed to constitutional law, administrative law, or case law).

Stock An equity (ownership) interest in a corporation, measured in units of shares.

Stock buyback Sometimes, publicly held companies use funds from their own treasuries to repurchase their own stock. The result is that the price of the stock usually goes up.

Stock certificate A certificate issued by a corporation evidencing the ownership of a specified number of shares in the corporation.

Stock warrant A certificate that grants the owner the option to buy a given number of shares of stock, usually within a set time period.

Subject-matter jurisdiction Jurisdiction over the subject matter of a lawsuit.

Subpoena A document commanding a person to appear at a certain time and place or give testimony concerning a certain matter.

Substantial performance Performance that does not vary greatly from the performance promised in a contract; the performance must create substantially the same benefits as those promised in the contract.

Substantive due process A requirement that focuses on the content, or substance, of legislation. If a law or other governmental action limits a fundamental right, such as the right to travel or to vote, it will be held to violate substantive due process unless it promotes a compelling or overriding government interest.

Substantive law Law that defines the rights and duties of individuals with respect to each other, as opposed to procedural law, which defines the manner in which these rights and duties may be enforced.

Substantive unconscionability Occurs when contracts, or portions of contracts, are oppressive or overly harsh. Courts generally focus on provisions that deprive one party of the benefits of the agreement or leave that party without remedy for nonperformance by the other.

Summary jury trial (SJT) A method of settling disputes in which a trial is held, but the jury's verdict is not binding. The verdict acts only as a guide to both sides in reaching an agreement during the mandatory negotiations that immediately follow the summary jury trial.

Superseding cause An intervening force or event that breaks the connection between a wrongful act and an injury to another; in negligence law, a defense to liability.

Supremacy clause The provision in Article VI of the Constitution that provides that the Constitution, laws, and treaties of the United States are "the supreme Law of the Land." Under this clause, state and local laws that directly conflict with federal law will be rendered invalid.

Symbolic speech Nonverbal conduct that expresses opinions or thoughts about a subject. Symbolic speech is protected under the First Amendment's guarantee of freedom of speech.

T

Tangible property Property that has physical existence and can be distinguished by the senses of touch, sight, and so on. A car is tangible property; a patent right is intangible property.

Technology licensing Allowing another to use and profit from intellectual property (patents, copyrights, trademarks, innovative products or processes, and so on) for consideration.

Tender An unconditional offer to perform an obligation by a person who is ready, willing, and able to do so.

Tender of delivery Under the Uniform Commercial Code, a seller's or lessor's act of placing conforming goods at the disposal of the buyer or lessee and giving the buyer or lessee whatever notification is reasonably necessary to enable the buyer or lessee to take delivery.

Third party beneficiary One for whose benefit a promise is made in a contract but who is not a party to the contract.

Tort A civil wrong not arising from a breach of contract. A breach of a legal duty that proximately causes harm or injury to another.

Tortfeasor One who commits a tort.

Trade dress The image and overall appearance of a product—for example, the distinctive decor, menu, layout, and style of service of a particular restaurant. Basically, trade dress is subject to the same protection as trademarks.

Trade name A term that is used to indicate part or all of a business's name and that is directly related to the business's reputation and goodwill. Trade names are protected under the common law (and under trademark law, if the name is the same as the firm's trademark).

Trade secret Information or a process that gives a business an advantage over competitors who do not know the information or process.

Trademark A distinctive mark, motto, device, or implement that a manufacturer stamps, prints, or otherwise affixes to the goods it produces so that they may be identified on the market and their origins made known. Once a trademark is established (under the common law or through registration), the owner is entitled to its exclusive use.

Transferred intent A legal principle under which a person who intends to harm one individual, but unintentionally harms a second individual, can be liable to that second person for an intentional tort. The law transfers the required intent to the second person.

Trespass to land The entry onto, above, or below the surface of land owned by another without the owner's permission or legal authorization.

Trespass to personal property The unlawful taking or harming of another's personal property; interference with another's right to the exclusive possession of his or her personal property.

Trespasser One who commits the tort of trespass in one of its forms.

Trial court A court in which trials are held and testimony taken.

Triple bottom line The idea that investors and others should consider not only corporate profits, but also the corporation's impact on people and on the planet in assessing the firm. (The bottom line is people, planet, and profits.)

Typosquatting A form of cybersquatting that relies on mistakes, such as typographical errors, made by Internet users when inputting information into a Web browser.

U

Ultra vires (pronounced *uhl*-trah *vye*-reez) A Latin term meaning "beyond the powers"; in corporate law, acts of a corporation that are beyond its express and implied powers to undertake.

Unanimous opinion A court opinion in which all of the judges or justices of the court agree to the court's decision.

Unconscionable (pronounced un-*kon*-shun-uh-bul) **contract or clause** A contract or clause that is void on the basis of public policy because one party, as a result of his or her disproportionate bargaining power, is forced to accept terms that are unfairly burdensome and that unfairly benefit the dominating party.

Undisclosed principal A principal whose identity is unknown by a third person, and the third person has no knowledge that the agent is acting for a principal at the time the agent and the third person form a contract.

Undue influence Persuasion that is less than actual force but more than advice and that induces a person to act according to the will or purposes of the dominating party.

Unenforceable contract A valid contract rendered unenforceable by some statute or law.

Uniform law A model law created by the National Conference of Commissioners on Uniform State Laws and/or the American Law Institute for the states to consider adopting. If the state adopts the law, it becomes statutory law in that state. Each state has the option of adopting or rejecting all or part of a uniform law.

Unilateral contract A contract that results when an offer can only be accepted by the offeree's performance.

Unliquidated debt A debt that is uncertain in amount.

Usage of trade Any practice or method of dealing having such regularity of observance in a place, vocation, or trade as to justify an expectation that it will be observed with respect to the transaction in question.

Usury Charging an illegal rate of interest.

Utilitarianism An approach to ethical reasoning in which ethically correct behavior is related to an evaluation of the consequences of a given action on those who will be affected by it. In utilitarian reasoning, a "good" decision is one that results in the greatest good for the greatest number of people affected by the decision.

V

Valid contract A contract that results when elements necessary for contract formation (agreement, consideration, legal purpose, and contractual capacity) are present.

Venue (pronounced *ven*-yoo) The geographical district in which an action is tried and from which the jury is selected.

Vicarious liability Legal responsibility placed on one person for the acts of another.

Virus A type of malware that is transmitted between computers and attempts to do deliberate damage to systems and data.

Void contract A contract having no legal force or binding effect.

Voidable contract A contract that may be legally avoided (canceled, or annulled) at the option of one of the parties.

Voluntary consent The element of agreement in the formation of a contract. The knowledge of, and assent to, the terms of a contract.

Voting trust An agreement (trust contract) under which legal title to shares of corporate stock is transferred to a trustee who is authorized by the shareholders to vote the shares on their behalf.

W

Waiver An intentional, knowing relinquishment of a legal right.

Warranty A promise that certain facts are truly as they are represented to be.

Warranty disclaimer A seller's or lessor's negation or qualification of a warranty.

Warranty of merchantability *See* Implied warranty of merchantability.

Warranty of title An implied warranty made by a seller that the seller has good and valid title to the goods sold and that the transfer of the title is rightful.

Watered stock Shares of stock issued by a corporation for which the corporation receives, as payment, less than the fair market value of the shares.

White-collar crime Nonviolent crime committed by individuals or corporations to obtain a personal or business advantage.

Winding up The second of two stages involved in the termination of a partnership or corporation. Once the firm is dissolved, it continues to exist legally until the process of winding up all business affairs (collecting and distributing the firm's assets) is complete.

Worm A type of malware that is designed to copy itself from one computer to another without human interaction. A worm can copy itself automatically and can replicate in great volume and with great speed.

Writ of *certiorari* (pronounced sur-shee-uh-*rah*-ree) A writ from a higher court asking the lower court for the record of a case.

TABLE OF CASES

Following is a list of all the cases mentioned in this text, including those within the footnotes, features, and case problems. Any case that was an excerpted case for a chapter is given special emphasis by having its title **boldfaced.**

INDEX